D0197539

Hiking in the
ROCKY MOUNTAINS

Clem Lindenmayer
Helen Fairbairn
Gareth McCormack

LONELY PLANET PUBLICATIONS
Melbourne • Oakland • London • Paris

US ROCKY MOUNTAINS STATES

GREATER YELLOWSTONE Hot springs, waterfalls and adventure – airy Teton Crest Trail, Yellowstone's own Grand Canyon and the aptly named Froze-to-Death Mountain.

CENTRAL & EASTERN WYOMING Islands in the sky and wild alpine valleys – spectacular Devil Canyon, a marvelous panorama from Cloud Peak, and hiking mecca Wind River Range, with favorites such as Titcomb Basin and Cirque of the Towers.

NORTHERN COLORADO & THE FRONT RANGE Landmarks and lakes – Rocky Mountain National Park, with landmark 14er, Longs Peak, and popular Flattop Mountain, plus jewel-like lakes in Glacier Gorge and Loch Vale.

SOUTHWEST MONTANA Wild, wild southwest – spectacular Blodgett Canyon, tiny heights and wildflowers at Trapper Peak, and large native trout and a taste of the Continental Divide Trail.

GREATER GLACIER Superb scenery and so different – glaciated peaks and abundant wildlife in Glacier National Park, and remote and rugged Bob Marshall Wilderness and Mission Mountains.

CENTRAL IDAHO Solitude and pristine wilderness – magnificent Bighorn Crags, Idaho's highest point, Mt Borah, and beautiful lakes.

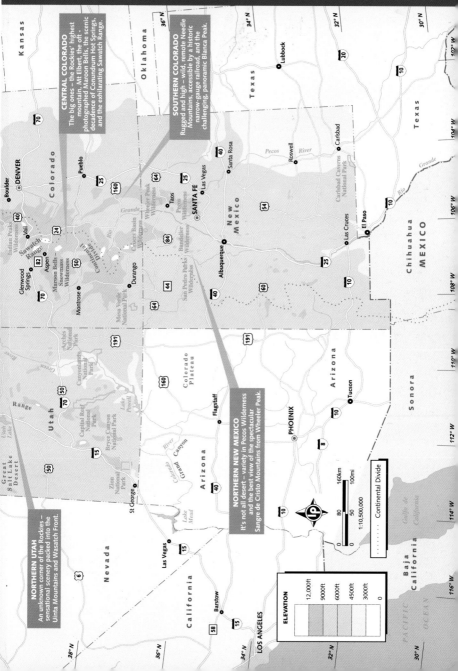

CENTRAL COLORADO
The big ones – the Rockies' highest mountain, Mt Elbert, the oft-photographed Maroon Bells, the scenic decadence of Conundrum Hot Springs, and the exhilarating Sawatch Range.

SOUTHERN COLORADO
Rugged and high – wild, remote Needle Mountains, accessible by a historic narrow-gauge railroad, and the challenging, panoramic Blanca Peak.

NORTHERN NEW MEXICO
It's not all desert – variety in Pecos Wilderness and the best view of the spectacular Sangre de Cristo Mountains from Wheeler Peak.

NORTHERN UTAH
An unknown corner of the Rockies – sensational scenery packed into the Uinta Mountains and Wasatch Front.

Continental Divide

1:10,500,000

ELEVATION
12,000ft
9000ft
6000ft
4500ft
3000ft
0

Hiking in the Rocky Mountains
1st edition – June 2002

Published by
Lonely Planet Publications Pty Ltd ABN 36 005 607 983
90 Maribyrnong St, Footscray, Victoria 3011, Australia

Lonely Planet Offices
Australia Locked Bag 1, Footscray, Victoria 3011
USA 150 Linden St, Oakland, CA 94607
UK 10a Spring Place, London NW5 3BH
France 1 rue du Dahomey, 75011 Paris

Photographs
Many of the images in this guide are available for licensing from
Lonely Planet Images.
|e| lpi@lonelyplanet.com.au
|w| www.lonelyplanetimages.com

Main front cover photograph
Moon over the Grand Tetons, Wyoming (David Meunch/Corbis)

Small front cover photograph
Hiker in the Bitterroot Mountains, Montana (Clem Lindenmayer)

ISBN 1 74059 333 2

**Although the authors
and Lonely Planet try
to make the informa-
tion as accurate as
possible, we accept
no responsibility for
any loss, injury or
inconvenience sus-
tained by anyone
using this book.**

Contents

2 Contents

NORTHERN NEW MEXICO 288

GLOSSARY 302

INDEX 306

MAP LEGEND back page

METRIC CONVERSION inside back cover

The Hikes	Duration	Standard	Transport
Greater Glacier			
Swiftcurrent Mountain Lookout	7½–10 hours	moderate–hard	car, bus
Highline Trail/Ptarmigan Tunnel Loop	6 days	moderate–hard	car, bus
Iceberg Lake	5–6 hours	easy–moderate	car, bus
Grinnell Glacier	4–5½ hours	easy–moderate	car, bus
Gunsight Pass	2 days	moderate–hard	car, bus
Boulder Pass	4 days	moderate–hard	car, ferry
Carthew Lakes	5½–7 hours	moderate	car, bus
Avion Ridge Loop	8½–9 hours	moderate–hard	car, bus
Jewel Lakes Loop	4½–5½ hours	easy–moderate	car
Mt Aeneas	3–4 hours	moderate	car
Mollman Lakes	6–8 hours	moderate–hard	car
Eagle Pass Loop	2 days	hard	car
Chinese Wall Loop	6 days	moderate	car
Upper Holland Loop	6–7½ hours	moderate–hard	car
Central Idaho			
Bighorn Crags	2 days	moderate	car
Sawtooth Lake	5½–7½ hours	moderate	car
White Cloud Loop	4 days	moderate–hard	car
Bear Valley Lakes	4½–6 hours	easy–moderate	car
Mt Borah	7–10 hours	hard	car, bus
Southwest Montana			
Blodgett Canyon	5½–7 hours	easy–moderate	car
Trapper Peak	4¼–5½ hours	hard	car
Pintler Loop	3 days	moderate	car
Torrey Lake	7–9 hours	moderate	car
Greater Yellowstone			
Beartooth High Lakes	3 days	easy–moderate	car
Froze-to-Death Mountain	3 days	hard	car
Black Canyon	2 days	moderate	car
Mt Washburn & Sevenmile Hole	5½–6½ hours	easy–moderate	car
Fairy Falls & Twin Buttes	3–4 hours	easy	car
Bechler River	4 days	moderate	car
Heart Lake	2 days	easy	car
Paintbrush Divide Loop	3 days	moderate	car
Teton Crest Trail	4 days	moderate–hard	car, bus
Teton Glacier Overlook	5½ hours	moderate	car
Taggart & Bradley Lakes Loop	3 hours	easy	car

The Hikes *continued*	Duration	Standard	Transport
Central & Eastern Wyoming			
Devil Canyon	4½–6 hours	moderate	car
Cloud Peak	3 days	hard	car
Cirque of the Towers	2 days	moderate	car
Titcomb Basin	3 days	moderate	car
Laramie Peak	4–5½ hours	easy–moderate	car
Snowy Range Loop	2 days	easy–moderate	car
Northern Utah			
Kings Peak Loop	4 days	moderate	car
Mt Timpanogos	8–10½ hours	moderate–hard	car
Northern Colorado & the Front Range			
Odessa Lake	2 days	easy–moderate	car
Flattop Mountain	2 days	moderate–hard	car, bus
Glacier Gorge	4½–5½ hours	easy–moderate	car
Longs Peak	9½–13½ hours	hard	car
Lawn Lake	7–8 hours	moderate	car
Pawnee Pass	2 days	moderate	car
Arapaho Pass & Arapaho Glacier Trail	2 days	moderate–hard	car
Gilpin Lake & Gold Creek Circuit	6½–7½ hours	moderate	car
Mt Zirkel	2 days	moderate–hard	car
Central Colorado			
Maroon Bells Loop	4 days	moderate	car, bus
Conundrum Hot Springs	2 days	moderate	car
Missouri Lakes	4–5 hours	easy–moderate	car
Mt Elbert	5½–7 hours	moderate–hard	car
Mt Belford	6–7 hours	moderate–hard	car
Brown's Pass	5–7 hours	moderate	car
Southern Colorado			
Powderhorn Lakes	3¾–5¼ hours	easy	car
Uncompahgre Peak	4½–6½ hours	hard	car
Needle Mountains Loop	4 days	moderate–hard	train
Rainbow Hot Springs	2 days	easy–moderate	car
Comanche-Venable Loop	2 days	moderate	car
Blanca Peak	3 days	hard	car
Northern New Mexico			
Cruces Basin Loop	4¼–5¼ hours	easy–moderate	car
Wheeler Peak	7–10 hours	moderate	car, bus
Around Chimayosos Peak	3 days	moderate	car
Winsor-Skyline Loop	2 days	moderate–hard	car

The Maps

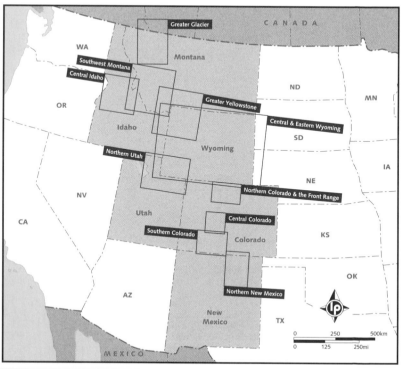

The Authors

Clem Lindenmayer
Clem has spent much of the past two decades exploring the earth's wildest mountain regions – pursuing a particular interest in alpine flora – on trips that have taken him to *almost* every continent (he still intends to trek across the Transantarctic Mountains). Clem authored Lonely Planet's *Walking in Switzerland, Trekking in the Patagonian Andes* and the Rocky Mountains chapter of *Hiking in the USA*. He has also helped update Lonely Planet guidebooks to China, South-East Asia and Europe.

Helen Fairbairn
A year spent teaching English on the French Caribbean island of Guadeloupe convinced Helen of the benefits of life in the sun, and she regularly escapes the dark winters of Ireland to rekindle her relationship with things more exotic. A mountain lover and a dedicated kayaker, the wild areas of the world seem to hold a particular attraction for her. This is Helen's third book for Lonely Planet.

Gareth McCormack
After finishing a degree in law in 1995 Gareth traveled, walked and climbed his way across Asia, Australia and New Zealand for 18 months. This trip inspired a radical career turnaround and he is now a writer and photographer based in Ireland. He is a regular contributor to the magazine *Walking World Ireland* and has co-authored five titles for Lonely Planet. Every year he tries to spend several months photographing wild and beautiful parts of the world.

FROM THE AUTHORS
Clem Lindenmayer Special thanks to the NPS and USFS staff for their consistent help and advice during my research.

Helen Fairbairn & Gareth McCormack Thanks first to the staff at Lonely Planet who helped out with queries and planning for this book: in particular Nick Tapp, Lindsay Brown and Sally Dillon. Thanks also to Clem Lindenmayer and to the multitude of park rangers and USFS staff who answered an array of obscure questions. The ground support provided by Diane and Dermot at home must also be acknowledged as an essential part of the operation. Helen would like to thank Sharon and Paul for company on hikes in Waterton, and Gareth would like to thank the grizzly he met in Glacier National Park for not attacking! Big thanks also to Aaron and Anita for their kindness and hospitality in London.

This Book

Avoiding angry bears, gallivanting around glaciers and climbing every mountain, the team of authors responsible for this 1st edition of *Hiking in the Rocky Mountains* was Clem Lindenmayer (coordinating author), who wrote the introductory chapters, as well as Central Idaho, Southwest Montana, Northern Utah, Southern Colorado, Northern New Mexico and part of Central & Eastern Wyoming; and Helen Fairbairn and Gareth McCormack, who together compiled Greater Glacier, Greater Yellowstone, Northern Colorado & the Front Range, Central Colorado and part of Central & Eastern Wyoming. Material from Lonely Planet's *Hiking in the USA* (1st edition) and *Rocky Mountains* (3rd edition) was used in this book.

From the Publisher

Back at base, the LP team responsible for the spit and polish included Eoin Dunlevy (coordinating cartographer/designer) and Jennifer Garrett (coordinating editor). Cartographic assistance was provided by Andrew Smith, Helen Rowley, Chris Klep and Karen Fry. Editorial assistance was provided by Andrew Bain, Miranda Wills, Angie Phelan and Janet Brunckhorst. Assembling and assisting with slides was the crew from Lonely Planet Images (LPI) and the cover was designed by Jamieson Gross. Handling administrative duties was Fiona Siseman. Making sure everything was up to LP standard and responsible for final checks were Glenn van der Knijff (senior cartographer/designer), Sally Dillon (senior editor) and Lindsay Brown (publishing manager). All deserve a relaxing soak in one of the Rockies' famous hot springs!

Foreword

ABOUT LONELY PLANET GUIDEBOOKS

The story begins with a classic travel adventure: Tony and Maureen Wheeler's 1972 journey across Europe and Asia to Australia. Useful information about the overland trail did not exist at that time, so Tony and Maureen published the first Lonely Planet guidebook to meet a growing need.

From a kitchen table, then from a tiny office in Melbourne (Australia), Lonely Planet has become the largest independent travel publisher in the world, an international company with offices in Melbourne, Oakland (USA), London (UK) and Paris (France).

Today Lonely Planet guidebooks cover the globe. There is an ever-growing list of books and there's information in a variety of forms and media. Some things haven't changed. The main aim is still to help make it possible for adventurous travelers to get out there – to explore and better understand the world.

At Lonely Planet we believe travelers can make a positive contribution to the countries they visit – if they respect their host communities and spend their money wisely. Since 1986 a percentage of the income from each book has been donated to aid projects and human rights campaigns.

UPDATES & READER FEEDBACK

Things change – prices go up, schedules change, good places go bad and bad places go bankrupt. Nothing stays the same. So, if you find things better or worse, recently opened or long-since closed, please tell us and help make the next edition even more accurate and useful.

Lonely Planet thoroughly updates each guidebook as often as possible – usually every two years, although for some destinations the gap can be longer. Between editions, up-to-date information is available in our free, quarterly *Planet Talk* newsletter and monthly email bulletin *Comet*. The *Upgrades* section of our website (**w** www.lonelyplanet.com) is also regularly updated by Lonely Planet authors, and the site's *Scoop* section covers news and current affairs relevant to travelers. Lastly, the *Thorn Tree* bulletin board and *Postcards* section carry unverified, but fascinating, reports from travelers.

Tell us about it! We genuinely value your feedback. A well-traveled team at Lonely Planet reads and acknowledges every email and letter we receive and ensures that every morsel of information finds its way to the relevant authors, editors and cartographers.

Everyone who writes to us will find their name listed in the next edition of the appropriate guidebook, and will receive the latest issue of *Comet* or *Planet Talk*. The very best contributions will be rewarded with a free guidebook.

We may edit, reproduce and incorporate your comments in Lonely Planet products such as guidebooks, websites and digital products, so let us know if you don't want your comments reproduced or your name acknowledged.

How to contact Lonely Planet:
Online: **e** talk2us@lonelyplanet.com.au, **w** www.lonelyplanet.com
Australia: Locked Bag 1, Footscray, Victoria 3011
UK: 10a Spring Place, London NW5 3BH
USA: 150 Linden St, Oakland, CA 94607

HIKING THROUGH THIS GUIDEBOOK

Hiking is an individual pursuit and we expect that people will use our guidebooks in individual ways. Whether you carry it in your backpack or read it as you hike along (not recommended near cliffs), a Lonely Planet hiking guide can point your wandering spirit in the right direction. Never forget, however, that the finest discoveries are those you make yourself.

What We've Packed All Lonely Planet guidebooks follow roughly the same path, including the hiking guides. The Facts about the Region chapter provides background information relevant to hikers, ranging from history to weather, as well as a detailed look at the plants and animals you're likely to encounter on the track. Facts for the Hiker deals with the hiking practicalities – the planning, red tape and resources. We also include a special Health & Safety chapter to help combat or treat those on-track nasties. The Getting There & Away and Getting Around chapters will help you make your travel plans.

The hiking chapters are divided into regions, encompassing the hikes in those areas. We start each hike with background, planning and how to get to/from the hike information. Each hike is detailed and highlights en route are included in the text. We also suggest where to rest your weary feet and fill your empty stomach. You will have earned it.

Maps These are a key element of any Lonely Planet guidebook, particularly hiking guides. The maps are printed in two colors, making route-finding a snap, and show everything from town locations to the peaks around you. We strive for compatability between word and image, so what you read in the text will invariably feature on the map. A legend is printed on the back page.

Navigating the Guidebook The traditional 'map and compass' for a Lonely Planet guidebook are the contents and index lists but, in addition, the hiking guides offer a comprehensive table of hikes, providing thumbnail information about every described hike, as well as a table of maps.

Lonely Planet gathers information for everyone who's curious about the planet – and especially for those who explore it firsthand. Through guidebooks, phrasebooks, activity guides, maps, literature, newsletters, image library, TV series and website we act as an information exchange for a worldwide community of travelers.

Introduction

Dividing the continent into the great Pacific and Atlantic (including the Arctic) watershed basins, the Rocky Mountains earn their title of the 'backbone of North America'. The US Rockies stretch from northern Montana to northern New Mexico, forming a broad and complex system of ranges and valleys.

Despite a steady encroachment of human infrastructure, the US Rockies remain the wildest and most pristine region in the Lower 48 states. These mountains constitute a large part of the country's natural heritage, with numerous unique and spectacular geological features – from the raw, glaciated ranges of northern Montana, to the volcanic phenomena of the Yellowstone country, Idaho's deeply eroded canyons, Colorado's concentration of 14,000ft peaks and New Mexico's vast, semiarid basins.

The Rockies' intact forest ecosystems, unpolluted rivers, wildlife rangelands and skies full of raptors represent one of the world's most important biosphere reserves. The Rockies are the birthplace of the national park system, an idea first conceived to protect the region's outstanding natural wonders. Today, more than one quarter of the protected wildlands in the Lower 48 are in the Rocky Mountains region, which boasts four of the country's great national parks: Glacier, Yellowstone, Grand Teton and Rocky Mountain.

An extensive network of hiking trails provides access to even the most remote, roadless areas throughout the Rocky Mountains. This guidebook aims to give a representative selection of the very best scenery and wildlife on offer.

US Rocky Mountains States

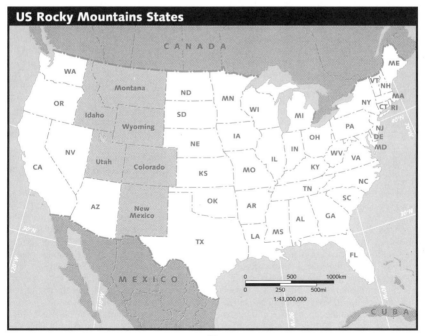

Facts about the Rocky Mountains

HISTORY
The First Americans

The first humans are believed to have reached North America from eastern Siberia more than 30,000 years ago during the Pleistocene Ice Age. Sea levels, as much as 450ft lower than today, allowed them to cross the broad ice-free plain of 'Beringia' (today's Bering Strait) to Alaska. There appear to have been separate waves of migration, the last of which ended some 12,000 years ago.

As they pushed down into the area that now comprises the Lower 48 US states, these first hunter-gatherers found a land of abundant wildlife. Spectacular megafauna (large, land-dwelling animals) included bear-sized beavers, enormous camels, giant moose, mastodons (extinct mammals related to elephants) and even bison that stood almost 20ft high. Archaeologists have identified two distinct cultures (known as Clovis and Folsom) among these ice-age hunter-gatherers, largely based on the differently shaped stone spearheads they fashioned.

Rising global temperatures around 9000 years ago led to rapid melting of the North American ice sheet. The combination of a warmer, drier climate and (probably) overhunting by humans caused a collapse of the ice-age ecosystem, wiping out almost all of the large game species on which these cultures depended. This catastrophe was the catalyst for social diversification and cultural specialization among the early peoples of the Rocky Mountains.

On the vast grasslands of the Great Plains, nomadic tribes began to follow the large, free-roaming herds of bison, which they killed by driving the animals over cliffs at so-called *pishkun*, or buffalo jumps. The peoples of the semiarid regions to the southwest gradually established agricultural settlements based on maize, pumpkins and beans. From around AD 900 the Pueblo peoples, including the Anasazi of southwest Colorado, constructed multistory dwellings that were centered around a subterranean kiva, where ceremonies were held. The best-preserved example of such Pueblo settlements is at Mesa Verde, where hundreds of families once lived. Mysteriously, the Pueblo towns were abandoned around 1200, perhaps due to a prolonged drought.

None of the tribes were truly at home in the high ranges of the Rocky Mountains – the winter was simply too harsh. Rather, tribes from the surrounding plains established summer camps in sheltered foothill valleys, making lengthy forays into the high mountains to hunt or collect medicinal substances and food.

Early European Influence

Well before their arrival in the west, Europeans had already begun to profoundly influence traditional cultures of the region.

From the late 1600s, the first tribes of the forested Great Lakes region acquired firearms. With this enormous advantage in battle they forced their traditional enemies southwest into the sparse Great Plains, causing a chain reaction of displacement that gradually engulfed the entire Rocky Mountains region. Fleeing Dakota (Sioux) drove established Mandan and Hidatsa tribes into the upper Missouri. In turn, Cheyenne and Arapaho tribes fled southwest into the Front Range of modern-day Wyoming and Colorado and pushed the local Kiowa tribe south, where it came into conflict with recently arrived Comanche. Newly armed Blackfoot people forced the Shoshone people off traditional tribal lands into the mountains of today's northern Montana. Almost every tribe in the region found itself forced to live in a new and unfamiliar environment.

The reintroduction of the horse (which had actually evolved in America but became extinct there at the end of the last Ice Age) by the Spanish around 1600 resulted in further upheaval. By the mid-1700s virtually all the Plains tribes, particularly the Comanche and the Dakota, had adopted horses and were already expert riders. The greater mobility, speed and pack-carrying capacity of horses made the Plains tribes true masters of the sparse grasslands, enabling them to cross vast, waterless areas, as well as follow and hunt the bison much more easily.

Europeans also introduced deadly foreign diseases. Long before the appalling massacres at the hands of settlers or the US Army, whole tribes were wiped out by epidemics of cholera, measles or smallpox.

Exploration

The Spaniards, pushing north from Mexico in the second half of the 16th century, were the first Europeans to reach the Rocky Mountains. They founded the city of Santa Fe, and pushed as far north as the Arkansas River. The Domínguez-Escalante Expedition of 1775–76 explored Utah and much of the Colorado Plateau. From the early 18th century French explorers and fur traders from eastern Canada reconnoitered the northern Great Plains. By the early 19th century, Spanish authority extended over Arizona, California, New Mexico, Nevada and Utah, as well as large parts of Colorado, Montana and Wyoming.

In 1803 President Thomas Jefferson accepted Napoleon's offer to sell France's vast, but poorly defined, territory of Louisiana to the US. The 830,000-sq-mile Louisiana Purchase – initially kept secret, as Napoleon feared the ire of his Spanish allies – included present-day Montana, most of Wyoming and eastern Colorado. Jefferson almost immediately commissioned an expedition to explore the new territory, commanded by Meriwether Lewis and William Clark (see the boxed text 'The Lewis & Clark Expedition', p16).

Lewis and Clark were the most successful of the early US explorers of the west. In 1806 Lieutenant Zebulon Pike led an expedition into the Front Range of today's Colorado, but the following year he was arrested by Spanish police on his way to Santa Fe. In 1807–08, John Colter, former member of the Lewis and Clark Expedition, explored the wonderful natural phenomena of the Yellowstone region. In 1820 Major Stephen Long led a scientific expedition to Colorado's Front Range, which included an ascent of Pikes Peak, but like Pike he produced unreliable accounts that described the west as a 'Great American Desert', discouraging settlement for decades. In the early 1820s, the trader William Becknell opened the first overland route into the Rocky Mountains region – the Santa Fe Trail from St Louis to Santa Fe in newly independent Mexico. Soon after, Jedediah Smith found a feasible westward passage via South Pass on the Continental Divide in present-day Wyoming.

High demand for beaver pelts (used to make fashionable European gentlemen's hats) attracted and sustained many Euro-American fur trappers. These 'mountain men' were often the first white people to visit many remote valleys and perhaps climb some of the peaks in the Rockies. In 1825 the first annual 'rendezvous' was held at Henry's Fork on Wyoming's Green River. Although these summer gatherings were also attended by suppliers, Native Americans and even early tourists, the rendezvous was largely an excuse for mountain men to do some hard drinking and showing off. With almost total collapse of the fur industry in the early 1840s (as hat fashion shifted from beaver to silk), the rendezvous became obsolete.

Between 1842 and 1845 the surveyor Captain John Frémont led several major expeditions into the Great Basin, crossing the Wasatch Range to reach Utah's Great Salt Lake. Defeat in the 1848 Mexican-American War forced Mexico to cede all of its vast northern territories, including Utah, New Mexico, southwestern Wyoming and most of Colorado, to the US. Two years earlier, the British had recognized US sovereignty over parts of Montana and Wyoming.

During the 1860s and '70s the federal government sponsored four major scientific expeditions into its new lands. Led by Clarence King (1867–78), Ferdinand Hayden (1867–72), George M Wheeler (1869–79) and John Wesley Powell (1869–79), these

The Lewis & Clark Expedition

William Clark | Meriwether Lewis

The ostensible purpose of the Lewis and Clark Expedition of 1804–06 was to seek a 'Northwest Passage' to the Pacific Ocean. Although a chain of 'stony mountains' was known to exist in the west, the magnitude and vastness of the Rocky Mountains had not been suspected – President Thomas Jefferson even assumed the existence of an all-water route to the Pacific.

Lewis and Clark set out from St Louis on May 14, 1804, pushing up the Missouri River, past the spectacular White Cliffs and the Great Falls of the Missouri. In August and September 1805 the expedition made an arduous crossing of the rugged Bitterroot Mountains, first via Lehmi Pass on the Continental Divide, then north over Lost Trail Pass and finally west across Lolo Pass. Lewis and Clark continued west down the Clearwater, Snake and Columbia Rivers to reach the Pacific Ocean on November 15, 1805. After overwintering near the mouth of the Columbia River, the expedition recrossed the Bitterroots and explored several upper tributaries of the Missouri. Upon their return to St Louis on September 23, 1806, Lewis and Clark received a heroes' welcome.

Lewis and Clark recorded the natural history and inhabitants of the west. They were the first Euro-Americans to describe and name hundreds of animals and plants, including bighorn sheep, grizzly bears and prairie dogs, and made contact with numerous Native American peoples. The expedition was accompanied by Sacagawea, the teenage Shoshone wife of a French trapper, who acted as an interpreter and helped gain vital assistance from the Shoshone and Nez Perce tribes. Despite bad weather, illness, malnutrition, rough terrain, dangerous wildlife and hostile tribes, only one member of the expedition died (of a ruptured appendix) during the epic 2½-year, 8000mi journey.

'Great Surveys' produced the first reliable maps of the Rocky Mountains and Great Basin. Hayden's expedition brought the uniqueness of Yellowstone to public attention, convincing Congress to establish it as the world's first national park in 1872.

Settlement

Resolution of the national sovereignty issue in 1848, along with the outbreak of the California gold rush the following year, greatly swelled the numbers of westbound settlers. Few of these 'overlanders' viewed the Rocky

Mountains region as much more than a transit corridor, however, and settlement was initially slow and sporadic. (An early exception was the Mormons, whose leader, Brigham Young, had arrived in Utah in 1847 to found Salt Lake City.) From the late 1850s, travel and postal services improved with the introduction of the Pony Express and overland coach routes.

Following the discovery of gold near Denver in 1859, a minerals boom spread throughout the region. Mining became the mainstay of many areas of the Rockies, but the industry has always been prone to severe fluctuations and eventual exhaustion of ore. Ranchers stocked the emptying Great Plains with cattle and sheep, but the largely semiarid country could not support large populations of livestock. The completion of transcontinental railroads from the late 1860s opened up the Rocky Mountains region to further settlement and development of its extractive (including lumber) industries. Congress encouraged settlement by enacting a wide variety of laws, including the Homestead Act of 1862, which granted 160 acres of public land to settlers after five years of residence.

After the massacre of the Cheyenne people at Colorado's Sand Creek in 1864, warfare gradually spread between the US Army and Native Americans. Despite notable battle successes, the tribes were overwhelmed by the vastly greater numbers and resources of the US Army. Native American hostility led the US government to build forts throughout the west to protect miners, overlanders and settlers. Huge reservations were also established for the tribes, but, without exception, these were steadily reduced in size or moved to less desirable areas. Bison were slaughtered in their millions – ostensibly for their hides, although destruction of the immense herds was probably tacit government policy aimed at depriving the Plains tribes of their sustenance – and by 1883 bison were almost extinct. When, in 1890, the US Census declared that 'the frontier has closed', Americans began to realize that the resources of the west were not limitless.

Conservation & Land Use

From the late 19th century, concern about uncontrolled exploitation of the Rockies' natural resources led to the early conservation movement, which then brought about a profound change in land management. Its advocates were as diverse as John Muir, who emphasized the spiritual value of wilderness, and Theodore Roosevelt, who believed that wildlands should serve both commercial and recreational needs.

Public lands were increasingly withdrawn from sale or settlement, particularly in the Rocky Mountains region, and used instead to establish forest reserves, wildlife refuges or national parks. Government regulation of hunting and fishing was introduced. In 1905 the United States Forest Service (USFS) was created; its counterpart and competitor, the National Park Service (NPS), was set up 11 years later. Congress also enacted laws strictly regulating commercial exploitation of public lands, including the Mineral Leasing Act of 1920 and the Taylor Grazing Act of 1934.

Wildland recreation rapidly grew in popularity during the early decades of the 20th century, largely due to increased prosperity and higher car ownership. In 1912 the Colorado Mountain Club, still the largest in the Rockies, was founded in Denver. Several new national parks were established in the first decades of the 20th century – Rocky Mountain (1916), Grand Teton (1929) and Glacier (1931). During the Depression years of the mid-1930s, the Civilian Conservation Corps (CCC) constructed thousands of miles of new hiking trails and other infrastructure in national parks and forests. The Bureau of Land Management (BLM) was created in 1946 to coordinate the 'multiple use' of public land.

In the mid-1950s, conservationists led by the Sierra Club fought successfully to stop a large dam at Echo Park in Utah's Dinosaur National Monument. Decades of lobbying by the Wilderness Society and others finally convinced Congress to pass the Wilderness Act of 1964, which gave primitive, roadless areas on public land permanent protection. In 1976 the Land Policy and Management Act officially declared an end to the further sale of public lands. The Reagan administration's *President's Commission on Americans Outdoors* of 1987 led to the establishment of National Scenic Byways and Recreational Trails programs, as well as the federally funded acquisition of privately owned wildlands. In January 2001 the outgoing Clinton administration announced long-term protection for 93,750 sq miles (around one third) of US national forests, but this proposal was shelved by the new Bush administration.

Since the 1980s, economic and social patterns have changed fundamentally throughout the Rocky Mountains. Many previously agricultural or lumber-based towns now rely heavily on tourists and outdoor recreationists – anglers, horseback riders, hikers, hunters and skiers. Resettlement from other parts of the US – often by people attracted to the region for aesthetic rather than economic reasons – has produced major population growth in most urban and many rural areas. Former cattle and sheep ranches are being turned into 'dude ranches' that cater to paying guests, or are subdivided into residential 'ranchettes'. A gulf in outlook and lifestyle often exists between recently arrived outsiders and long-time residents.

GEOGRAPHY

The Rocky Mountains extend some 3000mi through western North America, from the Cassiar Mountains near Canada's border with Alaska to the Sangre de Cristo Mountains of northern New Mexico. The southern half of the Rocky Mountains (although well over half of the Rockies' total area) lies within the US and is the focus of this guidebook.

Key Rocky Mountains states are Montana, Wyoming and Colorado, but major outliers extend deep into Idaho and Utah.

Geographers usually divide the US Rockies into three – northern, middle and southern – sections, which are offset slightly west-to-east and have considerable latitudinal overlap.

Northern US Rockies

The northern US Rockies extend south-southwest from the Canadian border through

Definitions of the Rockies

According to the narrowest definition, the Rocky Mountains consist only of those ranges crossed by the Continental Divide. A somewhat broader definition includes all the main mountain ranges of Montana, Wyoming and Colorado, but still excludes important ranges like the Bitterroots, Bighorns and Uintas. The broadest definition – used in this guidebook – includes all the 'cordilleran' ranges between the Great Plains to the east and the Columbia Plateau, Great Basin and Colorado Plateau to the west.

central-eastern Idaho and western Montana. They are lower than the middle and southern Rockies, with only a few summits rising much above 12,000ft, including Mt Borah (12,662ft) and Leatherman Peak (12,228ft), both in Idaho's Lost River Range.

The western ranges of the northern US Rockies form the higher eastern rim of the Columbia Plateau. The ranges consist of the Salmon River and Clearwater Mountains, as well as the more rugged Lost River and Sawtooth Ranges at their south, and are largely drained by the tributaries of the Snake River.

Further east are the Bitterroot Mountains, which form most of the Idaho-Montana border. The Rocky Mountains Trench, which extends 1000mi south from Canada's Yukon as far as the Bitterroot Valley in southwestern Montana, divides these western ranges from the mighty Front Ranges of the Greater Glacier region, which stand on, or close to, the Continental Divide. To the south, the Tobacco Root, Anaconda and Pioneer Ranges are cut by broad valleys up to 40mi wide. The eastern slopes of the northern US Rockies are drained by the Missouri and its upper tributaries, chiefly the Yellowstone River.

Middle Rockies

The middle Rockies (not synonymous with the *central* Rockies) extend south-southwest from Greater Yellowstone and northern Wyoming's isolated Bighorn Mountains into northeastern Utah. The middle Rockies' western slopes mark the eastern rim of the vast Great Basin (not to be confused with Wyoming's Great Divide Basin), a high, semiarid plateau extending west to the Sierra Nevada. The middle Rockies are higher than the mountains to their north but are also much less continuous, with their major ranges often separated by relatively low hills or even rolling prairies.

The middle Rockies' northwestern edge includes the volcanic Yellowstone Plateau and the Absaroka Range to its east. To the south are the granitic Teton and Wind River Ranges, with the middle Rockies' highest summits – Grand Teton (13,770ft) and Gannet Peak (13,804ft). Further south, the Wasatch Range fronts Great Salt Lake, intersecting with the Uinta Mountains – the Rockies' only west-to-east mountain chain – to form an 'L' where Utah meets southwestern Wyoming.

Southern Rockies
The extent of the southern Rockies is from Wyoming's Great Divide Basin – a broad, undrained depression completely enclosed by the Continental Divide – to as far south as northern New Mexico. They form the widest and highest section of the US Rockies, with numerous peaks rising to well above 14,000ft. The southern Rockies are the source of the eastward-flowing Rio Grande and Colorado River, which drain into the Pacific. The southern Rockies' western slopes gradually go over into the Colorado Plateau, a vast basin dissected by deep canyons stretching through southern Utah into northern Arizona.

The southern Rockies are dominated by two broad bands of mountains separated by several large basins, or 'parks', including South Park (at the headwaters of South Platte River) and the San Luis Valley (at around 7500ft the widest valley of its height in the world). The western band consists of the Sierra Madre, Elk, West Elk and Sawatch Ranges (the latter has the Rockies' highest summit, Mt Elbert, at 14,433ft); its southwestern end being formed by the San Juan Mountains, an irregular and rugged plateau

The Front Range

The Front Range extends along the eastern edge of the Rocky Mountains through Montana, Wyoming and Colorado. Geologically, it marks the easternmost extent of vertical uplifting in the ongoing mountain-building process. The Front Range can appear as little more than a high ridge among low foothills or it may rise like a massive blue wall almost directly out of the flat plains – the abrupt Colorado Front is particularly dramatic. In Utah, the western edge of the Rockies is characterized by the spectacular Wasatch Front Range.

RICHARD CUMMINS

The snowy peaks of Mt Olympus in Utah's Wasatch Range, the Rockies' western edge.

of volcanic origin crossed by high ranges with a dozen 14ers (peaks over 14,000ft). The eastern band takes in the Laramie, Medicine Bow, Wet and Sangre de Cristo Ranges, as well as the Front Range.

GEOLOGY
The creation of the Rockies began around 100 million years ago as the supercontinent of Pangea began to break apart. The newly separated North American plate drifted west (as it continues to do), gathering in its path isolated islands of earth crust (which compose California and much of the West Coast today).

In the so-called Laramide Orogeny, beginning around 60 million years ago, the North American plate started to collide with the Pacific plate. Under the enormous force, its thick, solid continental crust rode over the thinner and more brittle oceanic crust of the Pacific plate, forcing the latter downward in a process known as subduction. Compressed deep within the earth's semifluid mantle, molten sections of the subducted oceanic crust now pushed back upward.

Unable to withstand this enormous pressure, the continental crust itself uplifted in numerous places. Associated buckling and fracturing created the Rockies' complex system of ranges and caused its older sediments to slide over younger rock strata. Major volcanic eruptions occurred as molten mantle was forced through cracks in the continental crust, raising the mountains further as whole valleys were filled in by mineral-rich deposits. The intense volcanic activity seen today in Yellowstone National Park, which sits above an unusually large bubble of molten magma (known as a 'hot spot') lying just below the earth's surface, shows that this process is continuing.

While the formation of the Rocky Mountains progressed, an ancient sea on their eastern side was also gradually uplifted and filled in by erosion debris from the mountains. This exposed the thick marine sediments now widespread in the Rockies of Montana and more isolated ranges further south, such as the Maroon Bells of Colorado. As it shrank, the eastern sea gave way to a vast swampy floodplain that supported diverse vegetation and wildlife. The thick deposits of organic matter laid down during this period are the origin of the abundant coal and oil resources found on the eastern plains. The steady rise of the Rockies, however, formed an increasingly impenetrable barrier to rain clouds from the Pacific, and the eastern plains gradually turned into the dry, sparsely vegetated prairies seen today.

The Rocky Mountains were transformed by the (Pleistocene) cycle of ice ages, beginning some two million years ago. Enormous glaciers choked all but the higher ranges, grinding away at the bedrock to create deep, U-shaped valleys. Starting some 10,000 years ago, the large glaciers began to melt and the moraine (glacial debris) they left as they receded dammed up the rivers to create tens of thousands of lakes and tarns. See also the boxed text 'Glaciers & Glacial Landforms' (p91).

The Rockies' rugged features are a result of their young geological age and recent massive erosion. By contrast, the Appalachian Mountains to the east, which were created more than 150 million years earlier by a similar process, are lower and more rounded from eons of relentless erosion. The Rockies' position as a secondary range – well back from the point of contact between the Pacific and North American tectonic plates – has also given the Rocky Mountains a more complex topography than that of the Cascade-Sierra Nevada Ranges along the Pacific coast. Numerous ancient and recent secondary seismic faults run through the Rockies. Localized (though sometimes catastrophic) earthquakes occur as tension in the earth is released by the sudden slide of a relatively minor fault.

The Rocky Mountains have many diverging outliers with a complex system of ridges and isolated buttes (lone hills or mountains with steep sides). The Rockies' eastern slope is fringed by the Great Plains, composed of massive deposits of erosion (including glacial) material washed down from the mountains. This seemingly endless expanse of sparse, grassy steppes continues east, gradually dropping in elevation to meet the Mississippi River.

The Continental Divide – the ridgeline that sheds water either west to the Pacific or east to the Atlantic – wanders erratically through the Rocky Mountains, often a long way from the highest summits and ranges. This fuels debate as to which mountains should be considered part of the Rockies proper – see the boxed text 'Definitions of the Rockies', p18).

CLIMATE

Climate in the Rocky Mountains is determined primarily by altitude, latitude and proximity to the (Pacific) coast. The Rockies run roughly perpendicular to, and hence act as a massive barrier against, the prevailing westerly airstream. Even in summer,

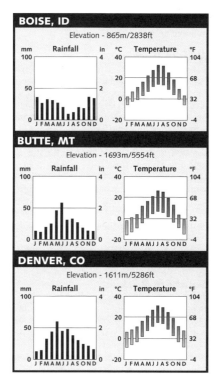

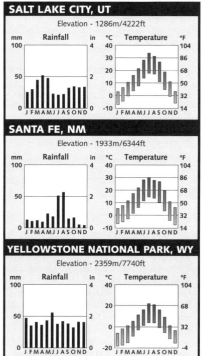

snow can fall anywhere in the Rockies, but much more frequent are thunderstorms that bring cold, drenching rain or hail and lightning, a major cause of forest fires. The Continental Divide has a major influence on microclimates and local weather, as storms drop most of their moisture as rain or snow on its western slopes, leaving ranges further east in a rain shadow. Individual mountains and ranges complicate the general pattern by casting their own rain shadows.

An elevation increase of 1000ft typically brings a temperature drop of 4°F or more – the climatic equivalent of a shift 200mi north. On a high summit the temperature may be 50°F or so cooler than at the valley floor. Above 9000ft, nightly frosts may occur at any time of the year.

Microclimate is also influenced by the period of exposure to the sun. The average temperature difference between shaded and sunny sites increases markedly with rising elevation – a south-facing slope may be as much as 50°F warmer than a north-facing slope. This explains why tiny, remnant glaciers still endure in sun-sheltered cirques and couloirs throughout the Rockies. Solar radiation also increases with both elevation and southerliness (proximity to the equator), and is at its most intense high up in the southern Rockies in midsummer.

Ridges and mountain slopes are especially exposed to winds, and tend to dry out more quickly – but due to their greater exposure they may also receive heavier falls of rain and snow. Areas on the Rockies' eastern slopes are also effected by the Chinook (see the boxed text, p22).

These varying influences make weather in the Rockies unpredictable and prone to rapid

The Chinook

The Rocky Mountains' famous Chinook is a warm westerly wind that is most pronounced in winter, although it blows at any time of the year. The Chinook occurs when a powerful airstream from the Pacific pushes across the Rockies, cooling as it climbs their western slopes and releasing its moisture as rain or snow. As the wind drops down the Rockies' eastern slopes, it rapidly compresses and warms. This brings a rapid and dramatic temperature rise – in extreme cases as much as 51°F, with a drop in relative humidity of 40% or more. For this reason, winter temperatures along the higher western edge of the Great Plains are actually somewhat warmer than along the plains' eastern side.

Locals generally welcome the respite from the winter chill brought by the Chinook. It particularly pleases ranchers, as it clears snow from cattle pastures, but the Chinook's effects can be devastating for plants and animals that rely on snow for insulation and protection from predators. The temporary warmth can also confuse vegetation, which may sprout only to be killed in the next freeze. Some people complain of headaches or the 'shakes' whenever the Chinook blows, while others find it energizes them – apparently due to the positively charged particles it carries.

change. For more specific local information, refer to Climate in the regional chapters.

Northern US Rockies

The northern US Rockies have a closer proximity to the Pacific Ocean and generally lower elevations, with few peaks rising much above 10,000ft. This gives them a moister but relatively moderate climate, with cold, snowy winters and cool summers interrupted by repeated thunderstorms and sporadic storm fronts. The prevailing westerly winds dump up to 100 inches of precipitation on the higher ranges annually, most of it falling as snow, which often supports dense rainforests on slopes west of the Continental Divide.

Temperatures in the northern Rockies average around 36.5°F.

Middle Rockies

In the middle Rockies, the Pacific influence is marginal (confined to the higher western ranges of the Greater Yellowstone region), and a predominantly dry continental climate prevails. Summers are warm to hot, while winters long and cold.

Significant precipitation falls as snow. Isolated high ranges stand as climatic islands, receiving virtually all of the moisture that westerly storms bring to the region, while the parched lowlands receive minimal precipitation. The ranges of southwestern Wyoming and Utah are particularly exposed to the searing, dry winds that blow from the Great Basin.

Average temperatures in the middle Rockies range around 43°F.

Southern Rockies

The southern Rockies are warmer and drier than the ranges further north, with hot summers. Overall precipitation levels are lower with a relatively even seasonal distribution, but this can vary widely from year to year. Summer precipitation comes mainly from convection thunderstorms and periodic advances of moist, tropical air from the south, while northwestern storms bring the snow in winter.

Although their higher altitude partly compensates for their closer proximity to the equator, the southern Rockies – where a valley may be higher than 9000ft – lie far inland and have a pronounced 'continental' climate with wide temperature fluctuations. These factors largely eliminate excessively high humidity, even when a midsummer thunderstorm is building up, which makes for less 'sticky' conditions in hot weather. Average temperatures in the southern Rockies are around 50°F.

The southern Rockies' more southerly latitude and greater elevations (and hence thinner atmosphere) do mean they also receive higher levels of ultraviolet radiation, which can lead to faster and/or more severe sunburn.

WATCHING WILDLIFE

PLANTS

Although hikers will note significant variations in the plant species found locally around the greater Rocky Mountains region, the overall patterns of forest composition are surprisingly consistent.

VEGETATION ZONES

Elevation is the most important factor determining which plant species are likely to be present. Botanists generally distinguish four vegetation zones in the Rocky Mountains – foothills, montane, subalpine and alpine. These zones are not strictly defined, and there is considerable overlap between them. The altitude and width of each zone also increases progressively as you move from the northern (Idaho-Montana) to the southern (New Mexico) Rockies.

The **foothills** of the Rocky Mountains (3000–4000ft in the north, 5500–8000ft in the south) are a transition zone between the dry prairies and the timbered montane zone. Here, plants take hold best on north-facing slopes, which are less exposed to the sun and hence retain moisture for longer. The vegetation is often scrubby, with light woodland, sparse grasses or sagebrush meadows.

In the **montane** zone (3500–5000ft in the north, 7500–9500ft in the south), warmer south-facing slopes (where winter snow melts more quickly) support botanically diverse forests with numerous berry and shrub species in a damp understory.

The **subalpine** zone (4500–6500ft in the north, 9000–11,500ft in the south) is dominated by so-called fir-spruce forest. While there are generally fewer species present, the subalpine zone is often wilder and more rugged.

The **alpine** zone (above 6000ft in the north, 11,000ft in the south) takes in all areas higher than tree line. The arctic-type 'tundra' vegetation includes a myriad of wildflowers, which are at their most magnificent from early June to late July.

WILDFLOWERS

Admiring and identifying wildflowers is one of the most pleasurable activities hikers can undertake. A breathtaking variety of native (and some exotic) wildflowers are found in the Rockies. The best time to see wildflowers is from June to July, although some species (like gentians) tend to be at their best in August. Below is a tiny selection of some of the more common, most striking and/or favorite wildflower species.

The flamboyant, yellow **alpine sunflower** is an interesting perennial of the high tundra. The San Juan Mountains of Colorado are one of the best regions to see it. Unlike true sunflowers, it stands less than 1ft high and continuously faces east – the direction of the rising sun. The alpine sunflower saves its reserves for many years until it can bloom, then sets seed and dies.

CLEM LINDENMAYER

Alpine sunflower

23

Beargrass is a hardy perennial found in well-drained montane and subalpine clearings. Fragrant, white, star-like flowers cluster around a central, 4ft-high stalk. Beargrass (actually a member of the lily family) has waxy, blade-like leaves that are tender and nutritious in spring, when they are eaten by bears.

The Rocky Mountains have more than a dozen species of **gentian** (usually pronounced 'jen-shun' in North America). Most have trumpet-like flowers that are at least partially blue or purple in color. They tend to bloom much later than most other Rockies wildflowers. The pretty arctic gentian has trumpeted, greenish-white flowers with purple stripes, and – like most of its cousins – prefers moist, open sites like alpine bogs or tundra slopes.

Columbines in the Rockies come in variants of blue, red, white and yellow, and are typically found at the edges of small, shaded clearings. The especially attractive Colorado columbine has purple-white flowers with delicate long spurs, resembling a bird in flight. The nectar in the spur tips attracts butterflies and hummingbirds.

CLEM LINDENMAYER

Beargrass

Fireweed is a perennial that grows as a single stem up to 8ft tall, topped by clusters of pink, four-petal flowers about an inch in diameter. As its name suggests, fireweed is a vigorous opportunist that typically colonizes recently burnt areas. Not surprisingly, this species is also found right across Europe and Siberia growing up to (sometimes well above) tree line.

The **globeflower** has dish-shaped flowers with five creamy (some-times pinkish) petals around a yellow center. It grows in waterlogged alpine areas such as stream banks, where it is often found in association with the similar-looking marsh marigold.

The succulent shoots of **Indian hellebore** (also commonly known as the corn lily) push up out of the melting snow in early summer, and quickly grow into a proud, 7ft-high stalk with large leather leaves and crowned by maize-like flower tassels. This plant, mainly found on moist, subalpine slopes, is extremely poisonous – Native Americans used it as a powerful insecticide – and hikers should even avoid drinking water that Indian hellebore grows in.

ANTHONY PHELAN

Fireweed

Scores of species of **Indian paintbrush** are found in the Rockies. They generally have a tightly packed flower head, sometimes vaguely reminiscent of a small artichoke. Most are reddish in color, but yellow and white varieties are also fairly common. Indian paintbrush hybridize readily to produce more variations in their form and color, making it hard even for botanists to identify individual species. Indian paintbrushes are semi-parasitic, often tapping the roots of their neighbors to draw nourishment.

Many species of **lupine** are found throughout the Rockies, generally favoring dry, open slopes from the foothills to the alpine zone. Lupines have palmate leaves and produce purplish-blue flowers that set into seed pods (some of which are poisonous).

The **yellow glacier lily** (also called dogtooth violet and snow lily) is a perennial subalpine to alpine species that thrives where winter snow lies longer. In early summer the bulb produces several bright yellow flowers with six petals curled upward. In places yellow glacier lilies cover entire tundra slopes, which bears dig over to extract the edible bulbs.

ANTHONY PHELAN

Lupine

SHRUBS

These small woody plants may grow as heaths, form thickets, or stand as single bushes on slopes and in meadows. Below are a few of the Rockies' main shrub species.

The **shrubby cinquefoil** grows in meadows from the foothills to the tundra, sometimes in association with sagebrush. Throughout summer, this multibranched bush up to 4ft high is covered in yellow, buttercup-like flowers with five petals (the name 'cinquefoil' comes from the French meaning 'five-leaf'). Both livestock and native mammals, such as deer, bighorn sheep and mountain goats, eat the foliage only when no other food is available, so nibbled cinquefoil bushes are a useful indication of overgrazing.

Several dozen species of small willow are found in the Rockies, but their diversity often makes precise taxonomical classification impossible. Willows can be identified by their typical fluffy-silky 'catkin' flowers, that look a bit like small bottle brushes. **Dwarf willows**, such as the tiny arctic willow, barely reach a few inches in height, and creep along heat-storing alpine rocks to form 'mats'. **Shrub willows**, including the common gray-leafed willow, form thickets along subalpine and alpine stream basins.

The large **blueberry** genus, includes species locally known as bilberry, cranberry, grouseberry, huckleberry and whortleberry. Almost all produce – in widely varying abundance – small, round fruits of bright red to deep purple that sustain bears and other wildlife throughout the Rockies. One of the most common species is the dwarf blueberry, which typically grows in lodgepole pine forest. It forms low mats with an enticingly fruity fragrance (even when there are very few berries to pick).

Junipers are cedar-like, aromatic conifers that generally thrive in dry, well-drained sites. Creeping juniper is a ground-hugging plant most common in the northern Rockies. Rocky Mountain juniper can grow to the size of a small tree, and older shrubs (which may reach 1500 years) are typically gnarled and knotted. Birds feed on juniper 'berries', allowing the seed to sprout by removing its fleshy covering. Two similar larger shrub species, oneseed juniper and Utah juniper, are found only in the southern Rockies.

The collective name for several strongly aromatic species of the wormwood genus, **sagebrush** grows on lowland prairies, foothills and drier montane meadows. Native hoofed animals and livestock shun the bitter foliage, so overgrazing tends to favor the spread of sagebrush. Hikers, on the other hand, enjoy the rich fragrance that wafts up as they cross a sagebrush meadow.

The **thimbleberry** (also called salmonberry) is a typical understory shrub found in moist, semi-shaded sites – such as along forest trails. It has thornless canes and vine-like leaves. In August it produces a small cluster of edible red berries with a fleshy seedy texture and sourish taste not unlike raspberries.

TREES

The harsher climatic conditions at higher elevations strongly favor coniferous tree species. With the partial exception of aspen, conifers

CLEM LINDENMAYER

Thimbleberry

dominate the forests of the Rocky Mountains. Pines are especially well represented, with two-needle, three- and five-needle species.

A beautiful, subalpine poplar species, **aspen** has radiant silver-white bark and rounded leaves that 'tremble' in the mountain breeze. Aspen foliage turns a striking orange-gold for just a few weeks in fall. It is a regeneration species that tends to reproduce by sending out root runners rather than by seeding, so a stand of aspen is likely to consist mainly of clones from an original parent tree.

Not a true fir at all, **Douglas fir** is a tall, adaptable and extremely wide-spread 'false hemlock', whose natural habitat ranges from the foothills to the subalpine zone and from very dry to quite moist locations. Douglas fir has flattened, irregularly arranged needles, four-inch-long cones with distinctive three-toothed bracts protruding between the scales, and thick, corky bark that protects it from fire. It is an outstanding lumber tree.

Firs bear a superficial resemblance to spruces, but can be easily differentiated by their flat, blunt needles and cones that point upward (like Christmas candles) on its upper branches. Easily the most abundant and widespread fir species in the Rockies, the subalpine fir is usually found in close association with Engelmann and/or blue spruce. Subalpine fir has characteristic silvery-gray bark with horizontal blister scars that often become cracked on older trees. Rocky Mountain white fir is found in the montane zone of Utah, Colorado and New Mexico, and has flatter needles more inclined to curl upward than to radiate around the branch as those of the subalpine fir.

Gambel oak, a very small, deciduous broad-leaved tree, forms dense thickets throughout much of the Rocky Mountains foothills of Utah, Colorado and New Mexico. Its starchy acorns provide important fodder for squirrels and other native animals.

Two species of **hemlock** are found in the Rockies of Idaho and Montana. The western hemlock is a very tall tree with yellowish needles arranged in two opposing rows (like a horizontal 'V' on either side of the branchlet) and tiny cones just one inch long. Mountain hemlock can be casually mistaken for Douglas fir, as its needles and cones are comparable in size and form, although its bark is more reddish and less rough.

Larch are deciduous conifers, and in the fall their needles turn a bright gold and drop off. Two larch species are found in the Rockies only as far south as Idaho and Montana. Western larch has needles up to two inches long in bunches of 12 to 40. Western larch is a montane forest tree that grows to 150ft, and Native Americans tapped its slightly bitter syrup. The much smaller subalpine larch has shorter needles in bunches of 30 to 40. It is found only near or at tree line, often in a twisted and stunted form.

SHELLEY FIRTH

Western hemlock

Forests of **lodgepole pine** and **ponderosa pine** (the latter is also known as (western) yellow pine) cover the Rockies' foothills, extending well into the montane zone. Both are dependent on periodic forest fires (without which they gradually lose ground to more shade-tolerant tree species).

Lodgepole pine has cones coated in resin that melts in high temperatures, ensuring its seeds disperse only when fire has prepared a fertile bed of ash. Lodgepole has needles in bunches of two and a

GARETH McCORMACK

Limber pine

straight, narrow 'pole-like' trunk that makes for a dense stand in recently regenerated forest.

A beautiful tree, ponderosa pine grows in spaced, park-like stands up to 180ft tall. It has long, three-needle bunches and scaly, textured bark that bleaches rusty red on the side exposed to the sun. Native Americans stripped away the bark to get at the sweet cambium (inner bark), and occasionally hikers may come across ancient ponderosa pine still scarred by this practice.

The five-needle **limber pine** is essentially a subalpine tree, and is always found at or near the tree line on exposed sites. As both its common and botanical names imply, the branches of the limber pine bend rather than break under the force of gales or heavy snowpack. The closely related **whitebark pine** looks similar to limber pine, but has smaller, almost round cones and is only found south of Idaho or northwestern Wyoming.

Another five-needle pine of the subalpine zone, the **bristlecone pine** is found only in the southwestern Rockies, where it can reach a staggering age. The most ancient specimens are believed to be more than 4600 years old – the oldest known living tree. The bristlecone pine has short, curved, resinous needles that radiate from the branchlets, giving them a 'bottlebrush' appearance.

The small **pinyon pine** is also a southwestern species and has thick, two-needle bunches. It is confined to the foothills and montane zones, where it often forms 'pigmy forests' together with juniper and gambel oak. Its oily nuts were once the staple food for Native American peoples of the southwest, and wild (ie, uncultivated) pinyon nuts are still harvested commercially – except, that is, when native birds, bears or wood rats get them first.

Engelmann spruce is a tall, cold-tolerant tree capable of withstanding winter temperatures of -50°F. It tends to be the dominant tree in subalpine forests throughout the Rockies. Like other spruce species, Engelmann has round, slightly pointed needles, and cones that hang downward from the branch. Its resonant wood is used to make piano sounding boards.

Blue spruce, also called Colorado spruce, shares many of its characteristics with Engelmann spruce, but its needles are slightly longer, more clustered and have a striking silvery-white or 'blue' tinge when young. Blue spruce cultivars are widely planted in parks and gardens around the world, and it is the state tree of Colorado.

Western red cedar is a towering giant of the wet montane forests of northwestern Montana and the Idaho panhandle. It has shiny, overlapping, scale-like leaves and tiny cones. Its fibrous, cinnamon-colored bark can be peeled off in strips. One of the world's great lumber trees, western red cedar can reach more than 200ft under ideal growing conditions, but it has been somewhat over-exploited.

ANIMALS
MAMMALS

The Rocky Mountains offer the best wildlife-viewing in the Lower 48, especially for larger mammals. Featured here are some species hikers are most likely to see – or would *most like* to see.

Rodents

Aside from those described, there are numerous other species of small native rodent in the Rockies, including gophers, ground squirrels, mice, voles and wood rats.

A frequent inhabitant of montane and alpine streams, the **beaver** attracted 18th-century fur trappers into the Rocky Mountains. This large, amphibious, paddle-tailed rodent is a great hydrological engineer, gnawing down whole forests in order to dam up mountain streams. Long-term beaver activity keeps open valley meadows that trees would otherwise soon recolonize. Beavers build island-like mounded dens (lodges) that keep the colony safe from predators and winter cold.

Chipmunk

A half-dozen or so species of **chipmunk**, some with very limited distribution, are found in the Rockies, although visual similarities make them hard to distinguish. All chipmunks are reddish-gray to ginger, and have several longitudinal black and white stripes extending from their noses down their backs (sometimes also along their tails). Unbelievably fast and able to stop or change direction instantaneously, chipmunks can afford to be daring in their pursuit of a meal. No Rockies campsite is without a resident chipmunk ready to snap up fallen crumbs or raid unhung food.

Marmots are large alpine rodents that establish extensive burrow systems in bouldery terrain. Marmots fatten up on forbs and grasses during their four frenetic months of summer, then hibernate over the long mountain winter. A sentinel keeps watch over the feeding colony and gives a loud warning whistle at the approach of an intruder. The aptly named **yellow-bellied marmot** is widely distributed through the Rockies, while the somewhat larger gray-white **hoary marmot** is found only in the northern Rockies.

The **red squirrel** has a gray-brown coat, often with a reddish tinge on its back and tail, and a white underbelly and eye rings. It is especially common in lodgepole and ponderosa pine forests of the montane zone, as it feeds largely on pine nuts. Red squirrels work feverishly to store enough cones for winter, dropping them off the trees (sometimes hitting passing hikers!) and burying the cones in numerous secret caches. Strongly territorial, the red squirrel furiously berates intruders with shrill chattering, often resuming its tirade hours after hikers arrive at a campsite. Also entertaining are its fall mating antics, when courting pairs streak madly around the branches and trunks.

Marmot

Pikas, Rabbits & Hares

The popular **pika** somewhat resembles a hamster in size and shape. It lives in alpine talus fields (often in close association with marmots) and also communicates using a distinctive high-pitched cheep. The pika energetically collects flowers and grasses, which it lays on rocks to dry before stacking them into bundles as winter fodder. Pikas are tolerant of humans and often turn up at hiker picnics.

The ubiquitous **snowshoe hare** (sometimes spotted on high tundra meadows dashing for cover) has a reddish-brown summer coat, which turns snowy white in the fall as camouflage. It is the main prey of the lynx, so when the snowshoe hare population declines (due to a shortage of feed or a very harsh winter) lynx numbers follow. The snowshoe hare is a prolific breeder, however, allowing populations of both species to quickly recover.

Goats & Sheep

Arguably the animal that best symbolizes the Rocky Mountains, **bighorn sheep** (commonly called bighorns) are robust, muscular beasts, colored grayish brown with a white muzzle tip, underbelly and rump patch. Bighorns grow up to 6ft long, stand almost 4ft at the shoulder and weigh well over 300lb. Their ideal habitat is alpine meadows or subalpine forests fringed by rocky ridges, which allow them to easily escape predators. Rams have thick, curled horns, which they use during the fall rut (from about mid-September to late October) in fierce head-butting bouts with rivals. Discreet hikers – at least those with good binoculars – can often closely observe bighorn herds (even dueling rams at the right time of year) around ridges or alpine valleys. The national parks, especially Glacier and Yellowstone, are some of the best places to see bighorns, although they inhabit most wilderness areas throughout the Rockies.

Bighorn sheep

HUGH D'ANDRADE

The **mountain goat** is found from the Canadian border through the Idaho-Montana Rockies as far south as the Greater Yellowstone region. Surefooted and confident in even the most precipitous terrain, the mountain goat is highly adapted to the harsh environment of the upper subalpine and alpine zones. It has a shaggy, snowy-white coat that includes a thin 'missionary' beard and narrow, almost straight black horns. Mountain goats can reach 5ft, stand 4ft at the shoulder and weigh up to 300lb. Mountain goats crave salt, and will chew up sweaty clothing or gnaw down vegetation where someone has urinated in order to get it – see Dangers & Annoyances (p57).

Bison

Vast herds of **bison** (often called buffalo) once grazed the eastern Great Plains as well as the western Great Basin, often migrating to the valleys and high plateaus of the Rocky Mountains over summer. Today, numerous small isolated herds exist throughout the Rocky Mountains region (an increasing number on private ranches), with the largest in Yellowstone National Park – generally the best place to observe them.

A truly majestic animal, full-grown bison may stand more than 6ft high, have a total length of 12ft and weigh 2000lb or more. Bison have a thick, shaggy coat of light brown and a high, rounded back. Both sexes have short black horns curved upward.

Despite their docile, hulking appearance and 'aloof' manner, bison are surprisingly agile and extremely fast. They become increasingly uneasy when approached – indicated by a raised tail – and may suddenly charge anyone who gets too close. Each year people are seriously injured, sometimes even killed, in bison attacks. Statistically, bison are actually more dangerous than grizzly bears! For more information see Animal Attacks (p74).

HUGH D'ANDRADE

Bison

Deer & Pronghorn

The largest deer species in the Rockies, **elk** (also called wapiti or red deer) can weigh 1000lb and stand 5ft tall at the shoulder. Their summer coats are golden-brown and the bulls have a darker throat mane. Each year bull elk grow impressive, multipointed antlers (up to 5ft long) for the fall rut (mating season), when they round up harems of breeding hinds and make resonant, bugling calls to warn off other males. Although elk populations were decimated in the 19th century, their numbers have largely recovered – well beyond sustainable levels in some areas. Elk are cautious and elusive, as they are prized by trophy hunters.

The largest of the world's deer species, **moose** stand up to 7ft at the shoulder, can reach 10ft in length and weight as much as 1200lb. They have a brownish-black coat and a thick, black horse-like muzzle. The bull produces massive, cupped antlers, each weighing perhaps 50lb, which are shed after the fall mating season. Moose mainly eat twigs and tiny branches (typically aspen or shrub willow), but also feed extensively on waterweeds in streams and lakes. They are excellent swimmers and can dive to depths of 20ft. Moose may become aggressive if cornered or defending calves, when they strike out with powerful blows of their front hooves. For more information see Animal Attacks, p74.

The **mule deer** is a stocky, gray-brown animal with a white rump patch and white, black-tipped tail. Its name comes from its large donkey-like ears. A buck typically reaches 5½ft in length, stands 3½ft at the shoulder and grows 3½ft antlers. Rutting bucks lock antlers, each trying to push the rival's head below its own. The mule deer's distinctive 'stotting' gait involves jumping with all four feet leaving and hitting the ground simultaneously (similar to the gait of an African springbok).

Like bison, the **pronghorn** is essentially a herd animal of the Great Plains, but it also inhabits the foothills and montane regions of the Rockies, such as Yellowstone National Park. It has a tan coat with a white underbelly and rump patch. The tips of its horns are 'pronged', curling backward to form a half-hook. The fastest animal in North America, the pronghorn can run up to 45mph, but its inability to jump fences is fatal on the ranch-covered plains.

White-tailed deer were originally rare in the region, but the clearing of forest by settlers enabled this adaptable species to spread throughout the northern Rockies. It remains absent in most of the southern Rockies, however. The white-tailed deer is similar in form to, but somewhat sleeker than, the mule deer (a close relative), and can be identified by its conventional gait, smaller ears, and reddish brown coat with distinctive white patches on its neck, snout, underbelly and underside of its tail, which it raises while running.

Mustelids

These small carnivores are members of the mustelid family (including weasels, skunks, otters and badgers).

About the size of a small dog, the **badger** avoids forest areas, mainly inhabiting stream environs, tundra meadows or open areas of the

Elk (wapiti)

Moose

Mule deer

Rockies' foothills. Its coat is yellowish-gray with fainter side stripes and a long white stripe running back from between its eyes. This expert excavator builds large burrows (which later provide shelter to other species) and chiefly feeds on gophers, ground squirrels, marmots and pikas, which it digs out of their burrows. The badger's search for food sometimes also brings it into campsites.

Once extensively trapped for its soft pelt, the chestnut-colored **pine marten** (also called the American sable) is a playful, weasel-like animal that lives in old-growth coniferous forests. It typically preys on the red squirrel, but sometimes ventures into the alpine zone to hunt marmots or pikas. The pine marten is closely related to the rare **fisher**, found only in wilderness areas of the Idaho-Montana Rockies and Wyoming's Wind River Range.

The largest member of the weasel family, the wily **wolverine** is typically 40 inches long and weights 30lb or more. Its coat is dark brown with a yellow-white stripe across its forehead and along each side. Confident in any terrain, this agile animal is an excellent climber, digger and swimmer. Despite its modest size, the wolverine can become incredibly vicious – there have been cases of wolverines seriously injuring bears and killing young deer.

Raccoons

The **raccoon** typically frequents forest lakes of the montane zone, but (as a non-hibernator) it cannot thrive in higher areas with a harsh winter. Its fur is brownish-black gray with a paler underbelly and characteristic black patches around each eye. The raccoon has an acute sense of touch in its front paws, which it uses to 'feel out' hidden food sources. It will eat anything.

Raccoon

Cats

The **bobcat** is a handsome feline – like a scaled-up version of the domestic tabby – with a brown-spotted, yellowish-tan coat and a short 'cropped' tail. It mainly eats birds and rodents, but when easier prey is scarce it may even take small deer or pronghorn antelopes. Bobcats are fairly common, and it is not unusual for hikers to sight one darting across a forest meadow or into a thicket of shrub willow – considered a consolation prize for *never* seeing a cougar.

The **lynx** is only slightly larger than the bobcat, but has a silvery-gray coat and prominent black tufts on the tips of its ears. Males often have a slight mane and a bib-like underside of white. The distribution of the lynx extends from Canada through the Idaho-Montana Rockies to the Greater Yellowstone region, with two isolated populations in the Uinta Mountains of Utah and Wyoming's Bighorn Mountains. The entire predatory focus of the lynx is on the snowshoe hare, and lynx numbers are largely determined by the size of the local snowshoe hare population.

The **cougar** (often called mountain lion) prefers remote, forested areas of the montane zone. With a size and shape similar to that of a smallish (African) lioness, the cougar may reach 9ft from nose to tail tip and can weigh up to 190lb. A solitary and highly elusive creature, the

Lynx

cougar is rarely seen even by the backcountry biologists who study it. Its typical prey is mule deer, elk and small moose, and it follows these animals as they migrate to higher ground in summer. It is also a curious animal known to secretly 'stalk' humans without harmful intent, however, cougars have occasionally made predatory – very rarely fatal – attacks on humans, and they should be regarded as dangerous animals. For more information see Animal Attacks, p74.

Foxes & Dogs

The small, nimble **red fox** grows to 3½ft, weighs up to 15lb and has a brilliant red coat. Although it is widely distributed around the Rockies (except for New Mexico) the red fox is not as abundant as the coyote, perhaps because the latter is such a strong competitor. The somewhat larger **gray fox** inhabits montane forest areas of the southern Rockies.

HUGH D'ANDRADE

Red fox

The **coyote** is actually a small opportunistic wolf species that eats anything from ground squirrels to insects and berries. Its sleek, reddish-gray form soon becomes familiar to Rocky Mountains hikers. Coyotes form small packs to hunt larger prey such as deer or livestock, for which they are detested by ranchers. While wide-scale coyote eradication programs have had no lasting impact, reintroduction of the gray wolf (which fills a similar ecological niche) tends to marginalize coyotes.

The **gray wolf** (also called the timber wolf) was once the main predator in the Rocky Mountains, but relentless persecution reduced its territory to a narrow belt stretching from Canada through the Idaho-Montana Rockies. It has recently been reintroduced into Yellowstone National Park, although plans for wolf reintroduction in other Rocky Mountains regions are very controversial.

The gray wolf looks rather like a very large, blackish German shepherd, and roams in close-knit packs ruled by a dominant 'alpha' male and female pair. Gray wolves tend to focus their predation skills on one particular species, such as elk in Yellowstone, sparing other potential prey. They communicate by making long, mournful howls that can be heard from miles away.

Coyote

Bears

The **black bear** lives in montane and subalpine forests throughout the Rockies and their foothills. It is an adaptable forager with a largely vegetarian diet and hunts (usually smaller animals) only sporadically. Rocky Mountains black bears can be quite pale (occasionally almost white), when they are often mistaken for grizzlies. Black bears are generally somewhat smaller than grizzlies, and have more tapered muzzles, larger ears and smaller claws. Although they are generally less aggressive and more tolerant of humans than grizzlies, black bears should always be treated as dangerous animals.

Like grizzlies, black bears hibernate in a den over the long winter, conserving energy by reducing their body temperature and metabolism. Worryingly, they are increasingly being poached for their gall bladders (and other body parts used in Chinese traditional medicine), which can fetch thousands of dollars on the black market.

The **grizzly bear** (also called brown bear) was once found right across the western US. Today its population in the Lower 48 has been reduced to less than 1200 individuals concentrated in the Greater Glacier and Greater Yellowstone regions. Plans to link genetically isolated populations by reintroducing grizzlies in key areas have met with vehement local opposition.

The grizzly grows to 8ft in length (from nose to tail) and 4ft high at the shoulder (when on all fours), and weighs more than 1100lb at maturity. Although some grizzlies are almost black, their coats are typically pale brown to cinnamon with 'grizzled', white-tipped guard hairs (the long, coarse hairs that protect the shorter, fine fur of the undercoat). They can be distinguished from black bears by their concave (dish-shaped) facial profile, slightly smaller and more rounded ears, prominent shoulder hump, and long, nonretractable claws (that show up clearly on their paw prints).

HUGH D'ANDRADE

Grizzly bear

An omnivorous opportunist and notorious berry-eater, the grizzly has an incredibly acute sense of smell – good enough to detect food sources many miles away. It will viciously defend a carcass, and hiking trails sometimes have to be closed temporarily because a grizzly is feeding on a dead bison, elk or moose close by.

Grizzlies are unpredictable and dangerous, as they become extremely agitated and aggressive if approached or surprised, but otherwise they will not normally attack humans. For more information see Animal Attacks (p74).

BIRDS

With several hundred species common in the region, the Rocky Mountains offer one of North America's most varied and intact environments for birds. A (scant) selection of Rockies bird species follows.

Small Birds

Centered on the Colorado and New Mexico Rockies, the tiny **broadtailed hummingbird** feeds in montane forests but breeds in alpine tundra. It has a radiant-green back, white underparts and a broad black tail; the male has a red bib. The broad-tailed hummingbird flies at amazing speeds for a bird with a wingspan of just four inches, and can stop, hover or change direction in a split second. It uses its long, narrow beak to suck out energy-rich flower nectar (which powers it's frenetic flight) and is an important pollinator for numerous wildflower species.

Clark's nutcracker, a boisterous member of the crow family, is light gray with black wings and a white tail. It inhabits subalpine forests, feeding largely on conifer nuts, which it breaks open with its long, black beak. Clark's nutcracker is named after Captain William Clark of the Lewis and Clark expedition, the first Euro-American to collect a specimen.

The small **mountain chickadee** is a titmouse species of the subalpine forests, where it gorges on insects. It has a black cap and throat bib, and its onomatopoeic name describes its distinct call.

Steller's jay has striking, lustrous-blue plumage, but for its black crest (the longest of any North American bird), head and nape. Its grating 'ack-ack-ack' call is also distinctive, if less attractive. Although its natural diet typically consists of pine nuts, berries and insects, this bird is also an incorrigible scavenger, and frequently raids campgrounds or picnic areas for scraps.

The **red-naped sapsucker** is a woodpecker species with a black back, white stripes running above and below each eye, and a red chin and forehead. It bores into tree bark (preferably willow or aspen), discharging gooey gum and entrapping insects, both of which it eats. Despite the damage it causes to the trees, the bird's activity helps control the even more destructive bark beetle as well as other noxious insects.

Steller's Jay

A true alpine grouse, the **white-tailed ptarmigan** forages for berries, buds and seeds on the high tundra. Unusual among birds, the white-tailed ptarmigan's plumage is white in winter and mottled brown in summer. It is so well camouflaged that a hiker could almost step on it before it scurries away.

Birds of Prey

This group of birds (also called raptors) includes eagles, falcons, harriers and hawks. Sweeping across lakes, forests or plains in search of fish or small game, they are some of the most interesting and 'watchable' birds.

The **bald eagle** is a large raptor with a wingspan up to 8ft. It has brown plumage and a distinctive white 'bald' head. Bald eagle pairs mate for life, building their nest close to water. The size of the nest grows with each breeding season to become a truly massive structure up to 12ft in diameter. The bald eagle often takes fish (or harasses an osprey until it drops its catch), but also preys on other birds or smaller mammals.

Bald eagle

The true 'king of the Rockies', the **golden eagle** can sometimes be spotted riding thermals high above craggy ridges. This majestic mountain bird was venerated by Native Americans, who used its golden-brown plumage in their headdresses. The golden eagle is only marginally smaller than the bald eagle, and typically nests on rocky cliff ledges that afford a bird's-eye view of potential predators or prey. The golden eagle's diet is also more varied, and it will swoop down on anything from fish and rodents to deer fawns.

The **great horned owl** is mottled gray-brown in color and has prominent, 'horned' ear tufts. It is found throughout the Rockies, although its camouflage is so effective that few hikers even notice when they pass one. A largely nocturnal hunter, the great horned owl preys mostly on rodents (including skunks!), but will also take grouse and other birds. It has a deep, resonant hooting call.

Golden eagle

The large, black **turkey vulture** (also called turkey buzzard) is a clumsy creature, but once airborne it becomes a superb glider with a

HUGH D'ANDRADE

HUGH D'ANDRADE

Osprey

wingspan up to 6ft. Although its featherless red face should be enough to scare animals to death, the turkey vulture is only a very sporadic predator. It takes the occasional small rodent but prefers to eat carrion, which it spots from the air.

The fish-eating **osprey** lives around larger lakes and rivers, nesting on treetops near the shore. Its upper body and wings are dark brown, while its underside is white on the body and inner wings and speckled brown-white on the outer wings. This well-adapted hunter has efficient water-shedding feathers and clamp-like feet with two pairs of opposing toes to better grasp slippery, wriggling fish.

Waterbirds

A vast number of waterbirds are (at least partial) inhabitants of the Rocky Mountains. Many migrate to the region only for the warmer months, arriving from around May and returning to their wintering grounds from about mid-September. They include species of coot, crane, gulls and teals.

HUGH D'ANDRADE

Great blue heron

Although not a true waterbird, the **American dipper** (also called the water ouzel) is amazingly well-adapted to life in subalpine streams. This otherwise unspectacular, small gray bird can sometimes be seen darting in and out of the icy rushing water, feeding on aquatic insects or fish fry. It has oily, insulating feathers, strong claws to keep its footing in a strong current and even 'flies' underwater.

The **great blue heron** is a large, gray-blue wading bird common around mountain lakes, marshes and rivers. Often mistaken for a crane, it quietly stalks in the shallows, waiting to pluck out fish, frogs or invertebrates. The bird's very long neck is kept fully recoiled while it roosts, and its even longer legs are stretched back awkwardly in flight.

The **loon** is more common in the northern US Rockies, where its beautiful mournful wail carries across tranquil backcountry lakes. It is a large bird up to 35 inches long, and has a black-green head with speckled upper body and white underparts. The loon's dense body mass enables it to dive to depths exceeding 150ft, but also requires it to make a long take off, which limits it to larger lakes.

The small **snow goose** has either white or bluish-white plumage and black wing tips. In one of North America's great natural events, in early spring (from April) enormous flocks of snow goose overfly the Rockies on their way north to their nesting grounds on the arctic tundra. In the fall (mid-September on) the birds return south to overwinter around the Mexico/US border, completing a journey of about 12,000mi.

The attractive **western grebe** is found on deeper lakes. It is recognizable by its mellow, lilting call and a distinctive long, slender neck with a white front and black back, and yellow, pointed beak. Its other plumage is whitish brown. In a complex courtship ritual, pairing western grebes 'dance' and flit together across the water, then build their floating nest moored to underwater plants.

ECOLOGY & ENVIRONMENT

Different interests compete for the natural resources of the Rocky Mountains. Agriculture, forestry, mining and ranching have driven the economies of many areas for generations, but local and national conservation groups have increasingly opposed unsustainable practices such as clear-cutting, overgrazing and strip mining. They have initiated the removal of ill-conceived dams and forced the cleanup of contaminated military sites.

Conservationists are now striving to protect the Rockies' remaining roadless areas, which are largely within national forest areas. Here, the role of the USFS as both an agent for the exploitation and protection of public lands is problematic. The USFS has tried repeatedly to sell land to timber or energy companies, and has found itself caught between powerful business interests and outraged environmental groups.

Many other factors continue to threaten ecosystems of the Rocky Mountains. Global warming is expected to produce a 5°F temperature rise over the next half-century, resulting in lower snowpack depths and faster spring melt-out. This would bring drier conditions, with more forest fires and greater seasonal fluctuations in river levels, which would reduce freshwater availability. Other ominous threats include acid rain (caused by industrial pollution from often very distant sources), introduced non-native weeds, insects or diseases, and proposed highway expansions that would further isolate habitat reserves. The Bush administration, concerned at the country's growing energy shortage, has endorsed a major expansion of natural gas exploration on both public and private lands throughout the Rocky Mountains.

Hikers should always practice the 'leave no trace' principles when in the Rocky Mountains backcountry – see Responsible Hiking, p55.

Conservation Groups

Numerous nongovernment organizations exist to promote conservation in the Rockies and the broader western region of the US, including:

Alliance for the Wild Rockies (AWR; ☎ 406-721-5420; Ⓦ www.wildrockiesalliance.org; PO Box 8731, Missoula, MT 59807) is dedicated to stopping further habitat destruction in the northern US Rockies.

Colorado Environment Coalition (CES; ☎ 303-534-7066; Ⓦ www.ourcolorado.org; 1536 Wynkoop Street #5C, Denver, CO 80202) is Colorado's largest grassroots environmental movement, and works to protect the state's wildlands, wildlife and quality of life.

Montana Wilderness Association (MWA; ☎ 406-443-7350; Ⓦ www.wildmontana.org; PO Box 635, Helena, MT 59624) is Montana's largest environmental grouping and was founded in 1958.

The Wilderness Society (TWS; ☎ 800-843-9453; Ⓦ www.wilderness.org; 1615 M St, NW, Washington, DC 20036), founded in 1935, is a national lobby working to protect America's wildlands.

The Nature Conservancy (☎ 800-628-6860; Ⓦ www.nature.org; 4245 North Fairfax Drive, Suite 100, Arlington, VA 22203-1606) supports and funds the acquisition of biologically significant lands (which currently total 143,750 sq miles worldwide or 19,688 sq miles in the US).

Sierra Club (☎ 415-977-5500; Ⓦ www.sierraclub.org; 85 Second St, 2nd Floor, San Francisco, CA 94105-3441) is the nation's largest outdoors organization. It organizes many hiking, backpacking trips and other activities, which are open to nonmembers.

NATIONAL FORESTS

The USFS administers approximately 75,000 sq miles of publicly owned national forest throughout the Rocky Mountains. Traditionally, national forests have been managed under a 'multiple use' system that allows some livestock grazing, logging and mining, but – even excluding designated wilderness areas – national forests throughout the Rockies still retain untouched wildlands of major ecological significance. A national forest may often consist of several sections that are separated by public or private lands, such as Montana's Beaverhead and Wyoming's Medicine Bow.

Fewer restrictions apply when visiting national forests. Many backcountry trails are open to ATVs (all-terrain vehicles) and trail bikes (off-road motorcycles). The USFS charges parking fees (typically $3 per

Fire in the Rockies

Forest fires burn out millions of acres of public and private lands in the Rocky Mountains in some years. Despite the enormous devastation they cause, fires are a natural and important element in the forest's life-cycles. Low-intensity fires prevent brush buildup in the forest understory and leave nutrient-rich ash that stimulates plant regrowth. Native Americans used fire to encourage new growth for grazing animals, and ranchers are learning to use 'cool' fires to restore their rangelands and ponderosa or lodgepole forests.

In recent years the importance of fire in regulating Rocky Mountains ecosystems has been better understood, and fires caused naturally (generally by lightning) are now usually allowed to burn if they are on public lands and do not endanger people or property.

To check current wildfire situations and other fire-fighting information online, go to w www.nifc.gov.

day or $7 per week) at some trailheads, which may also affect hikers heading to wilderness areas.

Wilderness Areas

Somewhat less than 20% of national forest lands are designated wilderness areas. The majority of hikes in this book are in such areas – roadless expanses established by Congress under the Wilderness Act of 1964. The dozens of designated wilderness areas in the Rocky Mountains lie within existing national forest boundaries and are administered by the USFS. Although their purpose and management are somewhat different, wilderness areas enjoy a degree of protection comparable to that of national parks, but generally offer a higher degree of challenge and solitude than national parks or other national forest lands.

Wilderness areas are closed to all mechanized forms of transportation (including mountain bikes and hang gliders), but dogs, horses and pack animals (sometimes also commercial livestock) are permitted in the backcountry. The only significant infrastructure in wilderness areas is (not always well maintained) hiking trails, including footbridges at major stream crossings; pit toilets occasionally exist at heavily visited places. Camping is generally not permitted anywhere within at least 200ft of lakes, streams or official trails, and campfires are often severely restricted (sometimes prohibited).

Limits also apply to group sizes and the length of stay. In some wildernesses, hikers must obtain a backcountry permit before setting out.

NATIONAL PARKS

Created by an act of Congress, national parks generally encompass spectacular natural features and cover hundreds of square miles. The Rockies' four main national parks are Glacier (Montana), Yellowstone (Wyoming), Grand Teton (Wyoming) and Rocky Mountain (Colorado), which all offer a great range of interesting and spectacular hiking routes. Two others in Colorado, the Black Canyon of the Gunnison and Great Sand Dunes National Parks, also have some excellent shorter hikes. Major roads penetrate most national parks, although large areas of wilderness accessible only to backcountry hikers also exist within park boundaries. Hiking trails in national parks are very well marked and maintained, often with restroom facilities at either end and sometimes with interpretive displays along the way.

All Rocky Mountains national parks require overnight hikers to carry backcountry permits. Hikers must use only designated campsites and dogs are not permitted in the backcountry. Shorter day hikes tend to be very popular among national park visitors and in midsummer trails can become overcrowded, while routes further from the trailheads normally receive only moderate use.

National Recreation Areas

Officially under the national park system, National recreation areas are often administered in close cooperation with the USFS. There are five national recreation areas in the Rocky Mountains – Curecanti (Colorado), Flaming Gorge (Utah), Glen Canyon (Utah), Hells Canyon (Idaho) and Sawtooth (Idaho) – of which only the latter is featured in this guidebook. Several are unique natural areas altered significantly by major dam projects. Mountain bikes are usually allowed on backcountry trails in national recreation areas. Some trails are also open to trail bikes, although usually not to ATVs or 4WDs.

POPULATION & PEOPLE

The greater Rocky Mountains region has a population rapidly approaching 10 million. Aside from the Denver–Colorado Springs sprawl along the foot of Colorado's Front Range, the region is generally thinly populated and decentralized. Most other areas of the Rockies are dominated by medium-sized regional centers rather than large cities.

The Denver–Colorado Springs area has the region's only large African-American population. The sizeable Latino populations of central and southern Colorado and (particularly) New Mexico include many descendants of settlers from the Spanish colonial period who have largely retained their culture and language, as well as large numbers of more recent Hispanic (largely Mexican) migrants. Native Americans live largely on reservations, which are governed by federal and tribal law.

Throughout the Rockies, religion plays an important part in people's lives. Native American worship is practiced at sacred sites such as Wyoming's Medicine Wheel. Roman Catholicism is particularly strong in parts of the southern Rockies. Protestants, including resilient Lutheran and Hutterite communities, are found widely across the region. Adherents of the Church of Jesus Christ of Latter Day Saints (Mormons) are centered in Utah, but Mormons are also well represented in Idaho, Montana and Wyoming (where their strictures on gambling and alcohol consumption are influential). Colorado's Front Range is a stronghold for various New Age communities, while northern Montana has thriving Buddhist groups.

Several small religious cults or even paramilitary groups exist in isolated areas of Idaho and Montana.

SOCIETY & CONDUCT
Traditional Culture

Native Americans throughout the Rocky Mountains region generally maintain firm bonds to their tribe and traditional culture. Over a dozen self-administering Native American reservations exist throughout the region, with commercial activities such as farming, tourism and (increasingly) gambling casinos. In the southern Rockies, most notably at Mesa Verde in Colorado and Bandelier in New Mexico, hikers can walk to ancient Pueblo settlements. Elsewhere you may occasionally come across ponderosa pine (see Watching Wildlife, p26) bark-stripped by local Native Americans more than 100 years ago. A good website dedicated to promoting Native American culture is Ⓦ www.nativeculture.com.

Dos & Don'ts

Dress standards are very informal in the backcountry – skinny dipping (nude bathing) is widespread but is frowned on at more popular 'family' spots.

Talking loudly, littering, cutting switchbacks, trampling vegetation (to put up a tent or otherwise), disregarding permit or fee payments, and taking more than your portion of a campsite are considered decidedly antisocial in the Rocky Mountains backcountry.

Always greet others you meet on the trail, and give advanced notice when passing someone. Hikers going uphill have the right of way.

Hikers should respect Native American cultural sites and obtain permission before visiting a reservation or entering tribal lands. Many tribes ban all forms of recording – photography, video, audio and drawing. Others permit these activities in certain areas only if you pay a fee. Obtain permission before you photograph anyone on a reservation, including children – a tip is usually expected.

Facts for the Hiker

When it comes to hiking in the Rocky Mountains, the highlights are difficult to select because so much depends on your own interests and experience. Following are a few ideas.

Spectacular Views
Gazing across sparkling, glaciated peaks from Swiftcurrent Mountain Lookout (p94) in Glacier National Park. Marveling at the awesome views of Cirque of the Towers (p204) from Jackass Pass in the Wind River Range. Looking across vast, semiarid plains around Santa Fe from the cool summit of Lake Peak on the Winsor-Skyline Loop (p299).

Tranquil Moments
Soaking away your aches in the Ferris Fork hot springs on the Bechler River hike (p177). Camping by the enchanting Mistymoon Lake near the foot of northern Wyoming's Cloud Peak (p200). Enjoying the solitude and delicate beauty of Gilpin Lake (p247) in northern Colorado's Mt Zirkel Wilderness. Strolling under majestic ponderosa pines in Montana's sheer-sided Blodgett Canyon (p149).

Flora & Fauna
Relaxing in alpine wildflower meadows directly beneath towering Mt Timpanogos (p223) in Utah's Wasatch Front Range. Watching herds of bighorn sheep graze the alpine tundra of Bighorn Flats on the Flattop Mountain hike (p233).

High Jinks
Spending four days above 11,000ft on the Maroon Bells Loop (p254) in central Colorado. Hiking toward the jagged skyline of central Idaho's Sawtooth Mountains en route to Sawtooth Lake (p136).

Different Tracks
Riding out on the historic narrow-gauge train after finishing the Needle Mountains Loop (p275) in southern Colorado's Weminuche Wilderness. Setting off along the ultra-scenic Highline Trail (p96) from the Going-to-the-Sun Rd in Glacier National Park.

SUGGESTED ITINERARIES
You probably won't have enough time to visit every hiking region of the Rocky Mountains in a single summer. Your travel plans will be determined largely by how much time you do have and your means of travel. Put together a list of the hikes or areas that most interest you – be realistic and flexible, as anything from bad weather to unavailability of preferred backcountry campsites may disrupt your itinerary. Remember to factor in time for organizing backcountry permits, buying provisions or sightseeing. Flying (with local car rental) may be the best option for ambitious hikers on a tight schedule. Those with less time are advised to focus on more accessible areas with better tourist infrastructure, such as national parks. The most convenient and popular way to travel around the Rockies is by private vehicle. Hikers relying on public transportation will have limited options and need more time.

One Week
Concentrate on one region close to your entry/exit point, such as Colorado's Rocky Mountain National Park or Greater Glacier in northern Montana.

Two Weeks
You should have enough time to travel between both of the regions mentioned above, and do a number of day and backpacking hikes within them. Alternatively, visit Yellowstone and Grand Teton National Parks, perhaps with a side trip to Central Wyoming's Wind River Range.

One Month
This is probably the minimum time necessary to get a bare overview of hiking in the Rockies, but you will still have to be fairly disciplined with your time. On top of the region's mentioned above, add the Greater Yellowstone region, plus either central Colorado or northern New Mexico, to your itinerary.

Two Months

This will give you a real opportunity to check things out, although there will still be plenty of places you can't visit. Explore some less-visited areas, such as Idaho's Sawtooth Wilderness, Wyoming's Bighorn Mountains, Utah's Wasatch Front or New Mexico's Pecos Wilderness. Another spectacular option is to hike the entire Colorado section of the Continental Divide Trail.

WHEN TO HIKE

Hiking in the Rocky Mountains is an activity essentially confined to summer. A few hardy hikers undertake trips from chilly early May until the lakes and streams freeze again in late October, but almost all traffic on the Rocky Mountains trails is in the period between mid-June and mid-September. Visiting outside the peak months of July and August will ensure fewer crowds and more affordable accommodations.

A brief outline of hiking conditions in each season follows – also see Climate (p20).

Spring

Hiking in spring (March through May) is rather limited. Snowpack levels vary from year to year and region to region (so it may be useful to check conditions in the region you intend to hike), but melting snow swells streams and makes trails slushy. Higher trails tend to be snowed-over before the end of May (sometimes until much later), but routes in lower mountain valleys are normally snow-free from late April.

Summer

Summer (June through August) is when almost all hikers visit. In June the weather is warm and backcountry use is not excessive. Alpine wildflowers also tend to be at their most splendid in June. The main vacation months of July and August bring an influx of hikers and other tourists to the Rocky Mountains. Expect large crowds and high rates as accommodations and campgrounds fill up, especially in and around national parks. Trails and backcountry campsites are often very heavily used.

Fall (Autumn)

Hikes can often be undertaken as late as mid-October. This time of the year has a special atmosphere, with gentle sunny days and golden aspen foliage. Campgrounds, backcountry campsites and trails are less frequented, but much of the tourist infrastructure (including restaurants and some hotels) shuts down from mid-September. Daylight hours are also fewer, which leaves less hiking time. Long periods of stable weather are common in early to mid-fall, but from late September hikers should be prepared for possible heavy snowfalls.

Winter

Winter begins from about mid-November, when the snow-smothered backcountry attracts a few adventurous snowshoers. Winter hiking is a more serious undertaking, however, and not really the subject of this guidebook. Snowshoeing requires proper equipment and sound knowledge of winter backcountry travel, including avalanche danger assessment, survival techniques in frigid temperatures, and navigation in poor visibility. A good guide to winter hiking is *The Essential Snowshoer* by Marianne Zwosta ($15.95). Online information is available at W www.backpacking.net/winter.html.

WHAT KIND OF HIKE?

Almost all hikers in the region organize their own informal trips, although quite a number of professional guiding companies lead groups throughout the Rocky Mountains (see Guided Hikes, p42). Sometimes livestock or llamas are used to carry gear (see the boxed text 'Hiking with Llamas', p41), but hiring porters is virtually unheard of in the Rockies.

As most routes lead through primitive backcountry areas, hikers must be self-reliant. Long hikes require more planning and provisions for sleeping, eating, discarding waste and keeping warm and well-hydrated; some also require a permit or registration at the trailhead. Overnight hikers will almost always have to carry the standard backpacking gear – tent, sleeping bag, sleeping mat (pad), stove and cooking utensils (see

Hiking with Llamas

Hiking with pack llamas has become quite popular throughout the Rocky Mountains, especially with families. Llamas originate from the Andes of South America, and are ideal mountain pack animals. Unlike other livestock, llamas are soft-footed and do not damage trails. Llama grazing also has little environmental impact (although curious deer and elk often hang around them).

Llamas are very cooperative and easy for a novice to safely handle – a few minutes' basic instruction is sufficient. They have stamina, and can carry loads of 80lb (including children too young to hike) over a long day.

For more information, see *Packing with Llamas*, by Stanlynn Daugherty ($19.95).

Quite a few companies throughout the Rockies rent llamas (around $40 per day) and/or organize guided 'llama treks' (from around $130/60 per day for adults/children). Some are listed here:

El Paso Llama (☎ 800-455-2627; W elpasollama.com; PO Box 2672, Taos, NM 87571) runs trips in New Mexico's Pecos and Wheeler Peak Wildernesses.
Great Northern Llama Company (☎ 406-755-9044; W www.gnllama.com; 600 Blackmer Lane, Columbia Falls, MT 59912) operates trips into Glacier National Park.
Idaho Teton Llama Hikes (☎ 800-398-0832; W www.llamagear.com; 9328 S 5th St W, Idaho Falls, ID 83404) covers eastern Idaho.
Lander Llama Company (☎ 800-582-5262; W www.wyomingadventure.com; 2024 Mortimore Lane, Lander, WY 82520) has llama treks in Wyoming's Wind River and Absaroka Ranges.
Redwood Llamas (☎ 970-560-2926; W www.redwoodllamas.com; PO Box 278, Dove Creek, CO 81324) offers hiking trips with pack llamas in the San Juan Mountains of southern Colorado and the Utah Canyonlands.
Timberline Llamas (☎ 303-526-0092; W www.timberlinellamas.com; 30361 Rainbow Hill Rd, Golden, CO 80401) runs trips throughout Colorado and southern Wyoming.
Yellowstone Llamas (☎ 406-586-6872; W www.yellowstone-llamas.com; PO Box 5042, Bozeman, MT 59717) specializes in guided 'gourmet' treks in Yellowstone National Park.

WADE EAKLE

Clothing & Equipment, p45) – but other equipment (such as climbing gear) is optional or unnecessary.

There are two basic approaches to overnight hikes: radial (where you walk in, set up a base camp, then do day hikes from there) and linear (where you move to a different camp each night). The radial model enables you to explore the backcountry with a day-pack and maximizes your time on the trail, as you don't have to set up a new camp each day. It's a good alternative for hikers with little time, limited backpacking experience or no desire to carry a heavy pack. The

linear model (which applies to loop, or circuit, hikes, as well as point-to-point, or destination, hikes) has the benefit of progressing through an area without backtracking. On long-distance trails this is the only option. If moving each day seems too arduous, plan several rest days.

Most hikes in this book are linear, but can be made radial by hiking the first (or last) leg and setting up a base camp. This is best done with hikes that have a side trip on the first or last day; if you don't find any in the region you are planning to visit, ask a ranger for suggestions.

GUIDED HIKES

A growing number of outdoor guiding companies organize (mostly five- to seven-day) hiking trips in the Rocky Mountains. These cover a wide range of tastes and territory. Upmarket trips essentially consist of day hikes based out of a (national park) mountain lodge, and include elegant accommodations and dining each evening. Others are guided backpacking trips, where participants *really* are expected to rough it. Many companies will custom-design a trip for 12 or more people. Most produce a glossy catalog which they'll send, free, to nearly anywhere on the globe.

American Adventure Expeditions (☎ 1800-288-0675; W www.americanadventure.com; 228 North F St, Salida, CO 81201) customizes backpacking trips in Colorado's Sawatch Range and Sangre De Cristo Mountains for $195/300 for one/three people per day.

Backroads (☎ 800-462-2848; W www.backroads .com; 801 Cedar St, Berkeley, CA 94710-1800) has high-end hiking/biking trips in the Greater Glacier and Greater Yellowstone regions from around $2000.

Big Wild Adventures (☎ 406-821-3747; W www .bigwildadventures.com; 5663 West Fork Rd, Darby, MT 59829) leads small groups into the Absarokas, Bitterroots, Frank Church and other wildernesses from $1100.

Country Walkers (☎ 800-464-9255; W www .countrywalkers.com; PO Box 180, Waterbury, VT 05676) guides small groups in Glacier, Yellowstone and Rocky Mountain National Parks, staying in mountain lodges, from $2000.

MountainFIT (☎ 406-585-3506, 800-926-5700; W www.mountainfit.com; PO Box 6188, Bozeman, MT 5977) integrates mind and body work with deluxe accommodations in Montana and Utah.

Wild Horizon Expeditions (☎ 888-734-4453; W www.wildhorizonsexpd.com; PO Box 7627, Jackson Hole, WY 83002) offers guided backpacking trips in Wyoming's Tetons and Wind River Range from $850.

ACCOMMODATIONS
Towns & Cities

Cities and larger regional centers have a broad spectrum of accommodations. Small towns offer a narrower choice, but generally have motels with rooms for less than $35/40 singles/doubles. Motel and hotel chains are commonly clustered near freeway exits. Free regional accommodations guides are available from tourist offices or at the entrances to shopping malls and even fast-food restaurants.

Private Campgrounds These offer tent sites from around $14 for two people, plus $1 to $3 for each extra person. RV (recreational vehicle) sites usually cost around $15 to $20, but prices of $25 or $30 are possible at peak times in popular locations. Facilities include hot showers, coin laundromat and usually a games area, playground and convenience store – sometimes even a swimming pool.

Kampgrounds of America (☎ 406-248-7444, W www.koa.com) has dozens of better campgrounds throughout the Rocky Mountains, with sites usually ranging from $14 to $20.

Public Campgrounds The National Park Service (NPS) operates campgrounds in all Rocky Mountains national parks. Sites typically cost $12, and hot showers (around $1 each) are often available. Sites can be reserved up to five months in advance by telephone on ☎ 800-365-2267 (☎ 301-722-1257 from outside the US) or online at W www .nps.gov.

The United States Forest Service (USFS) runs hundreds of basic campgrounds throughout the Rocky Mountains. These typically have only a pit toilet, and showers are rarely available. Each site has a fire pit and a picnic table with benches, and costs between $5 and $12 (occasionally free of charge). Drinking water is usually from a hand pump. Sites at USFS campgrounds can be reserved 240 days in advance under the National Recreation Reservation Service (☎ 877-444-6777, 518-885-3639, W www .reserveusa.com); a fee of $9 is charged for most reservations.

The Bureau of Land Management (BLM) has similar basic campgrounds, where all sites are available on a first-come, first-served basis. Arrive early, especially on weekends.

Hostels Offering generally the cheapest accommodations available, hostels are useful for meeting other hikers and finding out about the region. Hostels usually have a kitchen and laundry facilities, information and advertising boards, TV room and lounge area. Many will arrange excursions and offer transportation within the region for a minimal fee.

The best hostels tend to be those affiliated with Hostelling International/American Youth Hostels (HI/AYH, ☎ 202-783-6161, W www.hiayh.org). There are currently 14 HI/AYH hostels in the Rocky Mountains, mostly in Colorado. They charge from around $15 for a dormitory bed ($3 to $4 extra for nonmembers), and $25 to $30 for a private room – if they have any. If your sleeping bag looks like it's been on the trail for a few weeks, you'll probably have to rent bed linen for around $2.

Independent hostels, often called backpackers hostels, are usually a few dollars cheaper than HI hostels. Their standards widely vary.

Hotels & Motels Hotel and motel prices vary tremendously from season to season; prices quoted in this book are for the high season, unless otherwise noted. You can often get a cheaper rate for a stay of several days, but you may have to pay it all in advance. Simply asking about specials can often get you a discount.

The cheapest motels are usually small, independent (ie, nonchain) establishments with prices as low as $25. Rooms are usually small, and they normally have a private shower, toilet and TV. Many motel rooms have a stove (or microwave oven), fridge and sink.

Chain motels usually fall in the mid-range price category and maintain a consistent level of quality and style (sterile, both). The cheapest national chain is Motel 6, which charges from around $25 for a single in smaller towns, in the high $30s in larger towns, plus an extra $6 for each additional person. Motel chains in the next price level (Super 8, Days Inn, Econo Lodge) have cable TV and free coffee. Stepping up to the $45 to $80 range (Best Western, Holiday Inn, Comfort Inn) you'll find noticeably nicer rooms. At the highest end (Hilton, Hyatt, Radisson, Sheraton) are rooms for $100 or more.

Chain motels have central reservation systems and will take bookings days or months ahead. Normally, you have to give a credit-card number to hold the room. If you don't show up and don't call to cancel, you will be charged for the first night's rental.

On the Hike

With very few exceptions, undertaking a backpacking trip in the Rocky Mountains means camping out rather than overnighting in a hut or cabin.

Backcountry Camping National park backcountry camping is tightly regulated, with hikers permitted to camp only at the designated site shown on their backcountry permit. Backcountry campsites in national parks have a level area for tents, a fireplace (if permitted), a food-hanging pole (or bear-proof steel box) and a privy (pit toilet).

Although various restrictions and prohibitions always apply, camping out in USFS national forests and wilderness areas is generally free of charge and less strictly controlled. Hikers are free to choose their own campsites – but please try to find a spot already used by previous campers.

Backcountry Accommodations The USFS rents basic family cabins in some areas (usually close to trailheads), which cost from around $30 per night.

There are two historic backcountry chalets in Glacier National Park. Granite Park Chalet (☎ 406-387-5555) offers simple rooms with self-catering facilities for $60. Sperry Chalet (☎ 406-387-5654) has better rooms for $150/240 single/double.

Backcountry huts also exist in some parts of Colorado, but most are located along access roads and generally spaced too far apart for hikers to reach easily in one day. These huts cater mainly to ski tourers and mountain bikers and charge around $20 per night (in summer) for a dormitory bed. The 10th

Mountain Division Hut Association (☎ 970-925-5775; w www.huts.org; 1280 Ute Ave, Suite 21, Aspen, CO 81611) and the affiliated Summit Huts Association (☎ 970-453-8583; e summithuts@colorado.net; PO Box 2830, Breckenridge, CO 80424) manage a network of more than a dozen huts in central Colorado. The San Juan Hut System (☎ 970-626-3033; w www.sanjuanhuts.com; PO Box 773, Ridgway, CO 81432) runs a smaller network in southern Colorado.

Mountain lodges are sometimes found close to popular trailheads. Their standards vary considerably – some are luxurious and expensive, while others are rather rustic and simple – but they usually have a restaurant and some services. In national parks, lodges provide the only accommodations aside from camping, but park lodges tend to be overpriced for the quality they offer – around $100 for a double during the high season, when you need to make a reservation months in advance.

FOOD

Food doesn't rank with scenery as an outstanding feature of the Rockies. Most interesting is the Hispanic-influenced cuisine of New Mexico and parts of southern Colorado. Chinese (and more occasional Thai or Vietnamese) restaurants add some Asian flavor. Italian food is common, while French and similar Continental cuisines are available in cities and tourist centers. Otherwise, filling American food, such as bacon-and-egg breakfasts and hamburgers with fries, is easiest to find. Eat-all-you-like lunch and dinner specials for as little as $5 are common.

Bison (buffalo) meat is increasingly popular (and makes a more ecological and healthier dietary choice than beef cattle). Another regional specialty, Rocky Mountain 'oysters', is an appetizer that may cause some men to squirm upon learning precisely what a castrated bull has contributed to this dish! Freshwater trout and other local fish are found on restaurant menus.

On the Hike

Food is fuel for hikers and backpackers. As there will be no opportunity to buy food along the way (except at very occasional chalets and mountain huts – see Backcountry Accommodations, p43), you should carry plenty to eat, even on day hikes.

Health-food markets in larger towns stock bulk ingredients ideal for mixing up 'gorp' (good old raisins and peanuts), a favorite trail food that can include just about anything naturally dried, sweet or nutty. Supermarkets also sell a wide range of foods suitable for backpacking. When choosing food, try to balance bulk and weight against nutritional value. Plan for a daily weight of 2lb per person, but carry at least one extra day's rations on longer trips. Eating a big breakfast, such as muesli, will put you in good stead for the day's hiking.

Pre-prepared rice or noodle meals are tasty, but their long cooking times (especially at high elevations) use precious stove fuel. Potato powder and express rice (such as Uncle Ben's) requires only boiling water and a short wait. Beef jerky (or buffalo jerky) is a clean and lightweight source of protein. Peanut butter or eggs can be carried in special hard containers (available in hiking stores). It's advisable to avoid strong-smelling foods such as tinned fish or pungent cheeses in grizzly bear country, but tubes of cheese or salmon spread are bland enough. Firm pumpernickel-type bread is nutritious and will keep for many days in your pack.

Regional outdoor stores sell a wide variety of freeze-dried foods, which rapidly rehydrate when hot water is added. 'Freezies' are very convenient, but at up to $8 per packet – never enough for two hungry hikers – they are relatively expensive. Some of the leading brands are Backpacker's Pantry, Mountain House and Natural High, which all have quite flavorsome dishes.

Wild Food

Wild delicacies of the Rocky Mountains include a great assortment of berries (especially haws, huckleberries, saskatoons or serviceberries, and whortleberries), mushrooms (especially morels), pin cherries, pine nuts and even wild onions and prickly pears. Anglers can supplement their diet with fresh trout. The berry high season is

August, although in some years there is almost no fruit due to late frosts, low rainfall or other unfavorable conditions.

Wild food should be seen as an occasional treat, not as sustenance. Mushroom picking is no longer permitted in US national parks, and permits or other restrictions often apply on BLM and USFS lands. (Deaths sometimes occur when toxic mushrooms are mistaken for edible species.) Harvesting other wild fruit for personal use is generally allowed in national parks and other protected areas, but berry pickers must avoid trampling vegetation and should take only modest amounts of fruit (no more than one cup per person per day).

A good website for mushroomers is W www.fungaljungal.org. Also see Natural History under Books (p61).

DRINKS
Alcoholic Drinks
Parts of the Rocky Mountains states were formerly 'dry', and in Utah and some counties of Colorado only relatively weak 3.2% beer is available in supermarkets. In Utah, 'real' beer, wine and other alcohol can only be bought at state liquor stores (closed Sunday) or served at restaurants and private clubs (which casual patrons can 'join' for a small fee). There are wineries in southern Colorado and northern New Mexico.

People aged under 21 (minors) are prohibited from consuming alcohol in the US. Carry a driving license or passport as proof of age to enter a bar, order alcohol at a restaurant, or buy alcohol from a store.

On the Hike Although some hikers think the only alcohol that belongs in a backpack is in first-aid sterilization swabs or stove fuel, it is not against the law to enjoy a quiet beer or bourbon in the backcountry (unlike in neighboring Canada). Some campgrounds do not permit alcohol consumption, however, and it is illegal to drink alcohol on federal land while horseback riding or mountain biking. There are also possible safety issues, as alcohol misuse is often a factor in accidents and other mishaps in the backcountry. Alcohol impairs judgment and can mislead

a person into feeling warm in dangerously cold conditions (see Hypothermia, p68). You can be arrested for driving under the influence of alcohol even on the remotest backcountry roads.

Nonalcoholic Drinks
Vending machines that dispense all those familiar sticky, bubbly soft drinks are found everywhere from hostels and motels to gasoline stations and public library lobbies. Mineral water is a healthier way to rehydrate your body after a hike.

On the Hike It doesn't make much sense to backpack with bulky, heavy soft-drink bottles or cans, but clever day hikers have been known to pre-freeze fruit juice containers to keep perishable picnic food cool. Easier to pack are concentrate powders (such as Tang), which give an instant refreshing drink. People who sweat a lot on long, hot hikes will probably benefit from special sports drinks containing salts to restore the body's electrolyte balance, although their overall necessity tends to be exaggerated. Hot chocolate is another backpacking favorite, but it's best to avoid caffeinated beverages (especially tea and coffee) early in the day as they have a diuretic effect that will contribute to body dehydration. Hands-free 'hydration bags' (such those made by Nalgene and Platypus) have drinking tubes that allow hikers to sip as they go. All water from lakes or streams should be treated before drinking (see Water Purification, p65).

CLOTHING & EQUIPMENT
Clothing
Making the right choices in clothing will ensure you stay comfortable on the hike. Modern outdoor garments made from new synthetic fabrics (which are breathable and actively remove perspiration moisture) are better for hiking than anything made of cotton or wool. Hikers should practice 'layering' to cope with changing temperatures (see the boxed text, p47).

Warm Weather Wear In the warm, dry heat of midsummer, most hikers will want

Equipment Check List

This list is a general guide to the things you might take on a hike. Your list will vary depending on the kind of hiking you want to do – camping, the terrain, weather conditions and the time of year.

Equipment
- ☐ backpack with waterproof liner
- ☐ food (high-energy)
- ☐ flashlight (torch), spare batteries and globe
- ☐ map, compass and guidebook
- ☐ medical kit*, toiletries and insect repellent
- ☐ pocket knife (with corkscrew)
- ☐ sewing/repair kit
- ☐ small towel
- ☐ sunglasses and sunscreen
- ☐ survival bag or blanket
- ☐ water container
- ☐ whistle (for emergencies)

Clothes
- ☐ gaiters
- ☐ hiking boots and spare laces
- ☐ shorts and trousers
- ☐ socks and underwear
- ☐ sunhat
- ☐ sweater, fleece or windproof jacket
- ☐ thermal underwear
- ☐ training shoes (runners) or sandals
- ☐ T-shirt and long-sleeved shirt with collar
- ☐ warm hat, scarf and gloves

- ☐ waterproof jacket or cape
- ☐ waterproof overpants

Camping
- ☐ cooking, eating and drinking utensils
- ☐ dishwashing items
- ☐ matches or lighter, and candle
- ☐ portable stove and fuel
- ☐ sleeping bag
- ☐ sleeping mat
- ☐ sleeping sheet
- ☐ spare cord
- ☐ tent (check pegs, poles, guy ropes)
- ☐ toilet paper and toilet trowel
- ☐ water purification tablets, iodine or filter

Optional Items
- ☐ altimeter
- ☐ backpack cover (waterproof)
- ☐ binoculars
- ☐ camera, spare film and batteries
- ☐ cellphone (mobile phone)**
- ☐ day-pack
- ☐ GPS receiver
- ☐ hiking poles or stick
- ☐ lightweight groundsheet
- ☐ mosquito net
- ☐ notebook and pencil
- ☐ swimming costume

* see the First-Aid Check List (p65)
** see Safety on the Hike (p74)

to wear shorts and a short-sleeve shirt, with plenty of sunscreen smeared over arms, legs and face. For maximum protection from that burning Rocky Mountains sun, wear a broad-rimmed hat – baseball caps have only a face visor, and are *not* recommended. Maybe bring some bathers in case you get an urge to jump in a lake.

Cold Weather Wear Carrying sufficient warm clothing is essential, especially on longer hikes, as weather conditions can change rapidly in the mountains (see the boxed text 'The Layering Principle', p47).

A fleece sweater or jacket will keep the body warm even when wet. Also take gloves and something to keep your head warm, like a fleece cap.

Wet Weather Wear It is vital that hikers carry a completely windproof and waterproof rainjacket at all times. It should be properly seam-sealed and have a hood to keep the rain and wind off your head. Most experienced hikers prefer garments made from Gore-Tex or a similar breathable fabric. Plastic ponchos – or other cheap solutions – just won't do, as they tear easily, catch on branches and blow around in the wind. A pair of waterproof overpants is also highly recommended, although hiking in wet overpants is tiring and water tends to run into your boots – wearing gaiters helps prevent this.

Footwear

It is important to ensure that your boots are properly worn-in before you begin any serious hiking. Some hikers prefer the greater agility that lightweight boots allow, while others insist on (heavier) sturdy designs that give firm ankle support and protect feet in rough terrain. Hiking boots should have a flexible (preferably polyurethane) midsole, rather than a steel shank, and an insole that supports the arch and heel. A Gore-Tex inner lining (which allows perspiration to escape) will help keep your feet dry, but its effectiveness will gradually decrease as the boots wear. European models (such as Scarpa and Meindl) are among the best.

Equipment

Backpack A backpack that weighs on your shoulders as you hike is not just uncomfortable, it may be doing permanent injury to your back. The only good backpacks are those with robust, easily adjustable waistbelts that can comfortably support the entire weight carried, effectively transferring the load from your shoulders onto your hips. The shoulder straps should serve only to steady the backpack.

Backpacks with a relatively large capacity (at least 5500 cubic inches) are best for overnight hiking in the backcountry, although some people prefer to use a smaller backpack and strap their tent and/or sleeping mat to its outside. Until very recently, virtually all backpacks (including top brands such as Dana Design, Gregory or Osprey) were internal-frame models. Internal-frame backpacks fit snugly against your back, keeping the weight close to your center of gravity. Unfortunately, this allows for poor ventilation, so sweat soaks your shirt instead of evaporating to cool your body. Newer, redesigned external-frame packs largely solve this problem, but even the best

The Layering Principle

The layering principle involves adding or peeling off extra clothing as you start to feel cold or hot. This allows the body to maintain a comfortable and constant temperature.

Ideally, garments should be made from synthetic fabrics that wick away perspiration. On summer days, the base layer may be all you feel like wearing, although all layers should be carried in your pack.

For the upper body, the base layer is typically a light vest or T-shirt made of synthetic thermal fabric (eg, Polartec). The second layer is a long-sleeve shirt, and the third layer can be either a synthetic fleece sweater or pile jacket that continues to wick away moisture. The outer shell consists of a weatherproof jacket that also protects against strong cold winds.

For the lower body, shorts will probably be most comfortable in midsummer, although some hikers prefer long pants – light, quick-drying fabric (no more than 30% cotton) is best. As 'long-john' type underwear can't be easily removed, it is not recommended except when conditions are expected to remain very cold for the whole day (such as from mid-fall). Waterproof overpants form the outer layer for the lower body.

brands (eg, Mystery Ranch) are still slightly cumbersome and no cheaper than internal-frame backpacks.

For day hikes or side trips from camp, a small day-pack or 'bumbag' should hold all you need, although it's sometimes hard to justify the additional weight and bulk when your main pack can serve the same purpose.

Many hikers carry a utilities bag containing an assortment of useful things such as spare batteries, elastic bands, cords, plastic bags and spare lighter (or waterproof matches).

Sleeping Bag A three-season sleeping bag will probably be sufficient for normal midsummer conditions, but a four-season bag might be better if you are especially sensitive to cold or will be camping out in spring or fall. Using a fleece liner or sleeping with additional clothing may be a practical alternative. A design that allows good ventilation (such as a zip opening at the foot end) may improve comfort on warm nights. Most people prefer down-filled bags, which are more compact and give better insulation for their weight and bulk, but synthetic-filled bags have the advantage of retaining insulating properties even when wet. Quality three- and four-season down bags typically weigh around 2 to 3½lb respectively, while comparable synthetic bags can be twice as heavy.

Sleeping Mat Using a sleeping mat will give more comfort and better insulation from the cold ground. Closed-cell foam sleeping mats are lightest and cheapest, but are rather bulky. Inflatable sleeping mattresses (such as the Therm-a-Rest) are somewhat heavier but more comfortable and much less bulky (once you press all the air out). Air mattresses are also prone to puncture, so carry repair patches and adhesive.

Stove Hikers should carry their own stove and fuel rather than lighting campfires, which impact severely on the local environment. All of the following stove types are widely sold in outdoor-gear stores.

Multi-fuel stoves are small, very efficient and run on a variety of petroleum fuels (including automobile and aircraft fuel), making them ideal for use in places where a reliable supply of one type of fuel is hard to find. They tend, however, to be sootier, more prone to blockages from contaminated fuel, and require some care and experience to use and maintain.

Methylated spirit (ethyl alcohol) burners are slower and less efficient (requiring more fuel to be carried) but are safe, clean and easy to use. They often come as a complete cooking kit, with integrated compact pots, pans and kettles.

Butane gas stoves use disposable cartridges (which must be packed out when empty). While clean and reliable, they can be slow, awkward to pack and expensive to run over the long term.

Warning

It is illegal and irresponsible to carry any kind of stove fuel in checked or hand luggage on aircraft. Anyone caught doing so is liable to face criminal charges, and will almost certainly not be allowed to board.

Tent A tent is essential for virtually all overnight hikes in the Rockies, but cheaper, lower-quality tents are unlikely to offer safe protection in a storm. All modern mountain tents are supported by flexible (usually aluminum) poles, and come in a great variety of compact 'tunnel', lightweight 'single-hoop' or more robust 'dome' designs. Most tents are two-skin (with a waterproof outer fly), and one/two-person models typically weigh under 5/8lb. Breathable single-skin tents (such those made by Bibler) are lighter, but tend to be much more expensive. Vestibules (porches) are useful for stashing gear, but should never be used for cooking as this may attract bears to your tent (see Animal Attacks, p74). Carry a short section of aluminum tubing rod to temporarily repair broken tent poles.

Hiking Poles Giving stability and absorbing jolting on steep descents, hiking poles can help prevent knee pain, but tightly gripping the poles for long periods tires the hands. Better designs (such as Gabel Summit) have wrist-straps that largely eliminate this problem, but they can cost up to $100 a pair. Snow baskets can be fitted to some models, allowing their use in snow.

Lighting Even in the long daylight hours of summer, a flashlight (torch) is an essential safety item and should be carried even on day hikes. Headlamps (a good brand is Petzl) are best as they allow free use of your hands. Carry spare batteries.

Small (packable) candle or oil lanterns are a cheaper form of lighting, but should only be used outside the tent. Avoid spilling wax or oil on the ground. Citronella-scented candles will deter insects, but may attract bears.

Sunglasses Hiking in the mountains requires sunglasses with yellow/brown-tinted lenses that block out all UV (and most infrared) rays and stop glare from snow or water surfaces. Mountaineering 'glacier' sunglasses are often worn by hikers, but they tend to be poorly ventilated and uncomfortable in hot summer conditions.

Binoculars Compact lightweight binoculars (8x25 or 10x25) are more or less essential for bird-watching and wildlife-viewing, and useful for surveying the route ahead. Quality models (eg, Brunton) cost from around $100.

Buying & Hiring Locally

The large outdoor-gear retailers, Recreation Equipment Inc (REI; ☎ 800-426-4840, W www.rei.com) and Eastern Mountain Sports (EMS; ☎ 888-463-6367, W www.ems .com), have many stores throughout the region. In Denver, REI (☎ 303-756-3100, 1416 Platte St) has one of the world's biggest outdoor-gear stores. There is also a large EMS Denver store (870 S Colorado Blvd, Glendale). Sierra Trading Post (☎ 800-713-4534, W www.sierratradingpost.com) based in Cheyenne, Wyoming, has several retail outlets in the middle Rockies region and an excellent online store.

Even small towns usually have some kind of outdoor and backpacking supplier – many are given under Gateways, Access Towns and Nearest Towns in the regional chapters. Otherwise, check at large supermarkets (especially Wal-Mart) or hardware stores.

In some places (typically large cities or university towns) backpacking gear may be available for hire. Average daily rates are: tent ($10), backpack ($7), stove ($5), ice axe ($5) and crampons ($5).

MAPS & NAVIGATION

Carrying and using a topographic map will greatly increase the safety and appreciation of your hike. A good map enables hikers to easily identify landscape features and, if necessary, to navigate their way out of a lost situation. Maps become more important the further you venture into the backcountry. Although you don't necessarily have to buy

a whole stack of large-scale quads (see Large-Scale Maps below), some kind of up-to-date topographic map covering the core section of your hike should be carried. See also Maps in This Book (p52).

Small-Scale Maps

State tourism offices often distribute free state maps. GTR Mapping (W www.gtrmap ping.com) publishes an excellent and widely available series of 'recreational' state road maps ($3.95 each) that show national parks and wilderness areas as well as USFS campgrounds and access roads. Rand McNally (W www.randmcnally.com) also publishes road maps of each state; its *Central & Western United States* ($2.95) covers the greater Rocky Mountains region. The DeLorme Mapping (W www.delorme.com) atlas/ gazetteer series ($19.95 each) covers individual states with contoured maps scaled at between 1:160,000 and 1:250,000.

Large-Scale Maps

The United States Geological Survey (USGS), an agency of the federal Department of the Interior, publishes detailed topographic maps covering the entire Rocky Mountains region. The 7.5-minute topographic series is the USGS standard. (The USGS 15-minute series scaled at 1:62,500 has now been abandoned, although these older maps are sometimes still locally available.)

Most 7.5-minute maps, known as quadrangles or 'quads', are scaled at 1:24,000 (one inch = 2000 feet), although a (rather rare) metric version is scaled at 1:25,000. Due to their large scale, quads reproduce topographic detail quite accurately, but having to use numerous maps – especially for longer hiking routes – is inconvenient and expensive. Also many quads have not been revised for decades, so infrastructure such as trails, roads or buildings may be shown incorrectly.

The USGS also publishes a national 1:100,000 series, which is based on the 7.5-minute series, but shows all measurements in metric (ie, meters and kilometers). Although maps of the 1:100,000 series cover a much wider area than 1:24,000 quads, relief and detail is generally shown much less reliably, so they are not used much for serious backcountry travel. The USGS also has a very incomplete series of 'county' maps, scaled at 1:50,000 or 1:100,000, but these are seldom of any great use to hikers.

The United States Forest Service (USFS) produces topographic maps of national forest areas at a scale of 1:127,000 (one inch = 2mi). These maps are useful for a regional overview, but they are not really suitable for hiking purposes. The National Park Service gives out good park maps at park entrances, but these are also intended only for general orientation.

For information on where to find and how to order maps, see Buying Maps.

Special Hiking Maps

An increasing number of special high-quality topographic maps for hikers are available. Hiking maps are typically large-format, pre-folded, waterproof maps produced by private cartographic companies (occasionally by the USFS) at scales between about 1:40,000 and 1:140,000. They cover the most popular hiking areas, especially national parks and wilderness areas, and add features of special interest to hikers, such as campsites, backcountry regulations and trail distances. Hiking maps generally cost between $6 and $10. The series of hiking maps by National Geographic's Trails Illustrated (W maps.nationalgeographic.com /trails) is by far the largest, but Earthwalk Press (☎ 800-828-MAPS) and Drake Mountain Maps (☎ 505-988-8929) also produce useful hiking maps.

CD-ROMs

CD-ROMs containing hundreds of digitized USGS 1:24,000 quads and 1:100,000 topographic maps that cover entire regions or states are widely available from around $50. These maps can be printed out in color at a reasonably high resolution, and may work out to be a cheaper and more convenient way to buy maps for many hikers. Companies like iGage (W www.igage.com) and Maptech (W www.maptech.com) also sell

software that allows hikers using a GPS receiver (see GPS below) to plot their exact route on their computers.

Buying Maps

To order a USGS map index and price list, phone ☎ 800-435-7627, visit the USGS website at W www.usgs.gov, or write to USGS Distribution Branch, Building 810, Box 25064, Denver Federal Center, Denver, CO 80225. If you plan to order maps by mail, allow at least six weeks for delivery.

USFS regional offices, park visitor centers and outdoor stores in regional towns usually sell hiking maps (such as Trails Illustrated or Earthwalk Press), USFS maps and USGS quads. Otherwise try the local stationery store, hardware store or gas station. Quads cost $4 each when purchased from a federal agency; while many retail outlets charge the same price, some mark up quads as high as $7.

For advice on where to buy maps near trailheads, see the Information or Nearest Towns sections for each region or hike in this book.

GPS

The Global Positioning System (GPS) employs a network of satellites that beam encoded signals to special GPS receivers on the ground. GPS receivers decode the signals to determine the user's precise location to within 50ft, anywhere on the planet, at any time of day, in almost any weather. The cheapest hand-held GPS receivers now cost less than $100, but better (more expensive) models are able to work with digital mapping systems. Other important factors to consider when buying a GPS receiver are its weight and battery life.

A GPS receiver is of little use to hikers unless used with an accurate topographic map – the GPS receiver simply gives your position, which you must then locate on the map. GPS receivers will only work properly in the open. Directly below high cliffs, near large bodies of water or in dense tree cover, for example, the signals from a crucial satellite may be blocked (or bounce off rocks or water) and give inaccurate readings. GPS receivers are more vulnerable to breakdowns (including dead batteries) than the humble magnetic compass – a low-tech device that has served navigators faithfully for centuries – so don't rely entirely on them.

HIKES IN THIS BOOK

The hikes featured in this book (which represent years of research by the authors) are intended as a short-list selection of the best the Rockies have to offer. We have tried to provide a balance between day hikes, overnight hikes and longer backpacking trips. Although the general assumption is that readers will have their own vehicle, some of the routes can be undertaken by people dependent on public transportation. Hikes are recommended as described – although many side trips are included, alternative routes are not dealt with in depth. See the table (p4) for a full list of hikes.

For additional hike suggestions, see Other Hikes at the end of each regional chapter.

Route Descriptions

All multiday hikes are divided into 'Day' stages, each of which ends at a campsite or trailhead and can be easily walked in a single day. Other good camping possibilities along (or a short way off) the trail are noted either in the route description itself or under the occasional Alternative Campsites heading. Out-and-back hikes are described for each day of the return (backtrack) hike, even if it's only a sentence or two.

Hikes can usually be done in either direction, but there is often a strong argument for going one way instead of the other and this is explained in the text.

Level of Difficulty

Hikes in this guidebook are rated easy, easy–moderate, moderate, moderate–hard or hard. The grading appears in the summary box at the start of each hike. While there will often be disagreement regarding the difficulty of a hike, the authors have taken considerable care to ensure that gradings are at least consistent.

The level of difficulty tends to increase when a trail is wet or snowed over. Ratings for high-elevation hikes assume a reasonable degree of acclimation prior to starting. Hikers unfamiliar with a region are advised to do an initial day hike to acquaint themselves with local topography and climate. Remember, your own perception of a hike's difficulty is partially dependent on how you feel when you do it.

On the whole, designated (ie, official) hiking trails in the Rocky Mountains are well defined and sensibly routed, with numerous switchbacks that minimize the strenuousness (and erosion) on steep slopes.

While most of the hikes in this guidebook call for a good level of fitness, serious navigation is rarely necessary except in foggy, rainy or snowy weather. Although a bit of scrambling over boulders may be called for on some routes, none of the hikes require any special climbing gear, such as ice axe and crampons, if undertaken in normal summer conditions.

Hikes graded **easy** are suitable for anyone with a basic level of fitness and health. They are relatively short, have very mild gradients and present no navigational difficulties. Easy hikes can be done comfortably by a family with children aged 10 and up.

Hikes graded **moderate** are longer day hikes or shorter (overnight) backpacking trips that involve some ascending and descending. Ideally they should be undertaken by people with slightly more experience and better fitness.

Hikes graded **hard** are physically demanding. They generally take you into high, remote mountains where there is a strong possibility of encountering summer snow or bad weather (perhaps even grizzly bears). Long ascents and descents are common. Although the trail will be well trodden and not difficult to follow, it is important to have a basic knowledge of backcountry navigation.

Times & Distances

Average times needed to complete a day's hiking are given in the route description for each day stage, side trip and alternative route. Given times do not include rest stops or toilet breaks.

Maps in This Book
Small-scale maps at the start of every regional chapter give an overview of featured hikes. Each hike is detailed on a large-scale map that shows the route in continuous red stipple, and alternative routes or side trips in dashes of red stipple. Start and finish points are marked with boxes, and campsites, lookout points and other symbols are also indicated. The (varying) scale and contour intervals appear beneath the north arrow.

A map legend appears on the last page of the book.

Altitude Measurements
Elevations quoted in this book are largely based on USGS topographic maps (particularly 1:24,000 quads) or USFS maps. Where no official elevation was available, given heights were based either on the authors' own – not infallible – altimeter and/or GPS receiver measurements or estimations made by comparing map contour intervals.

Place Names & Terminology
Although the names of three states – Idaho, Utah and Wyoming – are derived from words of Native American languages, relatively little of that original nomenclature survives in the Rocky Mountains; some examples include Utah's Mt Timpanogos, Colorado's Sawatch Range and New Mexico's Chimayosos Peak. More often, Euro-Americans themselves have named land features after individual tribes, such as Montana's Flathead Lake or the Colorado Front Range's Indian Peaks.

Many place names commemorate early explorers, 'mountain men', prospectors or artists, including Montana's Lewis and Clark National Forest or Colorado's Longs Peak and Bierstadt Lake. Numerous mountains, lakes and streams are named – often with great repetition – after native animals or plants, as in Bighorn Peak, Elk Creek, Spruce Lake and the Bitterroot Valley. In the southern Rockies, Spanish places names are common, such as the Rio de los Pinos ('river of the pines'), and Spanish words are often combined with Anglo words, as in Truchas ('trout') Peak. Highly descriptive names,

such as Montana's Froze-to-Death Plateau or Colorado's Never Summer Mountains, hint at the rigors of the high mountains.

Readers may be unfamiliar with certain words in widespread usage throughout the Rockies, such as butte, snowpack or windthrow, which are listed in the glossary at the end of this book. Directional expressions, such as 'the east bank of the stream' (rather than, say, 'the true right bank of a stream'), are used throughout the text. Note also that terms like 'southwestward' are intended only as a general indication of direction, not as an exact compass bearing.

PERMITS & FEES
Entry Fees
All national parks in the Rockies charge an entry fee. These range from $5 to $10 for individual pedestrians or cyclists, and from $10 to $20 per vehicle. Fees are collected at park gates (cash and traveler's checks are the only accepted payment methods), and visitors receive a map and multiple-entry ticket valid for one week.

Under the federal Fee Demonstration Program, parking passes (typically $3/7 per day/week for each vehicle) must be purchased and displayed in vehicles parked at some trailheads (and other recreation areas) on lands administered by the BLM and USFS throughout the Rocky Mountains.

Hikers who enter Native American lands, including the Mission Mountains Tribal Wilderness in Montana and the Wind River Roadless Area in Wyoming, need to buy a 'fishing' or use permit from the local tribal authority.

Information on national park entry fees, trailhead parking passes and use permits for Native American land is given under Permits & Regulations in the regional chapters.

National Parks Pass & Golden Eagle Passport
The National Parks Pass makes excellent value for anyone who intends to visit more than one national park. The pass is issued per vehicle and costs $50 for one year's unlimited access to all national parks in the US, as well as most other areas administered by the National Park Service.

National Scenic Trails

Several of the US's long-distance National Scenic Trails (administered by the Department of Agriculture) pass through the Rockies. While few people ever have the time or energy to trek the entire distance of these long-distance trails, readers will often find themselves doing hikes that include small sections of the Continental Divide Trail or the Colorado Trail. Long-distance trails help popularize individual regions and form the principal arterial routes through many mountain ranges. Some trails, such as the Lewis and Clark National Historic Trail (which traces the explorers' epic journey) and the Mormon Pioneer National Historic Trail (which follows Brigham Young's flight from Illinois to Salt Lake City) are road-based routes intended mainly for motorized travelers.

The American Long Distance Hiking Association West (ALDHA-West; **w** www.aldhawest.org; PO Box 5286, Eugene, OR 97405-0286) promotes 'fellowship and communication among long distance hikers' in the western US.

American Discovery Trail

Distantly paralleling the I-50, the 4800mi American Discovery Trail (ADT) is a coast-to-coast route from Cape Henlopen State Park in Delaware to Point Reyes National Seashore near San Francisco. It connects many existing long-distance trails, including the Appalachian, North Country, Continental Divide and the Pacific Crest Trails. The two separate eastern branches of the ADT converge at Denver. The ADT then continues via sections of the Colorado Trail and Continental Divide Trail through Colorado National Monument. It exits the Rocky Mountains on Kokopelli's Trail, which leads west across the Colorado Plateau into the Utah Canyonlands.

The American Discovery Trail Explorer's Guide by Reese Lukei is a detailed guidebook to the route. *American Discoveries* by Ellen Dudley & Eric Seaborg ($24.95) gives an anecdotal introduction to the ADT. The official ADT website is at **w** www.discoverytrail.org.

Colorado Trail

The 474mi Colorado Trail (CT; see p260) stretches from Denver to Durango in the southwest corner of the state. Contiguous with the Continental Divide Trail for about 200mi, the CT crosses through seven national forests, five wilderness areas and eight mountain ranges – some of Colorado's finest scenery.

For more information contact the Colorado Trail Foundation (☎ 303-384-3729, ext 113, **w** www.coloradotrail.org, 710 10th Street, Suite 210, Golden, CO 80401-5843). It publishes the official guidebook, *The Colorado Trail* ($22.95).

Continental Divide Trail

The 3100mi Continental Divide Trail (CDT) leads along the crest of the Rocky Mountains from the Montana-Canada border to the New Mexico-Mexico border. The CDT follows the Atlantic-Pacific watershed as closely as possible, traversing along high ridges, over peaks, into mountain passes, past alpine lakes, through forests and meadows and across desert plateaus. Its route transits many of the Rockies' great wildland areas, including Glacier National Park, Bob Marshall Wilderness, Yellowstone National Park, Wind River Range, Rocky Mountain National Park, Indian Peaks Wilderness, Sawatch Range and the San Juan Mountains.

Barely a handful of people complete the entire six-month trek each year, but thousands of hikers use shorter sections of the CDT to do ascents of peaks, high traverses or loop combinations.

Westcliffe (**w** www.westcliffepublishers.com) publishes the official CDT guides in four separate volumes – *Montana/Idaho*, *Wyoming*, *Colorado* and *New Mexico* – that cost around $24.95 each. For additional information contact the Continental Divide Trail Alliance (☎ 888-909-2382, **w** www.cdtrail.org).

(By comparison, the Yellowstone-Grand Teton national park entry fee is $20/40 per week/year).

The National Parks Pass can be upgraded to a Golden Eagle Passport by purchasing and attaching a special $15 hologram sticker. The Golden Eagle Passport allows holders and accompanying passengers free access to *all* federal recreation areas that charge entrance fees, including on BLM, Fish and Wildlife Service and USFS lands.

These passes do not cover entry to Native American reservations, or fees for camping and parking on federal lands. The passes are sold at principle fee collection points, such as national park and USFS entrance gates or visitor centers, but can be also be purchased by telephone at ☎ 888-467-2757 or online at Ⓦ www.nationalparks.org.

Golden Age Passport & Golden Access Passport US senior citizens or permanent residents aged 62 or older may purchase a lifetime Golden Age Passport for a once-only fee of $10. US citizens or permanent residents who are blind or permanently disabled are entitled to a free lifetime Golden Access Passport.

Both passports cover entrance fees to all national parks, monuments, historic sites, recreation areas (including BLM and USFS lands) and national wildlife refuges. They also bring a 50% discount on fees for camping, parking, swimming and tours. Both the Golden Age Passport and the Golden Access Passport must be obtained in person at a federal area where an entrance fee is charged.

Hiking Permits

In all of the Rockies' national parks, you must have a backcountry permit to camp in backcountry areas. No permit is required for day hikes in national parks. Rules vary, but park authorities generally issue only a set number of backcountry permits per day for each backcountry camping area. In some national parks (eg, Yellowstone and Grand Teton) backcountry permits are issued free, while others (eg, Glacier and Rocky Mountain) a flat or per-day fee is charged. Making reservations well in advance is advisable

for all popular hiking routes. In most cases no more than half of the campsites can be reserved, with the remainder available the day before on a first-come, first-served basis. The backcountry permit lists the dates for which each campsite has been reserved – once issued, the itinerary cannot be changed without approval. Permits are regularly checked by patrolling park rangers and hikers caught camping out without a valid permit are likely to be fined.

With certain exceptions, such as Colorado's Indian Peaks Wilderness, hikers do not need a backcountry permit to camp in (USFS administered) national forests and wilderness areas. In some areas, such as Idaho's Sawtooth Wilderness and Wyoming's Cloud Peak Wilderness, hikers are merely required to self-register as they enter the wilderness.

Specific information on backcountry permits and self-registration requirements is given under Permits & Regulations in the regional chapters.

Fishing Licenses

All anglers must have a valid fishing license, regardless of where they fish in the Rocky Mountains. Fishing licenses are issued by, and are valid only within, each state (although limited reciprocal agreements sometimes exist). State fishing licenses are not valid on Native American reservations or in some national parks (eg, Yellowstone), where additional fishing permits are required. Regulations vary widely between states, and catch-and-release is mandatory on certain waterways.

If you'll be doing more than two week's fishing in any one state, it will probably work out cheaper to buy an annual license. Costs of fishing licenses also vary from state to state, but the higher the charge for nonresidents, the better the fishing seems to be! Nonresident fishing licenses cost $3 to $5 for one day, $17 to $23 for one week (if available) and $39 to $65 for one (usually calendar) year, although state residents will pay only a fraction of this amount.

For further information, contact these state fishing agencies:

Colorado Division of Wildlife (☎ 303-297-1192; W www.wildlife.state.co.us; 6060 Broadway, Denver, CO 80216)
Idaho Fish & Game (☎ 208-334-3700; W www.state.id.us/fishgame; 600 S Walnut, PO Box 25, Boise, ID 83707)
Montana Fish, Wildlife & Parks (☎ 406-444-2535, 1-800-TIP-MONT; W www.fwp.state.mt.us; 1420 E 6th Ave, Helena MT 59620)
New Mexico Department of Game & Fish (☎ 800-862-9310; W www.gmfsh.state.nm.us; 1 Wildlife Way, Santa Fe, NM 87505)
Utah Division of Wildlife Resources (☎ 801-538-4700; W www.wildlife.utah.gov; 1594 W North Temple St, Box 146301, Salt Lake City, UT 84114-6301)
Wyoming Game & Fish Department (☎ 800-842-1934; W gf.state.wy.us; 5400 Bishop Blvd, Cheyenne, WY 82006-0001)

RESPONSIBLE HIKING

Backcountry areas are fragile environments and cannot support insensitive or careless activity, especially with the increasing numbers of visitors. The aim of hikers should be to 'leave no trace' (see the boxed text, p56) as they move through the mountains.

Campsites

To preserve the environment, use old campsites instead of clearing new ones. Camp at least 200ft (70 steps) from the nearest lake, river or stream. Different hiking parties often have to share a common camping area. In such cases, have some regard for your neighbors. Pitch your tent a respectable distance from others – a 100ft buffer zone is about right. Keep your gear tidy and out of other people's way. Avoid intrusive noise, such as loud radios or singing.

Campfires

For many hikers, sitting around a fire is almost synonymous with a wilderness experience; however, campfires cause major environmental degradation in heavily used backcountry areas. Campfires are now severely restricted in many national parks and wilderness areas. In some places it is mandatory to light campfires in a fire blanket or fire pan. During a long dry spell, a local campfire ban may be imposed on public lands. We recommend that all hikers carry and use a lightweight stove. If you do light a fire, keep it at least 9ft away from flammable material (including grass and wood), watch it at all times and douse it thoroughly with water or dirt before going to sleep or leaving the site – always check it is fully out.

Water & Toilets

Water contaminated by careless or irresponsible hikers is a common cause of illness in the backcountry. Always use toilets established at trailheads, campsites or along trails, regardless of how smelly they are. Where no toilet exists, bury human waste in a 6-inch-deep 'cathole' at least 300ft from the nearest lake or water course. Pack out toilet paper in a sealed plastic bag. Salt in urine may draw wildlife that chew plants or dig up soil (see Dangers & Annoyances, p57) – urinate on unvegetated surfaces such as rocks or conifer needles.

Avoid using soaps and detergents – sand or a kitchen scourer will clean your pots remarkably well. Tip dishwater far from streams and remove residue food (it may attract bears) with a small basin or strainer.

Access

Access to some hikes is via private property, which may extend well beyond the trailhead. Roads or trails through freehold land are not automatically a right of way, however, and such public access may have been carefully negotiated by the BLM or USFS. The goodwill of local landholders depends on the continuing cooperation of all visitors. Please do not camp (or collect firewood) on private land without permission, and leave stock gates as you find them.

WOMEN HIKERS

While there are definitely some people who think a woman shouldn't be in the mountains, particularly without a male companion, rarely are these people encountered while hiking in the Rockies. If alone, in pairs or groups, or with partners, women actually seem to outnumber men on some routes. If there is an occasional remark, the best advice is not to react unless such behavior persists.

Leave No Trace

Leave No Trace (**w** www.lnt.org) is an educational and ethical code designed by conservation groups and federal agencies to minimize the impact of nonmotorized recreational use of public lands. Leave No Trace consists of seven basic principles:

Plan Ahead & Prepare

Poorly prepared hikers may encounter unexpected conditions that cause them to degrade natural resources and put themselves at risk.

Travel & Camp on Durable Surfaces

Don't short-cut switchbacks. When hiking off-trail keep to forested, rocky or snow-covered terrain and avoid fragile bogs or meadows. Don't mark your route in any way.

Dispose of Waste Properly

Pack out all garbage – don't burn or bury it.

Leave What You Find

Don't remove natural objects and archaeological or cultural artifacts – it is often illegal to souvenir antlers, petrified wood or colored rocks. Never pick wildflowers; berries and other wild food should be collected sparingly – leave enough for later hikers (and wildlife!). Do not dig trenches for tents or hammer nails into trees.

Minimize Campfire Impact

Refrain from lighting campfires. Otherwise use established fireplaces or protect the ground by making a 'mound fire' using a fire blanket or fire pan.

Respect Wildlife

Don't disturb wildlife – observe wild animals from a distance (carry binoculars) and keep down unnecessary noise (except when hiking in grizzly bear country, where noise warns bears of your approach). Never feed wild animals or let them eat food scraps. Hang all food in a strong sack at least 12ft above the ground and away from climbable trunks and tree limbs.

Be Considerate of Other Visitors

Be courteous and polite on the trail and at camping areas. Horses and pack animals have right of way – move downhill off the trail to avoid spooking livestock. Supervise dogs and use a leash where necessary.

If you feel uncomfortable hiking alone, stick to well-trodden trails where you are likely to meet people at campsites or try to hook up with a group or companion before hitting the trail; national park visitor centers and ranger stations often have bulletin boards specifically for this purpose.

Apart from the natural dangers of hiking in the mountains, the major safety issue for women hikers in the Rockies is bears. While it has not been proven that bears have an affinity for menstruating women, more than one woman has been attacked by a bear while in the middle of her menstrual cycle. If you have your period while hiking in bear country, be sure to carry plenty of tampons (pads are not recommended as they are more odorous and messy) and plenty of sealable plastic bags in which to dispose of them. If you accidentally bleed on clothing or gear, wash it out immediately when you get to camp. Women who have a heavy menstrual flow may want to try to schedule their trip for before or after their period. Also, perfumes or scented cosmetics, including deodorants, should not be worn in areas where you are likely to encounter bears, as the smell will attract them.

Resources & Organizations

Useful websites for outdoor women include the Climbing Femmes (W www.onr.com /user/hotrod/climbingfemmes), Journeywoman (W www.journeywoman.com) and Adventure Women (W www.adventure-women.com).

The National Organization for Women (NOW; ☎ 202-331-0066; W www.now.org; 1000 16th St NW, Suite 700, Washington, DC 20036) is a good resource. NOW can refer you to state and local chapters.

A Journey of One's Own by Thalia Zepatos ($16.95) contains travel tips, anecdotes and a long list of sources and resources for the independent woman traveler. *Adventures in Good Company*, also by Thalia Zepatos ($16), covers a huge range of adventure, outdoor and special interest tours and activities for women in the US and abroad.

For local resources, check in the Yellow Pages phone directory under 'Women's Organizations and Services'. Women's bookstores are very good places to find out about upcoming gatherings, readings and meetings and often have bulletin boards where you can find or place travel notices.

HIKING WITH CHILDREN

If your children enjoy hiking when they're young, there's a good chance they'll be hikers for the rest of their lives. All regions of the Rockies, especially the national parks, offer a good range of hikes suitable for families with children. Baby food, diapers (nappies) and creams are readily available in supermarkets and pharmacies throughout the Rocky Mountains region.

Children can be slow to adapt to changes of diet, temperature and altitude, so before undertaking a route of several days it might be wise to first establish a base camp and do a number of day- or half-day hikes to break yourselves in. It's important to choose hikes that have scope for lots of variety – a visitor center at which to spend some time, places for other related activities (lakes are perfect), unusual features such as archaeological sites, or somewhere there is a good chance of seeing wildlife. Tourist regions around large national parks such as Yellowstone and Glacier

are well equipped with children's entertainment such as go-kart tracks, minigolf and water slides. Keep in mind that spectacular views and interesting geological formations are usually more of an adult pastime. Hiking with llamas (see the boxed text, p41), which make gentle, easily managed pack animals, is ideal, even with quite young children.

Make sure you carry plenty of food and drinks, including the children's favorites. It's important to bring a generous range of warm clothing – children warm up and cool down very quickly. The distance and duration of the hike you choose should be firmly based on the children's capabilities, rather than your own with a bit taken off.

The Mountaineers (W www.moun taineers .org) publishes *Best Hikes with Children in Colorado* by Maureen Keilty and *Best Hikes with Children in New Mexico* by Bob Julyan (both $14.95). Lonely Planet's *Travel with Children* by Cathy Lanigan ($14.99) has lots of practical advice on the subject, along with first-hand travel stories from Lonely Planet authors and readers.

DANGERS & ANNOYANCES

On the whole, hiking in the Rocky Mountains is a safe and hassle-free activity, but you can further reduce risk and inconvenience by being aware of potential problems – see the Health & Safety chapter (p64–78) for more information.

Fire danger in the Rockies varies from year to year, but is often extreme in July and August. Local USFS offices can advise hikers about forest fires burning out of control, and fire warnings are usually posted at wilderness access points. Otherwise, contact the National Fire Information Center (☎ 208-387-5050, W www.nifc.gov).

Mountain animals, especially deer, marmots and mountain goats, crave salt and will often gnaw at sweaty garments or vegetation where humans have recently urinated. Although hardly what anyone could call attacks, minor 'incidents' sometimes occur when insistent animals, emboldened by their insatiable salt addiction, try to chew a backpack's strap or sneak off with a momentarily unwatched (and long un-washed!) hat. Hikers and campers can avoid such occurrences by hanging soiled gear and clothing well out of animals' reach, and by keeping an eye out for delinquent varmints. For information on more serious animal threats, see Animal Attacks (p74).

USEFUL ORGANIZATIONS

There are many organizations that administer or promote hiking and outdoor activities in the Rockies. Some are useful to join as they provide services such as handbooks and discounts for members. You may want to contact others for information. See also Conservation Groups, p36.

Gay & Lesbian Organizations

Gay Outdoors (W gayoutdoors.org) is a free Internet-based club for gay and bisexual outdoor enthusiasts.

Government Agencies

To find regional offices for government agencies listed below, check the blue section of the local White Pages directory under US Government, or call the Federal Information Center (☎ 800-688-9889).

Bureau of Land Management (BLM; ☎ 202-452-5125; W www.blm.gov; 1849 C St, Room 406-LS, Washington, DC 20240) is an agency of the US Department of Interior and manages public use of federal lands. BLM runs volunteer programs such as hosting campgrounds, monitoring animal or bird habitats, replanting vegetation and noxious weed control. There are numerous regional BLM offices throughout the Rockies, some of which are given under Gateways, Access Towns and Nearest Towns in the regional chapters.

National Park Service (NPS; ☎ 888-467-2757; W www.nps.gov; Department of Interior, PO Box 37127, Washington, DC 20013-7127), also an agency of the US Department of Interior, administers national parks and national recreation areas as well as national monuments and national historic sites.

United States Forest Service (USFS; ☎ 303-275-5310, 236-9431; W www.fs.fed.us; 11177 W 8th Ave, PO Box 25127, Lakewood, CO 80225), an agency of the Department of Agriculture, manages national forest lands, including most designated wilderness areas.

Hiking & Mountain Clubs

American Alpine Club (AAC; ☎ 303-384-0110; W www.americanalpineclub.org; 710 10th St, Suite 100, Golden, CO 80401) is essentially concerned with mountaineering. Yearly membership costs $75, which includes the annual *American Alpine Journal* (otherwise $30). The AAC's central office is in the American Mountaineering Center (currently under construction), which has a museum with exhibits on conservation, recreation, safety and mountaineering history.

American Hiking Society (AHS; ☎ 301-565-6704; W www.americanhiking.org; 1422 Fenwick Lane, Silver Spring, MD 20910) is the main national organization representing hikers, and acts as an umbrella for regional hiking clubs throughout the US. Membership costs $25/35 individual/family; members receive the club's bimonthly *American Hiker*.

Colorado Mountain Club (CMC; ☎ 303-554-7688; W www.cmc.org; 710 10th St, Suite 200, Golden, CO 80401) sponsors numerous mountain activities, including courses, conservation programs and trail work. It is also in the American Mountaineering Center, and has the US's largest mountaineering library. Annual membership costs $46/64 individual/family; members receive the CMC's monthly *Trail & Timberline* magazine (subscriptions otherwise $15).

Mountain Guides' Associations

American Mountain Guides Association (☎ 303-271-0984; W www.amga.com; 710 10th Street, Suite 101, Golden, CO 80401) represents certified US mountain guides.

TOURIST OFFICES

All larger centers and most towns have tourist offices (often run by volunteers) where you can get accurate information or advice. For the nearest tourist offices to your hike, see under Gateways, Access Towns or Nearest Towns in the regional chapters.

Tourist authorities publish free state maps as well as seasonal 'vacation guides', which are distributed through local tourist offices and include everything from accommodations to activities throughout the state or region. Listed here are the state tourist offices of the six states in the greater Rocky Mountains region:

Colorado Tourism Office (☎ 303-892-3840, 800-265-6723; W www.colorado.com; 1625 Broadway, Suite 1700, Denver, CO 80202)

Idaho Travel Council (☎ 208-334-2470, 800-842-5858; W www.visitid.org; 700 W State St, Boise, ID 83720-0093)

New Mexico Department of Tourism (☎ 800-733-6396; W www.newmexico.org; 491 Old Santa Fe Trail, PO Box 20002, Santa Fe, NM 87501)

Travel Montana (☎ 406-444-2654, 800-847-4868; W www.visitmt.com; 1424 9th Ave, PO Box 200533, Helena, MT 59620)

Utah Travel Council (☎ 801-538-1900, 800-200-1160; W www.utah.com; Council Hall/Capitol Hill, Salt Lake City, UT 84114-1396)

Wyoming Division of Tourism (☎ 307-777-7777, 800-225-5996; W www.wyomingtourism .org; I-25 at College Drive, Cheyenne, WY 82002)

DOCUMENTS
Travel Insurance
It is advisable to take out short-term travel insurance that covers you for emergency evacuation, medical expenses and later hospital treatment. Mountain rescue groups and law enforcement agencies may otherwise bill rescued hikers for expenses. Be sure to read the fine print, as many policies do not cover emergency evacuation or injuries incurred while engaged in 'mountaineering activities' (which can include hiking). Also check whether the policy covers ambulance or an emergency flight home.

Annual policies (around $150 per year) are a good option for hikers who travel frequently, as they provide up to $50,000 in medical-evacuation costs and usually do not exclude adventurous activities. Two established providers for US residents are Access America (☎ 800-284-8300, W www.acces samerica.com) and Travelex (☎ 888-407-5404, W www.travelex-insurance.com).

MONEY
Finding an ATM is rarely a problem. Even in out-of-the-way places, most gas stations and general stores have an ATM. Some national park lodges have currency exchange desks, but the rates are usually poor.

On the Hike
Unless you hike in the few areas with chalets or mountain huts (see Backcountry Accommodations, p43), there won't be much opportunity to spend money on the trail, although it's a good idea to carry some petty cash 'just in case'. Before setting out, you may also need to pay for a backcountry permit or trailhead parking pass at a ranger station or visitor center.

Security
Security is rarely an issue in the Rocky Mountains backcountry, and crime rates tend to be below the national average even in some of the region's larger cities. As a precaution against loss or theft, leave copies of all documents in your car but keep the originals with you in a waterproof bag. Most hotels and hostels provide safekeeping, so you can leave your valuables with them.

Costs
The cost of travel in the Rocky Mountains depends largely how much comfort you require and what you want to do. Generally, it's more expensive to travel alone than as a couple, a family or a small group. Spreading the cost of a national park entry fee, backcountry permit and topographic map among several people can greatly cut costs. The main expenses are transportation, accommodations, food, sightseeing and entertainment. In addition to permit and park entry fees, which vary from hike to hike, typical expenditures are:

item/service	cost
hostel bed	$17 (adult)
budget motel room	$32/36 singles/doubles
campground fee	$12 per site
budget restaurant	$9 per meal (adult)
glass of wine/beer	$4
loaf of bread	$2.30
brick of cheese	$3
instant noodle soup	$1
candy bar	$0.90
hiking map	$9
gasoline	$1.40 per gallon
local phone call	$0.35
major newspaper	$0.50

POST & COMMUNICATIONS
Post
The US Postal Service (W www.usps.com) is reliable and inexpensive. Post offices in

main towns are open weekdays 8am to 5pm, and Saturday 8am to 3pm. You can have mail sent to you c/o General Delivery at any post office that has its own zip (postal) code. Mail is usually held for 10 days before it's returned to sender.

Telephone

Local calls usually cost 25¢ or 35¢ at pay phones. Long-distance rates vary depending on the destination and which telephone company you use. International rates vary depending on the time of day and the destination. Call the operator (☎ 0) for rates.

The ☎ 800, ☎ 888, ☎ 877, ☎ 866 and ☎ 855 prefix codes are for toll-free numbers. If you are calling long-distance either from within the United States or from another country, dial ☎ 1 + the three-digit area code + the seven-digit number. To call Canada, simply dial ☎ 1 + the area code.

For local directory assistance (up to 90¢ per call) dial ☎ 411. For directory assistance outside your area code, dial ☎ 1 + the three-digit area code of the place you want to call + 555-1212. To obtain directory assistance for a toll-free number, dial ☎ 1-800-555-1212; these calls are free. To make an international call direct, dial ☎ 011, then the country code, followed by the area code and the phone number.

Lonely Planet's eKno global communication service (see Email & Internet Access opposite) provides low-cost international calls – for local calls you are usually better off with a local phonecard.

Cellphones (Mobile Phones) Cellphones have begun to revolutionize communications in the backcountry, although the mobile telephone network remains extremely patchy (often nonexistent) in large parts of the Rocky Mountains. While some hikers can't resist calling home to tell the folks about the great view from the summit, cellphones can also be vital in emergency situations (see also Rescue & Evacuation, p77).

Often only a 'roaming' or 'extended' cellphone service (if any) is available in the mountains. Where you have trouble accessing the network, moving a short way

along the slope or rigging up a small portable antenna (available from electronics retailers or telecom stores) may improve reception. Remember, most people find cellphones intrusive enough in the city, let alone in the backcountry, so try to make your calls discreetly.

AT&T (W www.att.com) has the widest coverage outside the urban centers, although Qwest (W www.qwest.com) and Verizon (W www.verizonwireless.com) also have a major regional presence. Local cellphone network coverages can be checked online at W www.wow-com.com/internet/coverage. Note that the US and Canada use the TDMA/CDMA standard for cellphones, while almost all other countries use the GSM standard, which means that standard cellphones from outside North America will not function.

Fax & Telegram

Fax machines can be found at shipping companies like Mail Boxes Etc, photocopy services like Kinko's and hotel business service centers, but be prepared to pay high prices (more than $1 a page). Telegrams can be sent from Western Union (☎ 800-325-6000).

Email & Internet Access

Most public libraries offer free Internet access, although users may have a lengthy wait and the online time limit is normally between 30 minutes and one hour. Cybercafes exist in major cities and larger regional centers, and charge from around $6 per hour. Some hostels also offer Internet access.

As well as low-cost international telephone calls, Lonely Planet's eKno offers free messaging services, email, travel information and an online travel vault, where you can securely store all your important documents. Join online at W www.ekno.lonelyplanet.com or by phone from the Rocky Mountains region by dialing ☎ 800-707-0031. Once you have joined, you can access eKno from anywhere in the Rockies by dialing ☎ 800-706-1333.

DIGITAL RESOURCES

Today, every important organization in the US has its own website. Some sites of particular interest to Rocky Mountains hikers are listed here:

American Parks Network (W www.american parknetwork.com) is one of the best non-official information sources for the major parks the US, with numerous useful links.

American Trails (W www.americantrails.org) has articles covering a wide range of issues of interest to hikers, with links to related private and government organizations in each state.

Cyberwest (W www.cyberwest.com) is an online magazine on the west for the outdoor-interested.

Great Outdoor Recreation Pages (W www.gorp.com) has interesting articles updated to reflect the seasons and draws a good crowd to its chat rooms.

Lightweight Backpacking (W www.backpacking.net) is a good place to find equipment information, hiking and packing tips, books and specifics on winter, ultralight and beginner backpacking skills.

Lonely Planet (W www.lonelyplanet.com) has information about most places on earth, linked to the Thorn Tree bulletin board and Postcards, where you can catch up on postings from fellow travelers. The website also has travel news and updates to many of Lonely Planet's most popular guidebooks, and the subWWWay section links you to the most useful travel resources elsewhere on the Internet.

Recreation on Public Lands (W www.recreation.gov) links eight federal land management agencies (including BLM, NPS and USFS) with information on hundreds of wildland recreation sites nationwide.

Rocky Mountain Nature Association (W www.rmna.org) assists land management agencies in education and research, and has useful links.

Wildernet (W www.wildernet.com) offers general background information about outdoor recreation.

BOOKS

Following are some in-print titles that may be of interest to Rocky Mountains visitors:

Lonely Planet

Rocky Mountain States ($24.99) is an extremely comprehensive guide covering the four main Rocky Mountains states of Colorado, Idaho, Montana and Wyoming.

Southwest US ($24.95) is a comprehensive guidebook to Arizona, New Mexico and Utah, covering parts of the middle and southern Rocky Mountains.

Hiking Guidebooks

Rocky Mountain Walks by Gary Ferguson ($15.95) has easy walks in Montana, Wyoming, Colorado and New Mexico.

Hiking the Great Northwest by Harvey Manning ($16.95) contains a selection of dozens of the best hikes in northwest US, including routes in the Idaho, Montana and Wyoming Rockies.

The Sierra Club Guide to the National Parks of the Rocky Mountains and the Great Plains, edited by Conger Beasley ($24.95), covers seven national parks in the region.

Travel & Exploration

Journal of a Trapper by Osborne Russell ($29.90) is a young fur trapper's account of his adventures in the Rocky Mountains between 1834 and 1843.

Lewis and Clark by Roy E Appleman ($14.95) is arguably the best-written and most readable history of the Lewis and Clark Expedition.

Exploring the American West ($6), a National Park Handbook, gives a concise introduction to Western history.

Native Americans

Bury My Heart at Wounded Knee by Dee Alexander Brown ($16) is a classic Native American history of the American West, ending with the massacre of the Sioux at Wounded Knee in South Dakota.

Indian Legends from the Northern Rockies by Ella E Clark ($17.95) provides good background on Native American culture.

The Wisdom of the Native Americans, edited by Kent Nerburn, ($32) is a compilation of quotes and writings of Native American leaders.

Natural History

Field Guide to the Rocky Mountain States by Peter Alden & John Grassy (National Audubon Society, $19.95) is comprehensive natural history field guide.

The Great Rocky Mountain Nature Factbook by Susan Ewing ($14.95) covers the region's animals, plants and natural features.

Alpine Wildflowers by Dee Strickler ($9.95) covers alpine and subalpine plants of the Rockies.

Forest Wildflowers by Dee Strickler ($9.95) is another straightforward Falcon guide to understory plants of the Rocky Mountains forests.

Plants of the Rocky Mountains by Linda Kershaw et al ($19.95) is the first of the excellent Lone Pine field guides, covering flora throughout the Canadian and US Rockies.

Rocky Mountain Wildflowers by JJ Craighead et al ($16.95) is a good general guide to Rockies flora.

Western Trees by Maggie Stuckey et al ($10.95) includes all the important tree species found in the US Rockies.

Birds of the Rocky Mountains by Chris C Fisher ($19.95) is a comprehensive guide to the hundreds of bird species found in the Canadian and US Rockies; its illustrations are of outstanding quality.

Mammals of the Rocky Mountains by Don Pattie et al ($18.95) is probably the best field guide to Rockies fauna, with excellent illustrations and information.

Rocky Mountain Wildlife by David Dahms ($11.95) is a good introduction to the animals of the region.

A Field Guide to Mammal Tracking in North America by James Halfpenny ($14.95) enables hikers to identify all those mysterious hoof and paw prints on the trail.

Best-Tasting Wild Plants of Colorado and the Rockies by Cattail Bob Seebeck ($17.95) tells you what and what not to eat in the Rockies.

Edible & Medicinal Plants of the Rockies by Linda Kershaw ($18.95) is a field guide to 'useful' flora.

Mushrooms of Colorado and the Southern Rocky Mountains by Vera Stucky Evenson ($25) is a well-illustrated guide with tips on avoiding poisonous species.

Wild Berries of the West by Betty Derig et al ($16) tells readers how to identify 150 berries and fruits of the wild west.

Fly Fishing the Rocky Mountain Backcountry by Rich Osthoff ($19.95) includes practical advice on planning a fishing trip in the Rockies.

Wisdom of the Guides: Rocky Mountain Trout Guides Talk Fly Fishing by Paul Arnold ($24.95) sees seasoned fishing guides let the spinners fly.

Buying Books

Check local bookstores and backpacking suppliers in regional towns for general guides as well as locally published books (which are often unavailable elsewhere). National park and USFS visitor centers or offices usually have a good selection of natural history publications for sale. Amazon (**W** www.amazon.com) has a vast catalog of books that can be viewed and ordered online. Nationwide booksellers such as Barnes & Noble, B Dalton and Crown Books can order unstocked titles for you.

Local titles of particular interest to hikers are given under Maps & Books in the regional chapters.

MAGAZINES

Two popular 'mainstream' outdoor magazines are *Backpacker* and *Outside*, which are widely available in bookstores and newsstands, and even libraries. *The Mountain Gazette* (☎ 970-453-4427, **W** www.mountaingazette.com) is a free monthly publication distributed throughout the Rockies and has an often eclectic mixture of topics, including conservation and the outdoors. *Rockies* (☎ 250-423-6693, **W** www.rockies.com) is a general-interest magazine on culture, natural history and golf (!) in the greater Rocky Mountains region.

WEATHER INFORMATION

Local weather updates are posted on bulletin boards at national park or USFS visitor centers and ranger stations.

Newspapers throughout the Rocky Mountains include weather forecasts for the local area. The daily *US Today* is widely available in regional towns and cities; its weather section has a national temperature map with forecasts for regional cities and a four-day outlook.

The Weather Channel (available in most motels and hotels with cable TV) has continuous weather reports. Watch out for roadside signs advertising local AM or FM radio weather broadcasts.

The National Oceanic and Atmospheric Administration (NOAA) Weather Radio (**W** www.nws.noaa.gov/nwr) broadcasts national and local weather information 24 hours a day on VHF-band frequencies between 162.400 MHz and 162.550 MHz. Unfortunately, these broadcasts cannot be received in many parts of the Rocky Mountains, and require a special NOAA Weather Radio receiver – available from retailers from around $30.

Telephone directories list local numbers (under 'Weather' in the 'US Government' sections), which provide updated weather information for the surrounding region.

Numerous websites offer weather information. The most accurate and detailed are the National Weather Service (**W** weather.noaa.gov) and UM Weather (**W** cirrus.sprl.umich.edu/wxnet).

The websites of the Climate Prediction Center (**W** www.cpc.ncep.noaa.gov/products/predictions), which issues long-term regional climate outlooks, and the National Water and Climate Center (**W** www.wcc.nrcs.usda.gov/water/snow/snow_rpt.html), which provides data on local snowpack depths, may be of use for advanced planning of hikes.

PHOTOGRAPHY

Print film and slide film are widely available at supermarkets and discount drugstores. In smaller towns or national park stores availability is more limited and prices are higher. Black-and-white film and is rarely sold outside of major cities. Drugstores are a good place to get your film processed cheaply and quickly.

Film can be damaged by excessive heat, so don't leave your camera or film in your car or in the top of your pack on a hot day. Bring a spare camera battery and a heavy-duty waterproof stuff bag to store your camera and film in wet weather.

TIME

Colorado, Montana, New Mexico, Utah, Wyoming are all on Mountain Time, seven hours behind GMT/UTC. Most of Idaho also lies within the Mountain Time zone, except for parts of northern Central Idaho and the Panhandle, which are on Pacific Time, eight hours behind GMT/UTC. All six states switch to Mountain Daylight Time (or Pacific Daylight Time), when clocks are moved forward one hour, from the first Sunday of April to the last Saturday of October.

Daylight In late June, the *maximum* period of daylight is around 16 hours (approximately 6:30am to 9:30pm) in northern Montana and Idaho, and around 14½ hours (approximately 5:50am to 8:20pm) in northern New Mexico. By late September, the period of daylight has decreased to just under 12 hours throughout the Rockies.

Check local sunrise, sunset and twilight times (plus other astronomical phases such as moonrise and moonset) at **W** aa.usno.navy.mil/data/docs/RS_OneYear.html.

Health & Safety

Generally a very healthy and safe region, the Rocky Mountains do have a few things to be aware of. The range of potential dangers discussed in this chapter can never be fully eliminated but can be minimized.

PREDEPARTURE PLANNING
Health Insurance
Health costs are extremely high in the US and some hospitals may refuse care unless you have some form of insurance (see Travel Insurance, p59).

Physical Preparation
If you're a bit out of shape, the best preparation for a hiking vacation is to start some regular, energetic exercise at least three weeks prior to travel – don't leave it until the week before you depart. In particular, build up your calves and quadriceps by doing squats and calf raises, or walking up stairs with a loaded pack. To minimize your chances of getting blisters and foot fatigue, wear in your boots thoroughly by undertaking long walks (at least 3mi, preferably in hilly areas). This will also allow you to try out different socks and lacing systems.

Visitors from other (generally much lower) regions of the US should wait several days after arrival before undertaking strenuous activity in the Rocky Mountains. Prepare your metabolism for acclimation to higher elevations by eating more carbohydrates and abstaining from alcohol – see also Altitude, p66.

Immunizations
No specific vaccinations are required for the Rocky Mountains region (or even to enter the US, although evidence of cholera and yellow fever vaccinations may be required if arriving in the US from an infected area). However, it's a good idea to make sure you are up to date with routine vaccinations such as diphtheria, polio and tetanus. It's particularly important that your tetanus is up to date – the initial course of three injections, usually given in childhood, should be followed by boosters every 10 years.

First Aid
Hikers should know what to do in the event of a serious accident or illness. Consider taking a basic first-aid course (preferably tailored to outdoor recreation) before you go. Although detailed first-aid instruction is outside the scope of this guidebook, some basic points are listed in Traumatic Injuries, p70. Prevention of accidents and illness is just as important – see Safety on the Hike, p74. You should also know how to summon help in case major accident or illness occurs – see Rescue & Evacuation, p77.

Hiking Health Guides
If you are planning to go hiking in remote areas, you may be interested in the following detailed health guides:

Medicine for the Backcountry by Buck Tilton & Frank Hubbell ($15) prepares you for just about any major or minor medical emergency in the outdoors.

Medicine for the Outdoors by Paul S Auerbach ($22) is a layperson's reference, giving brief explanations of many medical problems and practical treatment options.

Wilderness 911 by Eric A Weiss ($17) is a step-by-step guide to first aid and advanced care in remote areas with limited medical supplies and no professional help.

Online Resources
There are a vast number of websites dedicated to health issues. Some sites of particular interest to Rocky Mountain hikers are:

Centers for Disease Control & Prevention (W www.cdc.gov) represents US government agencies with a vast amount of information.

International Society for Infectious Diseases (W www.isid.org) is a world organization representing numerous agencies and individuals that work in infectious disease research.

Lonely Planet (W www.lonelyplanet.com/web links) has links to the World Health Organization (WHO) and many other useful sites.

Wilderness Medical Society (W www.wms.org) is a nonprofit organization dedicated to promoting outdoor and emergency knowledge and research.

STAYING HEALTHY
Hygiene

Maintaining a high standard of general hygiene will reduce your changes of contracting an illness. In particular, backcountry (pit) toilets can be rather unsanitary, so you should take special care to wash your hands after using them.

Water

Water from even the wildest mountain lakes and streams may contain harmful pathogens (especially those causing giardiasis and amoebic cysts) and should always be properly treated. Spring water – ie, water gushing straight out of the ground – is usually free of pathogens if taken directly from the source. Don't collect water downstream from abandoned mines or other human infrastructure such as ski resorts, as it may contain toxic impurities that cannot be removed by standard methods of purification. It is advisable not to rely on just one method of water purification.

Water Purification Normally, boiling water is the simplest way of treating it for human consumption. Water boils at lower temperatures with increasing elevation, however, so the higher up you go the longer it will take to kill pathogens. At an altitude of 8000ft, boil water for 10 minutes, and add about a minute for each 1000ft increase in elevation. If boiling is your main method of purification, carry plenty of stove fuel.

Chemical sterilization using chlorine tablets will kill many but not all pathogens. Iodine is very effective in purifying water and is available in tablet form (such as Potable Aqua), but follow the directions carefully and remember that too much iodine may be harmful. Adding vitamin C (which is in powdered drinks such as Tang) to iodized water eliminates the taste and

First-Aid Check List

Following is a list of items you should consider including in your first-aid kit – consult your pharmacist for brands available in your country.

- ☐ adhesive tape
- ☐ bandages and safety pins
- ☐ elasticized support bandage for knees, ankles etc
- ☐ gauze swabs
- ☐ nonadhesive dressings
- ☐ paper stitches
- ☐ reverse syringe – such as a Sawyer Extractor, to remove ticks or suck out poison from possible snake or scorpion bites
- ☐ small pair of scissors
- ☐ sterile alcohol wipes
- ☐ thermometer (note that mercury thermometers are prohibited by airlines)
- ☐ tweezers

Medications

- ☐ antidiarrhea and antinausea drugs
- ☐ antifungal cream or powder – for fungal skin infections and thrush
- ☐ antihistamines – for allergies, eg, hay fever; to ease the itch from insect bites or stings; and to prevent motion sickness
- ☐ antiseptic (such as povidone-iodine) – for cuts and grazes
- ☐ calamine lotion, sting-relief spray or aloe vera – to ease irritation from sunburn and insect bites or stings
- ☐ cold and influenza tablets, throat lozenges and nasal decongestant
- ☐ painkillers (such as aspirin or acetaminophen) – for pain and fever

Miscellaneous

- ☐ eye drops – for washing out dust
- ☐ insect repellent
- ☐ multivitamins – especially for longer hikes, when dietary vitamin intake may be inadequate
- ☐ rehydration mixture – to prevent dehydration, eg, due to severe diarrhea; particularly important when traveling with children
- ☐ sunscreen and lip balm
- ☐ water purification tablets or iodine

color of iodine, but wait until the iodine has had time to work.

Many backpackers carry a pump-filter unit capable of removing all water contaminants. Reliable pump-filters (such as those made by Katadyn, MSR and PUR) are available from outdoor stores from around $75, but ensure that the unit you buy will filter out pathogens such as Giardia. Other important considerations are the pump's output and ease of use – some models are cumbersome and tediously slow.

Food

Although travelers in the Rocky Mountains region are unlikely to be served contaminated food, from time to time unsanitary preparation (especially repeated reheating) or improper storage result in serious cases of food-poisoning. Self-serve bulk-food bins at supermarkets and food markets may be occasional sources of contamination, so look closely before scooping out nuts, trail mix or cereal.

Increasing dietary carbohydrates facilitates acclimation and improves physical performance at high elevations – see also Altitude (opposite) and Food (p44).

Nutrition Maintaining a balanced diet is particularly important during periods of hard physical exercise such as hiking. Eat foods with plenty of dietary fiber (such as nuts and dried fruits) and keep up your intake of fluids to facilitate digestion. Don't miss meals. Backpackers often carry vitamin and mineral supplements, especially on multiday trips.

Common Ailments

Blisters You can generally avoid getting blisters by properly wearing in boots before your trip. Ensure boots fit comfortably, with enough room to move your toes – boots that are too big or too small will cause blisters. Socks should also fit properly – wear only special, padded hiking socks but check, nevertheless, that there are no seams across the widest part of your foot. Wet and muddy socks can also cause blisters, so pack a spare pair even for a day hike. Keep your toenails clipped but not too short. If you feel

a blister coming on, treat it sooner rather then later. Apply either a simple sticking plaster or a 'second skin' plaster made specifically for the treatment of blisters.

Fatigue Note that hiking accidents tend to occur in the latter part of the day. After many hours' hard hiking, you may be impatient to reach your destination and fail to notice a steady decline in concentration and balance. This not only detracts from the appreciation of the hike, but in bad weather or in dangerous terrain it becomes life-threatening. If you're still on the trail by mid afternoon, make a deliberate effort to slow down and take regular rest stops. Keep up your stamina by snacking frequently on high-energy foods such as chocolate or gorp (good old raisins and peanuts).

Knee Pain Long, steep descents put a heavy strain on the knees. To reduce knee strain you should develop a proper technique for descent. Take short, controlled steps with the legs in a slightly bent position, placing your heels on the ground before the rest of the foot. Mountain trails usually negotiate steep slopes by making numerous switchbacks – which helps avoid erosion *and* knee strain! Hiking poles (see p48) take some of the load off the legs, and are recommended for hikers who are susceptible to knee pain.

MEDICAL PROBLEMS & TREATMENT
Environmental Hazards
Hikers are more at more risk than most groups from environmental hazards. Risks can significantly reduced, however, by applying simple common sense – and reading the following section.

Altitude The generally high elevations of the Rocky Mountains, particularly the middle and southern Rockies (from central Wyoming to northern New Mexico), present a serious risk to hikers. The potentially fatal condition known as acute mountain sickness (AMS) occurs because less oxygen reaches the muscles and the brain at high altitude,

Warning

Self-diagnosis and treatment can be risky, so you should always seek medical help. The local chamber of commerce should be able to advise you on where to get medical treatment. Although we do give drug advice in this section, it's for emergency use only. Correct diagnosis is vital.

Note that we have used generic rather than brand names for drugs throughout this section – check with a pharmacist for locally available brands.

requiring the heart and lungs to compensate by working harder.

There is no hard and fast rule about when 'true' cases of AMS can occur. Although serious cases of AMS at altitudes as low 8000ft have been documented, it more typically occurs above 11,000ft. The classic symptoms of AMS are headaches, nausea, dizziness, a dry cough, insomnia, breathlessness and loss of appetite. In more severe cases, lack of coordination, confusion, irrational behavior, drowsiness and unconsciousness can occur. Mild altitude problems will generally abate after a day or so of rest at the same altitude, but if the symptoms persist or become worse the only treatment is to descend – even 1000ft can help.

Prescription drugs, such as acetazolamide and dexamethasone, are recommended by some doctors for the prevention of AMS; however, their use is controversial. They can reduce the symptoms, but they may also mask warning signs. Severe and fatal AMS has occurred in people taking these drugs. In general we do not recommend them for hikers.

To help prevent AMS you should:

- Ascend slowly with frequent rest days.
- Drink extra fluids – in the mountains, moisture is more easily lost as you breathe; certain symptoms of body dehydration are easily mistaken for AMS.
- Eat light, high-carbohydrate meals for energy.
- Avoid alcohol as it may increase the risk of dehydration.
- Avoid taking sedatives.

Sun A large number of hikes described in this guidebook take you well above 10,000ft, where the sun can beat down with surprising intensity. Ultraviolet (UV) radiation rises with increasing elevation – at 13,000ft it is almost 50% higher than at sea level. Sunburn occurs more rapidly at higher elevations, even in overcast conditions. Despite being painful and unpleasant, sunburn permanently damages your skin and increases your risk of later developing skin cancer. Sunburn is a particular problem in early summer (June), as the sun's intensity is greatest and large snowdrifts remain to reflect the UV radiation. Protect your face by wearing a wide-brimmed hat – preferably not a baseball cap. Wear long pants and shirts with long sleeves or keep exposed limbs smeared with sunscreen. Calamine lotion is a good treatment for mild sunburn.

Snow Blindness This painful form of sunburn on the surface of the eye (cornea) occurs when the eyes are exposed to reflected snow glare for several hours. Placing a cold cloth on closed eyelids should relieve the pain and the eyes usually recover within a few days. A good pair of sunglasses, with UV-lenses, will help prevention.

Heat Despite the high elevation and relatively low humidity, hiking in the Rockies

Everyday Health

Normal body temperature is up to 98.6°F; more than 4°F higher indicates a high fever. The normal adult pulse rate is 60 to 100 per minute (children 80 to 100, babies 100 to 140). As a general rule the pulse increases about 20 beats per minute for each 2°F rise in fever.

Respiration (breathing) rate is also an indicator of illness. Count the number of breaths per minute; between 12 and 20 is normal for adults and older children (up to 30 for younger children, 40 for babies). People with a high fever or serious respiratory illness breathe more quickly than normal. More than 40 shallow breaths a minute may indicate pneumonia.

can be surprisingly hot, especially in July and August when temperatures in the mountains can reach 90°F. One way hikers can avoid the heat is by getting an early start, then taking it easy during the hottest part of the day.

Dehydration & Heat Exhaustion Dehydration is a potentially dangerous and generally preventable condition caused by lack of fluid. Sweating and inadequate fluid intake are the most common causes in hikers. It is easy to forget how much fluid you are losing via perspiration while hiking, particularly if a strong breeze is drying your skin quickly. The first symptoms are weakness, thirst and passing small amounts of very concentrated urine. This may progress to drowsiness, dizziness or fainting on standing up and, finally, coma. You should always maintain a good fluid intake while hiking. Dehydration and salt deficiency can cause heat exhaustion. Salt deficiency is characterized by fatigue, lethargy, headaches, giddiness and muscle cramps; salt tablets are overkill, just adding extra salt to your food is probably sufficient.

Heatstroke This is a serious, occasionally fatal, condition that occurs if the body's heat-regulating mechanism breaks down and the body temperature rises to dangerous levels. Long, continuous periods of exposure to high temperatures and insufficient fluids can leave you vulnerable to heatstroke. The symptoms are feeling unwell, not sweating much (if at all) and a high body temperature (102° to 106°F). Where sweating has ceased, the skin becomes flushed and red. Severe, throbbing headaches and lack of coordination will also occur, and the sufferer may be confused or aggressive. Eventually the victim will become delirious or convulse. Hospitalization is essential, but in the interim get victims out of the sun, remove their clothing, cover them with a wet sheet or towel and then fan continually. Give fluids if they are conscious.

Cold The arrival of a front or a sudden thunderstorm that drenches ill-prepared hikers in freezing rain is not just unpleasant but dangerous.

Hypothermia Also known as exposure, hypothermia is a real and ever-present threat to mountain hikers. It occurs when the body loses heat faster than it can produce it, causing the core temperature to fall.

It is surprisingly easy to progress from very cold to dangerously cold due to a combination of wind, wet clothing, fatigue and hunger, even if the air temperature is above freezing. Key signs of hypothermia include exhaustion, slurred speech, shivering, numb skin (particularly toes and fingers), irrational or violent behavior, lethargy, stumbling, dizzy spells, muscle cramps and violent bursts of energy. Irrationality may take the form of a sufferer complaining of being hot and trying to undress.

To treat hypothermia, first get the person out of the wind and/or rain, remove their clothing if it's wet and replace it with dry, warm garments. Give them hot liquids (not alcohol) and some simple sugary food. Do not rub the victim; instead allow them to slowly warm themselves. This should be enough for the early stages of hypothermia.

Watch for signs of impending bad weather and descend or seek shelter if conditions start to look threatening. Hikers should always carry a completely waterproof jacket (and preferably overpants) regardless of how good the weather seems when they set out. Also carry basic supplies, including food containing simple sugars (such as chocolate or gorp) to generate heat quickly, and lots of fluid to drink.

Infectious Diseases

Diarrhea While a change of water, food or climate may give travelers a case of the runs, serious diarrhea caused by contaminated water is an increasing problem in heavily used backcountry areas. If diarrhea does hit you, however, fluid replacement is the mainstay of management. Weak black tea with a little sugar, soda water, or soft drink allowed to go flat and 50% diluted with water are all good. With severe diarrhea, a rehydrating solution is necessary to replace minerals and salts. Commercially available oral rehydration salts (ORS) are very useful. You should stick to a bland diet as you recover.

Gut-paralyzing drugs such as diphenoxylate or loperamide can be used to bring relief from the symptoms, although they do not actually cure the problem.

Fungal Infections Fungal infections most commonly affect hikers between the toes (a condition known as athlete's foot). Another common complaint among hikers is 'jock itch', a painful rash between the legs caused by rubbing and sweating as you walk; simple solutions include wearing comfortable, nonabrasive clothing and keeping clean. Ringworm (a fungal infection, not a worm) is picked up from infected animals or by walking on damp areas such as shower floors. Fungal infections can be treated by exposing the infected area to air or sunlight, and/or applying an antifungal cream or powder such as tolnaftate.

Rabies Most human rabies cases in the US during the last few years have been transmitted by bats, although skunks and dogs have also infected humans. Rabies is caused by abrasive contact with an infected animal, so any bite, scratch or even lick from a warm-blooded, furry animal should be cleaned immediately and thoroughly. Scrub with soap and running water, and then clean with an alcohol solution. If there is any possibility that the animal is infected, medical help should be sought immediately. Even if the animal is not rabid, all bites should be treated seriously as they can become infected or can result in tetanus. Post-exposure prophylaxis (PEP) is administered to patients who may already be infected with rabies.

Tetanus Tetanus is caused by a bacterium that lives in soil and in the feces of horses and other animals. It enters the body via breaks in the skin. The first symptom may be discomfort in swallowing, or stiffening of the jaw and neck; this is followed by painful convulsions of the jaw and whole body. The disease can be fatal. It can be prevented by vaccination, so make sure your shots are up to date before you leave.

Insect-Borne Diseases

Several potentially life-threatening insect-borne diseases are prevalent throughout the US, although the overall risk of infection tends to be much lower in the Rocky Mountains region.

Colorado Tick Fever Sometimes called mountain fever, Colorado tick fever is a rare viral disease widely dispersed throughout the west. The disease is primarily transmitted to humans by the ground-squirrel tick, usually in the period between late May and early July. Typical symptoms are a sudden onset of fever accompanied by severe headache, photophobia (hypersensitivity to light) and myalgia (muscle ache). Virtually all patients make a complete recovery within a week, and no treatment apart from comforting the patient is required.

Human Babesiosis This uncommon, malaria-like illness is caused by a parasite that invades red blood cells. The prevalence of this disease in the Rocky Mountains region is somewhat unclear, but a large percentage of patients diagnosed with Lyme disease are also found to have human babesiosis. Within a week of being bitten by a tick, the patient may begin to feel unwell, with appetite loss and fatigue followed by fever, heavy sweating, muscle ache and headache. These symptoms can be mild with rapid recovery, or the disease may advance to severe hemolytic anemia, kidney failure, liver dysfunctions and hypotension (very low blood pressure). Patients with very severe cases may require a complete blood transfusion. Symptoms may persist for months. Human babesiosis is fatal in more than 5% of cases.

Lyme Disease A bacterial infection, in the Rocky Mountains Lyme disease is mainly transmitted by the deer (wood) tick. Although the number of cases reported in the US has skyrocketed during the last two decades, Lyme disease remains relatively uncommon over large parts of the Rockies. The early symptoms, which may take months to develop, are similar to those for influenza – headaches, stiff neck, tiredness and painful swelling of the joints. If left untreated, complications such as meningitis, facial palsy or heart abnormalities may occur, but fatalities are rare. A safe vaccination is not yet available, but Lyme disease responds well to antibiotics.

Rocky Mountain Spotted Fever The bacterial disease, Rocky Mountain spotted fever (RMSF), is widespread in the US (although its distribution is often localized in concentrated pockets). Humans usually contract the disease from the bite of an infected tick or through contact with fluid released after an infected tick is crushed against the skin, but RMSF can also be acquired through inhalation. Onset of the disease normally occurs two to eight days after infection. The initial symptoms are influenza-like headaches, fever, chills and muscle aches; a rash may appear several days later. RMSF may progress to confusion, shock and heart failure.

Children and young teenagers are more susceptible to RMSF infection, but the disease tends to be more serious in older people. Antibiotic treatment with tetracycline or chloramphenicol is usually effective but, of the 1000 or so cases that occur each year in the US, some 5% are fatal. As most RMSF deaths are the result of delayed treatment (sometimes caused by incorrect diagnosis), urgent medical attention should be sought in all suspected cases.

Tularemia Often called rabbit fever, tularemia is an uncommon disease mainly carried by rodents. Tick bites account for around half of all tularemia transmissions to humans, but infected (especially rabbit) meat and the bites of deer flies or mosquitoes are other transmission sources. After several days, there is a sudden onset of fever, chills, headache, myalgia (muscle aches), malaise (overall feeling of being ill) and fatigue. Tularemia has a fatality rate of up to 3%.

Traumatic Injuries

Sprains Hikers often suffer ankle and knee sprains, especially in rugged terrain. Sprained ankles can be avoided by wearing sturdy boots with adequate support. If you do suffer a sprain, immobilize the joint with a firm bandage, and relieve pain and swelling by keeping the joint elevated and applying an ice pack. If the sprain is mild, you may continue your hike after a few days. For more severe sprains, seek medical attention.

Major Accidents Head injuries or fractures caused during a serious fall or by rockfall (p77) are a small but significant danger to hikers. Detailed first-aid instruction is outside the scope of this guidebook but some basic advice on what to do in the event of a major accident follows:

1) make sure you and other people with you are not in danger
2) assess the injured person's condition
3) stabilize any injuries, such as bleeding wounds or broken bones
4) seek medical attention – see Rescue & Evacuation (p77) for more details

If the person is unconscious, check whether they are breathing (clear their airway if it is blocked) and check whether they have a pulse (feel the side of the neck rather than the wrist). If they are not breathing but have a pulse, you should start mouth-to-mouth resuscitation immediately. In these circumstances it is best to move the person as little as possible in case their neck or back is broken. Keep the person warm by covering them with a blanket or other dry clothing; insulate them from the ground if possible.

Check for wounds and broken bones – ask the person where they have pain if they are conscious, otherwise gently inspect them all over (including their back and the back of the head), moving them as little as possible. Control any bleeding by applying firm pressure to the wound. Bleeding from the nose or ear may indicate a fractured skull. Don't give the person anything by mouth, especially if they are unconscious.

Indications of a fracture (broken bone) are pain, swelling and discoloration, loss of function or deformity of a limb. Unless you know what you are doing, you shouldn't try to straighten an obviously displaced broken bone. To protect from further injury, immobilize a nondisplaced fracture by splinting it; for fractures of the thigh bone, try to straighten the leg gently, then tie it to the good leg to hold it in place. Fractures associated with open wounds (compound fractures) require more urgent treatment than simple fractures as there is a risk of infection. Dislocations, where the bone has come out of the joint, are very painful, and should be set as soon as possible.

Broken ribs are painful but usually heal by themselves and do not need splinting. If breathing difficulties occur, or the person coughs up blood, medical attention should be sought urgently, as it may indicate a punctured lung.

Internal injuries are more difficult to detect, and cannot usually be treated in the field. Watch for shock, which is a specific medical condition associated with a failure to maintain circulating blood volume. Signs include a rapid pulse and cold, clammy extremities. A person in shock requires urgent medical attention.

Some general points to bear in mind are as follows:

- Simple fractures take several weeks to heal, so they don't need fixing straight away, but they should be immobilized to protect them from further injury. Compound fractures need much more urgent treatment.
- If you do have to splint a broken bone, remember to check regularly that the splint is not cutting off the circulation to the hand or foot.
- Most cases of brief unconsciousness are not associated with any serious internal injury to the brain, but as a general rule of thumb in these circumstances, any person who has been knocked unconscious should be watched for deterioration. If they do deteriorate, seek medical attention straight away.

Burns
Immerse the burnt area in cold water as soon as possible, then cover it with a clean, dry sterile dressing. Keep this in place with plasters for a day or so in the case of a small, mild burn, but longer for more serious injuries. Medical help should be sought for severe and extensive burns.

Cuts & Scratches
Even small cuts and grazes should be washed and treated with an antiseptic such as povidone-iodine. Infection in a wound is indicated by the skin margins becoming red, painful and swollen. More serious infection can cause swelling of the whole limb and of the lymph glands. The patient may develop a fever, and will need medical attention.

Bites & Stings
Insects Numerous bloodsucking insects are found throughout the Rocky Mountain region, often reaching plague proportions in June and July. Biting insects may transmit disease (see Insect-Borne Diseases, p69), and can easily spoil your hike if you are unprepared.

To keep insects at bay, apply a repellent and wear light colored clothing with long sleeves and pants. The most effective insect repellents are those containing diethyltoluamide (DEET), but permethrin-based repellents can be sprayed on (synthetic) clothing. Citronella-based repellents are less noxious but need to be reapplied more often; they are also not advisable in grizzly bear country due to their strong, attractive aroma. Hats with mesh veils give added protection when insects are out in force. Skin ointments may relieve the pain and itching from bites.

Chiggers Minute, parasitic larva typically found in grassy or scrubby areas, chiggers attach themselves to a (mammal) host, gorging its blood and dropping off after several days. Affected areas of the skin may become red-blotched, remaining (intensely) itchy for many days and occasionally developing a form of dermatitis (trombidiosis). Chiggers tend to attack the ankles, crotch, waistline and armpits. If infestation occurs, wash the body thoroughly with soap.

Deer & Horse Flies These can be very bothersome in forested areas. They are attracted by movement, breathing (CO_2) and warmth, and will normally not enter deep shade.

The insects' salivary secretions can cause an allergic reaction (and possibly transmit diseases such as tularemia – see p70).

Mosquitoes These often reach near-plague proportions in early to mid-summer, particularly near marshes, bogs or lakes below tree line, but even up in the high tundra they can be almost unbearable. Mosquitoes tend to be worst in sheltered places during the evening. Some hikers carry mosquito coils, but these should not be used in bear country. Rocky Mountain mosquitoes are not carriers of malaria.

Ticks Found throughout the Rocky Mountains, ticks are known to be the main carriers of a range of diseases, especially Lyme disease (see Insect-Borne Diseases, p69). The period of greatest tick activity is from April through September. Ticks typically live in underbrush at the forest edge or beside hiking trails. The tick will crawl onto a passing animal or person, embedding its head in the host's skin in order to suck its blood. Slight itchiness around the bite may be the only indication of an attached tick.

Inspect your body – especially the warm, hairy parts – after traveling through grassy or brushy areas. Ticks are best removed by using a reverse syringe (such as a Sawyer Extractor). These are available at outdoor or backpacking stores, and draw the insect out safely and cleanly using suction. Otherwise, you can pull it out by pressing down around the tick's head with tweezers, grabbing the head and gently pulling upwards. Avoid pulling the rear of the body as this may squeeze the tick's gut contents through the attached mouth parts into the skin, increasing the risk of infection and disease. Smearing chemicals on the tick will not make it let go and is not recommended.

Poison Ivy & Poison Oak Closely related, poison ivy and poison oak are small shrubs or woody, ivy-like vines found mainly in the Rocky Mountains foothills. Both plants have egg-shaped, pointed leaflets arranged in threes at the end of each stalk and contain urushiol, an oily substance that produces a severe allergic reaction in most people. Contact typically occurs when hapless hikers brush against the leaves, causing an extremely itchy skin rash (often associated with swelling) to appear several hours later. This develops into blisters after one or two days, which may remain visible on the skin for up to a year.

Special 'barrier' lotions (such as Ivy Block) prevent or slow absorption of urushiol when applied to skin *before contact*. If you knowingly come into contact with poison ivy or poison oak, thoroughly wash the affected area within 10 minutes using alcohol, gasoline or cold water and soap. If a rash breaks out, do not scratch or cover blisters with Band-Aids, but apply a soothing lotion such as calamine. Strong topical steroids (available by prescription only) may help if used before the rash turns into blisters. An antihistamine might help you sleep.

Rattlesnakes Several species of rattlesnake are found in the drier foothills of the (particularly southern) Rocky Mountains. They are generally absent or very uncommon at higher elevations, however, and, due to the shy nature and nocturnal habits of rattlesnakes, hikers rarely even see them. Rattlesnake venom attacks the central nervous system and destroys blood tissue. The bite is extremely painful and can occasionally be fatal (especially in children, or elderly and unwell people), but antivenin is available.

To minimize your chances of being bitten, always wear boots, socks and long pants when hiking anywhere rattlesnakes may be present. Rattlesnake fangs can penetrate clothing, so wear loose-fitting garments. Don't put your hands into holes and crevices, and be careful when collecting firewood.

If someone is bitten by a rattlesnake, the best first aid is to immediately apply a reverse syringe (Sawyer Extractor) to slow the poison's spread. Keep the victim calm and still, wrap the bitten limb tightly (as you would for a sprained ankle) and then attach a splint to immobilize it. Tourniquets and sucking out the poison by mouth are now comprehensively discredited. Get the victim to a doctor as soon as possible.

Stinging Nettles Native and introduced stinging nettles grow throughout the Rockies, forming often dense patches. When the tiny hairs on the leaves and stem brush against a hiker's bare skin they release formic acid (the same toxin in ants' saliva), causing a painful, burning sensation that rapidly develops into a skin rash. The pain is most intense on tender skin surfaces, such as the backs of the hands, arms and legs. The sensation will normally only last an hour or so, but the effected area may later become very itchy.

Dousing the nettle burn with water will give relief – if available, add some sodium bicarbonate (baking soda) to neutralize the formic acid. In some people, formic acid can cause an allergic reaction. Nettle burn is sometimes mistaken for the effects of poison ivy (p72), but the itchiness (if any) is far less serious.

Women's Health

Hiking is not particularly hazardous to your health, however, women's health issues can be a bit trickier to cope with when you are on the trail.

Altitude Although little is known about the possible adverse effects of altitude on a developing fetus, almost all authorities recommend not traveling above 11,500ft while pregnant. There is a theoretical risk that side effects of oral contraceptives, such as blood clots in the legs or lungs, may be more likely if spending extended periods at high altitude. However, there are no conclusive examples to support this theory.

Menstruation A change in diet, routine and environment, as well as intensive exercise can lead to irregularities in the menstrual cycle. This in itself is not a huge issue and your cycle should return to normal when you return to your regular lifestyle. It is particularly important during the menstrual cycle to maintain good personal hygiene, and regularly change sanitary napkins or tampons. (Because they do not readily burn or decompose, and because they may attract bears, used sanitary napkins or tampons should be placed in a sealed plastic bag and carried out

for disposal – see also Women Hikers, p55). Anti-bacterial hand gel or premoistened wipes can be useful if you don't have access to water. Because of hygiene concerns and for ease while on an extended trip, some women prefer to temporarily stop menstruation. You should discuss your options with a doctor before you go. It is also important to note that failure to menstruate could indicate pregnancy! If concerned about irregularities seek medical advice.

Pregnancy If you are pregnant, see your doctor before you travel. Even normal pregnancies can make a woman feel nauseated and tired for the first three months. During the second trimester, the general feelings often improve, but fatigue can still be a constant factor. In the third trimester, the size of the baby can make hiking difficult or uncomfortable. While hiking, make sure you drink plenty of fluids but avoid water sterilized with iodine, maintain a comfortable pace and don't carry heavy packs.

Thrush (Vaginal Candidiasis) Antibiotic use, synthetic underwear, tight trousers, sweating and contraceptive pills can each lead to fungal vaginal infections. The most common is thrush. Symptoms include itching and discomfort in the genital area, often in association with a thick white discharge. The best prevention is to keep the vaginal area cool and dry, and to wear cotton, rather than synthetic, underwear and loose clothes. Thrush can be treated with clotrimazole pessaries or vaginal cream.

Urinary Tract Infection Dehydration and 'hanging on' can result in urinary tract infection and the symptoms of cystitis, which can be particularly distressing and an inconvenient problem when out on the trail. Symptoms include burning when urinating, and having to urinate frequently and urgently. Blood can sometimes be passed in the urine. Drink plenty of fluids and empty your bladder at regular intervals. If symptoms persist, seek medical attention because a simple infection can spread to the kidneys, causing a more severe illness.

SAFETY ON THE HIKE

Although hiking is generally one of the safest mountain activities, hiker injuries and deaths do occur – despite most serious accidents being preventable. Above all, hikers should avoid getting themselves into dangerous situations, especially when hiking off trails. Falls resulting from a slide on grass, autumn leaves, scree or icy trails are among the most common hazards.

Abandoned Mines

Tens of thousands of long-abandoned mines – up to 150 years old – exist throughout the Rocky Mountains backcountry. Although old mine workings hold great fascination and historical value, they are potentially very dangerous places that continually kill people. All mines are structurally unstable and prone to sudden collapse. Shafts may serve as dens for potentially dangerous animals such as bats (possible carriers of rabies), bears, cougars (mountain lions) and rattlesnakes. Mines may also contain suffocating carbon dioxide or poisonous gases (including radioactive radon), as well as live explosives. The best advice on old mines is simply 'stay out and stay alive'.

Animal Attacks

While the dangers should not be exaggerated, hikers in the Rocky Mountains backcountry occasionally have encounters with aggressive animals, which may lead to a serious attack. Watching Wildlife (p27) has more general information on the animals discussed here.

Bison & Moose Bison attacks can result in major injury or even death. Bison are deceptively tolerant of human approach, generally allowing people to get quite close before they show any obvious signs of annoyance – most notably, a raised tail. If their immediate 'private sphere' is encroached upon, however, bison may charge without warning, severely goring or trampling a victim.

Moose can also inflict severe injuries by striking out with their powerful front hoofs (rarely their antlers). Moose generally do not allow themselves to be approached and

---

Hiking Safety – Basic Rules

- Allow more than enough time to complete each leg of the hike before nightfall, especially late in the season when days are shorter.

- Always be prepared to turn back if you don't feel confident about continuing.

- Avoid hiking alone – two is the minimum number for safe hiking in the mountains.

- Inform a responsible person – a family member, park or national forest office – of your hiking route, and try to stick to your plans. Sign the trailhead register or summit logbook (if available).

- Carry an accurate topographical map, compass and whistle.

- Check the latest weather forecast before setting off – while you hike, keep a careful watch on the weather.

- Never leave the marked trails in foggy conditions. With care, most trails can be followed even in thick fog – otherwise wait until visibility improves.

---

will move away from intruding humans. If a moose feels cornered or threatened, however, the animal may suddenly charge a person. Moose cows with calves are especially dangerous, as they will aggressively defend their young.

Like all large, wild animals, bison and moose should be observed from a safe distance – never any closer than 100ft. If you happen to encounter a bison or moose on or near the trail, back off and either allow the animal plenty of time to move away or skirt well around it.

Black & Grizzly Bears Due to their greater number and wider distribution throughout the Rocky Mountains, black bear attacks on humans are much more common than those of grizzlies but tend to result in less serious injury, while deaths are very unusual.

Grizzlies are very shy and intolerant of humans, and can become aggressive if surprised at close range. Sow (female) grizzlies with cubs are especially defensive, and likely to charge anyone who gets too close – the minimum safety buffer is about 400yd. In serious attacks, grizzlies bite savagely into the victim's head (especially face) and inflict severe wounds with their claws – an experience well worth avoiding.

When hiking in grizzly country, always stay alert and make plenty of noise on the trail. Never hike after dusk. While grizzlies have a highly acute sense of smell, they may not catch your scent if you approach from downwind. Some hikers wear 'bear bells' on their packs to announce their approach, but bears are generally better able to hear deeper sounds like shouting or clapping. Hikers should restrain their dogs, which may disturb a grizzly and provoke an attack. If you happen to encounter a black bear or (especially) a grizzly at close range:

- Do not run – bears can easily outrun humans and will instinctively pursue a fleeing animal.
- Do not drop your pack as a decoy – this may teach the bear that threatening humans is a good way to get food.
- Back away slowly, talking soothingly to the bear while avoiding direct eye contact.

Bears very often 'bluff charge' an intruder, veering away at the last instant. Using a pepper spray (see the boxed text) may deter a charging bear, but if an attack does ensue:

- Do not resist or fight back.
- Lie down and pull your knees against your chest, and (if not wearing a large backpack) pull in your head and shield your neck with your hands.
- Remain as quiet and motionless as possible, even if you are clawed or bitten.
- In most cases the attacking bear will eventually leave the scene once it is certain that you present no danger.

Bears & Food

Bears are obsessed with food, and rarely 'unlearn' knowledge acquired in finding it. In the past, bears were regularly fed (often as a spectacle for tourists) and allowed to pick over garbage dumps. Conditioned to associate humans with food, large numbers of these so-called 'habituated' bears harassed picnickers or aggressively raided camps. Some grizzlies even began to prey on people – in a few chilling cases, sleeping campers were dragged from their tents. Such behavior, atypical for wild grizzly bears, is the ultimate consequence of habituation.

Nowadays, even mildly troublesome bears are usually destroyed. For their own welfare, bears must be prevented from eating any kind of human food.

All campers must hang food (including garbage and aromatic items such as toothpaste, soap or sunscreen) at least 12ft above the ground and 200ft away from their tent. Carry a robust stuff-sack attached to a 50ft length of rope for this purpose. First weight the sack with a rock and throw it over a high, sturdy limb at least 4ft away from the tree trunk, then gently lower it on the rope. Stash *everything* that might be attractive to bears in the sack, then pull it back up on the rope close to the tree limb. Finally, tie off the end of the rope on another trunk or tree limb well out of the way. National park backcountry campgrounds invariably have a food pole that simplifies the food hanging process.

Pepper Sprays

Pepper sprays contain the severe irritant oleoresin capsicum. Their effectiveness in deterring charging or attacking bears remains controversial, but many backcountry travelers now carry pepper spray as a last line of defense. The smallest (3oz) canisters (such as those made by UDAP) cost around $15, and are widely available in backpacking stores. The spray jet can reach up to 30ft, but is less effective in windy conditions. Pepper spray must be carried within easy and immediate reach – not in your pack. Remember that carrying pepper spray is not a substitute for vigilance or other safety precautions. Pepper spray is *not* a repellent – it may actually attract bears if sprayed on tents or packs.

In extremely rare cases, grizzly bears have attacked humans with clear predatory intent. Such attacks tend to occur around campsites at dusk or at night, and are the only time when you should fight back against a grizzly.

The excellent *Bear Attacks – Their Causes and Avoidance* by Stephen Herrero ($16.95) provides comprehensive information on avoiding dangerous encounters of the bruin kind. See also Women Hikers (p55) for information on women and bears.

Cougars (Mountain Lions) Although your chances of encountering an aggressive cougar remain extremely small, cougar attacks on humans appear to be on the increase. In prime cougar habitats, hikers should avoid hiking alone. Keep children within view at all times. If you happen to encounter a cougar:

- Do not run or approach it.
- Do not crouch down.
- Do not turn your back on the cougar.
- Raise your arms and back away slowly, facing the cougar.
- Pick up any small children (as their behavior may make them vulnerable).
- If a cougar appears aggressive, wave your hands, try to look as big as possible and speak firmly or shout.
- If attacked, remain standing and fight back fiercely!
- Report any cougar sightings to a park or forest ranger as soon as possible.

Wolves Wild wolf attacks on humans are exceptionally rare, but not entirely unheard of. While there have been no reliable documented cases of fatal wolf attacks on humans for more than a century – if ever – in North America, wolves have very occasionally attacked children, forest workers and even sleeping campers in Canada and Alaska. All attacks on humans by wild wolves are believed to be attributable to either rabies infection (see Infectious Diseases, p69) or habituation – when a wolf has lost its fear of people.

Avalanches

Snow avalanches are largely a winter phenomenon, but occasionally there may be some risk of avalanches on trails through narrow or steep-sided alpine valleys early in the hiking season – contact the local park or forest ranger station for advice on current conditions. Online information is available at W www.avalanche.org.

Fording Rivers

Most popular hiking trails in the Rockies have footbridges across larger streams. Footbridges are often dismantled in fall (when river levels tend to be very low anyway) and re-erected in spring. Sometimes, especially in late spring, when thawing snow swells streams, or after heavy summer rain, a serious ford may be necessary. Remember that while heavy rain quickly makes rivers impassable, mountain streams fall almost as fast as they rise. Glacial or snow-fed streams reach their highest level in late afternoon.

Hikers should be well-practiced in rivercrossing techniques. The safest place to ford a river is usually just downstream from a long pool. Undo the waist buckle and loosen the shoulder straps of your pack so that you can easily slip it off if you stumble or are swept off your feet. Groups should undertake a serious ford by linking arms and moving together in a line at right-angles to the current. Lone hikers should use a sturdy pole (or improvise with a tree branch) for support, leaning sideways into the current.

Hunting Accidents

The hunting season opens about mid-September (first for archers, then for musketeers and only later for hunters with rifles). Hunting is permitted on most public lands, including many wilderness areas but excluding national parks and other nature or wildlife reserves. Safety conscious hikers and hunters wear luminescent orange vests and/or caps to alert others (but rarely game) of their presence. Keep your wits about you, particularly if you leave the main trails, as accidents occasionally occur. Inquire at Bureau of Land Management (BLM) or United States Forest Service (USFS) offices and ranger stations about popular local hunting areas.

Lightning & Thunderstorms

Intense electrical storms are very common in the Rockies in summer. Rapid cloud build-up from around noon often produces drenching, cold thunderstorms that bring the danger of hypothermia (p68). Especially in high, exposed places the danger of being struck by lightning often becomes extreme.

To minimize the risk, hikers should note these basic safeguards:

• In open areas where there is no shelter, find a depression in the ground and take up a crouched-squatting position with your feet together.
• Do *not* lie flat on the ground.
• Avoid contact with metallic objects such as pack frames, ice axes and crampons.
• Never seek shelter under objects that are isolated or higher than their surroundings.
• You are reasonably safe in an evenly high forest as long as you keep a fair distance from each tree.
• If a thunderstorm catches you on an exposed ridge or summit, look for a concave rock formation to shelter in – but avoid touching the rock itself.
• Swimmers should get out of the water immediately. Anglers should quickly put down their fishing rods and retreat from the shore.
• Should anyone actually be struck by lightning, immediately begin first-aid measures such as mouth-to-mouth resuscitation and treatment of burns (p71). Get the patient to a doctor as quickly as possible.

Rockfall

Even a small falling rock could shatter your hand or crack your skull, so always be alert to the danger of rockfall. Trail sections most obviously exposed to rockfall lead below cliffs fringed by large fields of raw talus – don't hang around in such areas. If you accidentally let loose a rock, loudly warn other hikers below. Mountain goats and bighorn sheep sometimes dislodge rocks, so animal watchers should be especially vigilant.

Rescue & Evacuation

Hikers should aim to manage emergency situations themselves – self-evacuation should be your first consideration. However, even the most safety-conscious hikers may be involved in a serious mountain accident requiring urgent medical attention. If a person in your group is injured or falls seriously ill, leave someone with them while others seek help. If there are only two of you, leave the injured person with as much warm clothing, food and water as it's sensible to spare, plus a whistle and flashlight (torch). Mark the position with something conspicuous – a yellow bivy sack or perhaps a large stone cross on the ground. Remember, the rescue effort may be slow, perhaps taking some days to remove the injured person.

Emergency Communications The national emergency telephone number is ☎ 911. Only call out a rescue team in a genuine emergency – not for a relatively minor discomfort such as a lightly sprained ankle.

Park ranger stations and USFS guard stations or fire lookouts usually have a two-way radio that can be used in an emergency situation. In areas where they exist, backcountry huts may also have a two-way radio. There are generally public telephones at ski resort trailheads and upper chairlift or aerial tramway stations.

Cellphones (mobile phones) are an invaluable asset to mountain safety, as they enable direct communication between hikers in distress and emergency services. All US cellphones sold after October 2001 are equipped with GPS-based location-tracking technology that can help rescuers locate overdue or missing hikers.

Cellphones should not be relied upon too heavily, however. They will often not function in remote backcountry areas and batteries run down quickly – on long hikes, keep the cellphone turned off to save power for emergencies. Remember that when reporting an emergency by cellphone you will have to give your exact position. See also Cellphones, p60.

If no other emergency communications are available, use the international distress signal. This is six whistles, six calls, six smoke puffs – ie, six of any recognizable sign you can make – followed by a pause (equaling the length of time taken to make the six signs) before you repeat the signal. If your distress call is heard/seen (and understood), you should receive a reply consisting of three signals, each separated by a long pause.

Search & Rescue Organizations Backcountry search and rescue (SAR) is normally handled by the local county sheriff using (civilian) volunteers, but state police, Game & Fish services, local firefighters or even the military may also be called upon. Volunteer emergency rescues are generally free of charge (although donations are graciously accepted). Especially where irresponsibility, negligence or unlawful activity is a factor, however, rescued persons may be billed for major expenses.

The Mountain Rescue Association (**W** www.mra.org) is the umbrella organization for local volunteer SAR services throughout the US.

Helicopter Rescue & Evacuation When the rescue helicopter arrives, it is important to be familiar with several conventions. Standing face on to the chopper:

• Arms up in the shape of a letter 'V' means 'I/We need help'.
• Arms in a straight diagonal line (like one line of a letter X) means 'All OK'.

In order for the helicopter to land, there must be a cleared space of 80ft x 80ft, with a flat landing pad area of 20ft x 20ft. The helicopter will fly into the wind when landing. In cases of extreme emergency, where no landing area is available, a person or harness might be lowered. Take extreme care to avoid the rotors when approaching a landed helicopter.

Getting There & Away

AIR

Domestic airfares in the US vary tremendously depending on the season you travel, the day of the week you fly, the length of your stay and the flexibility of the ticket, allowing for flight changes and refunds. While airlines don't maintain set low- and high-season airfares, prices do rise during the summer season from mid-June to mid-September, which is when most Americans go on vacation.

Airports & Airlines

The major gateway airports to the Rocky Mountains are Denver and Salt Lake City International Airports, with flights to destinations throughout the region.

Many of the best air connections to regional cities in the northern Rockies (such as Billings or Kalispell in Montana, and Boise in Idaho) are from Minneapolis-St Paul in the east and Seattle or Portland in the west.

Numerous major international and domestic airlines have services to the Rocky Mountains states.

Buying Tickets

It pays to do a bit of research and shop around for your air ticket. Start shopping for a ticket early – some of the cheapest tickets must be bought months in advance, and some popular flights sell out early. Most major newspapers in the US produce weekly travel sections with numerous travel agents' advertisements. You may decide to pay more than the rock-bottom fare by opting for the safety of a better-known travel agent. Established firms such as Council Travel (☎ 800-226-8624, W www.counciltravel.com) and STA Travel (☎ 800-777-0112, W www.statravel.com) are valid alternatives and offer good prices to most destinations.

Those coming from outside the US might start by perusing travel sections of magazines such as *Time Out* and *TNT* in the UK, or the Saturday edition of newspapers such as *The Sydney Morning Herald* and *The Age* in Australia.

Phoning a travel agent is still one of the best ways to dig up bargains. However, airlines have started to cater more to budget travelers and can sometimes offer the same deals you'll get with a travel agent. Airlines often have competitive low-season, student and senior citizens' fares. Find out not only the fare, but the route (is it direct or are there lots of stops?), the duration of the

Round-trip International Fares

Prices for the US summer are:

from	to Denver	to Salt Lake City
Auckland	NZ$2655	NZ$2280
Frankfurt	€694	€708
London	£610	£712
Paris	€746	€792
Sydney	A$1838	A$1590
Tokyo	¥124,890	¥106,480
Toronto	C$806	C$880
Vancouver	C$760	C$804

Round-trip Domestic Fares

Prices for the US summer are:

from	to Denver	to Salt Lake City
Chicago	$250	$325
Dallas	$250	$310
Los Angeles	$200	$180
Miami	$500	$580
New York	$300	$355
San Francisco	$200	$180

journey (how long are the layovers?) and any restrictions on the ticket.

You can also use the Internet to hunt for low fares and the latest specials. Cheap Tickets (W www.cheaptickets.com) and Travelocity (W www.travelocity.com) are two services that can help. To buy a ticket via the Web you'll need a credit card.

Some airlines now offer special deals on the Internet. United Airlines (W www.ual.com) offers e-fares, with tickets for selected routes and dates at substantial discounts. The ticket conditions are highly inflexible, so read the directions and requirements carefully.

The cheapest tickets are often nonrefundable and require an extra fee for changing your flight. Many insurance policies will cover this loss if you have to change your flight for emergency reasons. Round-trip (return) tickets are usually cheaper than two one-way fares – often *much* cheaper.

Departure Tax

Airport departure taxes are normally included in the cost of tickets bought in the US, although tickets purchased abroad may not have this included.

The US

Buy domestic air tickets in the US as early as possible, since this is the main way to get the cheapest fares. The lowest priced tickets are 21-day advance purchase, followed by 14-day and seven-day advance purchase. Tickets between major destinations (such as New York to Denver) that are purchased within seven days of departure can become ridiculously expensive, usually ranging from $1000 to $1300, compared to $250 to $500 if you buy three weeks in advance. Note that direct flights often cost more, so bargain tickets may involve one or more stopovers and thus a longer flight.

Canada

Travel CUTS (☎ 888-838-2887, W www.travelcuts.com) has offices in all major Canadian cities. Toronto's *The Globe and Mail* and *The Vancouver Sun* carry travel agents' advertisements.

Australia & New Zealand

STA Travel (W www.statravel.com) and Flight Centre International (W www.flightcentre.com.au) are major dealers in cheap airfares; check the travel agents' ads in the Yellow Pages and call around. Qantas offers flights to Los Angeles from Sydney, Melbourne and Cairns. United flies to San Francisco from Sydney and Melbourne, as well as to Los Angeles.

The cheapest tickets often have a 21-day advance-purchase requirement, a minimum stay of seven days and a maximum stay of 60 days. Flying with Air New Zealand is slightly cheaper, and both Qantas and Air New Zealand offer tickets with longer stays or stopovers, but you pay more.

The UK

Check the ads in magazines such as *Time Out,* plus the *Evening Standard* newspaper. Also check the free magazines, such as *TNT,* widely available in London – start by looking outside the main railway and tube stations.

London is arguably the world's headquarters for bucket shops, which are well advertised and can usually beat published airline fares. Good, reliable agents for cheap tickets in the UK are Trailfinders (☎ 020-7628-7628; W www.trailfinder.com; 1 Thread Needle St, London, EC2R 8JX), STA Travel (☎ 020-7581-4132; W www.statravel.com; 86 Old Brompton Rd, London SW7 3LQ) and Council Travel (☎ 0171-437-7767; W www.counciltravel.com; 28a Poland St, London, W1). Their websites are good research tools.

Continental Europe

The most common route to the Rocky Mountains states from Europe is west via New York, but other gateway cities such as Miami and Atlanta are alternatives. In Paris, try Council Travel (☎ 01 44 55 55 65; 22 rue des Pyramides, 75001).

Asia

Hong Kong and Bangkok are the region's best spots to buy discount tickets, but some bucket shops can be unreliable. Ask the advice of other travelers before buying a ticket. STA Travel, which is dependable, has branches in Hong Kong, Tokyo, Singapore, Bangkok, Manila and Kuala Lumpur.

Of all the carriers serving the US from Asia, United Airlines and Northwest Airlines have the largest number of routes and flights. Some of the lowest fares are offered by Malaysia Airlines and Korean Airlines, which serve southeast and northeast Asia respectively, as well as Hong Kong.

LAND

Unless you're one of the few who travel by train, you'll probably be using one of several interstate highways to reach the Rockies. Running nearly the entire length of the USA, I-70 and I-80 pass through central Colorado and southern Wyoming respectively. Passing north-south from New Mexico through Colorado, I-25 ends at a junction with I-90 in northern Wyoming. In turn, I-90 runs north and then heads west to span most of southern Montana before continuing on through northern Idaho and on to Seattle (Washington). Southern Idaho is linked to Portland (Oregon) by I-84, while I-15 connects southeast Idaho and western Montana with Salt Lake City (Utah) and Las Vegas (Nevada).

Two road routes provide access from Canada to the northern US Rockies. Running south from Banff National Park to Coeur d'Alene (Idaho) and Kalispell (Montana) are Hwy 93 and Hwy 95 respectively. From Calgary (Alberta), Hwy 2 (which becomes US 89 after crossing the border at Carway) gives direct access to the east side of Glacier National Park. Non-US citizens may not be allowed to cross into the US unless they carry a 'sufficient' amount of ready cash. People without US dollars have been sent back (there are no ATMs or exchange facilities at the border crossings), so try to have at least US$50 in notes when you arrive.

Bus

The nationwide bus company, Greyhound (W www.greyhound.com) runs cross-country buses between San Francisco and New York via Wyoming, Denver and Chicago; between Seattle and New York via Minneapolis, St Paul and Chicago; and between Los Angeles and New York via Las Vegas, Denver and Chicago. There are also bus services from other eastern seaboard cities, including Philadelphia and Washington (DC) and southern cities such as Atlanta and Miami.

Because buses are so few, schedules can be inconvenient. Fares are relatively high and bargain airfares can undercut buses on long-distance routes; on shorter routes it can be cheaper to rent a car than to ride the bus. However, very long-distance bus trips are often available at bargain prices by purchasing or reserving tickets three days in advance. For more information see Bus (p83).

Train

Amtrak (☎ 800-872-7245 or ☎ 800-523-6590, W www.amtrak.com) provides cross-country passenger service between the West Coast and Chicago; travelers to or from the East Coast must make connections in Chicago. Routes are limited and fares can be expensive.

The northernmost route is the daily *Empire Builder*, which runs from Seattle through northern Montana to Minneapolis and Chicago. This train makes 12 stops in Montana (including East Glacier and Whitefish) and one stop in Idaho at Sandpoint.

The daily *California Zephyr* from San Francisco (via Emeryville, California) passes through Colorado en route to Chicago. Stops in Colorado include Denver, Fraser-Winter Park, Glenwood Springs and Grand Junction.

The *Southwest Chief* goes from Los Angeles via Albuquerque and the southern Colorado towns of Trinidad, La Junta and Lamar to Kansas City and Chicago.

Amtrak tickets may only be purchased aboard the train *without penalty* if the station is not open 30 minutes prior to boarding. Rail travel is generally cheaper if you purchase tickets in advance. Round trips are the best bargain, but even these are usually as expensive as airfares, if not more so.

The 30-day North America Rail Pass gives unlimited travel on Amtrak and VIA Rail Canada trains; in peak season (June 1 to October 15) it costs $674, or $607 for seniors (over 60), children (aged two to 18) and students. For permanent residents of countries *outside* the US and Canada, Amtrak offers various US Rail Passes. The National Rail Pass costs $440/550 for 15/30 days in peak season (June 1 to September 5) and gives unlimited rail travel throughout the US. The West Rail Pass costs $325/405 for 15/30 days (peak) and covers travel throughout the entire west.

Car & Motorcycle

If you are driving into the US from Canada or Mexico, remember to bring the vehicle's registration papers, liability insurance, your international driving permit and home driving license. Canadian and Mexican driving licenses are valid in the US. Customs officials along the entry points between Canada and Montana can be strict, and wary of anything that doesn't look straight-laced.

If you plan to drive to the Rockies from within the US, see Car & Motorcycle (p85) for road rules and rental and purchase advice.

HIKE OPERATORS ABROAD

Some European-based outdoor guiding companies organize hiking tours to the Rocky Mountains and other regions of the US. Arrangements are similar to those of US-based outdoor companies (see Guided Hikes, p42), but prices generally also include airfares to and within the US.

UK-based Ramblers Holidays (☎ 01707-331133; w www.ramblersholidays.co.uk; Box 43, Welwyn Garden City, AL8 6PQ) is one of the best. It offers two-week hiking tours to Glacier, Yellowstone and the Tetons from around UK£1800. Switzerland-based Baumeler Reisen (☎ 41-418-6565; w www .baumeler.ch; Zingeltorstrasse 1, CH-6002 Lacerne) runs an all-inclusive, 14-day tour of national parks throughout the Rocky Mountain region (from Sfr8980, ex Zurich, Basel or Geneva).

Getting Around

The Rocky Mountains region is fairly well connected by commuter flights, although the cost may deter some. On the ground, public transportation leaves much to be desired and many hiking areas are accessible only by private vehicle. Even hikes considered accessible by public transportation often involve an additional hiker shuttle (or lengthy walk) just to reach the trailhead.

AIR
International Airports
Two main air hubs serve the region – Colorado's Denver (DIA) and Utah's Salt Lake City international airports.

The enormous DIA (☎ 303-342-2000, 800-AIR2DEN, W www.flydenver.com), 24mi from downtown Denver, is served by about 20 airlines. United Airlines, which has made DIA one of its two main national hubs, has most of the services. There are connecting flights from DIA to most major regional cities throughout the Rockies.

Salt Lake City International Airport (☎ 801-575-2400, 800-575-2442, W www .slcairport.com), 10mi west of downtown, is also very large and served by almost a dozen major carriers.

Regional Airports
In Colorado, there are commercial airports at Alamosa, Aspen, Colorado Springs, Cortez, Durango, Fort Collins, Grand Junction, Gunnison, Montrose, Pueblo, Telluride, Vail and Yampa Valley (serving Steamboat Springs). All have connections to Denver, and Grand Junction also has flights to Salt Lake City.

Idaho's main airport is in Boise. Airports at Challis, Hailey, Lewiston, McCall, Salmon and Stanley have connections to Boise. Idaho Falls, Pocatello and Twin Falls have flights to Boise, Denver and Salt Lake City.

Montana's commercial airports are at Billings, Bozeman, Glacier National Park (between Whitefish and Kalispell), Great Falls, Helena, Lewistown, Missoula and West Yellowstone. Most airports are connected with out-of-state destinations such as Salt Lake City, and some have intrastate flights such as Helena-Great Falls and Missoula-Kalispell.

New Mexico's main airport is in Albuquerque. The other main airport in the north is in Santa Fe, with flights to Denver.

Utah's principle airport is in Salt Lake City, but in the northern part of the state there are also regional airports at Moab and Vernal.

Wyoming's airports are at Casper, Cody, Cheyenne, Gillette, Jackson Hole, Laramie, Riverton, Rock Springs, Sheridan and Worland. Most of Wyoming's airports are not connected to each other but do have flights to Denver.

Tickets & Fares
Most short flights within the region carry high price-tags. The best way to cut the cost is to link your regional flight to your flight into Denver or Salt Lake City, in which case the commuter connection is often a fraction of what it would cost to book separately.

BUS
Although long-distance buses connect most main cities and many towns along major highways, the network barely penetrates many parts of the Rocky Mountains.

Greyhound (W www.greyhound.com) has extensive fixed routes and its own terminal in most large cities. Texas, New Mexico & Oklahoma Coaches (TNM&O) is affiliated

Round-trip Regional Airfares		
from	to Denver	to Salt Lake City
Aspen	$295	NA
Bozeman	$456	$283
Durango	$304	$506
Kalispell	NA	$303
Jackson	$377	$462
Santa Fe	$410	$554
West Yellowstone	NA	$258

with Greyhound and serves the same routes in Colorado and parts of Wyoming. Powder River Coach USA primarily serves eastern Wyoming, but also goes to Denver and Billings. Rim Rock Stages serves Montana.

Scheduled minibus services also operate on some routes – such as Idaho Falls–Jackson and Idaho Falls–Missoula – connecting towns and cities on the main long-distance bus routes. These Idaho Falls services are run by CART (☎ 800-258-4937).

Tickets & Fares
Greyhound tickets can be bought over the phone (☎ 800-229-9424) or online with a credit card (American Express, MasterCard or Visa), and are then mailed out or can picked up at the bus terminal. Discounts apply to advance-purchase fares.

Special Fares Greyhound occasionally introduces a mileage-based discount fare program that can be a bargain, especially for very long distances, but it's a good idea to check the regular fare anyway. Greyhound offers a free companion ticket (child or adult) for any round-trip ticket purchased at least three days prior to travel.

Bus Passes
Passes allow you to stop whenever you like, for as long as you like, providing you finish travel while your pass is still valid.

Greyhound's Ameripasses give unlimited travel throughout the entire US. For all residents of Canada and the US, the Domestic Ameripass costs $349/195/310 adult/child/

Hiker Shuttles

People who undertake a destination (point-to-point) hike, or don't have their own means of transportation, will probably need to be dropped off (and/or picked up) at one of the trailheads. Hiker shuttle services are available on demand in many regional cities and towns. Ask in local outdoor stores about companies or individuals that do hiker shuttles. Expect to pay up to $2 per mile.

National park lodges and some hostels also do hiker shuttles. In some of the region's national parks, regular (mini) bus services run past popular trailheads.

Local taxi services will usually take you to/from trailheads (provided access roads are suitable for conventional vehicles); see 'Taxi' in the Yellow Pages for phone numbers.

Information on local hiker shuttles is given in the regional chapters.

---

concession for 21 days, and $549/315/486 for 60 days. For non-residents, the International Ameripass costs $324/182/288 for 21 days or $494/287/437 for 60 days.

Greyhound's 21-day Westcoast Discovery Pass, which gives unlimited travel throughout western US and western Canada, costs $324/182/288 for residents of Canada and the US, and $284/162/252 for non-residents.

Passes for residents can be bought at any bus terminal or purchased online (at least 14 days in advance). Passes for non-residents can also be purchased online (at least 21 days in advance) or at selected travel agencies abroad.

One-Way Regional Bus Fares

from	to Denver	to Salt Lake City
Aspen	$42*	$71*
Bozeman	$115	$83
Durango	$62	$76
Jackson	$135*	$69*
Kalispell	$132	$102
Santa Fe	$56	$125
West Yellowstone	NA	$58
*includes local bus or shuttle services		

TRAIN
Rail services within the Rocky Mountains region are limited. Amtrak's long-distance trains are few and serve only a small number of destinations. Trains are more likely to be useful in getting to the region than getting around it (see Land, p81).

Several tourist railroads in the Colorado Rockies provide access to wilderness trailheads. These are the Durango & Silverton Narrow Gauge Railroad (☎ 970-247-2733,

888-872-4607, W www.durangotrain.com) and the Cumbres & Toltec Scenic Railroad (☎ 719-376-5483, W www.cumbrestoltec .com), both in the San Juan Mountains; and the Pikes Peak Cog Railway (☎ 719-685-5401, W www.cograilway.com) from Manitou Springs. These historic trains are popular in July and August, so it is advisable to make reservations.

CAR & MOTORCYCLE

Having your own set of wheels is almost indispensable for travel in the Rocky Mountains region – hikers reliant on public transportation face frustrating limitations. Trailheads are generally accessible by conventional cars, although 4WD vehicles may sometimes be preferable, especially when roads are muddy or snowy.

The American Automobile Association (AAA; ☎ 866-625-3601, W www.aaa.com), with offices in all major cities and many smaller towns, gives travel advice and free material such as road maps. Membership offers discounts for some accommodations, car rentals and admission charges. The AAA also provides emergency roadside service (☎800-222-4357). AAA has reciprocal rights with other motoring associations – such as the UK Automobile Association and the RACV in Australia – bring your membership card and a letter of introduction from your home organization.

Road Rules

Seat belts are mandatory for the driver and passengers in all six Rocky Mountains states. Apart from Colorado, where there are no helmet laws, motorcycle riders under the age of 18 (19 in Wyoming) must wear a helmet. However, all motorcycle riders are strongly urged to wear a helmet. The maximum legal blood alcohol concentration (BAC) for drivers is 0.10% in Colorado and Wyoming, but 0.08% in Idaho, Montana, New Mexico and Utah.

Rental

The major car rental companies, such as Avis, Budget, Enterprise, Hertz and National, have offices throughout the region,

but there are also local rental agencies. Prices vary greatly according to region, season and type or size of the car you rent, but weeklong rental rates are typically around $240 for a compact car or $310 for a full-sized model (eg, Ford Taurus). Especially outside the summer peak season (from early July until the second half of August), cheaper rates are generally available. Members of a frequent-flyer program are often entitled to discounts.

Smaller local rental companies (such as Rent-a-Wreck) are generally quite a bit cheaper, but drivers are normally not permitted to take the car outside a specified area (eg, the state boundaries or a 200mi radius). Companies such as RV Central (☎ 562-266-1814, W www.rvcentral.com) rent RVs (recreation vehicles) from around $750 per week in the peak season (mid-May to early September). Adventures On Wheels (☎ 800-943-3579, W www.wheels9.com) rents older cars (from $165 per week) and RVs (from $230 per week) that can be dropped off in several locations on the east and west coasts of the US.

To rent a vehicle, you generally need to be at least 21 (often 25) years old and present a major credit card or a large cash deposit. Basic liability (third party) insurance covering any damage you may cause to another vehicle is included in the rental price, but you may wish to purchase a Collision Damage Waiver (CDW) covering any damage you cause to the rented vehicle. If you have collision insurance on your personal auto insurance policy, this may also cover rental cars. Some credit-card companies will cover certain types of insurance if you charge the full cost of rental to your card.

Purchase

Buying a used car becomes a much cheaper option for visitors who intend traveling for longer than several months. The market is quite well stocked with (functional) older cars, but there is the usual risk of paying too much and of additional repair costs in case of a major breakdown. Buying a car can also get a little complicated and requires some patience. To get an idea of current used-car prices, refer to the *Kelly Blue Book*, available in public libraries or online at

W www.kbb.com – this website even allows you to check a used car's history using its Vehicle Identification Number (VIN).

Before a vehicle can be registered (which costs up to $130), the owner must show proof of current liability insurance and, in some areas (eg, Denver), that the vehicle has passed an exhaust emissions test (about $20). Premiums for liability insurance, which is now compulsory in all US states, are far higher (up to $90 per month) for non-resident drivers, but if you obtain a US state driving license – generally a quick and straightforward procedure – premiums drop considerably. Your total, on-road cost for a (reliable) car is unlikely to be less than $2000.

The AAA or the local Department of Motor Vehicles in each state can give general advice on buying and/or registering a vehicle.

Road Safety

The Rocky Mountains region is largely open-range country where livestock (especially cattle) and large ungulates (including deer or moose) graze along roads and highways. A collision with a large animal can wreck a car and severely injure or kill the occupants (not to mention the animal), so pay attention to the roadside ahead – especially at night.

Backcountry roads are invariably unsurfaced and often of poor standard. On narrow, winding mountain roads, turnouts (widened sections) provide the only opportunity to pass other vehicles – always stop when meeting another vehicle on a single-lane road. Logging (or occasionally mining) trucks use some backcountry roads, even on weekends.

Icy or snowy conditions can make mountain roads hazardous for several days at a time (even in midsummer), when tire chains may be declared mandatory for all non-4WD vehicles. Current road conditions can be checked online at W www.usroadconditions .com or by phone in each state:

Colorado	☎ 303-639-1234, 303-573ROAD
Idaho	☎ 888-432-7623
Montana	☎ 800-226-7623, 800-332-6171
New Mexico	☎ 800-432-4269, 505-827-5118
Utah	☎ 800-492-2400, 801-964-6000
Wyoming	☎ 307-635-9966

Vehicles left at trailheads are very occasionally broken into. If you must leave expensive items such as cameras or sunglasses in your car, put them out of sight, preferably in the trunk.

BICYCLE

Cycling is an excellent way to travel around the Rocky Mountains region. Spare parts are widely available and repair shops are numerous. Some counties and cities do not require helmets, but they should always be worn anyway.

Mountain biking has become popular throughout the Rockies, although it is *not* permitted on national park trails or anywhere within designated wilderness areas. Two books of particular interest to mountain bikers are *Bike and Brew: Rocky Mountain Region* by Todd Mercer ($16.95), describing numerous mountain bike trips (each via a microbrewery!), and *Cycling the Great Divide* by Michael McCoy ($14.95), a guidebook to the 2470mi (60-day) Great Divide biking route from Canada to New Mexico along (or close to) the Continental Divide.

HITCHING

It is never entirely safe to hitchhike, regardless of where you are, and we do not recommend it. However, because public transportation is so limited in most areas of the Rockies, some hikers resort to thumbing a ride to or from the trailhead. If you do choose to hitch, it is safer to travel in pairs and let someone know where you are planning to go. You should keep a close watch on your possessions – 'friendly' drivers have been known to abscond with an innocent hitchhiker's gear while the latter visited the bathroom during a gasoline stop.

In Colorado, hitching is illegal (although widely tolerated in Rocky Mountain National Park) and pedestrians on the highway must walk in the opposite direction of traffic. Hitching is legal in Montana, but restricted in areas near state prisons. It is also legal in Wyoming (although against regulations in Grand Teton National Park). In Idaho, hitching is illegal on interstate highways, although it's allowed on all other roads.

Greater Glacier

The Greater Glacier area occupies a large portion of the northwest corner of Montana. At its heart is Glacier National Park, where hikers enjoy some of the most striking mountain scenery and easily seen wildlife in the Rocky Mountains. With beautiful wildflower meadows set against a backdrop of spectacularly glaciated peaks and a network of well-constructed trails offering a multitude of different hiking possibilities, this park attracts swarms of hikers in the summer months. Glacier adjoins Canada's much smaller and quieter Waterton Lakes National Park, and together the two form an International Peace Park. Some of the best hikes in Waterton are also described in this chapter.

To the south of Glacier National Park, the huge Bob Marshall Wilderness provides a radically different experience, offering long and remote outings into less spectacular, but arguably wilder, country. To the west of the 'Bob', the relatively unfrequented Mission Mountains challenge serious hikers with rugged terrain, thick brush and often-difficult trails. And if all that sounds a bit too much, Jewel Basin Hiking Area, just to the north of Mission Mountains, provides straightforward and relatively easy day hikes with distant views of Glacier National Park's most impressive peaks.

CLIMATE

The Greater Glacier area normally experiences warm, settled summers (June to August) with average, daytime temperatures in the low 70s and plenty of fine, clear days. Summer daytime temperatures can exceed 90°F and overnight temperatures in the valleys can drop as low as 20°F. Even in August, lying snow is not unknown, especially on the passes. Cold winters with significant snowfall are the norm, restricting mountain activities of all, but the most intrepid, to ski resorts.

The region is often influenced by weather systems in the northeast Pacific, which bring cloud and rain (snow in winter) down through British Columbia and Alberta. The

Highlights

GARETH McCORMACK

Majestic, glaciated beauty around Boulder Pass attracts many backcountry hikers.

- Looking out over rows of superb, glaciated peaks from Swiftcurrent Mountain Lookout (p94) in Glacier National Park

- Traversing some of Glacier National Park's most impressive scenery on the Boulder Pass trail (p103)

- Hiking along the base of the majestic Chinese Wall escarpment (p120) in Bob Marshall Wilderness

- Escaping from the crowds in the Mission Mountains (p114)

Canadian Rockies and the Pacific coastal ranges take the sting out of many of these systems before they reach Greater Glacier. This is particularly the case in summer, when these fronts may only produce cloudy conditions with showers.

On a more local level, the east side of the mountain ranges often experience slightly drier conditions than the west (although the

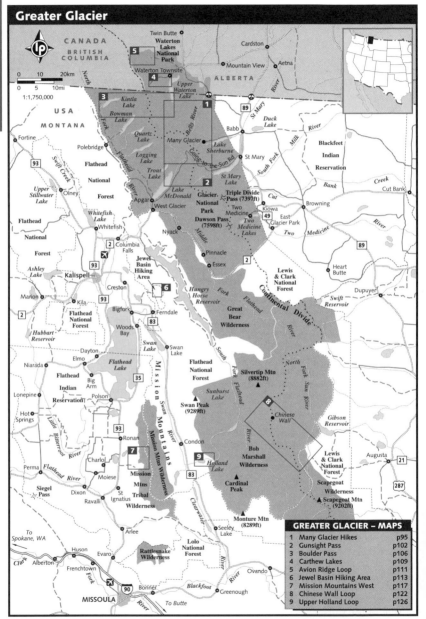

Greater Glacier

difference is not as marked as in Colorado). On wet days in Glacier National Park for example, it is often worth crossing Logan Pass to find drier conditions on the east side of the park.

INFORMATION
Maps
For travel within Montana, pick up the Montana Department of Transport Highway Map, available free from gas stations and supermarkets throughout Montana.

Information Sources
Montana's statewide tourist board is Travel Montana (☎ 406-444-2654, 800-847-4868; W www.travelmt.com; 1424 9th Ave, PO Box 200533, Helena, MT 59620). Another good online resource for planning is Discovering Montana (W www.discoveringmon tana.com).

GATEWAYS
Kalispell
A small, unexciting center, Kalispell lies at the intersection of US 2 and US 93, southwest of Glacier National Park and at the head of the Flathead valley. Flathead National Forest Headquarters (☎ 406-758-5204, 1935 3rd Ave E) has information on hiking in the Greater Glacier area, and sells local hiking

---

> ### Warning
>
> Many hikes and areas described in this chapter are in prime grizzly habitat – in particular all the hikes in Glacier National Park, where bear concentrations can be high. While maulings are rare and deaths from bear attacks even rarer (one to two a year in the US), encounters and sightings are relatively frequent. The author was bluff-charged by a sow grizzly in Glacier National Park (see the boxed text, p104).
>
> Stay alert, make lots of noise and be meticulous with food storage; taking the right precautions in bear country can reduce the chances of an encounter and acting appropriately in the event of an encounter can prevent a mauling or worse. See Animal Attacks (pp74–6) for more information about hiking in bear country.

---

guides and maps. Sportsman & Ski Haus (☎ 406-755-6484, cnr US 2 & US 93) is the best, all-round outdoor store in town. The chamber of commerce (☎ 406-758-2800, W www.kalispellchamber.com, 5 Depot Park) has local accommodations listings.

Amtrak's daily *Empire Builder* train stops at Whitefish, 13mi north of Kalispell. Intermountain Transport (☎ 406-755-4011) runs a daily bus between Whitefish and Missoula via Kalispell. Several airlines have flights between Missoula, Salt Lake City, Spokane, Seattle and the local Glacier Park International Airport (☎ 406-527-5994), located half way between Kalispell and Whitefish on US 2.

Missoula
This small, university city on I-90 is well positioned as a gateway to the Mission Mountains and Bob Marshall Wilderness. It is also home to the United States Forest Service (USFS) Northern Region Headquarters (☎ 406-329-3511, 200 E Broadway). Pipestone Mountaineering (☎ 406-721 1670, 101 S Higgins Ave) is a good source of outdoor gear and maps. For accommodations contact the chamber of commerce (☎ 406-543-6623, W www.missoulachamber.com, 825 E Front St).

The Greyhound depot (☎ 406-549-2339, 1660 W Broadway) has regional buses to Whitefish (via Kalispell), Billings (via Butte) and Bozeman (via Anaconda and Butte), as well as interstate services to San Francisco, Seattle and Denver. Intermountain Transport (☎ 406-755-4011) also runs a daily bus between Missoula and Whitefish via Kalispell.

Missoula airport (☎ 406-728-4381), 5mi west of the city, has flights to/from Kalispell, Seattle, Salt Lake City, Minneapolis and Washington (among others).

Glacier National Park

The 1583-sq-mile Glacier National Park extends south along the Continental Divide from the Canadian border. The entire Greater

Glacier area is regarded by many ecologists as the most important biosphere reserve in the Lower 48 states, largely because animal populations on both sides of the border can readily migrate. Its outstanding wilderness scenery and wildlife attract hordes of tourists during the short summer season, although most visitors leave their cars only briefly (if at all) on their way across the Going-to-the-Sun Rd between West Glacier and St Mary.

HISTORY

At the time of first European contact, the Blackfoot people occupied most of northern Montana. After a series of land-grabs and dishonored treaties throughout the latter 19th century, the Blackfoot people finally sold the area now comprising the national park to the US government in 1896. The construction of the Great Northern Railway in the 1890s led to rapid settlement and often-rapacious exploitation of the region's resources, especially timber.

In 1895 Waterton Lakes National Park was established just across the border in Canada. Having long recognized the area's uniqueness, Dr George Bird Grinnell (a co-founder of the Audubon Society and a campaigner for the interests of the Blackfoot people) finally convinced the US government to create Glacier National Park, which came into being in 1910. In the early 1910s the Great Northern Railway built a series of hotels and mountain chalets in the park, but the completion of the Going-to-the-Sun Rd over Logan Pass in 1927 and the rising popularity of motorized transportation brought to an end Glacier's short era of 'railroad tourism'.

NATURAL HISTORY

The moderating influence of the moist Pacific winds is particularly pronounced on the slopes west of the Continental Divide. For this reason many of the more temperate tree species found in the Greater Glacier area do not grow much further south in the Rockies, most notably western red cedar, mountain hemlock, western hemlock and western yew, as well as grand fir and white spruce. Tree species more readily associated with upper montane and subalpine forests of the Rocky

Mountains include Engelmann spruce and subalpine fir.

These rich forests support a diverse bird population. The varied thrush is typically present in the moist, lower forests of western red cedar and hemlock on the western side of the park. Steller's jay can be found in Engelmann spruce, while the gray-crowned rosy finch favors subalpine, shrub-willow thickets. The well-camouflaged spruce grouse is found in the coniferous montane and subalpine forests. White-tailed ptarmigans live mostly in the tundra, largely feeding on wildflowers and the buds of alpine shrub willows.

In early summer the park's alpine wildflowers bloom with almost unparalleled splendor. The diverse alpine flora species include the hardy, creamy-white globeflower, yellow blanket flower, deep-blue mountain bog gentian and purple pasqueflower, which pop out of the ground as the winter snows melt. Yellow glacier lilies carpet the highest alpine meadows, and their tubers are dug out and eaten by grizzly bears. Coarse, blade-like beargrass produces fragrant white flowers on a long stalk, eaten by elk and bighorn sheep.

Viewing wildlife is one of the great pleasures of Glacier National Park. Moose browse on saplings, shrubs and other plants in the waterlogged valleys, at times even diving to feed on the aquatic vegetation in lakes. Herds of bighorn sheep graze the alpine tundra in summer. Mountain goats are another of the park's often-sighted larger mammals (partly because salt-addicted mountain goats frequent many backcountry campsites). These remarkably agile animals pick their way through the steepest slopes in search of alpine grasses, shrubs or lichen.

The Greater Glacier area is an important breeding ground for grizzly bears. Local grizzlies are largely vegetarian, but sometimes take old or sick mammals and are quickly attracted by animal carcasses. Grizzlies are by nature solitary animals, but will congregate anywhere food is abundant, such as alpine berry fields. In late fall grizzlies dig out hollows, typically under tree roots just below tree line, where they hibernate

Glaciers & Glacial Landforms

Many of the world's finest hikes are through landscapes, which have been – or are being – substantially shaped by glaciers. As a glacier flows downhill its weight of ice and snow creates a distinctive collection of landforms, many of which are preserved once the ice has retreated (as it is doing in most of the world's ranges today) or vanished.

The most obvious is the *U-shaped valley* (1), gouged out by the glacier as it moves downhill, often with one or more bowl-shaped *cirques* (2) at its head. Cirques are found along high mountain ridges or at mountain passes or *cols* (3). Where an alpine glacier – which flows off the upper slopes and ridges of a mountain range – has joined a deeper, more substantial valley glacier, a dramatic *hanging valley* (4) is often the result. Hanging valleys and cirques commonly shelter hidden alpine lakes or *tarns* (5), such as those featured in so many of the hikes in this book. The thin ridge that separates adjacent glacial valleys is known as an *arête* (6).

As a glacier grinds its way forward it usually leaves long *lateral moraine* (7) ridges along its course – mounds of debris either deposited along the flanks of the glacier or left by sub-ice streams within its heart (the latter, strictly, an *esker*). At the end – or *snout* – of a glacier is the *terminal moraine* (8), the point where the giant conveyor belt of ice drops its load of rocks and grit. Both high up in the hanging valleys and in the surrounding valleys and plains, *moraine lakes* (9) may form behind a dam of glacial rubble.

The plains that surround a glaciated range may feature a confusing variety of moraine ridges, mounds and outwash fans – material left by rivers flowing from the glaciers. Perched here and there may be an *erratic* (10), a rock carried far from its origin by the moving ice and left stranded when it melted.

View of area before glacier's retreat

until winter snows are gone. Researchers keep track of local grizzlies by nailing short lengths of barbed wire to tree trunks. The barbed wire collects bear hair as the animals rub against the tree to mark their territory.

Other wildlife includes whitetail deer, mule deer and Rocky Mountain elk (or wapiti). Cougars (or mountain lions), lynx and bobcats also live in the park, but are rarely seen.

Glacier Geology: A Window to the Past

The rocks of Glacier and Waterton Lakes National Parks have a unique place in the geological world. Along many trails, especially in alpine areas and close to the bases of receding glaciers, you may notice strange patterns in the rock. These are the incredibly well-preserved impressions of sedimentation processes that took place around one billion years ago, and might include features such as ripple marks, mud cracks and fossils. The presence of such clear geologic evidence on the surface owes much to the Lewis Overthrust, a huge zone of severe faulting, which in turn was only part of the greater event that created the Rockies by driving two of the earth's plates together. The Lewis thrust eventually pushed a thick wedge of ancient (Proterozoic) sedimentary rock to the surface. Erosion, particularly glaciation, then stripped away the surface layers of this rock to reveal the subtly preserved features beneath.

In other parts of the world, rocks of this age have generally been greatly altered over time and no longer show their earlier characteristics, and it's for this reason that the mountains of Glacier and Waterton have a unique place in the geological world. A variety of fossilized algae known as stromatolites (also unique to the area in terms of variety and degree of preservation) allow geologists to estimate what conditions were like on earth one billion years ago, and to glean valuable information about the earth's climate changes over time.

PLANNING
Maps & Books
Most hikers use Trails Illustrated's 1:142,747 map No 215 *Glacier/Waterton Lakes National Parks* ($9.95), which covers the whole of Glacier National Park and includes a 1:83,930 inset map of the Many Glacier area. The USGS 1:100,000 *Glacier National Park* map ($5) covers the entire park at a smaller scale, but is rather unwieldy.

Hiking Glacier and Waterton Lakes National Parks by Erik Molvar ($14.95) details over 850mi of trails and is probably the most comprehensive hiking guide to the area.

Information Sources
Information about Glacier National Park (including a free 'Glacier Trip Planner') can be obtained from park headquarters (☎ 406-888-7800; W www.nps.gov/glac; Glacier National Park, West Glacier, MT 59936). Central Reservations (☎ 406-226-5551) takes bookings for the park's lodges. For campsite availability in the 13 National Park Service (NPS) campgrounds in the park, call ☎ 406-888-7800.

Permits & Regulations
Park entry fees (valid for seven days) are $5/10 for individuals/private vehicles or motorcycles.

Backcountry permits are required for all overnight trips within the park ($4 per person, per night from June through September, otherwise free). Up to 50% of backcountry sites are available for advanced reservation after April 15 for an additional fee of $20. For backcountry information and reservations, contact the park headquarters (☎ 406-888-7800; W www.nps.gov/glac; Glacier National Park, West Glacier, MT 59936). Details and forms are also available in the park's free *Backcountry Guide* (available at visitor centers within the park). There are backcountry offices at Apgar, Many Glacier, St Mary visitor center, Two Medicine, Polebridge and Waterton Lakes visitor center.

GETTING AROUND
During summer Glacier Park Inc (☎ 406-755-6303) operates a shuttle service between

Many Glacier and West Glacier via St Mary, Logan Pass and Apgar. There are three services in both directions each day and no reservations are taken. A one-way ticket between Many Glacier and Logan Pass costs $16.75. Apart from this service, public transportation options are very limited. Sun Tours (☎ 406-226-9220), which operates guided tours in the park, can offer private transportation.

ACCESS TOWNS

Surprisingly none of the access towns, with the exception of West Glacier and St Mary, have any reliable quantities of camping supplies or equipment for sale. You should bring all equipment, fuel and freeze-dried foods with you.

West Glacier

Just outside the park on US 2, at the western end of the Going-to-the-Sun Rd, West Glacier is the park's main entry point. Park headquarters (☎ 406-888-7800) is on the road toward Apgar. The nearest camping with all facilities is at *Glacier Campground* (☎ 406-387-5689), 2mi west of the park entrance (sites $17). The *Vista Hotel* (☎ 406-888-5311), 1mi west of the park entrance, has doubles for $67.

Amtrak's *Empire Builder* train, which runs the 2200mi between Chicago and Seattle/Portland daily in both directions, stops (around 8:30am eastbound and 7:30pm westbound) at West Glacier's Belton station. This train line connects West Glacier to Whitefish, where there are frequent bus connections to Kalispell (see Gateways, p89). West Glacier is 37mi northeast of Kalispell via US 2.

Apgar

Just inside the park boundary at the scenic southern shore of Lake McDonald, Apgar is 2mi from West Glacier. There is a small visitor center and a separate backcountry office (for permits). There is camping at the basic NPS *Apgar campground* ($14), doubles at *Apgar Village Inn* (☎ 406-888-5632) from $95, and a *general store*. See Getting Around (p92) for transportation options.

Many Glacier

Off US 89 in the park's northeastern sector, Many Glacier is 12mi west of Babb. With at least six excellent routes in the surrounding mountains, this scattered, summer-only village is probably the best base for hiking in Glacier National Park. The village's ranger station can provide trail and backcountry information.

The basic NPS *Many Glacier campground* has sites for $14. First opened in 1914, the large *Many Glacier Hotel* (☎ 406-732-4411, 602-207-6000), on the north shore of Swiftcurrent Lake, has doubles from $106. About 1.2mi on, at the end of the road, is the *Swiftcurrent Motor Inn* (☎ 406-732-5531), which serves as an annex for Many Glacier Hotel, and offers doubles from $41. The motor inn also has a *restaurant* and a *general store*, which sells tokens for the nearby shower and laundromat but, apart from maps, few backpacking supplies. See Getting Around (p92) for transportation options.

St Mary

At the intersection of US 89 and the Going-to-the-Sun Rd is St Mary. The visitor center at the park entrance sells maps and guidebooks, has natural history exhibits and issues backcountry permits. There is a reasonably well-stocked outdoor store. The *KOA campground* (☎ 406-732-4122), 1mi west of the village, has tent sites with full facilities for $22, while the NPS *St Mary Campground* (☎ 800-365-2267) is 1mi inside the park and charges $17. *St Mary Lodge* (☎ 406-732-4431) has doubles from $99. The village also has an expensive *supermarket*. See Getting Around (p92) for transportation options.

East Glacier Park

At the intersection of Hwy 49 and US 2, East Glacier Park gives access to the southeast side of the park. The small chamber of commerce (☎ 406-226-4403) offers local accommodations advice. *Firebrand Campground* (☎ 406-226-5573, Linhe Ave) has little shade but offers tent sites with full facilities for $13. The HI-AYH hostel *Brownies* (☎ 406-727-4448, Hwy 49) has dorm beds and doubles for $12/30. The *Whistling*

Swan Motel (☎ 406-226-4412, US 2) has doubles from $60.

Amtrak's *Empire Builder* train, which runs the 2200mi between Chicago and Seattle/Portland daily in both directions, stops (around 9am eastbound and 7pm westbound) at Glacier Park Station in East Glacier Park.

Swiftcurrent Mountain Lookout

Duration	7½–10 hours
Distance	15.8mi (25.4km)
Standard	moderate–hard
Start/Finish	Many Glacier
Transport	car, bus

Summary One of the most panoramic lookouts anywhere in the Rockies, following a long and tiring, yet unceasingly scenic, trail.

This spectacular route transits the upper valley of Swiftcurrent Creek in a long hike from Many Glacier with an elevation gain of almost 3500ft. Note that the upper Swiftcurrent valley is a summer feeding ground for grizzly bears – so be 'bear aware' at all times. Some hikers take two days to cover the route, staying overnight at Granite Park Chalet or campground, a short distance west of Swiftcurrent Pass. The route described is also the first (or last) day of the Highline Trail/Ptarmigan Tunnel Loop (p96).

PLANNING
When to Hike
It is unlikely that the upper sections of the trail will be clear much before the end of June or after September. Afternoon thunderstorms are a danger from June through August so try to get an early start. The trails around Many Glacier are heavily used during summer, even on weekdays.

Maps
Trails Illustrated's 1:142,747 map No 215 *Glacier/Waterton Lakes National Parks* is probably sufficient, but for more detail use two USGS 1:24,000 quads: *Many Glacier* and *Ahern Pass*.

NEAREST TOWN
See Many Glacier (p93).

THE HIKE (see map opposite)
The trailhead is 120yd past the Swiftcurrent Motor Inn on the northwestern side of the large parking area. Follow the Swiftcurrent Pass Trail left (west) at the junction a few paces from the trailhead, and cross the footbridge over Wilbur Creek. This low, lodgepole forest sprinkled with aspen is regrowth following the 1936 fire that burnt out much of the upper Swiftcurrent valley.

After passing largely hidden Fishercap Lake, the trail rises gently through beargrass meadows to Redrock Lake and then heads up beside Redrock Falls, where the inlet cascades in several stages over red mudstone. Continue through wildflower fields and brush willow, past an unnamed lake, to cross a side stream (the outlet of Windmaker Lake) on a suspension bridge. The view north is dominated by Mt Wilbur, Iceberg Peak and the North Swiftcurrent Glacier. The trail continues past greenish Bullhead Lake, then follows the small inlet almost to the base of the sheer headwalls at the head of the valley, two to three hours from the trailhead.

The climb now begins in earnest as the trail, in places cut into the precipitous rock, winds its way up past meltwater cascades from nearby Swiftcurrent Glacier. Now, high above the valley, you get a spectacular overview of the landscape you've just passed through. Cut up over mountain meadows to reach **Swiftcurrent Pass** (6770ft), 1½ to two hours after you began climbing. This broad, low saddle, scattered with yellow glacier lilies, is bordered by stands of battered firs, and gives the first views of Heavens Peak (southwest) and other peaks in the southern Livingston Range (west).

The signposted 1.4mi trail to the lookout turns north just west of the pass. Climb in repeated switchbacks along the steep shingle ridge to arrive at the summit shelter on **Swiftcurrent Mountain** (8436ft) from 45 minutes to one hour from the pass. The sublime panorama includes several dozen of Glacier National Park's classic stratified peaks; the sight of the north wall of Mt

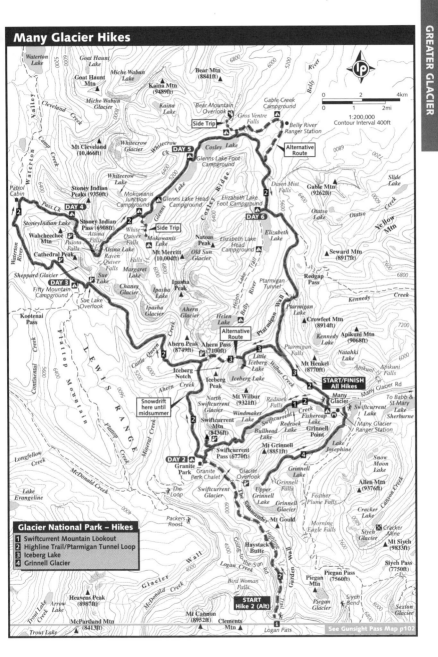

Many Glacier Hikes

Waterton
Lake

Goat Haunt
Lake

Goat Haunt
Mtn

Miche Wabun
Lake

Miche Wabun
Mtn

Kaina Mtn
(9489ft)

Kaina
Lake

Bear Mtn
(8841ft)

Bear Mountain
Overlook

Gros Ventre
Falls

Side Trip

Gable Creek
Campground

Belly River
Ranger Station

**Alternative
Route**

Cleveland Creek

Mt Cleveland
(10,466ft)

Whitecrow
Glacier

Whitecrow
Lake

Whitecrow Ck

DAY 5

Cosley Lake

Glenns Lake Foot
Campground

Dawn Mist
Falls

Gable Mtn
(9262ft)

Slide
Lake

Patrol
Cabin

Stoney Indian
Peaks (9350ft)

Mokowanis
Junction
Campground

Glenns Lake Head
Campground

Elizabeth Lake
Foot Campground

DAY 6

Otatso
Lake

Yellow
Mtn

Pass Ck

DAY 4

Stoney Indian
Pass (6908ft)

White
Quiver
Falls

Atsina
Falls

Side Trip

Mokowanis
Lake

Natoas
Peak

Elizabeth Lake
Head Campground

Elizabeth
Lake

Seward Mtn
(8917ft)

Stoney Indian Lake

Wahcheechee
Mtn

Cathedral Peak

Paiota
Falls

Aisina Lake

Raven
Quiver
Falls

Mt Merritt
(10,004ft)

Old Sun
Glacier

Redgap
Pass

Kennedy
Creek

Sheppard Glacier

DAY 3

Fifty Mountain
Campground

Sue
Lake

Margaret
Lake

Chaney
Glacier

Ipasha
Lake

Ipasha
Peak

Crowfeet Mtn
(8914ft)

Apikuni Mtn
(9068ft)

Kootenai
Pass

Sue Lake
Overlook

Ipasha
Glacier

Ahern
Glacier

Helen
Lake

Ptarmigan
Tunnel

Ptarmigan
Lake

Kennedy
Lake

Natahki
Lake

Apikuni
Falls

Ahern Peak
(8749ft)

Ahern Pass
(7100ft)

**Alternative
Route**

Ptarmigan
Falls

Mt Henkel
(8770ft)

**Snowdrift
here until
midsummer**

Iceberg
Notch

Iceberg
Peak

Little
Iceberg
Lake

Iceberg Lake

Wilbur Creek

**START/FINISH
All Hikes**

Many
Glacier

To Babb &
St Mary

Many Glacier Rd

North
Swiftcurrent
Glacier

Mt Wilbur
(9321ft)

Windmaker
Lake

Redrock
Falls

Fishercap
Lake

Swiftcurrent
Lake

Many Glacier
Ranger Station

Swiftcurrent
Mtn
(8436ft)

Redrock
Lake

Bullhead
Lake

Grinnell
Point

Lake
Josephine

DAY 2

Granite
Park

Swiftcurrent
Pass
(6770ft)

Granite
Park Chalet

Glacier
Overlook

Mt Grinnell
(8851ft)

Grinnell
Lake

Grinnell
Falls

Allen Mtn
(9376ft)

Snow
Moon
Lake

The
Loop

Swiftcurrent
Glacier

Upper
Grinnell
Lake

Grinnell
Glacier

Feather
Plume Falls

Cracker
Lake

Cracker
Mine

Packers
Roost

Mt Gould

Morning
Eagle Falls

Siyeh
Glacier

Mt Siyeh
(9833ft)

Haystack
Butte

Piegan
Mtn

Piegan
(7560ft)

Siyeh Pass
(7750ft)

Heavens Peak
(8987ft)

Bird Woman
Falls

Piegan
Glacier

Siyeh
Bend

Sexton
Glacier

McPartland Mtn
(8413ft)

Mt Cannon
(8952ft)

Clements
Mtn

**START
Hike 2 (Alt)**

Logan Pass

See Gunsight Pass Map p102

Glacier National Park – Hikes

1 Swiftcurrent Mountain Lookout
2 Highline Trail/Ptarmigan Tunnel Loop
3 Iceberg Lake
4 Grinnell Glacier

0 2 4km
0 2mi
1:200,000
Contour Interval 400ft

Grinnell rising up from Swiftcurrent Glacier is especially impressive. Far below in the Swiftcurrent valley you can easily make out Many Glacier Hotel. Exercise caution, however, as the summit drops away abruptly into cliffs on its northern side.

Reverse the route to return to the trailhead at Many Glacier.

Highline Trail/ Ptarmigan Tunnel Loop

Duration	6 days
Distance	50.2mi (80.8km)
Standard	moderate–hard
Start/Finish	Many Glacier
Transport	car, bus

Summary Also called the 'North Circle', this spectacular route around the northern Lewis Range probably offers the most varied scenery of any longer hike in the park.

This route combines several popular trails – Highline, Stoney Indian Pass and Ptarmigan Tunnel – to give up to a week of marvelous hiking. Some segments also make excellent shorter hikes. Another alternative is to begin at Logan Pass on the Going-to-the-Sun Rd and take the Highline Trail to Granite Park (see Alternative Start). Although there are a number of long, undulating sections, this route involves several strenuous ascents.

PLANNING
When to Hike
Due to heavy winter snow, the Highline Trail (particularly a tricky section near Ahern Pass that may require an ice axe and crampons; check at Many Glacier ranger station for the state of the trail), Stoney Indian Pass and the western approach to Ptarmigan Tunnel may remain closed well into July. From June through September thunderstorms with heavy lightning often occur in the early afternoon.

Maps
Use Trails Illustrated's 1:142,747 map No 215 *Glacier/Waterton Lakes National Parks*.

NEAREST TOWN
See Many Glacier (p93).

THE HIKE (see map p95)
Day 1: Many Glacier to Granite Park
4–5½ hours, 7.5mi, 2223ft ascent
The trailhead is 120yd past the Swiftcurrent Motor Inn on the northwestern side of the large car park. Follow the route directions for Swiftcurrent Mountain Lookout (p94) as far as Swiftcurrent Pass. From here the trail continues 0.9mi down through low firs to intersect with the Highline Trail, just above the historic *Granite Park Chalet* (☎ 406-387-5555). This stone-built hut (and annex) is open July 1 to September 12 and offers basic accommodations for 34 hikers ($60 per person). The chalet stands on a tiny plateau giving superb views toward Heavens Peak (southwest) and Logan Pass.

Another trail drops for several minutes down to *Granite Park campground*, with four clustered sites. The campground lies along a transit corridor for grizzlies, so be particularly attentive to hanging your food.

Alternative Start: Logan Pass to Granite Park
3–4 hours, 7.6mi, 830ft ascent
The alternative first day, via the Highline Trail, begins from the car park atop Logan Pass. Head north around sheer cliffs above the Going-to-the-Sun Rd (groaning traffic noise blends strangely with the rushing of Logan Creek). Across the valley, Bird Woman Falls dives down from hanging glaciers on Clements Mountain and Mt Cannon. Leaving the road behind, the trail traverses seepage streamlets, emerging from the craggy Garden Wall ridge to cross a broad saddle between Haystack Butte and Mt Gould, 1½ to two hours from Logan Pass.

Cross the high terraces that fall away left into a deep glacial trough draining southwest into Lake McDonald. Mountain goats, ground squirrels, marmots and pikas frequent these meadows of coarse alpine grasses and hardy wildflowers. The trail gradually descends along the upper tree line to pass the Garden Wall Trail turnoff. This 0.8mi side trail (about 40 minutes out-and-back) makes a steady diagonal climb up scree slopes to **Glacier Overlook**, a scenic gap in the Garden Wall that offers excellent views of Grinnell and Swiftcurrent Glaciers. The Highline Trail skirts briefly around the mountainside to arrive at *Granite Park Chalet* (see Day 1, p96), 1½ to two hours from the saddle near Haystack Butte.

Day 2: Granite Park to Fifty Mountain

4¼–5½ hours, 11.8mi, 1908ft ascent

From the chalet, the Highline Trail cuts north for five minutes to a small crest, where it is joined by a trail leading up from the campground. Proceed north, traversing up and down alpine meadows, and dipping occasionally into low stands of whitebark pine and subalpine fir at the upper forest fringe. There are almost uninterrupted views to the glaciated peaks of the Livingston Range to the west. After mounting a minor spur the trail momentarily turns right along a cliff face. A steep snowdrift here often blocks the way until midsummer and may require an ice axe (and perhaps crampons) to cross safely.

The trail continues into a shallow cirque and crosses Ahern Creek, 1½ to two hours from Granite Park. Here it meets the 0.3mi turnoff to Ahern Pass (7100ft), an easy 45-minute (out-and-back) side trail. **Ahern Pass** falls away dramatically on its eastern side (where it may be dangerously corniced). For clearer views walk onto coarse talus slopes looking out over Ahern Glacier. Waterfalls gush from this spectacular icefall, which drops occasional ice chunks into the tarns above Helen Lake.

The Highline Trail skirts the mostly open mountainsides into the grassy amphitheater of **Cattle Queen Creek**, where early season snow may be tricky to cross. Head steadily up over sparse meadows opposite the ridge of Flattop Mountain to reach a high crest. Here, a short side trail cuts up right to **Sue Lake Overlook**, an abrupt shelf commanding an impressive view of this wild lake in a deep glacial trough 500ft below. Mountain goats are often spotted on the far side of the lake.

Back on the Highline Trail, cut down left (southwest) over stabilized scree slopes into rich wildflower meadows to reach **Fifty Mountain** – a panoramic alpine slope below the ridge from which, supposedly, you can see 50 mountains – 2¾ to 3½ hours from Ahern Creek. There are six sites at *Fifty Mountain campground*, right at tree line, although a number of firs were killed in the 1988 fire. Grizzly bears frequent this area in summer – evidenced by the dug-over ground where they grub for glacier-lily tubers.

Day 3: Fifty Mountain to Stoney Indian Lake

3¼–4¾ hours, 7mi, 1787ft ascent

Follow the trail northwest from the campground through glorious wildflower tundra strewn with boulders to reach a crest at the foot of **Cathedral Peak**. Here, by the ruins of an old stone shelter, you get the best and last views back along the Lewis Range and across to the peaks of the adjacent Livingston Range. The trail drops into subalpine fir mixed with beargrass, then begins a long descent over scrubby avalanche slopes overlooking the wild, upper Waterton valley to meet the Waterton River. The trail leads on through rich spruce forest along the river, passing an NPS patrol cabin at Pass Creek, just before it comes to the signposted Stoney Indian Trail junction, two to 2½ hours from Fifty Mountain.

Turn right (east) and start a steady climb over shrubby slopes, which soon give way to dwarf birch and willow thickets. The trail follows Pass Creek past a cascade to arrive at **Stoney Indian Lake**, 1¼ to 1¾ hours from the junction. This beautiful emerald lake lies in a classic cirque underneath Wahcheechee Mountain. The frost-burnt tips of the low firs around the lake show the effects of harsh winds and winter avalanches. *Stoney Indian campground* has three sites just across the small lake outlet.

Day 4: Stoney Indian Lake to Glenns Lake Foot

3–4¼ hours, 8.5mi, 598ft ascent

Skirt the eastern shore to the lake head, then switchback your way up to **Stoney Indian**

Pass (6908ft) after 30 to 45 minutes. The pass overlooks Stoney Indian Lake and presents inspiring new views into the head of the pristine Mokowanis valley. The local, salt-addicted marmots pounce on *anything* left unattended.

Cut down southeast into the alpine basin filled with white globeflowers and Indian hellebore. The trail leads around a large, shallow tarn and across its outlet to cross another side stream descending from Sue Lake in the leaping cascades of Raven Quiver Falls. Ahead, a series of lakes snake along the bottom of the U-shaped valley like a wide, meandering river. Continue past the twin **Paiota** and (further back) **Atsina Falls**, gushing over an escarpment shelf, before winding down to cross the young Mokowanis River just above where it enters Atsina Lake.

Head through shrub willow and dwarf birch fringing the lake's northern side before dropping steeply past a series of waterfalls into the forest to reach *Mokowanis Junction campground* (five sites).

The trail proceeds past the Mokowanis Lake Trail turnoff (see Side Trip) to *Glenns Lake Head campground* (three sites with fireplaces). It then rises and dips through old spruce forest some distance from the lake's northern shore to arrive at *Glenns Lake Foot campground*, 2½ to 3½ hours from the pass. There are four pretty lakeside sites here.

Side Trip: Mokowanis Lake
1–1½ hours, 2mi
The detour to this beautiful lake in a tiny side valley, surrounded by craggy spires, is short and very easy. The trail quickly crosses footbridges over the Mokowanis River and the outlet of Mokowanis Lake, where **White Quiver Falls** rushes over a natural rock spillway into Glenns Lake. It then gently rises to two lovely (but mosquito-infested) sites at *Mokowanis Lake campground* on the lake's northeastern shore. An overgrown trail goes on to a churning waterfall descending from the outlet of Margaret Lake and fed by the eternal snows of the valley head.

Day 5: Glenns Lake Foot to Elizabeth Lake Foot
2¼–3 hours, 5.8mi
The trail heads northeast across the swift-flowing Whitecrow Creek then along the shore of Cosley Lake to *Cosley Lake campground* (four sites). Cosley Lake is a nesting area for bald eagles and public access to parts of the shore is restricted. Continue toward the lone rump of Chief Mountain and take the right-hand Ptarmigan Trail turnoff (east) leading directly to a ford at the lake outlet. (If the ford seems risky, take the Alternative Route.) After this serious wade the trail turns southeast through lush forest with sporadic stands of white spruce. The trail meets the Belly River just before the turnoff to the Belly River ranger station, then climbs up past **Dawn Mist Falls**, which sprays fine droplets into the air as it crashes 45ft.

The trail leads up along the west bank of the river through berry fields and firs to reach the scenic *Elizabeth Lake Foot campground*. The six sites here along the lake's pebbly north shore look toward the towering crags of Ptarmigan Wall. The mournful call of loons and other waterbirds often resonates across these tranquil waters.

Alternative Route: via Belly River Ranger Station
2–2½ hours, 4.8mi
If the ford seems risky, take the (one hour longer) left-hand detour leading past Bear Mountain Trail (see Side Trip) and the thundering Gros Ventre Falls to cross Belly River on a suspension bridge. The historic Belly River ranger station is on the uphill side of the fenced paddock here; **Gable Creek campground** (four sites) lies below it. Continue south above the east bank of the river, recrossing on another suspension bridge to intersect with the trail below Dawn Mist Falls.

Side Trip: Bear Mountain Overlook
2–2½ hours, 3.4mi, 1130ft ascent
The trail up to this scenic overlook turns west near a perennial golden eagle's nest on

the Alternative Route, five minutes from the Ptarmigan Trail junction. It climbs through Douglas fir and stands of hardy whitebark pines on steep scree slopes to a high ridge top. From here there are fine views both up and down the Mokowanis valley.

Alternative Campsites
Elizabeth Lake Head campground (with four sites) is at the southwest corner of the lake. Alternatively, the *Helen Lake campground* (two sites) is at the east end of Helen Lake.

Day 6: Elizabeth Lake Foot to Many Glacier
3¾–4¾ hours, 9.6mi, 2515ft ascent
Cross the lake outlet on a suspension bridge and begin climbing through fir-spruce forest to high above Elizabeth Lake. The trail passes the Redgap Pass Trail turnoff and continues along steep slopes of fir and whitebark pine, many of which show the signs of avalanche damage. There are excellent views down to Helen Lake in the upper Belly River valley, as well as across to the majestic, glaciated forms of Natoas Peak, Mt Merritt and Ipasha Peak.

The trail now skirts left (southeast) into a scree-filled cirque to reach the base of Ptarmigan Wall. At this point there is a stone-walled path cut into the cliff face; this leads up under the surrounding craggy spires to **Ptarmigan Tunnel** (7200ft). This damp, 120ft-long shaft was blasted through the ridge in 1931. You are now two to 2½ hours from Elizabeth Lake.

The tunnel takes you into the Swiftcurrent drainage basin. Descend steep, eroding slopes to Ptarmigan Lake, then drop more gently through forest of fir and spruce to the Iceberg Lake Trail turnoff.

The trail continues past Ptarmigan Falls, then traverses open berry fields above the broadening valley (these are prime grizzly bear feeding grounds, so beware) to a fork. Here, either cut down (right) back to the *Swiftcurrent Motor Inn*, which is 1¾ to 2¼ hours from the tunnel, or continue ahead (left) for about 25 minutes to the *Many Glacier Hotel*.

Iceberg Lake

Duration	5–6 hours
Distance	9mi (14.5km)
Standard	easy–moderate
Start/Finish	Iceberg Lake Trailhead
Nearest Town	Many Glacier
Transport	car, bus

Summary Justifiably one of the most popular day hikes in Glacier National Park, the 3000ft headwalls enclosing this glacial lake are stunning.

Enclosed by towering, vertical headwalls on three sides, Iceberg Lake is one of the most impressive glacial lakes anywhere in the Rockies. The 1200ft ascent is gentle and the approach is mostly at or above tree line, affording great views. Wildflower lovers will enjoy the meadows near the lake.

The lake was named in 1905 by George Grinnell, who saw icebergs calving from the glacier at the foot of the headwalls. The glacier is no longer active, but surface ice and avalanche debris still provide sizeable flotillas of bergs as the lake melts out in early summer. The trail was built in 1914 and the Great Northern Railway (which was promoting tourism in the park at the time) tried to attract visitors to the lake with fabricated stories of the 'furred' trout that could be caught in its frigid waters.

PLANNING
When to Hike
The trail should be largely free of snow by the end of June, depending on the snowpack. Go early in the season to see icebergs.

Maps
The trail is adequately covered by a 1:83,930 enlargement on Trails Illustrated 1:142,747 map No 215 *Glacier/Waterton Lakes National Parks*.

NEAREST TOWN
See Many Glacier (p93).

GETTING TO/FROM THE HIKE
The hike starts and finishes at Iceberg Lake Trailhead. From the end of the road, just past

the Swiftcurrent Motor Inn in Many Glacier, follow the signposts for the trailhead.

THE HIKE (see map p95)
The trail climbs steeply at first and passes a couple of signposted trail junctions before emerging onto scrubby slopes with great views across the valley to Grinnell Point. Climb steadily through open meadows and patches of stunted pine, gaining better views of the rock walls encircling Iceberg Lake. About 2mi from the trailhead the path enters mature forest and arrives at Ptarmigan Creek, just upstream from Ptarmigan Falls. By mid-summer you can forgo the footbridge and easily step across the creek. The trail continues to climb gently through mature pine to the junction with the Ptarmigan Tunnel Trail, which heads off right. (It is 4mi out-and-back and 1700ft of ascent to reach magnificent views on the other side of the tunnel – see Day 6, p99). Shortly after the junction, the Iceberg Lake Trail reaches the first of several beautiful meadows under Ptarmigan Wall. Continue through these meadows, descending for a short distance to cross Iceberg Creek via a footbridge, and then climb up past Little Iceberg Lake before dropping down to the shores of **Iceberg Lake** itself.

It is difficult to fully appreciate the scale of the lake and its surrounding cliffs without the figures: the lake is 150ft deep; around 0.75mi across; and the headwalls average around 3000ft in height, easily on a par with the big walls of Yosemite.

Retrace your steps to the trailhead.

Alternative Route: Iceberg Notch
2–3 hours, 1mi, 2300ft ascent
This route climbs out of the Iceberg Lake cirque via a steep and potentially dangerous ascent to Iceberg Notch. This is the gap at the top of the prominent snow gully north of Iceberg Lake. Leave the main trail just east of Little Iceberg Lake and find a faint track that climbs a steep ramp. Use this to reach scree-covered slopes beneath a rock wall just to the right of the snow gully. From the right side of this wall, a ledge system (more commonly used by mountain goats) allows a diagonal scramble up to the notch. The

ascent to Iceberg Notch is only suited to hikers with the utmost confidence and route-finding ability on steep ground.

On the other side lies a much easier descent, leading to Ahern Pass and the Highline Trail (p97). Hikers can then follow the Highline Trail in either direction and perhaps return to the Many Glacier area via Swiftcurrent Pass.

Grinnell Glacier

Duration	4–5½ hours
Distance	10.4mi (16.7km)
Standard	easy–moderate
Start/Finish	Swiftcurrent picnic area
Nearest Town	Many Glacier
Transport	car, bus

Summary A hike up to Grinnell Glacier, the largest in the park, and awesome alpine scenery, with a minimum of time and effort.

This highly scenic out-and-back hike has enough steep gradient to be challenging without becoming too strenuous, although the elevation gain is almost 1600ft. Bighorn sheep and other wildlife can usually be seen on the alpine slopes at the valley head. Taking shuttle boats across Swiftcurrent and Josephine Lakes cuts 1.5mi each way off the hike. From Many Glacier Hotel, Glacier Park Boat Co (☎ 406-257-2426) operates the boat service across Swiftcurrent Lake, connecting with boats on Lake Josephine. Backcountry camping is not possible on this route.

PLANNING
When to Hike
Large snowdrifts normally block the upper Grinnell Glacier Trail at least until early July. The trail remains closed until manual clearing work is completed. The trail may become dangerously icy after mid-September. This hike is extremely popular, and the trail becomes crowded on fine, summer days.

Maps
Use the 1:83,930 inset on Trail Illustrated's general *Glacier/Waterton Lakes National*

Parks map, or the USGS 1:24,000 *Many Glacier* map.

NEAREST TOWN
See Many Glacier (p93).

GETTING TO/FROM THE HIKE
The trailhead is at Swiftcurrent picnic area, roughly 300yd east of Many Glacier campground. There is a large car park here.

THE HIKE (see map p95)
The first part of the hike follows the Swiftcurrent Nature Trail through fir-spruce forest, across the Swiftcurrent Creek footbridge, then around Swiftcurrent Lake to the upper Swiftcurrent boat dock at its southern shore. (A minor route alternative is to leave from the trailhead car park above Many Glacier Hotel, and hike around the eastern side of Swiftcurrent Lake, before skirting right across the Grinnell Creek (inlet) bridge past the upper boat dock.)

A short, paved path lined by corn lilies and thimbleberry bushes brings you to another dock on a serene pebble beach at the north end of the turquoise **Lake Josephine**. The trail heads around the lake's western side over wildflower meadows of yellow columbines, Indian paintbrush and cinquefoil bushes, alternating with slopes of birch scrub and low firs battered by the avalanches that crash into the valley during winter. Continue steadily up (past a minor turnoff that heads diagonally back to the lakeshore) to a junction above the southwestern shore of Lake Josephine, 40 to 50 minutes from the trailhead. Note how the lake deepens dramatically beyond the narrow shelf of sediment swept in by the inlet.

Turn right (southwest) along the Grinnell Glacier Trail (the left trail drops to the upper Josephine boat dock, just across the inlet footbridge) and begin a winding ascent high above Grinnell Lake. These steep slopes look south toward Piegan Pass and give the first views of the spectacular cirque ahead. The trail traverses the almost sheer mountainside, passing through a splashing waterfall and persistent patches of snow to reach a picnic area with a pit toilet just below tree

line. A final climb leads to the moraine dam wall of **Upper Grinnell Lake**. You are now 1½ to 2¼ hours from the trail junction. This dramatic lookout lies below the narrow ice-shelf called The Salamander and the spectacular, fractured Grinnell Glacier; until quite recently these two features were joined together.

Retrace your steps to the trailhead.

Gunsight Pass

Duration	2 days
Distance	19.8mi (31.9km)
Standard	moderate–hard
Start	Jackson Glacier Overlook
Finish	Lake McDonald Lodge
Nearest Towns	Apgar, West Glacier, St Mary
Transport	car, bus

Summary The hike over Gunsight Pass is arguably Glacier National Park's most scenic pass route, with snowfields, glaciers and the particularly lovely Lake Ellen Wilson.

This classic east-to-west crossing of the Continental Divide is a shuttle hike, involving a gradual, but long, ascent totaling around 3700ft (easiest going east to west). The Gunsight Pass area is real mountain-goat country, and hikers are virtually assured of seeing the animals. The popularity of this hike is lessened by its length, which makes it a rather challenging day hike.

PLANNING
When to Hike
Gunsight Pass normally melts out by mid-July; before then the trail can be dangerously icy, especially on the northern approach to Gunsight Pass. Watch the sky for approaching electrical storms, a common hazard in summer.

Maps
Trails Illustrated's 1:142,747 map No 215 *Glacier/Waterton Lakes National Parks* covers the route. Alternatively use three USGS 1:24,000 quads: *Logan Pass*, *Mt Jackson* and *Lake McDonald East*.

GREATER GLACIER

NEAREST TOWNS
See Apgar, West Glacier and St Mary (p93).

GETTING TO/FROM THE HIKE
The hike starts at the Jackson Glacier Overlook (Piegan Pass Trailhead), roughly 4mi east of Logan Pass on the Going-to-the-Sun Rd, and ends at Lake McDonald Lodge, 6.8mi from West Glacier on the Going-to-the-Sun Rd. See Getting Around (p92) for details on the bus shuttle service along Going-to-the-Sun Rd.

THE HIKE
Day 1: Jackson Glacier Overlook to Sperry Chalet
6–9 hours, 13.4mi, 3283ft ascent

The Piegan Pass Trail cuts down southeast through fir-spruce forest to meet Reynolds Creek, following it downstream past Deadwood Falls to reach a trail junction after 25 to 30 minutes. Here, take the (right) Gunsight Pass Trail leading over a sturdy footbridge past *Reynolds Creek campground* (two sites with fireplaces). Head southwest along the northern side of St Mary River, which flows through waterlogged meadows and small beaver ponds past the 0.6mi

(right) turnoff to Florence Falls, a cascade that drops in several stages.

Continue upvalley below the sheer walls of Citadel (east) and Fusillade (west) Mountains through avalanche clearings of thimbleberry shrubs and pearly everlastings. There are fine views (south) of the six glaciers clinging to the high ridge between Blackfoot Mountain and Mt Jackson as you pass *Gunsight Lake campground* (seven sites), a short distance before Gunsight Lake and 1¾ to 2½ hours from Reynolds Creek.

Cross the lake outlet (St Mary River) on a suspension bridge and pass a rough turnoff that leads left (south) to the base of Jackson Glacier, then ascend numerous switchbacks through chest-high cow parsnip and alder shrub.

The reassuringly well-constructed and broad trail makes a winding, upward traverse via cliff ledges high above the lake, opposite interesting folded ripples in the multicolored rock strata on Gunsight Mountain, to arrive at **Gunsight Pass** (6946ft) about two to three hours from Gunsight Lake campground. A basic, emergency stone shelter (day-use only) stands on this narrow, high saddle.

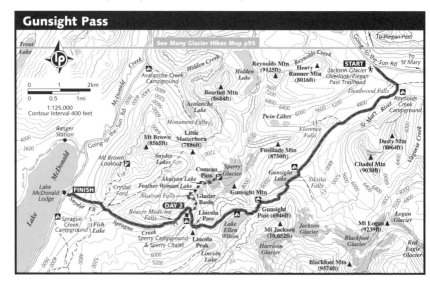

Drop in steep switchbacks almost to the north shore of **Lake Ellen Wilson**, a spectacular alpine lake lying in a deep trough ringed by sheer, glaciated rock walls. The trail continues around the lake's western shore over grouseberry meadows, passing above *Lake Ellen Wilson campground* (four sites).

Skirt diagonally up the slope to a high shelf of glacier-scratched slabs overlooking Lincoln Lake. The trail turns gradually west to cross the highest point of the hike, **Lincoln Pass** (7050ft), just north of Lincoln Peak, then winds its way down past *Sperry campground*, 1½ to 2½ hours from Gunsight Pass. There are four scenic sites here on a bench overlooking Lake McDonald far below. Mountain goats regularly visit the camp, so always use the pit toilet. (Water taken from the stagnant pond should be treated.)

The trail leads (five to 10 minutes) to the historic *Sperry Chalet* (☎ 406-387-5654; PO Box 188 West Glacier, MT 59936), several stone buildings dating from 1913 (open July 1 to mid-September). Rooms cost $150/240 for one/two people.

Day 2: Sperry Chalet to Lake McDonald Lodge
2¼–3 hours, 6.4mi
Drop quickly past the Sperry Glacier Trail (see Side Trip) and across the small Sprague Creek. The trail leads down into fir-spruce forest scattered with columbines, past Beaver Medicine Falls. It continues 2.5mi downvalley, mostly well above the creek, to cross Snyder Creek on a footbridge at Crystal Ford. Pass in quick succession turnoffs to Fish Lake (left), Snyder Lakes (right), where there is a scenic backcountry *campground*, and Mt Brown Lookout (right). The trail descends through mossy montane forest rich in cedar, hemlock, grand fir, larch and yew to reach the Going-to-the-Sun Rd, just above the upmarket *Lake McDonald Lodge* (☎ 406-888-5431).

Side Trip: Sperry Glacier Overlook
3½–5½ hours, 7.5mi, 1615ft ascent
From the turnoff below Sperry Chalet, follow the Sperry Glacier Trail up into the heavily glaciated upper valley of Sprague Creek. The often-steep trail ascends past Akaiyan Falls, Feather Woman Lake and Akaiyan Lake, before climbing a stairway blasted into the cliff face to reach **Comeau Pass** overlooking Sperry Glacier. Cairns lead to meltwater tarns at the edge of the glacier, from where a mountaineers' route continues north along the range to Hidden Lake, itself accessible via a highly popular trail from Logan Pass.

Boulder Pass

Duration	4 days
Distance	31.4mi (50.5km)
Standard	moderate–hard
Start	Boulder Pass Trailhead
Finish	Goat Haunt ranger station
Nearest Towns	Polebridge, Waterton Townsite
Transport	car, ferry

Summary A challenging hike featuring beautiful glacial lakes, an alpine pass and stunning mountain scenery.

Boulder Pass lies in Glacier National Park's isolated northwest corner and is one of the most spectacular hikes in the park. On most summer days the majestic, glaciated beauty of Boulder Pass attracts a full quota of backcountry hikers, so you should get to the permit office early or consider paying the reservation fee to ensure backcountry campsites.

The route skirts the north shores of Kintla and Upper Kintla Lakes, climbing steeply over Boulder Pass, before descending via the superb Hole-in-the-Wall cirque to Brown Pass. From here there are two main routes. Either continue east to Goat Haunt on Upper Waterton Lake, where you can walk or catch a boat to Waterton Townsite in Canada (this is the route described here). Alternatively it is possible to hike to Brown Pass and then drop southwest to the trailhead at the southern end of Bowman Lake; a better option for those with limited time and transportation options.

Grizzly Encounter

I heard the sow before I saw her. I looked up to see a silver-gray grizzly charging fast along the trail toward me, head lowered, eyes fixed on me, muscles and fur rippling as she tore across a bank of snow less than 200ft away. I tried to look away and not make eye contact, but otherwise I was struggling for options. In the apparent absence of the usual explanatory factors for a bear charge (cubs, food, close-quarters surprise), it appeared this bear was coming for me – and I had no pepper spray and there were no trees. I would have to take what was coming. Then, abruptly, the bear stopped short about 100ft away, sat up on her hind legs and thrust her nose into the air. It was then that I saw the cubs.

Perched on a rock ledge just above and out of sight of the trail, two tiny dark cubs watched their mother, now placed between them and this strange human threat. My mind scrambled for the right thing to do. I crouched, bowed my head and tried to appear submissive, watching out of the corner of my eye, waiting for the bear to make up its mind. A few tense moments passed before she dropped to all fours and started moving again. For a second I thought she was going to attack, but instead she turned and headed for the cubs, rounded them up and, with a final backward glance at me, shepherded them off in the opposite direction. My legs were shaking uncontrollably as I turned and walked as fast as I could toward Boulder Pass, mumbling expletives as I went.

By the end of the day I had run into another brown bear at fairly close range, but it had turned and fled as most wild grizzlies do. I finished the day with nerves in tatters, but at the same time elated, and feeling incredibly alive at having had such a remarkable and intense experience. With hindsight I would have done a few things differently. Firstly I would have carried bear spray because, despite question marks over its effectiveness, you'd sell your soul to have it in a confrontation. Secondly I would have been noisier and more alert – the two main rules of travel in bear country.

I had been complacent for two reasons. Because I had been above tree line I trusted that I could see everything between my camp and the pass – but patently I couldn't see a grizzly and two cubs. Second I was laboring under a common misapprehension that bears don't come up that high; a ranger later told me that grizzlies have been spotted near the summits of Glacier National Park's highest peaks. Perhaps the notion of bear danger is just too abstract until you've had a firsthand experience.

Gareth McCormack

PLANNING
When to Hike
Snow can persist on the pass until late July.

Maps
The Trails Illustrated 1:142,747 map No 215 *Glacier/Waterton Lakes National Parks* is quite adequate for the hike. Three USGS 1:24,000 quads also cover the route: *Kintla Lake*, *Kintla Peak* and *Mt Carter*. For the Upper Waterton Lake section add *Porcupine Ridge*; for Bowman Lake add *Quartz Ridge*.

NEAREST TOWNS
See Waterton Townsite (p108).

Polebridge
This tiny settlement is around 28mi north of Apgar. It has a general store with enough groceries to stock up for the trail, but bring fuel and camping essentials with you. Polebridge ranger station, a couple of miles north of the village, also has a backcountry office. The *Northfork Hostel* (☎ 406-888-5241) offers tent sites ($8 per person), cabins (from $31) and dorm beds ($15). The hostel is open year-round and provides kitchen facilities and free use of mountain bikes, cross-country skis and snowshoes. The owners will collect you from the West Glacier Amtrak station for $25.

GETTING TO/FROM THE HIKE
To reach Boulder Pass Trailhead at the start of the hike, drive north from Apgar via the park's Camas Creek Entrance, continuing along the North Fork Rd to Polebridge. Then follow Glacier Route 7 to the trailhead near Kintla Lake.

The hike finishes at Goat Haunt ranger station on the southern shore of Upper Waterton Lake. Waterton Inter-Nation Shoreline Cruise Co (☎ 403-859-2362) has daily boat services from Waterton Townsite to Goat Haunt from early May to October 8. During July and August, boats leave Goat Haunt at 10:35am, 11:25am, 2:25pm, 5:25pm and 8:05pm. A one way fare is US $9. You'll need to telephone Canadian immigration at Chief Mountain (☎ 403-653-3535) upon arrival in Waterton Townsite.

For those who want to finish on foot, a relatively flat trail runs from Goat Haunt along the western shores of Upper Waterton Lake to Waterton Townsite. This 6mi stretch will take three to four hours; there are *campgrounds* at Bertha Bay and Boundary Bay.

THE HIKE
Day 1: Kintla Lake to Upper Kintla Lake
5–6 hours, 11.6mi, 400ft ascent
If you have arrived late there is a *campground* very close to the trailhead ($14 per site). The trail quickly reaches the forested shore of Kintla Lake and there is a fine view along almost the entire length of the lake to Kinnerly Peak. The trail continues along the shore for a few miles and then climbs away from the water before dropping back down to it about 2mi from the lake's head and two hours from the start.

Passing the *Head of Kintla Lake campground*, plunge through some dense vegetation and pass a patrol cabin before starting the ascent to Upper Kintla Lake. Climb steadily along a winding trail that is vegetated in places and provides occasional glimpses of Kintla Creek. The trail climbs into a meadow with great views of the Kintla Glacier (south) and the ring of peaks surrounding it: Parke, Kintla and Kinnerly. Swathes of dead trees on that side of the valley are testament to a wildfire. Reach Upper Kintla Lake in one to 1½ hours from the head of Kintla Lake. The trail now follows the north shore of this lake to arrive at *Upper Kintla campground* after another 1½ hours, with stunning views of Kinnerly Peak and Gardner Point as you progress.

Day 2: Upper Kintla Lake to Boulder Pass Campground
3½–4½ hours, 5.6mi, 2800ft ascent
The strenuous ascent to Boulder Pass campground only takes a few hours but will constitute a full day's effort for most hikers. With a bit of determination you could continue for an extra two hours, crossing Boulder Pass to reach the even more dramatically sited Hole-in-the-Wall campground. But why rush?

The trail leaves Upper Kintla Lake and crosses Kintla Creek on a swing bridge. For the next 2mi the trail climbs steadily through forest with views opening up across the cascades on Agassiz Creek to the Agassiz Glacier. The fantastic east faces of Kinnerly and Kintla Peaks loom over the valley. The trail begins to climb more steeply, switchbacking through lush vegetation, which frequently encroaches on the trail. Past this section the gradient eases as the trail crosses a forested depression and then enters a series of long, drawn-out switchbacks around outcrops of steep rock. Eventually the trail goes south, through some lovely **wildflower meadows** before reaching tree line and *Boulder Pass campground*, just below the trail to the right.

Day 3: Boulder Pass Campground to Lake Francis
4–5 hours, 7.6mi
It's a short and gentle climb from Boulder Pass campground to the top of **Boulder Pass**. Even in late July you may have to tramp across some small patches of snow. The view from the pass itself is restricted by the steep slopes and cliffs of Boulder Peak and Mt Custer. Descend into the beautiful cirque on the east side of the pass, where several small tarns have formed in the wake of Boulder Glacier's retreat. Here, you get your first glimpse (south) of the spectacular summit of Thunderbird Mountain, which dominates the view for the next few miles.

Continue across a small rise and then descend steeply over ice scoured rock slabs (potentially dangerous if still under snow) into another basin covered by wildflower meadows. Traverse across the basin and pass a trail junction, where a path leads right, to *Hole-in-the-Wall campground*, which is one of the most popular and spectacular back-country sites in the park. Continue to traverse around increasingly steep slopes, with tremendous views across the 3000ft cliffs that drop into Bowman valley from Thunderbird Mountain. Next is a short section of very exposed rock ledge only a few feet wide (care is required). The trail then descends across meadows to **Brown Pass** (6253ft) on the Continental Divide, two to three hours from Boulder Pass. The *Brown Pass campground* is nearby, and hikers returning to the west side of the park via Bowman Lake should turn right here. Goat Haunt is 8.6mi east of Brown Pass (all downhill), and hikers who have reached the pass early and feel fresh could continue to the finish.

Descend steeply on switchbacks to a small, unnamed lake beneath Thunderbird Glacier, and then descend more gently through mature forest, past a *campground* to *Lake Francis campground*.

Day 4: Lake Francis to Goat Haunt
3 hours, 6.6mi
Continue to descend gently from Lake Francis, traversing largely forested ground

all the way, past *Lake Janet campground* to Goat Haunt. Two miles before reaching Goat Haunt the trail begins to descend more steeply, reaching a trail junction 0.9mi from Goat Haunt. Hikers wishing to walk to Waterton Townsite can continue straight ahead, reaching the town after 6mi (there are two *campgrounds* – Boundary Bay and Bertha Bay – en route). Turn right for Goat Haunt, crossing a big swing bridge over the Waterton River (a good swimming hole) before arriving at the ranger station and *campground*. The boat launch is a few hundred yards further along the lakeshore.

Waterton Lakes National Park

Waterton Lakes National Park adjoins Glacier National Park to the north. Although separated by the Canadian border, the two parks banded together in 1932 to form the world's first International Peace Park. There is very little difference topographically or in terms of ecology between the two parks, and the animal populations move freely between

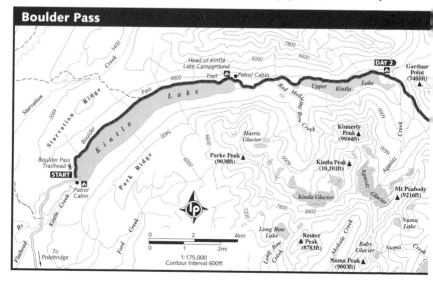

Boulder Pass

them. (See Natural History for Glacier National Park, p90) The parks are managed in close cooperation and several popular hiking routes (including the Boulder Pass hike, p103) cross the border. For many visitors to Greater Glacier, Waterton offers a wonderful opportunity for an 'international hike'.

PLANNING
Maps & Books
The Trails Illustrated 1:142,747 map No 215 *Glacier/Waterton Lakes National Parks* provides an overview of Waterton, but it is insufficiently detailed for most hikes. The Canadian Parks Service 1:50,000 *Waterton Lakes National Park* map also covers the entire area (and a section of northern Glacier National Park), and is much better for hiking (US$9.50, C$12.95). Note that distances are metric.

Hiking Glacier and Waterton Lakes National Parks by Erik Molvar (US$14.95) details most of the best routes in the park.

Information Sources
For details on Waterton Lakes National Park contact the visitor center (☎ 403-859-2224; W www.parkscanada.pch.gc.ca/waterton;

Waterton Lakes National Park, Alberta, TOK 2MO, Canada).

Permits & Regulations
Visiting Waterton entails crossing the US/Canadian border. The most frequently used customs station is along the Chief Mountain International Highway (US Hwy 17/Canadian Hwy 6) on the eastern side of the parks. All travelers need identification, and citizens of countries other than the US or Canada need a passport and a visa if appropriate. There are special restrictions on crossing with some pets, firearms, bear sprays, alcohol and firewood. For more information about crossing the border, call ☎ 800-320-0063 from the US or ☎ 206-553-4676 from Canada. Hikers who cross the border in the backcountry should also carry ID, and are required to register their arrival at the nearest customs station by telephone as soon as possible.

The entrance fee for Waterton is US$3 (C$4) per person, per day, with groups of two to seven people paying US$6 (C$8) per day. All commercial outlets in Waterton accept US currency and traveler's checks. An overnight wilderness permit is required for all

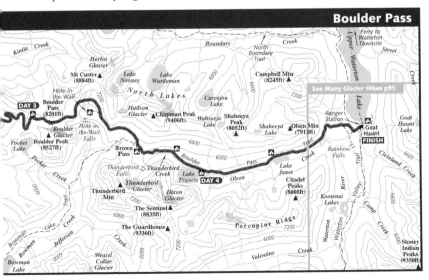

backcountry camping, and camping is only permitted in designated campgrounds. Permits cost US$4 (C$6) per person, per night, and can be obtained from the visitor center just north of Waterton Townsite (☎ 403-859-5133 mid-May to early October, otherwise ☎ 403-859-2224). Permits are issued up to 24 hours in advance and can be reserved for a fee of US$15 (C$10) up to 90 days in advance. Open fires are only permitted in fire boxes where provided. Pets must be kept on a leash at all times within the park.

GETTING AROUND

Waterton Sports & Leisure (☎ 403-859-2378; Tamarack Village Square, Mountview Rd, Waterton Townsite) operates a hiker shuttle from outside the shop to destinations within the park. The only scheduled service runs up Akamina Parkway to Cameron Lake at 8:30am, and will drop hikers off at trailheads along the road (US$5/C$7.50 one way). Advance reservation is recommended and additional services are available upon arrangement.

Several hikes also leave from the shores of Upper Waterton Lake, with the trailheads accessible by boat. Waterton Inter-Nation Shoreline Cruise Co (☎ 403-859-2362) has regular services from Waterton Townsite marina to popular points around the lake.

ACCESS TOWN & FACILITIES
Waterton Townsite

Waterton Townsite is the main settlement within the park. The visitor center (☎ 403-859-5133 mid-May to early October, otherwise ☎ 403-859-2224; W www.waterton chamber.com), is just north of town alongside Hwy 5. Waterton Sports & Leisure (☎ 403-859-2378; Tamarack Village Square, Mountview Rd) sells an excellent selection of outdoor gear and maps.

Numerous accommodations in Waterton Townsite include the *International Hostel* (☎ 403-859-2151), off Cameron Falls Drive, where dorm beds cost US$14/17 (C$21/25) for members/nonmembers.

Greyhound Canada (☎ 403-627-2716) operates a scheduled bus service from Calgary to Pincher Creek several times daily.

From Pincher there is a connecting shuttle to Waterton. Waterton is 40mi north of St Mary via US Hwy 17/Canadian Hwy 6.

Park Campgrounds

The park-operated *Townsite Campground* (☎ 403-859-5133) has tent and RV sites with showers from US$10 (C$15). Approximately 10mi from Waterton Townsite along Red Rock Parkway, *Crandell campground* (☎ 403-859-5133) costs US$9 (C$13) per site. Although there are no showers, campers can use the Townsite Campground facilities for free.

Carthew Lakes

Duration	5½–7 hours
Distance	11.8mi (19km)
Standard	moderate
Start	Cameron Lake Trailhead
Finish	Waterton Townsite
Transport	car, bus

Summary Arguably *the* classic hike in Waterton, this varied route leads over a ridge with wonderful mountain views before descending via a network of subalpine lakes.

Ask any number of seasoned Waterton hikers what their favorite route in the park is, and a good number will probably answer 'Carthew Lakes'. Despite the large number of hikers using the trail, the quality of scenery on offer and the fact that the climb of 1440ft is offset by a descent of 3150ft makes this a trip with a whole lot of gain for relatively little pain. Views over the summits of northern Glacier National Park are unsurpassed, and several interesting lakes are also explored. Most people take advantage of the high starting point at Cameron Lake and complete the route in a single day. There is camping available at dramatic Alderson Lake for those who want to take two days.

PLANNING
When to Hike

The route should be free of snow by mid-June.

Maps

Use the Canadian Parks Service's 1:50,000 *Waterton Lakes National Park* map.

NEAREST TOWN

See Waterton Townsite (p108).

GETTING TO/FROM THE HIKE

The hike begins at Cameron Lake, 10mi southwest of Waterton Townsite on the Akamina Parkway. Waterton Sports & Leisure (☎ 403-859-2378) operates a daily hiker shuttle to and from Cameron Lake (see Getting Around, p108). The hike ends at the Cameron Falls parking area on Evergreen Ave, a short walk from the center of Waterton Townsite.

THE HIKE

The trail heads southeast from the Cameron Lake boat ramp and enters the pines along the eastern shore, climbing steadily through a series of switchbacks for 2.5mi to **Summit Lake**. This pool, surrounded by meadow and pine, marks the top of the steepest climb and is an ideal place for a break.

The Carthew Lakes Trail is signed left (northeast) at a junction shortly after Summit

Lake. The ascent eases slightly as the trees give way to scrub and then grass, before all vegetation disappears and the trail climbs onto shale-covered hillside. Views over Lake Wurdeman and Carcajou Lake, stunning turquoise pools in the basins of steep rock cirques to the south, become more and more arresting. A narrow path switchbacks up the maroon-colored scree to the ridgeline (approximately 2½ hours from the start of the hike), where an even more expansive panorama is revealed. To the south, the spectacular summits of northern Glacier National Park cover a 180° sweep, while the Carthew Lakes lie among the barren, scree-covered mountains to the north. Just a few minutes off the trail to the right, an **outcrop** at the southeast end of the ridge provides an ideal overlook.

With all the climbing completed, the trail descends from the ridge and weaves between the two starkly located **Carthew Lakes**. A steep cliff is negotiated at the exit of the Carthew basin before Alderson Lake comes into sight below, dramatically set at the base of towering cliffs. The trail re-enters the trees shortly before the lake, and there is a signed detour of 0.3mi to reach the water itself.

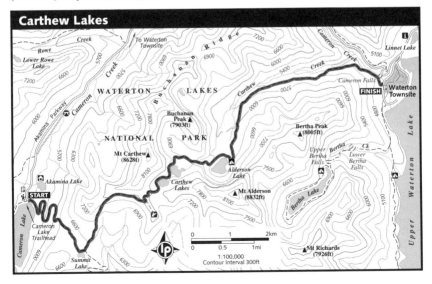

From here the trail follows the Carthew Creek valley, making a gradual descent of 6.1mi through the forest to Waterton Townsite. The first sign of civilization is the road on the opposite side of the valley and then the roofs of the town itself come into view. The final stretch of the trail runs rather unscenically along a barrier. A fitting end to the day is the sight of the impressive Cameron Falls, where some of Waterton's oldest rocks are visible (1200–1500 million years old). See the boxed text 'Glacier Geology: A Window to the Past', p92.

Avion Ridge Loop

Duration	8½–9 hours
Distance	14mi (22.5km)
Standard	moderate–hard
Start/Finish	Red Rock Canyon Trailhead
Nearest Town	Waterton Townsite
Transport	car, bus

Summary An unusual route that traverses a high, scree-covered ridge and offers spectacular views of the peaks of Waterton and southern British Columbia.

The Avion Ridge offers one of the best, and most remote, high-elevation hikes in the park. Although the trail is well-worn, signposted and generally easy to follow, it is only partly maintained and is not fully marked on most maps. This, in addition to the 3218ft elevation gain, means the route is suited to experienced hikers. There are backcountry campsites at Snowshoe after 5.1mi and at Goat Lake after 10.2mi for those who want to take two days. There is no water on the ridge itself, so collect enough at Snowshoe campground or soon afterwards to last the 5mi to Goat Lake. This is also prime bear habitat, so stay alert.

PLANNING
When to Hike

The ridge may be partly covered by snowdrifts until late June. It is also exposed to the elements, so avoid windy conditions and plan to be off the ridge early if afternoon thunderstorms are a possibility.

Maps

The 1:50,000 *Waterton Lakes National Park* map published by Canadian Parks Service is recommended, although the trail is not marked between Avion Ridge and Goat Lake. Note also that the trail does not follow the ridgeline as indicated on the map, but works around the southern slopes of the main summit (unnamed at 7950ft and approximately 1.5mi east of Castle River Divide) and around the western slopes of the next peak (to the south of Newman Peak).

NEAREST TOWN
See Waterton Townsite (p108).

GETTING TO/FROM THE HIKE
The hike begins at Red Rock Canyon parking area, 9mi from Waterton Townsite at the end of Red Rock Parkway. Waterton Sports & Leisure's (☎ 403-859-2378) shuttle service can provide trailhead transportation.

THE HIKE
From the trailhead, cross the bridge over Red Rock Creek and take the trail that continues straight ahead up Bauerman Creek. This is an easy, well-worn section of trail that undulates gently along the forested creek. Pass the Goat Lake Trail junction after 2.4mi and continue west to the wide clearing of **Snowshoe campground**, reached approximately two hours from the start.

The Avion Ridge Trail makes an abrupt (but signed) right turn here onto a smaller path. Climb through the forest and keep right at a signed junction 0.5mi from Snowshoe campground, where the trail to Lost Lake veers to the left (a side trip of just over 1mi). The ascent gradually steepens until a point just before the saddle of Castle River divide (the watershed between Bauerman Creek and Castle River). The Avion Ridge is signed to the right from the main trail and the climb continues up the shoulder to the east. As the trees begin to dwindle in size, there are views over Lost Lake and the peaks of northwest Waterton.

The trail flattens out for a section, crosses a saddle in a clearing and then passes the first marker indicating the northern boundary of

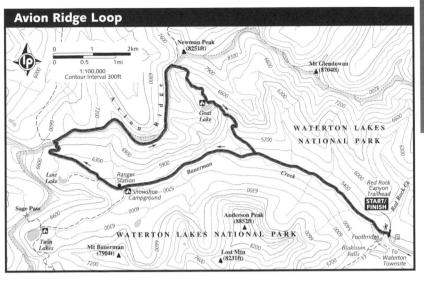

Avion Ridge Loop

Waterton Lakes National Park. The trail more or less follows this boundary for the next 2mi. There is another ascent through pine forest before the trail re-emerges from the trees for the last time. The climb is more gradual now and the trail picks its way along the southern side of scree slopes, heading toward the main summit of the ridge. This peak is bypassed to the south, with the trail passing around scree slopes to avoid the steep cliffs to the north. The path returns to the **airy ridge** just east of the peak (around five hours from the start) and more magnificent views are revealed. A sheer drop falls away to the fertile Castle River valley to the north, with the peaks of British Columbia visible in the distance. To the south lies a panorama of the Waterton mountains.

Make a short, steep descent along the ridge to a saddle. Avoid the temptation to drop into the cirque below as there is no safe descent. Instead cross the saddle and begin to contour around the western slopes of the scree-covered mountain ahead. Follow the sometimes narrow trail to the next saddle and, from this point, Goat Lake is clearly visible in the cirque to the southeast. The descent route is signed to the lake, 1mi away.

The steep, twisting descent cuts across scree slopes to the left (north) of the saddle, before dropping down to the basin floor. A cliff wall is negotiated on the left side of the valley and then a dry creek is followed to the beautiful turquoise waters of **Goat Lake**. Pass around the northeastern shore of the lake and begin to descend through steep switchbacks. The trail uses some narrow ledges and somehow manages to find a way down through the cliffs at the entrance to the cirque. The path re-enters the pines as it descends, joining the Bauerman Creek Trail 1.5mi from Goat Lake. Turn left along this trail, and retrace your initial steps to the trailhead.

Jewel Basin Hiking Area

In the Swan Range, between Kalispell and Glacier National Park, the 15,349-acre Jewel Basin Hiking Area is one of Montana's most heavily visited outdoor recreation areas. The basin's 'jewels' are its two-dozen-odd, scattered glacial lakes. The area is unique in the US in that it is the country's only specifically

GREATER GLACIER

designated backcountry area outside a wilderness boundary. A specially constructed access road climbs more than 1500ft, which cuts the on-foot ascent from valley to peak by roughly half. Jewel Basin's 35mi of trails are generally used for day-hiking, although overnight routes are also possible.

NATURAL HISTORY

Among the patches of spruce and fir, the 27 alpine lakes of Jewel Basin shelter a wide range of aquatic life ranging from simple invertebrates to westslope cutthroat trout. A management plan is in place to preserve these native species by removing hybrid cutthroat trout from the area. You may be lucky enough to see mountain goats in the higher reaches of the area and particularly on the slopes of Mt Aeneas. Although Jewel Basin is considered to be bear country, sightings of brown and black bears are not common. However, you should still hang food and take the usual precautions if you plan to camp in the basin.

PLANNING
When to Hike

Routes in the Jewel Basin should be free of snow by early July, depending on the snowpack. The basins themselves are generally sheltered, although the summit ridge of Mt Aeneas is exposed to the elements, so avoid hiking here in strong winds and plan to summit before noon if afternoon storms are forecast.

Maps

The USFS 1:25,000 *Jewel Basin Hiking Area* ($2) is a very basic topographical map with a guide to the area, and is sufficient for hiking use. Two USGS 1:24,000 quads also cover most of the basin: *Jewel Basin* and *Crater Lake*.

Information Sources

Jewel Basin falls within the boundaries of Flathead National Forest. For further information contact the forest service headquarters in Kalispell (☎ 406-758-5200; W www.fs.fed .us/r1/flathead; 1935 3rd Ave E, Kalispell, MT 59901).

Permits & Regulations

No permits are required for hiking or camping in Jewel Basin. The advantage of the designated hiking ethos is that trails are left solely for human use – no horses, bicycles or motorized vehicles are permitted within the hiking area. Open fires are generally discouraged, and are forbidden within the 500ft no-camping zones around Birch, Crater, Picnic and Twin Lakes. Due to the area's small size, hiking groups no larger than four to six people are recommended and there is a 12-person limit on group size. Permits are not needed for fishing, but you still need a Montana fishing license.

GETTING AROUND

Jewel Basin Hiking Area is most easily accessible from the west. From Bigfork, follow Hwy 35 north for 3mi before turning right on Hwy 83. It is a further 3mi before the Echo Lake Rd turnoff, signed to Jewel Basin. In another 3mi a signed right turn leads up the Jewel Basin Rd (No 5392). From here it is seven steep miles up a gravel road to the Camp Misery Trailhead, the start and finish point for both routes described here.

ACCESS TOWN
Bigfork

Fifteen miles southeast of Kalispell on the northern shore of Flathead Lake, Bigfork is a small town with a pretty marina area. It is home to the Swan Lake USFS office (☎ 406-837-7500, 200 Ranger Station Rd) where local hiking maps are available. The visitor center (☎ 406-837-5888, W www.bigfork .org) is 0.5mi to the north of town off Hwy 35. Two River Gear and Outfitter (☎ 406-837-3841, 603 Electric Avenue) stocks a limited amount of hiking gear, but no maps or guidebooks.

The *Wayfarers's State Park campground* (☎ 406-752-5501) is on the southern edge of town off Hwy 35, and shady RV or tent sites cost $12. *Timbers Motel RV & Park*, adjacent off Hwy 35, has doubles ($72) and camping sites ($7 per person).

Bigfork is a stop on the daily Missoula-Kalispell-Whitefish bus route operated by Intermountain Transport (☎ 406-755-4011).

GREATER GLACIER

Jewel Lakes Loop

Duration	4½–5½ hours
Distance	10.2mi (16.4km)
Standard	easy–moderate
Start/Finish	Camp Misery Trailhead
Nearest Town	Bigfork
Transport	car

Summary A scenic hike exploring the hidden lakes and passes of the Jewel Basin.

This route is probably the best circuit in the Jewel Basin and makes for a very pleasant hike with plenty of scope for variation. It could easily be combined, for instance, with the Mt Aeneas hike (p114) to create a long and fairly tough day hike, featuring the airy views from the Mt Aeneas ridge and the forested lakes in the Jewel Basin. Although the trail is well maintained, you should consult a map at the many junctions (signposting refers to trail numbers only).

PLANNING
Maps
The USFS 1:25,000 *Jewel Basin Hiking Area* map covers this hike.

NEAREST TOWN
See Bigfork (p112).

GETTING TO/FROM THE HIKE
See Getting Around (p112).

THE HIKE
Set out on Trail 8 and climb steadily away from the parking area. Turn right (southeast) at the first trail junction and left (northeast) at the second. The ascent is now quite steep as it passes through meadows that are alive with beargrass in summer, reaching a pass near Picnic Lakes about an hour from the trailhead. Keep left (north) here and then turn right, then left, at the next two trail junctions before beginning the descent toward Black Lake, which sits beautifully in the large hollow beneath Mt Aeneas. On a clear day you should also be able to make out the ragged profile of Glacier National Park on the northeastern skyline. Keep left at the next two trail

Jewel Basin Hiking Area

Jewel Basin – Hikes
1 Jewel Lakes Loop
2 Mt Aeneas

junctions, passing a side trail down to the shores of Black Lake and the trail to Handkerchief Lake. The main trail flattens out as you approach the first of the **Jewel Lakes**, which is a good option for a lunch break and some two hours from the trailhead.

After winding between the Jewel Lakes, the trail descends steeply and then contours some steep and rugged slopes to reach the outlet of Blackfoot Lake. Climb gently around the slopes to the north of the lake and then follow switchbacks on the long, steady climb to the Twin Lakes Pass. The Twin Lakes are set in a deep hollow well below the main trail, and can be reached via a short side trip.

Emerging on the west side of the pass, vast views across the Flathead valley open up again. The trail contours across the steep slopes, loosing height gradually as it returns to the parking area. Take a right turn at the trail junction and follow the last steep switchbacks back to the trailhead.

Mt Aeneas

Duration	3–4 hours
Distance	6mi (9.7km)
Standard	moderate
Start/Finish	Camp Misery Trailhead
Nearest Town	Bigfork
Transport	car

Summary A moderate climb and a wonderfully airy ridge give access to panoramic views from the summit of this modest mountain.

The hike to the summit of Mt Aeneas is probably the most popular trip in the hiking area, and justly so. Although it demands 1778ft of ascent and is also the most strenuous short walk in Jewel Basin, the hike up the area's second-highest peak is full of character. In clear weather views extend across many of the mountain ranges of the Greater Glacier area and the path along the airy summit ridge is a real treat. The descent also leads through the basin itself and past some of its watery jewels. At the end of the day, it is difficult to imagine a route that could offer more in such a relatively short time. Note that no water is available until Picnic Lakes on the descent route, so make sure to carry plenty.

PLANNING
Maps
The USFS 1:25,000 *Jewel Basin Hiking Area* map covers this hike.

NEAREST TOWN
See Bigfork (p112).

GETTING TO/FROM THE HIKE
See Getting Around (p112).

THE HIKE (see map p113)
Begin by following Trail 717, which leads off to the right of the trailhead information board. The wide, graveled track climbs southwest to a saddle on a ridge, where a footpath leads right on a short side trip to the top of an unnamed peak at 6437ft. The main route sweeps back to the southeast onto the other side of the ridge and the track soon narrows to a footpath. The trail then contours around the hillside, with fine views to the southwest over Flathead Lake, before reaching a junction of several trails. Signs at the junction are a little confusing, but take the second right (the trail that leads most steeply uphill) and a marker on a tree within a few yards confirms the trail as No 717.

From here it is another 1.5mi of ascent to Mt Aeneas, with several wide switchbacks leading to the microwave tower and the beginning of the summit ridge. Veer right, following the undulating and narrow ridgeline over a wonderfully, airy section of trail. Views over the scattered high lakes of Jewel Basin are enticing, although loose ground in one or two places demand care. From the **summit**, reached after 1½ to two hours from the start, the panorama is even better. To the south lie the peaks of the Mission Mountains and Bob Marshall Wilderness, to the east and west are the waters of Hungry Horse Reservoir and Flathead Lake, and to the north rise the angular peaks of Glacier National Park and the southern Canadian Rockies.

The descent east from the summit is initially steep and loose, and demands attention. The terrain becomes easier after a sharp left (north) turn, where the trail leads across a saddle and begins the descent into **Jewel Basin**. Pines provide shade and a trail junction just before Picnic Lakes is soon reached. Turn left here, following Trail 392 west to cross a log bridge between the two lakes. A short climb then leads to a saddle and another three-way trail junction. Keep left here, crossing the saddle to begin the descend through switchbacks on Trail 7. The most direct return route to the trailhead turns right onto Trail 68 in a little over 0.5mi, passing through pine forest before making a final left turn onto Trail 8. This descends the final 0.6mi to the car park, arriving 1½ to two hours from the summit of Mt Aeneas.

Mission Mountains

When viewed from the rolling farmland along US 93 on their western fringe, the high crags and deep lateral valleys of the Mission Mountains are striking. The central spine of the Mission Mountains runs north-south for more than 40mi. To the west of this divide the land is owned and managed by the Federated Salish and Kootenai Tribes as the Mission Mountains Tribal Wilderness, while the Mission Mountains Wilderness, part of the Flathead National Forest, is to the east.

Hiking more than a short distance from trailheads is a challenging and rugged undertaking, especially in the tribal wilderness where trails are cleared infrequently and signposting is not common. Most significant hikes demand a reasonable fitness, confidence and experience of backcountry hiking.

NATURAL HISTORY

Low levels of human intrusion have meant that the Mission Mountains have managed to maintain a small, but significant, population of several dozen grizzlies. A special Grizzly Bear Conservation Zone has been established around McDonald Peak in the tribal wilderness, and the area is closed annually to allow grizzlies to feed on a seasonal concentration of lady bugs and cut worms. Although it is tempting to think the bears remain conveniently within this boundary, they do roam extensively and you should be alert, especially in the frequent areas of thick brush. Black bears, mountain goats, elk, mule deer and sometimes white-tailed deer are found in the wilderness, but are difficult to see. The Mission Mountains area also supports around 50 different species of bird.

PLANNING
Maps

The USFS 1:50,000 *Mission Mountains and Mission Mountains Tribal Wildernesses* ($6) covers the entire range.

Information Sources

The USFS Mission Mountains Wilderness falls within the boundaries of Flathead National Forest. For details contact the USFS office (☎ 406-758-5200; [W] www.fs.fed.us/r1/flathead; 1935 3rd Ave E, Kalispell, MT 59901). For details on the Mission Mountains Tribal Wilderness, contact the office of the Salish and Kootenai Tribes (☎ 406-675-2700; PO Box 278, Pablo, MT 59855).

Permits & Regulations

To enter the tribal wilderness each hiker needs a permit ($8/12 for three days/one year) and a $10 camp stamp is also needed for overnight stays. Permits are available from the tribal office (☎ 406-675-2700; Hwy 93, Pablo), regional Montana Fish & Wildlife offices, local outdoor stores and some local accommodations. No permits are required for hiking or camping in the USFS Mission Mountains Wilderness.

Camping restrictions operate within 0.25mi of several popular lakes in both wilderness areas – these areas are marked in pink on the USFS 1:50,000 map. A sizeable section of the tribal wilderness in the vicinity of McDonald Peak is also designated a Grizzly Bear Conservation Zone, and is closed for all recreational use from July 15 to October 1.

GETTING AROUND

Getting around in the Mission Mountains, particularly to trailheads, usually means using private transportation. Two main roads, US 93 and Hwy 83, run along the west and east side of the range respectively. Intermountain Transport (☎ 640-755-4011) operates a daily Missoula-Kalispell-Whitefish bus service, which passes through Ronan and the other towns on US 93. There is no public service along Hwy 83.

ACCESS TOWNS & FACILITIES
Ronan

Ronan is situated about halfway up the Mission Valley on US 93. The town's visitor center (☎ 406-676-8300; 207 Main St SW) is small, but friendly. Ronan Sports & Western Store (☎ 406-676-3701, US 93), near the visitor center, sells outdoor gear and tribal wilderness permits.

'S' RV Park & Campground (☎ 406-676-3641, Hwy 93), at the north end of town, has tent sites for $18. The nearest hostel accommodations is 14mi south along Hwy 93 at the excellent *St Ignatius Campground & Hostel* (☎ 406-745-3959), where dorm beds and tent sites both cost $12. *Starlite Motel* (☎ 406-676-7000, 18 Main St) has doubles for $54.

See Getting Around (p115) for details of public transportation to and from Ronan. Intermountain Transport (☎ 640-755-4011) operates a daily Missoula-Kalispell-Whitefish bus service, which passes through Ronan and the other towns on US 93. Ronan is around 66mi south of Kalispell and 49mi north of Missoula via US 93.

Condon

A small settlement spread out along Hwy 83 in the heart of the Swan Valley, Condon is approximately midway between Seeley and Swan Lakes. Condon serves as an access point for both Mission Mountains Wilderness and Bob Marshall Wilderness. The town's USFS office (☎ 406-754-3137) off Hwy 83, sells local trail maps and offers hiking advice.

Swan Valley Super 8 Lodge (☎ 406-754-2688), at the north of town alongside Hwy 83, offers the only accommodations, with doubles from $72. Condon is roughly 84mi northeast of Missoula via Hwy 200 and Hwy 83, and 66mi southeast of Kalispell via US 93 and Hwy 83.

Campgrounds

There are five USFS or Fish & Wildlife campgrounds between Condon and Seeley Lake, 25mi to the south, most cost around $11. *The Filling Station RV Park (☎ 406-677-2980)*, behind the gas station in Seeley Lake, is the closest private campground.

Mollman Lakes

Duration	6–8 hours
Distance	10.4mi (16.7km)
Standard	moderate–hard
Start/Finish	Mollman Trailhead
Nearest Town	Ronan
Transport	car

Summary A rewarding route that climbs over the Mission Mountain ridge to a group of high lakes in a spectacular situation.

This route climbs through the tribal wilderness to Mollman Pass, where it enters the USFS Mission Mountains Wilderness. The pass gives access to an alpine plateau surrounded by soaring cliffs, with Mollman Lakes sitting spectacularly in the hollows beneath. With a total ascent of 3371ft, the route makes a reasonably challenging day hike, or can be appreciated over two or more days by camping on the plateau in the vicinity of the lakes, which also offer good cutthroat trout fishing.

If two vehicles are available, this route can also be completed as a 17mi, A-to-B hike that completely crosses the Mission range. From Mollman Lakes, descend east through the lush Elk Creek valley and finish at a trailhead on FR 10291. The last 2.8mi of walking is along a 4WD track where vehicle access is restricted. The trailhead is accessed via a warren of gravel roads beginning with a west turn onto FR 903 from Hwy 83, 23mi south of Swan Lake. The hefty road shuttle of more than 80mi between start and finish points may deter some.

PLANNING
When to Hike

The pass is usually snow-free by mid-June, however, snow can be a problem until early July depending on conditions.

Maps

The USFS 1:50,000 *Mission Mountains and Mission Mountains Tribal Wildernesses* map is recommended, although note that access to the trailhead is incorrectly marked (see Getting To/From the Hike).

NEAREST TOWN

See Ronan (p115).

GETTING TO/FROM THE HIKE

Getting to the Mollman Trailhead is one of the biggest challenges of the route. The USFS map does not show the access correctly, although staff at Sports & Western Store (☎ 406-676-3701; US 93, Ronan) are so used to dealing with lost hikers that they can provide a photocopy of a sketch map detailing the route to the trailhead.

Take Mollman Trail Road east off US 93, 3mi south of Ronan. A small sign indicates the trailhead left off this road opposite

Mountain Shadow Ranch. The gravel road soon deteriorates into a rough track that is just passable without a high-clearance vehicle. Follow signs over the feeder canal and turn right at a junction into a makeshift car park. There are no official markings because the trailhead itself is still 0.5mi away, accessible only by foot.

THE HIKE (see map below)

Follow an overgrown track south from the car park for 0.1mi to a junction with a 4WD track. Turn left here and climb for around 0.5mi to the rusted trailhead board and the

official start of the route. The 4WD track ends at this point and a trail continues into the pines, passing over a short, steep section before easing into a steadier ascent. The lodgepole forest is so thick here that no vegetation can grow on the woodland floor, giving the place a rather primeval feel.

The trail climbs along the north bank of Mollman Creek, before crossing the stream on a series of felled logs. Wide switchbacks then lead up the southern bank before the path levels off and crosses the creek once more, this time via a single log bridge. The trail then ascends through more switchbacks,

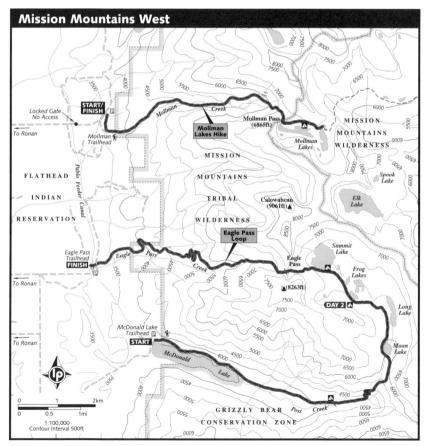

Mission Mountains West

climbing high above the creek, until the gradient eases and the path contours above the valley floor. As the trees dwindle in size, there are increasing glimpses of the steep valley headwall, and it is only after exiting the trees completely that two small lakes become visible among the trees behind you.

The next section can be a bit of a bushwhack, passing through meadows of vegetation that can grow to shoulder height. A climb over a short rock bluff provides a break between the meadows, and an elegant waterfall tumbling down the valley headwall marks the end of the jungle.

The trail re-enters the pines and a final climb, initially over steep, eroded ground and then over a series of switchbacks, leads to **Mollman Pass**. An information board at the ridgeline marks the boundaries between the tribal and the USFS wildernesses, and there are *camping sites* nearby. The first of the **Mollman Lakes** is a short distance away across the beautiful **plateau**, and the second is soon afterwards. Both are spectacularly located beneath the sheer, jagged rock walls that make the pass so dramatic, and offer *camping sites*. The trip from the trailhead to the first of the lakes will take three to four hours.

Retrace your steps to the trailhead.

Eagle Pass Loop

Duration	2 days
Distance	15mi (24.1km)
Standard	hard
Start	McDonald Lake Trailhead
Finish	Eagle Pass Trailhead
Nearest Town	Ronan
Transport	car

Summary A strenuous and challenging circuit visiting several remote lakes and crossing a beautiful subalpine pass.

You should expect to emerge from this route with more than a few scratches and bruises. At the time of writing the trail had not been cleared for some time, and you'll frequently find yourself clambering over fallen trees and wading through sections of chest-deep vegetation. The effort is worth it though; after a tough ascent through forests of western hemlock, stunning views of Calowahcan (9061ft) are suddenly revealed. In late July and August the wildflower meadows on the way to Eagle Pass are wonderful. The route skirts the northern boundary of the Grizzly Bear Conservation Area and, although bears are concentrated here, they range throughout the Mission Mountains. Be bear alert and make plenty of noise.

Although the route can be completed in a single day by fit and determined hikers, a more relaxed approach is to spend at least a night at Frog Lakes or Summit Lake, or even on the pass itself, before committing to the long and unrelenting descent of more than 4000ft. Times given for individual days allow for hiking with an overnight pack – expect a day trip to take eight to 10 hours.

PLANNING
When to Hike

Eagle Pass should be clear of snow by late June depending on the snowpack. Inquire locally as to the mosquito situation and either postpone your trip or take the necessary repellent and clothing to combat the swarms that plague the lakes and Eagle Pass area for a couple of weeks each summer.

Maps

Use the USFS 1:50,000 *Mission Mountains and Mission Mountains Tribal Wildernesses*, or two USGS 1:24,000 quads: *Fort Connah* and *Mt Harding*.

NEAREST TOWN

See Ronan (p115).

GETTING TO/FROM THE HIKE

The hike starts at McDonald Lake, which is easily reached by taking a signposted right turn off US 93, 5mi north of St Ignatius and 9mi south of Ronan. Follow the gravel road up to the north end of the dam.

The finish on the Pablo Feeder Canal is tricky to find. Take a right turn off US 93 at Allentown, 6mi south of Ronan. Follow this road (which turns to gravel after 2mi) to a small bridge over the Pablo Feeder Canal. Take the left turn just before the bridge and follow the narrow dirt road for a few hundred yards to a parking area on the left. There is a rickety footbridge crossing the canal just a short distance further along the road.

THE HIKE (see map p117)
Day 1: Lake McDonald to Frog Lakes
5–6 hours, 9mi, 2800ft ascent

Follow the undulating trail along the northern shore of McDonald Lake, passing occasional bluffs with views across the lake. After 30 to 45 minutes descend into mature hemlock forest and continue along a broad trail for the next 0.5mi. The trail then climbs gently, moving back into more vegetated terrain, reaching a huge stand of western hemlock and a *camping area* beside Post Creek 1½ hours from the start. This is a good spot to have a break and admire the **waterfall** just upstream.

The trail leaves Post Creek and climbs on switchbacks through dense hemlock forest and then through rock outcrops (caution needed), before crossing the outlet creek of Moon Lake just beneath another impressive waterfall. Continue to climb steeply, encountering some awkward vegetation and tree limbs and then recross the outlet of Moon Lake just before reaching the shores of the lake itself (four to five hours from the trailhead). Climb away from Moon Lake and negotiate a difficult section of trail to reach the southern Frog Lake after another hour (between these two lakes a rough side trail leads right to Long Lake, hidden among the trees; the lake can be visited with difficulty along an indistinct trail which is overgrown and very hard to find). The suddenly open views across **Frog Lakes** to Calowahcan are splendid. *Campsites* have been established where the trail reaches the water, although you should consider camping further back from the lakeshore.

Day 2: Frog Lakes to Eagle Pass Trailhead
6 hours, 6mi, 1200ft ascent, 4100ft descent

The trail continues in the same vein as you head for Summit Lake, crossing more fallen trees and sections of thick vegetation. Look out for a point where the trail swings to the right across a small stream. (A false trail continues along the left side of the stream but soon disappears.) **Summit Lake** and some small *campsites* are reached after 30 to 45 minutes. The views from the shores of Summit Lake are, if anything, even better than those from Frog Lakes.

The trail continues (poorly defined) along the southern shore of the lake and then begins the long, steep ascent to Eagle Pass. It is very easy to lose the trail as it leaves the lake, and other unmarked trails head across the meadows to the west of the lake. The proper trail heads toward the left edge of the prominent cliffs, which appear to bar progress to the pass. Once established on the steep slopes beneath these cliffs the trail becomes better defined and climbs in tight switchbacks, working around the cliffs and up into a dramatic rock basin. The meadows both here and beneath the cliffs are fantastic, especially when the beargrass is in bloom. Cross the basin and follow the trail as it switchbacks up the steep slopes, arriving suddenly at narrow **Eagle Pass**, where there is evidence of hikers having camped (two to 2½ hours from Frog Lakes).

The descent from the pass begins immediately and the trail drops steeply through the narrow Eagle Pass Creek valley. Flatter sections come in the form of lush beargrass meadows, which seriously overgrow the trail in places. After around an hour from the pass, the trail drops into taller forest and then begins to contour out of the valley before dropping through a long series of switchbacks. Continue down a small forested ridge and then drop into a thickly forested gulch with a small creek. Cross the creek and continue to descend north along what was once a fully benched cart track. At a switchback the trail leaves this old access route and drops steeply through thick hemlock to reach a riding track close to the finish. Turn left onto this, but only for a few yards. Look carefully for a hole in a fence and follow the trail through this to a rickety footbridge crossing the Pablo Feeder Canal. The car park is just across this and to the left.

Bob Marshall Wilderness

Named in honor of Robert Marshall, one of America's greatest advocates of wilderness protection, the 1577-sq-mile Bob Marshall Wilderness straddles the Continental Divide, taking in the headwaters of the Flathead River to its west and the Sun River to its east. Two smaller wilderness areas adjoin the Bob: Great Bear Wilderness, bordering on Glacier National Park to the north, and Scapegoat Wilderness in the south. Together they form the second largest contiguous tract of officially gazetted wilderness in the Lower 48.

NATURAL HISTORY

The Bob is dissected by massive, tilted limestone escarpments running north to south, of which the finest example is the Chinese Wall. Mountain goats and bighorn sheep find shelter in these inaccessible precipices. Grizzly bears in the Bob migrate with populations in adjoining Glacier National Park, although the local black bears, which tend to be large and brownish, are often mistaken for grizzlies. Other wildlife includes wolverines, deer, elk, moose and cougars. Bob Marshall Wilderness is an important habitat for the grayish-blue-and-chestnut harlequin duck, which winters on the Pacific coast but breeds here along fast-flowing streams, feeding on insect larvae.

PLANNING
Maps & Books

The 1:100,000 USFS map *Bob Marshall, Great Bear, and Scapegoat Wilderness Complex* ($6) covers the entire area; note that contours are shown in metric measurements. *Hiking Montana's Bob Marshall Wilderness* by Erik Molvar ($19.95) is a comprehensive guide to the area and includes the Great Bear and Scapegoat Wildernesses, as well as Jewel Basin Hiking Area.

Information Sources

Bob Marshall Wilderness falls within the boundaries of Flathead National Forest. For information contact the USFS office (☎ 406-758-5200; 1935 3rd Ave E, Kalispell, MT 59901) or see W www.fs.fed.us/r1/flathead.

Permits & Regulations

Permits are not required for overnight hikes in Bob Marshall Wilderness. Anglers will need a Montana fishing license. Camping is not allowed within 100ft of waterways or 200ft of trails.

ACCESS TOWNS
See Condon (p116).

Augusta

This pleasant little town, 26mi south of Choteau and 53mi west (via Vaughn and Simms) of Great Falls, is at the intersection of US 287 and Hwy 21, and is the eastern gateway to the Bob. The USFS office (☎ 406-562-3247, 405 Manix St) is open daily in summer and sells local hiking maps (check here for fire warnings). The town also has a chamber of commerce (☎ 406-562-3493). *Bunkhouse Inn (☎ 406-562-3387, 122 Main St)* charges from $42 for doubles, while *Wagons West (☎ 406-562-3295)* has tent sites with full facilities for $10.

There is no public transportation to Augusta. If driving from Helena, follow I-15 north 2mi past Wolf Creek, then turn north along US 287.

Chinese Wall Loop

Duration	6 days
Distance	60.5mi (97.3km)
Standard	moderate
Start/Finish	Benchmark
Nearest Town	Augusta
Transport	car

Summary This hike circumnavigates the Bob's most striking geological formation, the Chinese Wall, a 1000ft-high tilted limestone escarpment extending 22mi along the Continental Divide.

This long hike crosses the Continental Divide at the north and south ends of the Chinese Wall, and its highlight is the exhilarating high-level trail along the base of the wall. With the exception of the long ascent to White River Pass, gradients are fairly unchallenging, but the trail is often badly chewed up due to excessive horse traffic. A no-camping zone is in force along the base of the wall to protect the area's sensitive alpine environment; hikers should camp on the sections before and after the Chinese Wall. Grizzlies roam the area, so stay alert.

PLANNING
When to Hike
Hiking in the Bob can be rather hot in July and August. In summer hikers will also encounter numerous (often large) horseback-riding parties. Trails can be appallingly boggy in June.

Maps
The USFS 1:100,000 *Bob Marshall, Great Bear, and Scapegoat Wilderness Complex* covers the entire route. Alternatively use six USGS 1:24,000 quads: *Benchmark* (optional), *Pretty Prairie*, *Prairie Reef*, *Slategoat Mountain*, *Amphitheater Mountain* and *Haystack Mountain*.

NEAREST TOWN & FACILITIES
See Augusta (p120).

USFS Campgrounds
There are two basic USFS campgrounds at Benchmark: *South Fork Sun* ($6, 15 sites) at the trailhead, and *Benchmark* ($5, 18 sites) 1mi further back. The *Wood Lake USFS campground* ($5, 10 sites), 6.2mi before the trailhead, is also attractive. These fill quickly on July and August weekends.

GETTING TO/FROM THE HIKE
The hike begins and ends at Benchmark, 31mi from Augusta. Take the road signed to Nilan Reservoir, then continue west.

THE HIKE
Day 1: Benchmark to Indian Point Meadows
3½–4½ hours, 10.3mi
Follow the initially broad Sun River Trail from the *South Fork Sun campground* over a sturdy pack bridge over the South Fork Sun River (a summer nesting site for harlequin ducks) to intersect with a trail diverging left. Proceed right (downstream) well above the river through mixed forest of mostly lodgepole pine, Douglas fir and Engelmann spruce dotted with purple lupines, yellow groundsels and low huckleberry brush. The often-muddy trail passes the Bighead Creek Trail turnoff and crosses the wilderness boundary (register trip details here), before it swings west through dry clearings to cross the West Fork Sun River on another pack bridge.

Pick up the West Fork Sun River Trail at the junction on the river's north bank and continue left (west) across Wapiti Creek. The crags of Nineteen Ridge emerge up to your left as you head over moist, riverside meadows of yellow cinquefoils and pink wild roses alternating with drier slopes of sagebrush and Rocky Mountain juniper. The trail passes pleasant *campsites* among the trees on the left as the rusty ridges of Red Butte (8590ft) come into view ahead. A gentle climb through thickets of regenerating lodgepole brings you to the Prairie Reef Fire Lookout Trail (see Side Trip), three to four hours from Benchmark. Here, a well-worn path also leads down left to attractive *campsites* on the sunny river flats of the West Fork.

The trail continues a further 20 minutes through forest and grassy river flats to the Camp Creek Pass Trail turnoff at **Indian Point Meadows**. There are good *campsites* here.

Side Trip: Prairie Reef Fire Lookout
3½–4½ hours, 4.8mi, 3482ft ascent
The hike up to the fire lookout atop the limestone summit known as Prairie Reef – the highest point in the Bob accessible by trail – is strenuous but rewarding. Carry plenty of water, as none is normally available en route.

Climb steeply to wildflower terraces overlooking the West Fork valley, then swing northwest over rocky meadows and through fir-spruce forest. The views open out steadily as you get higher, and after crossing the (usually dry) bed of White Bear Creek the trail

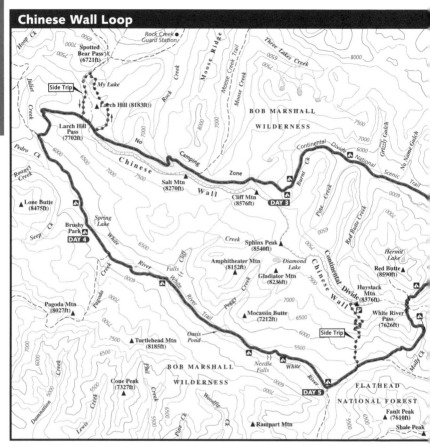

comes into a minor saddle. A steep ascent brings you out of the stunted limber pines, where a final, gentler climb across rocky tundra slopes sprinkled with mountain buttercups and globeflowers leads to the **Prairie Reef fire lookout** (8858ft), two to three hours from the turnoff. The superb panorama takes in the highest summits of Bob Marshall Wilderness and associated ranges, and the white outline of the adjacent Chinese Wall is particularly impressive. The lookout is staffed (in summer only) by a friendly USFS warden who enjoys the intermittent visits of day hikers.

Day 2: Indian Point Meadows to Chinese Wall

3½–4½ hours, 8.1mi, 975ft ascent

Make your way over a small stream, where the USFS Indian Point guard station can be seen up to the right, to meet the intersecting White River Pass Trail. There are more good *campsites* here. Proceed right (north) and follow the often boggy trail through riverside forest scattered with blue gentians. The trail crosses Black Bear Creek and No Name Gulch before fording the West Fork, about two hours from Indian Point Meadows. In summer this is a shallow wade but there is

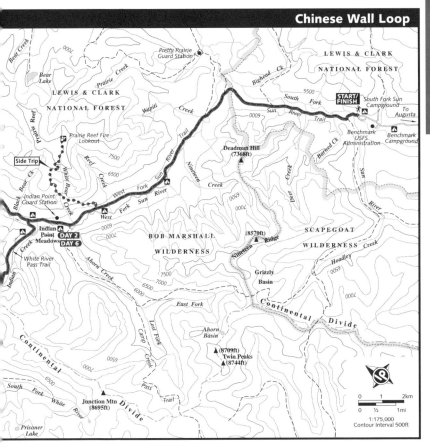

Chinese Wall Loop

a makeshift log bridge 10yd upstream. There are a few damp *campsites* on the east bank. Continue 1mi along the west bank before recrossing and following Burnt Creek, its headwater tributary. *Campsites* can be found along upper West Fork and Burnt Creek.

The trail gradually steepens as it crosses the creek and turns west, making a second crossing before it climbs through limber pine and subalpine fir onto beautiful, flowery meadows under the spectacular, towering face of the **Chinese Wall**. There are scenic *campsites* among the trees here, just before the (signposted) no-camping zone.

Day 3: Chinese Wall to Brushy Park

4¾–6¼ hours, 12mi, 908ft ascent

Head up through the trees to a saddle on a ridge buttressing Cliff Mountain. This point offers marvelous views along the escarpment in both directions, and you also get a different perspective on Prairie Reef across the valley. The trail drops through fir and whitebark pine to cross the outlet of a long, shallow tarn, then continues over lovely meadows under the towering precipices. Seepage springs emerge from the rubbly cliff base, where colonies of whistling marmot shelter. Higher up are picturesque, isolated clumps of stunted trees clinging to narrow terraces between the bluffs. After one to 1½ hours you meet the Moose Creek Trail.

Head north over a ridge crest descending from Salt Mountain, before dipping into the upper valley head of Rock Creek. The trail sidles up steeper slopes above the creek's northern tributaries, from where there are good views east toward the Sawtooth Range. After rising over two more low grassy crests, the trail makes a steeper ascent through spruce forest to intersect with the Spotted Bear Pass Trail (see Side Trip). Head left here and climb on briefly to reach **Larch Hill Pass** (7702ft), two hours from the Moose Creek Trail junction. The pass, which marks the northern extent of the Chinese Wall, gives a first view northwest to the snow-capped Silvertip Mountain and (a few paces down) southwest to Pagoda Mountain.

Cut down northwest onto open, fire-cleared ridge tops past a second turnoff to Spotted Bear Pass, then wind your way down into the lodgepole forest to join the White River Trail on the banks of Juliet Creek. Turn left and proceed south through narrow clearings beside the (usually dry) gravel creek bed into an extended strip of forest burnt in the mid-1990s. Up to your right, idyllic alpine lawns on Lone Butte contrast with the starkness of the charred trees. The trail fords the **White River** by a small grassy pasture, where there are good *campsites* at the edge of the spruce forest, then crosses channels of the river as it passes through the string of meadows known as **Brushy Park**, two to 2½ hours from the pass. Hummingbirds visit the good *campsites* here.

Side Trip: My Lake
1½–2 hours, 5mi
The attractive My Lake is reached from the trail junction below Larch Hill Pass. Take the Spotted Bear Pass Trail up around the eastern side of Larch Hill to a minor saddle, then descend northeast. My Lake is closed to camping due to past over-use. Continue around the lake to a trail junction and turn left (northwest), following it back to the main trail, just beyond Larch Hill Pass.

Day 4: Brushy Park to South Fork White River Junction
3½–4¾ hours, 10.5mi
Head downvalley through intact fir-spruce forest. The tracks of bears and other animals that frequent this more isolated part of the valley show up on the often-muddy trail, which descends only slightly as it passes the Pagoda Mountain Trail turnoff and skirts a shallow, marshy lake. The trail fords the cold, knee-deep river at some *campsites* on its stony western bank, 1¼ hours from Brushy Park.

Continue down along the white-pebbled, meandering river through flowery herb fields in the lodgepole forest, which would make ideal *campsites*. Note as you go how the direction of tilt on the eastern side of the valley – part of the so-called White River Syncline – is opposite to that of the surrounding ranges. The rock strata lean down into the valley, so there is no escarpment. The trail skirts the reedy Oasis Pond to cross Peggy Creek, then climbs past swirling pools to reach a scenic overlook high above the river, 1½ to two hours from the ford. Here, the thundering **Needle Falls** flow beneath a natural rock bridge before plummeting 100ft into a pool in the ravine far below. There is also a good view south along the valley toward Fault Peak.

Descend gradually through Douglas fir and Rocky Mountain juniper. After meeting the river again the trail follows the east bank – one of the best fishing spots in Montana – to reach a confluence at the much smaller **South Fork White River**, about one hour on. The large horse-outfitters' encampment here between the two forks is occupied throughout the summer. There are also *campsites* along the forested flats of the White River.

Day 5: South Fork White River Junction to Indian Point Meadows
4–5¼ hours, 9.3mi, 2180ft ascent
Turn left along the White River Pass Trail and climb steadily east into the wild South Fork valley past the Haystack Mountain turnoff (see Side Trip, p125). The trail continues high above the steep-sided gulch

through lodgepole and Douglas fir past another turnoff, where the (largely disused) South Fork White River Trail goes right. Ascend in steep switchbacks, before sidling up southeast into the tiny valley head of Molly Creek. There are scenic *campsites* among fir-spruce forest on the south bank.

The trail rises gently along the creek's north bank, then begins a steep winding climb northeast over fire-denuded slopes that lead up to a saddle. Take a last look southwest to the Flathead Alps before cutting right around the slope into the rocky gully that is **White River Pass** (7626ft), about 2½ hours from the trail junction at White River. The pass offers a sudden view of tilted limestone crags ahead and a final glimpse of Silvertip Mountain to the northwest.

The trail drops left into the upper valley of Indian Creek. Here, semi-sheltered *campsites* can be found among the regenerating subalpine firs and whitebark pines, where boisterous Clark's nutcrackers, a black-and-white jay, can sometimes be seen (or heard). A side trail detours 0.5mi north up to the small saddle overlooking the wild upper valley of Red Butte Creek.

Cross the tiny Indian Creek and follow its north bank down through heath and wildflower meadows past a waterfall splashing down over the trail from the red mudstone slopes. As the valley broadens, the trail dips into lodgepole forest and passes several more streamside *campsites* to ford the West Fork Sun River in a knee-high wade, about two hours from White River Pass. Climb the embankment to rejoin the West Fork Sun River Trail 0.5mi north of Indian Point guard station (see Day 2, p122).

Side Trip: Haystack Mountain
3–4 hours, 6.5mi, 3631ft ascent
Haystack Mountain (8376ft) is the best lookout point for the Chinese Wall. From the South Fork turnoff, the trail climbs steeply northwest in numerous switchbacks out of the lodgepoles and up the open western slopes of Haystack Mountain, before cutting southeast to gain the summit. From here the views stretching along the mighty escarpment are breathtaking.

Day 6: Indian Point Meadows to Benchmark
3½–4½ hours, 10.3mi
Reverse the Day 1 route to Benchmark.

Upper Holland Loop

Duration	6–7½ hours
Distance	13.3mi (21.4km)
Standard	moderate–hard
Start/Finish	North Holland Lake Trailhead
Nearest Town	Condon
Transport	car

Summary A strenuous ascent, a rock portal and beautiful Sapphire and Upper Holland Lakes.

This circular hike explores the subalpine terrain just beneath the western crest of the Swan Range. The first part involves a tough and continuous ascent of 3630ft to the high and remote Sapphire Lakes. The return is by a long, gentle descent past Upper Holland Lake and along Holland Creek. It is also possible to hike the route in the opposite direction, if the idea of a long ascent and steep descent is more appealing. For those who prefer to take two days, there are established backcountry campsites at Sapphire Lakes and Upper Holland Lake, although the former sites are the quieter and more scenic.

The Holland Creek Trail is a major access route for extended backcountry trips into the heart of the Bob and receives heavy use by both hikers and stock animals (it is the second busiest trailhead to the wilderness after Benchmark). Although the official boundary of the Bob currently makes a detour around the Holland Creek valley – to allow for potential hydroelectric schemes – there are also proposals to make the area an addition to the wilderness and so ensure the valley's protection.

PLANNING
When to Hike
The trail should be free of snow by mid-June. If hiking in counterclockwise, an early start is recommended to avoid the horses and stock that use the Holland Creek Trail.

Maps

The USFS 1:100,000 map *Bob Marshall, Great Bear, and Scapegoat Wilderness Complex* covers the route, as does the more detailed USGS 1:24,000 quad *Holland Lake*.

NEAREST TOWN & FACILITIES

See Condon (p116).

Holland Lake

Recently refurbished ***Holland Lake USFS campground*** ($12), at the western end of Holland Lake 1mi before the trailhead, is a convenient base for the hike. Also on Holland Lake Rd, ***Holland Lake Lodge*** (☎ 406-754-2282, [e] *cnd2208@blackfoot.net*) has rooms from $60 and campsites for $10.

GETTING TO/FROM THE HIKE

Turn west from Hwy 83, 9mi southeast of Condon, onto FR 44 (Holland Lake Road). The trailhead is at the end of the gravel road (4mi) on the north side of Holland Lake.

THE HIKE

The path forks a couple of hundred yards from the car park, and a sign indicates Upper Holland Lake to the right. Take the left trail, which then crosses the undulating forested shores at the northeastern end of Holland Lake, before a steady ascent begins and switchbacks lead to a four-way junction. Take the sharp right here (along Trail 415) and continue to climb for 0.25mi to another junction. Turn left along the Sapphire Lakes Trail (No 42), and begin the long ascent up the slopes of an unnamed peak (8053ft). The climb is continuous and the trail consists largely of wide switchbacks, although fine views back over the ever-receding Holland Lake offer some relief.

The switchbacks eventually lead to a ridge just south of the summit, where the Sapphire/Holland route is signed straight ahead at a junction (follow Trail 42). This junction is reached approximately 2½ hours from the start. The trees have thinned at this point, and a vista of the Mission Mountains to the west is added to the view. The trail then contours around the southern slopes of the mountain before a final short climb leads to the southeastern ridge – the highest point of the route. A break in the ridgeline offers an impressive portal through which the trail passes.

Switchbacks descend from the ridge into the heart of the Sapphire basin. Pass a left

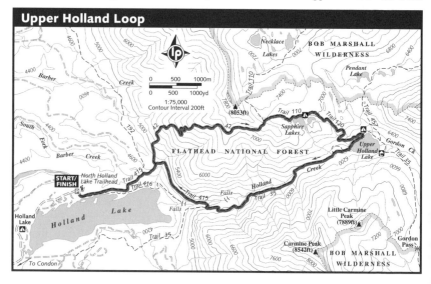

Upper Holland Loop

turn (and possible side trip of 3mi return) to Necklace Lakes. The trail weaves a path through the rock outcrops and scattered trees of the basin and passes Sapphire Lake and its smaller sibling. The lakes are signed to the right from the main trail and are only a short detour. The trail to Upper Holland Lake (now No 120) turns left (a detour from the old lakeshore trail marked on the USGS map), and begins a steady descent. The dark waters of Upper Holland Lake come into view amid the trees below and a steeper descent through switchbacks leads to the Holland-Gordon Trail (No 35), and the lake itself. Turn right to pass along the northwestern edge of the lake, and several well-established *campsites*, four to five hours from the start.

The descent from Upper Holland Lake follows the impressive falls and rapids of Holland Creek most of the way back to Holland Lake. The modest gradient makes for relatively easy hiking. The creek is crossed twice on log bridges, and there is an overflow path offering an alternative route when this heavily used access trail is crowded. If using the main trail, turn right at a junction around 2.2mi from Upper Holland Lake and follow Trail 415 to the second log bridge. The overflow path avoids this junction and leads directly to the bridge. The trail leaves the creek after this second crossing and climbs over the top of steep cliffs at the eastern end of Holland Lake. Care is needed on some parts of this narrow scree-covered trail, but there are great views over the length of the lake. Descend back into the forest, where the trail soon joins the Sapphire Lake Trail, followed earlier on the route. Keep straight ahead and retrace your initial steps to the trailhead.

Other Hikes

GLACIER NATIONAL PARK
Cracker Lake

Cracker Lake, a lovely tarn nestled against the valley headwall below towering Mt Siyeh, makes a relatively unstrenuous but long (12mi return) day hike from Many Glacier Hotel. The trail climbs 1100ft as it follows the Canyon Creek drainage to the scenic (if rather unsheltered) backcountry

campground on the lake's eastern side below the long-disused Cracker Mine. Use the enlargement on the Trails Illustrated 1:142,747 map No 215 *Glacier/Waterton Lakes National Parks* or three USGS 1:24,000 quads: *Many Glacier*, *Lake Sherburne* and *Logan Pass*.

Triple Divide Pass

This 7397ft pass lies on the eastern side of Triple Divide Peak, the meeting point of North America's vast Atlantic, Pacific and Arctic drainage basins. From Cut Bank ranger station, 17mi north of East Glacier Park (see p93), Triple Divide Pass makes an easy–moderate (14.5mi return) hike with a gradual 2400ft ascent. A worthwhile two- or three-day extension is to continue north along Hudson Bay Creek and Red Eagle Creek to St Mary, camping at Atlantic Creek campground and/or Red Eagle Lake. Use the Trails Illustrated 1:142,747 map No 215 *Glacier/Waterton Lakes National Parks* or two USGS 1:24,000 quads: *Cut Bank Pass* and *Mt Stimson*.

Dawson Pass

Dawson Pass is directly west of Two Medicine, 13mi from East Glacier Park. The out-and-back, 11.5mi hike to the 7598ft pass offers wonderful vistas of Mt Phillips and adjacent peaks in the southern Lewis Range. Take the North Shore Trail from the trailhead just north of Two Medicine campground, or a boat from the east end of Two Medicine Lake, to the lake's western side, then continue northwest past No Name Lake to Dawson Pass. A more adventurous loop – just feasible as a rather long (19mi) day hike, but best done as an overnighter – follows the exhilarating, high-level trail north along the western flank of Flinsch Peak and Mt Morgan to Pitamakan Pass. Return to Two Medicine by dropping to Oldman Lake and following Dry Fork valley. There are backcountry campgrounds at No Name and Oldman Lakes. Use the Trails Illustrated 1:142,747 map No 215 *Glacier/Waterton Lakes National Parks* or three USGS 1:24,000 quads: *Squaw Mountain* (optional), *Mt Rockwell* and *Cut Bank Pass*.

WATERTON LAKES NATIONAL PARK
Crypt Lake

Once voted Canada's top hike, the 10.8mi round trip to Crypt Lake on the border of Waterton and Glacier National Parks is still one of the most popular routes in the park. Access to the trailhead is by boat: Waterton Inter-Nation Shoreline Cruise Co (☎ 403-859-2362) departs from Waterton Townsite at 9 and 10am, returning from Crypt Landing at 4 and 5:30pm (C$12/US$8). Escaping the mass of people disembarking at once is a challenge, but the hike itself is unique, leading past several spectacular waterfalls and lakes, passing along narrow ledges, and negotiating a 60ft rock tunnel. Although the trail is well-worn, a total ascent of 2,300ft means that this is a hike of at least moderate difficulty. The recommended map is the Canadian Parks Service's 1:50,000 *Waterton Lakes National Park*.

Carthew Lakes Loop

A two- or three-day, 22.2mi loop from Waterton Townsite is possible by hiking south along the western shores of Upper Waterton Lake to Boundary Bay campground (4.5mi). This short first day reduces the effort needed to reach the next campground at Alderson Lake 13.4mi further on. An ascent of around 3000ft is also involved on the second day as you climb past Cameron Lake and begin to follow the route described in the Carthew Lakes hike (p108). After a night at Alderson Lake you can descend the final 4.2mi back into Waterton Townsite. Use the Canadian Parks Service's 1:50,000 *Waterton Lakes National Park* map.

JEWEL BASIN HIKING AREA
Crater Lake

This popular, 10mi round trip leads to a high lake in a rocky, glacier-scoured basin with excellent fishing. It is an easy–moderate route with a total ascent of just 570ft, and with good camping close to the lake, it is perfectly suited as a family overnighter. From Camp Misery Trailhead, follow Trail 707 past Birch Lake to reach Crater Lake. The USFS *Jewel Basin Hiking Area* map covers the route, as do two USGS maps: *Jewel Basin* and *Crater Lake*.

MISSION MOUNTAINS
Cold Lakes

An easy 5mi round trip to the Cold Lakes in the Mission Mountains Wilderness makes a pleasant two- to three-hour excursion perfect for families. The trail involves 600ft of ascent and crosses forest and meadows to reach the lakes. Access the trailhead via the Cold Creek turnoff, 23mi south

of Swan Lake on Montana Hwy 83, and continue 7mi to the end of the gravel road. Use the USFS 1:50,000 map *Mission Mountains and Mission Mountains Tribal Wilderness* or two USGS 1:24,000 quads: *Piper-Crow Pass* and *Peck Lake*.

BOB MARSHALL WILDERNESS
Sunburst Lake

This impressive alpine lake sits in a cirque at the foot of glacier-studded Swan Peak in the Bob's most northwesterly corner. Sunburst Lake makes a long day or overnight hike of moderate difficulty (15mi round trip). The lake offers excellent fishing.

The Sunburst Lake Trailhead is accessible via the town of Hungry Horse, on US 2 roughly 20mi northwest of Kalispell; drive south around Hungry Horse Reservoir to the junction near the USFS Spotted Bear campground, then follow the Bunker Creek Rd (2826). The USFS 1:100,000 map *Bob Marshall, Great Bear, and Scapegoat Wilderness Complex* is adequate, but USGS 1:24,000 quads *Meadow Creek*, *String Creek* and *Sunburst Lake* also cover the route.

Gateway Pass & Gateway Gorge

This moderate–hard, 32mi route passes through some of the most beautiful alpine scenery the Bob has to offer, taking in awesome Gateway Gorge along the way. The hike explores the area west of Swift Reservoir, a part of the Rocky Mountain Front that is a recent addition to Bob Marshall Wilderness. The circuit follows the Gateway Creek, Strawberry Creek and East Fork Trails, involves 1600ft of gain, and generally takes three days to complete. There are good campsites 1mi beyond Gateway Pass at Big River Meadows (14mi from the trailhead), and shortly after the junction with the East Fork Trail at 20mi. To reach the trailhead, turn west off US 89 at Dupuyer onto a gravel forest road signed to Swift Dam. Turn right at the dam and follow the north shore of the reservoir for 2mi to the end of the road. Use the USFS 1:100,000 *Bob Marshall, Great Bear, and Scapegoat Wilderness Complex* map, or four USGS maps: *Swift Reservoir*, *Gateway Pass*, *Gooseberry Park* and *Morningstar Mountain*.

Top Left: Heading up to Iceberg Lake, enclosed by towering 3000ft headwalls, in Montana's Glacier National Park. **Top Right:** Meadows and mountains near Logan Pass, the starting point for several hikes in Glacier National Park. **Bottom:** Spectacular hiking, following the 1000ft-high limestone escarpment known as the Chinese Wall, in Montana's Bob Marshall Wilderness.

Top: The jagged granite ridges of Bighorn Crags, the result of intense glacial shearing, in the Salmon River Mountains, Idaho. **Bottom Left:** Sawtooth Lake, in the far north of Idaho's Sawtooth Wilderness, lies in a deep basin. **Bottom Right:** Blodgett Canyon, with majestic ponderosa pines and towering granite walls, in Montana's Bitterroot Mountains.

Central Idaho

Central Idaho is probably the wildest and most sparsely inhabited part of the US Rockies. Stretching north-south from the lower Idaho panhandle to the rim of Snake River Plain, and west-east from Boise Front Range to meet the Montana Bitterroots, central Idaho takes in most of the state's classic mountains, including the Salmon River Mountains, and the Lost River and Lemhi Ranges, as well as the Boulders, White Clouds and Sawtooths. This vast and rugged territory is almost 80% public land, mainly national forest and/or designated wilderness. There is virtually nowhere in central Idaho where you cannot find solitude and pristine surroundings within a short drive. Not surprisingly, the region has a special place in the hearts and minds of US conservationists and outdoor enthusiasts.

CLIMATE
Despite the moderating influence of the nearby Pacific Ocean, central Idaho has a continental climate with relatively short, mild summers and long, chilly winters. However, the region experiences the great local climatic variation typical for most mountain regions. As little as 15 inches of precipitation falls in the valleys of the Frank Church River of No Return Wilderness, while as much as 50 inches may fall on the mountain tops – producing up to 150 inches of winter snow. Summer temperatures in the mountains can occasionally reach more than 90°F but nights are typically quite cool.

INFORMATION
Maps & Books
GTR Mapping's 1:800,000 *Recreational Map of Idaho* ($3.95) gives an overview of national forest, park and wilderness areas.

Trails of Western Idaho by Margaret Fuller ($14.95) and *Trails of Eastern Idaho* by Margaret Fuller & Jerry Painter ($13.95) give excellent coverage of the region. *Hiking Idaho* by Ralph & Jackie J Maughan ($19.95) is also very good. *Easy Hiking*

Highlights

CLEM LINDENMAYER

Beautiful Fourth of July Lake, below pink Patterson Peak, on the White Cloud Loop.

- Standing under the fabulous pinnacles and spires of the Bighorn Crags (p132)

- Taking a quick dip in the chilled waters of Sawtooth Lake (p136)

- Hiking past the dozen Boulder Chain Lakes on the White Cloud Loop (p137)

- Breathing the alpine air among eroding ridges on the summit of Mt Borah (p143)

Near Sun Valley by Gloria Moore ($11.95) covers more than 50 day hikes in Idaho.

Information Sources
Idaho's official website is at W www.state.id.us. For general information contact Idaho Travel Council (☎ 208-334-2470, 800-842-5858; W www.visitid.org; 700 W State St, Boise). The state office for the Bureau of Land Management (BLM; ☎ 208-373-4000; W www.id.blm.gov; 1387 S Vinnell Way, Boise) manages vast areas of public land.

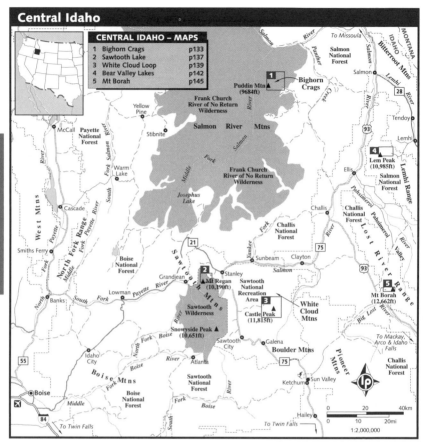

Central Idaho

CENTRAL IDAHO – MAPS

1	Bighorn Crags	p133
2	Sawtooth Lake	p137
3	White Cloud Loop	p139
4	Bear Valley Lakes	p142
5	Mt Borah	p145

CENTRAL IDAHO

GATEWAYS
Boise

Boise (population 170,000) is the state capital and a 'small big town' on the Boise River north of I-84. For information contact the visitor center (☎ 208-344-5338, 850 Front St), the US Forest Service (USFS; ☎ 208-343-2527, 5493 Warm Springs Ave) or the BLM Boise district office (☎ 208-384-3300, 3948 Development Ave).

Places to Stay & Eat The *On the River RV Park* (☎ 208-375-7432, 800-375-7432, 6000 N Glenwood St) has tent/RV sites for $15/20. *Sands Motel* (☎ 208-343-2533, 1111 W State St) has singles/doubles for $35/40. *Boise Center Guest Lodge* (☎ 208-342-9351, 1314 Grove St) charges $45/50. *Boise Co-op* (☎ 208-472-4500, 888 W Fort St) sells natural and bulk foods.

Getting There & Away There are daily flights from Denver, Las Vegas, Minneapolis, Salt Lake City, Phoenix, Portland, Seattle and St Louis. Greyhound (☎ 208-343-3681, 1212 W Bannock St) buses between Salt Lake City and Portland, Salt Lake City and Bozeman, and Reno and Spokane stop in Boise.

Salmon River Mountains

Salmon River Mountains is a term given to the diverse and remote ranges clustered along either side of the Middle Fork Salmon River as far north as its confluence with the main branch of the Salmon River. They are characterized by high, rugged ridges dissected by large, wild rivers that have often eroded spectacularly deep canyons. The Salmon River Mountains lie within the Payette and Challis National Forests, and form the southernmost section of the vast (3698 sq mile) Frank Church River of No Return Wilderness. The most outstanding scenery is found in the magnificent Bighorn Crags area.

NATURAL HISTORY
The Salmon River Mountains are largely composed of granitic Idaho batholith (the local form of which is often known as Bitterroot batholith), mixed with volcanic rocks such as andesite and rhyolite from ancient eruptions.

Ponderosa pine forests cover the lower slopes, giving way to lodgepole pine mixed with Douglas fir, then Engelmann spruce and subalpine fir with increasing elevation. Whitebark pine is abundant on the high, exposed, dry slopes and ridge tops.

Since their reintroduction into northern Idaho in the mid-1990s, gray wolves have moved south into the Salmon River Mountains, but plans to reintroduce grizzly bears have been stalled due to strong local opposition. Black bears, bighorn sheep, deer, mountain goats, lynx and wolverines are also found in the region. Salmon and steelhead trout swim from the Pacific Ocean to spawn in the high mountain tributaries of the Salmon River.

PLANNING
Maps
The USFS 1:126,720 *Challis-Salmon National Forest* map ($7) is good for a general overview.

Information Sources
The regional USFS website is ⓦ www.fs .fed.us/r4.

Permits & Regulations
Backcountry permits are not required for Frank Church River of No Return Wilderness, but hikers should register by filling out an itinerary card at the trailhead. Camp at least 200ft from lakes and streams.

ACCESS TOWNS
Challis
On US 93, north of the Hwy 75 intersection, Challis is 52mi northeast of Stanley. The USFS district office (☎ 208-879-4101) gives advice but sells only USFS maps (no topos). Outdoor Outlet (☎ 208-879-4814) sells topographic maps at marked-up prices.

Places to Stay With hot springs access, *Challis Hot Springs (☎ 208-879-4442)*, 4.5mi from town via a road south of the US 93-Hwy 75 intersection, has sites from $14.

Getting There & Away CART (☎ 208-879-2448, 800-258-4937) runs twice-daily buses on Tuesday and Friday southeast to Idaho Falls and north to Salmon.

Salmon
At the intersection of US 93 and Hwy 28, Salmon is 55mi from Challis. The USFS office (☎ 208-756-2215, 756-5100) and BLM office (☎ 208-756-5400, 756-2201) are beside each other on US 93, just south of town. Silver Spur Sports (☎ 208-756-2833, 403 Main St) sells outdoor gear and quads.

Places to Stay The *Salmon Meadows Campground (☎ 208-756-2640, 400 N St Charles St)* has tent/RV sites for $15/20. *Heritage Inn B&B (☎ 208-756-3174, 510 Lena St)* and *Solaas B&B (☎ 208-756-3903, 3 Red Rock Stage Rd)* have rooms from $35.

Getting There & Away CART (☎ 208-756-2191, 800-258-4937, 206 South Saint Charles St) runs twice-daily buses on Tuesday and Friday along the Salmon-Challis-Idaho Falls route.

Bighorn Crags

Duration	2 days
Distance	17.4mi (28km)
Standard	moderate
Start/Finish	Crags USFS campground
Nearest Towns	Challis, Salmon
Transport	car

Summary A loop hike through a remote and wild area, with incredible craggy formations and numerous lovely alpine lakes.

The Bighorn Crags area lies in the south-eastern corner of Frank Church River of No Return Wilderness. Here glacial and other natural erosion has carved the hard granite into remarkable hump and fin shapes that rise out of gentle, forested slopes or jut abruptly up from smooth, slab-rock ridges, touching 10,000ft. True to its name, herds of bighorn sheep roam the area. The Bighorn Crags stand among a dozen strikingly beautiful glacial tarns, most notably the large Ship Island Lake, considered one of Idaho's best backcountry fishing lakes.

These ranges typically experience hot, dry summers and snowy winters. The Clear Creek Fire of July to October 2000 – the largest blaze in the US that year – burnt more than 313 sq miles of southern Frank Church River of No Return Wilderness. The flames repeatedly threatened, although never quite reached, the Bighorn Crags area, but charred ranges are visible to the north.

Despite unusual and outstanding scenery, the area's relative remoteness and rough, dusty access seem to discourage potential visitors. Bighorn Crags are best visited as a radial hike, with a base camp at one of the lake basins.

PLANNING
When to Hike
Access to Bighorn Crags is usually possible from late June to late September.

What to Bring
Carry some water (from the trailhead campground pump) as there is almost none until the end of the thirsty first day's hike.

Maps
USGS's 1:24,000 quads, *Mount McGuire*, *Aggipah Mountain* and *Hoodoo Meadows*, cover the hike but do not always show trails accurately. A 1:100,000 metric map, *Bighorn Crags*, published by Idaho Fish & Game, gives a wider overview, although it is not really suitable for serious navigation.

NEAREST TOWNS & FACILITIES
See Challis and Salmon (p131).

USFS Campgrounds
Immediately below the trailhead is the basic *Crags USFS campground* with 14 sites ($4). There are several other USFS campgrounds nearby, including *Yellowjacket*.

GETTING TO/FROM THE HIKE
From Challis drive approximately 9mi north of town on US 93, turning left (west) along the Morgan Creek Rd (signposted 'Cobalt 40'). Follow this for 32mi, then continue left along FR 112, bearing right along the rough FR 113 after 7mi. After 8.3mi take the even rougher and narrower FR 114 right and continue a final 17.4mi just past the Crags USFS campground to the trailhead car park, where there is space for around 12 vehicles.

From Salmon drive about 6mi south on US 93 then turn right (west) along Williams Creek Rd (FR 21). Continue for 12mi to the Panther Creek Rd intersection, then go south for 10.6mi to the FR 112 turnoff.

THE HIKE
Day 1: Crags USFS Campground to Gentian Lake
3¾–4¾ hours, 7.7mi, 816ft ascent

Fill out an 'itinerary card' and drop it in the trailhead registration box. Take the Crags Trail (No 21) up north into the mixed forest across the wilderness boundary, then northwest around the slope above Golden Trout Lake. Views of incongruous domed formations and fortress-like towers rising out of granite-slab ridges develop ahead as you proceed along the ridge top to a junction, where the alternative 'horse trail' and the Yellowjacket Trail (No 38) enter from the left, 40 to 50 minutes from the trailhead.

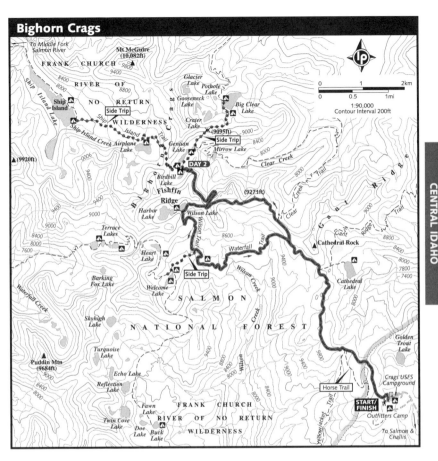

Bighorn Crags

Continue along (or just below) the broad, undulating, sandy-gravel ridge top, directly past those bizarre-shaped granite outcrops to meet the Gant Ridge Trail (No 29) on the right. Good *campsites* at Cathedral Lake (visible before the trail junction) can be reached by taking Trail 29 down east for 0.4mi, then turning southeast. The main trail (No 21) cuts down left to avoid the imposing **Cathedral Rock**, a bulky hulk marking the southwestern end of Gant Ridge, passing above a tiny, trickling spring just before it intersects with Waterfall Trail (No 45), 1¼ to 1½ hours from the Yellowjacket Trail junction.

Climb steeply north back to the ridge and follow it past the Clear Creek Trail (No 22) turnoff (right), high above the wild basin of Clear Creek, the lower section of which exhibits major fire damage. The route climbs through whitebark pine and fir growing out of polished slab rock to a point at 9271ft, then traverses west above the upper basin of Wilson Creek into a small saddle (9220ft), that gives the first views west of the jagged columns and pinnacles of Bighorn Crags. Switchback down west to meet the Wilson Trail (No 144) junction in a narrow gap, 1¼ to 1½ hours from the Waterfall Trail junction.

Turn right and contour northeast along steep slopes opposite the magnificent Fishfin Ridge, a row of pillars and columns that juts out of massive glacier-smoothed slabs. Trail 21 doubles back under Fishfin Ridge and skirts high above Mirrow Lake before spiraling down to meet Ship Island Trail (No 30) beside Birdbill Lake, 40 to 50 minutes from the gap. Beyond the junction is **Gentian Lake**. There are pleasant *campsites* among the meadows, dotted with blue gentians, around the lake, which can be reached by taking either the left or right trail. This lake basin makes a good base to explore the Bighorn Crags area on day hikes.

Side Trip: Ship Island Lake
3½–4½ hours, 6.9mi, 1415ft ascent
Take Ship Island Trail (No 30) from the junction near Birdbill Lake. It climbs to the scenic ridge top (around 8940ft), then winds around northwest and descends almost to the shore of Airplane Lake. A short trail leads left (southeast) to some lakeside *campsites* among the spruce. Continue more gently down through the forested valley, meeting a small stream just before you reach **Ship Island Lake** at a pebble beach, 1½ to two hours from Birdbill Lake. There is a great view across the water past a ship-shaped island to a strikingly rugged, high rock ridge at the lake's western end. *Campsites* can be found near the inlet and around the eastern shore.

Side Trip: Big Clear Lake
1½–2 hours, 3.5mi, 730ft ascent
From the trail junction near Birdbill Lake head north, skirting the revegetated lateral moraine along the east side of the elongated Gentian Lake and continue around an unnamed tarn on its north side, past the Mirrow Lake Trail (No 12; also called Ship Island Lake Trail) junction. Ascend northeast in switchbacks to reach a pass (9095ft) between the two lake basins, then wind your way down through the boulders across the trickling inlet to reach **Big Clear Lake**, 45 minutes to one hour from Birdbill Lake. Attractive *campsites* can be found around the pebbly shore of this very attractive but less-visited lake.

Day 2: Gentian Lake to Crags USFS Campground
5–6½ hours, 9.7mi, 800ft ascent
You can retrace your steps from Day 1 to the trailhead but a more interesting option is via Wilson Lake.

From Birdbill Lake return to the narrow gap and the Wilson Trail (No 144) junction. Turn right (west), following the trail for 10 to 15 minutes down to the right over the slabrock slope to **Wilson Lake**. This picturesque lake lies directly under 800ft glacier-carved walls, which are crowned by the pinnacles and columns of Fishfin Ridge. The best *campsites* are among the fir and spruce near the western shore or a short way on beside the larger Harbor Lake.

Trail 144 cuts south from midway around Wilson Lake, winding down beside the trickling Wilson Creek to join Waterfall Trail (No 45) at a larger tributary, 30 to 40 minutes from the lake. Follow Trail 45 southeast past *campsites* along the creek. Gradually climb away from the water, heading northeast over low slab shelves littered with small boulders to meet Trail 21 at the junction below Cathedral Rock, 1¼ to 1½ hours from the Wilson Trail junction.

Turn right (southeast), retracing the first section of the Day 1 hike back to the trailhead (1¾ to 2¼ hours).

Side Trip: Welcome Lake
30–40 minutes, 1.4mi
A worthwhile detour is to head right (southwest) at the Wilson and Waterfall Trails junction, climbing gently to **Welcome Lake**. This elongated lake is ringed by moist lawns frequented by moose. Scenic extensions lead west across to Terrace Lakes (four hours, 7.4mi) and south into the Reflection Lake basin (eight hours, 11mi).

Sawtooth National Recreation Area

Situated far to the west of the Continental Divide, the 1178-sq-mile Sawtooth National Recreation Area (SNRA) marks the approximate geographical center of Idaho. It is named after the spectacular Sawtooth Mountains, an amazingly jagged range that stretches along the Salmon River's west side, climaxing at Thompson Peak (10,751ft) near the town of Stanley. Sawtooth Wilderness, a 339-sq-mile area inside the SNRA, takes in the entire Sawtooth Mountains, while the somewhat higher White Cloud Mountains extend along the east side of the Salmon River valley, reaching their highest point at Castle Peak (11,815ft). Hundreds of delightful glacial lakes and tarns lie in the valleys and cirques of these superb ranges.

HISTORY
The Sheepeaters, a branch of the Shoshone people, inhabited the Salmon River basin when the first Euro-American fur trappers arrived in the early 1820s. The first gold strike in the Stanley Basin was in 1863 and mining continued until 1879. In the 1920s, the photographer and mountain guide Robert Limbert explored the mountains around Stanley and built the Redfish Lake Lodge.

Creating a national park in the area was first proposed in the early 1910s. In 1937 Congress established an initial, primitive area in the Sawtooths, which in 1972 was expanded into the SNRA (including Sawtooth Wilderness). A federal proposal in 1976 for the creation of two large national parks in the region is unlikely to ever come to fruition.

NATURAL HISTORY
The jagged peaks of the Sawtooths are composed of 70-million-year-old gray granite (known as Idaho batholith), with intrusions of younger pink granite (called Sawtooth batholith). Bands of marble-like metamorphosed limestone mixed with silica give the White Cloud Mountains their name. The lower foothills are largely composed of glacial moraine.

Broad, sagebrush plains cover the lowest valleys. Extensive forests of lodgepole and ponderosa pine thrive in the dry foothills of the SNRA, but in recent years a (native) bark beetle infestation has killed a large number of these trees. The drier climate also favors whitebark pine, which is usually the dominant tree species on well-drained ridges, although fir-spruce forest is also widespread on moister slopes and valleys. The rare Idaho ground squirrel is not often found outside the SNRA, which is also the most southerly extent of the Columbian ground squirrel.

PLANNING
Maps & Books
USFS's 1:126,720 *Sawtooth National Forest*, a metric map available in paper ($4) and plastic ($7), gives a good overview. Another USFS map, the 1:192,000 *Sawtooth National Forest*, is distributed free at USFS offices, but is less useful.

Trails of the Sawtooth and White Cloud Mountains by Margaret Fuller ($14.95) describes more than 100 hikes in the area.

Information Sources
SNRA's main office (☎ 208-727-5000), 8mi north of Ketchum on Hwy 75, is open 8am to 5pm daily throughout summer (to 4:30pm in winter). The Sawtooth Society (☎ 208-387-0852, Ⓦ www.sawtoothsociety.org) is a local organization dedicated to protecting the SNRA.

Permits & Regulations
Passes are required for all vehicles parked at designated trailheads in the Sawtooth Wilderness and National Recreation Area. Passes cost $5 for three days or $15 for one year, and can be purchased at any local ranger station, USFS office or visitor center, as well as many stores and other commercial enterprises in the area.

Hikers in Sawtooth Wilderness must have a self-issued permit (available free of charge at all designated trailheads); drop the white slip into the trailhead deposit box and attach the registration copy to your pack.

Campfires are prohibited in many popular areas of the SNRA, including Alpine Lake, Chamberlain Lakes, upper Boulder Chain Lakes, Four Lakes Basin, Sawtooth Lake and along the entire Toxaway Loop hike. Where permitted, all campfires in the Sawtooth Wilderness should be made only on a fire blanket or fire pan.

ACCESS TOWN
Stanley

An enclave within the SNRA, Stanley is an excellent base for exploring the area. It is on the Salmon River at the junction of Hwy 21 (Ponderosa Pine Scenic Byway) and Hwy 75 (Sawtooth Scenic Byway), 61mi north of Ketchum and 52mi southwest of Challis.

For information contact Stanley-Sawtooth Chamber of Commerce (☎ 208-774-3411, 800-878-7950, w www.stanleycc.org) in the community building on Hwy 21. Stanley ranger station (☎ 208-774-3000, Hwy 75), 1.9mi south of town, and Redfish Lake visitor center (☎ 208-774-3376), 0.8mi further south, give advice and sell trailhead parking passes and maps (quads $4.20).

Riverwear (☎ 208-774-3592, w www .riverwear.com, Hwy 21), which is opposite the Mountain Village Mercantile, and River One (☎ 208-774-2270) sell hiking gear. *Elk Mountain RV Resort (☎ 208-774-2202, 800-428-9203, Hwy 21)*, 4mi west of Stanley, has a few tent sites ($15) and RV hookups ($30). *Cole's Sawtooth Hotel & Cafe (☎ 208-774-2282, Ace of Diamonds Ave)* has rooms from around $30/35.

River Rat Express (☎ 208-774-2265, 800-831-8942) operates a shuttle service mostly for rafters, but can drop hikers off at trailheads.

Sawtooth Lake

Duration	5½–7½ hours
Distance	10.9mi (17.5km)
Standard	moderate
Start/Finish	Iron Creek Trailhead
Nearest Town	Stanley
Transport	car
Summary	A hike up to a tranquil alpine tarn surrounded by high, craggy ranges.

Sawtooth Lake lies in the far north of the Sawtooth Wilderness, in a deep basin with sheer slab sides formed by intense glacial action. It makes a rewarding and popular day hike, although some heavy switchbacking on sunny slopes can make it rather hot in summer. The hike has a total ascent of 1720ft (another 60ft up to the pass). Backpackers should note that campfires are not permitted along this route.

PLANNING
Maps

Use either the USGS 1:24,000 *Stanley Lake* quad or the Earthwalk Press 1:48,000 *Sawtooth Wilderness* waterproof hiking map.

NEAREST TOWN & FACILITIES

See Stanley (this page).

Iron Creek USFS Campground

Next to the trailhead, this *campground* has around a dozen sites for $11.

GETTING TO/FROM THE HIKE

Drive 2.5mi north of Stanley on Hwy 21, turn left (west) and continue 3.1mi to Iron Creek Trailhead (also known as Iron Creek Transfer Camp). A trailhead parking pass is required.

THE HIKE

After lodging your wilderness-use permit, head southwest through lodgepole forest along the flat north side of Iron Creek. Pass the turnoff (left) to Marshall Lake at the edge of a long soggy clearing. Avalanche runs descend the steep slopes on the opposite side of the valley. Climb gradually north 0.6mi to reach another junction, 45 minutes to one hour from the car park. Turn left (the right branch continues 7mi north to Stanley Lake), heading west up through tall stands of graceful Douglas fir to ford the small Iron Creek, 30 to 40 minutes from the trail junction.

Ascend steeply southward in tight switchbacks, opposite impressive towers of granite-slab on the craggy ridge across the valley, to reach a turnoff (left) after 30 to 40 minutes. This short side trail leads down (five minutes) to **Alpine Lake**, a beautiful, greenish tarn in a deep cirque below the soaring 2000ft north wall of Alpine Peak (9861ft). There are some scenic *campsites* around to the left, back from the northern shore; campfires are not permitted anywhere in the lake basin.

On the main trail continue up switchbacks southwest, through slopes of whitebark pine

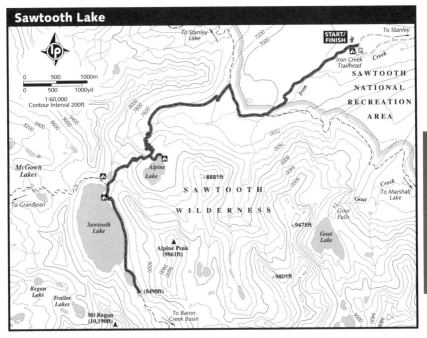

Sawtooth Lake

high above Alpine Lake, where the town of Stanley comes briefly into view. The route rises over a minor crest past a tiny tarn, re-crossing the stream to reach a trail junction at the northeast shore of tranquil **Sawtooth Lake**, 45 minutes to one hour from the Alpine Lake turnoff. (The right trail climbs 1.5mi west over a pass to McGown Lakes.) *Camp-sites* can be found in the firs between the tarn and Sawtooth Lake.

Sawtooth Lake lies just below tree line in a deep glacial trough enclosed by high peaks that drop straight into the lake's west side. Patches of permanent snow cling to the north face of Mt Regan (10,190ft), which rises directly from the southern shore. Sawtooth Lake can be explored in 1¼ to two hours. Cross the outlet and cut left past a small outcrop, then traverse around to attractive meadows fringing its southern shore. The trail leads gently up past a small tarn to a moraine-choked pass (8490ft) that gives a good view south to Baron Peak (10,291ft).

The (downhill) hike back to the car park takes two to 2½ hours.

White Cloud Loop

Duration	4 days
Distance	28.1mi (45.2km)
Standard	moderate–hard
Start/Finish	Fourth of July Trailhead
Nearest Town	Stanley
Transport	car

Summary A wild, backcountry trip that circum-navigates Castle Peak, the highest of the White Cloud Peaks.

The White Cloud Peaks area, in the heart of White Cloud Mountains, attracts a large number of hikers every summer. The area's surprising concentration of subalpine and alpine lakes, often accessible via unmaintained 'social' trails leading up through wild valleys, are a delight to explore and fish. The string of 12 beautiful tarns (Boulder Chain Lakes), sitting on separate benches stretching up a narrow alpine valley, is one of the most popular backpacking destinations in Idaho.

Some lower access trails used for this hike are open to mountain bikes and trail motorbikes (although not ATVs – All Terrain Vehicles), but such nonpedestrian traffic is relatively moderate. This route – especially the remoter section between Windy Devil and Born Lakes – is better suited to hikers experienced in backcountry travel.

PLANNING
When to Hike
The trail is likely to be out of condition before mid-July (the high passes, especially, will have snow) and after late September.

Maps
Two USGS 1:24,000 quads, *Washington Peak* and *Boulder Chain Lakes*, cover the hike but do not accurately show all sections of the route. A 1:100,000 metric map, *White Cloud Peaks*, published by Idaho Fish & Game, shows the route in poor detail but may be useful for a general overview.

NEAREST TOWN & FACILITIES
See Stanley (p136).

Campsites
There is no campground near the trailhead, but many attractive (free) *campsites* exist along the creek beside the access road.

GETTING TO/FROM THE HIKE
Drive 15.6mi south from Stanley on Hwy 75, then turn east just south of Fourth of July Creek and continue 20mi to the Fourth of July Trailhead car park. There is space here for around 30 vehicles. A trailhead parking pass is required.

THE HIKE
Day 1: Fourth of July Trailhead to Chamberlain Lakes
3½–4¾ hours, 7.3mi, 1375ft ascent
After signing the register book, cross the Fourth of July Creek bridge and proceed east

across a dirt road. The trail climbs smoothly through dry lodgepole and fir-spruce forest, recrossing the creek to pass the Born Lakes turnoff (left) just before it reaches **Fourth of July Lake**. This tranquil, greenish tarn contrasts with the red crags of Patterson Peak (10,872ft) rising directly behind it. There are *campsites* among the trees around the shore. Skirt the lake's western side and head southeast over a broad watershed (9570ft) to arrive at **Washington Lake**, 1¼ to 1¾ hours from the trailhead. The area between the trail and the shore is closed to camping for rehabilitation, but some good *campsites* can be found further back from the lake.

Continue down to a junction in a meadow below chalky cliffs. Head left (the right trail goes to Germania Creek) across the babbling Washington Lake Creek and then south, up through occasional sagebrush clearings and pine forest active with squirrels. The route passes another turnoff (right) to Germania Creek before it swings northeast and climbs to a saddle (9785ft), 1½ to two hours from Washington Lake. From here you get a sudden and impressive view across Chamberlain Basin to Castle Peak (11,815ft).

Descend northeast over old scree slopes, which are colonized by tiny yellow arnicas, pink-yellow asters, blue harebells, yellow saxifrage and other wildflowers. The trail dips past *campsites* above a small, undrained tarn in a deep trough, then continues down to reach the lower of the **Chamberlain Lakes**, 45 minutes to one hour from the saddle. This attractive lake sits directly below Castle Peak. More *campsites* can be found in the fir-spruce forest around the lake's southern shore.

Day 2: Chamberlain Lakes to Lodgepole Lake
3¾–5 hours, 7.9mi, 1664ft ascent
Head across the tiny stream flowing out of lower Chamberlain Lake and follow the trail 0.4mi east (past a gushing spring on your right) to a junction. Turn left and traverse northeast through grassy avalanche runs scattered with light pine forest, then into a dry gully leading to **Castle Divide** (9990ft), one to 1¼ hours from the lake. This pass looks

White Cloud Loop

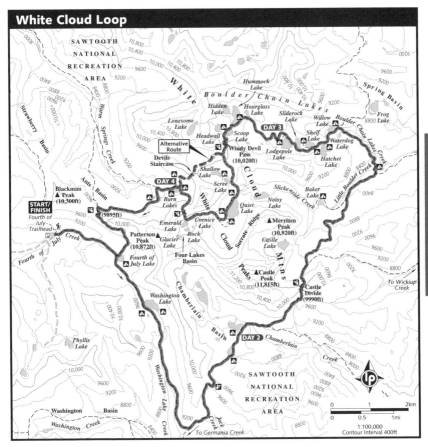

northwest to the tilted slabs on Castle Peak's precipitous 2000ft east face, and the craggy turrets on Serrate Ridge and Merriam Peak.

Switchback down over slopes of fragrant lupines, past a minor turnoff (right) to Wickiup Creek. The trail makes a long winding descent through the forest, past the (unmaintained) turnoff (left) to Baker Lake, where tailings of an old mine are visible on the other side of the valley.

Continue downvalley through narrow meadows, turning left at another trail junction just before you ford the (very little) Little Boulder Creek, 1¼ to 1¾ hours from

Castle Divide. There are several pleasant *campsites* in a grassy clearing on the creek's north bank.

Ascend steeply northwest beside Boulder Chain Lakes Creek, passing the trail (right) to Frog Lake just before you come to **Willow Lake**. This is the lowest of the beautiful Boulder Chain Lakes, most of which have *campsites* hidden around their shores. Climb on to **Hatchet Lake**, crossing and recrossing the tiny creek past **Shelf Lake**, a sparkling green tarn underneath craggy pinnacles, then traverse boulder fields to reach **Sliderock Lake**. The trail skirts the northern side of **Lodgepole Lake**, 1½ to two hours from the Little Boulder Creek ford. The fifth in the 'chain', this deep lake is popular with anglers and has excellent *campsites* on its upper (west) shore. Hikers should not light campfires anywhere in the valley above Lodgepole Lake.

Day 3: Lodgepole Lake to Born Lakes
3¾–5 hours, 7mi, 1822ft ascent
The trail makes a steady ascent through bouldery granite, crossing and recrossing the creek to reach **Hourglass Lake** after 30 to 40 minutes. This small, shallow tarn fringed by whitebark pines is the first of the upper group of Boulder Chain Lakes.

Continue gently up to the larger **Hummock Lake**, with nice *campsites* on the eastern shore. Hidden Lake is just visible on Hummock's far side against talus slopes. A short climb through granite boulders brings you to **Scoop Lake**, sitting on its own little shelf not far below tree line. Continue around the lake's western shore past more *campsites* above a tiny peninsula, then switchback south up through rock rubble to arrive at **Windy Devil** (10,020ft), 40 to 50 minutes from Hourglass Lake. This pass offers fine views of the surrounding peaks and scenery.

Traverse 300yd right (southwest) to the top of a ridge scattered with whitebark pines. (Here more experienced hikers can opt for the Devils Staircase route – see Alternative Route.) A poorly defined trail, marked only by occasional cairns, leads south down open, shallow gullies in the broad ridge. As the gradient steepens, cut right (southwest) to meet a rough social trail on the shore of Scree Lake, 30 to 40 minutes from Windy Devil.

Head steeply down the left side of the lake outlet through a small gap in low cliffs, crossing the tiny stream before you cut easily right (south) over polished rock and open forest to reach Slickenside Creek. A social trail leads upvalley to **Quiet Lake**, skirting around its western side past excellent *campsites* among tall spruce, 30 to 40 minutes from Scree Lake. The aptly named Quiet Lake is a deep, tranquil tarn lying under the towering crags of Serrate Ridge and Castle Peak.

From Quiet Lake's inlet, you can either follow vague walking pads up the splashing creek or shortcut southwest through a little gully to the uppermost meadow. From here climb more steeply out of the trees beside the cascading, mossy stream, which disappears just before you reach the stark, glaciated upper-valley area known as **Four Lakes Basin**. Follow the social trail around Cornice Lake, but as you approach Emerald Lake cut steeply up right (northwest) to the left of a minor spur to reach a flat shelf (10,240ft), one to 1½ hours from Quiet Lake. To the west, the jagged line of the Sawtooth Mountains marks the horizon.

From the middle of this flat area, drop sharply right (northeast) through an eroding rubble field. Stay left as you move back into the forest to arrive at the largest of the **Born Lakes**, 30 to 40 minutes from the shelf. Good *campsites* can be found on its northern shore, or by following the inlet up to the upper Born Lake. These lakes lie on a wide, undulating bench ringed by craggy ridges fringed by scree slides.

Alternative Route: via Devils Staircase
1¾–2¼ hours, 1.6mi, 208ft ascent
This shorter, little-used route to Born Lakes is much more hazardous and misses the scenic Quiet Lake and Four Lakes Basin. From the ridge below Windy Devil, traverse southwest past a tiny tarn (not the same pools visible on Windy Devil's southeast side) across the moraine-filled basin. The route cuts up diagonally left (south) over the slope and makes a final, steep climb 100yd through scree to reach a gap (10,300ft) just north of a sharp rock spire on the narrow ridge top. The route drops down through extremely steep scree slides to the upper Born Lake.

Day 4: Born Lakes to Fourth of July Trailhead
2¼–3 hours, 5.9mi, 340ft ascent
Take the designated trail 10 minutes downvalley beside the tiny Warm Springs Creek (which drains the Born Lakes) past a small, reedy tarn to a (usually dry) shallow sink. Turn left off the main trail and head south

for 150yd to recross the creek between the two lowest lakes, where there are attractive *campsites*. A prominent social trail leads southwest, first down through talus fields and then up onto the high grassy shelf called **Ants Basin**. There are more sheltered *campsites* around here among the spruce and fir. Cut right, across the shelf, passing a little-used trail (right) to Warm Springs Canyon, before you make a steep, diagonal ascent southeast to a **pass** (9895ft), 50 minutes to 1¼ hours from the lower Born Lakes. There are good views northwest to the interesting folded slabs and chalky ridges on Watson Peak (11,314ft) and back northeast over the Born Lakes.

Briefly follow the ridge top, then sidle down along the slope to a tiny undrained tarn. The trail swings southwest past meadows to reach a junction just west of Fourth of July Lake, 30 to 40 minutes from the pass. Retrace your steps for a further 40 to 50 minutes to arrive back at the Fourth of July Trailhead.

Lemhi & Lost River Ranges

Situated within Salmon, Targhee and Challis National Forests, the Lemhi and Lost River Ranges run parallel for 100mi through central Idaho. These are Idaho's highest mountains, with numerous summits over 11,000ft, including Mt Borah (12,662ft) and Leatherman Peak (12,228ft) in the Lost River Range, and Flatiron Mountain (11,019ft) in the Lemhi Range. The remote, twin ranges are demarcated by Lemhi Valley to the east, Pahsimeroi-Little Lost River Valley (which separates them) and Big Lost River Valley to the west.

A French-Canadian fur trapper, Antoine Godin, ventured into the valleys of the Lost River and Lemhi Ranges in the early 1820s, and at one time the Big Lost River was called Godin's River.

NATURAL HISTORY

These two great, faulted ranges rise abruptly from semiarid valleys. The higher Lost River Range somewhat shelters the more easterly Lemhi Range from the harsh dry winds blowing off the volcanic desert of the Columbia Plateau (the upper Snake River basin) to the southwest. This gives the Lemhi Range a slightly moister climate, supporting forest of spruce and fir on its upper slopes. The dusty slopes of the Lost River Range, on the other hand, are more sparsely forested with white-bark pine and Douglas fir, giving way to dry-land shrub on the lower slopes.

PLANNING
Maps
The free USFS 1:8,500,000 *Challis National Forest* map covers most of the Lehmi and Lost River Ranges, and can be picked up at local tourist or USFS offices.

Permits & Regulations
No permits are normally required to climb, camp or light campfires in the Challis and Salmon National Forests of the Lemhi and Lost River Ranges. It's advisable to check the fire-danger rating before leaving, however, as the fire danger is often extreme in summer and campfires may be prohibited.

ACCESS TOWN
See Challis (p131).

Bear Valley Lakes

Duration	4½–6 hours
Distance	10.2mi (16.4km)
Standard	easy–moderate
Start/Finish	Bear Valley Lakes Trailhead
Nearest Town	Salmon
Transport	car

Summary A hike to lovely lake basins in the Lehmi Range.

This hike leads into the upper Bear Valley at the foot of Lem Peak (10,985ft) in the northern Lehmi Range. Proposed for wilderness designation, this pristine and quiet area receives only a modest number of visitors. Elk, mule deer and mountain goats can all sometimes be spotted around the ridges,

CENTRAL IDAHO

and there is good trout fishing in the lakes and streams. The hike follows a national recreation trail open to mountain bikers as well as motorized trail bikes and ATVs, although the volume of wheeled traffic is normally fairly light. The route involves an ascent of 2335ft.

PLANNING
Maps
The USGS 1:24,000 *Lem Peak* quad covers the route, although some trail sections are not up-to-date and the Buck Lakes Trail is not shown at all. The adjoining (west) *Allison Creek* map may be useful for reference.

NEAREST TOWN & FACILITIES
See Salmon (p131).

Bear Valley USFS Campground
This tiny, very basic *campground* (free) is right at the trailhead.

GETTING TO/FROM THE HIKE
Drive 28mi southeast along Hwy 28 from Salmon (or 0.9mi northwest from Lemhi) and turn southwest along Hayden Creek Rd. At the fork just past Hayden Fish Hatchery

(2.4mi from Hwy 28) go left along Hayden Creek Road (FR 08) and continue 5.8mi before turning right (west) along Bear Creek Rd (FR 09). Continue 4.7mi across Bear Creek to the trailhead parking area at the end of the road on the creek's southern bank.

THE HIKE
Sign the trailhead register at the meadow, about 100yd downstream from the campground. Immediately cross the footbridge to the north bank of Bear Valley Creek, then head upvalley over sagebrush slopes past the Basin Creek Trail turnoff (right). Never far above the stream (where sporadic *campsites* can be found), the trail rises at a steady but pleasantly moderate gradient through Douglas fir and lodgepole forest, alive with scrambling squirrels, to meet the Buck Lakes Trail (see Side Trip, p143) turnoff (left) after 1¼ to 1½ hours.

The main trail steepens as it climbs over spring-fed side streams and past the Bear Valley High Trail turnoff (right) to reach a fork after 50 minutes to 1¼ hours from the Buck Lakes Trail junction. Here the Upper Bear Valley Lakes Trail (see Side Trip, p143) goes right.

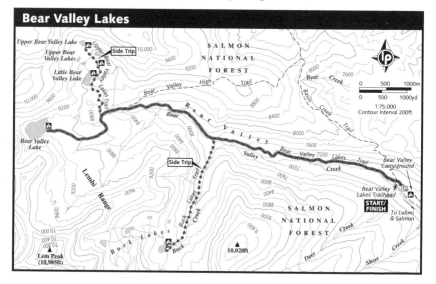

Continue left (south) to recross the creek, sidling briefly before you ascend gently along the right side of a broad ridge. The trail almost levels out as you continue past tiny, boggy meadows among beautiful, open stands of fir and whitebark pine to arrive at **Bear Valley Lake**, 30 to 40 minutes from the fork. This breathtakingly spectacular alpine tarn is embedded in coarse talus and scree fields, enclosed by rough, towering walls. In places, stands of valiant trees are recolonizing the rubble. There are excellent *campsites* in the forest back from the much kinder eastern shore.

Side Trip: Buck Lakes
1½–2 hours, 3.5mi, 809ft ascent
The Buck Lakes Trail cuts quickly down to cross the Bear Valley Creek on a makeshift log bridge (otherwise an easy ford), then makes a steady climb along the west side of Buck Creek. Head up past a talus slide sweeping down the opposite slope, then, just after crossing Buck Creek's west fork, cut away briefly northwest to reach the lowest and largest of the **Buck Lakes**, 45 minutes to one hour from the trail turnoff. This elongated tarn lies in the subalpine forest below craggy ridges and offers good *camping* on its east side. Very rough social trails lead from its northern shore through the forest to the higher Buck Lakes under Lem Peak.

Side Trip: Upper Bear Valley Lakes
1–1¼ hours, 2mi, 580ft ascent
This short route goes up to an attractive, although less spectacular, group of lakes in the upper basin. From the fork with the main trail, climb moderately steeply northwest for 15 to 20 minutes past *campsites* by the pleasant **Little Bear Valley Lake**. The trail climbs gently to the edge of a meadow, then continues up through a narrow open strip beside a tiny brook clustered with yellow arnicas and groundsels to reach **Upper Bear Valley Lake** after another 15 to 20 minutes. This smaller tarn, tucked against the base of a ridge, also has *campsites* on its eastern shore.

Mt Borah

Duration	7–10 hours
Distance	7.2mi (11.6km)
Standard	hard
Start/Finish	Mt Borah Trailhead
Nearest Towns	Arco, Challis, Mackay
Transport	car, bus
Summary	A strenuous climb to a superb lookout peak.

The highest point in Idaho, the 12,662ft Mt Borah (alternatively known as Borah Peak) crowns the Lost River Range. Mt Borah falls away steeply on all four sides (its northern face is cloaked by Idaho's only glacier) but the summit is accessible to fit and agile hikers via its southwest ridge. This climb is not technically difficult, but it does include some challenging rock-hopping (on Chicken-out Ridge) and is very long and fatiguing. The views of the surrounding mountains and valleys make the exertion worthwhile. Mt Borah is named after long-serving Idaho Senator William E Borah.

PLANNING
Maps & Books
The USGS 1:24,000 *Borah Peak* quad covers the described route, although it does not show the trail itself. The USFS brochure, *Climbing Guide – Mount Borah*, is available from the BLM office in Mackay.

Warnings

- There is no water anywhere en route, and each hiker should carry at least two quarts.

- Camping options on the mountain are limited.

- Be alert to the danger of falling rocks, particularly when hikers are on ridges directly above you.

- If you're not acclimated to high altitude, take it easy.

- Hikers making the climb early or late (outside mid-July to mid-September) may need an ice axe and crampons. Watch the weather.

NEAREST TOWNS & FACILITIES

See Challis (p131).

Arco

Best known as the world's first town to be powered by nuclear energy, Arco is on US 20/26 at the intersection with US 93. *DK Motel* (☎ *208-527-8282, 800-231-0134)* and *Arco Inn* (☎ *208-527-3100)* have rooms from around $32/38 single/double.

CART (☎ 208-527-9944, 800-258-4937) runs buses east to Idaho Falls, and north to Salmon via Mackay and Challis.

Mackay

Midway between Arco and Challis on US 93 (27mi in each direction) is Mackay. The USFS Lost River Ranger District (☎ 208-588-2224, 716 W Custer St) sells USGS 1:24,000 quads.

The municipal *Tourist Park*, on the northwest side of town by the Mackay River, has free camping with tables, toilets and drinking water (no showers). The *Wagon Wheel Motel & RV Park* (☎ *208-588-3331, 809 W Custer St)* has singles/doubles from $33/43 and RV sites for around $12.

CART (☎ 208-756-2191, 800-258-4937) operates twice-daily buses on Tuesday and Friday to/from Salmon and Idaho Falls (both around $15 one-way).

USFS Campgrounds

Mt Borah Trailhead USFS campground has four sites among the scrub ($5 each); this tiny campground is popular and often full. There are a number of other BLM and USFS campgrounds in the area, including *Ironbog*, *Mill Creek*, *Park Creek*, *Phi Kappa*, *Starhope*, *Timber Creek* and *Wildhorse* (sites $5).

GETTING TO/FROM THE HIKE

Drive 22mi north from Mackay or 32mi south from Challis on US 93, then turn northeast and follow the dirt road 2.5mi to the Mt Borah Trailhead. There is space for around 25 vehicles. Hikers may also be able to arrange to be dropped off at the trailhead turnoff by the regional CART (☎ 208-756-2191, 800-258-4937) bus service.

The 1983 Earthquake

Hikers approaching the Mt Borah Trailhead may notice what looks like an old road running across the slope at the base of the Lost River Range. This is actually the fault line of the October 1983 earthquake, which extends for more than 20mi along the edge of the Lost River Valley. This earthquake, which measured 7.3 on the Richter scale, tilted the range upward by about 1ft and pushed down the valley by as much as 9ft. The sudden shift in pressure forced billions of gallons of groundwater to gush out in countless (mostly short-lived) springs. The quake caused major infrastructure damage and two deaths in the area, but it was typical of the destructive-formative earth movements that over the past few million years have shaped the Lost River Range into the highest section of the northern US Rockies.

It's worth stopping at the nearby Earthquake Interpretation Site (turn off 2mi north of the Mt Borah Trailhead access road).

THE HIKE

Head up east through the trailhead gate into scrub of spiky mountain mahogany and the occasional pinyon pine or juniper. The trail climbs right (south) of a dry stream gully, crossing it to reach a minor saddle on a forested spur (where there are a few dry *campsites*), 50 minutes to 1¼ hours from the trailhead.

Follow the eroding spur east, climbing steeply through gnarled old whitebark pine and Douglas fir with thick corky bark to reach tree line, 50 minutes to 1¼ hours from the spur. From this point you get the first clear views over the broad dry valley dotted with large green irrigated circles. More dry *campsites* can be found on tiny leveled areas among the stunted trees a short way over to the right.

Ascend steeply southeast to attain Mt Borah's long southwestern ridge, the edge of which plummets into a deep ravine under the mountain's mighty west wall. The gradient eases slightly as the trail traces the ridge top scattered sparsely with snow cinquefoils,

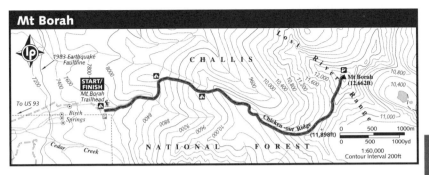

mountain avens and tiny dwarf willows to the start of the narrow, craggy section known as Chicken-out Ridge, 50 minutes to 1¼ hours from tree line. There are already great views from here, and some hikers decide not to proceed any further.

Scramble over the rough rock for about 400ft (you will have to use your hands continually), then cut down left and skirt below the ridge top through a snowy couloir. (Note there is some danger of rockfall on the latter section, especially if other hikers are above you.) The route immediately cuts back left and traverses below point 11,898ft into a high, usually heavily corniced saddle at around 11,780ft. A small tarn comes into view down in the moraine gully to the southeast.

Cut left again, then sidle up north past ancient seashell fossils. The route picks its way up through the boulders and loose rock of the upper west face to arrive at the top of **Mt Borah** (12,662ft), 1¼ to 1¾ hours from the start of Chicken-out Ridge.

There is a USGS survey marker and a steel box (which *may* contain a log book) on the tiny summit area. From here you get a spectacular panorama that includes the Salmon River Mountains to the north, the Lemhi Range to the east, the Boulder, Sawtooth and White Cloud Mountains to the west, and the Pioneer and White Knob Mountains to the southeast. Leatherman Peak (Idaho's second-highest summit) stands nearby to the southeast.

Return to the trailhead by retracing the route of ascent.

Other Hikes

SALMON RIVER MOUNTAINS
Soldier Lakes
The Soldier Lakes lie at around 7000ft near the southern boundary of the Frank Church River of No Return Wilderness. This small group of sub-alpine tarns offers excellent fishing, and can be easily visited in four to five hours (6mi) round-trip from Josephus Lake. The route leads southwest via Soldier Creek Pass (8088ft). A worthwhile 3mi extension to the hike can be made to the nearby Cutthroat Lakes.

The USGS 1:24,000 *Soldier Creek* quad covers the route; the adjoining 1:24,000 quad, *Big Soldier Mountain*, is useful for the Cutthroat Lakes hike. To reach the trailhead, drive 19mi northwest from Stanley on Hwy 21, then turn right (north) and continue for another 21mi, via Vanity Summit, to Josephus Lake.

PIONEER MOUNTAINS
Hyndman Valley
The beautiful Hyndman Valley is the most popular hiking area in the Pioneer Mountains, a high range northeast of Ketchum. Two excellent out-and-back routes exist from the Hyndman Creek Trailhead, each offering views of Hyndman Peak (12,009ft), the Pioneer Mountains' highest summit, at the valley head. A five-hour (9mi) round-trip hike follows Trail 166 northeast up the main branch of Hyndman Creek to the base of Cobb Peak (11,650ft). A seven-hour (8mi) round-trip hike goes up the North Fork Hyndman Creek to scenic Hyndman Lake (8640ft).

USGS's 1:24,000 *Hyndman Peak* quad covers both routes. To reach the trailhead, turn off Hwy 75 5.7mi south of Ketchum. Drive 6mi up the East Fork Wood River Rd, then turn left along Hyndman Creek Rd and continue for 4mi. An SNRA trailhead parking pass is required.

CENTRAL IDAHO

Southwest Montana

Occupying the area between Greater Glacier and Greater Yellowstone, the less-visited southwest corner of Montana makes a surprisingly exciting destination for hikers. This region is largely defined by the rugged Bitterroot Mountains, a long, winding arc of peaks topping 10,000ft that stretches along the Idaho and Montana border, although the mountains to their east (the Anaconda Range and the Pioneer Mountains) reach comparable or greater heights. Almost half of southwest Montana lies within the Bitterroot, Deerlodge and Beaverhead National Forests, which include large areas of (all-too-often undesignated) wilderness offering superb scenery and marvelous hiking opportunities. An almost-300mi section of the great Continental Divide Trail leads through the Anacondas and along the crest of the southern Bitterroots, providing access to some of Montana's most remote and pristine places.

CLIMATE

In the valleys of southwest Montana, summer daytime temperatures average 70° to 85°F, dropping to 40° to 50°F overnight. At higher elevations temperatures may be more than 25°F lower, and frosty nights or even snowfalls are possible at any time of year. June tends to be fairly moist, but July and August are typically dry and warm, with extended periods of little or no rainfall. Precipitation in many valleys averages little more than one inch per month. Thunderstorms are frequent in the mountains through July and August. Snow usually starts to accumulate from late October and may last until July at higher elevations. Snowpack levels on the Bitterroots' eastern slopes can reach more than 10ft but the ranges to the east receive lighter falls.

INFORMATION
Maps & Books

Most of this region is covered by the USFS 1:126,720 *Southwest Montana* map, published in separate east and west sections ($6 each). Also available is GTR Mapping's

Highlights

The Bitterroots distinctive crown, Trapper Peak, can be reached in a long day hike.

- Strolling under majestic ponderosa pines in the sheer-sided Blodgett Canyon (p149)

- Sitting atop the lofty summit of Trapper Peak (p151) among endless rows of rugged ranges

- Reeling in 14-inch native cutthroat trout in the wild lakes of the Anaconda-Pintler Wilderness (p152)

- Admiring twilight on the spectacular slab ridges above Torrey Lake (p157)

1:800,000 *Recreational Map of Western Montana* ($3.95), which covers all of Greater Glacier and Southwest Montana.

Falcon Guides' *Hiking Montana* by Bill & Russ Schneider ($15.95) describes hikes throughout the state.

Information Sources

Contact Travel Montana (☎ 406-444-2654, 800-847-4868; Ⓦ www.visitmt.com; 1424

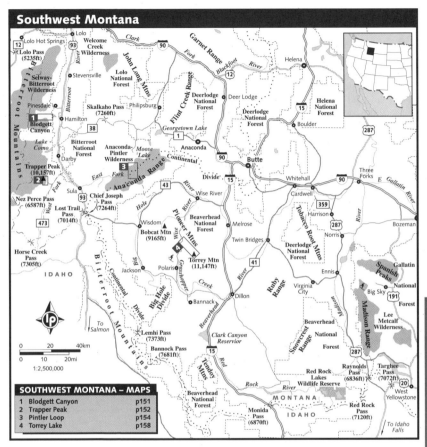

Southwest Montana

SOUTHWEST MONTANA – MAPS

1	Blodgett Canyon	p151
2	Trapper Peak	p152
3	Pintler Loop	p154
4	Torrey Lake	p158

SOUTHWEST MONTANA

9th Ave, PO Box 200533, Helena, MT 59620) for state-wide information. General tourist information for Montana is available at W www.discoveringmontana.com.

GATEWAY
Butte

The old mining town of Butte (population 35,000) is clustered around the intersection of I-90 and I-15. For information contact the visitor center (☎ 406-723-3177, 1000 George St). Pipestone Mountaineering (☎ 406-782-4994, 829 S Montana St) sells hiking gear and USGS quads.

Places to Stay The *Butte KOA* (☎ 406-782-0663), one block north and one block east of I-90 exit 126, charges $18/23 for tent/RV sites. The *Capri Motel* (☎ 406-723-4391, 220 N Wyoming St) has rooms from $36. The *Historic Finlen Hotel* (☎ 406-723-5461, 100 E Broadway) charges $50/55 singles/doubles.

Places to Stay Greyhound and Rimrock Bus, which both use Butte's Greyhound depot (☎ 406-723-3287, 101 E Front St), have daily runs to Dillon, Missoula, Helena, Bozeman and Billings.

Bitterroot Mountains

The Bitterroot Mountains extend more than 300mi from the Clark Fork River, in the northern Idaho panhandle, southeast as far as the Yellowstone country. Their watershed forms most of the Idaho-Montana border, as well as a lengthy portion of the Continental Divide itself. The central Bitterroots – a rugged section between Lolo Pass (on US 12) and Lost Trail Pass (on US 93) – are the highest and wildest in the range. They lie inside Selway-Bitterroot Wilderness, an enormous (2031-sq-mile) expanse of wildland stretching deep into Idaho. The central Bitterroots are most easily accessed from the Montana side. They are typified by long, deep glacial canyons splayed eastward from jagged peaks and high cirques to meet the broad Bitterroot Valley.

HISTORY

The Bitterroot Valley was the ancestral home of the Salish (Flathead) people, who hunted bison, fished salmon and harvested bitterroot (see the boxed text). In 1805 the Lewis and Clark Expedition (see the boxed text, p16) journeyed through the valley and across the Bitterroot Mountains. The first Euro-American trappers ventured into the Bitterroot Valley in the early 1820s.

In 1841 Father Pierre Jean De Smet established a mission at Stevensville, which John Owen, a trader with the US Army, bought in 1850 and turned into a thriving trading post. In 1877, after fleeing east via the Lolo Trail through the Bitterroots, the nontreaty Nez Perce people fought running battles with the US Army in the Bitterroot Valley. Despite earlier promises to recognize the Salish people's claims to the Bitterroot Valley, by 1891 pressure from settlers finally persuaded the US government to relocate all Salish to the Flathead Reservation (near the Mission Mountains).

Congress established the first Bitter Root Forest Reserve in 1897, out of which Selway-Bitterroot Wilderness was created in 1964. In the 1930s the Citizen's Conservation Corp (CCC) built dozens of small dams and canals in the mountains for irrigation to the Bitterroot Valley, cutting many access trails into the high valleys that now serve as hiking routes.

During the summer of 2000, wildfires burned vast tracts of the central Bitterroots and surrounding ranges. While the flames spared some of the Bitterroots best hiking routes, many trails were devastated and will probably require a generation or so to fully recover.

NATURAL HISTORY

The forests of the Bitterroots are the richest in southwest Montana. The foothills are fringed by sagebrush, juniper and paintbrush, broken in places by graceful stands of ponderosa pine that quickly give way to lodgepole forest. The higher ranges receive more moisture, encouraging stands of Douglas fir mixed with pockets of alder, birch and mountain hemlock. The highest subalpine forests are dominated by Engelmann spruce and subalpine fir, while whitebark pine, subalpine larch and western larch often form the uppermost tree line.

The Bitterroot Plant

The Bitterroot Mountains get their name from the bitterroot plant, a ground-hugging perennial that produces bright yellowish-pink flowers from late April to early June. Montana's state flower, the bitterroot takes its scientific name *(Lewisia)* from the explorer Captain Meriwether Lewis – the first Euro-American to collect a specimen. The astringent tubers of the bitterroot were a staple food of the Salish people. Each spring, near today's Missoula, they hosted a large bitterroot harvest festival attended by the neighboring Kalispell, Kootenai, Nez Perce, Pend d'Oreille and Spokane tribes. This important regional gathering served to renew alliances and celebrate the passing of winter (although raids by hostile Blackfoot warriors were a constant threat). Early Euro-American settlers also had a fondness for bitterroot but it is now seldom eaten.

Large mammals, such as mule deer, white-tailed deer, elk, bighorn sheep, mountain goats, cougars (mountain lions), moose and black bears, are all fairly common in the Bitterroots, but plans to reintroduce grizzly bears (which became locally extinct in the 1950s) have been postponed indefinitely due to fierce local opposition.

PLANNING
Maps & Books

The USFS uncontoured 1:126,720 *Bitterroot National Forest* map, available in paper ($4) and plastic ($7), gives a good overview of the Bitterroots.

Hiking in the Bitterroots by Mort Arkava ($12.95) describes more than 40 hikes in Selway-Bitterroot Wilderness accessible from Bitterroot Valley. Falcon Guides' *Hiking the Selway-Bitterroot Wilderness* by Scott Steinberg ($18.95) concentrates on the Montana Bitterroots, but also features many routes on the Idaho side of the range.

Information Sources

For online information about the Bitterroots, visit the USFS website at W www.fs.fed .us/r1/bitterroot.

Permits & Regulations

No permits are required to hike in either Bitterroot National Forest or Selway-Bitterroot Wilderness. As many of the Bitterroots' canyons are heavily impacted by a large number of visitors, hikers should strictly adhere to the Leave No Trace principles (p56). At popular Lake Como there is a day-use and parking fee ($2 per vehicle).

Due to an increase in mushroom-picking in the wake of the 2000 fires, a permit (issued free at local USFS offices) is currently required to remove wild fungi from Bitterroot National Forest.

ACCESS TOWN
Hamilton

Located on US 93, about 50mi south of Missoula, this rapidly growing town is the main center of the Bitterroot Valley. The Bitterroot Chamber of Commerce (☎ 406-363-2400, W www.bvchamber.com, 105 E Main

St) gives tourist advice. The USFS regional office (☎ 406-363-7161, 1891 N First St), on the north edge of town, sells only USFS maps. USGS quads ($4) and other topographic maps are available at The Paper Clip (☎ 406-363-5480, 228 W Main St). Bob Ward & Sons (☎ 406-363-6204, 1120 N 1st St) sells outdoor and fishing supplies.

Deffy's Motel (☎ *406-363-1244, 321 S 1st St*) and *City Center Motel* (☎ *406-363-1651, 415 W Main St*) have singles/doubles from around $35/40.

Valley Taxi (☎ 406-961-4400) can shuttle hikers to trailheads ($1 per mile). CART (☎ 800-258-4937) runs buses several times each week to/from Missoula ($7) and Salmon ($13); the latter connects to another CART service to Idaho Falls.

Blodgett Canyon

Duration	5½–7 hours
Distance	12.6mi (20.3km)
Standard	easy–moderate
Start/Finish	Blodgett Canyon USFS campground
Nearest Town	Hamilton
Transport	car
Summary	Hike into a spectacular, sheer-sided canyon with impressive rock formations.

One of the Rocky Mountains' best examples of a deep, heavily glaciated valley, Blodgett Canyon lies between the towering granite walls of the Printz and Romney Ridges. This majestic area is frequented by mountain goats and moose, while prairie falcons and golden eagles build their nests on ledges along the canyon's high ramparts. The fires of summer 2000, which devastated much of the forest in surrounding valleys, caused only minor damage in the canyon.

Although a long trail leads through Blodgett Canyon into the remote heart of Selway-Bitterroot Wilderness, most people visit the canyon's more accessible lower section (excluded from the wilderness because a dam was once planned for the lower valley) as a day hike. The described route (as far as the High Lake trail junction) involves an ascent of 1200ft. For hikers inclined to continue, the trail leads on another 5.5mi up through the canyon (past the turnoff to Blodgett Pass) to Blodgett Lake.

PLANNING
When to Hike
Due to its relatively low elevation, the hike can be undertaken early or late in the season (usually at least from late May to late October).

Maps
Two 1:24,000 USGS quads, *Hamilton North* and *Printz Ridge*, cover the hike; if you continue into the upper canyon you will also need the *Blodgett Mountain* map.

NEAREST TOWN & FACILITIES
See Hamilton (p149).

Blodgett Canyon USFS Campground
This basic *campground* is on the north bank of Blodgett Creek, 150yd past the trailhead at the end of the road; it has six free sites and a five-day limit applies.

GETTING TO/FROM THE HIKE
From the center of Hamilton drive 2mi north along US 93, then (just after the bridge) turn left (west). Proceed 0.9mi along Bowman Rd before turning left (south) along Ricketts Rd for 2mi through a four-way intersection into Blodgett Camp Rd. This road leads 3.8mi (past the left turnoff to Blodgett Overlook) to the terminus at Blodgett Canyon USFS campground, where there is space for about 12 vehicles. The trailhead itself is about 120yd back across the bridge.

THE HIKE
Head up through the forest for five minutes, past the **Don Mackey Memorial**. This bronze statue is dedicated to a local 'smoke jumper' who died in 1994, along with 13 other firefighters, on Colorado's Storm King Mountain. Most of the Douglas fir and ponderosa pine around here were blackened and singed by the fires of 2000, although the flames killed relatively few of these thick-barked trees.

The trail leads on through more severely burned stands of fir and western red cedar, past *campsites* near anglers' pools in Blodgett Creek, then cuts across the base of a boulder field kept tree-free by avalanches. From here you get spectacular views of the sheer-sided, 600ft bluffs, crowned by craggy rock columns, fronting Blodgett Canyon's northern rim. The trail proceeds over largely open slopes, colonized by wild raspberries and other shrubs, to cross the creek on a wooden footbridge, 1¼ to 1½ hours from the trailhead. Up to your left (southwest), on a sharp ridge top, stands a natural, angular 'hole' in the rock, which is known as Gothic Arch.

Continue upvalley past *campsites* and old beaver dams, through meadows sprinkled with pearly everlastings. The trail climbs past a series of cascades into fir-spruce forest, cutting through a narrow, open avalanche chute (where you get more good views of craggy spires and impressive rock walls on both sides) shortly before it reaches the High Lake turnoff (left), 1¾ to 2¼ from the footbridge. This junction (around 5455ft) is about 6mi from the trailhead and there are *campsites* nearby.

Return to the start by retracing your steps.

Side Trip: High Lake
3¼–4 hours, 4.8mi, 1930ft ascent
This strenuous side trip follows a lightly trodden and not-always-well-marked trail. Ford two pebbly channels of the small Blodgett Creek, then begin a steep climb south along the eastern side of the gushing lake outlet. The gradient eases as you pass craggy spires on the ridge up to your left. The trail now cuts left (northeast), below broken boulders and scree, before ascending steeply right (southeast) to make a long, high traverse along the base of the cliffs. From here there are fine views back across Blodgett Canyon to Printz Ridge.

The trail becomes less distinct as you reach scattered stands of subalpine larch. Ignoring a rougher route that breaks away

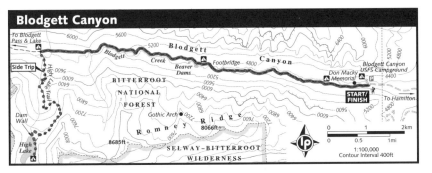

Blodgett Canyon

left over the ridge, continue right (north-west) and skirt slightly down to the old dam wall of **High Lake**, 1¾ to 2¼ hours from the junction. This melancholic tarn lies in a deep glacial basin under the 9153ft Canyon Peak. Fair *camping* exists around the shore.

Trapper Peak

Duration	4¼–5½ hours
Distance	12mi (19.3km)
Standard	hard
Start/Finish	Trapper Peak Trailhead
Nearest Town	Darby
Transport	car

Summary A steady ascent to a the superb, lookout summit of Trapper Peak.

At 10,157ft, Trapper Peak is the highest summit (and the only peak above 10,000ft) in both the Bitterroots and Selway-Bitterroot Wilderness. When viewed from the east, Trapper Peak presents a strikingly sharp, horn-like outline, but it can be climbed via a nontechnical route involving a 3807ft ascent and requiring good physical condition.

Trapper Peak was named in the 1870s by a local prospector (evidently more impressed by the area's wealth of furry animals than its mineral deposits).

Mountain goats and bighorn sheep sometimes visit its higher slopes, where uncommon wildflowers, such as purple fleabane and pink Parry primroses, shelter among the rocks.

PLANNING
When to Hike
The trail is generally passable from early July, although upper sections may sometimes remain snowed-over until early August.

Maps
Two USGS 1:24,000 quads cover the route: *Boulder Peak* and *Trapper Peak*; an adjoining map, *Piquet Creek*, shows the trailhead access road but is not really necessary.

Information Sources
For information and USFS maps, West Fork Ranger Station (☎ 406-821-8269, 6735 West Fork Rd) is several miles north of the Trapper Peak Trailhead turnoff and Sula Ranger Station (☎ 406-821-3201, US 93) is about 18mi south of Darby.

NEAREST TOWN & FACILITIES
Darby
Darby is a small town about 17mi south of Hamilton on US 93. USFS' Darby Ranger Station (☎ 406-821-3913, 712 N Main St) is helpful but sells only USFS maps. *Wilderness Motel (☎ 406-821-3405, Main St)*, south end of town, has tent/RV sites from $7/18 and singles/doubles from $35/45. CART (☎ 800-258-4937) buses pass through Darby.

USFS Campgrounds
There are several basic USFS campgrounds accessible from West Fork Rd (CR 473), including the free *Sam Billings Memorial campground*, several miles southwest of the Trapper Peak Trailhead turnoff.

GETTING TO/FROM THE HIKE

Drive 4.7mi south from Darby on US 93 and then turn right (southwest), following West Fork Rd (CR 473) for 11.5mi before taking the turnoff (right), signposted to 'Trapper Peak Trailhead'. Bear left at a fork 1mi on and follow the rough, winding FR 5630-A for 4mi up to the few roadside parking spaces beside Trapper Peak Trailhead. Park wisely here to avoid blocking the road.

THE HIKE

The ascent begins immediately, as the trail cuts up steeply through lodgepole pine and Douglas fir, carpeted with low grouseberries and juniper, to gain Trapper Peak's long southeast ridge. There are some first fine views west into the wild, U-shaped valley of Boulder Creek, where Boulder Falls spouts over a precipice. The trail climbs steadily northwest, steepening as it rises through sporadic meadows fringed by subalpine fir and Engelmann spruce. Proceed up the broadening ridge through stands of gnarled whitebark pine, which finally give way to battered, subalpine larch at tree line (around 9000ft). Follow cairns northwest over rocky tundra and occasional large snowdrifts to reach a broad, sparse saddle, 1¾ to 2¼ hours from the trailhead.

Only a rough route continues west along the crest of the bare ridge top, where delicate alpine wildflowers shelter in rock crevices. Scramble over reddish granite boulders, up past a minor outcrop, then cut through a tiny, grassy gap to arrive at the 10,157ft summit of **Trapper Peak**, 30 to 45 minutes from the saddle. The glorious panorama encompasses seemingly endless rows of craggy ranges. Prominent peaks include the unique, long and narrow ridge of El Capitan to the northwest, and the closer Boulder Point (7753ft), crowned by a USFS fire-lookout tower, a few degrees east of due south. Trapper Peak's sharply tilted north face plummets through moraine-filled cirques into the canyon-like valley of Trapper Creek 4000ft below – Cave Lake sits perched about halfway down the mountain. Proud summiteers can sign the logbook (protected in a metal box) before returning via the ascent route.

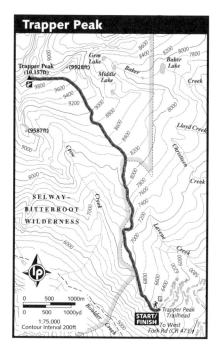

Anaconda-Pintler Wilderness

The 248-sq-mile Anaconda-Pintler Wilderness is within the (jointly administered) Deerlodge and Beaverhead National Forests. The wilderness takes in most of the Anaconda Range, a 45mi-long mountain chain on the Continental Divide, bordered by the basins of Big Hole River (south), Bitterroot Valley (west) and Clark Fork River (east). Although some craggy peaks rise from its forested slopes to above 10,000ft, the range is characterized by a relatively mellow topography. Many lovely tarns lie in isolated cirques.

HISTORY

The Salish people would move up from Bitterroot Valley in early summer to gather camas bulbs in the Anaconda Range and Big Hole Valley, which they knew as the 'Land of the Big Snows'. From the 1840s hunters and trappers were active in the area. Beginning in the late 1800s Charles Ellsworth Pintler, a homesteader in the Big Hole Valley, explored large parts of the Anacondas. (An early USFS cartographer misspelled his name as 'Pintlar' but the USFS finally corrected this in the late 1970s at the urging of Pintler's descendants.) Extraordinary copper riches around the town of Anaconda attracted many prospectors from the 1880s, although only the northern end of the Anaconda Range – outside today's wilderness and national forest – was heavily mined.

From 1887 the reclusive Martin Johnson lived more than five decades in the Anacondas, hunting, trapping and capturing wild animals for zoos, until a fatal fall. Johnson guided early tourists into the backcountry and single-handedly built a network of mountain trails; like Pintler, he is honored in the local nomenclature (eg, Johnson Lake). The first Anaconda-Pintler Primitive Area was set aside in 1937, and became part of the new National Wilderness System in 1964.

NATURAL HISTORY

The Anacondas are largely composed of Idaho batholith – the easternmost extension of this granitic rock type. The range is an important habitat for black bears, cougars, elk, mountain goats, moose, white-tailed deer and wolverines, as well as many smaller mammals and birds. Forest types are fairly typical for the northern US Rockies. Lodgepole pine is the dominant tree species at lower elevations, but gives way to dense forest of Engelmann spruce and subalpine fir above 7000ft. Stands of whitebark pine with pockets of larch are found at tree line. The Bitterroot Valley fires of summer 2000 ravaged southwestern Anaconda-Pintler Wilderness, but most other areas were untouched.

PLANNING
Maps & Books

USFS's 1:50,000 *Anaconda-Pintler Wilderness* map ($7) covers the whole wilderness at a scale suitable for navigation. The USFS 1:126,720 *Deerlodge National Forest* map ($6) is good for a regional overview.

Hiking the Anaconda-Pintler Wilderness by Mort Arkava ($14.95) describes 48 routes in the Anacondas.

Information Sources

For online information about the Deerlodge and Beaverhead National Forests, visit the USFS website at W www.fs.fed.us/r1/b-d.

Permits & Regulations

Permits are not required for Anaconda-Pintler Wilderness, but hikers should fill out a visitor registration card (available at major trailheads). Camping is not permitted within 200ft of lakes and water courses – this is especially important at places such as Johnson Lake, which is showing signs of heavy impact.

ACCESS TOWN
Anaconda

The famed but rather unsightly former mining town of Anaconda (population 9721) is on Hwy 1, 9mi west of I-90. There is a visitor center (☎ 406-563-2400, Cherry St), but nowhere to buy USGS maps or hiking supplies. *Rainbow Sporting Goods* (☎ 406-563-5080, 605 E Park Ave) sells fishing gear. The *Marcus Daly Motel* (☎ 406-563-3411, 119 W Park St) charges around $45/58 for singles/doubles.

Pintler Loop

Duration	3 days
Distance	25.5mi (41km)
Standard	moderate
Start/Finish	Middle Fork Trailhead
Nearest Town	Anaconda
Transport	car

Summary A lake-to-lake trip that crosses passes on the Continental Divide and circumnavigates the Pintler Peaks in the heart of the wilderness.

Despite its length and several up-and-down sections, this lollipop loop leads through gently contoured terrain. The central section was burned in summer 2000 and now serves as an educational example of the results of forest fire. The deeper lakes along the hike generally offer good fishing for cutthroat (and other) trout. The route includes a 7mi stretch on the classic Continental Divide Trail (CDT). Giardia is prevalent in the wilderness – all water should be treated before being consumed.

PLANNING
When to Hike
The route is normally passable from early July until late September.

Maps
Use either USGS 1:24,000 quads, *Kelly Lake* and *Warren Peak*, or the USFS 1:50,000 *Anaconda-Pintler Wilderness* map.

NEAREST TOWN & FACILITIES
See Anaconda (p53).

USFS Campgrounds
Basic *Copper Creek*, accessible via Frog Pond Rd (go right at the fork 9.9mi off CR 38), is free of charge. There are other USFS campgrounds along Hwy 1 and CR 38.

GETTING TO/FROM THE HIKE
From Anaconda drive 23mi west on Hwy 1 (Pintler Scenic Hwy) past Georgetown Lake, then take CR 38 (Skalkaho Pass Rd) south-west for 10mi before turning left (south) on Moose Creek Rd (FR 80). After 9.9mi bear left at a fork on FR 5106 (signposted 'Moose Lake') and continue 5.1mi to the large parking loop at Middle Fork Trailhead.

From Hamilton (p149), turn left (east) off US 93 about 2mi south of town, then drive 42mi along CR 38 before turning right into Moose Creek Rd.

THE HIKE
Day 1: Middle Fork Trailhead to Kelly Lake
3–4 hours, 6.1mi, 1990ft ascent

Take the Middle Fork Trail (No 28) from the south end of the car park (not Trail 29 from its east side) and walk through low lodgepole pine to cross the Middle Fork Rock Creek on a footbridge. The trail soon crosses the wilderness boundary and begins

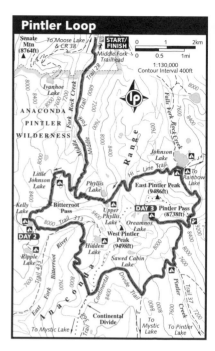

a gentle but steady climb along the east side of the creek through fir-spruce forest to a junction at the edge of a meadow cleared by avalanches, 1¾ to 2¼ hours from the trailhead. From here the Hi-Line Trail (No 111) goes left to the Phyllis Lakes.

Follow Trail 28 right (west) and wind your way up past the shallow, weedy **Little Johnson Lake**, 30 to 45 minutes from the junction; there are *campsites* on a tiny shelf above its east side. Trail 28 ascends south through whitebark pine to **Bitterroot Pass** (8400ft), then drops past the little-used Copper Creek Trail (No 313) to end at **Kelly Lake**, 40 to 50 minutes from Little Johnson Lake. Ideal *campsites* can be found in the forest back from the grassy shore of this attractive tarn.

Day 2: Kelly Lake to Oreamnos Lake
3¾–5 hours, 8.6mi, 1843ft ascent

Take Trail 313 and head down southeast through a beargrass meadow, past a turnoff (right) to Ripple Lake (a lovely tarn with good *camping* and fishing). Continue east down into the charred, dead trees of the upper valley of the East Fork Bitterroot River, which was devastated by the fires of 2000, past Trail 433 (going down the East Fork) to reach a turnoff (left) at around 7730ft. This side trail leads up steeply to the picturesque Hidden Lake in a craggy cirque; its shore escaped significant fire damage and offers excellent *camping* and fair fishing.

Continue above the blackened valley, then switchback up to follow a broad ridge southeast before intersecting with the **Continental Divide Trail** (see the boxed text 'National Scenic Trails', p53), 1½ to two hours from Kelly Lake. Go left along the CDT (No 9) and sidle northeast out of the scorched trees. The CDT heads gradually southeast to pick up a ridge leading down to a trail junction in a saddle, where Trail 368 diverges right to Mystic Lake. Continue along the CDT, cutting down northeast to reach Pintler Creek, 1½ to two hours after joining the CDT. There is pleasant *camping* here on grassy flats among the fir-spruce forest, although insects can be bothersome.

Continue on the CDT (ignoring Trail 37 leading downvalley to Pintler Lake) across the tiny creek, then climb north for 30 to 40 minutes to meet a (probably unsignposted) side trail on the left. Follow this 0.8mi west, over a grassy shelf strewn with pink-yellow asters, to arrive at **Oreamnos Lake** after 15 to 20 minutes. This delightful, subalpine tarn nestles in a hollow between East Pintler Peak (9486ft) and West Pintler Peak (9498ft) – the latter's northeast face eroded into coarse scree slopes. *Campsites* can be found back from the shore across the outlet.

Day 3: Oreamnos Lake to Middle Fork Trailhead

4¾–6¼ hours, 10.8mi, 1283ft ascent

Retrace your steps to the CDT and follow it east and then north, climbing several switchbacks to reach **Pintler Pass** (8738ft). This pass, on the Continental Divide, brings a fresh view down the upper Falls Fork Rock Creek to Johnson Lake (visible only from the south side of the pass). Drop through stands

of subalpine larch and moist slopes of yellow groundsels, skirting the tiny valley's eastern slopes, to meet the Hi-Line Trail (No 111) on the southern shore of **Johnson Lake**, a beautiful, large tarn, 1¼ to 1¾ hours from Oreamnos Lake. The fires of 2000 hit the lake's northern edge, although the area was otherwise unaffected. There are many wonderful *campsites* but, as the area is already heavily impacted, camp on the *uphill* side of trails.

Leave the CDT and follow Trail 111 left (west) to Johnson Lake's southwest corner. Passing Trail 29 (leading down the Falls Fork Rock Creek) climb steeply west over a bouldery crest, giving a good view across the lake to McGlaughlin Peak (9487ft). Trail 111 makes a winding traverse up southwest onto a minor saddle (8540ft), overlooking the wild, forested basin of the Phyllis Lakes, before it cuts down southwest to reach **Upper Phyllis Lake**. This small tarn lies among talus fields and high craggy cliffs, 1½ to two hours from Johnson Lake. There are fair *campsites* back from the east shore. Continue up west across another small saddle (around 8260ft), then drop in switchbacks through the forest to rejoin Trail 28 in the avalanche meadow, 45 minutes to one hour from Upper Phyllis Lake. Return to the Middle Fork Trailhead, as described on Day 1 (1¼ to 1½ hours).

Pioneer Mountains

The highest range in southwest Montana, the Pioneer Mountains take in an area of roughly 780 sq miles within the Beaverhead National Forest. Surrounded by the Big Hole River on three sides, the Pioneers are divided into two distinct ranges by the Wise River and Grasshopper Creek drainages. The eastern Pioneers rise to more than 11,000ft, while the western range is much lower with a gentler topography. The narrow, 49mi Pioneer Mountains Scenic Byway runs through the valleys. Parts of the Pioneers have been proposed for inclusion in the National Wilderness System but, as national forest lands, the area has only minimal level protection. Many trails are open to motorbikes and ATVs, and in certain areas cattle are grazed in July and August.

HISTORY

Native American peoples, including the Salish to the west and the Shoshone to the south, regularly visited the Pioneers, bathing in the hot springs or harvesting the sweet bulbs of the blue camas. Journeying up the Beaverhead River in August 1805, Lewis and Clark passed the Pioneers and members of their expedition were probably the first Euro-Americans to see the mountains.

In 1873 silver was discovered at Elkhorn Creek in the eastern Pioneers, and a bustling town (Coolidge) developed at the mine site. A huge processing mill and a narrow gauge railroad linking Coolidge with the main Utah & Northern Railroad (via Wise River and Divide) were later constructed. In 1927 the Pattengail (Pettengill) Creek dam in the western Pioneers collapsed, damaging the railroad and scouring the Wise River (the river's ecology still hasn't fully recovered).

With the mine's closure in the 1930s, Coolidge was abandoned and today only curious tourists on the Scenic Byway visit this unrestored ghost town (4mi on from the Mono Creek Trailhead at the start of the Torrey Lake hike). Since the 1970s a modest ski resort has been developed on Maverick Mountain at the south end of the Pioneers.

NATURAL HISTORY

The eastern Pioneers largely consist of a granitic rock called Pioneer batholith, believed to have formed 68 million years ago as molten intrusions pushed upward. Superheated water percolated in the rock and, as the batholith cooled and solidified, quartz and pyrite was gradually deposited on the sides of rock fissures to form crystals, such as amethyst. Today novice rock hounds can dig their own crystals (free) at Crystal Park, on the Scenic Byway about 5mi south of the Coolidge turnoff. The hard batholith was chiseled and shaped by glaciers to create the many dramatic cirques and alpine tarns seen today, particularly in the eastern Pioneers.

Along with lodgepole and ponderosa pine, Douglas and subalpine fir and Engelmann spruce, the Pioneers harbor the otherwise locally rare blue (Colorado) spruce. Camas grow at lower elevations, producing blue, lily-like flowers from May to June. Wolverines can occasionally be spotted hunting for squirrels or hoary marmots, while elk, mule deer, moose and other large game animals are plentiful in the Pioneers (attracting a large number of hunters during the season). Grayling and trout abound in the waterways and are sometimes taken by bald eagles.

PLANNING
Maps

The USFS 1:126,720 *Southwest Montana – West Half* map ($6) gives a good overview of the area but is not suitable for serious navigation.

Information Sources

For information on Beaverhead National Forest go to W www.fs.fed.us/r1/b-d.

Permits & Regulations

No permit is required to camp or hike in the Pioneer Mountains backcountry and few restrictions apply – arguably, regulations are too lax. Hikers should, nonetheless, practice Leave No Trace principles (p56), especially those relating to camping and food hanging. During periods of extreme fire danger, a total ban on campfires may apply – check at local USFS offices.

ACCESS TOWN
Dillon

This small town is 65mi south of Butte at the intersection of I-15 and Hwy 41. Dillon's visitor center (☎ 406-683-5511, S Montana St) is between Sebree and Glendale Sts. The regional USFS office (☎ 406-683-3900, 420 Barrett St) gives advice but sells only USFS maps. Sagebrush Outdoor Gear (☎ 406-683-2329, 36 N Idaho St) sells hiking supplies and USGS quads. Tim Tollett's Frontier Angler (☎ 406-683-5276, 680 N Montana St) can provide hiker shuttles.

KOA (☎ 406-683-2749, 735 Park St) has riverside tent/RV sites for $23/35. The *Hotel Metlen (☎ 406-683-2335, 5 S Railroad Ave)* has very basic singles/doubles for $16/18. The *Sundowner Motel (☎ 406-683-2375, 800-524-9746, 500 N Montana St)* has rooms for $40/42.

Torrey Lake

Duration	7–9 hours
Distance	16.4mi (26.4km)
Standard	moderate
Start/Finish	Mono Creek Trailhead
Nearest Town	Wise River
Transport	car

Summary A long, out-and-back hike to an exceptionally scenic alpine lake between stunning 11,000ft peaks.

The route up to Torrey Lake takes you to the remotest and most spectacular part of the Pioneer Mountains. The lake is often visited in a long day hike based at Mono Creek campground, although many people do it as an overnight backpacking trip. Horseback riders sometimes use this route and it is open to trail motorbikes (although not to ATVs) from mid-July to mid-October, which more or less corresponds to the snow-free period. The hike involves an ascent of 1979ft – relatively modest considering its length.

PLANNING
Maps
Four USGS 1:24,000 quads cover the hike: *Elkhorn Hot Springs*, *Torrey Mountain*, *Mount Tahepia* and *Maurice Mountain*.

NEAREST TOWN & FACILITIES
Wise River
This tiny settlement is about 12mi west of I-15 at the intersection of Hwy 43 and the Pioneer Mountains Scenic Byway. The USFS office (☎ 406-832-3178, Hwy 43), just east of town, gives friendly advice and has a good range of USGS quads. The ***Wise River Club*** *(☎ 406-832-3258, Hwy 43)*, about 0.5mi west of town, has cabins and rooms from around $40 and RV sites from around $15.

USFS Campgrounds
The basic ***Mono Creek campground***, right beside the trailhead, has six sites for $7 each. About half a dozen other USFS campgrounds are spaced along the Pioneer Mountains Scenic Byway; the closest is ***Little Joe***, north of the trailhead, just off the Scenic Byway.

GETTING TO/FROM THE HIKE
From Wise River drive 21.5mi south along Pioneer Mountains Scenic Byway, then take the left (east) turnoff (signposted 'Coolidge Ghost Town'), which leads to Mono Creek Trailhead. There is space for about 30 cars. At the time of research, the USFS was planning to establish an information board with a registration book at the trailhead.

THE HIKE
Follow the Jacobson Creek Trail (No 2) along the old narrow-gauge railroad grading behind the campground, then climb southeast past a grassy moor to the attractive **Jacobson Meadows**. Here, Jacobson Creek meanders through soggy, natural pastures grazed by elk, deer – and cattle. Trail 2 skirts the meadows' dry northeast side, which is fringed by dwarf willow and sagebrush, passing ***campsites*** before it comes to a trail junction, 50 minutes to 1¼ hours from the trailhead.

Turn right onto the Torrey Lake Trail (No 56) and cross the small Jacobson Creek on a footbridge. The trail leads up the east bank of David Creek, rising at an easy gradient for 4mi through open lodgepole forest carpeted with low whortleberry heath and juniper – there are continual opportunities for ***camping*** along the lower valley – before it finally crosses the creek. Continue for 1mi up through fir-spruce forest under impressive, jagged white ridges to recross the stream, two to 2½ hours from the trail junction. Trail motorcycles are not permitted beyond this point.

Now begin a steeper 700ft ascent, winding your way southeast into stands of graceful old whitebark pine, opposite superb, raw ridges topped by 10,000ft peaks. As the gradient eventually eases, the trail sidles under the crags of the 11,154ft Tweedy Mountain to arrive at **Torrey Lake**, 50 minutes to 1¼ hours after recrossing David Creek. This magnificent tarn lies just below tree line and is surrounded on three sides by massive, granite-slab ridges rising like a gigantic stone wave. To the southwest is 11,147ft Torrey Mountain, with a craggy form that glows red in the late evening light. Picturesque

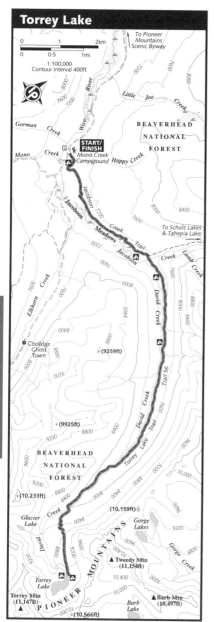

Torrey Lake

0   1   2km
0   0.5   1mi
1:100,000
Contour Interval 400ft

SOUTHWEST MONTANA

campsites can be found on both sides of the lake outlet on moist meadows or hidden among slab rocks. Torrey Lake is well stocked with golden trout.

Return to Mono Creek Trailhead via the ascent route.

Other Hikes

FLINT CREEK RANGE
Trask Lakes
The six lovely tarns known as the Trask Lakes lie in the Flint Creek Range north of Anaconda. They can be visited in an excellent, two-day, easy–moderate route leading up the South Fork Rock Creek. Three USGS quads cover the hike: *Rock Creek Lake, Pikes Peak* and *Pozega Lakes*. To reach the trailhead, exit I-90 at Deer Lodge and drive west toward Montana State Prison Farm, but after 1.9mi turn right along FR 006. Continue about 5mi to a three-way division, then go left and follow the road another 5mi around Rock Creek Lake to the small trailhead parking area.

TOBACCO ROOT MOUNTAINS
Lake Louise & Lost Cabin Lake
Lake Louise and Lost Cabin Lake lie in small cirques just below tree line in the Tobacco Root Mountains, which extend south from Whitehall (on the I-90). These beautiful tarns can be reached in separate (long day or overnight) hikes from the Lost Cabin/Lake Louise Trailhead. One USGS 1:24,000 quad, *Noble Peak*, covers these routes. To reach the trailhead, exit I-90 at Cardwell and drive south on CR 359 for 4mi, then follow South Boulder Rd (FR 107) for 18mi via the tiny settlement of Mammoth to the small, disused Bismark Reservoir; a 4WD or high-clearance vehicle is best for the final (rough!) section.

SNOWCREST RANGE
Snowcrest Loop
This 20mi circuit from the upper East Fork Blacktail Deer Creek follows the panoramic Snowcrest Trail along the spine of the Snowcrest Range, in the southeastern sector of Beaverhead National Forest. Much of the route is above 9500ft and may be impassable before mid-July. Two USGS 1:24,000 quads cover the route: *Antone Peak* and *Stonehouse Mountain*. From Dillon, take Blacktrail 158Deer Rd (which becomes FR 1808) southeast for about 35mi, then turn left and continue 1mi past the BLM campground to the East Fork Blacktail Deer Creek Trailhead.

Greater Yellowstone

The Greater Yellowstone area encompasses some of the most famous landscapes in the Rockies. Foremost has to be Yellowstone itself – the world's first national park and the most visited area in the US national park system. Not surprisingly it offers unique hiking experiences, with several routes visiting thermal hot spots or exploring the dramatic Grand Canyon of the Yellowstone. Chances of meeting bison and elk are probably higher than anywhere else in the county.

For many keen hikers, however, Grand Teton National Park, just south of Yellowstone, is an even more impressive destination. Its jagged fins of rock lurch abruptly skyward from relatively flat surrounds. Although the serious nature of the terrain means several of the highest summits are the preserves of climbers and mountaineers, some hiking routes manage to penetrate the high ground – with spectacular views and terrain.

To the northeast of Yellowstone, across the Montana border, lies yet a different landscape. Absaroka-Beartooth Wilderness is less visited than either of the national parks, and so it is possible to escape the crowds and immerse yourself in the wild granite mountain scenery.

CLIMATE

The Greater Yellowstone area experiences long and harsh winters, but June to September is warm, with daytime maximums in the high 70s and frequently reaching the high 80s.

Afternoon thunderstorms are common in June and July, especially in Yellowstone itself and the Beartooths. During this kind of weather expect to encounter morning fog and mist in Yellowstone where the basin-like topography of the park encourages cool, moist air to sink into the valleys at night.

INFORMATION
Maps

The Greater Yellowstone area straddles three states (Wyoming, Idaho and Montana), so it can be difficult to find a single map that

Highlights

ROB BLAKERS

Spectacular Teton Crest Trail leads through the wild heart of Wyoming's Teton Range.

- Exploring the snowfields and looking for mountain goats on Froze-to-Death Plateau (p166) in Absaroka-Beartooth Wilderness

- Taking the short stroll to Fairy Falls and Twin Buttes (p176) in famous Yellowstone National Park

- Bathing in the unspoiled Ferris Fork hot springs, beside scenic Bechler River (p177) in Yellowstone National Park

- Admiring the views from the Teton Crest Trail (p187), one of the most spectacular high routes in the Rockies

covers the entire area at a reasonable scale. Wyoming state maps (for example, the free highway map issued by the state's Department of Transport) cover the Grand Tetons and to the boundary of Yellowstone National Park. A Montana state map (such as the equivalent free highway map from Montana Department of Transport) is needed for the

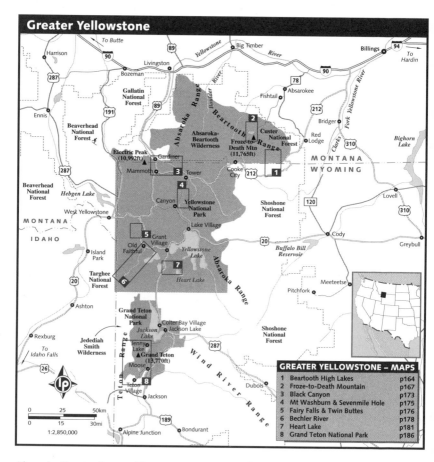

Greater Yellowstone

Absaroka-Beartooth area. These maps can be obtained at visitor centers in the particular states.

GATEWAYS
Cody

Situated 51mi east of Yellowstone's east entrance at the intersection of US 14/16/20 and Hwy 120, the 'Wild West' town of Cody is within easy driving distance of Greater Yellowstone's national parks and wilderness areas.

The visitor center (☎ 307-587-2777, 836 Sheridan Ave) is open daily. The US Forest Service's (USFS) Shoshone National Forest Wapiti Ranger District (☎ 307-527-6921, 203A Yellowstone Ave) is open from 8am to 4:30pm weekdays. The Bureau of Land Management (BLM) office (☎ 307-587-2216, 1002 Blackburn St), east of town, does not sell USGS maps. The Wyoming Game & Fish Department (☎ 307-527-7125, 2820 Hwy 120) gives information and issues fishing licenses. Sierra Trading Post (☎ 307-578-5802, ⓦ www.sierratradingpost.com, 1402 8th St) stocks a wide range of outdoor equipment, including topographic maps for the region.

GARETH McCORMACK

GARETH McCORMACK

Top: Dawn mist over Mt Washburn, all that remains of a volcano that exploded about 600,000 years ago, in Wyoming's famous Yellowstone National Park. **Bottom:** The Tetons, which rise with stunning abruptness in a row of 'witch-hat' peaks, reflected in a tarn in Grand Teton National Park, Wyoming.

Top Left: Evening at beautiful Senaca Lake on the Titcomb Basin hike in Wyoming's Wind River Range. **Top Right:** Dawn over Titcomb Basin and the spiky peaks of the mighty Wind River Range. **Bottom:** The lovely Island Lake at the foot of Titcomb Basin.

GARETH McCORMACK

GARETH McCORMACK

CLEM LINDENMAYER

Places to Stay & Eat There are shady campsites at *Gateway Campground* (☎ 307-587-2561, 203 W Yellowstone Ave), which has tent sites for $12 and RV hookups for $17. Historic *Pawnee Hotel* (☎ 307-587-2239, 1032 12th St) has singles/doubles for $32/36. Both *Uptown Motel* (☎ 307-587-4245, 1562 Sheridan Ave) and *Big Bear Motel* (☎ 307-587-3117, 139 W Yellowstone Ave) charge from around $38/46.

Whole Foods Trading Company (☎ 307-587-3213, 1239 Rumsey Ave) has natural bulk and backpacking foods. *Proud Cut Saloon* (☎ 307-527-6905, 1227 Sheridan Ave) is big on beef. *Maxwell's Fine Food & Spirits* (☎ 307-527-7749, 937 Sheridan Ave) serves up bistro dinners.

Getting There & Away SkyWest/Delta connects Cody and Salt Lake City with daily flights out of Yellowstone Regional Airport (☎ 307-587-5096), just south of town. Powder River Coach USA (☎ 800-442-3682) buses stop at Daylight Donut (1452 Sheridan Ave) en route to Casper and Billings, and also do Yellowstone tours ($50).

Bozeman

Bozeman is on Montana's I-90 north of Yellowstone National Park, surrounded by the Absaroka, Beartooth, Bridger, Crazy and Gallatin Mountains. For information and local accommodations advice contact the chamber of commerce (☎ 406-586-5421, W www.bozemanchamber.com, 2000 Commerce Way).

Regional and interstate bus connections, including to West Yellowstone, leave from the Greyhound depot (☎ 406-587-3110, 625 N 7th Ave). Several airlines fly into the local Gallatin airport (☎ 406-388-8321) from Salt Lake City, Washington and Alaska.

Jackson

The southern gateway to Grand Teton National Park, Jackson is at the intersection of Hwy 22 (to Teton Pass) and US 26/89/191. The USFS and Grand Teton National Park have a joint counter at the Jackson Hole and Greater Yellowstone visitor center (☎ 307-733-3316, W www.jacksonholechamber.com,

---

> ## Warning – Bear Country
>
> Many of the hikes described in this chapter are situated in bear habitat – current estimates suggest there are up to 550 grizzlies living in Yellowstone National Park alone. While maulings are rare and deaths even rarer (one to two per year in the entire US), encounters and sightings are more frequent. Taking the right precautions in bear country can reduce the chances of an encounter, and acting appropriately in the event of an encounter can prevent a mauling or worse.
>
> For advice on hiking in bear country see Animal Attacks (p74). For more advice and specific information about bears in Yellowstone National Park, including a list of related books, see W www.yellowstone-bearman.com/bearman/bears.

532 N Cache Dr). The National Museum of Wildlife Art, 3mi north of town, has works by important US outdoor painters, including Bierstadt and Rungiers. Teton Mountaineering (☎ 307-733-3595, 170 N Cache Dr) has a good range of backpacking gear.

The *El Rancho Motel* (☎ 307-733-3668, 215 N Cache Dr) has budget rooms ($75) and runs *The Bunkhouse* in the basement, with hostel-style accommodations ($22).

Jackson Hole Express (☎ 307-733-1719) runs shuttles to Salt Lake City ($49) via Idaho Falls ($26), both of which have Greyhound connections. Jackson Hole airport (☎ 307-733-7682) is 7mi north of town, with connections to Salt Lake City, Denver and Chicago.

Absaroka-Beartooth Wilderness

Covering 1474-sq-miles, Absaroka-Beartooth Wilderness stretches along Montana's southern border with Wyoming (a small section on its eastern side lies inside Wyoming) in the Gallatin, Custer and Shoshone National Forests. The wilderness area takes in two distinct mountain ranges, the Absarokas and the Beartooth Plateau (the Beartooths). The Absarokas are characterized by steep, forested valleys and craggy peaks, while the Beartooths are essentially high plateaus dotted with more than 1000 lakes and tarns. The Absaroka-Beartooth offers a solitude and serenity not easily found in other wilderness areas of the Rockies.

NATURAL HISTORY

The Beartooths are composed of uplifted granite, some three billion years old. Most of the wilderness consists of rock and ice peaks or high plateau above 10,000ft – an arctic type of environment where the vegetation and wildlife depend on a comparatively short growing season. Forests of Engelmann spruce scattered with subalpine fir cover the less elevated valleys, with limber pine in higher, more exposed places. Grizzly and black bears are not common in the wilderness; hikers have a better chance of seeing bighorn sheep, mountain goats or elk. The Beartooths are a paradise for anglers, with brook, cutthroat, golden, lake and rainbow trout abounding in the many streams, rivers and lakes.

PLANNING
When to Hike

The Beartooths' hiking season is very short. Snow is likely to be encountered in many places above tree line at least until the end of July and starts to accumulate again after mid-September. Localized afternoon thunderstorms, with hail, are common in the Beartooths during June and July.

Maps & Books

The contoured USFS 1:63,360 *Absaroka Beartooth Wilderness* map ($9.75) covers the whole area and is adequate for most hikes. *The Trail Guide to the Beartooths* by Bill Schneider ($14.95) offers descriptions of more than 300mi of trails.

Information Sources

Information about the Beartooths can be obtained from the Beartooth Ranger District headquarters (☎ 406-446-2103; W www.fs .fed.us/r1/custer; HC 49, Box 3420, Red

Lodge, MT 59068). For information on the Absaroka Range, in Gallatin National Forest, contact the supervisor's office (☎ 406-522-2520; W www.fs.fed.us/r1/gallatin; PO Box 130, 10 East Babcock Ave, Bozeman, MT 59771).

Permits & Regulations

Permits are not required for hiking in the Absaroka-Beartooth Wilderness. In order to protect the fragile alpine vegetation, however, hikers should not light campfires above tree line (preferably not at all). Note that the southern area of the wilderness is part of a grizzly bear management zone and, although bears rarely venture into the higher country, encounters with grizzlies occasionally occur.

GETTING AROUND

The Red Lodge Shuttle (☎ 406-446-2257) will taxi hikers to trailheads in the vicinity of Red Lodge.

ACCESS TOWNS & FACILITIES
Red Lodge

This quaint mining town is on the scenic Beartooth Hwy (US 212) in southern Montana. Contact the local chamber of commerce (☎ 406-446-1718, W www.redlodge.com, 601 N Broadway Ave) for information. Sylvan Peak Mountain Shoppe (N Broadway Ave) sells backpacking gear and some maps, but USGS maps are available only at Red Lodge Office Supply (12 N Broadway Ave). The USFS office (☎ 406-446-2103), 2mi south of town on US 212, is open daily from May through September.

Perry's Campground (☎ 406-446-2722), 3mi south of town on US 212, has sites for $12. *Eagle's Nest Motel (☎ 406-446-2312, 702 S Broadway Ave)* has doubles from $40.

Red Lodge Shuttle (☎ 406-446-2257) runs between Red Lodge and Billings ($46, less for several people), where there is a Greyhound bus station (☎ 406-245-5116) and domestic airport (☎ 406-238-3420).

Cooke City

This small, isolated town lies on US 212 near the northeastern entrance to Yellowstone National Park. The general store sells topographic maps. *Yellowstone Yurt Hostel* (☎ *406-586-4659*) has dorm beds for $14 and *High Country Motel* (☎ *406-838-2272*) offers double rooms from $62.

Along Beartooth Highway

There are 13 basic USFS *campgrounds* along the Beartooth Hwy (US 212) between Red Lodge and Cooke City, most charging $8 or $9. *Top of the World Motel* (☎ *307-899-2482*), on the highway about 1mi east of the Island Lake turnoff, offers rooms from $48.

Beartooth High Lakes

Duration	3 days
Distance	20.6mi (33.2km)
Standard	easy–moderate
Start/Finish	Island Lake
Nearest Towns	Red Lodge, Cooke City
Transport	car

Summary This hike leads from the gentle lake landscape of the southern Beartooth Plateau into the varied, raw terrain around the glaciated peaks on the main Beartooth Range. It is an adventurous route for hikers who are well acclimated.

This lollipop loop through a high alpine landscape dotted with lakes. Waymarkings and signposts are unreliable, numerous unofficial trails exist and off-trail (side) trips are easy. Hikers should be acclimated to the high altitude. The first section of the route to Becker Lake (perhaps even as far as Albino Lake) makes an excellent and easy day hike with gentle gradients, and is ideal for children.

PLANNING
Maps

The USFS 1:63,360 *Absaroka Beartooth Wilderness* map covers the route. Alternatively use the four USGS 1:24,000 quads: *Beartooth Butte*, *Silver Run Peak*, *Castle Mountain* and *Muddy Creek*.

NEAREST TOWNS

See Red Lodge and Cooke City (p162).

GETTING TO/FROM THE HIKE

The trailhead is at Island Lake, 38mi southwest of Red Lodge (3.7mi west of Beartooth Pass) along the scenic Beartooth Hwy (US 212). There is parking on the east side of the boat ramp for around 50 vehicles (the $3 day-use fee for Island Lake Recreational Center does not apply to hikers).

THE HIKE
Day 1: Island Lake to Becker Lake

1½–2 hours, 3.6mi

Follow the Beartooth High Lakes Trail over fields of purple fleabane and yellow aster along the western shores of Island and Night Lakes. The trail continues northwest across a minor watershed and on past some reedy tarns and **Flake Lake**, where an inlet stream splashes down over polished pink slabs. There are enticing views toward the flat-topped ranges ahead, as you rise gently over grassy meadows to an unsigned trail junction by some boggy ponds, about one hour from the trailhead.

Take the right trail (not shown on USFS maps as it is not official) and head north between Jeff and Mutt Lakes, crossing the short outlet/inlet on stepping stones. The trail skirts marshy grassland on Jeff Lake's northern shore, before climbing over a slight crest to reach **Becker Lake**, around 35 minutes from the trail junction. Walking pads (well-worn trails created by animals or humans) lead left, down to a tiny peninsula with grassy *campsites*. Left by ancient glaciers, boulders lie stranded among smooth granite slabs around the shore, and sheer cliffs drop 150ft directly into the lake's western side.

Alternative Campsites

Camping is possible along most of the Day 1 route, including *campsites* on the forested terraces just across the inlet to Jeff Lake.

Day 2: Becker Lake to Wright Lake

3½–4½ hours, 7.5mi, 1777ft ascent

Head around the eastern side of Becker Lake past several more *campsites* in the low forest. The trail cuts north across tundra meadows

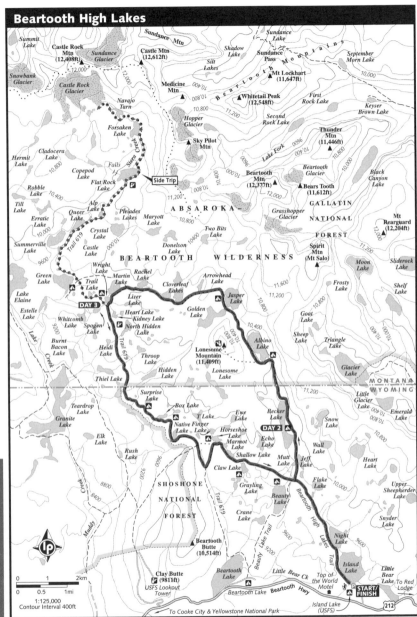

Beartooth High Lakes

GREATER YELLOWSTONE

and follows the east bank of the inlet stream up through a lovely, grassy valley leading to Albino Lake at the upper tree line. Rising from its western shore is Lonesome Mountain (11,409ft); its rounded summit can be scaled with little difficulty via its broad southern ridge (one hour return). Sheltered *campsites* can be found among stands of spruce and limber pines at the lake's southeastern corner.

Cross the outlet just below Albino Lake and skirt its western shore. The trail ascends more steeply to an almost bare, rocky **saddle** overlooking Jasper Lake, a deep trough in a stark landscape of glacier-polished slabs, littered with boulders and other moraine rubble. Beartooth Mountain and Bears Tooth jut from behind the divide to the northeast. Drop for several minutes, crossing stepping stones over the outlet that flows directly into Golden Lake. The trail peters out at Jasper Lake's northwestern corner. From here a vague route darts west over a rocky ridge to reach the southern shore of **Arrowhead Lake**, another deep alpine lake in raw, glacial surroundings, around two to 2½ hours from Becker Lake.

Cut down left (southwest) beside the trickling outlet then through a dry, rocky gully that curves west to meet the lovely **Cloverleaf Lakes**. A faint trail leads around the southern shores of these deep-blue lakes over bouldery talus and moist meadows of marsh marigold. Follow the left (south) bank of the cascading outlet down past small escarpments, then around the waterlogged southern side of Rachel Lake. Lower down the stream flows subterraneously beneath dry rock rubble, allowing an easy crossing just before you descend to **Martin Lake**, a picturesque sight with its island hillock. In summer, bluebell and yellow arnica bloom in the watery meadows around the inlet, and good *campsites* can be found around the lake. A well trodden trail leads around the southern shores of Martin Lake and the smaller, almost adjoining Wright Lake to intersect with Trail 619 a short way below the outlet, 1½ to two hours from Arrowhead Lake.

A 30-minute alternative from Martin Lake is to take a rough trail leading around

its northern shore, then up west through a small grassy gap before descending beside a forested streamlet to meet Trail 619 at the eastern shore of Green Lake (see Side Trip).

Alternative Campsites
Even above tree line, sheltered *campsites* can be found in many places among the boulders, such as the pleasant alpine lawns between Jasper and Golden Lakes.

Side Trip: Castle Rock Glacier
5½–7½ hours, 15mi, 1770ft ascent
This excellent moderate–hard side trip into the headwaters of the Sierra Creek makes a long day hike or can be enjoyed in shorter stages by camping almost anywhere along the way.

The trail crosses Wright Lake outlet and climbs northwest above a waterfall streaming into Spogen Lake on the left. After rising to tranquil Trail Lake, on a flattened ridge high above Whitcomb Lake, begin a gradually steeper descent past a tarn on boulder-strewn slopes to reach a damp meadow on the eastern shore of Green Lake.

Head around to the start of some grassy clearings on Green Lake's north side and follow a trail (unsignposted) that cuts up over the forested ridge. From here you get a fleeting glimpse of Summerville Lake, before descending to where the lake outlet splashes down the granite rock into Sierra Creek. Head upstream through meadows of yellow arnica and dandelion-like agoseris, past Queer Lake below glacier-smoothed rock walls. To avoid a small gorge, the route moves up right through a tiny, open gully and steers left to Alp Lake. After crossing the inlet, return to the creek and head up past waterfalls splashing through the cracked granite to reach **Flat Rock Lake**. From this deep, greenish lake among reddish, scree-covered mountains you get clear views of Sky Pilot Mountain up to the right and the small glaciers around 12,612ft Castle Mountain directly to the north.

Head past the whale-shaped island on the lake's eastern side, then cut across flowery meadows and follow the rubble-choked gully of the inlet stream to Forsaken Lake (shown on USFS maps as Varve Lake). This stark lake lies just below the upper vegetation line and is surrounded by craggy ranges. Trace the eastern shore, then ascend steeply beside the lake's main inlet to make an icy ford just below the stream's exit from the turgid, turquoise Navajo Tarn. After skirting around the tarn's shore, a short, steep climb over raw moraine, glacial mud and lingering snowdrifts brings you to **Castle Rock Glacier**, which slides smoothly down into a large meltwater pool from below Castle Rock Mountain (12,408ft).

Return to Wright Lake by the same route.

Day 3: Wright Lake to Island Lake

5¼–6½ hours, 9.5mi, 420ft ascent

From halfway around Wright Lake, the trail climbs southeast past Kidney Lake onto an undulating granite plateau, granting excellent views north to the glaciers and flat-topped summits of the Beartooth Mountains. The trail picks its way past tarns in this glaciated landscape high above Heidi and Granite Lakes to the southwest. Beyond them the fin-like summits around Pilot Peak fall abruptly into the Yellowstone Valley, beginning an arc of jagged ranges that stretches along the southern horizon.

The trail (often badly eroded) winds down through fir-spruce forest carpeted with shin-high grouseberry shrubs. Continue high above Thiel Lake before dropping to cross several channels flowing into Mule Lake at an attractive grassy meadow. The trail heads up past sporadic tarns to Surprise Lake, ascends high above Box Lake and passes the slimy-green Native Lake. Reach a broad, boulder-strewn saddle at the northern foot of the impressively craggy rock ridge marking the wilderness exit point, 2½ to three hours from Wright Lake. A signposted turnoff leads southwest to Clay Butte, where a staffed USFS lookout tower is open to the public. (There is also a rough shortcut to Horseshoe Lake going east across largely open, glaciated terrain from the saddle.)

Hike south down open hillsides of pink asters to a turnoff (signposted 'Island Lake') below the castle-like formations (Trail 619

continues to Beartooth Lake). The turnoff trail leads northeast through bouldery woods to intersect with the Beartooth High Lakes Trail above the beautiful **Horseshoe** and **Finger Lakes**; scenic *campsites* exist on the moraine bar separating the lakes. Sidle down over grassy slopes of yellow arnica and shrub willow above Marmot and Shallow Lakes.

The trail crosses the stream where it enters Claw Lake, then leaves this charming valley as it rises and dips over low forested ridges and stream gullies to reach Beauty Lake. Cross the twin inlets on stepping stones to a turnoff, where the Beauty Lake Trail departs south to Beartooth Lake. Make a short, steep ascent east to arrive back at the junction with the Becker Lake turnoff, around two hours from the saddle above Native Lake. Retrace your steps from Day 1 to reach Island Lake in a further hour.

Alternative Campsites

Camping is possible almost anywhere on Day 3, but good *campsites* can be found on the eastern side of Surprise Lake, near the trail high above Box Lake, on the southwestern shore of Claw Lake and around the Beauty Lake outlet.

Froze-to-Death Mountain

Duration	3 days
Distance	15.5mi (24.9km)
Standard	hard
Start/Finish	West Rosebud Trailhead
Nearest Towns	Red Lodge, Absarokee, Fishtail
Transport	car

Summary A strenuous and challenging ascent to an exposed and beautiful alpine plateau. The summit of Froze-to-Death Mountain offers views encompassing much of the Beartooth Range.

This is one of the best alpine outings in the Beartooths and demands a good level of fitness as around 5000ft of ascent is required. The route is also a popular jumping-off point for ascents of Montana's highest summit, Granite Peak (12,799ft). This is an irresistible goal for many Beartooth hikers, but it is essentially a mountaineering route (requiring ice axe and crampons) and beyond the scope of this book. The summit of Tempest Mountain (12,478ft), 1mi northeast of Granite Peak, is more easily reached and offers comparably marvelous views.

PLANNING
Maps & Books
The USFS 1:63,360 *Absaroka Beartooth Wilderness* map covers the route. Alternatively, use two USGS 1:24,000 quads: *Granite Peak* and *Alpine*. The USFS has a free brochure on climbing Granite Peak, which is available from the Beartooth Ranger District office in Red Lodge (see Information Sources, p162).

NEAREST TOWNS & FACILITIES
See Red Lodge (p162).

Absarokee
About 33mi northwest of Red Lodge along Hwy 78, Absarokee is a small town but a convenient gateway for the Granite Peak area of the Beartooths. Outdoor Supply (☎ 406-328-4904, 19 Woodard Ave) stocks local maps and a limited supply of outdoor goods, while *The Stillwater Lodge (☎ 406-328-4899, 28 Woodard Ave)*, just opposite, has doubles from $52.

Fishtail
Just off Hwy 78 and 1mi east of the turnoff onto West Rosebud Rd, Fishtail is the closest settlement to the trailhead but has no accommodations.

However, Fishtail is home to the *Cowboy Bar and Supper Club (☎ 406-328-4288)*, where you can get a bite to eat. You can also participate in the club's infamous 'Chickenshit Game', where participants place bets on which square of a marked grid certain chickens will choose to grace with their droppings. There is also a pleasant, creek-side *cafe* with a shaded verandah.

USFS Campgrounds
There are several USFS campgrounds along West Rosebud Rd. Best positioned is the *West Rosebud Creek campground*, only 2mi from the trailhead.

GETTING TO/FROM THE HIKE
West Rosebud Trailhead is reached via a turnoff to the west from Hwy 78, roughly 30mi north of Red Lodge and 3mi south of Absarokee. At the subsequent fork, 1mi west of Fishtail, proceed left (south) along West Rosebud Rd to the Mystic Lake hydroelectric plant.

THE HIKE
Day 1: West Rosebud Trailhead to Froze-to-Death Plateau
5–6 hours, 6mi, 3200ft ascent
The trail climbs past the hydroelectric plant and winds through forest close to the West Rosebud Creek, before arriving at a footbridge some 20 minutes from the trailhead.

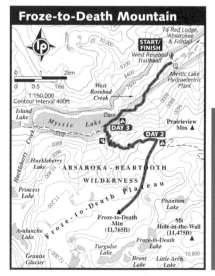

The trail continues gently through a growth of lodgepole pine before crossing the boundary of the wilderness area and beginning a long, winding climb. The lodgepole pine gives way to aspen growing among large boulders. Climbing higher, the trail becomes stony but reveals great views across the West Rosebud valley. Ahead the talus slopes steepen into huge cliffs and the trail heads west, traversing a steep slope, with airy views into the canyon below, before emerging onto a spur just above **Mystic Lake** (1½ to two hours from the trailhead).

Descend to the lakeshore and continue along the broad trail, enjoying views of the high cliffs on the northwestern edge of the Froze-to-Death Plateau. Enter a swathe of fir-spruce forest, where there are several good *campsites* set back from the lake. Turn left at a signposted junction and begin the long ascent to the Froze-to-Death Plateau. The climb is gentle at first, making long switchbacks through the forest. As the trees thin out the gradient steepens and excellent views are revealed west along the length of Mystic Lake. After one to 1½ hours the trail sweeps across to the east, contouring steep slopes. Cross a small stream and climb steeply through a beautiful grove of limber pine. Eventually the gradient eases and a rock cairn marks the beginning of the **plateau**.

Continue to follow the trail as it climbs gently to the east (wet in places – collect water for camping here) onto a broad saddle between Prairieview Mountain and Froze-to-Death Mountain. There is plenty of flat ground close to this saddle to make a *camp*.

Day 2: Froze-to-Death Plateau to Mystic Lake (via Froze-to-Death Mountain)
4½–5½ hours, 6.5mi, 1700ft ascent
The summit of Froze-to-Death Mountain is not quite visible from the saddle but soon comes into view as you climb gently to the southwest, following small rock cairns. The route climbs into a shallow basin, with the summit of Froze-to-Death Mountain sitting prominently above it. Aim for the shoulder just east of the summit and climb strenuously across boulder fields before reaching

the **summit** (11,765ft), 1½ to two hours from the saddle. The view on a clear day is fantastic, encompassing much of the Beartooth Range, which breaks up the horizon in almost every direction. Only to the northeast, where you can see the distant plains, is the alpine scene interrupted. You can see Tempest Mountain across the plateau to the southwest. Partially hidden behind Tempest Mountain is the highest summit in Montana – Granite Peak.

Return to the *campsites* at Mystic Lake by retracing you steps.

Day 3: Mystic Lake to West Rosebud Trailhead
1–2 hours, 3mi
Retrace your steps from Day 1 along the Mystic Lake Trail.

Yellowstone National Park

The 3472-sq-mile Yellowstone National Park in the northwest corner of Wyoming is the world's oldest national park and the largest in the Lower 48 states. This vast, intensely active volcanic plateau has an incredible range and concentration of fascinating volcanic phenomena, from geysers and fumaroles to hot springs, thermal pools and boiling mud pots. Millions of visitors are attracted to this volcanic wonderland each year, although only a tiny percentage ever hike into the Yellowstone backcountry.

HISTORY
Although the Yellowstone basin was traversed by the Shoshone and Absaroka (Crow) people, who sometimes hunted its bighorn sheep and fished the local rivers, only small numbers of Native Americans lived permanently in the area. The Lewis and Clark expedition of 1804–06 bypassed Yellowstone without an inkling of its remarkable geology, but soon after John Colter, a trapper who had accompanied the explorers, ventured into this strange country. His accounts of finding bubbling mud pools, steaming brooks and

jets of boiling water were ridiculed back in St Louis, but returning frontiersmen continued to tell these fantastic stories.

In 1871 Dr Ferdinand Hayden, director of the US Geological Survey, resolved to lead an expedition into the Yellowstone area. His party included landscape painter Thomas Moran and photographer William Jackson. Their paintings and photographs provided crucial evidence of Yellowstone's outstanding features, which, together with Hayden's exhaustive report, convinced Congress to establish Yellowstone as the world's first national park the following year.

The nontreaty Nez Perce people, fleeing the US Army in a desperate attempt to reach Canada, crossed Yellowstone in the summer of 1877, briefly seizing several tourists. As poaching and other illegal activities began to get out of hand, the US Army assumed administration of the park in 1886, a role it held until the formation of the National Park Service (NPS) in 1916. In 1972 Yellowstone became a UN-designated World Heritage Site.

NATURAL HISTORY
Around 80% of Yellowstone is forested. Lodgepole pine is easily the most widespread tree species, largely due to the high silica content of the common rhyolite (volcanic) rock, which breaks down into infertile soils unfavorable to other species. Subalpine fir and Engelmann spruce forests cover the higher ranges, especially in the park's moister southwestern quarter, where Colorado blue spruce is also present.

Much of Yellowstone's forest was destroyed or damaged in the catastrophic fires of 1988, which left behind vast areas of charred trees. The shocking severity of the 1988 fires was due to the park's natural fire policy, which allows naturally occurring fires to burn themselves out. Being the driest summer in the park's recorded history the various fires soon got out of hand. Finally, on July 21, the decision was made to fight, but it wasn't until rain fell in September that park management gained any control. See the boxed text 'Regeneration after the Fire' (p179) for details on the park's flora and fauna post-1988.

Having been protected from human hunters for over 100 years, Yellowstone's wildlife is less wary of people than elsewhere in the Rockies. The park also shelters the Rockies' largest numbers of bison and elk, and herds of these muscular animals graze in the valleys. Bull elk gather on lower ridges in the rutting season, when their bugling calls resonate through the mountains as they challenge far-off rivals. In winter bison and elk often leave the park in search of food, and many are killed for fear they will infect domestic livestock with brucellosis, a bovine disease carried by the animals. Moose frequent bogs and shallow lakes; each year the males grow massive antlers (weighing 100lb or more) to impress the moose cows during mating season (September–early October).

Wolves were reintroduced in the mid-1990s (having previously been eradicated by the NPS). Although biologists believed this would re-establish natural control of the high number of elk, which had created an imbalance in the Yellowstone ecosystem, there has (still) been no significant impact on Yellowstone's elk population. Coyote numbers have declined, however, as wolves force them back into a more typical scavenging role. At times wolves take sheep and cattle from neighboring ranches and, although livestock producers are compensated for such losses, many locals continue to oppose the spread of wolves.

Yellowstone's large number of mammals ensures plenty of carrion for scavenging black-billed magpies, easily identified by their shiny greenish-black backs and long, black tails. The common American robin (actually an adaptable thrush species, found throughout the Rockies) often overwinters around the park's hot springs.

Yellowstone's lakes and streams contain five species of trout, plus mountain whitefish and grayling. Biologists are concerned about the recent (illegal) introduction of the lake trout into Yellowstone Lake, one of the last sanctuaries for the native Yellowstone cutthroat trout. The competition and predation of this aggressive species has already caused an alarming decline in the number of cutthroat trout, which in turn provides food

Wildlife Management – A Contentious Issue

How best to conserve environments and their wildlife is a contentious issue and Yellowstone National Park has traditionally been one of the US' primary sites for debate. A simple, historical case is bear management. Prior to 1970 bears were considered one of the park's greatest tourist attractions and were routinely encouraged to visit garbage dumps and hotels, where they were sometimes fed in front of the guests under the guard of an armed park ranger. Only in 1970 was a program adopted that changed the tack of bear management, discouraging the habituation of bears to human foods.

Such management decisions may seem archaic today, but, in fact, many similar issues are ongoing in the park. Elk management is one current debate. Yellowstone's large population of elk traditionally moves north to the lower elevations of the Lamar Valley for winter. Past theories suggested that the accumulation of animals grazing in this area damaged vegetation. As a result, a proportion of Yellowstone's grazers (including bison and pronghorn) were routinely trapped or killed. The official slaughtering of thousands of ungulates on national park land eventually led to a public outcry, and the practice ceased in 1968. A system of 'natural regeneration' has been experimented with since then, and results have tended to show that the Lamar Valley is able to self-regulate and winter grazing does not have a significant effect on overall biodiversity.

One of the main obstacles to sound management remains the fact that decisions are often fuelled more by political and public pressure than by scientific information. A prime example of this point is bison management. The park's current management scheme caps its bison population at 3000 animals, based largely on local political pressure to control the herd and protect adjoining ranch land. Given that the total number of bison in the US fell to less than 800 animals around the 1890s (reduced from an estimated population of 65 to 80 million before the arrival of Euro-Americans), the issue of genetic diversity in surviving animals is a major worry. Today's Yellowstone herd is thought to have descended from between eight and 50 individuals. Current management programs restrict the free movement of bison – members of the Yellowstone herd are discouraged from wandering beyond park boundaries and outside creatures are not allowed in. Annual culling based on number and disease tends to remove animals of certain characteristics only, leading to fears that unnatural selection could be compounding the problem of low genetic diversity.

Controversy surrounds the management of Yellowstone's bison – one of many park attractions.

in spring for threatened grizzly bears and bald eagles, as well as many other predators.

PLANNING
Maps & Books
Trails Illustrated's 1:168,500 map No 201 *Yellowstone National Park* ($2.95) covers the whole park in a single sheet, as does the Earthwalk Press 1:106,250 Hiking Map and Guide ($3.95) of the same name. However, neither are ideal for hiking (see individual hikes for recommended maps).

Hiking in Yellowstone National Park by Bill Schneider ($14.95) describes more than 100 routes in the area and is one of the best of the wide range of trail guides.

Information Sources
Park information can be obtained from the NPS visitor services office (☎ 307-344-7381; W www.nps.gov/yell; PO Box 168, YNP, WY 82190). To reserve lodges or campsites (not backcountry) contact Yellowstone National Park Lodges (☎ 307-344-7901; W www .travelyellowstone.com; PO Box 165, YNP, WY 82190).

Permits & Regulations
Park entry fees (valid for seven days and also giving access to Grand Teton National Park) are $20 for private vehicles, $15 for motorcycles (one person only) and $10 for individuals on foot or bicycle.

Backcountry camping permits are required for all overnight trips in Yellowstone. Permits are free unless you book more than 48 hours in advance ($20 fee). There are backcountry offices at Canyon, Grant Village, Lake Village, Mammoth, Bechler, Tower, West Entrance, Old Faithful and South Entrance. Reservations are accepted by mail to Backcountry Office, PO Box 168, Yellowstone National Park, WY 82190. For details call the central backcountry office (☎ 307-344-2160).

Anglers (16 years and over) need only a park fishing permit ($10/20 for 10 days/full season). Free permits are required for anglers aged between 12 and 15. Permits are available at backcountry offices and Hamilton General Stores. State fishing licenses are not required.

Warning
Bathing in natural hot pools not only carries the risk of scalding burns, but is not permitted in the park except at three sites: Boiling River (between Gardiner and Mammoth), Madison Hot Pot (near Madison) and Ferris Fork (on the Bechler River).

GETTING AROUND
Yellowstone has no public transportation, so getting to/from remote trailheads without a car can be problematic. Amfac buses do make daily sightseeing trips around the Grand Loop Rd, although only scheduled stops are permitted. For tour timetables call ☎ 307-344-7311 or visit one of the park visitor centers.

ACCESS TOWNS
Gardiner
Gardiner straddles the Yellowstone River on US 89 at the northwestern boundary of Yellowstone National Park. For information contact the chamber of commerce (☎ 406-848-7971, Park St) or the local USFS office (☎ 406-848-7375, S Yellowstone St).

Rocky Mountain campground (☎ 406-848-7251, 14 Jardine Rd) has sites with facilities from $20, while *Yellowstone River Motel (☎ 406-848-7303)* charges from $54.

West Yellowstone
This small, tourism-based town serves as the western gateway to the park. For information contact the chamber of commerce (☎ 406-646-7701; W www.westyellowstonechamber .com; Grizzly Park, Canyon St) or the park information center (☎ 406-646-7332, Canyon St). Eagle's Store and Tackle (☎ 406-646-9300, W Yellowstone Ave) sells backpacking supplies.

There are two USFS campgrounds within 8mi of West Yellowstone, both charging $12 for a site. The closest is *Baker's Hole*, 3mi north of town on US 191. *Hideaway RV Campground (☎ 406-646-9049, cnr Gibbon Ave & Electric St)* charges from $20 for a tent site. *Madison Hotel (☎ 406-646-7745, 139 W Yellowstone Ave)* has double rooms with shared/private bathroom from $36/42.

Greyhound buses to/from Bozeman and Idaho Falls stop at the Western Union office (☎ 406-646-1111, 126 Electric St), also the home of Yellowstone Taxi.

Mammoth

Mammoth, at the northwest corner of the Yellowstone, is the park headquarters. The village lies at the foot of the fascinating Mammoth Hot Springs, where calcium-rich thermal waters have formed an extensive system of limestone terraces. The visitor center (☎ 307-344-2263), in a section of the old Fort Yellowstone, has exhibits on the establishment and early history of the park. Sites at the USFS *Mammoth campground* cost $12. *Mammoth Hot Springs Hotel & Cabins (☎ 307-344-7311)* has double rooms from $96 and four-person cabins from $56.

Black Canyon

Duration	2 days
Distance	18.5mi (29.8km)
Standard	moderate
Start	Hellroaring Trailhead
Finish	Gardiner
Nearest Towns	Tower, Gardiner
Transport	car

Summary A rewarding route that escapes the crowds to explore the meandering waters and thundering rapids of the Yellowstone River.

Despite its lack of thermal activity, the Black Canyon is one of Yellowstone National Park's classic hikes. The route leads downstream through a little-visited valley, where the Yellowstone River alternately surges into rapids, plunges over waterfalls or just drifts gently along. Following the river downstream also has the advantage of giving a descent for the route of 1060ft.

The route can be extended to 22mi by starting from Tower, or shortened to a more manageable day hike of 12.1mi by starting at Blacktail Creek Trailhead, 6.8mi east of Mammoth. There are 18 designated backcountry campsites along, or in close proximity to, the route, so a number of overnight

permutations are possible. Sites 1R2 to 1Y1 are all beside the river in good spots, although this description suggests site 1Y7 (roughly halfway) as a good stopping point. If you are keen on fishing then any number of days could be happily spent along the trail.

PLANNING
When to Hike

The trail is at a relatively low altitude and should be free of snow by early June. The ford of Hellroaring Creek can be dangerous in anything but low water (see Warning) and the final section (near Gardiner) also crosses steep and eroded slopes that become slippery and dangerous after rain.

What to Bring

The meadows at the start of the route are haven to a whole range of insects and the grasses can be thigh-high in places. Bug spray and long pants might be appreciated.

Maps

Two Trails Illustrated 1:83,333 maps cover the hike: No 304 *Tower/Canyon* and No 303 *Mammoth Hot Springs*.

NEAREST TOWNS
See Gardiner (p171).

Tower

Sited along the road above Tower Falls, there is a *general store* and the *Tower Fall*

Warning

The map indicates a ford across Hellroaring Creek toward the start of the hike. A signpost on the trail at this point advises against crossing the river here, and indicates the trail northeast along Hellroaring Creek where there is a stockbridge 1.5mi further up. At normal summer levels the water at the ford is thigh deep at most and should be passable with care by most adults (preferably with the help of a stick or pole). If the water is in any way high, or if you are hiking with children or large packs, the detour to the bridge is advised (add 3mi to the total hike distance).

campground. A short distance along the road, the ***Roosevelt Lodge*** *(☎ 307-244-7311)* has cabins with bath for $83.

GETTING TO/FROM THE HIKE
The turnoff for Hellroaring Trailhead is 3.5mi west of Tower on the Upper Loop Rd and there is adequate parking 0.5mi along the access road.

At the end of the hike in Gardiner, the trail exits at the back of Rocky Mountain campground, situated on the first road going east from town on the north side of the Yellowstone River. The trail is not signposted from the road and no parking is available in the campsite itself; campsite staff can advise on suitable parking nearby.

THE HIKE
Day 1: Hellroaring Trailhead to Campsite 1Y7
3½ hours, 9mi
The trail begins by descending through scattered trees to a metal **suspension bridge** across a rock gorge, with the mighty Yellowstone River thundering through a series of white-water rapids below. This first impressive encounter with the river is also the last

for 2½ hours, because the trail veers away from the water after the bridge to cross over a sagebrush-covered hill. On the far side of the rise lies Hellroaring Creek, which can be forded in low water. See Warning (p172) for safety information before attempting the ford. To ford you turn left and then quickly right to reach the river bank.

Once over the creek the path crosses a series of grass and sagebrush meadows, with abundant insect life. A short, steep climb leads up and around a dirt-covered hill, and the ascent continues to some stark, fire-blackened tree stumps. This marks the beginning of a long, gradual descent back to the bank of the Yellowstone, which is green and calm at this stage. Shortly after reaching the river you arrive at ***campsite 1Y9*** (a little over three hours from the start), with ***campsites 1Y7*** and ***1Y5*** 20 and 40 minutes further on respectively.

Day 2: Campsite 1Y7 to Gardiner
4 hours, 9.5mi
After a flat stretch along the riverbank, the second day continues with a short climb to another suspension bridge, where the Blacktail Creek Trail crosses the river. Do not

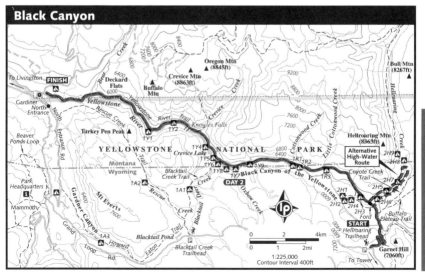

GREATER YELLOWSTONE

cross here but descend through pine trees to the deep, green oval of **Crevice Lake**, about 30 minutes from the start. The pines provide shade around the shore of the lake as far as the footbridge over Crevice Creek.

The Yellowstone changes character as it enters a small canyon. The trail climbs high above the water, weaving over a boulder field. Switchbacks drop to an overlook for the short but impressive **Knowles Falls**. A section of flat bank then leads to more continuous white water, where the trail is forced to make a steep climb over a rocky shoulder as the river thunders along below a steep cliff.

Scattered pines lead down to the riverbank again, before the trail negotiates a rock outcrop via a narrow ledge. From here it is a gentle climb away from the river to the first of many posts marking the boundary of Yellowstone National Park, 1½ hours from Crevice Lake.

The trail now undulates along the dry slopes of Deckard Flats, crossing Bear Creek on a wooden footbridge. Steep, mud-covered hillsides force the path to contour along a sometimes narrow ledge that is slippery in the wet. The town of Gardiner eventually comes into view around a right-hand bend in the river. The last 0.5mi of trail before the town crosses private land, so stick to the trail.

Mt Washburn & Sevenmile Hole

Duration	5½–6½ hours
Distance	16.6mi (26.7km)
Standard	easy–moderate
Start	Dunraven Pass
Finish	Canyon Village
Nearest Towns	Gardiner, Canyon Village
Transport	car

Summary This hike climbs 1400ft to the summit of Mt Washburn, then continues along the rim of the spectacular Grand Canyon of the Yellowstone.

Mt Washburn (10,243ft) is all that remains of a volcano that exploded 600,000 years ago, forming the vast Yellowstone Caldera

(see the boxed text 'Hot Spot', p175). A popular short hike (3.2mi out-and-back) goes to the fire lookout tower on Mt Washburn's summit, which overlooks the caldera basin to its south. An excellent addition to the described hike drops down to Sevenmile Hole (see Side Trip, p175) on the impressive Grand Canyon of the Yellowstone, an area of hot springs, high waterfalls and superb eroded cliffs.

PLANNING
When to Hike
Bear in mind that there are lots of grizzlies in the Mt Washburn area around August and September. Also be wary of lightning associated with afternoon thunderstorms.

Maps
Trails Illustrated's 1:83,333 map No 304 *Tower/Canyon* covers the hike. Two USGS 1:24,000 quads also cover the route: *Mount Washburn* and *Canyon Village*.

NEAREST TOWNS
See Gardiner (p171).

Canyon Village
Canyon is at the southern end of the Grand Canyon of the Yellowstone, at the eastern intersection of the Upper and Lower Grand Loop Rds. The visitor center (☎ 307-242-2550) includes a backcountry office and has exhibits devoted to the ecology of bison. *Canyon Campground* costs $15 and cabins are available.

GETTING TO/FROM THE HIKE
The hike starts from Dunraven Pass, on the Grand Loop Rd, 4.8mi north of Canyon Village; there is trailhead parking for around 20 vehicles only. An alternative start is the larger Chittenden parking area, from where a somewhat steeper hike (mostly along a road) joins the main route described below.

THE HIKE
The wide trail (along a rough, disused road) makes a comfortable, steady ascent through forest of subalpine fir to a minor gap. Continue northeast up broad switchbacks, then

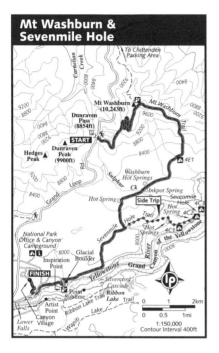

Mt Washburn & Sevenmile Hole

boiling mud pools and fumaroles. It may be dangerous to leave the trail here. Proceed past more minor thermal springs to reach the junction with the Sevenmile Hole Trail (see Side Trip), 1¼ hours from campsite 4E1.

Turning right, the trail is broader now and leads along the northern rim of the almost-1300ft-deep **Grand Canyon of the Yellowstone**, passing through lodgepole forest carpeted with fragrant, low grouseberry shrub. The views become increasingly spectacular as you continue past the long, thin **Silvercord Cascade**, which falls through its own precipitous little chasm. The amazing yellow, white and red columns of the canyon's eroding sides stretch to the Glacial Boulder Trailhead near **Inspiration Point**, 1¼ hours from the Mt Washburn Trail junction. It is a 1.3mi walk along the sealed road to Canyon Village.

Side Trip: Sevenmile Hole
3½–4½ hours, 5.2mi, 1382ft ascent
Sevenmile Hole is a small field of geysers and hot springs at the bottom of the Grand Canyon of the Yellowstone. Unattended food must be out of reach of bears – do not just dump your pack at the junction as you begin this side trip.

The trail drops in switchbacks through Douglas fir, passing a 10ft-high geyser cone

follow a narrow rock ridge, scattered with a few stunted whitebark pines, to meet the gravel road from the Chittenden parking area at the Mt Washburn Trail turnoff. The road curves around to the left after a few minutes to reach the fire-lookout tower on **Mt Washburn** (10,243ft). From the public observation room (which has a free telescope) there are majestic views across the Yellowstone basin south to the Tetons and north to the Beartooths.

The Mt Washburn Trail drops southeast along an undulating ridge of alpine wildflower meadows. After dipping through a saddle to another little gap at tree line, cut down right and make a winding descent through tiny clearings to reach *campsite 4E1*, about 1¼ hours from Mt Washburn. Keep your wits about you as you are now in prime grizzly bear habitat.

The trail continues southwest through areas of boggy grassland grazed by deer and elk to **Washburn Hot Springs**, a small field of

Hot Spot

Yellowstone's intense volcanic activity is caused by a massive bubble of molten magma close to the earth's crust (known as a 'hot spot'), which is floating gradually northeast. The Yellowstone hot spot is extraordinary, as it sits below thick continental crust rather than relatively thin oceanic crust (such as Hawaii).

The present topography of the park was created some 600,000 years ago by a massive volcanic explosion. The force blew out the immense Yellowstone Caldera, which takes in a 1316-sq-mile area between Mt Washburn and Mt Sheridan. Geologists believe the gradual, upward bulging of the Yellowstone Caldera indicates that another major eruption will occur some time in the future.

GREATER YELLOWSTONE

in the forest before arriving at another area of hot springs. Continue down among these bubbling pools and small geysers, past *campsite 4C1* (right), crossing a tiny, thermal stream to pass *campsite 4C2* beside the **Yellowstone River**. Large springs emerge from the reddish chalky cliffs on the river's east side. To reach *campsite 4C3* cross the small Sulphur Creek, then hike along the edge of the river past a tiny hot pool in the rock bed.

Fairy Falls & Twin Buttes

Duration	3–4 hours
Distance	6mi (9.7km)
Standard	easy
Start/Finish	Fairy Falls Trailhead
Nearest Town	Old Faithful
Transport	car

Summary An easy hike to one of Yellowstone's most beautiful waterfalls. Explore two seldom-visited geysers and climb the Twin Buttes for excellent views across the Geyser Basin.

The 197ft Fairy Falls is the highest waterfall in Yellowstone and, perhaps, one of the most beautiful. Tucked away in a corner of the Geyser Basin, the waterfall receives relatively few visitors even though it is only a very short hike from the trailhead. Beyond Fairy Falls the trail continues to a thermal area at the base of the Twin Buttes – two conspicuous bald hills severely burned in the 1988 fires. The two geysers are undeveloped and you are likely to have them to yourself, in stark contrast to the crowds at the Grand Prismatic Spring only a few miles away.

Maps
Trails Illustrated's 1:83,333 map No 302 *Old Faithful* covers the hike.

NEAREST TOWN
Old Faithful
This large complex in the central-west of the park is focused on the famous Old Faithful geyser, which pleases the crowds by erupting (more or less) every 80 minutes. The visitor center (☎ 307-344-7353) has a film on the

park's geothermal features. Grandiose *Old Faithful Lodge* (☎ 307-344-7311) has rooms from $70 and cabins from $45.

GETTING TO/FROM THE HIKE
The trailhead is just off the Grand Loop Rd, about 1mi south of the Grand Prismatic Spring.

THE HIKE
Head northwest along the Old Freight Rd, which is now a wide cycle and hiking path. The colored steam rising from the Grand Prismatic Spring draws your attention to the right, but you can't reach the viewing boardwalk from this trail. Continue on to a trail junction after about 20 minutes and turn left onto the narrower Fairy Creek Trail. The trail winds through an area burned in the 1988 fires (see the boxed text 'Regeneration after the Fire', p179), which at first is uninteresting but, as you near Fairy Falls, wet ground has encouraged an increasing quantity and variety of plants and wildflowers to grow among the blackened stumps.

Fairy Falls is reached about 40 minutes from the trail junction. At 197ft it is the highest in the park, but the volume of water is

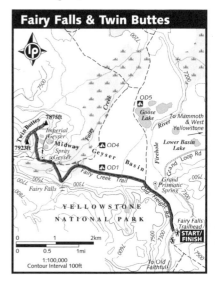

hardly on a par with the falls on the Yellowstone River! Still, the streaks of white water falling across the dark lower rocks create a beautiful pattern set off by the clumps of fireweed growing around the plunge pool.

The trail (not marked on the Trails Illustrated map) continues northwest from Fairy Falls, toward the two prominent buttes and the conspicuous plumes of steam rising from beneath each one. Cross some wet ground with the aid of logs and head for the closest plume emanating from **Spray Geyser**, erupting frequently to a height of 6ft to 8ft. Return a little way along the trail, and then continue west, following the outlet from Imperial Geyser, which is lined with orange bacteria. **Imperial Geyser** is also in near-perpetual activity, sending up blasts of water to around 20ft. If you want to climb onto the Buttes, locally known as the Dolly Parton Hills for obvious reasons, simply head across the open slopes behind Imperial Geyser. After discovering the collection of little pools set in the hollow between the two summits, you can continue to either summit without much difficulty. The views to the east encompass the Fairy Creek Valley and the Lower and Midway Geyser Basins, while to the west, the wild and trail-free Madison Plateau stretches off to Yellowstone's western boundary.

Retrace your steps to the Fairy Falls Trailhead.

Bechler River

Duration	4 days
Distance	29.7mi (47.8km)
Standard	moderate
Start	Lone Star Trailhead
Finish	Bechler River ranger station
Nearest Town	Old Faithful
Transport	car

Summary This long but largely downhill hike is to southwestern Yellowstone's wild Cascade Corner, the area least affected by the 1988 fires.

Known for its numerous waterfalls, this area receives higher levels of precipitation than elsewhere in the park and the extensive wetlands of the Bechler Meadows support numerous water birds, including sandhill cranes and great blue herons. The Bechler's Ferris Fork side stream is the only place in the Yellowstone backcountry where hikers can (legally) bathe in natural hot springs.

PLANNING
When to Hike
Bechler River is popular with anglers and backcountry campsites can be difficult to get, even outside the busy months of July and August. The mosquitoes can be appalling along the river until the end of July. The route also requires a serious ford, which may be impassable in early summer or after heavy rain, so inquire about river levels before departing.

Maps
Trails Illustrated's 1:83,333 map No 302 *Old Faithful* is recommended. Five USGS 1:24,000 quads also cover the route: *Old Faithful*, *Shoshone Geyser Basin*, *Trischman Knob*, *Cave Falls* and *Bechler Falls*. The approximately 1:100,000 *South Yellowstone Park* map, published by the American Adventures Association, is another acceptable alternative.

NEAREST TOWN
See Old Faithful (p176).

GETTING TO/FROM THE HIKE
The hike begins at the Lone Star Trailhead, which is around 2mi (about 30 minutes' hike) southeast along the Grand Loop Rd from Old Faithful village. There is parking for around 30 cars.

The hike ends at Bechler River ranger station, accessible (via Grassy Lake Reservoir) from the turnoff just north of Flagg Ranch in the John D Rockefeller Jr Memorial Parkway, 2mi south of the South Entrance. A car shuttle is required.

THE HIKE
Day 1: Lone Star Trailhead to Bechler River Trail Junction
2¼–2¾ hours, 5.8mi, 900ft ascent
The easy, 2.3mi hike from Grand Loop Rd to Lone Star Geyser (the first section of this

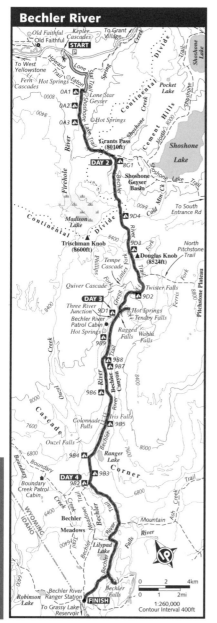

Bechler River

day's hike) is very popular with day hikers. To avoid the crowds, the Howard Eaton Trail from near Old Faithful offers an alternative (if less interesting) starting point.

From Lone Star Trailhead, situated immediately above Kepler Cascades where the Firehole River flows through a spectacular little gorge, take the old road (closed to public vehicles since 1972) past a tiny weir diverting water to Old Faithful village. The road crosses the Firehole River bridge, following the stream up past the Spring Creek Trail turnoff (and a route diverging right) to end at **Lone Star Geyser** after 45 minutes. This isolated geyser erupts for 10 to 15 minutes at intervals of around three hours, sending a jet of boiling water up to 40ft into the air. A foot trail continues 0.3mi north to intersect with the Shoshone Lake Trail.

Turn left and proceed southwest, past *campsite OA1*, recrossing the river on a footbridge around a small thermal field of scalding hot pools and hissing steam vents. The trail passes *campsites OA2* and *OA3*, then climbs south over the broad rolling ridge top to cross **Grants Pass**, which lies on the Continental Divide at 8010ft. Head down through superb stands of tall, old-growth Engelmann spruce and whitebark pine to reach the Bechler River Trail junction, 1½ to two hours from Lone Star Geyser. *Campsite 8G1* is a short way down by the meadows around Shoshone Creek.

From here a worthwhile (3mi) hike can be made to the **Shoshone Geyser Basin** at the western end of Shoshone Lake, the largest lake in the park and its shore is untouched by a road. Trails provide easy access to the main areas of thermal activity.

Day 2: Bechler River Trail Junction to Three River Junction
3½–4½ hours, 9.2mi, 620ft ascent

Take the right (southwest) Bechler River Trail and cut briefly through meadows before making a steady (but rarely steep) climb into montane forest interspersed with small moors. The undulating trail crosses the (approximately 8500ft) watershed of the Continental Divide before descending past *campsites 9D4* and *9D3* (no fires allowed).

Cross a shallow, marshy basin at the northern foot of the prominent Douglas Knob and continue down past *campsite 9D2* to cross the small Gregg Fork.

The trail follows the stream past the 20ft-high, lightly tumbling **Twister Falls** (a short way over to the right), then drops along a fir-covered ridge to a left turn (not shown on most maps) under the northwestern rim of Pitchstone Plateau.

Don't miss the short trip from here to some interesting bubbling thermal pools and spurting geysers along the Ferris Fork. A vigorous hot spring gushes out of the stream bed itself in one of the park's few permitted **bathing sites** – but beware of scalding as the boiling water mixes erratically with the stream. A rough route goes upstream to Tendoy Falls.

Bechler River Trail continues to *campsite 9D1* and past **Ragged Falls**, crossing the Ferris Fork on a footbridge before arriving at Three River Junction. Here the Gregg and Ferris Forks merge with the Phillips Fork to form the **Bechler River**. The river has plentiful rainbow trout and attracts backcountry fly fishers.

Day 3: Three River Junction to Bechler Meadows Trail Junction
3–4 hours, 7.7mi

Make your way over the lovely river flats of the wild upper valley past a string of steaming, algae-rich pools opposite Bechler River patrol cabin to *campsite 9B9* (no fires), near a pretty waterfall. The trail continues downstream into the steep-sided **Bechler Canyon**, past *campsite 9B8*, to ford the river below an area of burned forest. Follow the often muddy trail across numerous cold springs and ford the river again (a slightly more serious wade) just upstream of *campsite 9B6*. The trail leads through old fir-spruce forest past gliding cataracts with picturesque islets to reach the spectacular **Iris Falls**, a 40ft-high curtain of water spraying thick mist into the air, about two hours from Three River Junction.

Descend quickly past the damp *campsite 9B5* to a short turnoff (northwest), leading down to a scenic overlook of **Colonnade Falls**, where the Bechler drops another 85ft in two stages. The trail continues close to the river, through fir-spruce forest alternating with boulder fields and meadows fringed by birch or native cherry scrub to *campsite 9B4*. It then breaks away from the river southwest, past *campsite 9B3* at the edge of a broad clearing to meet the Bechler Meadows Trail turnoff. This is a slightly shorter (5mi) but less interesting route to Bechler River ranger station; it leads directly past *campsite 9B2* to ford the Bechler River, then continues southwest across the boggy Bechler Meadows.

Day 4: Bechler Meadows Trail Junction to Bechler River Ranger Station
3–4 hours, 7mi

Proceed left (south) along the open grassy plains of the meandering river. The trail then leads southeast through forest patches to pass the Mountain Ash Creek Trail turnoff after about one hour. Turn right (southwest) here

Regeneration after the Fire

The huge fires of 1988 burned around 1240 sq miles, or 36%, of Yellowstone National Park. Almost 15 years on, evidence of the fires is still very obvious. But the long-term effects and the subsequent regeneration of the forests have been closely monitored by conservationists. Far from marking a disaster, ecologists have come to see the fires as a natural event heralding a new cycle of growth in Yellowstone.

Many plants and trees depend on high temperatures to trigger the release of their seeds, and it was estimated that there were as many as one million seeds per acre on the ground during the fall of 1998. It was also found that only 390 large mammals perished in the fires, the vast majority being elk. The year after the fires, populations of all grazing and browsing mammals flourished, thanks to succulent new vegetative growth. Birds thrived on increased numbers of insects living on dead wood. Ten years later grasses, wildflowers and shrubs were clear winners, aided by increased sunlight and soil nutrients. Tree saplings were also well established. It is estimated that most of the remaining dead trees will have fallen by 2008.

GREATER YELLOWSTONE

for 1mi to make a last (normally knee-high) ford of the Bechler River. The trail follows the river's right bank for 2mi to another trail junction, from where a rewarding detour (30 minutes out-and-back) leads downstream to **Bechler Falls**, the largest and most impressive of the Bechler's many waterfalls. The main trail cuts right (roughly west) to arrive at the remote Bechler River ranger station in Yellowstone's southwestern corner.

Heart Lake

Duration	2 days
Distance	16mi (25.7km)
Standard	easy
Start/Finish	Heart Lake Trailhead
Nearest Town	Grant Village
Transport	car

Summary An interesting and uncomplicated out-and-back hike to a lake rich in wildlife and flanked by a geothermal field.

Although large parts of the area were hit by the 1988 fires, Heart Lake has retained much of its charm. Stretching around its northwestern shore is an extensive thermal field, which includes boiling pools and a large geyser. Its tranquil waters are a rich habitat for waterbirds, and there are plentiful stocks of cutthroat and lake trout.

Mt Sheridan (10,308ft), the highest point in the small Red Mountains range, rises from the lake's western shore and provides a wonderful panorama. Although very fit people hike to Heart Lake and climb Mt Sheridan in a long, out-and-back day hike, it makes more sense to camp a night (or two) at Heart Lake.

Note that the Heart Lake area is prime grizzly bear country, so stay alert. There is also no water available on the route until Heart Lake, so carry plenty.

PLANNING
When to Hike
Due to the high bear activity in the area, the trail to Heart Lake does not open until July 1. Hikers may encounter heavy snow on the way up to Mt Sheridan until mid-July or later.

Maps
Trails Illustrated's 1:83,333 map No 305 *Yellowstone Lake* adequately covers the hike. Alternatively use two 1:24,000 USGS maps: *Mount Sheridan* and *Heart Lake*.

NEAREST TOWN
Grant Village
Grant Village, near West Thumb (bay) on Yellowstone Lake, is at the intersection of the Lower Grand Loop Rd and South Entrance Rd. The visitor center (☎ 307-242-2650) deals with effects of forest fires on Yellowstone's ecology. The separate backcountry office is beside the gas station. *Grant Village Campground* ($15) is by the lake shore. *Grant Village Motel (☎ 307-344-7311)* has rooms from $94.

GETTING TO/FROM THE HIKE
The hike begins 5.3mi south of Grant Village on South Entrance Rd. There is trailhead parking for around 25 cars.

THE HIKE
Day 1: Heart Lake Trailhead to Heart Lake
3½–4½ hours, 8mi, 342ft ascent

Follow the wide trail southeast through lodgepole forest severely affected by the 1988 fires and the voracious mountain bark beetle. The trail rises very slightly over a minor watershed to the first group of smoking fumaroles at the northern foot of bald-topped Factory Hill (9607ft), 1½ to two hours from the trailhead. From here you get your first view of the lake, still 2mi away.

Wind your way down into the intensely active **Heart Lake Geyser Basin** past numerous spurting hot springs and boiling pools, most of which are a short way off to the right. The trail crosses and recrosses the tepid Witch Creek to reach Heart Lake ranger station, just back from the northern shore of **Heart Lake**. In summer this log hut is usually occupied by a park ranger. From here Trail Creek Trail departs left (east) around the lake's northeastern side.

The Heart Lake Trail continues right, first following the gray sand beach to cross the inlet, then tracing the lake's western

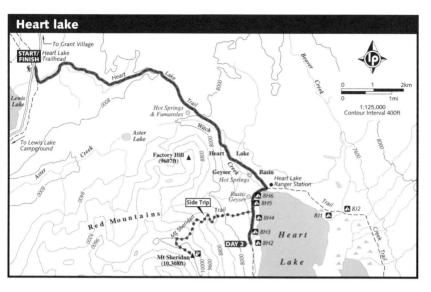

Heart lake

shore to reach ***campsite 8H6***. This is the first of five sites along the unburned strip of firs and spruces fringing the shore. A path leads a few paces off right to another small but fascinating thermal area. Here, the **Rustic Geyser** shoots up at irregular intervals, while other hot springs bubble up into large calcified bathtubs. Tread carefully in these fragile and dangerous places.

The trail leads past ***campsite 8H5*** to meet the Mt Sheridan Trail turnoff (see Side Trip) and continues 20 minutes south past ***campsites 8H4*** and ***8H3*** to ***8H2***. There are good views across the placid waters east to Overlook Mountain and southeast to flat-topped Mt Hancock. In the evenings, courting pairs of grebes can be seen diving and calling to each other in mellow, lilting voices.

Side Trip: Mt Sheridan
4–5½ hours, 7mi, 2858ft ascent
Mt Sheridan Trail cuts up briefly over open meadows before beginning a spiraling ascent along a steep spur largely covered by whitebark pine. The spur leads into a saddle among wind-battered fir. Continue left (southeast) up the narrowing tundra ridge over old snowdrifts to reach the 10,308ft summit of

Mt Sheridan. The fire lookout (staffed in summer, otherwise locked) enjoys a complete panorama encompassing Pitchstone Plateau to the west, Shoshone Lake to the northwest, Yellowstone Lake to the northeast and the jagged Tetons to the south.

Day 2: Heart Lake to Heart Lake Trailhead
3½–4½ hours, 8mi, 342ft descent
Retrace your Day 1 steps to the trailhead.

Alternative Campsites
There are six other campsites around Heart Lake: ***8J1*** and ***8J2*** on its eastern side; ***8J6*** and ***8J4*** on the southeastern shore; ***8J3*** nearby along Surprise Creek; and ***8H1*** at the lake's southwestern corner.

Grand Teton National Park

Grand Teton National Park lies south of Yellowstone National Park in northwestern Wyoming. On its western boundary the park merges with Jedediah Smith Wilderness (within Targhee National Forest). The park stretches 40mi along the spectacular but compact 15mi-wide Teton Range.

Unlike any other range in the Rockies, the Tetons rise with stunning abruptness in a row of 'witch-hat' peaks that tower 1.5mi above the saltbush plains to the east. Gradual westward tilting has created numerous escarpments separating high 'belvedere' terraces that serve as marvelously scenic walkways. The Teton Range boasts a dozen peaks over 12,000ft and a similar number of high hanging glaciers. The Tetons' highest (and Wyoming's second-highest) peak is 13,770ft Grand Teton itself.

The vast majority of hikers visit the especially picturesque and easily accessible southern Tetons, having a severe impact on the most heavily used or fragile areas. Backcountry visitors should keep to designated trails and established campsites.

HISTORY

The Blackfoot, Shoshone and Gros Ventre Native American tribes all frequented Jackson Hole (the broad valley at the eastern foot of the range) over the summer season, but moved to lower elevations to avoid harsh winters. Ranchers began settling in the area from the late 19th century. The Carrington expedition of 1879 proposed that the Teton Range be incorporated into Yellowstone National Park, but it took until 1929 for the area to gain protection as a separate Grand Teton National Park. This original park excluded Jackson Hole but much of the land in the valley was secretly purchased by the billionaire John D Rockefeller Jr, who donated it to the US government in 1950 to form the present boundary of Grand Teton National Park.

NATURAL HISTORY

Although they are composed of some of the most ancient (Precambrian) rocks in North America, the Tetons are the youngest mountain range in the Rockies. The Tetons' classic, pointed forms are due to the relatively recent uplifting of the range, a process that began only nine million years ago, and the even more recent ice-age glaciations that sharpened their summits.

Elk, mountain goats, bighorn sheep, mule deer, moose and black bears are common in these mountains. Grizzly bears are found in the northern half of the park (beyond Mt Moran).

The Tetons' beautiful montane and subalpine forests preserve the largest whitebark pines found anywhere in North America. These slow-growing conifers have reached heights exceeding 80ft and diameters of 6ft at the base. Other typical forest species are Douglas fir, Engelmann spruce and subalpine fir, with stands of cottonwood, lodgepole pine and aspen on better-drained lower slopes.

Wildflowers of the moist forests include delicate, yellowish-white, three-petaled western trilliums, white corn-lilies, star-flowered false Solomon's seals and fairybells – the twin red 'pom-pom' berries, which are eaten by grouse and rodents. Yellow arnica and pink and white phlox are found in forest clearings and subalpine meadows. Scarlet paintbrush, the floral emblem of Wyoming, is abundant in the moraine soil of the Tetons' canyon valleys.

Gray jays dart around the spruce forests, audaciously pecking for leftovers around campsites, while the dark-eyed junco hops through the underbrush. Here you may also hear the distinctive calls of ruby-crowned kinglets (otherwise recognizable by the male's red crest, raised when wooing the female) and the white-crowned sparrow. Water birds, including American coots, sandhill cranes and double-crested cormorants, are common on the park's lakes, especially the shallows of the large Jackson Lake.

PLANNING
Maps & Books

Two waterproof maps covering the whole park are the Earthwalk Press 1:72,500 *Hiking Map and Guide, Grand Teton National Park* ($7.95), with a 1:48,000 inset of its popular southern sector, and Trails Illustrated's 1:78,000 No 202 *Grand Teton National Park* ($9.95), with a 1:24,000 inset of the Grand Teton climbing area.

Jackson Hole Hikes by Rebecca Woods ($16.95) is a recommended trail guide to the area.

Cougars

Cougars, or mountain lions as they are also known, are making a comeback in the US. The big cat population had plummeted during the middle part of last century due to bounty hunting. There has, however, been increased conflict with humans as a result of people living and recreating more frequently in cougar habitat. In 1999 near Jackson, just outside Grand Teton National Park, a female cougar with three cubs set up den on Millar Butte, in full view of Elk Refuge Rd, and stayed there for six weeks. It is estimated that 15,000 people visited the area to see and photograph the cougar family during its brief stay.

Although the increase in the local cougar population was met with an increase in hunting quotas (the Wyoming State Game and Fish Department more than doubled the cougar mortality quota for the Teton area to 12 animals just a few weeks after the disappearance of the Jackson lion family), the animal appears to be thriving. This is particularly the case in areas where its preferred prey of deer, elk, bighorn sheep and occasionally moose are protected.

Cougars are generally very shy animals and wary of humans, however, they are also very powerful and potentially dangerous. Males can weigh up to 190lb and measure 9ft from nose to tip of tail, and both males and females are capable of vertical jumps of 15ft. Adults can drop noiselessly 60ft to the ground and land running. There have been no fatal cougar attacks on humans to date in Wyoming, although neighboring Colorado and Montana have both suffered big-cat killings. Cougar attacks are different to bear attacks in that the mountain lion's primary reason for attacking is generally predatory rather than defensive. The course of action suggested for cougar encounters is also different: make noise, make yourself seem big, confront the animal and fight hard if necessary to let it know that you are not an easy meal. It is also thought that moving quickly through cougar habitat (ie, running or skiing) can trigger a predatory response, especially around the prime activity periods of dawn and dusk. For more information see Animal Attacks (p74).

MATT SWINDEN

Information Sources

Information is available from the park headquarters (☎ 307-739-3300, fax 739-3438; W www.nps.gov/grte; Grand Teton National Park, Draw 170, Moose, WY 83012).

Permits & Regulations

Park entry fees (valid for seven days and also giving access to Yellowstone) are $20 for private vehicles, $15 for motorcycles and $10 for individuals on foot or bicycle.

Backcountry permits are required for all overnight trips in Grand Teton. Backcountry permits are free, although for bookings there is a $15 fee. Reservations are accepted by fax or mail at the park headquarters (see Information Sources) from January 1 to May 15. Permits can be obtained in person from the backcountry offices at Moose and Colter Bay visitor centers or Jenny Lake ranger station.

In southern Grand Teton, backcountry camping is restricted to camping zones. Hikers (with backcountry permits) can choose their own sites but in the most heavily used zones all sites are designated (indicated by marker posts). Fires are prohibited and campsites must be at least 200ft from waterways.

GETTING AROUND

Alltrans (☎ 307-733-1112) can do hiker shuttles within the park. Teton Boating Company (☎ 307-733-2703) runs frequent boats from the southern shore of Jenny Lake to the dock near Hidden Falls on its western shore; the one-way fare is adults/children $3.25/2.

ACCESS TOWNS

Colter Bay Village

Colter Bay is on the east side of Jackson Lake on US 89/191/287. The backcountry office (☎ 307-739-3595) is at the visitor center (☎ 307-739-3594). *Colter Bay campground* sites cost $12. *Colter Bay Village* (☎ 307-543-2828) has a range of accommodations, from tent village ($35) to cabins (from $35). A gas station, *grocery store*, laundromat and hot showers are also available in the village.

Jenny Lake

The village of Jenny Lake is 7mi north of the park entrance on the lake's southeast shore. The backcountry office is open in summer only. Sites at *Jenny Lake campground* cost $12.

Moose

Moose, roughly 10mi north of Jackson at the Teton Park Rd turnoff, is the park headquarters. The backcountry office (☎ 307-739-3309) is at the visitor center (☎ 307-739-3399). The village also offers a shopping center and a gas station.

Teton Village

This modern ski resort lies at the foot of Rendezvous Mountain, 12mi northwest of Jackson. The village has several *grocery stores* and a wealth of outdoor sports shops. The Jackson Hole Aerial Tram (☎ 307-739-2753) runs up 4139ft to Rendezvous Mountain, providing easy access to the high trails of southern Grand Teton National Park. The aerial tram operates daily from 9am to 5pm between late May and late September (to 7pm between late June and early September). Uphill fares are $16/13/6 for adults/seniors/children but (hikers note!) the downhill trip is free.

Hostel X (☎ 307-733-3415) has no dorm beds but basic double rooms cost $48. *Teton Village KOA Campground (☎ 307-733-5354)*, 1.5mi north of Hwy 22 on Hwy 390, has tent sites with full facilities from $26.

Local START buses (☎ 307-733-4521) run regularly between Teton Village and Jackson.

Paintbrush Divide Loop

Duration	3 days
Distance	17.8mi (28.6km)
Standard	moderate
Start/Finish	South String Lake Trailhead
Nearest Town	Jenny Lake
Transport	car

Summary A circuit route crossing a scenic high pass offering marvelous views of the park's classic summits.

The high shelf known as Paintbrush Divide (10,645ft) stands between the deep Paintbrush and Cascade Canyons. This superb natural lookout gives outstanding vistas of the surrounding peaks, particularly Mt Moran. A minor variant is to finish at the South Jenny Lake Trailhead. The hike can also be linked with the Teton Crest Trail to make a fantastic five-day hike.

PLANNING
When to Hike
Paintbrush Divide usually remains snowbound well into July. Between late June and early September thunderstorms often bring heavy rain, and the danger of lightning strike is acute on high-level routes such as this.

Maps
Use either of the maps mentioned under Maps & Books (p182). For more detail, two USGS 1:24,000 quads cover the route: *Jenny Lake* and *Mount Moran*.

NEAREST TOWN
See Jenny Lake (p184).

GETTING TO/FROM THE HIKE
The hike begins at South String Lake Trailhead, near Jenny Lake Lodge. There is a large car park at the trailhead.

THE HIKE (see map p186)
Day 1: South String Lake Trailhead to Holly Lake
3–4½ hours, 6.2mi, 2540ft ascent
Cross the String Lake outlet on a footbridge, near the trailhead car park. Bear right at the junction a few minutes later and follow the String Lake Trail around the lake's western shore. The trail rises steadily north over avalanche slopes of snapped firs, from where String Lake's unusually narrow, elongated form becomes apparent, to reach a junction, about 40 minutes from the trailhead. Turn left along the Paintbrush Canyon Trail and climb through fir-spruce forest (with a generous scattering of Douglas fir and occasional white fir). The trail swings west into the deep, enclosed valley of **Paintbrush Canyon**, under the towering walls of Rockchuck Peak to meet Paintbrush Canyon Creek. Continue up into the *Lower Paintbrush Camping Zone* (eight campsites),

crossing the creek just before you pass the two uppermost sites. As you get higher, fine views open out downvalley to Leigh Lake and Spalding Bay in Jackson Lake.

The trail ascends through rocky avalanche chutes colonized by wild raspberry shrubs, and small meadows sprinkled with columbines and Indian paintbrush, the flamboyant red wildflowers that lend their name to the canyon. After passing the *Outlier campsite* (a reservation-only site not marked on most maps) the trail forks. The left trail climbs an old lateral moraine ridge covered by whitebark pine, past a scree-filled tarn, while the more scenic right trail leads up to **Holly Lake**, a beautiful alpine lake directly below Mt Woodring. There are a number of designated *campsites* at the lake's southeast corner.

Day 2: Holly Lake to North Fork Cascade Camping Zone
2½–3 hours, 3.2mi, 1235ft ascent
From Holly Lake make a steep, 300ft climb to join a trail coming in on the left, the alternative from the end of Day 1. The main trail leads northwest through the *Upper Paintbrush Camping Zone* into the treeless tundra of the upper basin to reach a high, flat shoulder. Traverse quickly (as this slope is prone to rockfall) over persistent snowdrifts above icy tarns, then make a short, winding ascent through the coarse rubble to arrive at **Paintbrush Divide** (10,645ft), one to 1½ hours from Holly Lake. The views from the pass include the amazing slab walls on Mt Moran to the north, and the rock needles of the Jaw, Mt St John, and Rock of Ages poking up along the southern rim of Paintbrush Canyon.

The trail descends west in broad switchbacks to reach **Lake Solitude**, an enchanting tarn in a snowy cirque surrounded by grassy lawns, after about one hour. Head down through the U-shaped glacial valley toward the north faces of Mt Owen and (later) Grand Teton, the two highest peaks in Grand Teton National Park.

Cross Cascade Creek to enter the *North Fork Cascade Camping Zone*, with 10 campsites scattered among moraine boulders and old firs.

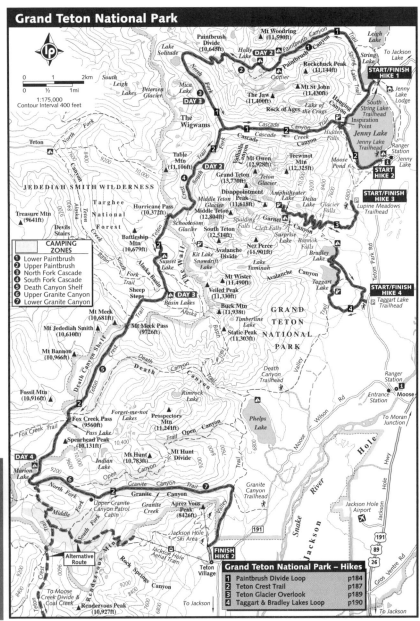

Grand Teton National Park

Mt Woodring
(11,590ft) ▲

Paintbrush
Divide
(10,645ft)

Holly
Lake

DAY 2

Lake
Solitude

South
Leigh
Lakes

Petersen
Glacier

Mica
Lake

DAY 3

The Jaw
(11,400ft) ▲

Rock of Ages

Lake
Solitude

Leigh
Lake

String
Lake

To Jackson
Lake

Rockchuck Peak
(11,144ft) ▲

Outlier

**START/FINISH
HIKE 1**

Mt St John
(11,430ft) ▲

Lake of
the Crags

South
String Lake
Trailhead

Jenny
Lake
Lodge

Inspiration
Point

Jenny Lake

The
Wigwams

Table
Mtn
(11,106ft) ▲

DAY 2

Cascade

Cascade

Cascade
Creek

Hidden
Falls

Jenny Lake
Trailhead

Ranger
Station

Jenny
Lake

**START
HIKE 2**

Mt Owen
(12,928ft) ▲

Teewinot
Mtn
(12,325ft) ▲

Moose
Pond

Grand Teton
(13,770ft) ▲

Disappointment
Peak

Amphitheater
Lake

Delta
Lake

**START/FINISH
HIKE 3**

JEDEDIAH SMITH WILDERNESS

Targhee

National

Forest

Treasure Mtn
(9641ft) ▲

Devils
Stairs

Hurricane Pass
(10,372ft)

The Wall

Schoolroom
Glacier

Middle Teton
Glacier

Middle Teton
(12,804ft) ▲

South Teton
(12,514ft) ▲

Spalding
Falls

Cleft Falls

Garnet
Canyon

Surprise
Lake

Glacier
Falls

Lupine Meadows
Trailhead

**START/FINISH
HIKE 4**

Battleship
Mtn
(10,679ft) ▲

Sunset
Lake

Alaska Basin

Kit Lake

Avalanche
Divide

Snowdrift
Lake

Nez Perce
(11,901ft) ▲

Lake
Taminah

Bannock
Falls

Bradley
Lake

Mt Wister
(11,490ft) ▲

Avalanche Canyon

Taggart
Lake

**START/FINISH
HIKE 4**

Taggart Lake
Trailhead

Sheep
Steps

South
Fork
Trail

Veiled Peak
(11,330ft) ▲

Basin Lakes

DAY 3

Buck Mtn
(11,938ft) ▲

Timberline
Lake

Static Peak
(11,303ft) ▲

GRAND

TETON

NATIONAL

PARK

CAMPING
ZONES
1 Lower Paintbrush
2 Upper Paintbrush
3 North Fork Cascade
4 South Fork Cascade
5 Death Canyon Shelf
6 Upper Granite Canyon
7 Lower Granite Canyon

Mt Meek
(10,681ft) ▲

Mt Jedediah Smith ▲
(10,610ft)

Mt Meek Pass
(9726ft)

Mt Bannon
(10,966ft) ▲

Death

Canyon

Shelf

Fossil Mtn
(10,916ft) ▲

Fox Creek Pass
(9560ft)

Spearhead Peak
(10,131ft) ▲

DAY 4

Marion
Lake

Fox Creek Trail

Forget-me-not
Lakes

Prospectory
Mtn
(11,241ft) ▲

Pass Lake

Indian
Lake

Mt Hunt
(10,783ft) ▲

Mt Hunt
Divide

Rimrock
Lake

Death
Canyon

Open Canyon

Phelps
Lake

Death
Canyon
Trailhead

Ranger
Station

Entrance
Station

Moose

To Moran
Junction

Granite

Canyon

Open

Granite
Canyon
Trailhead

Granite

Canyon

Trail

Upper Granite
Canyon Patrol
Cabin

Granite
Creek

Aprez Vous
Peak
(8426ft) ▲

Jackson Hole
Ski Area

Jackson Hole
Aerial Tram

**FINISH
HIKE 2**

Teton
Village

Alternative
Route

Rock Springs
Canyon

To Jackson

Rendezvous Peak
(10,927ft) ▲

To Moose
Creek Divide
& Coal Creek

Jackson Hole
Airport

Snake River

Jackson

Hole

Jackson Hole
Hwy

To Jackson

Grand Teton National Park – Hikes

0   1   2km
0   ½   1mi
1:175,000
Contour Interval 400 feet

GREATER YELLOWSTONE

Day 3: North Fork Cascade Camping Zone to South String Lake Trailhead

3½–4 hours, 8.4mi

The trail crosses and recrosses the creek, descending through forest to an intersection a short way above the confluence of Cascade Creek's North and South Forks, one hour from Solitude Lake. Here Teton Crest Trail heads south along the creek's South Fork.

Follow the Cascade Canyon Trail east, gently descending through pockets of spruce and lodgepole forest past stream ponds, where you have an excellent chance of spotting moose. You should reach **Inspiration Point** (7200ft), an overlook with views across Jenny Lake to the Gros Ventre mountains, in two to 2½ hours. Continue the short distance, past the trails to Hidden Falls and South Jenny Lake Trailhead, to the boat dock. From here head north across the stream from Hanging Canyon and proceed around the lake's northwestern shore through fir-spruce forest to arrive back at South String Lake Trailhead, about 45 minutes from the boat dock.

Teton Crest Trail

Duration	4 days
Distance	31.4mi (50.5km)
Standard	moderate–hard
Start	South Jenny Lake Trailhead
Finish	Teton Village
Nearest Town	Jenny Lake
Transport	car, bus

Summary One of the most spectacular hikes in the Rockies, the Teton Crest Trail leads over several passes and along broad, high terraces with sheer drop-offs.

This is an exhilarating, high-level route (often above 9000ft) through the wild heart of Grand Teton, offering some superb vistas. As its name suggests, this trail follows a high-level, scenic route, dipping in and out of the neighboring Jedediah Smith Wilderness. Numerous side routes lead up the canyons or passes on either side of the trail, allowing easy access and exits. Various additions are possible, including the Paintbrush Divide route (p184), the Valley Trail (north from the Granite Canyon Trail junction to Jenny Lake), or the continuation of the Teton Crest Trail to Hwy 22.

PLANNING
When to Hike

The sustained altitude of this route means that it is often impassable well into July. Between late June and early September afternoon thunderstorms are also common – try to time your trip to avoid them and avoid exposed ridges if caught out.

Maps

Use either of the maps mentioned under Maps & Books (p182). For more detail, three USGS 1:24,000 quads cover the route: *Jenny Lake*, *Mount Bannon* and *Grand Teton*.

NEAREST TOWN

See Jenny Lake (p184).

GETTING TO/FROM THE HIKE

The hike starts at Jenny Lake (and can be shortened slightly by taking the boat – see Getting Around, p184) and finishes at Teton Village. Shuttle hikers can park vehicles at Jenny Lake and Granite Canyon Trailhead (on the Moose-Wilson Rd, 2mi northeast of Teton Village). From Teton Village there are regular buses back to Jackson. Hitchhiking is officially against park regulations but is not uncommon.

THE HIKE (see map p186)
Day 1: Jenny Lake to South Fork Cascade Camping Zone

3½–4¾ hours, 7.4mi, 1437ft ascent

The trail heads around the western shore of Jenny Lake, then follows Cascade Creek up past small ravines to a footbridge. A short side trail leads upstream to the concealed cascades of **Hidden Falls**. Ascend in spectacular switchbacks through a precipice to **Inspiration Point** (7200ft), an overlook with views across Jenny Lake to the Gros Ventre mountains, to meet the Cascade Canyon Trail, about 1½ hours from the trailhead.

Continue left (west) up into the lower canyon, where the summit of Grand Teton can be seen pushing up behind Mt Owen and Teewinot Mountain. The trail rises gently through meadows alternating with pockets of spruce and lodgepole forest past stream ponds, where you have an excellent chance of spotting moose. Continue to Cascade Creek Forks Junction, two to 2½ hours from Inspiration Point.

Head up the forested western bank of the South Fork, where American dippers can sometimes be seen ducking in and out of the cascading water. The trail soon enters the *South Fork Cascade Camping Zone* after about 20 minutes.

Day 2: South Fork Cascade Camping Zone to Alaska Basin
2¾–3¾ hours, 6.1mi, 1992ft ascent

The trail continues upvalley, switchbacking briefly as it makes a mainly gentle climb over almost level stages below abrupt spurs coming off the Tetons and Table Mountain. A junction in the upper valley is reached after 1½ to two hours from the camping zone. The left trail is a worthwhile hike (1.6mi) south to Avalanche Divide (10,600ft), a scenic lookout above Snowdrift Lake at the edge of the escarpment known as the Wall.

Follow Teton Crest Trail (right), directly past the zone's two uppermost *campsites*, over slopes of purple aster and stunted shrub willow. The trail makes an increasingly steep, zigzagging ascent past the now much diminished Schoolroom Glacier (a murky tarn has formed within the circular moraine walls in the wake of the glacier's recession) to arrive at **Hurricane Pass** (10,372ft), 30 to 45 minutes from the Avalanche Divide junction. The pass offers unsurpassed views of Grand, Middle and South Teton, as well as west across interesting stratified ranges.

Head briefly south along the top of the range, then cut down right past limestone sinkholes into Jedediah Smith Wilderness. The trail gently descends a broad ridge past the striking, mesa-like outcrop of Battleship Mountain before switchbacking down over alpine meadows of blue lupines to Sunset Lake.

Continue south past several turnoffs – two that lead left (east) over Buck Mountain Pass (a shortcut route to Moose or Teton Village via Phelps Lake) and a right trail that goes 7.7mi down the canyon to the *USFS Teton campsite*. The Teton Crest Trail skirts around into scenic Alaska Basin (at roughly 9500ft), where a scattering of shallow tarns known as the **Basin Lakes** look out across the tiers of massive escarpments that fall directly into Teton Canyon.

Sheltered *campsites* can be found in the low trees above Sunset Lake and around the tarns of Alaska Basin. This area is extremely popular with campers (partly because it is outside the national park and backcountry permits are not required). Remember you must camp at least 300ft from lakes and 50ft from streams. Campfires are not allowed.

Day 3: Alaska Basin to Marion Lake
3¼–4¾ hours, 8.2mi

Continue west to cross the small South Fork Teton Creek on stepping stones. After switchbacking steeply up Sheep Steps, make a smoother climb over open, rolling slopes past another turnoff to Teton campsite (via Devils Stairs) to reach the wide grassy saddle of Mt Meek Pass (9726ft) after one to 1½ hours.

The trail dips to re-enter the park at the start of **Death Canyon Shelf**. This remarkable terrace stretches nearly 3mi between two great precipices, offering breathtaking 'belvedere' views of Prospectors Mountain and adjacent peaks across the 1500ft-deep canyon. For most of the way the trail transits *Death Canyon Shelf Camping Zone* (unrestricted), rising and dipping through clusters of whitebark pine and subalpine fir alternating with meadows of cow parsnip. A final, easy climb past the Death Canyon Trail (east) and Fox Creek Trail (west) turnoffs brings you up to **Fox Creek Pass** (9560ft), about 1½ hours from Mt Meek Pass.

Continue southwest across open, undulating slopes west of Spearhead Peak. To the north, just left of the elongated pyramid of Fossil Mountain, steep ravines have cut through the forested mountainside to create a series of narrow, green bands. The Teton

Crest Trail cuts up gradually right (west) to follow a broad, flowery ridge into a vague saddle (9600ft), then drops south to arrive at **Marion Lake**, one to 1½ hours from Fox Creek Pass. This lovely emerald lake lies just below tree line under the stratified east face of Housetop Mountain; there are a number of designated *campsites* across the outlet.

Day 4: Marion Lake to Teton Village
4–5¼ hours, 9.7mi

Head southwest over a low ridge, then sidle down across trickling streams of the upper North Fork Granite Creek to a trail junction.

Turn left (east) along the Granite Canyon Trail and commence the gentle descent through *Upper Granite Canyon Camping Zone*. There is excellent, unrestricted camping (with backcountry permit) among the fir-spruce forest and wildflower meadows of this charming alpine valley. The trail leads past turnoffs (northeast) to Mt Hunt Divide and (south), near the Upper Granite Canyon patrol cabin, to Rendezvous Mountain. The patrol cabin is 1¼ hours from Marion Lake.

Proceed down into *Lower Granite Canyon Camping Zone* (unrestricted) through old Douglas fir below the high granite cliffs. The slope's steepness makes it hard to find good campsites until near the end of the canyon, where elk, moose, mule deer and black bears frequent meadows fringed by thickets of mountain ash and Rocky Mountain maple. The trail intersects with the broad Valley Trail, about two hours from the patrol cabin.

Follow the Valley Trail right (south) across Granite Creek and past the Granite Canyon Trailhead turnoff (which goes 1.5mi southeast to recross Granite Creek before cutting east over sagebrush plains to the trailhead car park). The Valley Trail rises over slopes of aspen overlooking the wide, flat plain of Jackson Hole. Go right (southwest) at a fork on the national park boundary and continue to a gravel road, following this down left (south) under ski lifts to arrive at Teton Village, one to 1½ hours from the Granite Canyon Trail turnoff.

Alternative Finishes
From North Fork Granite Creek trail junction on Day 4, you can continue along the spectacular Teton Crest Trail heading south for 13.5mi across Moose Creek Divide and Phillips Pass to the southern trailhead at Coal Creek, 2mi west of Teton Pass.

The trail to the upper station of the Jackson Hole Aerial Tram on Rendezvous Mountain turns left (east) off the Teton Crest Trail, 1.4mi from the North Fork Granite Creek trail junction.

Teton Glacier Overlook

Duration	5½ hours
Distance	10.2mi (16.4km)
Standard	moderate
Start/Finish	Lupine Meadows Trailhead
Nearest Town	Jenny Lake
Transport	car

Summary A sustained ascent leads past two high lakes to one of the most spectacular lookout points in the Tetons.

This trail makes a strenuous and continuous 3000ft ascent to perhaps the most impressive spot in the Tetons that is easily accessible to hikers. On its way the route passes two lakes carved into a rocky cirque high on the slopes of Disappointment Peak. The route's views and accessibility make it very popular so don't expect to be alone on the trail. There are several designated campsites between Surprise and Amphitheater Lakes for those who want to stay overnight, although because of heavy use several regeneration areas are in effect.

PLANNING
When to Hike
The route should be free of snow by late June.

What to Bring
No water is available between the trailhead and the two lakes, which are almost at the top of the long climb, so make sure to bring plenty.

Maps
Use Earthwalk Press' 1:48,000 *Hiking Map and Guide, Grand Teton National Park*.

NEAREST TOWN
See Jenny Lake (p184).

GETTING TO/FROM THE HIKE
The Lupine Meadows parking area is about 1mi along an unpaved road, just to the south of Jenny Lake. There is adequate parking for about 30 vehicles.

THE HIKE (see map p186)
The well-worn trail begins by gently winding through pine trees, until it mounts a shoulder and the ascent begins in earnest. A junction with the Taggart and Bradley Lakes trail lies at the top of the shoulder, 1.7mi and 40 minutes from the start. Keep right and begin to climb the series of wide switchbacks that ascends (2200ft) the flank of Disappointment Peak. As you climb there are expansive views over Jackson Hole to the east, and a signed junction with the Garnet Canyon Trail is passed around 1½ hours from the start.

The switchbacks ease shortly before the lakes, and the inviting green waters of **Surprise Lake** are finally reached after 2¼ hours of solid climbing. The beauty of the pool, set in a hollow beneath jagged white rocks and cliffs, makes it an ideal place to recover from the exertion of the ascent. The slightly bigger and starker **Amphitheater Lake** is just 0.2mi further along the trail.

To reach the overlook continue to follow the trail around the northeastern shore of Amphitheater Lake and keep right at several indistinct forks. Climb between the rocks to the top of a shoulder. The view into the next valley, which sweeps down from Grand Teton, is breathtaking. The razor-sharp spires and shattered ridgeline between Teewinot Mountain and Mt Owen to the north contrast with the flatlands of Jackson Hole that are visible between sheer valley walls south. The sense of vertical height is impressive, and will leave more than a flutter in the heart of vertigo sufferers.

Retrace your steps to the trailhead.

Taggart & Bradley Lakes Loop

Duration	3 hours
Distance	5.9mi (9.5km)
Standard	easy
Start/Finish	Taggart Lake Trailhead
Nearest Towns	Moose, Jenny Lake
Transport	car

Summary This short and easy loop provides fine, close-up views of the Tetons without having to negotiate difficult trails.

This pair of glacial lakes sit at the base of the Tetons in an area badly affected by wildfire. Despite the absence of forest (the only significant remaining forest on this hike is around Bradley Lake) the burned areas provide their own interest. Numerous species of wildflower and insect flourish in the open areas, and you could easily spend an extra couple of hours on the trail with an identification guidebook. The hike is well suited to children.

PLANNING
When to Hike
The trail should be clear of snow from mid-May. It is best to plan an early start if you don't like the heat, since much of the trail lacks shade.

Maps
Use the Earthwalk Press 1:48,000 *Hiking Map and Guide, Grand Teton National Park*.

Permits & Regulations
Day hikers visiting Taggart and Bradley Lakes are not permitted to camp at Bradley Lake. Sites are reserved for hikers on multi-day loops.

NEAREST TOWN
See Jenny Lake and Moose (p184).

GETTING TO/FROM THE HIKE
The huge parking lot for the Taggart Lake Trailhead is just off Teton Park Rd, 5mi north of Moose.

THE HIKE (see map p186)

Follow the trail northwest, away from the parking area, and turn left at a junction after 0.2mi. The trail winds around several small ridges, skirts a patch of wetland, and after 1.4mi reaches a junction with the Valley Trail (which runs along the base of the Tetons all the way to Teton Village). Turn right at the junction and climb open slopes to a point on the moraine wall overlooking **Taggart Lake**. Descend the short distance to the lakeshore and use a wooden footbridge to cross the outlet creek. The views of the Tetons from the shore are fantastic.

The trail winds around the shores of Taggart Lake and passes a trail junction signposted for the parking area (a shortcut back if you are tired). Climb steadily away from Taggart Lake across slopes that can be festooned with the cocoons of butterfly larvae during the summer. After about 20 minutes the path reaches patches of forest at the crest of the moraine wall separating Taggart and Bradley Lakes. Descend through the trees to reach the forested shores of **Bradley Lake** – a considerable contrast from the burned area around Taggart Lake. Just before the trail reaches the shores of Bradley Lake there is a trail junction. Turn right to begin the trip back to the parking area, or continue ahead to explore the shores of Bradley Lake before returning to this junction. The return trail climbs briefly to reach the top of the moraine wall before descending steadily across an area of wildfire burn to the parking area.

Other Hikes

ABSAROKA-BEARTOOTH WILDERNESS
Lake Plateau

This delightful plateau in the western Beartooths contains 24 lakes. This easy–moderate, 24mi hike departs from Box Canyon guard station, roughly 50mi south of Big Timber on the Boulder River Rd, and gradually climbs 12mi to the Rainbow Lakes. From here a side trip can be made to Lake Pinchot. Lake Plateau offers excellent camping and fishing. USFS' 1:63,360 *Absaroka Beartooth Wilderness* map covers the route. Alternatively use the USGS 1:24,000 quads *Mount Douglas*, *Tumble Mountain* and *Haystack Peak*.

Sundance Pass

This popular trail is one of the most scenic in the Beartooths, leading past numerous lakes to a wonderful vista of the 12,000ft peaks that surround the pass itself. The moderate–hard, 21mi trip is a hike of at least two days, although numerous side-trip possibilities mean that allowing three days is a more attractive option. The route has a total ascent of 3900ft and is often snowbound until mid-July. The A-to-B format also necessitates arranging shuttle transportation. Begin at the Main West Fork of Rock Creek Trailhead (turn west along FR 70 from Hwy 212 just south of Red Lodge, and continue 14mi to the end of the road). The route ends at the Lake Fork of Rock Creek Trailhead (signed to the right 10mi southwest of Red Lodge along US 212). The USFS 1:63,360 *Absaroka Beartooth Wilderness* map covers the route.

YELLOWSTONE NATIONAL PARK
Electric Peak

One of the higher summits in the park, Electric Peak (10,992ft) overlooks the town of Gardiner. The summit is reached via a 3mi side trail off the Sportsman Lake Trail, 4.8mi north from the Glen Creek Trailhead (itself roughly 4mi south of Mammoth on the Grand Loop Rd or hike directly from Mammoth via Snow Pass). The strenuous route involves almost 3000ft of ascent along the mountain's rocky southern spur, requiring some minor scrambling. There are no really dangerous drop-offs except for the summit itself. Although Electric Peak is sometimes climbed as a long day hike, it is better to book campsite 1G3 or 1G4 and take two days. Trails Illustrated's 1:83,333 map No 303 Mammoth Hot Springs covers the route. Otherwise, use three USGS 1:24,000 quads: *Mammoth*, *Quadrant Mountain* and *Electric Peak*.

Mary Mountain Trail

The 21mi Mary Mountain Trail runs southwest to northeast across Yellowstone's wild Central Plateau, passing several thermal fields. The area is frequented by large herds of bison, elk and deer, and is an important habitat for grizzly bears and wolves. As camping is not permitted anywhere along the route, the full Mary Mountain Trail makes a very long day hike, requiring an early start and a late finish. Many hikers explore the valleys on shorter day hikes from either trailhead.

The western trailhead is just south of Nez Perce Creek on the Grand Loop Rd, 6mi south of Madison or 9.5mi north of Old Faithful. The eastern trailhead is on the Grand Loop Rd just north of Alum Creek, 4.5mi south of Canyon. Use two

Trails Illustrated 1:83,333 maps, No 302 *Old Faithful* and No 305 *Yellowstone Lake*; or three USGS 1:24,000 quads, *Lower Geyser Basin*, *Mary Lake* and *Crystal Falls*.

Avalanche Peak

This moderate, 4mi round-trip climbs 2100ft to reach an exposed and rocky summit with superb views into the heart of Yellowstone. The trailhead is 19mi east of Fishing Bridge Junction near the east entrance to the park. Allow around four hours for the hike and use Trails Illustrated's 1:83,333 map No 305 *Yellowstone Lake*.

GRAND TETON NATIONAL PARK
Table Mountain

The summit of Table Mountain affords perhaps the park's best view of the Teton Range. Only the very top of the peak lies within the park boundary, with most of the hike crossing through the Targhee National Forest on the less-visited west side of the park. The strenuous, 12mi hike to the summit involves 4100ft of ascent and takes eight hours to complete. Start and finish at the Teton Campsite Trailhead (with adjacent campsite), 25mi northwest of Jackson along Hwy 22 and then Hwy 33 to Driggs, and then 5mi east to the end of the road toward Grand Targhee. Use the Earthwalk Press 1:72,500 *Hiking Map and Guide, Grand Teton National Park*.

Death Canyon

This 8mi, five-hour hike through a narrow portal into upper Death Canyon passes through some of the most extraordinary rock scenery in the park. The moderate, out-and-back trip involves 1450ft of ascent, and starts and finishes at the Death Canyon Trailhead and parking area. To reach the trailhead, drive 3mi southwest of Moose along Moose Wilson Rd, and then 1.5mi to the end of the first road on the right (last mile of road is unpaved). Use the Earthwalk Press 1:48,000 *Hiking Map and Guide, Grand Teton National Park*.

Central & Eastern Wyoming

If Wyoming's name comes from a Native American word meaning 'rolling prairies and mountains', then it best describes the state's central and eastern parts. Within this enormous region, isolated mountain ranges rise up like islands towering over the vast, undulating plains. Even the Continental Divide skims along the 13,000ft spine of the mighty Wind River Range only to fall away into lowly steppes of barely 7000ft around the Great Divide Basin.

The Wind River Range is the undisputed hiking mecca of central Wyoming. This formidable chain of mountains is characterized by bare rock walls, jagged spires and numerous glaciers, and boasts the state's highest summit – Gannett Peak (13,804ft).

The Bighorn Mountains form the Front Range of eastern Wyoming – the last high range before the Rockies start to drop away into the lowland plains extending into the Dakotas and Nebraska. The Bighorns are a fascinating area of wild alpine valleys between broad plateau-like ridges that culminate in classic Cloud Peak.

The Laramie Mountains and the Snowy Range of Medicine Bow National Forest rise abruptly from the plains of southeastern Wyoming and include the superb lookout summits of Laramie Peak and Medicine Bow Peak.

CLIMATE

Central and eastern Wyoming have a drier climate than either the neighboring Greater Yellowstone region or Colorado to the south. (Due to their relative height and isolation, the higher mountain ranges tend to catch and cause cloud buildup, which produces much moister conditions.)

Summer highs are usually around 80°F followed by cool nights, often below 40°F. From June through August, daytime heating can trigger heavy afternoon thunderstorms. In the harsh winters, only skiers and intrepid snowshoers venture into the mountain backcountry.

Highlights

GARETH McCORMACK

Sheer, craggy ridges enclose the glaciated valleys and isolated tarns of Titcomb Basin.

- Admiring the panorama from the summit of Cloud Peak (p200)

- Gazing in awe from Jackass Pass at the staggering Cirque of the Towers (p204)

- Exploring the intricate network of lakes, tarns and pools in Titcomb Basin (p206)

- Standing on the narrow ridge between North Gap and South Gap Lakes on the Snowy Range Loop (p212)

PLANNING
Maps & Books

GTR Mapping's 1:800,000 *Recreational Map of Wyoming* ($3.95) provides an overview of national forest, national park and wilderness areas throughout the state.

Falcon Guide's *Hiking Wyoming* by Bill Hunger ($15.95) focuses heavily on the Greater Yellowstone area, but features a fair range of hikes in both central and eastern Wyoming.

CENTRAL & EASTERN WYOMING

Central & Eastern Wyoming

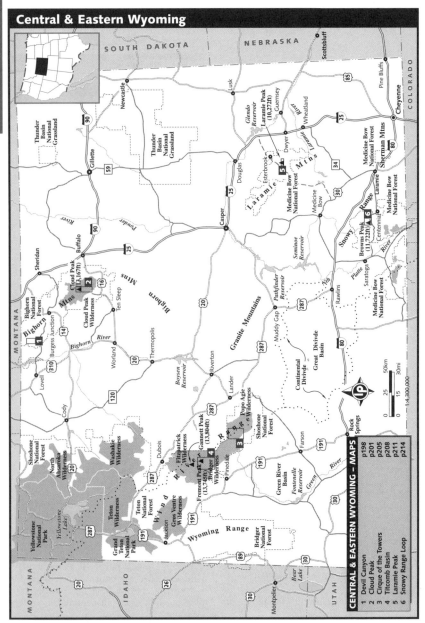

SOUTH DAKOTA

NEBRASKA

Scottsbluff

Pine Bluffs

COLORADO

Newcastle

Lusk

Glendo
Reservoir

Laramie Peak
(10,272ft)

Guernsey

Wheatland

Cheyenne

85

Thunder
Basin
National
Grassland

Thunder
Basin
National
Grassland

Dwyer

Medicine Bow
National Forest

Sherman Mtns

80

Gillette

Douglas

Esterbrook

5

Medicine Bow
National Forest

Laramie

Medicine Bow
National Forest

59

25

Medicine
Bow

L a r a m i e

M t n s

34

30

Casper

Seminoe
Reservoir

Snowy

Range

Browns Peak
(11,722ft)

6

Buffalo

Powder

River

90

25

Sheridan

Pathfinder
Reservoir

Centennial

Saratoga

Platte

River

Medicine Bow
National Forest

Cloud Peak
(13,167ft)

2

Ten Sleep

B i g h o r n

M t n s

Granite Mountains

287

Nis

Rawlins

Bighorn
National
Forest

16

Cloud Peak
Wilderness

Muddy Gap

80

MONTANA

Bighorn

14

Burgess Junction

1

River

Worland

Thermopolis

20

Continental
Divide

Great
Divide
Basin

310

Lovell

Bighorn

River

Boysen
Reservoir

120

Cody

Riverton

20

Lander

287

Farson

191

Rock
Springs

Shoshone
National
Forest

North
Absaroka
Wilderness

Washakie
Wilderness

20

Dubois

Popo Agie
Wilderness

Shoshone
National
Forest

50km

25

30mi

0

15

1:4,300,000

Gannett Peak
(13,804ft)

4

R a n g e

3

Fitzpatrick
Wilderness

W i n d

Fremont Peak
(13,745ft)

Bridger
Wilderness

Green River
Basin

Green

River

30

Teton
Wilderness

Teton
National
Forest

287

Pinedale

Fontenelle
Reservoir

Yellowstone
National
Park

Yellowstone
Lake

Gros Ventre
Wilderness

Jackson

191

Grand
Teton
National
Park

J a c k s o n

287

Wyoming   Range

Bridger
National
Forest

MONTANA

IDAHO

26

89

30

Bear
Lake

UTAH

30

Montpelier

CENTRAL & EASTERN WYOMING – MAPS

Information Sources

For general tourist information, contact the Wyoming Division of Tourism/Wyoming Information Center (☎ 307-777-2883, 800-225-5996, W www.wyomingtourism.org). Also check the official Wyoming website at W www.state.wy.us.

Wyoming State Bureau of Land Management (☎ 307-775-6256; W www.wy.blm.gov; 5353 Yellowstone Rd, Cheyenne) manages more than 28,000 sq miles of public land. Anglers should try the Wyoming Game and Fish Department (☎ 307-777-4600; W gf .state.wy.us; 5400 Bishop Blvd, Cheyenne) for information on fishing.

GATEWAYS

See Jackson (p161).

Cheyenne

Cheyenne, 100mi north of Denver and 50mi east of Laramie, is Wyoming's state capital and largest city. Its well-preserved historic downtown is surrounded by museums and parks.

For information contact Cheyenne Area Convention and Visitors Bureau (☎ 307-778-3133, 800-426-5009, W www.cheyenne.org, 309 W Lincolnway). The Sierra Trading Post (☎ 307-775-8090, 800-713-4534, W www .sierratradingpost.com, 5025 Campstool Rd) sells outdoor clothing and gear.

Places to Stay For those wanting to pitch a tent, *AB Camping (☎ 307-634-7035, 1503 W College Dr)* has sites from $13. The *Home Ranch Motel (☎ 307-634-3575, 2414 E Lincolnway)* has singles/doubles for around $30/35. The *Plains Hotel (☎ 307-638-3311, 1600 Central Ave)* charges from $35/45.

Getting There & Away United Express (☎ 800-241-6522) has daily flights to Denver. Armadillo Express (☎ 307-632-2223, 888-256-2967) runs daily shuttles to/from Denver International Airport ($28 one way). Greyhound (☎ 307-634-7744), TNM&O (☎ 307-634-7744) and Powder River Coach USA (☎ 307-635-1327, 800-442-3682) run frequent bus services to/from Billings, Dallas, Denver, Chicago and San Francisco.

Rock Springs

A former mining town with a gritty feel, Rock Springs is on I-80 in southwestern Wyoming. The chamber of commerce (☎ 307-362-3771, W www.rockspringswyoming.net, 1897 Dewar Dr) provides a range of local visitor information. The Rock Springs/Sweetwater County Airport (☎ 307-382-4580) is 7mi east of town and has regular connections to/from Denver International Airport. The Greyhound depot (☎ 307-362-2931, 1655 Sunset Dr), has connections to Denver, Cheyenne and Salt Lake City among others.

Bighorn Mountains

Part of eastern Wyoming's wavering Front Range, the Bighorn Mountains form an arc stretching south from the Montana border almost to Riverton. The far-higher northern half of the range lies within the 1700-sq-mile Bighorn National Forest and is of more interest to outdoor recreationists than the drier, less angular ridges that characterize the southern Bighorns.

Deep canyons formed by powerful thrust faults penetrate both the eastern and western edges of the Bighorns. The superb 295-sq-mile Cloud Peak Wilderness takes in an almost 30mi-long section of the range, including eastern Wyoming's highest peaks and some of the US's most majestic alpine scenery. Most of the wilderness lies above 9000ft and, its highest point, the mighty Cloud Peak rises to 13,167ft. Each year many thousands of enthusiastic hikers and anglers experience the Bighorns' solitude and beauty on several hundred miles of maintained trails through the mountains.

HISTORY

The Bighorns were considered sacred by Native Americans tribes – Cheyenne, Crow, Sioux, Arapaho and Eastern Cheyenne – and the mountains were the backdrop to some of their bloodiest and most desperate battles against the US Army. Although famous pioneers, including Lewis and Clark, Jim Bridger and Buffalo Bill, had explored the range, Native American resistance kept settlers out of the Bighorns until the 1870s. In the 1890s gold fever attracted prospectors into upper Little Horn River and Porcupine Creek, but by 1900 poor yields led to most claims being abandoned. In 1932 the Cloud Peak Primitive Area was established, which in 1994 was designated by Congress as Cloud Peak Wilderness.

NATURAL HISTORY

The Bighorns are largely composed of the one-billion-year-old, quartz-rich, pink granite rock found in many parts of the west. During the most recent Ice Age, some 20 glaciers splayed out from the main range of the Bighorn Mountains, gouging out the bedrock and laying down gravelly sediments or rough boulder fields along their course. This intense glaciation created the Bighorns' sheer rock faces, U-shaped valleys and glacial lakes.

Even so, with their characteristic broad, plateau-like ridges, the Bighorns are topographically gentler than other major ranges in Wyoming. Today the only surviving glacier in the Bighorns is on the eastern face of Cloud Peak, although much of the high ground still remains snowbound until July.

The Bighorn Mountains are named for their once-abundant bighorn sheep, which were decimated by overhunting. More recent restocking has revived the herds, meaning the Bighorns are again the most easterly place in Wyoming where you can view wild bighorn sheep.

Large wildlife populations, including black bears, cougars (mountain lions), coyotes, elk (wapiti), moose and mule deer, inhabit Cloud Peak Wilderness. The Bighorns are also home to an isolated population of lynx, which are slightly larger than bobcats with silvery-gray coats and prominent black tufts on the tips of their ears.

Several hundred lovely lakes cover the landscape, many offering excellent trout fishing. Fringing the streams and canyons you'll see attractive open forests of lodgepole and ponderosa pine. Higher up these give over to Engelmann spruce and subalpine fir interspersed by meadows, moors and valley bogs.

Although far from any major industrial center, the Bighorns occupy a kind of acid-rain fallout zone, which is threatening sensitive amphibians, including the northern leopard frog, and negatively affecting other areas of the local ecology.

PLANNING
Maps & Books

USFS' 1:126,720 *Bighorn National Forest* map ($7.50) covers the hikeable northern half of the Bighorns.

The pamphlet *Bighorn Bits and Pieces*, available free at US Forest Service (USFS) offices in Sheridan (p197) and Buffalo (p197), provides information on all the trails and campgrounds in Bighorn National Forest.

The Beauty of the Bighorns by Ester McWilliams ($24.95 hardback, $19.95 softcover) is an attractive book for the coffeetable. Falcon Guide's *Hiking the Cloud Peak Wilderness* by Erik Molvar ($16.95) details almost 80 hikes throughout Bighorn National Forest – not just within the wilderness. *Cloud Peak Wilderness* by M Melius ($14) is better suited to adventurous backcountry hikers.

Information Sources

Contact the regional USFS office in Sheridan (p197) for information on the Bighorn Mountains. You can also visit the USFS website at ☒ www.fs.fed.us/r2/bighorn.

Permits & Regulations

All hiking parties that enter Cloud Peak Wilderness must have a backcountry permit. These are free and can be picked up and deposited at trailhead registration boxes either in the wilderness or the USFS offices in Sheridan (p197) and Buffalo (p197).

Within Cloud Peak Wilderness, it is prohibited to camp within 100ft or to light any campfires within 300ft of lakes, streams or designated trails. Campfires are also prohibited anywhere above 9200ft; campfires below 9200ft must be contained in a fire blanket or fire pan.

Permits are not required for hikes in Bighorn National Forest outside the Cloud Peak Wilderness area.

ACCESS TOWNS
Sheridan
The largest regional center in Wyoming's central-north, Sheridan lies at the eastern foot of the Bighorn Mountains on I-90, 31mi north of Buffalo.

For information contact Wyoming Information Center (☎ 307-672-2485, 800-453-3650, Valley View Dr). Wyoming Game and Fish Department (☎ 307-672-2790, E 5th St) has exhibits on regional ecology and issues fishing licenses. Almost next door is the USFS Bighorn National Forest headquarters (☎ 307-672-0751). Bighorn Mountain Sports (☎ 307-672-6866, 333 Main St) has a good range of hiking gear, and sells books and maps.

The *Guest House Motel (☎ 307-674-7496, 800-226-9405, 2007 N Main St)* has rooms for less than $35.

United Express (☎ 307-674-8455) has flights to Denver. Powder River Coach USA (☎ 307-674-6188) runs buses twice daily to Billings, Cheyenne and Denver.

Buffalo
The historic town of Buffalo is at the intersection of I-90 and I-25, and is 31mi south of Sheridan, 68mi west of Gillette and 109mi north of Casper.

For information consult the visitor center (☎ 307-684-5544, 800-227-5122, W www .buffalowyoming.org, 55 N Main St). For advice on hikes in the area contact the USFS Bighorn National Forest Buffalo Ranger District or the Bureau of Land Management Buffalo Resource Area, which share the same office (☎ 307-684-1100, 1425 Fort St). Sports Lure (☎ 800-684-7682, W www.sportslure .com, 66 S Main St) sells USGS quads ($4) and has a good range of backpacking and fishing gear; ask here about shuttles to the trailheads.

The shady *Indian Campground (☎ 307-684-9601, 660 E Hart St)* charges $16/21 for campsites/full hookups. *Canyon Motel (☎ 307-684-2957, 800-231-0742, 997 Fort St)* offers rooms from $36.

Powder River Coach USA (☎ 800-442-3682) has twice daily buses to Sheridan, Billings, Casper and Cheyenne.

Devil Canyon

Duration	4½–6 hours
Distance	11.7mi (18.8km)
Standard	moderate
Start	Bucking Mule Falls Trailhead
Finish	Forest Road 14 (0.8mi south of FR146)
Nearest Town	Sheridan
Transport	car

Summary This hike skirts the rim of a deep canyon past spectacular waterfalls.

Devil Canyon is a spectacular gorge of Porcupine Creek (which drains north to meet the Bighorn River in southern Montana's Bighorn Canyon National Recreation Area) lined by often-sheer 1000ft bluffs on both sides. Although the area is not officially designated 'wilderness', difficult-to-access Devil Canyon is a wild habitat for elk, mule deer, black bears and other game – which accounts for the numerous trailers parked at trailheads in the fall hunting season.

The trail as far as Bucking Mule Falls is often done as an easy (5.2mi) day hike. The route from the falls is rather more strenuous and less trodden, with an ascent of around 2300ft, but it is popular with horse riders.

PLANNING
When to Hike
The route is normally snow-free from mid-June until early October. Hikers visiting during the fall hunting season should stay on the trails and wear bright clothing.

Maps
Two 1:24,000 USGS quads, *Mexican Hill* and *Medicine Wheel*, cover the hike, although minor sections of trail are not shown accurately in several places.

NEAREST TOWN & FACILITIES
See Sheridan (this page).

Burgess Junction
This is the name of a general locality around where US 14 (Bighorn Scenic Byway) and US 14 Alternate (Medicine Wheel Passage)

meet, 47mi from Sheridan. Burgess Junction's USFS visitor center, 0.5mi east of the intersection, has a free museum and sells (only) USFS maps.

Bear Lodge (☎ 307-752-2444, W www .bearlodgeresort.com), 250yd west of the intersection along US 14 Alternate, has tent sites from $7.50, rustic cabins from $30 and double rooms from $79. *Arrowhead Lodge (☎ 307-655-2388)*, 2mi east of the intersection, offers a similar deal.

USFS Campgrounds

The basic *Porcupine Creek campground* is 1.8mi along Forest Rd (FR) 13, left from the four-way intersection on FR 14 (past the USFS Porcupine Creek Ranger Station). The *Bald Mountain campground* is on US 14 Alternate, 0.2mi east of the FR 14 turnoff. Both have about 12 sites for $10 and are open June through September. The *Five Spring Falls campground* ($6), is several miles west along US 14 Alternate from the FR 14 turnoff, is open May through September.

GETTING TO/FROM THE HIKE

Drive 18.8mi west on US 14 Alternate from Burgess Junction (or 40mi east from Lovell), then turn off along Devil Canyon Rd (FR 14). Proceed through a four-way intersection and on past the Porcupine Falls turnoff (FR 146) to reach the Bucking Mule Falls Trailhead, 9.7mi from the highway. The small parking loop has space for around 25 vehicles.

The hike finishes on FR 14, about 0.8mi south of the Porcupine Falls turnoff (FR 146), where there is poor roadside parking only. Parties able to do a two-vehicle shuttle may prefer to continue to the Porcupine Creek Trailhead (see Alternative Finish, p199).

THE HIKE

From the southern side of the car park loop, head gently down through lodgepole forest (past a disused road going left) to cross the tiny **Tepee Creek** on a footbridge. The trail climbs away left and follows sagebrush clearings along a terrace above the stream to reach a junction about 45 minutes from the trailhead. Turn right (northeast) here and walk a few minutes to an overlook on a

rocky outcrop high above **Bucking Mule Falls**. This neat, narrow waterfall tumbles 400ft over a precipice where the stream has cut a gorge through jagged granite cliffs. It's a spectacular scene, but tread carefully as there are sheer drop-offs.

Backtrack to the junction and continue to the right (northwest) along the **Devil Canyon Trail**. This less-trodden trail follows a steepening ridge down through stands of old Douglas fir to a tiny, grassy saddle among bluffs fronting Devil Canyon. Cut down left (southwest) in switchbacks over steep, sun-exposed slopes of juniper trees and limber pine to some *campsites* on the northern bank of **Porcupine Creek**, about one hour from Bucking Mule Falls.

Cross the creek on a footbridge and climb away out of thickets of pin cherry and gooseberry (visited by black bears). The sometimes overgrown trail winds around to the right (southwest) through forest largely destroyed by bark beetle above the ravine of

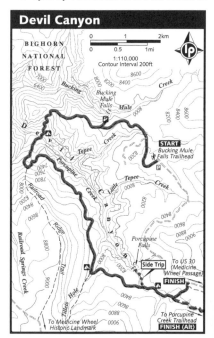

Railroad Springs Creek, then winds up steeply to a junction on a forested spur. Proceed left along the Devil Canyon Trail (the Railroad Ridge Trail continues up the spur, while the right way goes west to Mexican Hill). The route traverses briefly then makes a steep, muddy descent leading to a high, open terrace, 1¼ hours from the Porcupine Creek bridge. This spot grants a wonderful first clear view of Devil Canyon.

Pick up the trail at the upper edge of the trees and begin a long upward traverse close to the canyon's rim, which drops 800ft to the roaring stream. Although you are in the forest for much of the way, occasional tiny shelves offer surprising vistas of the mighty bluffs and cascades on the other side. The route moves gradually away to the right through narrow clearings with attractive *campsites*, passing the (right) Tillets Hole Trail turnoff just before it crosses the tiny Tillets Hole stream. Continue on through damp fir and spruce and a broad meadow then sidle down through a wire gate to re-cross Porcupine Creek on a bridge (the Side Trip begins from here), one to 1½ hours from the high, open terrace. There are more *campsites* here on the right (east) bank of the creek.

Hike up the eastern bank of the creek through gentle meadows that contrast with the more grandiose scenery of Devil Canyon. The trail leads past *campsites* near the confluence with the aptly named Long Park Creek, which runs through a narrow, grassy, park-like strip below Medicine Mountain (see the boxed text 'The Medicine Wheel') to the south. Atop this 9962ft summit is a conspicuous domed radio station.

Head up across a little brook flowing down through a meadow scattered with shrub willow, then turn up left along an unmarked trail (shown as a 4WD track on the USGS 1:24,000 quad; see also Alternative Finish). Where the meadow divides, cut up to the right and pick up a rough path leading directly up through the forest to arrive back on FR 14 (around 8575ft), 30 minutes from the Porcupine Creek bridge. The 3.7mi hike back to Bucking Mule Falls Trailhead takes around 1½ hours.

The Medicine Wheel

Medicine Mountain was named for the Medicine Wheel that sits on a ridge just west of its summit. A designated National Historic Landmark, this near-perfect 70ft-wide circle of flat stones with 28 spokes radiating from its center was constructed sometime between 1200 and 1700. Its makers and significance are matters of speculation, but the wheel is believed to represent a likeness of the Sun Dance Lodge of Crow legend. For today's Native Americans, the Medicine Wheel symbolizes humanity's connection to the earth. Religious ceremonies are conducted at the site, when flags or offerings may be left about the wheel.

Medicine Mountain is accessible from US 14 Alternate via the unsurfaced FR 12 – the turnoff is 1mi west of FR 14. The site is closed for a few days around the summer solstice and during other Native American religious festivals. Respect the Medicine Wheel as you would any place of worship.

Side Trip: Porcupine Falls
30 minutes, 0.8mi
If water levels are not too high, you can easily hike downstream from the upper Porcupine Creek bridge to the top of Porcupine Falls, where the creek spouts through a little gap and plummets 150ft into the upper Devil Canyon.

Follow cattle pads 300yd downstream along the right (east) bank, then ford the creek and continue along the streamside. Traces of mining machinery are visible in the stream bed immediately above the falls. Be very careful close to the cliff face. (For a full view of Porcupine Falls, do the 0.5mi round-trip hike from the trailhead at the end of FR 146, just off FR 14.)

Alternative Finish: Porcupine Creek Trailhead
1–1¼ hours, 2.2mi
Shuttle hikers may prefer to continue up the eastern bank of Porcupine Creek to Porcupine Creek Trailhead. The trail transits sagebrush meadows and stands of lodgepole

pine in the upper valley lined by low bluffs to reach the end of FR 137 near some private cabins. Follow the road briefly to the trailhead parking area.

Cloud Peak

Duration	3 days
Distance	21.4mi (34.4km)
Standard	hard
Start/Finish	West Tensleep Trailhead
Nearest Town	Ten Sleep
Transport	car

Summary An often strenuous, but otherwise nontechnical ascent of the Bighorns' highest summit, which offers a wonderful panorama of northeast Wyoming.

Rising to 13,167ft, Cloud Peak is the Bighorns' highest summit and – apart from the nearby Black Tooth Mountain (13,006ft) – the only 13er in the range. The route takes you past several delightful alpine lakes, then follows the southwest ridge of Cloud Peak to its summit. Day 1 of the hike is easy and very pleasant, and recommended even to hikers who do not wish to tackle the strenuous ascent.

The West Tensleep Creek basin has to cope with a large number of hikers. Please try to minimize the ecological impact of your visit to this fragile area.

PLANNING
When to Hike
The optimum period is July through September, although the upper route is likely to be in fair condition a month earlier or later.

Heavy thunderstorms with lightning are a major summer hazard, but snowfalls are also quite possible in summer.

What to Bring
Storms are frequent and furious on the Bighorns' higher slopes, so remember your waterproofs. Hikers who make the ascent very early in the season (before June) may appreciate the aid of an ice axe (and possibly even crampons).

Maps
Two 1:24,000 USGS quads cover the hike: *Lake Helen* and *Cloud Peak*. Otherwise use Trails Illustrated's 1:43,635 map No 720 *Cloud Peak Wilderness*.

NEAREST TOWN & FACILITIES
Ten Sleep
The tiny town of Ten Sleep (population 311) is on US 16 (Cloud Peak Scenic Skyway), 16mi west of the trailhead turnoff. It has basic shopping facilities and a laundromat. *Ten Sleep Valley Motel* (☎ 307-366-2321, 412 2nd St) has singles/doubles from around $37/46.

West Tensleep Area
Along FR 27 are several USFS campgrounds, *Boulder Park*, *Island Park*, *Deer Park* and, close to the trailhead, *West Tensleep Lake*. All cost $9 per site but there are also many free places to camp beside the road.

Big Horn Mountain Resorts (☎ 888-244-4676, 307-366-2424, [W] www.thebighorn.com) runs three lodges nearby on US 16. The closest is *Deer Haven Lodge* at the FR 27 turnoff. Several miles east is *Meadowlark Lake Lodge* and *Bighorn Ski Resort*. These offer double, motel-style rooms from $65 and rustic cabins from $45. RV sites cost $15. Meadowlark also has cottages from $84.

GETTING TO/FROM THE HIKE
The hike begins at West Tensleep Trailhead, accessible from US 16, via by the unsurfaced FR 27 turnoff 16.2mi east from Ten Sleep or 11.5mi west from Powderhorn Pass. Bear right on FR 27 at a fork after 1mi, then continue 6.4mi past a USFS guard station to the trailhead car park. There is space for at least 50 vehicles – park in the overnight section.

THE HIKE
Day 1: West Tensleep Trailhead to Mistymoon Lake
2½-3¼ hours, 6.5mi, 1141ft ascent
Sign the registration book at West Tensleep Trailhead (*not* West Tensleep Falls Trailhead) at the top of the road loop. Bear left at the fork a few steps on and proceed through open lodgepole forest around the east shore

of **West Tensleep Lake**, a shallow lake filled with aquatic plants that attract waterbirds.

Cut northwest across streamside meadows, passing some *campsites* and crossing a footbridge over tiny **West Tensleep Creek**, before entering Cloud Peak Wilderness. The trail rises gently north into fir-spruce forest growing among granite slabs, passing boggy beaver dams and the Bald Ridge Trail (No 97) turnoff to reach beautiful **Lake Helen**, about two hours from the trailhead. This is a deep glacial tarn, with rock islands and *campsites* on its southern, western and northwest shores.

The trail leads around the west of Lake Helen, through rock and grass meadows and small pockets of low fir-spruce forest, to reach **Lake Marion**. The best *campsites* here are at the lake's northern end, with more *campsites* on some small slab ridges around its southern end. Climb over regenerated moraine mounds scattered with shrub willow. Cloud Peak and Bomber Mountain (see the boxed text 'The Bomber Mountain Crash') increasingly dominate the northeast skyline as you come to **Mistymoon Lake**, about 45 minutes after reaching Lake Helen. This austere alpine tarn lies at tree line in a round grassy basin visited by mule deer and surrounded by raw ridges. Here you meet the Solitude Trail (No 38) coming from Florence Pass to the east. There are some semi-sheltered *campsites* on Mistymoon Lake's southern side.

The Bomber Mountain Crash

On June 28, 1943, at the height of WWII, an Army Air Force B-17 (Flying Fortress) bomber, en route to England, crashed high in the Bighorn Mountains on the ridge known today as Bomber Mountain. The entire crew of 10 was killed and, in August 1945, a memorial plaque was erected at the crash site (the coordinates of which are N 44° 21' 17.7" W 107° 11' 3.2"), where much scattered wreckage still lies. A locally produced book, *The Bomber Mountain Crash Story: A Wyoming Mystery* by R Scott Madsen, gives the full history.

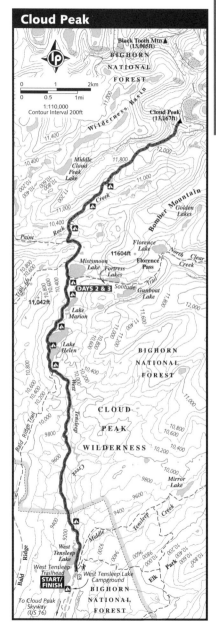

Cloud Peak

Day 2: Mistymoon Lake Return (via Cloud Peak Summit)

5–7 hours, 8.4mi, 2931ft ascent

Take the Solitude Trail around the western shore of Mistymoon Lake past the left Trail 66 turnoff before climbing gently northeast over grassy slopes to cross a broad pass scattered with several small tarns. The trail winds gently down west, above the meandering **Paint Rock Creek**, to reach a minor saddle. Leave the trail here, descending into the waterlogged valley floor and cutting across to where the stream tumbles in an attractive waterfall, 40 minutes from Mistymoon Lake.

Cross Paint Rock Creek below the waterfall (normally an easy ford after mid-July) and follow well-trodden walking pads leading up past *campsites* among stunted firs on the opposite (southern) bank. Climb beside the rushing creek into the narrow upper valley abutted by steep, raw-rock sides, then skirt left through a level meadow. *Campsites* can also be found here among the boulders. Cairns mark the way up left into the drainage of a tiny side-stream, leading along a slab ridge strewn with coarse glacial rubble to a second level grassy area with more *campsites* by a tiny tarn.

Head up through a gap to another boggy meadow. Follow the tiny splashing streamlet more steeply (requiring minor rockhopping) until the gradient eases and a rough trail reappears. Now practically above the vegetation line, cut north across the broad slope to a small gap in the southwest ridge, 1¼ to two hours from the waterfall. The northern side of the ridge plummets 1500ft directly into the savagely glaciated Wilderness Basin, a complex of cirques covered by the series of superb elongated tarns known as the Cloud Peak Lakes.

Make your way to the right (northeast) along the ridge through a short, narrow section, then continue almost north jumping rock-to-rock to arrive on the tiny summit plateau of **Cloud Peak**, reached about one hour from the ridge gap. A large boulder marks the Bighorns' highest point (13,167ft), where the summit logbook can be found in a plastic tube. From here the marvelous panorama includes the adjacent Bomber Mountain and Wilderness Basin, and then stretches away across much of northeastern Wyoming. Cloud Peak's precipitous northeast edge slides away onto a small, heavily crevassed glacier that calves into Glacier Lake – this spectacular overlook is best approached with caution.

Day 3: Mistymoon Lake to West Tensleep Trailhead

2¼–3 hours, 6.5mi, 1141ft descent

Retrace you steps from Day 1.

Wind River Range

Extending some 100mi northwest-southeast along the Continental Divide through central western Wyoming, the spectacular Wind River Range offers some of the Rockies' best hiking. Virtually the entire range is protected wilderness, divided into four large, contiguous tracts comprising some 1400-sq-miles. Bridger Wilderness takes in most of the range's western side, while the Fitzpatrick and Popo Agie Wilderness Areas and the Wind River Roadless Area (part of the Wind River Indian Reservation managed by the Shoshone and Arapaho tribes) take in its

A Long Human History

Humans have moved through the Wind River area for more than 10,000 years. The earliest visitors would have been hunters and gatherers, drawn by the abundance of plants and wildlife. These groups passed through the mountains following the migrations of large mammals and the seasonal availability of edible plants. The Eastern Shoshone and Northern Arapaho tribes call this area home, and their ancestors would probably have been among the first human visitors. In many cases the trails established by these (and other) Native Americans were later used by Euro-American trappers, explorers and emigrants, with some of the traditional paths even providing the basis for hiking routes today.

eastern slopes. Few roads penetrate the range, and hikes into the remote heart of the 'Winds' generally necessitate long approaches.

NATURAL HISTORY

Past ice ages have left a stunningly glaciated landscape of hundreds of jagged peaks, ice-ground cirques and lakes. The Winds have several dozen 13ers, including Wyoming's highest summit, Gannett Peak (13,804ft). The higher northern half of the Wind River Range also boasts seven of the 10 largest glaciers in the Lower 48. This remarkable topography makes the Winds one of the Rockies' best regions for mountaineering and alpine rock climbing.

Forests of lodgepole pine, sometimes mixed with ponderosa pine, cover the Winds' lower slopes, giving way to fir-spruce forest in moister and/or higher areas. Limber pine is fairly common up to tree line. Wildlife in the Winds, especially elk and mule deer, is subject to hunting and, hence, wary of humans. Pronghorn antelopes are common on the sagebrush plains fringing the range, and moose are often spotted in the waterlogged valley floors or around lakes. Bighorn sheep, which were almost wiped out in the Winds by overhunting and the introduction of livestock, are now so abundant they are used to restock other wilderness areas. There are plans to re-establish grizzly bears in the Winds. The range is also home to the rare fisher, which is closely related to the pine marten.

PLANNING
Maps & Books

USFS' contoured 1:126,720 *Teton-Bridger National Forest* ($4.50, waterproof edition $6.50) takes in almost all of the Wind River Range; it is useful as an overview map, but insufficiently detailed for accurate navigation. Two waterproof 1:48,000 hiking maps *Southern Wind River Range* and *Northern Wind River Range*, published by Earthwalk Press, cover the Winds at a more practical scale for hiking purposes ($7.95 each).

Walking in the Winds by Rebecca Woods ($14.95) is one of the best hiking guides to the area.

Information Sources

USFS information about the Bridger Wilderness can be obtained from Pinedale Ranger District headquarters (☎ 307-367-4326; PO Box 220, Pinedale, WY 82941), or W www.fs.fed.us/btnf/bridger. For information about the eastern part of the range contact Fitzpatrick Wilderness headquarters in Dubois (☎ 307-455-2466), Popo Agie Wilderness headquarters in Lander (☎ 307-332-5460) or Wind River Indian Reservation (Joint Council of the Shoshone and Arapaho Tribes) in Fort Washakie (☎ 307-332-7207).

Permits & Regulations

No permit is needed for trips in the USFS-administered national forest areas of the Winds. Camping is not permitted within 100ft of streams or 200ft of trails and lakes (within 0.25mi of certain heavily visited lakes); fires are prohibited above tree line.

ACCESS TOWN
Pinedale

The beef and timber town of Pinedale lies at the western foot of the Wind River Range on US 191. The town's chamber of commerce (☎ 307-367-2242, 32 E Pine St) can provide accommodations listings, or you can visit W www.pinedaleonline.com. The USFS office (☎ 307-367-4326, 210 W Pine St) has information on the Wind River Range and also sells local hiking guides and maps. The Great Outdoor Shop (☎ 307-367-2440, 332 W Pine St) sells gear and maps, and rents ice-climbing equipment and pack llamas.

Pinedale campground (☎ 307-367-4555, 204 S Jackson Ave) has grassy, but unshaded, tent sites for $12; showers are available for nonguests and cost $4. *Rivera Lodge (☎ 307-367-2424, 442 W Marilyn St)* has double rooms starting at $65. *Fremont Lake campground*, 7mi northeast of town on that lake's eastern shore, is the closest USFS campground (sites $7).

GETTING AROUND

Pinedale Taxi (☎ 307-360-8313) and The Great Outdoor Shop (☎ 307-367-2440) can both provide hiker shuttles to local trailheads.

Cirque of the Towers

Duration	2 days
Distance	20.4mi (32.8km)
Standard	moderate
Start/Finish	Big Sandy campground
Nearest Town	Pinedale
Transport	car

Summary An out-and-back hike (with a loop option via Texas Pass) to a spectacular, sheer-sided amphitheater ringed by more than a dozen granite towers.

The Cirque of the Towers, one of the Rockies' most spectacular cirques, is a favorite hiking destination. The hike begins with a long, steady ascent of around 2000ft to Jackass Pass, which is also one of the few places in the Winds where the Continental Divide can be reached in a day hike (15mi out and back). Many hikers on the longer route (especially families) make a base camp at Big Sandy Lake and explore the cirque and other nearby features on day hikes.

PLANNING
When to Hike
Jackass Pass normally melts out by mid-July, but the higher Texas Pass (optional) takes somewhat longer. Lightning from summer electrical storms is a major hazard, especially anywhere above tree line. Mosquitoes can be extremely bothersome in summer.

What to Bring
Early in the season hikers tackling the Texas Pass may need an ice axe and crampons (available for hire at the Great Outdoor Shop in Pinedale, p203). As this is a heavily impacted area, hikers should carry a fuel stove and refrain from lighting campfires.

Maps
Earthwalk Press'1:48,000 *Southern Wind River Range* hiking map covers the entire area. Alternatively use two USGS 1:24,000 quads: *Temple Peak* and *Lizard Head Peak*; if you do the optional Texas Pass loop you will also need the *Mount Boneville* and *Big Sandy Opening* maps.

NEAREST TOWN & FACILITIES
The nearest town is Pinedale (p203), more than 40mi away.

Near the Trailhead
The free USFS *Big Sandy campground* at the trailhead has 10 primitive sites; treat water collected from the river. *Big Sandy Lodge (☎ 307-382-6513)* at Mud Lake (take the turnoff 1mi south of Big Sandy campground) offers cabins from $45 and may be able to arrange transportation for guests.

GETTING TO/FROM THE HIKE
Turn off Hwy 353 at Boulder, 12mi south of Pinedale, and take the left turn just after the sealed road ends (17mi from the highway). Proceed across Big Sandy River to take another turnoff (26mi from the highway) and continue past Dutch Joe guard station to Big Sandy campground. There is trailhead parking for several dozen cars, but space is scarce on summer weekends.

THE HIKE
Day 1: Big Sandy Campground to Lonesome Lake
4¾–6 hours, 10.2mi, 2332ft ascent
This is most direct route to the cirque. From the campground parking area, follow the Big Sandy Trail along the banks of Big Sandy River, bearing right at its junctions with the Mud Lake Trail and the Diamond Lake Trail. The trail rises incrementally through lodgepole pines and narrow meadows of pink asters and lupines above the alternately meandering and tumbling river. Climb gently away to the left into spruce forest past the second Diamond Lake Trail turnoff, continuing upvalley through stands of limber pine to reach the southern shore of **Big Sandy Lake**, two to 2½ hours from the trailhead.

Sheltered *campsites* can be found among boulders in the forest along the lake's southern shore, as well as on its western side on terraced meadows looking out over a picturesque island toward the massive slabs of Haystack Mountain's western face. Marauding black bears were a major problem at both camping areas until steel food storage containers were put in place – use them.

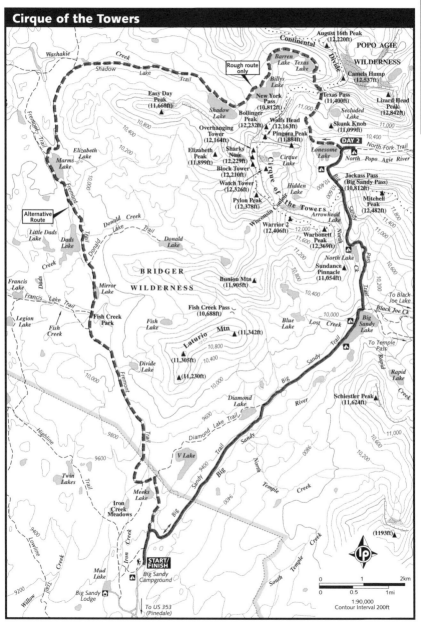

Cirque of the Towers

Washakie
Shadow
Creek
Lake
Trail

Continental

August 16th Peak
(12,220ft)

POPO AGIE
WILDERNESS

Barren
Lake
Texas
Lake

Camels Hump
(12,537ft)

Rough route
only

Billys
Lake

Easy Day
Peak
(11,660ft)

Shadow
Lake

New York
Pass
(10,812ft)

Texas Pass
(11,400ft)

Lizard Head
Peak
(12,842ft)

Bollinger
Peak
(12,232ft)

Wolfs Head
(12,163ft)

Seeluded
Lake

Skunk Knob
(11,099ft)

Overhanging
Tower
(12,164ft)

Pingora Peak
(11,884ft)

North Fork Trail

Fremont
Trail

Elizabeth
Lake

Elizabeth
Peak
(11,899ft)

Sharks
Nose
(12,229ft)

Lonesome
Lake

DAY 2

North Popo Agie River

Marms
Lake

Block Tower
(12,210ft)

Cirque
Lake

Jackass Pass
(Big Sandy Pass)
(10,812ft)

Fremont
Trail

Watch Tower
(12,326ft)

Hidden
Lake

Mitchell
Peak
(12,482ft)

Alternative
Route

Donald
Creek
Trail

Pylon Peak
(12,378ft)

Cirque of the Towers

Arrowhead
Lake

Little Dads
Lake

Dads
Lake

Donald
Lake

Donald
Lake

Warrior 2
(12,406ft)

Warbonnet
Peak
(12,369ft)

North Lake

Francis
Lake

Mirror
Lake

BRIDGER
WILDERNESS

Bunion Mtn
(11,905ft)

Sundance
Pinnacle
(11,054ft)

To Black
Joe Lake

Black Joe Ck

Legion
Lake

Fish Creek
Park

Fish
Creek

Fish
Lake

Fish Creek Pass
(10,688ft)

Blue
Lake

Lost
Creek

Big
Sandy
Lake

To Temple
Pass

Laturio Mtn
(11,342ft)

Rapid
Lake

(11,305ft)

Divide
Lake

(11,230ft)

Big
Sandy
River

Schiestler Peak
(11,624ft)

Diamond
Lake

Diamond Lake Trail

V Lake

Fremont
Trail

North
Temple
Creek

Twin
Lakes

Highline
Trail

Meeks
Lake

Iron
Creek
Meadows

Big
Sandy
Trail

(1193ft)

Mud
Lake

START/
FINISH

Big Sandy
Campground

Iron
Creek

South
Temple
Creek

Big Sandy
Lodge

To US 353
(Pinedale)

Willow
Creek

Lowline
Trail

0   1   2km
0   0.5   1mi

1:90,000
Contour Interval 200ft

Make your way to a junction on the lake's northern shore. The right turnoff leads to Little Sandy Lake and Clear Lake, then to Temple Pass – a scenic moderately difficult 12mi side trip (5–6½ hours) that leads past several lakes in the glacial trough between Haystack Mountain and East Temple Peak.

Bear left and climb north onto meadows beside North Creek. As you ascend, clear views open out southeast toward Temple Pass, with the slanting beret form of East Temple Peak, the tooth-like Lost Temple Spire and Steeple Peak on the northern side of the pass. After fording the creek the trail enters a wilder glacial landscape, where hardy conifers cling to the polished rock or shelter among raw boulders, before sidling down to cross a minor inlet to **North Lake** on moist lawns at the lake head. There are a few pleasant *campsites* around the shore here.

Climb steeply past some gnarled, old limber pines onto rubbly slopes. The trail follows sporadic cairns over open slab shelves and up low bluffs to reach an (unofficial) junction high above the emerald-green Arrowhead Lake, which lies in a deep trough below the sheer walls of Warbonnet Peak. Cut to the right – the left turnoff leads across the ridge to Hidden Lake – up the eroding slope to reach **Jackass Pass** (10,812ft), also known as Big Sandy Pass, about two hours from Big Sandy Lake. The pass, where you cross into Popo Agie Wilderness, offers an excellent overview of the spectacular Cirque of the Towers. The broad amphitheater is ringed by more than a dozen jagged towers of gray granite running around to Lizard Head Peak (12,842ft) at its northeastern rim.

Descend (with a brief glimpse of Hidden Lake to the left) into meadows scattered with shrub willows and stands of subalpine firs to arrive at **Lonesome Lake** after 30 minutes. This beautiful tarn lies in a forested glacial bowl below the striking horn-shaped Pingora Peak (11,884ft). Moose are sometimes spotted around the shore or swimming in the lake. Camping is not permitted within 0.25mi of Lonesome Lake due to the high number of visitors, but suitable (legal) *campsites* can be found on the slopes well up from its southern shore or beside meadows 10 minutes

downstream along the small North Popo Agie River (the lake outlet).

Day 2: Lonesome Lake to Big Sandy Campground
4–5 hours, 10.2mi, 2332ft descent
Return to the trailhead by hiking Day 1 in reverse.

Alternative Route: Texas Pass Loop
7–10 hours, 16mi, 1230ft ascent
This moderate–hard alternative loops back to Big Sandy campground. The (unofficial) route climbs up along the northwestern inlet of Lonesome Lake to (11,400ft), then descends to Texas Lake and follows the Washakie Creek drainage down past several lakes to meet the Fremont Trail. The trail leads south past **Marms Lake**, **Dads Lake** and **Mirror Lake** back to Big Sandy campground.

Titcomb Basin

Duration	3 days
Distance	30.6mi (49.2km)
Standard	moderate
Start/Finish	Elkhart Park Trailhead
Nearest Town	Pinedale
Transport	car

Summary A lengthy access trail leads to an intensely glaciated alpine valley at the base of some of Wyoming's highest peaks.

Titcomb Basin, a narrow valley enclosed on three sides by superb craggy ranges, is probably the most visited backcountry area in the Winds. Most parties base themselves at lovely Island Lake, at the foot of Titcomb Basin, and explore the area on day hikes. It is a relatively long, undulating hike (with 2090ft elevation gain) to access the heart of the area, although the wild and remote feel of the basin makes the effort worthwhile. Numerous other side trips radiate from Island Lake, and a stay of four or five days could easily be justified. See Other Hikes (p215) for details of the trip up Fremont Peak, Wyoming's third highest summit.

This area is notorious for its mosquitoes during the summer, so bring a good supply of bug repellent and possibly also a bug net.

PLANNING
When to Hike
The route is likely to be free of snow by mid-June or early July at the latest.

What to Bring
There is limited running water available from the trailhead to Barbara Lake, halfway to Island Lake, so be sure to carry enough.

Maps
Earthwalk Press' 1:48,000 *Northern Wind River Range* map covers the vast majority of the route, with just a short section near Elkhart Park on the 1:48,000 *Southern Wind River Range*. Two USGS 1:24,000 quads, *Bridger Lakes* and *Gannet Peak*, cover the Titcomb area, while two others, *Fremont Peak North* and *Fremont Peak South*, take in the area immediately to its east.

NEAREST TOWN & FACILITIES
See Pinedale (p203).

Near the Trailhead
Along with plenty of informal *campsites* along the access road there is also the basic *Trails End USFS campground* ($7 per site) at the trailhead itself.

GETTING TO/FROM THE HIKE
To reach the trailhead, take Fremont Lake Rd near the USFS office in Pinedale (signposted 'Museum of the Mountain Man') and continue 15mi to the end of the road. There is trailhead parking for around 100 cars.

THE HIKE
Day 1: Elkhart Park Trailhead to Island Lake
7 hours, 11.7mi, 1840ft ascent
The first section of Pole Creek Trail entails the most sustained ascent on the hike and, although the gradient is not steep, the climb is continuous to **Photographers Point**, 4.5mi into the hike. Several wildflower meadows offer some respite along the way.

After taking in distant views of Titcomb Basin from Photographers Point descend to a meadow with three pools, where there is a junction with the Sweeney Creek Trail some 2½ hours from the trailhead. At another junction 0.5mi further on, the Pole Creek Trail turns right, but keep to the left, following signs to Senaca Lake. Hike around the western shore of Barbara Lake, and then make a steep descent to a meadow and up to Hobbs Lake, which is also skirted to the west. The trail descends to a creek, which is forded on stepping stones, and after climbing through a short series of switchbacks, you descend once again past three small lakes. At the third lake the trail veers east, and a continuous 0.75mi ascent leads to the top of a rocky spur overlooking beautiful **Senaca Lake** some five hours from the trailhead. There are several scenic *campsites* just off the trail along its northwestern shore.

Island Lake is still two hours away, however, and the route continues around the northern shores of Senaca Lake before making a short climb to Little Senaca Lake. Climb steeply above this to where the trail rounds a corner (keeping left at the Highline Trail junction) and enters a series of switchbacks surmounting a short but steep rocky pass. This pass is the gateway to the most beautiful alpine scenery, and within 1mi the trail drops down to the shore of **Island Lake**, backed by the peaks of Titcomb Basin. There are several good *campsites* along the southern shore.

Day 2: Island Lake Return (via Titcomb Basin)
4–5hours, 7.2mi, 250ft ascent
The trip to Titcomb Basin continues around the southeast shore of Island Lake. The trail to Indian Pass veers off right after about 1mi. Keep left for Titcomb Basin and cross a creek using some large boulders. The trail meanders around alpine moraine before squeezing through a narrow rock portal and entering Titcomb Basin proper. It is little more than 2mi to the north shore of Upper Titcomb Lake, with the flat terrain and spectacular rock surrounds making the trip both relaxing and memorable. There are

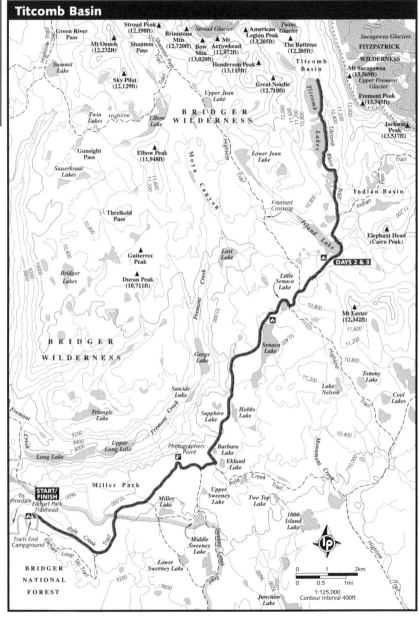

Titcomb Basin

Green River Pass

Mt Oeneis (12,232ft)

Summit Lake

Stroud Peak (12,198ft)

Shannon Pass

Sky Pilot (12,129ft)

Brimstone Mtn (12,720ft)

Stroud Glacier

Bow Mtn (13,020ft)

Mt Arrowhead (12,972ft)

Henderson Peak (13,115ft)

American Legion Peak (13,205ft)

Twins Glacier

The Buttress (12,205ft)

Titcomb Basin

Sacagawea Glaciers

FITZPATRICK

WILDERNESS

Mt Sacagawea (13,569ft)

Upper Fremont Glacier

Fremont Peak (13,745ft)

Twin Lakes

Highline

Elbow Lake

Upper Jean Lake

B R I D G E R

W I L D E R N E S S

Great Needle (12,710ft)

Titcomb Lakes

Jackson Peak (13,517ft)

Gunsight Pass

Sauerkraut Lakes

Elbow Peak (11,948ft)

Moya Canyon

Highline Trail

Lower Jean Lake

Island Lake

Indian Basin

Indian Pass

Threlkeld Pass

Bridger Lakes

Guiterrez Peak

Duran Peak (10,711ft)

Fremont Creek

Lost Lake

Fremont Crossing

Little Senaca Lake

Elephant Head (Cairn Peak)

DAYS 2 & 3

B R I D G E R

W I L D E R N E S S

Gorge Lake

Senaca Lake

Mt Lester (12,342ft)

Lake Nelson

Tommy Lake

Cool Lakes

Triangle Lake

Snicide Lake

Fremont Creek

Sapphire Lake

Hobbs Lake

Highline Trail

Monument Creek

Fremont Creek

Long Lake

Upper Long Lake

Photographers Point

Barbara Lake

Eklund Lake

Pole Creek

Miller Park

START/ FINISH

To Pinedale

Elkhart Park Trailhead

Trails End Campground

Pole Creek Trail

Elkhart Loop Ski Trail

Miller Lake

Upper Sweeney Lake

Two Top Lake

1000 Island Lake

Sweeney Creek

Middle Sweeney Lake

BRIDGER

NATIONAL

FOREST

Lower Sweeney Lake

Junction Lake

Highline Trail

0   1   2km

0   0.5   1mi

1:125,000
Contour Interval 400ft

plenty of good spots for low-impact *camping*. Return to Island Lake via the same trail when you have had your fill of the scenery.

Day 3: Island Lake to Elkhart Park Trailhead
6 hours, 11.7mi, 1840ft descent
Reverse the Day 1 hike to return to Elkhart Park Trailhead.

Medicine Bow National Forest

Medicine Bow National Forest stretches across southeastern Wyoming along the North Platte, Medicine Bow and Laramie river basins. It is divided into separate northeast (Laramie Mountains), southwest (Snowy Range and Sierra Madre) and southeast (Pole Mountain) units and includes the small Savage Run, Platte River, Huston Park and Encampment River Wilderness Areas.

HISTORY
Various Native American nations originally occupied southeastern Wyoming – Shoshone, Crow, Arapaho, Cheyenne, (Sioux) Oglala and Brulé. Euro-American fur trappers were active in the region by the early 1800s and were soon followed by other explorers, including Jim Bridger, Kit Carson and John Fremont. From the 1860s pioneers on the Overland Trail passed through today's Medicine Bow National Forest. The arrival of the Union Pacific Railroad in 1867 allowed the exploitation of local timber resources. In 1902 President Theodore Roosevelt established Medicine Bow National Forest.

In the first half of the 20th century, gold, platinum, palladium and later copper were sporadically mined; in the 1970s there was even a short-lived uranium rush. In the late 1930s and early 1940s the Civilian Conservation Corps built campgrounds, trails and Hwy 130 (Snowy Range Scenic Byway). Despite the designation of four wilderness areas during the last few decades, lumber remains a significant industry in Medicine Bow National Forest.

NATURAL HISTORY
The ranges of Medicine Bow National Forest were formed by uplifting (the so-called Laramide Orogeny) some 100 million years ago, although they are composed of rocks more than 2.5 billion years old. The southern extension of the Wyoming Front Range, the Laramie Mountains are characterized by granite ridges eroded into bizarre formations in places. The higher and more rugged Snowy Range is typified by ridges of hard quartzite (with minor intrusions of marble or limestone) shaped by heavy glaciation that has left behind numerous alpine tarns.

Medicine Bow supports strong populations of elk, bighorn sheep, black bears, mule deer, white-tailed deer and pronghorn antelopes (which also attract many autumn trophy hunters).

Summer livestock are grazed in Medicine Bow (especially in the Snowy Range). There is good trout fishing in the lakes, with anglers out in force in summer.

PLANNING
Maps
Two USFS 1:126,720 maps, *Medicine Bow National Forest* ($6) and *Medicine Bow National Forest – Laramie Peak Unit* ($6) are useful for access and a general overview.

Information Sources
Visit the USFS offices in Casper or Laramie (p210), or visit W www.fs.fed.us/mrnf.

Permits & Regulations
Permits are not required to hike or camp in Medicine Bow National Forest, but parking fees ($2 or $3 per day) apply at many popular trailheads – drop the money (or a check) in the trailhead deposit box.

ACCESS TOWNS
Casper
Casper is on the North Platte River at the intersection of I-25, US 20/26 and Hwy 220, 178mi northwest of Cheyenne and 112mi south of Buffalo.

For information contact the chamber of commerce (☎ 307-234-5362, 500 N Center St) or the BLM office (☎ 307-261-7600, 1701

East E St). Dean's Sporting Goods (☎ 307-234-2788, [e] deanssg@surfbest.net, 260 S Center St) sells maps as well as some backpacking gear. Mountain Sports (☎ 307-266-1136, [e] bruce@wyomap.com, 543 S Center St) has a better range of outdoor gear.

Fort Caspar Campground (☎ 307-234-3260, 888-243-7709, 4205 Fort Caspar Rd) has sites from $11. The *Royal Inn (☎ 307-234-3501, 440 East A St)* has singles/doubles for $30/40. *Super 8 (☎ 307-266-3480, 888-266-0497, 3838 Cy Ave)* charges $45/50.

There are daily flights to/from Salt Lake City (SkyWest/Delta) and Denver (United Express). Powder River Coach USA (☎ 307-266-1904, 800-442-3682) runs daily buses to/from Douglas, Cheyenne/Denver, Cody and Billings.

Laramie

The vibrant University of Wyoming town of Laramie lies between Medicine Bow Mountains to the west and Laramie Mountains to the east, 50mi west of Cheyenne and 99mi east of Rawlins.

For information contact the chamber of commerce (☎ 307-745-7339, 800 S 3rd St), the USFS office (☎ 307-745-2300, 2468 Jackson St) or visit [W] www.laramie-tourism.org. The Geological Survey of Wyoming (☎ 307-766-2286, [W].www.wsgsweb.uwyo.edu, 11th St), opposite Engineering on the university campus, stocks topographic maps. Cross Country Connection (☎ 307-721-2851, 222 S 2nd St) sells a good range of outdoor supplies. Rocky Mountain Sports (☎ 307-742-3220, 221 E Grand Ave) rents backpacking gear.

Laramie KOA (☎ 307-742-6553, 800-562-4153, 1271 W Baker St) has sites from $15 and cabins for $30. *Motel 6 (☎ 307-742-2307, 621 Plaza Lane)* offers singles/doubles for $38/45, while *Motel 8 (☎ 307-745-4856, 888-745-4800, 501 Boswell Dr)* charges $42/50. For bulk and backpacking foods visit the *Whole Earth Grainery (☎ 307-745-4268, 800-368-4268, 111 E Ivinson Ave)*.

Platte Valley Shuttles & Tours *(☎ 307-326-5582, [W] www.plattevalleyshuttles.com)* does airport pick-ups and provides trailhead drop-offs.

United Express (☎ 307-742-5296) has daily flight to/from Denver. Armadillo Express (☎ 307-632-2223, 888-256-2967) runs shuttles between Denver International Airport and Laramie ($52 one-way). Greyhound (☎ 307-742-5188) eastbound buses stop four times daily; westbound buses stop five times daily. Powder River Coach USA (☎ 800-442-3682) departs for Denver ($30 one-way) twice daily.

Laramie Peak

Duration	4–5½ hours
Distance	10.2mi (16.4km)
Standard	easy–moderate
Start/Finish	Friend Park Trailhead
Nearest Towns	Douglas, Esterbrook
Transport	car
Summary	A straightforward, but energetic climb to a panoramic lookout summit.

The 10,272ft Laramie Peak is the highest summit in the Laramie Mountains, both of which are named after an obscure early-19th-century French-Canadian trapper, Jacques La Ramie, who was killed by the Shoshone tribe. The hike has an ascent of about 2700ft, but follows a well-graded trail through shady forest for most of the way. Trail bikes and all-terrain vehicles (ATVs) are permitted on this route, although motorized traffic is not excessive.

PLANNING
When to Hike

Early in the season – usually until mid-June – large snow patches lie on the upper sections of the trail. In July and August the going can be rather hot, but a September climb is ideal. Despite the hike's short length, don't rely on the weather – thunderstorms are somewhat less common in the Laramie Mountains than in other ranges of Wyoming, but can build up with surprising suddenness.

Maps

The USGS 1:24,000 *Laramie Peak* quad shows the route fairly accurately.

NEAREST TOWNS & FACILITIES
Douglas
Douglas (4815ft) is 46mi east of Casper along I-25. For information contact the Chamber of Commerce (☎ 307-358-2950, 121 Brownfield Rd). The USFS Medicine Bow/Routt National Forest office (☎ 307-358-4690, 2250 Richards St) is open 7:30am to 4:30pm weekdays.

Riverside Park along the North Platte River has free camping (showers available). The *Plains Motel (☎ 307-358-4484, 628 Richards St)* has rooms from around $33. The *Chieftain Motel (☎ 307-358-2673, 815 Richards St)* charges $38/45 single/double.

Powder River Coach USA (☎ 307-358-4484) stops at Plains Cafe (☎ 307-358-4489, 628 Richards St). Daily buses depart Douglas for Billings, via Gillette; Billings via Casper and the Bighorn Basin; and Cheyenne and Denver.

Esterbrook
This is a scattered locality some 29mi from Douglas. The USFS Esterbrook Ranger Station (☎ 307-358-4690) is near the turnoff to Friend Park. *Esterbrook USFS campground* (sites $5) is nearby. Rustic *Esterbrook Lodge (☎ 307-351-7568)* offers campsites for $8 and two-person cabins from $45 (only $8 for subsequent nights); there is a bar-restaurant.

Friend Park USFS Campground
This *campground* near the trailhead has six sites for $5. From Douglas take Esterbrook Rd (Hwy 91) south to a fork, then continue left. From Glendo, south of Douglas on I-25, drive 12mi west to the intersection 1mi north of Esterbrook.

GETTING TO/FROM THE HIKE
At the intersection near the USFS Esterbrook ranger station, go right (west), bearing left at a fork after 4.7mi, then take a left turnoff (the right-hand way is signposted 'Rock River') another 10.3mi on. Follow this road 3.5mi past the Friend Park USFS campground to the small parking area at the Friend Park Trailhead, where a $2 daily parking fee applies. The road from Esterbrook can be rather rough in places, but is normally passable to conventional vehicles.

THE HIKE
At Friend Park Trailhead sign the register book and take the Laramie Peak Trail (No 602) down east over juniper-sagebrush clearings. The trail dips quickly into light ponderosa forest past a short connector path to the campground to cross the small **Friend Creek** on a footbridge after 20 minutes. A picnic table and bench have been erected here by the shady stream.

Begin the long climb through lodgepole forest, switchbacking up beside the creek to reach **Friend Creek Falls**, a tiny cascade splashing down among aspen, after about 30 minutes. Aside from a trickling streamlet some way above, this is the last running water.

The trail winds up through fields of round granite boulders into stands of Engelmann spruce and subalpine fir, then makes

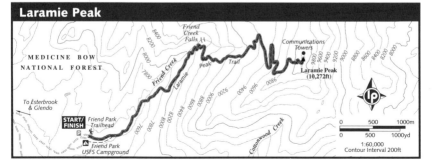

Laramie Peak
To Esterbrook & Glendo

MEDICINE BOW NATIONAL FOREST

Friend Creek Falls

Friend Creek

Laramie Peak Trail

Communications Towers

Laramie Peak (10,272ft)

Cottonwood Creek

START/FINISH Friend Park Trailhead

Friend Park USFS Campground

0   500   1000m
0   500   1000yd

1:60,000
Contour Interval 200ft

a final steeper ascent through limber pine to arrive at the summit of **Laramie Peak** (10,272ft), about 1½ hours from Friend Creek Falls. Some short but serious bouldering is then required to reach the summit proper. A telecommunications mast, cable lines and small maintenance huts crowd the ridge top among jumbled rock blocks.

Easily the highest point in the vacinity, Laramie Peak's west side falls away into the plains of the Medicine Bow River. There is an excellent view south across the Wheatland Reservoirs toward the Medicine Bow Mountains.

Return to the trailhead via the ascent route (1¾ to 2½ hours).

Snowy Range Loop

Duration	2 days
Distance	13.1mi (21.1km)
Standard	easy–moderate
Start	Sheep Lake Trailhead
Finish	Brooklyn Lake Trailhead
Nearest Towns	Centennial, Saratoga
Transport	car

Summary This short overnight (or longer day) hike circumnavigates the eastern half of the Snowy Range, which it crosses via a scenic pass known as The Gap.

Marking the northern limit of the Medicine Bow Mountains (which extend 40mi northwest from near Cameron Pass in Colorado), the 832-sq-mile Snowy Range is an area of broad-summit peaks among raw ridges and dozens of tarns.

Despite the Snowys' name, only one tiny remnant glacier and a few patches of permanent snow remain throughout the summer. The area has been proposed as a wilderness, but until now its small size (and some local opposition) has prevented such designation.

Although intense glaciation is visible everywhere, the Snowys are surprisingly gentle country for hiking, with few long climbs and plenty of opportunities for camping or resting.

PLANNING
When to Hike

Try to avoid coming on any weekend in July or August, when trails can get rather congested. Hikers should be mindful that this is still a high-level route where weather can quickly turn nasty at any time of year.

Maps

Four USGS 1:24,000 quads cover the hike, *Centennial*, *Morgan*, *Sand Lake* and *Medicine Bow Peak*, but the last sheet does not show the route between Lost Lake and Brooklyn Lake. The USFS 1:126,720 *Medicine Bow National Forest* gives a broader overview of the entire Medicine Bow area, and includes a contoured inset map (scaled at approximately 1:50,000) covering the Snowy Range Loop.

NEAREST TOWNS & FACILITIES
Centennial

The tiny gold-rush town of Centennial lies at the eastern foot of the Medicine Bow Mountains on Hwy 130 (Snowy Range Scenic Byway), 33mi west of Laramie. Medicine Bow National Forest's Centennial visitor center (☎ 307-742-6023, Hwy 130), 1.6mi west of town, sells books and maps; ask for the free USFS brochure *Snowy Range Trails*.

Basic *Friendly Motel (☎ 307-742-6033)* has singles/doubles for $37/45 and cabins for six for $75. *Old Corral Motel (☎ 307-745-5918, 800-678-2024)*, has rooms for $40/60 and a popular restaurant. *Trading Post Restaurant (☎ 307-721-5074)* serves steaks and seafood, and has live music on weekends. There are also rustic cabins with kitchenettes for $50.

Saratoga

Saratoga is at the western foot of the Medicine Bow Mountains on Hwy 130, about 49mi from Centennial and 20mi south of I-80. Saratoga Hot Springs (entry is free) are locally famous.

The USFS ranger station (☎ 307-326-5258, Hwy 130), just south of town, sells maps. The USFS Brush Creek visitor center (☎ 307-326-5562, Hwy 130), 20mi east of Saratoga also sells maps. The Great Rocky

Mountain Outfitters (☎ 307-326-8750, W www.grmo.com, 216 E Walnut St) sells outdoor (mostly fishing) supplies.

Deer Haven RV Park (☎ 307-326-8746, 706 N 1st St) offers sites from $5. Historic *Wolf Hotel (☎ 307-326-5525, 101 E Bridge Ave)* has singles/doubles from $30/35 and a good restaurant.

Platte Valley Shuttles & Tours (☎ 307-326-5582, W www.plattevalleyshuttles.com) drives hikers to/from trailheads.

Snowy Range Area

There are several USFS campgrounds (in the Snowy Range: *Sugarloaf, Nash Fork* and, at the trailhead, *Brooklyn Lake*; sites at each cost $9, but all are closed between mid-September and early to mid-June.

Mountain Meadows Cabins (☎ 307-742-6042, e mtmeadowcabins@cs.com), just off Hwy 130 along the Brooklyn Lake access road (first right turnoff), has two-person cabins from $48 and is open all year. Just west of the Brooklyn Trailhead turnoff is *Brooklyn Lodge (☎ 307-742-6916)* which also has rooms (reservations required).

GETTING TO/FROM THE HIKE

From Hwy 130 take the Brooklyn Lake campground turnoff, 8.6mi west from Centennial or 4.5mi east from Snowy Range Pass. Continue 1.9mi to the small Glacier Lakes Trailhead car park beside the campground.

Alternatively, leave your car at the small Sheep Lake Trailhead car park 0.2mi before the campground. There is currently no parking fee at either trailhead.

THE HIKE
Day 1: Sheep Lake Trailhead to Deep Lake

2¼–2¾ hours, 5.4mi, 470ft ascent
From the parking area, take the Sheep Lake Trail (No 309) and cut across grassy alpine meadows. The trail leads north near shallow pools in fir-spruce forest, then rises through a minor gap into a small hollow where permanent snowdrifts hug the slope. There are *campsites* nearby down around tarns at tree

line. Following orange marker poles, skirt over a minor crest to reach the **North Twin Lakes**, 40 to 50 minutes from the trailhead, where there are more *campsites*.

Climb on gently into meadows scattered with shrub willow, then traverse west above tarns in the upper South Fork Rock Creek valley. The trail skirts down northwest through a broad open basin with clumps of battered spruce to reach a trail junction just above **Sheep Lake**, about one hour from the North Twin Lakes. This shallow, bowl-like highland lake is fringed by grassy lawns.

Here, turn left (west) along the North Gap Lake Trail, which transits an undulating plateau with more small tarns nestling among natural pastures to meet the (right) Deep Lake Trail turnoff after 30 minutes. Follow this down 15 minutes (0.6mi) past the somber, waterweed-choked **Black Spotted Lake** to **Deep Lake**, a rounded tarn with good fishing. There are very attractive *campsites* among the spruce a few minutes on the left around the shore.

Day 2: Deep Lake to Brooklyn Lake Trailhead

3¼–4 hours, 7.7mi, 590ft ascent
Backtrack to the North Gap Lake Trail and continue up gently around the western shore of **Cutthroat Lake** – there are mediocre *campsites* near the tiny outlet – past the (right) Quealy Lake Trail turnoff. Climb southwest up a flat ridge covered by weathered alpine shrubbery past the elongated **Crescent Lake** to reach **North Gap Lake**. Head around the east side of this dramatic glacial tarn directly under almost 1200ft walls of a (nameless) 11,761ft peak past the (left) Shelf Lakes Trail turnoff. Ascend quickly through boulder rubble to arrive at **The Gap** (10,950ft), about 1½ hours (3mi) from Deep Lake. This narrow pass gives an immediate view of South Gap Lake – wider and deeper than its northern sibling – and the conical Sugarloaf Mountain (11,398ft) beyond.

Cut down around the east side of **South Gap Lake** to its oozing outlet, then break away left. Over to your right there are improving views of Klondike, Lewis and Libby

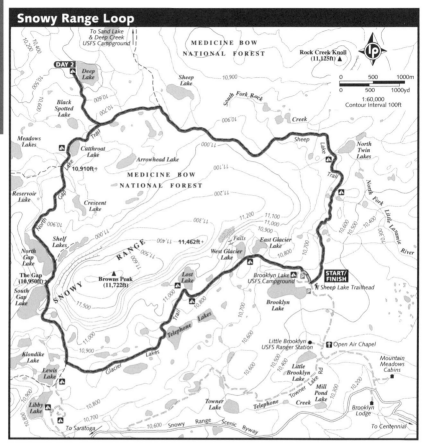

Snowy Range Loop

Lakes as well as the domed summit of Medicine Bow Peak, at 12,013ft the highest point in both the Snowy Range and Medicine Bow National Forest, as you sidle south along the slope to intersect with the **Glacier Lakes Trail** (No 395).

Go left and head east past several tarns before cutting up above the larger of the two **Telephone Lakes**. These slopes offer a fine view south across the plateau-like Libby Flats and the Platte River basin. The trail continues northeast through the low fir and spruce forest to reach **Lost Lake**, about 1¼ hours from The Gap. Pleasant *campsites*

can be found around the lake's southern shore below the eroding white limestone ridge of the Snowy Range.

The trail swings briefly southeast then climbs gently northeast to **West Glacier Lake**, which is fed by a small, but resilient hanging glacier with its gushing melt-water stream cascading over slab rocks. A slight rise leads on to the equally scenic **East Glacier Lake**, which has nice *campsites* back from its southern shore. Head down 0.5mi through the forest above **Brooklyn Lake** to arrive at the small car park near the USFS campground, 45 minutes from Lost Lake.

Other Hikes

BIGHORN MOUNTAINS
Lake Geneva

This lake is a beautiful elongated tarn in a deep glacial trough among slab-crag mountains in Cloud Peak Wilderness, roughly 7mi directly northwest of Cloud Peak. The lake can be visited as in an easy–moderate 8mi day hike from the (basic and free) Coffeen Park USFS campground. A good trail makes a steady rise up the East Fork Big Goose Creek (which in spring may require an almost knee-high ford) to Lake Geneva. There are lovely campsites at the lake head, but camp well back from the shore and do not light a fire.

A worthwhile (backpacking) hike is the 12mi lollipop loop to Cliff Lake via Geneva Pass.

Use the Trails Illustrated 1:43,635 map No 720 *Cloud Peak Wilderness* or the three USGS 1:24,000 quads: *Park Reservoir*, *Shell Lake* and *Cloud Peak*.

Lake Geneva's popularity is reduced by the relatively long and rough trailhead access. From Sheridan drive south on Hwy 335 to Bighorn, then continue 30mi along FR 26 to Big Goose Park (1mi before Big Goose USFS campground) and take FR 293 for 7mi to Coffeen Park. The last section of FR 26 is not suitable for low-clearance two-wheel-drive vehicles, but parking is possible near many roadside campsites.

WIND RIVER RANGE
Fremont Peak

At 13,745ft, Fremont Peak is the third highest peak in Wyoming, but it is the highest summit accessible to hikers without mountaineering expertise. It is still a hard climb to the top, suitable for experienced hikers only. You may also need to wait until mid-July for the snow to melt out sufficiently. From Island Lake (see the Titcomb Basin hike, p206), it is a further 10mi (with 3385ft of elevation gain) to the summit and back. From the lake, follow the Indian Pass Trail to the northwest inlet of an unnamed lake at 11,008ft. Then climb northwest along a faint path marked by cairns to gain the southern ridge. Follow this ridge to the summit from where there are dramatic views across Wind River Range. Use the 1:48,000 Earthwalk Press map *Northern Wind River Range*.

Green River Lakes

This is a popular and easy 6.5mi loop hike that explores the shores of Lower and Upper Green River Lakes. This largely flat hike allows great views of Square Top and Flat Top Mountains, probably the most photographed peaks in the Wind River Range. An early start is preferable to avoid the heat (there is little shade), and for the best chance of reflections in the lakes. Green River Lakes Trailhead (with adjacent camp-ground) is situated 51mi north of Pinedale at the end of State Road 352. Use the 1:48,000 Earthwalk Press map *Northern Wind River Range*.

MEDICINE BOW NATIONAL FOREST
Sherman Mountains

An absurd jumble of granite formations that attracts the momentary attention of motorists whizzing past on nearby I-80, the Sherman Mountains lie southeast of Laramie in the isolated Pole Mountain unit of Medicine Bow National Forest. A popular, easy–moderate hike from the Summit visitor center (accessible from I-80 via Exit 323) leads over juniper slopes and meadows among aspen forests and limber pine to the south-ern trailhead on FR 707. Another popular area for day hikes is Vedauwoo Glen, around which are interesting ice age rock formations (take Exit 329 from I-80). In summer carry plenty of liquids. Use either the USGS 1:24,000 quad, *Sherman Mountains West*, or the basic USFS map *Pole Mountain Unit*.

North Platte River

The North Platte River flows through the western side of the 35-sq-mile Platte River Wilderness. Along its roughly 9mi winding course the river offers leisurely hiking through sagebrush slopes alternating with stands of Douglas fir, cotton-wood and ponderosa pine. The fishing is best early in the season when meltwater swells the river, but note that special catch rules apply.

USGS map *Elkhorn Point* covers the route. Also ask for the free USFS brochure *Platte River Wilderness*. The trailhead is just past the Sixmile Gap USFS campground, 2.2mi off Hwy 230 on FR 492. From Saratoga, drive south 17.5mi to Riverside, then continue 22.5mi along Hwy 230. From Laramie, the distance is roughly 65mi.

Northern Utah

Representing the middle Rockies' most distant outliers, the mountains of Utah consist essentially of the Uinta Mountains and the Wasatch Range, which intersect at right-angles to form an inverted 'L'. These are the only well-watered, forested areas in a state better known for its desert canyons and salt pans. The Uintas and the Wasatch may make up only a small fraction of the Rockies' area, but they have all the classic vistas – massive rock walls, high rolling plateaus and glacial lakes, as well as plenty of 'spottable' wildlife (mountain goats, elk, black bears and deer).

CLIMATE
Up to 40 inches of precipitation, mostly snow, falls annually on the Uintas and the Wasatch. Summer temperatures higher than 80°F are unusual at elevations higher than 10,000ft and nights often drop below 40°F – but freezing weather is possible at any time. Afternoon thunderstorms are less common than in other parts of the Rockies, but fierce downpours can occur, with little warning, from June to late September.

INFORMATION
Maps & Books
GTR Mapping's 1:800,000 *Recreational Map of Utah* ($3.95) shows wilderness areas, trails and campgrounds throughout the state. *Utah's Favorite Hiking Trails* by J David Day and *Hiking Utah* by David Hall (both $14.95) cover a wide range of routes.

Information Sources
Online information is available at W www.utah.com and W www.go-utah.com. The USFS website covers Ashley (W www.fs.fed.us/r4/ashley) and Wasatch-Cache (W www.fs.fed.us/wcnf) National Forests.

GATEWAY
Salt Lake City
Salt Lake City, with a population of 1.1 million, sprawls along the southeastern shore of Great Salt Lake at the foot of the Wasatch

Highlights

Setting your sights on Utah's loftiest point – Gunsight Pass on the Kings Peak Loop.

- Rock-hopping to Utah's highest summit on the Kings Peak Loop (p219)

- Lazing on the wildflower meadows beside Emerald Lake under the Wasatch Range's beautiful Mt Timpanogos (p223)

Range. It is the state capital and international headquarters of the Mormon Church.

For information contact Salt Lake Convention & Visitors Bureau (☎ 801-521-2822, 800-541-4955; W www.visitsaltlake.com; 90 S West Temple). The US Forest Service (USFS; ☎ 801-524-5030; 8th Floor, Federal Building, 125 S State St) has maps and information on all national forest areas in Utah. The Public Lands Information Center (☎ 801-466-6411, W www.publiclands.org, 3285 East 3300 South) can also provide useful advice on outdoor recreation opportunities. REI (☎ 801-486-2100, W www.rei.com, 3285 East 3300 South) sells a wide range of outdoor gear.

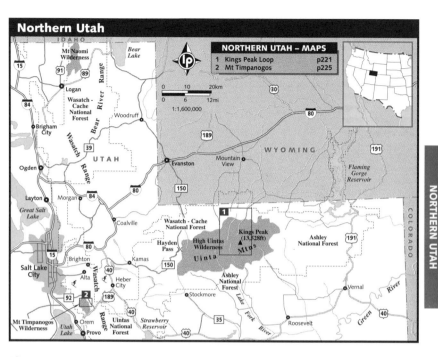

Northern Utah

NORTHERN UTAH – MAPS
1 Kings Peak Loop   p221
2 Mt Timpanogos   p225

Places to Stay The enormous *Camp VIP* (☎ 801-328-0224, 800-226-7752, 1400 W North Temple) charges $20/26 for tents/RV hookups. *Avenues Youth Hostel* (☎ 801-359-3855, ⓔ hisaltlakecity@sisna.com, cnr 107 F St & 2nd Ave) has dorm beds for $15/18 for youth hostel members/nonmembers, and private rooms for $30. *Deseret Inn* (☎/fax 801-532-2900, 50 W 500 South) charges $41/47 for singles/doubles. The *Historic Peery Hotel* (☎ 801-521-4300, Ⓦ www.historicpeeryhotel .com, 110 W Broadway) has rooms from $60.

Getting There & Away Salt Lake City international airport (see International Airports, p83) has many flights to/from major US cities. Greyhound (☎ 801-355-9579, 160 W South Temple) runs daily westbound and eastbound buses. Amtrak (☎ 801-531-0188) has a daily train service between Chicago and Salt Lake via Denver. Utah Transit Authority (☎ 801-287-4636) runs buses to nearby Provo, Tooele and Ogden ($2).

High Uintas Wilderness

The 714-sq-mile High Uintas Wilderness encompasses the high, wild and scenic core of the Uinta Mountains within the Ashley and Wasatch National Forests. Unlike any other range in the Lower 48 states, the Uintas run in an east-west direction. They present a formidable barrier, stretching some 100mi along Utah's border with Wyoming, from near Colorado almost as far as Salt Lake City.

The lofty Uinta (pronounced 'yoo-in-tuh') Mountains are characterized by magnificent upper-valley canyons ringed by remarkable staggered cliffs and tapered summits, including Kings Peak (13,528ft), Utah's highest point. The Mirror Lake Scenic Byway (between Kamas and Evanston) runs along the western edge of the wilderness, but the higher eastern Uintas are accessible only via dead-end roads from the north and south. The Highline Trail, which the Kings Peak Loop briefly follows, leads along the southern slope of the High Uinta Mountains from near Hayden Pass, on the Mirror Lake Scenic Byway, to Leidy Peak Trailhead, at the eastern end of the wilderness.

HISTORY

Centered in the Uinta Basin on the southern side of the Uinta Mountains, the ancient Fremont Culture experienced a similar development and decline to the better-known Anasazi (see The First Americans, p14) of the Four-Corners region (where Utah, Colorado, Arizona and New Mexico meet). When Europeans arrived the Ute people had been the principal inhabitants of the area for many centuries.

A party of Spanish explorers from Santa Fe, led by Father Silvestre Velez de Escalante and Father Francisco Atanasio Domínguez, were probably the first Europeans to see the Uinta Mountains in 1776. In the late 1820s the traders Etienne Provost and Antoine Robidoux established outposts in the Uinta Basin. In 1825 General Ashley journeyed through the nearby Flaming Gorge of the Green River and explored the Uinta Mountains. He was followed by the expeditions of Captain John Fremont in the 1840s and Major John Wesley Powell from the late 1860s.

In 1861 the entire south slope of the Uinta Mountains was made part of the vast Uintah and Ouray Indian Reservation, where most of the Ute people in the Uinta Basin were soon relocated. From the 1870s, however, pressure from ranchers and miners gradually saw these Native American lands opened to settlement and development.

In 1905 President Theodore Roosevelt reparceled the reservation lands, transferring almost the entire area of the Uinta Mountains into the new Uinta Forest Reserve, from which the separate entities of the Wasatch, Uinta and Ashley National Forests were later created. The High Uintas Wilderness was formally established by Congress in 1984.

NATURAL HISTORY

The Uinta Mountains are composed of 600-million year old quartzite, with sandstone and shale, that has been uplifted to near-vertical faults. Their east-west aspect produces a drier climate, because the range is less of a barrier to the moist, westerly airstream. These conditions tend to favor lodgepole pine, which dominates the foothills and the montane zone. In places lodgepole encroaches into the subalpine forests of Engelmann spruce and subalpine fir to as high as 11,000ft (where it holds a rather more graceful posture than at lower elevations). Cushion (mat) plants and sedges are found in alpine and subalpine plant communities.

Elk, bighorn sheep, cougars (mountain lions), moose, mule deer and black bears all inhabit the wilderness. The Uinta ground squirrel, a species found only in the middle Rockies, thrives in the higher summer temperatures. The High Uintas are also one of the few areas in the middle Rockies where the lynx is found. The white-tailed ptarmigan has been successfully reintroduced to the area.

PLANNING
Maps & Books

BLM's 1:100,000 *Kings Peak* map ($4) covers the entire wilderness area and is good for a general overview.

High Uintas Backcountry by J & B Probst ($13.95) and *High Uinta Trails* by Mel Davis & John Veranth ($11.95) cover routes throughout the Uinta Mountains. The *Lakes of the High Uintas*, published by the Utah Wildlife Resources Division (☎ 801-538-4700; 1594 W North Temple, Salt Lake City, UT 84114), provides information for anglers.

Permits & Regulations

Permits are not required to hike or camp in the High Uintas Wilderness. Camping within 200ft of all trails and waterways is prohibited. To avoid further environmental degradation, fires are not permitted in many heavily used lake basins or popular sections of the trail. A total fire ban may be imposed throughout the wilderness during long summer dry-spells.

Vehicles parked at picnic areas and trailheads along the Mirror Lake Scenic Byway must display a valid recreation pass; these cost $3/6/25 per day/week/year. Elsewhere, trailhead parking fees ($2 per vehicle, good for five consecutive days) apply at all major USFS trailheads in Utah and Wyoming. A self-serve system applies for recreation passes and trailhead fees – drop your fee envelope into the deposit box.

ACCESS TOWN
Evanston
Evanston (population 12,000) is along I-80, at the intersection of Hwys 89 and 150, 3mi east of the Wyoming-Utah state line. For information contact the chamber of commerce (☎ 307-789-2757, 800-328-9708, 36 10th St) or the USFS office (☎ 307-789-3194; 1565 Hwy 150 South, Suite A). Bear River Books (☎ 307-789-5111, 1008 Main St) sells quads. There is no outdoor store in Evanston, but Wal-Mart has some basic backpacking supplies.

Phillips RV & Trailer Park (☎ 307-789-3805, 800-349-3805, 225 Bear River Dr) has shaded tent sites ($16) and full hookups ($18). *Prairie Inn Motel (☎ 307-789-2920, 264 Bear River Dr)* and *Motel 6 (☎ 307-789-0791, 261 Bear River Dr)* have singles/doubles from around $35/45.

Regular Greyhound (☎ 307-789-2810) buses run from/to Salt Lake City and Denver.

Kings Peak Loop

Duration	4 days
Distance	35.5mi (57.1km)
Standard	moderate
Start/Finish	China Meadows Trailhead
Nearest Town	Mountain View
Transport	car

Summary A beautiful route with many highlights including a climb of Utah's highest summit, Kings Peak.

This wonderful backpacking lollipop loop leads into the wildest, highest and most spectacular part of the High Uinta Wilderness. The route crosses several scenic passes on either side of the 13,528ft Kings Peak, which is 12mi from the closest road. The area also boasts the only population of white-tailed deer in the state. Many of the lake basins have been severely impacted by large numbers of campers, so please practice Leave No Trace principles (p56).

PLANNING
When to Hike
The hike can normally be undertaken from July through September.

Maps
Recommended is Trails Illustrated's 1:75,000 *High Uintas Wilderness* map. Otherwise use the four USGS 1:24,000 quads; *Gilbert Peak*, *Mount Powell*, *Bridger Lake* and *Kings Peak*.

NEAREST TOWN & FACILITIES
Mountain View
This tiny town lies well inside Wyoming, north of the Uintas at the junction of CR 410 and Hwy 414, about 10mi south of I-80. The USFS Mountain View Ranger District (☎ 307-782-6555, Hwy 414) can advise on local conditions. Mountain View has gas stations and a large *supermarket*, but the nearest accommodations are in Evanston (this page).

USFS Campgrounds
Two USFS campgrounds, the small *Trailhead*, right beside the trailhead itself, and *China Meadows*, on the access road about 0.7mi north, have basic sites for $7. Several other USFS campgrounds, costing between $9 and $10, exist along the access road: *Stateline* (just inside Utah), *Bridger Lake*, *East Marsh Lake* and *West Marsh Lake*.

GETTING TO/FROM THE HIKE
From Mountain View drive 6mi south along CR 410, then turn left at a sharp bend (signposted 'Wasatch National Forest'). Follow CR 283 south for 12mi to a fork, then continue left along FR 77 for 4mi to the China Meadows Trailhead, where there is space for around 50 vehicles. A trailhead parking fee is payable (see Permits & Regulations, p218).

NORTHERN UTAH

THE HIKE
Day 1: China Meadows Trailhead to Broadbent Meadow

2¾–3¾ hours, 7.5mi, 1002ft ascent

After signing the trailhead register take Trail 110 and head south through the stock gate into low lodgepole forest. The trail leads along the west bank of the East Fork Smiths Fork into the wilderness, crossing the stream on a sturdy footbridge after 1.6mi. Continue beside boggy clearings, passing through a gate in a log fence before meeting the left (southeast) branch of Trail 105 at Stillwater Junction, 1½ to two hours from the trailhead.

Continue along Trail 110, passing where Trail 105 turns right (to West Fork Smiths Fork) in 0.5mi. The well-maintained trail rises only incrementally past attractive *campsites* along the extensive, sometimes boggy **Broadbent Meadow** until it recrosses the East Fork Smiths Fork, 1¼ to 1¾ hours from Stillwater Junction. From here you get a sudden, spectacular view of Red Castle, a massive fortress-like rock that divides the tiny head of the valley into east and west sides. There are pleasant *campsites* back from the streamside.

Day 2: Broadbent Meadow to Yellowstone Creek

3–3¾ hours, 8.5mi, 1450ft ascent

Switchback up beside the stream's cascading west branch, ignoring the right (northwest) Trail 111 (to East Fork Blacks Fork), to continue south for 200yd before turning left (east) onto Trail 111. (Trail 110 continues to Red Castle Lake – see Side Trip.) Trail 111 recrosses the tiny stream and cuts southeast onto a wide, low ridge, rising past tiny tarns among light stands of spruce on the east side of Red Castle. There are sporadic *campsites* along this section of trail. Climb past tiny waterfalls out of the trees to arrive at **Smiths Fork Pass Lake**. Isolated stands of weather-beaten spruce above the lake's west side offer scenic but rather bleak *camping*.

Climb through the rocky tundra to reach the **ridge top** (11,790ft), around 350yd west of Smiths Fork Pass, two to 2½ hours from Broadbent Meadow. From here you get good views west to Wilson Peak and ahead

into the upper valley of Yellowstone Creek, a broad basin fronted by high, precipitous ridges. The trail cuts down briefly right, then turns southeast past a tarn among regenerated moraine mounds to intersect with the Highline Trail (No 25). Go left (northeast) and continue down over shrub willow slopes just above tree line to cross the tiny **Yellowstone Creek**, 50 minutes to 1¼ hours from the pass. Sheltered *campsites* can be found among the spruce on the opposite side of another small brook a few minutes on.

Side Trip: Red Castle Lake

1¾–2¼ hours, 4.5mi, 545ft ascent

From the upper junction of Trails 111 and 110, continue right (south) through meadows along the stream's west side to the scenic **Lower Red Castle Lake**, the shore of which is an (overly) popular spot for *camping*. The trail skirts the lake, beginning a moderate climb southwest to **Red Castle Lake**, a grandiose alpine lake nestling against the west face of Red Castle. This lake is one of the largest – and arguably the most spectacular – of the High Uintas tarns. A social trail leads around the eastern shore to Upper Red Castle Lake. *Camping* is very poor around both of the latter lakes. Note that fires are not permitted anywhere in the Red Castle Lakes basin.

Day 3: Yellowstone Creek to Henrys Fork Lake

4½–6 hours, 9.8mi, 2472ft ascent

The Highline Trail climbs northeast out of the trees over more moraine, leading onto boulder-strewn alpine lawns. Switchback steeply up north through rubbly scree before making a final upward traverse east to reach **Anderson Pass** (12,670ft), 1½ to two hours from Yellowstone Creek. This narrow gap of broken rock is the starting point for the Kings Peak ascent (see Side Trip, p222).

Drop eastward into alpine meadows dotted with harebells and western yellow paintbrush, crossing and recrossing a small stream as you wind down to a trail junction in Painter Basin, which is drained by Atwood Creek, an upper tributary of the Uinta River. Turn left along Trail 68 and hike northwest

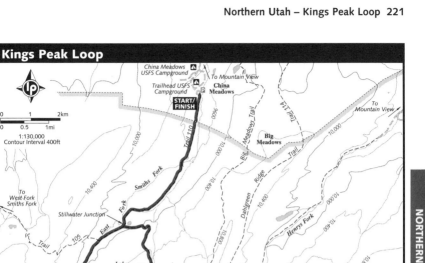

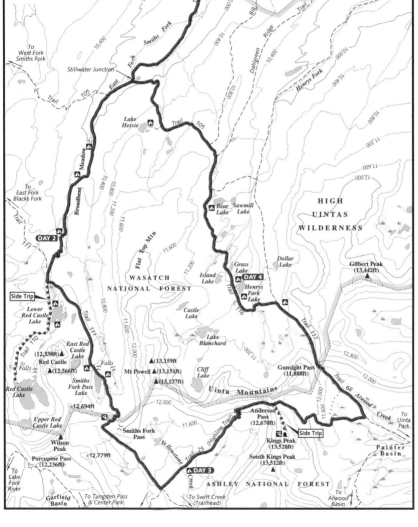

past battered fir-spruce groves and picturesque grassy ponds in the waterlogged valley, rising steadily through limestone rock to arrive at **Gunsight Pass** (11,888ft), 1¾ to 2¼ hours from Anderson Pass. Gunsight Pass looks back into Painter Basin but offers only limited views ahead.

Descend northwest (now on Trail 117) for 1.6mi over meadows scattered with shrub willow to a trail junction. There are pretty *campsites* at the forest edge here. Take Trail 116 left (west) over streamlets of **Henrys Fork**, past a tiny log cabin and a small tarn, to reach **Henrys Fork Lake**, 1¼ to 1½ hours from Gunsight Pass. Henrys Fork Lake lies in a beautiful alpine valley basin, the rim of which is defined by an almost continuous wall of stratified, red-rock ridges. The trail traces the west side of the lake, past scenic and secluded *campsites* (five minutes off to the right) where moose can often be seen browsing around the water's edge. Campfires are not permitted anywhere within the lake basin.

Side Trip: Kings Peak
1½–2 hours, 1.6mi, 858ft ascent
Despite its short distance, the climb to the 13,528ft summit of Kings Peak is exhausting as it requires a lot of scrambling over boulders. Watch out for afternoon thunderstorms – in July and August it's advisable to avoid the summit area after 1pm. There is no real trail to speak of, although heavy traffic has worn rough routes in places.

From Anderson Pass head southeast, well to the east side of the ridge crest, then cut up right to reach the top of Kings Peak after 45 minutes to one hour. The exhilarating views include the tarns of the Garfield Basin to the southwest and Lake Atwood in the upper basin of the Uinta River to the southeast.

Day 4: Henrys Fork Lake to China Meadows Trailhead
3½–5½ hours, 9.7mi, 373ft ascent
Trail 116 heads northwest through the forest, past the aptly-named **Grass Lake** in watery meadows under more red-crag ridges. Continue over low ridges around the small but deep **Bear Lake**, where the west shore has

appealing *campsites*. Climb 300yd to meet Trail 105 (left) and follow it north, traversing steadily up along the valley side until you come out onto a sloping tundra plateau (11,140ft) at the northern edge of **Flat Top Mountain**, 1¼ to 1¾ hours from Henrys Fork Lake. In summer sheep are driven up to graze on these lovely alpine pastures.

Follow large marker cairns down northwest past the (right) Dahlgreen Ridge (No 114) and Big Meadows Trails into stands of park-like alpine lodgepole pine – some of the most elevated lodgepole anywhere in the Rockies – to pass the **Lake Hessie** turnoff (left), 50 minutes to 1¼ hours from the plateau. This tarn, hidden in the trees just 400yd over to the west, offers very pleasant *camping*; fires are not permitted. Trail 105 makes a slightly steeper descent northwest past a large lily pond to intersect with Trail 110 at Stillwater Junction, 25 to 30 minutes from the Lake Hessie turnoff.

Retrace your steps to China Meadows Trailhead (1½ to two hours).

Wasatch Range

The 200mi-long Wasatch Range stretches along the eastern rim of the Great Basin, from north-central Utah into southeast Idaho. Its highest summits, including Mt Nebo (11,877ft) and the superb Mt Timpanogos (11,750ft), tower almost 5000ft above vast, arid plains and saline lakes, forming the Wasatch Front. The range largely lies within Wasatch-Cache and Uinta National Forests, and harbors five small designated wilderness areas. Situated right beside one of the most rapidly developing locations in the Rocky Mountains region, the Wasatch Range is a sensitive area that receives extremely heavy recreational and commercial use.

HISTORY
People associated with the ancient Fremont Culture, and later the Shoshone and Ute peoples, inhabited the eastern Great Basin and the lower valleys of the Wasatch – a word that means 'high mountain pass' in the Ute language. In summer Native Americans

would venture into the higher mountains to fish or hunt large game. From the 1820s trappers and explorers, including early 'mountain men' like Peter Skene Ogden and John Weber (now well remembered in local nomenclature), were attracted by the abundant wildlife of the Wasatch.

In the mid-1840s settlers bound for California began crossing the Wasatch Range (via Weber Canyon). The first Mormon settlers, led by Brigham Young, arrived at Salt Lake City in 1847. Their community was able to thrive only because of the resources of the Wasatch – above all water for irrigation – and early Mormon mines, kilns and sawmills are still visible throughout the mountains. The devastating effects of overgrazing and uncontrolled fires on the water catchment led to the creation of the Wasatch National Forest in 1906 and the Cache National Forest the following year. Since 1973 the two have been jointly administered as the Wasatch-Cache National Forest.

NATURAL HISTORY

Utah's most ancient rocks – around two billion years old – are found along the Wasatch Front and can be best seen in outcrops near the mouth of Farmington Canyon. Great Salt Lake and Utah Lake were originally part of a far larger lake, known as Lake Bonneville. Today ancient terraces are still visible in places where the lake waters lapped against the foothills of the Wasatch Front.

The searing desert winds ensure that dryland vegetation dominates the lower and middle slopes of the Wasatch. Gambel oak and canyon maple (also called wasatch maple) form woody thickets in the lower valleys and mountainsides, often in association with gnarled, old Rocky Mountain juniper. A 1500-year-old specimen found in the northern Wasatch Front, known as the Jardine Juniper, is believed to be the oldest living tree in the Rockies. Aspen occurs in scattered patches on moister (shaded) slopes at lower elevations. Stands of Engelmann spruce, usually with subalpine fir or the rarer Rocky Mountain white fir, grow up to tree line. Mountain goats graze on the alpine wildflower meadows.

PLANNING
Maps & Books

The Trails Illustrated 1:90,000 *Wasatch Front* map covers many of the best hiking routes in the Wasatch.

Hiking the Wasatch by John Veranth ($14.95) outlines great routes throughout the range. Falcon Guide's *Best Easy Day Hikes Salt Lake City* by Brian Brinkerhoff ($6.95) also deals mainly with hikes in the Wasatch.

Permits & Regulations

Permits are not required to hike or camp on public land in the Wasatch Range. However, as the Wasatch provides most of the drinking water for Salt Lake and other nearby cities, swimming in, or camping closer than 200ft to, lakes and streams is prohibited. Pets are not allowed in many areas.

Recreation passes ($3/10 for three/14 days, $25 for one year) are required to access some popular trailheads, including Mt Timpanogos Trailhead.

Mt Timpanogos

Duration	8–10½ hours
Distance	11mi (17.7km)
Standard	moderate–hard
Start/Finish	Mt Timpanogos Trailhead
Nearest Town	Salt Lake City
Transport	car
Summary	A vigorous but rewarding hike up Utah's most beautiful mountain.

Towering above the sprawling conglomerate of Salt Lake City and Provo, Mt Timpanogos' distinctive, stratified form makes it the most grandiose summit in the Wasatch Range. Mt Timpanogos is the Wasatch's second highest peak and nurtures the state's only glacier. Mountain goats, reintroduced into the Mt Timpanogos Wilderness in 1981, now wander about the mountain's upper slopes.

The climb to the summit of Mt Timpanogos, which requires a vertical ascent of 5500ft, is very popular, although many hikers are quite satisfied once they reach the scenic Emerald Lake (more than halfway up the mountain). Timpanogos is derived from a Ute word meaning 'rocky creek' and is believed to have originally referred to the American Fork. Most people do the climb as a *long* day hike, although camping out may be a better option for slower parties – but please consider the environment in this sensitive, heavily visited area.

PLANNING
When to Hike
The trail is normally passable (at least as far as Emerald Lake) from late June to early October.

Maps
Recommended is Trails Illustrated's plastic 1:48,000 *Uinta National Forest* map. Otherwise use two 1:24,000 USGS quads: *Aspen Grove* and *Timpanogos Cave*.

Information Sources
The Pleasant Grove USFS Ranger District (☎ 801-785-3563, 390 North 100 East) can advise on local conditions, and sells Trails Illustrated maps (but not USGS quads).

NEAREST TOWN & FACILITIES
See Salt Lake City (p216).

Near the Trailhead
Very basic *Mt Timpanogos USFS campground*, just uphill from the trailhead car park, has 12 attractive sites for $11; it fills quickly on weekends. More *campgrounds* are along American Fork (near Timpanogos Cave). Upmarket *Sundance Resort (☎ 801-225-4107, W www.sundanceresort.com, Hwy 92)*, about 3mi south of the trailhead, has accommodations from $225.

GETTING TO/FROM THE HIKE
Take exit 275 off I-15 south of Salt Lake City, following Hwy 52 (8th North) and then US 189 via Provo Canyon for 14mi before turning left along Hwy 92 (American Fork Alpine Loop). Continue for 5mi, past the Sundance Resort and Aspen Grove Family Camp (beyond which you must purchase a recreation pass – see Permits & Regulations, p223), to the parking lot at Mt Timpanogos Trailhead.

Warning
This route (especially the lower sections) is exposed to the summer sun, and can be very hot going in July and August. Wear a wide-brimmed hat and sunscreen. Carry plenty of fluids as there is little running water (which must be filtered or chemically treated) for much of the way. Hikers should aim to set off early (before 9am).

THE HIKE
Take the gravel/bitumen path west through light aspen forest, past a small USFS information booth (open daily in July and August), to a waterfall, then begin the long climb into gambel oak and maple scrub with isolated Douglas fir. Switchback up and traverse the massive, terraced cliffs of **Primrose Cirque**. Cross and recross a tiny, splashing stream, through thickets of fireweed and purple mountain bluebells, until you finally emerge onto a broad, grassy shelf under soaring, two-tiered bluffs. There are *campsites* among small stands of spruce down to the left, near Hidden Lakes.

The trail skirts above a small pond in the meadow and then follows the stream over moraine to reach **Emerald Lake**, three to four hours from the trailhead. This meltwater tarn lies at the snout of the tiny, rubble-covered **Timpanogos Glacier**, which fills a deep, narrow trough directly under Mt Timpanogos. Mountain goats can be spotted roaming around this high alpine basin. Some people *camp* among the last trees on the ridge just east of the lake.

Hike west up the alpine wildflower slopes, past a basic emergency shelter, to where the Timpooneke Trail (No 53) cuts down right into the sparse Timpanogos Basin. Continue left, traversing along a high, bouldery ledge under the north wall of Mt Timpanogos, before cutting up southwest, past the intersecting Trail 54, into a narrow gap in the ridge (11,140ft). The trail now makes a final ascent along the southwest side of the shingly ridge to arrive at the tiny steel hut atop **Mt Timpanogos** (11,750ft), 1½ to two hours from Emerald Lake. The summit offers a stunning

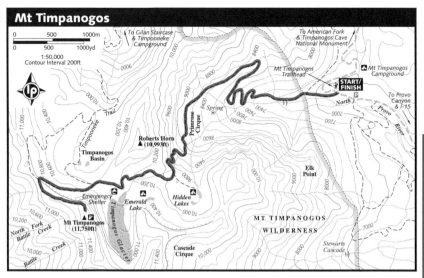

panorama stretching across Provo and Utah Lake to the west, and the high mountains of the Wasatch Range.

Experienced hikers sometimes continue southeast along the narrow ridge before descending along the north side of the glacier back to Emerald Lake. Otherwise return to the trailhead via your ascent route (3½ to 4½ hours).

Other Hikes

HIGH UINTAS WILDERNESS
Naturalist Basin
Naturalist Basin, a high alpine basin dotted with a dozen or so delightful tarns, lies at the western end of the High Uintas Wilderness. It can be visited easily as a 13mi round-trip day hike (or leisurely overnight backpacking trip) from the Highline Trailhead, 120yd south of Hayden Pass on the Mirror Lake Scenic Byway. Campfires are not permitted in Naturalist Basin. Use either USGS's 1:24,000 *Hayden Peak* quad or Trails Illustrated's 1:75,000 *High Uintas Wilderness* map.

WASATCH RANGE
Brighton Basin
The low ranges around the small Brighton Ski Resort in the Wasatch Range offer easy, laid-back hiking. A 3.4mi loop leads from Silver Lake (information office) via Twin Lakes and Lake Mary, from where an excellent 3.6mi side trip can be made up to the lookout summit of Sunset Peak (10,648ft). Longer (including backpacking) options are also possible in the area. The best map is the 1:24,000 *Hiking the Wasatch*, produced by the Wasatch Mountain Club, but Trails Illustrated's 1:90,000 *Wasatch Front* map also covers the route. To reach Brighton turn off I-15 (just south of the intersection with I-215) and drive along Hwy 190 for 22mi through Big Cottonwood Canyon.

Northern Colorado & the Front Range

For the two million-plus citizens of Denver and Boulder, the mountains of northern Colorado's Front Range provide a back-garden playground of monumental proportions. The gradual upward sweep of Colorado's plains changes abruptly just west of Denver, as a wall of peaks stretches from north to south across the horizon. It is an arresting sight and at its heart is the superb glacial landscape of Rocky Mountain National Park, dominated by Longs Peak, the most-climbed 14er in the Rockies. A network of well-maintained trails explores the park's cirques and alpine plateaus, providing an opportunity for the large number of hikers who visit this park to spread out amid the stunning scenery.

Blessed with the same alpine scenery as its prestigious neighbor, Indian Peaks Wilderness runs contiguously to the south of Rocky Mountain National Park. It is a local's favorite and hikers use the beautiful Arapaho Pass and Pawnee Pass Trails to cross the main spine of the Indian Peaks (thereby crossing the Continental Divide).

Moving west from the Front Range, the character of the mountains softens and the number of hikers on the trails drops dramatically. North of the pleasant ski and spa town of Steamboat Springs, Mt Zirkel Wilderness is a wonderful getaway for hikers who seek a little more solitude but still want a taste of the dramatic rock scenery that is so characteristic of northern Colorado.

CLIMATE

The great height of the mountains in northern Colorado (which frequently rise above 13,000ft) is perhaps the biggest single factor determining climate in the area. Precipitation tends to drop off markedly as you move east across the mountains. Average annual snowfall near Granby on the western side of Rocky Mountain National Park is 145 inches, while only 30mi away, in the eastern lee of the

Highlights

GARETH McCORMACK

A Rocky Mountains icon – bighorn sheep graze the alpine tundra of Bighorn Flats.

- Watching herds of bighorn sheep grazing on the alpine tundra near Flattop Mountain (p233) in Rocky Mountain National Park

- Savoring the spectacular view from Longs Peak (p237) after the challenging ascent of this famous 14er

- Taking in the fine summits of Indian Peaks Wilderness from Pawnee Pass (p241)

- Enjoying the solitude and delicate beauty of Gilpin Lake (p247) in Mt Zirkel Wilderness

range, Estes Park averages a mere 34 inches. The towns are at comparable altitudes.

Because of the high elevations the thaw of snowfields can last well into July and high passes can be difficult to negotiate until then. The moisture from this melt fuels afternoon thunderstorms – a real consideration when

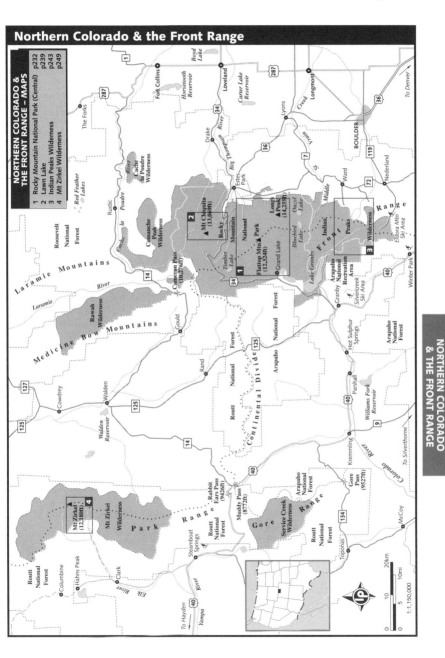

NORTHERN COLORADO &
THE FRONT RANGE – MAPS

1 Rocky Mountain National Park (Central)   p232
2 Lawn Lake   p239
3 Indian Peaks Wilderness   p243
4 Mt Zirkel Wilderness   p249

NORTHERN COLORADO
& THE FRONT RANGE

planning a hike in June or July, when they are a daily occurrence. Winters are harsh and almost all hiking ends in late September or October when the first heavy snows fall.

Recorded weather and road information for the Indian Peaks and Rocky Mountain National Park area can be heard on ☎ 970-586-1333.

INFORMATION
Maps & Books
Most Colorado state maps, including the *Colorado Recreation Map* ($3.95), give good overviews of the area and smaller-scale topographic maps for hiking are widely available.

The Complete Guide to Colorado's Wilderness Areas by John Fielder & Mark Pearson ($24.95) includes background information and hike descriptions for Indian Peaks Wilderness and Mt Zirkel Wilderness. *The Best Hikes of Colorado* by Christina Williams ($29.95) includes a selection of hikes in Rocky Mountain National Park and around Steamboat Springs. Kent & Donna Dannen's *Hiking Rocky Mountain National Park – Including Indian Peaks* ($12.95) is the most comprehensive guide dedicated to trails in those areas.

GATEWAYS
Denver
Sprawling across the rolling prairies at the eastern foot of the Front Range, Denver is a pleasant city with a broad range of attractions. The Convention and Visitors Bureau (☎ 303-892-1112; W www.denver.org; Tabor Center, 1668 Larimer St) is open from 8am to 5pm Monday to Saturday, and from 10am to 2pm Sunday.

Places to Stay The large *Denver International Hostel* (☎ 303-832-9996, 630 E 16th Ave) charges $8.60 for a dorm bed. Alternatively, the HI/AYH *Melbourne International Hotel & Hostel* (☎ 303-292-6386, 607 22nd St) charges $12/15 for members/nonmembers. *Motel 7* (☎ 303-592-1555, 930 Valley Hwy, cnr US 6 and I-25 exit 209C) is one of the most convenient budget motels, with basic double rooms from $46.

Getting There & Away Amtrak's *California Zephyr* (☎ 303-825-2583) runs daily between Chicago and San Francisco via Denver's Union Station (cnr 17th & Wynkoop Sts). From the downtown bus terminal (☎ 303-293-6555, cnr 19th & Arapahoe Sts) Greyhound and others offer frequent connecting services to/from all major US cities.

Denver International Airport (☎ 303-342-2000, 800-247-2336) is the Rockies' main point of entry for air travelers. See International Airports (p83) for more details.

Boulder
Boulder sits right under the slab-rock mountainsides of the Front Range, 27mi northwest of Denver. This pleasant, laid-back university city is the gateway to the Rocky Mountain National Park and Indian Peaks Wilderness. The Boulder Convention and Visitors Bureau (☎ 303-442-2911, W www.bouldercoloradousa.com, 2440 Pearl St) offers maps, brochures and assistance, and is open 9am to 5pm weekdays.

Places to Stay Boulder is an expensive place to stay but among the cheaper options are the shaded campsites ($14) at the *Boulder Mountain Lodge* (☎ 303-444-0882, 91 Four Mile Canyon Rd), 4mi west of town on Hwy 119. The *Boulder International Youth Hostel* (☎ 303-442-0522, 1107 12th St) has $15 dorm beds with a surcharge of up to a $4 a night for linen.

Getting There & Away RTD (☎ 303-299-6000) buses run at least hourly between Boulder and downtown Denver.

Rocky Mountain National Park

The 415-sq-mile Rocky Mountain National Park lies northwest of Denver. Packed into an area hardly one tenth the size of Yellowstone, 'Rocky' is a superb alpine landscape of granite summits, high tundra plateaus, tiny relict glaciers and more than 150 lakes accessible by over 345mi of scenic trails.

HISTORY

The Rocky area was originally inhabited by groupings of the Ute people. Immediately prior to the arrival of Europeans, however, Ute territory was increasingly encroached upon by Arapaho and Cheyenne tribes displaced from the eastern plains by advancing pioneers. In 1820, while leading an expedition on the South Platte River, Major Stephen Long sighted the prominent 14er (14,000ft peak) that today bears his name.

In 1859 Joel Estes tried unsuccessfully to settle the open 'park' meadows along the Big Thompson River. Twelve years later the Irish earl Lord Dunraven established a private hunting estate here, depicted in 1877 by the great landscape artist Albert Bierstadt in the work *Estes Park*. The inventor FO Stanley purchased Dunraven's estate and in 1909 opened the luxurious Stanley Hotel, establishing Estes Park as a vacation destination for wealthy tourists. Alarmed by the unrestrained development and expansion of the pastoral and logging industries, the conservationist Enos Mills campaigned for the preservation of the area and in 1915 Congress finally passed the act creating Rocky Mountain National Park. The Fall River Rd over the Continental Divide was completed in 1920 but was largely replaced by the more scenic, high-level Trail Ridge Rd, which opened in 1932.

NATURAL HISTORY

Lodgepole and ponderosa pine forest predominates in the lower, drier edges of the park. As the altitude increases, the Douglas fir mingles with subalpine fir, Engelmann spruce and aspen. These montane and subalpine forests are often carpeted by fragrant heath-like grouseberry (known locally as whortleberry) shrubs. Colorado blue spruce, readily recognized by its striking bluish-green foliage, grows along mountain streams. Wildflowers such as the radiant red Indian paintbrush, purple monkshood and blue-and-white Colorado columbine are found in the subalpine forest clearings, while in moist areas pink moss campion, primrose and white marsh marigold are common. Glacier lilies, mountain gentians and alpine sunflowers bloom on the alpine tundra, which makes up more than one quarter of the park's area.

In summer red squirrels and chipmunks busily work the lodgepole and fir-spruce forests, harvesting nuts and seeds (or picking over crumbs left by picnickers). Yellow-bellied marmots and pikas shelter in coarse talus slopes, feeding on grasses or lichen in the alpine tundra. Nuttall's cottontail rabbits and snowshoe hares shelter in alpine shrub willows. These herbivores are kept under control by various small predators, including martens, red foxes and bobcats. Rocky's black bears are small and shy, but can occasionally be spotted in meadows munching berries or digging grubs out of rotted trunks in the forest. Mule deer browse in the forests while elk graze in the meadows around dawn and dusk.

Rocky's range of mountain environments supports a diverse bird population. Red crossbills – note the male's orange-red (especially breast) plumage – constantly move around the ponderosa and lodgepole forests in search of pine nuts. Radiant green broad-tailed hummingbirds feed on flowers in the lower montane forests, although they breed in the alpine zone. Greenish-yellow Wilson's warblers and mountain chickadees flit about the alpine krummholz (stunted forest).

Streams in Rocky Mountain National Park have been restocked with the threatened Colorado River cutthroat trout, a subspecies originally distributed throughout the headwaters of the Colorado River.

PLANNING
Maps & Books

Trails Illustrated's 1:59,000 No 200 *Rocky Mountain National Park Recreation Map* ($9.95) covers the entire park. A nonwaterproof version ($1.95) is also available. The USGS 1:50,000 *Rocky Mountain National Park* map ($7) also covers the whole park, but routes are not always shown clearly and it is not as widely available. Trail Tracks Panoramic Hiking Maps' *Rocky Mountain National Park* ($9.95) is a colorful overview of the area and includes brief route descriptions but is not a good topographic reference.

Rocky Mountain National Park by Patrick Soran & Dan Klinglesmith ($14.95) is a colorful handbook detailing the practical and natural aspects of the park.

Information Sources

Information packs about the park are available from the park headquarters (☎ 970-586-1206; RMNP, Estes Park, CO 80517) or can be requested via the National Park Service (NPS) website (W www.nps.gov/romo).

Permits & Regulations

The park entry fee (valid for seven days) for private vehicles is $15, while individuals entering on foot, bicycle, motorcycle or taxi pay $5. Annual passes (individual or private vehicle) cost $30.

Backcountry permits are required for all overnight trips in Rocky. These cost $15 from May through October (otherwise free), regardless of the number in the hiking party and the length of hike (maximum six nights). There are backcountry offices at Estes Park (near the NPS visitor center), Grand Lake (West Unit office) and the Kawuneeche visitor center. Backcountry permits can be reserved after March in writing (Backcountry Office, Rocky Mountain National Park, Estes Park, CO 80517) or by telephone from March to May 20 (☎ 970-586-1242). Otherwise reservations are only accepted one day prior to pick-up. Fires are not permitted at most backcountry campsites.

Anglers need park fishing licenses. Certain streams are catch-and-release only.

GETTING AROUND

Within the park, two free shuttle buses make frequent trips (every 10 minutes during peak periods) from near Glacier Basin campground to Bear Lake and Fern Lake, stopping at many of the most popular trailheads along the way. For less-used trailheads your only option is Charles Limousine (☎ 970-586-5151), a local taxi service.

ACCESS TOWNS
Estes Park

The main access point for Rocky Mountain National Park, this sprawling town lies at the eastern foot of the Front Range just outside the park boundary. The visitor center (☎ 800-443-7837, W www.estesparkresort.com, 500 Big Thompson Ave) can advise on accommodations, while the national park headquarters and visitor center (☎ 970-586-1206, US 36) is 2.5mi west of Estes Park. The US Forest Service (USFS) office (☎ 970-586-3440, 161 Second St) is also open daily from May through September.

Outdoor World (☎ 970-586-2114, 156 Elkhorn Ave) is one of several stores with a good range of backcountry gear.

Places to Stay The *Glacier Basin campground (☎ 800-365-2267)* and *Estes Park campground (☎ 970-586-4188, 3420 Tunnel Rd)*, at East Portal, have tent sites for $16 and $20 respectively. *Colorado Mountain School (☎ 970-586-5758, 351 Moraine Ave)* offers dorm beds for $25, while the huge *YMCA of the Rockies (☎ 970-586-3341, Tunnel Rd)* has rooms from $40.

Getting There & Away Jeff Norton (☎ 303-589-5489) runs a shuttle between Boulder and Estes Park for $17/22 one way/return. Estes Park Shuttle (☎ 970-586-5151) has four services daily to/from Denver International Airport for $39/75 one way/return.

Grand Lake

This attractive, if touristy, town lies on the north shore of Grand Lake. For information try the chamber of commerce (☎ 970-627-3402, W www.grandlakechamber.com, cnr US 34 & W Portal Rd). Never Summer Mountain Products (☎ 970-627-3642, 919 Grand Ave) sells hiking gear and maps.

Places to Stay Just west of US 34, *Elk Creek campground (☎ 970-627-8502, Golf Course Rd)* has sites from $18. The excellent and homely *Shadowcliff Mountain Lodge (☎ 970-627-9220, 405 Summerland Park Rd)* is at the northeast end of town; dorm beds start from $10 and private rooms from $32. The historic *Grand Lake Lodge (☎ 970-627-3967, W www.grandlakelodge.com, US 34)* has cabins with views from $75 a double.

Getting There & Away A shuttle from Denver (and Denver International Airport) via Granby to Grand Lake is run by Home James (☎ 970-726-5060) three times daily from the end of June to the beginning of September ($58).

Odessa Lake

Duration	2 days
Distance	12.4mi (19.9km)
Standard	easy–moderate
Start	Bear Lake Trailhead
Finish	Glacier Basin
Nearest Town	Estes Park
Transport	car

Summary This relatively easy but rewarding, hike leads past half a dozen or so of the park's loveliest lakes.

This hike, possible in one long day, crosses two minor watersheds (with one moderately steep climb) as it circles Mt Wuh past pretty subalpine lakes. Although much of the route is forested, there are some spectacular views.

PLANNING
When to Hike
The relatively low elevation of this hike means it can usually be undertaken from early June until early October.

Maps
Trails Illustrated's 1:59,000 No 200 *Rocky Mountain National Park Recreation Map* covers the route. Alternatively use the USGS 1:24,000 *McHenrys Peak* map.

NEAREST TOWN
See Estes Park (p230).

GETTING TO/FROM THE HIKE
The hike begins at the very popular Bear Lake Trailhead, at the end of Bear Lake Rd. The car park fills quickly in busy periods. From July to mid-August the free shuttle (see Getting Around, p230) runs to/from the larger Glacier Basin parking area, where the hike ends, so it is best to leave your car there.

THE HIKE (see map p232)
Day 1: Bear Lake Trailhead to Fern Lake
2–2½ hours, 6mi, 1150ft ascent

A broad path from the trailhead leads almost immediately to **Bear Lake** (9475ft). With a backdrop that includes Longs Peak and Pagoda Mountain, this lovely tarn is possibly the most visited place in the park. The short circuit of the lake is worth hiking if you have time.

Take the Flattop Mountain Trail turnoff on the lake's northeast side, climbing away through bouldery terrain colonized by hardy aspen and conifers, passing a turnoff to Bierstadt Lake. There are some good views south into the valley of Glacier Gorge before you reach another trail junction among fine stands of aspen.

Turn right and swing northwest up into the Mill Creek catchment, passing through winter avalanche chutes and old limber pines among jumbled boulder moraines. Pass the *Sourdough campsites* and Two Rivers Lake just before crossing a minor watershed, where the gushing Grace Falls come into view. Here an unsigned foot track goes left to Lake Helene, a broad, shallow tarn on a small shelf below Flattop Mountain, which makes a rewarding 10-minute side trip.

Return to the main trail (avoiding a hazardous, old side trail that drops directly from Lake Helene into the basin). The trail sidles down above the spectacular Odessa Gorge through coarse talus slides to meet Fern Creek. Here a short side trail leads left, crossing the stream on a footbridge to reach *campsites* near the northern shore of **Odessa Lake** (10,020ft). This sapphire lake fills a small but deep glacial trough overlooked by the striking craggy peaks of Notchtop Mountain and the Little Matterhorn. The main trail continues down, quickly curving east past *campsites* by the tranquil **Fern Lake**, where, just across the outlet, you come to an NPS patrol cabin.

Side Trip: Spruce Lake
1 hour, 1.6mi

A trail to Spruce Lake leaves from just below the NPS cabin at Fern Lake. The

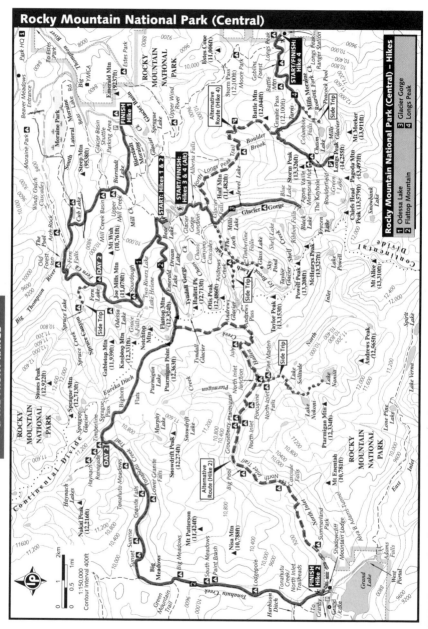

Rocky Mountain National Park (Central)

Rocky Mountain National Park (Central) – Hikes

1 Odessa Lake
2 Flattop Mountain
3 Glacier Gorge
4 Longs Peak

unimproved trail climbs west over a ridge (with some minor boulder hopping) to this picturesque tarn. There are **campsites** on Spruce Lake's northeast shore.

Day 2: Fern Lake to Glacier Basin Shuttle Parking Area
3–4 hours, 6.4mi, 1250ft ascent

Drop more steeply through fir-spruce forest carpeted with grouseberry shrubs past the pleasant if unspectacular Fern Falls. The path descends between the deep gullies of Spruce and Fern Creeks, recrossing the latter and passing the **Old Forest Inn campsites** to reach The Pool, where the two streams meet the Big Thompson River. Don't cross the river here, but take the right-hand trail and sidle up high above the valley opposite sheer granite cliffs to a route junction. Here it's worth making the short detour to the reedy, lily-covered Cub Lake (8620ft); there are **campsites** near the outlet.

As you continue ascending there are some good views back northwest across the wild valley of Spruce Creek to Stones Peak, identifiable by the snowdrift near its summit. Pass through lodgepole and occasional bristlecone pines (regenerating after the 1972 fires) before dropping into **Mill Creek Basin**.

Head through this pretty little meadow bordered by stands of aspen, passing a trail departing left to Hollowell Park (a shorter, 1.7mi alternative exit that comes out on Bear Lake Rd closer to the YMCA complex) and the **Mill Creek Basin campsite**. Continue across the wooden bridge over **Mill Creek**, past a second left turnoff, to reach the **Upper Mill Creek campsite**.

Climb gently for 0.5mi then go left (east) at the first turnoff, which leads onto the foot track ringing **Bierstadt Lake**. Short trails run through the forest to the lakeshore itself, from where you get great views of Longs Peak and other mountains on the Continental Divide.

Two alternative routes can be taken from here: the 1.4mi trail leading southwest back up to Bear Lake; or the 1.2mi trail southeast down the Bierstadt Moraine to the Bierstadt Trailhead on Bear Lake Rd.

Otherwise, continue down east through more lodgepole pine forest, where mule deer browse on herbs and fungi, to reach Glacier Basin shuttle parking area. **Glacier Basin campground** is a five-minute hike across Bear Lake Rd (a 1.3mi trail to the **YMCA of the Rockies** leaves from near campsite No 21).

Flattop Mountain

Duration	2 days
Distance	18.3mi (29.5km)
Standard	moderate–hard
Start	Bear Lake Trailhead
Finish	Grand Lake
Nearest Towns	Estes Park, Grand Lake
Transport	car, bus

Summary The hike to Flattop Mountain and the extensive undulating plateau known as Bighorn Flats is unquestionably one of the most scenic in the park.

This is a marvelous, high-level crossing of the Continental Divide, although the round-trip hike up to the high, sweeping plains of Flattop Mountain is itself a popular day trip. Those wanting an even longer hike can make a loop by returning to Bear Lake via the North Inlet Trail.

The area is a vital summer pasture for bighorn sheep and elk, and sizeable herds graze these high tundra plains from June to August.

PLANNING
When to Hike
Except for possible smaller drifts on the upper slopes, the trail is normally snow-free from late June to mid-September.

Warning
The central part of this hike crosses open and exposed alpine terrain. In summer, severe electrical storms bring the danger of cold, wet conditions as well as lightning – hikers have been fatally struck on Flattop Mountain – so keep a close watch on the weather. Be prepared to retreat if the weather looks threatening.

NORTHERN COLORADO & THE FRONT RANGE

Maps

Trails Illustrated's 1:59,000 No 200 *Rocky Mountain National Park Recreation Map* covers the route. Alternatively use the two USGS 1:24,000 quads: *McHenrys Peak* and *Grand Lake*.

NEAREST TOWNS

See Estes Park and Grand Lake (p230).

GETTING TO/FROM THE HIKE

The hike begins at Bear Lake Trailhead (see the Odessa Lake hike, p231).

The hike finishes just past Tonahutu Creek Trailhead at Grand Lake. There are two parking areas with space for 30 vehicles across the Tonahutu Creek bridge, a short way past the trailhead; if full park along West Portal Rd. North Inlet Trailhead is at the smaller, lower car park.

THE HIKE (see map p232)
Day 1: Bear Lake Trailhead to Haynach Lakes Trail Junction

3¾–5½ hours, 8.9mi

Follow the directions for Day 1 of the Odessa Lake hike (p231) as far as the Odessa Lake turnoff. Continue ahead here, with the trail curling up to reach an overlook high above the elongated Dream Lake, about one hour from the trailhead.

The trail then zigzags up the broad ridge through steadily thinning alpine scrub of prostrate limber pine and dwarf birch to reach another, more spectacular overlook. From here Emerald Lake is visible directly below in the 1300ft-deep, talus-filled Tyndall Gorge, while there are fine views northeast down the valley to both Bierstadt and Sprague Lakes.

Climb into rocky alpine tundra. Pikas scurry about with mouthfuls of lichen and yellow-bellied marmots sound a shrill alarm as you approach. Over to your left is Tyndall Glacier, now a tiny remnant of its former self, and behind it Hallett Peak, with its rounded summit that makes a straightforward and worthwhile one-hour side trip. The gradient eases as you come onto **Flattop Mountain** (12,324ft), a grassy plateau dotted with yellow avens and other alpine wildflowers,

to reach a signposted trail junction, 1½ to two hours from the Dream Lake overlook. Day hikers should turn around here.

Turn right and follow the Tonahutu Creek Trail northwest, above tarns at the head of Fern Creek past Ptarmigan Point. From here a short deviation left gives a spectacular view of (otherwise unseen) Ptarmigan Lake, set in a glacial cirque. As the names suggest, the white-tailed ptarmigan, a flightless alpine grouse, inhabits these treeless highlands and (although well camouflaged by its speckled plumage) can sometimes be spotted here. The main path rises on past Knobtop Mountain and Eureka Ditch, a small canal dug in 1902 to divert water west, before making a long, gentle descent through the lovely rolling tundra of **Bighorn Flats**.

Sidle down into the fir-spruce forest of the charming Tonahutu Creek, where six cascading streamlets merge in a steep-sided alpine valley. The path crosses a larger side stream near *Timberline campsite* (groups only) shortly before reaching the **Haynach Lakes** Trail turnoff (right). Take this side trail up northwest for about 10 minutes to *Renegade campsite* or continue another 700yd on a forested lateral moraine to *Haynach campsite*. A less prominent trail proceeds to the head of the valley and **Haynach Lakes**, situated in an imposing setting below Nakai Peak.

Alternative Route: North Inlet Trail

4¾–6 hours, 11.8mi

From the Flattop Mountain Trail junction, follow cairns south across the plateau of alpine tundra. Andrews Peak stands in front of you and there are great views northwest to the summits of the Never Summer Mountains. Skirt above a deep basin on your right, then drop down through heath of dwarf birch and shrub willow cropped by browsing ungulates. The well-formed trail zigzags down through wildflower slopes into the first trees, crossing Hallett Creek after one to 1¼ hours.

A quick side trip north into the beautiful upper valley – recommended even if you haven't reserved one of the idyllic *July campsites* (individual and group) – leads up past old, stout-trunked firs to near the base of a waterfall splashing down from the Bighorn Flats.

Back on the main trail, head down past a swathe of avalanche-cleared forest littered with uprooted trees and snapped trunks. A steeper descent on broad switchbacks, past the *North Inlet Junction campsites*, brings you to a turnoff (left) at North Inlet Junction, 40 to 50 minutes from the Hallett Creek crossing.

The main trail continues downvalley under sheer cliffs past *Porcupine campsite* to cross Ptarmigan Creek. This restocked stream is a refuge for the threatened Colorado River cutthroat trout and presently a no-fishing zone. The muddy trail passes the *Ptarmigan*, *Grouseberry* and (on the creek's south side) *North Inlet campsites*, skirting the water-logged meadows to reach **Big Pool**, a small, churning pond popular with fly fishers and with an attractive *campsite*. Drop steadily beside the gushing torrent to Cascade Falls, 1½ to two hours from the Lake Nanita turnoff. Here North Inlet dives 50ft in several stages; take care as the moist rocks are dangerously slippery. A *campsite* is just above the falls.

The path is cut into the cliff in places and leads to the lower valley, a glaciated landscape with ice-polished bedrock and the occasional erratic boulder. The fir-spruce woods are plentiful in wild fungi and gradually give way to lodgepole pine forest as you meet a dirt road (closed to unauthorized traffic) near a vacation cabin. Follow the road across the riverside flats of Summerland Park, where there are pleasant *campsites*. The road leads past the rustic log fence of a private ranch until it comes out at the lower car park at North Inlet Trailhead, 1½ to two hours from Cascade Falls.

From here it's a five-minute hike down to the West Portal Rd just above Grand Lake.

Side Trip: Lake Nanita

1½–2 hours, 3.5mi

From North Inlet Junction on the Alternative Route (p234), this side trail leads across the North Inlet stream and winds its way up through the forest past the *North Inlet Falls*

and *Pine Marten campsites* to Lake Nokoni, before rising more gently to **Lake Nanita**. This picturesque tarn nestled at tree line below the craggy outlines of Ptarmigan Mountain and Andrews Peak is probably Rocky's loveliest lake.

Day 2: Haynach Lakes Trail Junction to Grand Lake

3½–3¾ hours, 9.4mi

Back on the Tonahutu Creek Trail, cross a side stream (the Haynach Lakes outlet) and proceed down the narrow, enclosed valley through moist forest draped with lichen, past *Tonahutu Meadows campsite* to Granite Falls, a series of small cascades that fall a total of about 60ft. Two campsites are nearby, *Granite Falls* just above the falls and *Lower Granite Falls* on attractive river flats below them.

The trail continues past *Sunrise* and *Sunset campsites* along the northern bank of the Tonahutu Creek, the Arapaho name alluding to the open grassy flats known as **Big Meadows**, through which the stream now meanders. After passing the Onahu Creek Trail turnoff (right) and the ruins of two cabins built by settler Sam Stone in the early 1900s, the route intersects with the Green Mountain Trail, 1½ to two hours from the Haynach Lakes turnoff.

The 1.8mi Green Mountain Trail is a shorter exit route to Trail Ridge Rd. It leads west over a minor watershed then follows a brook down to reach the trailhead car park after about 45 minutes.

The Tonahutu Creek Trail continues downvalley through lodgepole pine forest fringing the soggy meadows. The easy, if rather monotonous, trail passes the *Big Meadows* (for groups or with pack animals only), *South Meadows*, *Paint Brush* and *Lodgepole campsites* to meet a trail leading right, 1½ to two hours from the Green Mountain Trail turnoff. This 0.5mi route leads along the small Harbison Ditch to arrive at the Kawuneeche visitor center after about 15 minutes.

The main trail continues, passing a turnoff (right) to *Grand Lake Lodge* a short way on and then following the creek to terminate by the water-treatment plant at Tonahutu Creek Trailhead, about 15 minutes from the last turnoff. From here it's a five-minute hike down the dirt road past *Shadowcliff Mountain Lodge* and across the West Portal Rd to Grand Lake.

Glacier Gorge

Duration	4½–5½ hours
Distance	10.2mi (16.4km)
Standard	easy–moderate
Start/Finish	Glacier Gorge Junction
Nearest Town	Estes Park
Transport	car

Summary This hike leads up into the enclosed valley of Glacier Gorge. A longer side trip into the adjacent Loch Vale is also covered.

The alpine valleys of Glacier Gorge and Loch Vale have an almost magical beauty. Easily accessible (but not overly crowded) trails lead up to jewel-like lakes and tarns in these wild valley heads, where small remnant glaciers cling to the peaks of the Continental Divide. Backcountry camping is possible but limited.

PLANNING
When to Hike
The trail normally melts out by mid-June and remains passable into October. Winter hikers sometimes make the climb to Mills Lake and the Loch on snowshoes.

Maps
Trails Illustrated's 1:59,000 No 200 *Rocky Mountain National Park Recreation Map*, covers the route. Alternatively use USGS 1:24,000 *McHenrys Peak* map.

NEAREST TOWN
See Estes Park (p230).

GETTING TO/FROM THE HIKE
The hike begins and ends at Glacier Gorge Junction, a sharp bend on the Bear Lake Rd. The small car park here fills very quickly, so it is best to park at Glacier Basin Shuttle parking area and take the free shuttle bus to the trailhead (see Getting Around, p230).

THE HIKE (see map p232)
At the trail junction immediately above the car park head left across Chaos Creek. The trail leads south, first into mixed aspen and fir-spruce forest growing on ancient, bouldery moraine, then climbs beside Glacier Creek to the impressive **Alberta Falls**, where the creek spills over the pink granite bedrock. Continue up slopes that are still regenerating from a fire in 1900 past the North Longs Peak Trail turnoff (left) to reach a three-way fork, about 45 minutes (or 1.9mi) from the trailhead.

Take the left trail (the right and middle branches go to Lake Haiyaha and Loch Vale – for the latter, see Side Trip), which crosses Icy Brook and Glacier Creek before ascending past Glacier Falls to reach Mills Lake after about 30 minutes. Arriving hikers are wonder-struck by the sudden views up **Glacier Gorge**, dominated by massive scree-strewn slabs below the rump of Longs Peak and the sheer valley headwalls under Pagoda Mountain and Chiefs Head Peak.

Continue around Mills Lake, with its shore of smoothed rocks fringed by erratic blocks and weathered limber pines. The trail leads upvalley past boggy **Jewel Lake** and the *Glacier Gorge campsites*, beginning a steady climb beside Glacier Creek past Ribbon Falls to reach **Black Lake** after about 1¼ hours. This tarn lies in a spectacular cirque under the east face of McHenrys Peak.

Return to the trailhead by the same route.

Side Trip: Sky Pond & Andrews Glacier
3–4 hours, 4.8m, 1112ft ascent/descent
The middle trail (from the three-way fork) rises above the Icy Brook in a few minor switchbacks to reach the Loch at the start of enchanting **Loch Vale**. The trail proceeds around the lake's north side and through the valley to *Andrews Creek campsite*. From here a steepening side trail climbs 1mi west along the Andrews Creek drainage to a tarn fed by the meltwater from **Andrews Glacier** (one hour return). The main trail crosses

moist meadows before making a moderate ascent past Timberline Falls to **Glass Lake**. More often called Lake of Glass, in still conditions this tarn in the raw bedrock gives a classic mirror reflection of the surrounding peaks. The trail rises on smoothly to arrive at **Sky Pond**, nestled under the abrupt east wall of Taylor Peak (13,153ft).

To return to the three-way junction on the main route, retrace your steps along the Loch Vale trail.

Longs Peak

Duration	9½–13½ hours
Distance	13.6mi (21.9km)
Standard	hard
Start/Finish	Longs Peak ranger station
Nearest Town	Estes Park
Transport	car

Summary This long, strenuous hike, with an ascent of almost 5000ft, climbs to the broad summit of the park's highest peak.

The distinctive box shape of Longs Peak (14,255ft) is Rocky's great landmark, and rises almost 1000ft higher than any other summit in the park. Longs Peak is also the most-climbed 14er in the Rockies, and can be reached in a very long day hike, either via the standard (eastern) route or the longer (western) route from Glacier Gorge Junction (see Alternative Start, p238).

Hikers making the ascent in a day usually make a pre-dawn start (using a headlamp), and should carry plenty of water and carefully watch the weather. The route is not suited to sufferers of vertigo. The climb involves a total ascent of 4855ft via the normal route (or just over 5000ft from Glacier Gorge Junction). Camping is possible but backcountry sites are often heavily booked.

PLANNING
When to Hike
The upper route may be snowed over or dangerously icy before July or after late September, when ice axe and crampons are often required for a safe ascent.

Maps
Trails Illustrated's 1:59,000 No 200 *Rocky Mountain National Park Recreation Map* covers the route, as does two USGS 1:24,000 quads: *McHenrys Peak* and *Longs Peak*.

NEAREST TOWN & FACILITIES
See Estes Park (p230).

Longs Peak NPS Campground
This *campground (☎ 800-365-2267)*, near the trailhead, makes an excellent base camp for the hike (sites $16).

GETTING TO/FROM THE HIKE
Most hikers set out from Longs Peak ranger station, 1mi from the turnoff on Hwy 7, 9mi south of Estes Park. From July to mid-August the large car park often fills up before dawn.

THE HIKE (see map p232)
From the ranger station begin a gentle ascent through mostly fir and spruce forest, past the Storm Pass turnoff (right), to Alpine Brook. Climb past *Goblins Forest campsite*, in a stand of thick-trunked limber pine.

The trail winds up past the idyllic *Battle Mountain campsite*, crossing the stream before it rises above tree line onto open wildflower slopes. There are some good views of Longs Peak left, while behind the Twin Sisters Peaks (11,413ft) rise beyond the Tahosa Valley. The winding trail skirts up the side of Mills Moraine to reach a ridge-top trail junction, 1½ to two hours from the trailhead.

The main trail sides (northwest), above shallow pools in a soggy basin down to your right, to arrive at **Granite Pass** (12,100ft), about 30 minutes from the Chasm Lake junction. The pass offers no good views of Longs Peak but note the interesting cairn-like outcrop to your right.

Head southwest up steep switchbacks, then climb more smoothly and cross the now-tiny Boulder Brook to reach Boulder Field, a jumble of glaciated granite blocks under the abrupt north wall of Longs Peak. The nine sheltered *Boulderfield campsites* are at around 12,800ft – by far the highest in the park.

The trail climbs on past the Agnes Vaille Memorial Hut, a stone emergency shelter dedicated to two mountaineers who died in 1925 during the first winter ascent of Longs Peak, to reach the **Keyhole** after about two hours. This gap in the ridge, at around 13,000ft, gives you a first spectacular view down into Glacier Gorge, a valley head ringed by McHenrys Peak, Chiefs Head Peak and Pagoda Mountain.

From here the terrain becomes much more serious. Be wary of rockfall – watch for falling debris from climbers above and avoid dislodging rocks yourself. Be alert to approaching bad weather and be prepared to turn back; thunderstorms bring an extreme danger of lightning strikes.

Follow red-and-yellow paint markings on rocks southeast into the (often snow-filled) gully of the **Trough**. The route continues up the so-called **Narrows**, a sheer-edged shelf with some exhilaratingly tight and exposed sections. Give way to descending hikers you may encounter on this narrow trail. A final, steeper ascent over the polished-granite slabs known as the **Homestretch** leads onto the broad open top of **Longs Peak** (14,255ft), two to three hours from the Keyhole.

The summit area is bigger than a football field and, fortunately, easily accommodates the scores of climbers here on an average summer day. Sign the register book and explore the panoramic views taking in much of the northern Colorado Rockies. Begin your descent before noon.

Side Trip: Chasm Lake

45 minutes, 2mi

From the ridge-top trail junction, the trail to the left leads to **Chasm Lake**. The narrow path dips slightly past **Columbine Falls**, where Roaring Fork Creek cascades 100ft to Peacock Pool, then continues across the stream to a patrol cabin at the end of a lovely meadow. Follow cairns up a rough moraine ridge for a stunning vista of this highland tarn nestled right at the granite foot of Longs Peak's east face.

Alternative Start: Glacier Gorge Junction

3–4 hours, 7mi, 2850ft ascent

At the trail junction immediately above the car park at Glacier Gorge Junction (see Getting to/from the Hike, p236) head left across Chaos Creek. The trail leads south, first into mixed aspen and fir-spruce forest growing on ancient, bouldery moraine, then climbs beside Glacier Creek to impressive **Alberta Falls**, where the creek spills over the pink granite bedrock. Continue up slopes still regenerating from a fire in 1900 to the North Longs Peak Trail turnoff. Bear left and cross Glacier Creek just above an impressive water slide. The trail rises gently over regenerating slopes high above the valley to cross Boulder Brook, where there are *campsites*, 1½ to two hours from the trailhead.

Sidle around the mountainside, then climb several switchbacks through the last stands of stunted limber pine, from where there are the first close-up views of Longs Peak. A final, long, sweeping rise brings you to **Granite Pass** and the main Longs Peak trail, 1½ to two hours from Boulder Brook.

Lawn Lake

Duration	7–8 hours
Distance	12.4mi (20km)
Standard	moderate
Start/Finish	Lawn Lake Trailhead
Nearest Town	Estes Park
Transport	car

Summary An enjoyable out-and-back hike on a well-graded trail. Climb to a picturesque alpine lake surrounded by the high peaks and granite cliffs of the Mummy Range.

Set apart from the main focal points of Rocky Mountain National Park, the Mummy Range is a compact mountain group with some well-maintained trails and idyllic back-country campgrounds. The Lawn Lake Trail follows the deeply scoured gully of Roaring River, climbing steadily to Lawn Lake and its sublime surround of rock peaks. Although this trail can be hiked in a day, it is common for hikers to camp at Lawn Lake. The extra effort required to haul a tent, stove and food up the 2500ft of ascent is well worthwhile. The campsites above Lawn Lake are hidden in the trees and it is not uncommon to think you are completely alone in the basin. Such solitude encourages wildlife, and it is worth spending a day watching out for deer and other animals.

HISTORY

The hike to Lawn Lake is both attractive and educational. On July 15, 1982, the dam wall, built across the lake outlet in 1902 to provide water to farms around Estes Park, burst. This released a catastrophic flood that killed several campers downstream and covered central Estes Park in a thick layer of mud. The trail follows the gully of Roaring River (the outlet of Lawn Lake), along which those tremendous floodwaters once poured. The evidence of their passing is still on display.

PLANNING
When to Hike

The trail should be largely free of snow by late June or early July.

Maps

Trails Illustrated's 1:59,000 No 200 *Rocky Mountain National Park Recreation Map* covers the route.

NEAREST TOWN

See Estes Park (p230).

GETTING TO/FROM THE HIKE

The hike begins at the Lawn Lake Trailhead just off the Old Fall River Rd, close to the junction with US 34, and approximately 5mi east of Estes Park.

THE HIKE

The trail begins quite steeply, mounting a series of switchbacks above the parking area.

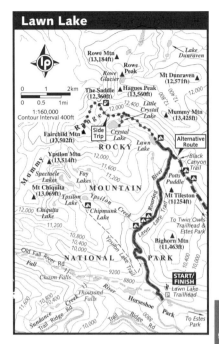

It then climbs steadily northwest, passing a cleared area where you can look down across the debris still evident from the 1982 dam collapse (see History). Some 30 minutes from the start the trail swings around into the Roaring River valley and climbs gently through pine and aspen, with occasional views of the river and the impressive gorge cut by the 1982 flood. At various points it is possible to scramble down to the river to collect water.

An hour from the start you pass the turnoff to Ypsilon Lake (a 6mi side trip). A further 15 minutes of gentle ascent brings you to a long switchback, where the gradient increases slightly and the trail climbs away from the river. The path returns to the river at a signpost for three *campgrounds* on the opposite bank. The main trail keeps to the eastern bank, climbing steeply for 10 minutes to a clearing beside the river, where there are good views toward the head of the valley. Ahead, the river descends over rocky slabs; from this point the gradient of the trail becomes steeper and the surface rougher.

Climb through occasional switchbacks and across two small streams to reach a clearing on the left close to the river. Deer can often be seen here rooting for nutritious forage. The gradient eases somewhat between this clearing and the junction with the Black Canyon Trail some 15 minutes further up (see Alternative Route).

From this junction the tree cover begins to thin noticeably and a short climb brings you to **Lawn Lake**. The impressive view extends from the southeast spur of Fairchild Mountain, through the Saddle to Mummy Mountain. Copses of stunted pine, bare granite slabs and patches of remnant snow complete the scene.

There are signs directing you to the *Lawn Lake campsites* hidden in the trees to the southeast of the lake. A less defined trail continues through the trees along the east shore of the lake, headed for Crystal Lake, the Saddle, Fairchild Mountain and Crystal Lake (see Side Trip).

Return to the Lawn Lake Trailhead by retracing your steps.

Side Trip: Crystal Lake, The Saddle & Fairchild Mountain
5–6 hours, 7mi, 2500ft ascent
Using Lawn Lake as a base, a second day can be spent either climbing Fairchild Mountain or making a shorter trip to Crystal Lake. Sections of both routes may be covered by snow until mid-July.

From the Lawn Lake campsites follow the small trail that winds along the eastern shore and then climbs onto the open slopes beneath Hagues Peak. Turn left at a trail junction to reach **Little Crystal** and **Crystal Lakes**, set dramatically beneath the granite cliffs of Fairchild Mountain.

Continue straight ahead at the junction to climb steeply for 1mi to the **Saddle**, a broad pass at 12,360ft on the spine of the Mummy Range.

From here a steady climb leads southwest up a broad shoulder to the 13,502ft summit of **Fairchild Mountain**, with its fine panoramic views.

Alternative Route: Black Canyon Trail
4–5 hours, 9.4mi
Hikers without their own transportation can start the Lawn Lake hike from the Twin Owls Trailhead (just 2mi north of Estes Park), and use the Black Canyon Trail to reach the main trail to Lawn Lake.

Indian Peaks Wilderness

The 114-sq-mile Indian Peaks Wilderness lies 15mi west of Boulder in the Colorado Front Range. Its eastern half lies in Roosevelt National Forest, while the western side takes in Arapaho National Forest. On its northern boundary Indian Peaks Wilderness merges with Rocky Mountain National Park (whose early advocates pushed unsuccessfully for its inclusion). Most of its highest summits bear the names of Native American tribes.

Indian Peaks Wilderness is an interesting landscape of wild, forested valleys and large expanses of alpine tundra, mountain cirques with tiny relict glaciers, and more than 50 lakes and tarns. It is also subject to extremely heavy recreational use due to its proximity to the sprawl of the Boulder and Denver metropolitan areas.

PLANNING
Maps & Books
Trail Tracks Panoramic Hiking Maps' *Indian Peaks* ($10.95) is a colorful overview of the area and includes brief route descriptions, but is not useful as a topographic reference. Much better for hiking purposes is the Trails Illustrated 1:40,680 map No 102 *Indian Peaks Gold Hill* ($10.95).

Colorado's Indian Peaks by Gerry Roach ($16.95) is the most comprehensive hiking guide to the wilderness.

Information Sources
Indian Peaks Wilderness falls into the Arapaho and Roosevelt National Forests. For information contact the district headquarters

(☎ 303-541-2500; 2140 Yarmouth Ave, Boulder, CO 80301) or W www.fs.fed.us/r2/arnf.

Permits & Regulations

Between June 1 and September 15 a backcountry permit is required for overnight trips in Indian Peaks Wilderness. The USFS offices in Boulder (☎ 303-444-6600), Estes Park (☎ 970-586-3440) and Granby (☎ 970-887-4100), as well as Ace Hardware in Nederland (see Access Town), issue backcountry permits ($5 per group) for 17 of the Indian Peaks' 18 travel zones. Only a limited number of permits are available for each zone per day. Specific USFS campsite reservations must be made at least five days in advance and can be arranged at any of the area offices, as well as via a centralized system (☎ 800-280-2267, 1877-444-6777, W www.reserveusa.com). You do not need a backcountry permit for hikes that do not involve an overnight camp.

Camping is not permitted in the Four Lakes Travel Zone (the eastern approach to Pawnee Pass) and is only permitted in designated campsites (with backcountry permit) in the Diamond Lake, Crater Lake, Caribou Lake and Jasper Lake Travel Zones. Outside these areas campers with backcountry permits are free to choose their own sites. Campfires are not allowed anywhere on the east side of the Continental Divide, nor around most lakes on its west side. Tents and fires must be at least 100ft from lakes, streams and trails.

ACCESS TOWN
Nederland

Nederland stands at the junction of Hwy 119 and Hwy 72, on the eastern foot of Indian Peaks Wilderness. The town is 17mi west of Boulder (via Boulder Canyon Dr). Ace Hardware (☎ 303-258-3132), open daily at the Village shopping mall, sells maps and guidebooks and issues state fishing licenses and backcountry permits for Indian Peaks Wilderness. The Nederland visitor center (☎ 303-258-3936) is diagonally opposite the Village shopping mall. The Bucking Brown Trout Co (1st St) has hiking and fishing supplies.

Nederland International Hostel (☎ 303-258-7788, 8 W Boulder St) has dorm beds ($17) and double rooms ($40). RTD buses (☎ 303-299-6000) run up to 12 times a day between Nederland and Boulder.

Pawnee Pass

Duration	2 days
Distance	15mi (24.1km)
Standard	moderate
Start	Brainard Lake (Long Lake Trailhead)
Finish	Monarch Lake
Nearest Town	Nederland
Transport	car
Summary	This east-west crossing of the Continental Divide is one of the most beautiful and popular hikes in the wilderness and includes excellent views from 12,541ft Pawnee Pass.

This hike from Long Lake makes a stiff ascent over Pawnee Pass before following the Cascade-Buchanan drainage to Monarch Lake. The route involves an ascent of 2500ft and can be combined with the Arapaho Pass hike to make a wonderful semi-loop tour.

In 1882 Pawnee Pass was surveyed as a possible railroad route, which was ultimately built over Rollins Pass, but a trail was constructed over the pass in the 1930s by the Civilian Conservation Corps. Although fit hikers manage to complete this route in a single day, it's best to get a backcountry permit and take at least two days. Pawnee Pass is often also visited as an out-and-back day hike from Brainard Lake.

PLANNING
When to Hike

Pawnee Pass usually melts out by the beginning of July, and the route is often already out of condition by early October. From late June to mid-September thunderstorms bring heavy rain and extreme danger of lightning strike.

Maps

The 1:40,680 Trails Illustrated map No 102 *Indian Peaks Gold Hill* is recommended.

Two USGS 1:24,000 quads also cover the route: *Ward* and *Monarch Lake*.

NEAREST TOWN & FACILITIES
See Nederland (p241).

Pawnee Lake USFS Campground
This *campground* (for reservation details see Permits & Regulations, p241) at Brainard Lake makes a convenient base for the start of the hike (sites $12).

GETTING TO/FROM THE HIKE
The hike begins at the Long Lake Trailhead in the Brainard Lake Recreation Area. To get there follow Hwy 72 8mi north from Nederland to Ward, then drive 5mi west to Brainard Lake. The large trailhead car park is 0.5mi on, west of the lake. There is an entry fee of $5 per vehicle but free parking exists at the recreation area entrance, 2.5mi before Brainard Lake.

The hike ends at the western shore of Monarch Lake. From Granby take US 34 to the Arapaho National Recreation Area, then drive 10mi east on the unpaved US Forest Service Rd 125. Pass the southern shore of Lake Granby to reach the large car park at Monarch Lake Trailhead.

THE HIKE (see map opposite)
Day 1: Long Lake Trailhead to Pawnee Lake
3¼–4½ hours, 6.6mi, 2540ft ascent
The Pawnee Pass Trail heads through fir-spruce forest (past a lefthand trail from Brainard Lake) to Long Lake, continuing around its north shore before climbing over a crest to reach **Lake Isabelle**. This lake lies slightly below tree line in a horseshoe of craggy peaks. From here a popular side trip (two hours return) leads left along the lake's northern shore, then follows the drainage of the inlet (South St Vrain Creek) to a tarn under Shoshone Peak, Isabelle Glacier and Navajo Peak.

On the main trail turn right and climb beside a stream, then follow a revegetated moraine ridge out of the trees. Steep switchbacks cut into the rock lead to a rocky shelf high above the lake. Ascend tundra slopes that look east over the smoggy sprawls of Boulder and Denver to reach the broad and blustery ridge of **Pawnee Pass** (12,541ft), about 2½ hours from the trailhead.

Drop west (where Lake Granby comes briefly into view) to begin a long, spiraling descent through rough, bouldery rubble underneath mushroom-like outcrops on the western flank of Pawnee Peak. The trail leads out onto meadows before cutting down to the north end of **Pawnee Lake**, a lovely, subalpine lake nestling in a cirque one to 1½ hours from the pass. Good *campsites* (undesignated, fires prohibited) can be found across the outlet among tall spruces.

Day 2: Pawnee Lake to Monarch Lake Trailhead
3–4 hours, 8.4mi
Head downvalley opposite glistening glaciers under the jagged summit of Mt George, passing the turnoff to Crater Lake. (This is another spectacular lake, ringed with abrupt rock ridges, that makes a worthwhile side trip of 1½ hours round-trip; eight backcountry permits are available per day for the designated *campsites* in the surrounding Crater Lake Travel Zone.) The main trail descends along Cascade Creek past the tumbling, 40ft-high Cascade Falls, crossing and recrossing the stream as it passes occasional beaver dams and *campsites* in the lodgepole forest.

Proceed down to Buchanan Creek and pass the Buchanan Pass Trail turnoff (on the right). The trail leads on across Hell Canyon Creek to intersect with the Southside Trail (this is a 0.6mi cutoff that crosses the creek, then goes southwest through lodgepole to Arapaho Creek – see the Arapaho Pass hike, p244). The trail continues on to the eastern end of **Monarch Lake** (8351ft), skirting its northern shore to arrive at Monarch Lake Trailhead.

Alternative Campsites
There is undesignated *camping* along Cascade Creek Travel Zone (16 backcountry permits available per day), which extends from Pawnee Lake almost to Monarch Lake. *Arapaho Bay campground*, at the northeastern end of Lake Granby, is 1.5mi from Monarch Lake Trailhead.

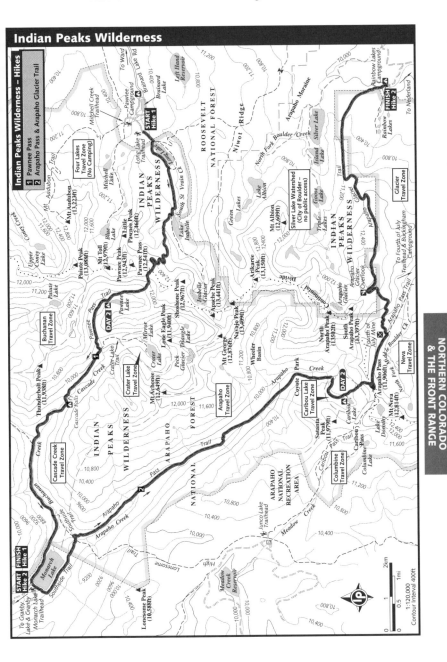

Arapaho Pass & Arapaho Glacier Trail

Duration	2 days
Distance	18.9mi (30.4km)
Standard	moderate–hard
Start	Monarch Lake Trailhead
Finish	Rainbow Lakes campground
Nearest Town	Nederland
Transport	car

Summary The 11,906ft Arapaho Pass is another of the Indian Peaks' scenic pass routes, offering open ridges and fine views, including over the southernmost glacier in North America.

This combined route, involving two lengthy ascents, approaches the pass from the wild Arapaho Creek, west of the Continental Divide, and continues across open ridges overlooking the interesting string of artificial lakes along North Fork Boulder Creek. It is easily combined with the Pawnee Pass route. In 1904 work began on a road over the pass from the Fourth of July Mine on its eastern side, but the road was never completed further than Arapaho Pass itself.

PLANNING
When to Hike
Before July deep snow blocks the upper pass area and higher ridges, as it does after mid-October. Remember, you must have a backcountry permit if you want to camp in Indian Peaks Wilderness between June 1 and September 15.

Maps
The Trails Illustrated map 1:40,680 No 102 *Indian Peaks Gold Hill* is recommended. Two USGS 1:24,000 quads also cover the route: *East Portal* and *Monarch Lake*.

NEAREST TOWN & FACILITIES
See Nederland (p241).

Campgrounds
Rainbow Lakes campground, at the end of the hike, has 12 sites ($12). The basic USFS *Buckingham campground* at the Fourth of July Trailhead also has 12 sites ($12). See Permits & Regulations (p241) for reservation details for both campgrounds.

GETTING TO/FROM THE HIKE
The hike begins at Monarch Lake Trailhead (see Getting to/from the Hike, p242). The hike finishes at Rainbow Lakes campground, 6mi west along the unpaved USFS Rd 298 from the turnoff on Hwy 72, roughly 6.5mi north of Nederland. Parking at the Rainbow Lakes Trailhead, 100yd on at the end of the road, is very limited.

Another option is to finish the hike at the Fourth of July Trailhead, on the east side of Arapaho Pass. This trailhead is reached from Nederland via the road to Eldora (CR 130), taking the Buckingham campground turnoff (CR 111) just west of Eldora.

THE HIKE (see map p243)
Day 1: Monarch Lake Trailhead to Caribou Lake
4½–6 hours, 9.3mi, 2799ft ascent
Follow the Southside Trail through lodgepole forest around the southern shore of Monarch Lake. Proceed across Arapaho Creek, then turn right along the Arapaho Pass Trail. The trail begins a long, gradual climb with occasional switchbacks through the bouldery spruce forest of the narrow valley, crossing numerous streamlets before it fords the small creek below its confluence with the stream from Wheeler Basin.

Recross to the creek's northern bank a few minutes further on, then continue up more steeply opposite white craggy ridges around Mt George. After cutting through the grassy marshes of Coyote Park, the trail climbs away southwest (right) through attractive alpine meadows, crossing and recrossing the now tiny creek to reach **Caribou Lake**. This delightful tarn at tree line is perched on a high shelf ringed by spectacular peaks. Six backcountry permits are available per day for the designated *campsites* in the surrounding Caribou Lake Travel Zone.

Alternative Campsites
Numerous (undesignated) campsites can be found within the Arapaho Travel Zone (10 backcountry permits available per day),

which extends upvalley from near Monarch Lake to just below Caribou Lake.

Day 2: Caribou Lake to Rainbow Lakes Campground

4½–6 hours, 9.6mi, 1795ft ascent

The trail heads southeast across the meadow to make a 750ft ascent up numerous steep switchbacks onto the tundra ridge top, then follows this briefly right to reach the scenic **Arapaho Pass** (11,906ft) after about 45 minutes. For better views of Mt Neva (12,814ft) and Lake Dorothy, follow the Caribou Pass Trail right (west) a short way.

The main trail traverses gently down slopes above the North Fork of Middle Boulder Creek to pass shafts and tailings – even an old steam engine – from the long abandoned **Fourth of July Mine** to reach the Arapaho Glacier Trail turnoff after about 30 minutes. (From here you can simply continue 1.8mi on the Arapaho Pass Trail down to the Fourth of July Trailhead – see Getting To/From the Hike, p244.)

Turn left and begin a sustained eastward ascent through switchbacks high above the valley to reach **Arapaho Glacier Overlook** after one to 1½ hours. This gap in the ridge southeast of South Arapaho Peak gives an awesome (if incomplete) view of Arapaho Glacier – the most southerly glacier in North America – with its snout fringed by moraine masses damming a tiny melt-water tarn.

Head east over rolling tundra, which gives wonderful views south toward Rollins Pass and southeast to Nederland, before cutting through a minor saddle (12,085ft) to the north side of the ridge. These slopes overlook the picturesque chain of small reservoirs in the upper North Fork Boulder Creek, which supply water to the City of Boulder. (Public access to this watershed is prohibited – trespassers risk a $100 fine.)

The trail sidles down toward the dozen or so lowland ponds called the Rainbow Lakes, ducking into the first stunted limber pines to make a long descent beside a wire fence (marking the watershed boundary) to arrive at the USFS *Rainbow Lakes campground*, 2½ to three hours from Arapaho Glacier Overlook.

Alternative Campsites

This section passes through the Neva Travel Zone (upper valley of North Fork Middle Boulder Creek; nine backcountry permits) and the Glacier Travel Zone (along the Arapaho Glacier Trail; seven permits), both of which have undesignated *camping*.

Mt Zirkel Wilderness

Mt Zirkel Wilderness on Colorado's northern border encompasses 250 sq miles of roadless backcountry in the Routt National Forest. It is one of the five original wilderness areas designated in the state in 1964, and includes a 36mi stretch of the Continental Divide. Characterized by alpine lakes and broad valleys, the natural beauty of the area is not the only attraction for hikers. The wilderness receives far fewer visitors than more popular spots in the Rockies, and a certain solitude accentuates the outdoor experience on most of the area's 155mi of trail. Tracks are smaller and less eroded, and peak-baggers are rarely tempted by 12,180ft Mt Zirkel, the highest peak in the wilderness, so the summits and their views are left (thankfully!) to those connoisseurs who do seek them out.

The wilderness and its highest peak are named after a German petrologist who accompanied Clarence King (the famed mountaineer and first director of the USFS) when the pair made the first reconnoiter of the area in 1874.

PLANNING
Maps & Books

Trails Illustrated's 1:40,680 maps No 116 *Hahn's Peak Steamboat Lake* and No 117 *Clark Buffalo Pass* (both $9.95) cover Mt Zirkel Wilderness. *Hiking the Boat II* by Diane White Crane is the hiker's bible to the area ($21.95).

Information Sources

For information about Medicine Bow-Routt National Forests, which encompass Mt Zirkel Wilderness, contact the Hahns Peak/Bears

Ears Ranger District headquarters (☎ 970-879-1870; 925 Weiss Dr, Steamboat Springs, CO 80487) or see W www.fs.fed.us/r2/mbr.

Permits & Regulations

No permits are required for hiking or camping in Mt Zirkel Wilderness, although group sizes are limited to 15 people. Camping and campfires are not permitted within 0.25mi of Gilpin, Gold Creek and Three Island Lakes, or within 100ft of any stream, lake or trail. It is strongly recommended that all water be filtered or treated before drinking.

Routt Blowdown

On October 25, 1997 winds in excess of 120mph swept over the Continental Divide and laid waste to over four million trees in the Routt National Forest. Much of the flattened area of forest was within Mt Zirkel Wilderness. The species of spruce and fir making up this forest have shallow root systems that had developed in a way that offered maximum purchase against the prevailing westerly winds. The winds on October 25, 1997 came from the east and even the mutual shelter created by thousands of trees growing close together couldn't prevent this huge 'blowdown' event.

Since 1997 most of the popular trails and campgrounds have been cleared of debris, however, rangers still warn hikers to be wary of potentially unstable tree limbs. Most of the fallen forest has been left to recover slowly over time. A slow succession of ecosystems is expected to develop over the coming centuries before the original climactic species of mature spruce and fir once again establish themselves. Apart from aesthetic damage to forests, the only major complication of blowdowns comes from the modest, but multitudinous, spruce beetle, which favors fallen trees. After other blowdown events in the Rocky Mountains, spruce beetles have reached epidemic proportions, spreading destructively into remaining stands of trees where they cause their own damage and also promote the growth of a fungi that can rapidly destroy healthy trees.

GETTING AROUND

The free Steamboat Springs Transit (☎ 970-879-5585) runs around town and also stops adjacent to the Greyhound set-down point. For hikers without their own transportation, Alpine Taxi (☎ 970-879-2800) may be able to provide a shuttle service between Steamboat Springs and local trailheads.

ACCESS TOWN & FACILITIES
Steamboat Springs

Steamboat Springs is a friendly, low-rise ski resort set among a backdrop of forested hills. The USFS Hahns Peak ranger office (☎ 970-879-1870) is off US 40 at the southern end of town. There are several outdoor stores in downtown Steamboat Springs, which are located on Lincon Ave between 6th and 10th Sts, all selling gear and maps. The town's visitor center (☎ 970-879-0880, W www.steamboat-chamber.com, 1255 S Lincoln Ave) can help with accommodations, although beds are not cheap and you'll be lucky to find anything for under $45 per person.

Places to Stay The closet camping with full facilities is *Ski Town KOA Campground* (☎ *970-879-0273, US 40)*, 2mi west of downtown, with sites from $20. *Nordic Lodge Motel* (☎ *970-879-0531, 1036 S Lincoln Ave)* is one of the less expensive places (doubles from $65).

Getting There & Away Yampa Regional Airport (☎ 970-276-3669) is 22mi west of Steamboat Springs, and Greyhound's US 40 service between Denver and Salt Lake City stops just outside town. Alpine Taxi (☎ 970-879-2800) also has two to three shuttle services daily between Steamboat Springs and Denver International Airport ($65/120 one way/return).

USFS Campgrounds

There are nine USFS backcountry *campgrounds* in the area, most charging $10. The most convenient for the routes described is *Seedhouse Campground*, which is 29mi north of Steamboat Springs, 1mi before the Slavonia Trailhead.

Gilpin Lake & Gold Creek Circuit

Duration	6½–7½ hours
Distance	9mi (14.5km)
Standard	moderate
Start/Finish	Slavonia Trailhead
Nearest Town	Steamboat Springs
Transport	car

Summary A beautiful circuit taking in two lakes and an alpine pass.

On their own the Gilpin Lake and Gold Creek Lake Trails are two of the most popular trips within Mt Zirkel Wilderness, and walked together they form a classic loop hike. Winding up through thick spruce-fir forests and passing over an alpine saddle, the trail's highlight is 29-acre Gilpin Lake, sitting dramatically in the hollow of a deep glacial cirque. The hike is enlivened by a couple of entertaining creek crossings, neither of which are serious as long as the creeks are not in flood. This hike can also be completed in conjunction with the Mt Zirkel hike (p248), with the ascent of this fine peak forming a substantial side trip. This combination will require a minimum of two days on the trail.

PLANNING
When to Hike

Numbers of hikers in this area are low compared to other regions in Colorado; hike midweek and you should find yourself almost alone. The saddle on this route is likely to be snowbound until late June or early July, but is normally passable with care a couple of weeks before the thaw is complete. The route also necessitates two creek crossings that may become dangerous or impassable after heavy rain.

Maps

Trails Illustrated's 1:40,680 map No 116 *Hahn's Peak Steamboat Lake* covers the hike. However the trail is not marked correctly on the map, and some of the creek crossings and trail junctions are actually in a different position to their location on the map.

NEAREST TOWN & FACILITIES

See Steamboat Springs and USFS Campgrounds (p246).

GETTING TO/FROM THE HIKE

Slavonia Trailhead is around 30mi north of Steamboat Springs. Follow US 40 west out of town for 2mi, turn right up the CR 129 and continue for 18mi to Clark. Turn right onto USFS Rd 400 just past the bridge over Elk River, and continue for 10mi to the end of the road and the trailhead.

THE HIKE (see map p249)

Shortly after leaving Slavonia Trailhead the path forks; bear left and follow the Gilpin Lake Trail. There is a beaver dam on the left shortly before some fine aspen woodland. After about 1mi the path crosses the boundary of Mt Zirkel Wilderness and enters spruce-fir forest. The ascent becomes steadier, and after an hour of hiking the Mica Basin Trail turns off to the left – a side trip of 5mi return. Remaining close to Gilpin Creek, the route enters an area that was affected by the 1997 blowdown (see the boxed text, p246), although the trail itself has been cleared. A creek crossing leads toward alpine habitat, with wildflowers becoming more frequent and views of Mt Zirkel dominating the head of the valley. A series of switchbacks then leads to a crossing of Gilpin Creek, where boots and socks may have to be removed. There is then a final climb of 0.5mi (with several *campsites* soon after the start of the ascent) before **Gilpin Lake** is revealed in a cirque below, around three hours from the trailhead.

The steep slopes leading to the saddle are on the opposite side of the lake and a path follows around the eastern shore to reach them. Note that, once on the climb to the saddle, there is no water until Gold Creek on the opposite side, so make sure to bring enough. It is a 45-minute climb up steep switchbacks to the top of the **saddle**, with its fine views back over Gilpin Lake. The descent down the other side is initially steep, but the trail soon re-enters the forest and becomes more even. Keep right at a trail junction 30 minutes below the saddle (the Mt Zirkel side trip heads left here) and follow the path through the trees for 1mi to a crossing of Gold Creek, passing *campsites* along the way. Once again footwear will need to be removed to wade across the water. The shallow green waters of **Gold Creek Lake** are just a short distance further on. The 2.5mi descent back to Slavonia Trailhead is through forest and entails two further stream crossings, although stepping stones and a log bridge offer an easy way across both.

Mt Zirkel

Duration	2 days
Distance	15mi (24.1km)
Standard	moderate–hard
Start/Finish	Slavonia Trailhead
Nearest Town	Steamboat Springs
Transport	car

Summary A beautiful, peaceful alpine valley leads to the Continental Divide and the highest summit in Mt Zirkel Wilderness.

Although relatively modest in height, the summit of Mt Zirkel (12,180ft) is a wonderful place, characterized as much by its fine views as by the atmosphere of undisturbed calm that pervades its surrounds. The relatively long ascent (3680ft) is tempered by the beauty of the scenery and, in particular, by the experience of camping in alpine meadows near the head of the approach valley.

PLANNING
When to Hike
Snow patches may persist on the slope leading to Red Dirt Pass and around the summit of Mt Zirkel until early July. The route also necessitates a creek crossing that becomes dangerous or impassable after heavy rain. The final climb from Red Dirt Pass to Mt Zirkel is over open terrain (no path) and route finding may be difficult in poor visibility.

Maps
Trails Illustrated's 1:40,680 map No 116 *Hahn's Peak Steamboat Lake* covers the hike.

NEAREST TOWN & FACILITIES
See Steamboat Springs and USFS Campgrounds (p246).

GETTING TO/FROM THE HIKE
See Getting To/From the Hike (p247).

THE HIKE (see map opposite)
Day 1: Slavonia Trailhead to Slavonia Mine
4–5 hours, 5.5mi, 2000ft ascent
From Slavonia Trailhead take the right-hand trail and follow the Gold Creek Lake Trail for 4mi to the junction with Gilpin Lake Trail, reversing the second half of the route described in the Gilpin Lake and Gold Creek Circuit (p247). At this junction keep straight ahead on the Gold Creek Trail and continue over fairly even terrain to the junction with the Red Dirt Pass Trail. Follow the Red Dirt Pass Trail to the left. The climb becomes steeper as you approach the beautiful meadows at **Slavonia Mine** (reached about an hour after the Gilpin Lake Trail junction).

There is good *camping* here on the firmer ground. The old cabin and rusty relics of machinery that mark the former mine are just above tree line. There are fine views of the upper valley and its surrounding peaks, and a short distance to the north a beautiful creek winds through a meadow. Red Dirt Pass is clearly visible to the north.

Day 2: Slavonia Mine to Slavonia Trailhead via Mt Zirkel
7–8 hours, 9.5mi, 1680ft ascent, 3680ft descent
From the Slavonia Mine the path contours northeast across the head of the valley before making the ascent to **Red Dirt Pass** on a series of switchbacks. In early summer much of this trail will be under extensive snowfields. There is no proper trail for the final 1mi to **Mt Zirkel** but the route is obvious given good visibility. A broad shoulder leads up to a grassy, rock-strewn plateau, which in turn leads toward Mt Zirkel's jagged summit ridge. Negotiating this final ridge is probably the trickiest part of the route, with some loose rock and a high level

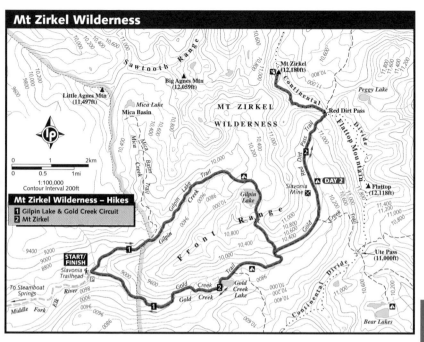

Mt Zirkel Wilderness

Mt Zirkel Wilderness – Hikes
1 Gilpin Lake & Gold Creek Circuit
2 Mt Zirkel

of exposure making it a challenge best suited to hikers free from vertigo. The official summit is the northernmost of the three ragged peaks and offers extensive views across the entire wilderness area (it is also possible to enjoy similar views without progressing onto the more difficult terrain around the summit). Count on taking about two hours to reach the summit from the Slavonia Mine.

Retrace your steps to the Slavonia Mine (1¼ hours) and then return to the trailhead by reversing the first day's hike.

Other Hikes

ROCKY MOUNTAIN NATIONAL PARK
Ouzel & Bluebird Lakes
This easy–moderate day or overnight hike (9.2mi return) in the park's less-visited southern end involves a climb of around 1500ft. From the trailhead just east of Wild Basin ranger station, the route traverses above the valley of North St Vrain Creek to Ouzel Falls. It then follows Ouzel Creek up to the lovely Ouzel Lake, where there are backcountry campsites. A short (2.4mi return) continuation leads to Bluebird Lake. Use the Trails Illustrated 1:59,000 No 200 *Rocky Mountain National Park Recreation Map*.

East Inlet Trail
This out-and-back route on the park's western side sees fewer hikers than routes on the more popular eastern side. Start at West Portal, 2mi east of Grand Lake, and follow the marked trail for 6mi as far as Spirit Lake, passing several other scenic lakes and a set of waterfalls beneath Mt Cairns on the way. Ascents are relatively gentle and total ascent is a little less than 2000ft, giving a six- to eight-hour hike of moderate difficulty. Use the Trails Illustrated 1:59,000 No 200 *Rocky Mountain National Park Recreation Map*. More adventurous hikers could consider the option of continuing on a poorly defined trail across Boulder-Grand Pass, with possible side trips to Mt Alice (13,310ft) or Tanima Peak (12,420ft), before descending steeply to Thunder Lake and then on down to Ouzel Falls and the Ouzel Falls Trailhead. This hard, eight- to 10-hour hike covers a distance of 11.6mi.

Timber Lake Trail

This out-and-back day hike on the western side of the park has its trailhead 11.4mi north of Grand Lake on the Trail Ridge Rd. Follow a marked trail through forest, climbing steadily to reach Timber Creek and then Timber Lake (11,000ft), set in a beautiful rocky cirque. Several campsites are passed en-route, including Snowbird campground just below the lake. Total distance for the return trip is 9.2mi, and with just over 2000ft of ascent this moderate–hard hike should take between four and six hours. Use the Trails Illustrated 1:59,000 No 200 *Rocky Mountain National Park Recreation Map*.

INDIAN PEAKS WILDERNESS
Mt Audubon Trail

This moderate–hard hike offers a rewarding and relatively straightforward ascent of a 13,000ft summit. The route can be crowded, especially on weekends and vacations. The trailhead is accessed from Ward; drive west on Brainard Lake Rd for around 4mi and then turn right for the Mitchell Creek Trailhead. Follow the signs for the Mt Audubon Trail and climb steeply for 2700ft to reach the summit of Mt Audubon at 13,223ft, with superb views of Indian Peaks Wilderness. Allow five to six hours for the 7.8mi return trip. Use the 1:40,680 Trails Illustrated map No 102 *Indian Peaks Gold Hill*.

Buchanan Pass

This A-to-B route crosses the Continental Divide several miles north of Pawnee Pass at a height of 11,837ft. Sawtooth Mountain (12,304ft), just south of the pass, is a possible side trip. Access on the west side is shared with the Pawnee Pass route. The finish on the east side is at Peaceful Valley Campground, just north of Ward. This moderate–hard hike will take one to two days, with a total distance of 18.4mi and an ascent of 3277ft. Use the 1:40,680 Trails Illustrated map No 102 *Indian Peaks Gold Hill*.

MT ZIRKEL WILDERNESS
Bear Lakes/Ute Pass Loop

A moderate 13.5mi hike, this circuit leads past two alpine lakes and crosses the continental divide on the eastern flanks of Mt Zirkel. Ute Pass, the high point of the route, is at 11,000ft and some people chose to split the eight- to nine-hour trip into two days – there is good camping between upper and lower Bear Lakes. The route starts at the Grizzly Helena Trailhead on USFS road 640, about 18mi west of Walden. Follow Bear Lake Trail (it is about 5.5mi to the lakes themselves) to Ute Pass, and descend back to the trailhead using the Ute Creek and Grizzly Helena Trails. Optional side trips include Twin Lakes and Blue Lake. Use Trails Illustrated maps No 116 *Hahn's Peak Steamboat Lake* and No 117 *Clark Buffalo Pass*.

Central Colorado

If you are one of those mountain hikers who thinks that size matters, then central Colorado is for you. The region boasts the highest concentration of 14,000ft peaks in the contiguous US. Almost as many hikers come here in their quest to 'conquer the 14ers' as come to sample the area's less lofty delights. A network of wilderness areas and national forests link to ensure that almost all of this region is protected.

This chapter begins with two walks in the Maroon Bells–Snowmass Wilderness near Aspen. The Elk Mountains provide the rugged spine of this wilderness, with the often-photographed Maroon Peaks serving as the undoubted focal point. A four-day loop circumnavigates these peaks, while another hike takes in the scenic decadence of the Conundrum Hot Springs to their east.

The real superlative-collector of the area is the Sawatch Range. Often referred to as the 'backbone of the country', the range contains several of the highest and largest mountains in the Lower 48 states, and offers a multitude of choices for hikers who relish the exhilaration of standing atop high peaks. Despite the heights of the summits, the fact that many of the hikes begin from around 10,000ft makes the tops quite accessible within a day. However, to concentrate solely on the peaks would be to miss out – the mountains also hide some scenic jewels in the valleys and on their flanks, which are as worthy of exploration as any summit.

CLIMATE

Central Colorado experiences warm and sometimes hot summers, with valley highs often in the 70s or 80s, and overnight lows from 30° to 40°F.

The great height of the mountains in central Colorado is, perhaps, the biggest single factor determining local climate. The ranges block moisture and storm systems coming from the west, and precipitation drops off markedly as you move east across the mountains. While average annual snowfall

Highlights

Admiring the spectacular Maroon Peaks in the Maroon Bells–Snowmass Wilderness.

- Spending four days above 11,000ft on the Maroon Bells Loop (p254)

- Taking a soak in the Conundrum Hot Springs (p258) amid the alpine splendor of the Maroon Bells–Snowmass Wilderness

- Exploring the watery beauty of Missouri Lakes basin (p261)

- Looking out across hundreds of peaks from the summit of Mt Elbert (p263), the highest mountain in the Rockies

near Crested Butte, on the western side of the Sawatch and Elk Mountains, is 198 inches, only 50mi away, in the eastern lee of the ranges, Buena Vista averages a mere 39 inches. It is quite possible to leave rain in the Maroon Bells and enjoy dry conditions on the eastern slopes of the Collegiate Peaks on the same day.

Because of the high elevations, the thaw of snowfields can last well into July and

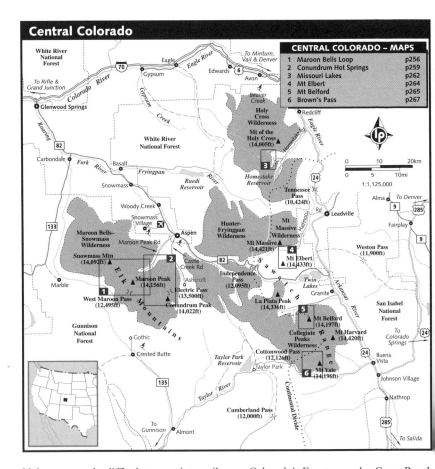

Central Colorado

CENTRAL COLORADO – MAPS

1	Maroon Bells Loop	p256
2	Conundrum Hot Springs	p259
3	Missouri Lakes	p262
4	Mt Elbert	p264
5	Mt Belford	p265
6	Brown's Pass	p267

high passes can be difficult to negotiate until then. All the moisture from this late melt fuels frequent afternoon thunderstorms – a daily occurrence during June and early July, and a real consideration when planning a hike. Winters tend to be harsh and almost all hiking comes to an end in late September or October when the first heavy snows fall.

INFORMATION
Maps & Books
Most Colorado state maps, such as the *Colorado Recreation Map* ($3.95), give good overviews of the area.

Colorado's Fourteeners by Gerry Roach ($18.95) has descriptions of routes up all the highest summits in the state, many of which are clustered in the area covered by this chapter. *The Complete Guide to Colorado's Wilderness Areas* by John Fielder & Mark Pearson ($24.95) includes background information and hike descriptions for the Maroon Bells–Snowmass, Holy Cross, Mt Massive and Collegiate Peaks Wildernesses.

GETTING AROUND
For trailhead shuttles in the Aspen area call High Mountain Taxi (☎ 970-925-8294) or

Warning

As an area packed with 14,000ft mountains, central Colorado is a region with a high risk of acute mountain sickness (AMS). Hikers who come from low elevations and drive directly to a trailhead (many of which are around 10,000ft), then start up a peak, are likely to suffer at least some of the symptoms of this potentially lethal condition. See Altitude (p66) for more details on the causes and prevention of AMS.

Alpine Express (☎ 800-822-4844). Town Taxi (☎ 970-349-5543) runs hiker shuttles between Aspen and Crested Butte; Aspen Aviation (☎ 970-925-2522) does the same by air. In the Leadville area, Dee Hive Tours & Transportation (☎ 719-486-2339) offers a drop-off service to many trailheads and campgrounds.

GATEWAYS
Aspen
About 41mi southeast of Glenwood Springs on Hwy 82, Aspen is a former mining town. It has become one of the Rockies' premier ski resorts, as well as a second home for the rich and famous. Staff at the visitor center (☎ 970-925-1940, W www.aspenchamber.org, 425 Rio Grand Place) are helpful and friendly, as are the people at the US Forest Service (USFS) office (☎ 970-925-3445, 806 W Hallam St), where free brochures on local hikes are available. Ute Mountaineers (☎ 970-925-2849, 308 S Mill St) is one of several outlets that sells outdoor gear, books and maps.

Places to Stay There are six basic *USFS campgrounds* (☎ 877-444-6777) near Aspen, along Maroon Creek and Roaring Fork River Rds (sites cost from $10 to $14). The closest camping with full facilities is at *Aspen-Basalt campground* (☎ 800-567-2773), on Hwy 82 about 20mi north of Aspen, where sites cost from $25 for a tent and two people. Hostel-type accommodations are scarce, although *St Moritz Lodge* (☎ 970-925-3220, 334 W Hyman Ave) offers beds in shared rooms for around $37.

Getting There & Away Aspen is one of the Rockies' few hiking centers accessible by public transportation. RFTA buses (☎ 970-925-8484) run regularly between Aspen and Glenwood Springs, which is on the Greyhound bus and Amtrak rail networks. Several airlines also have regular flights between Denver and Aspen airport (☎ 970-920-5384), 4mi north of town on Hwy 82. Alternatively, a one-way shuttle from Denver International Airport to Aspen costs $100 with Colorado Mountain Express (☎ 970-949-4227).

Leadville
A former mining town nicknamed 'Cloud City' for its 10,200ft altitude, Leadville is 38mi south of Vail. The visitor center (☎ 719-486-3900, W www.leadvilleusa.com, 809 Harrison Ave) offers maps and brochures covering the local area, while the USFS Leadville ranger station (☎ 719-486-0749, 2015 N Poplar St) sells local hiking maps and offers backcountry advice. Bill's Sport Shop (☎ 719-486-0739, 225 Harrison Ave) sells topographic maps and other hiking equipment.

Places to Stay There are more than 10 USFS campgrounds in the Leadville area, most charging around $10. Of these, *Halfmoon campground*, 10mi southwest of the town along Halfmoon Rd, is one of the most popular with hikers. *Sugar Loafin' campground* (☎ 719-486-1031), 4mi west of Leadville on Lake County Rd 4, is the closest campground with facilities. Tent sites cost $22.

Leadville Hostel & Inn (☎ 719-486-9334, 500 E 7th St) is friendly, has great facilities and is the cheapest place to stay in town; dorm beds cost from $15.

Getting There & Away Dee Hive Tours & Transportation (☎ 719-486-2339, 506 Harrison Ave) charges $135/245 for one person/four people one way to Denver. Alternatively, Eco Transit (☎ 970-328-3520) has daily shuttle buses between Leadville and Vail, which is on the Greyhound bus network.

Maroon Bells–Snowmass Wilderness

The 283-sq-mile Maroon Bells–Snowmass Wilderness lies within the White River and Gunnison National Forests, just south of Aspen. It is one of Colorado's five original wilderness areas, designated in 1964. The sheer majestic presence of the region impressed legislators then and has lost none of its impact.

Forming the spine of the wilderness, the mighty Elk Mountains include six 14ers, among them the famous Maroon Bells. The deep red cliffs of these iconic mountains are typical of the rock that is so characteristic of the area; colored by a mixture of sand and iron-rich mud laid down more than 200 million years ago. Massive ice-age glaciations also had a huge affect on the landscape, producing some classic glacial lakes and tarns. Today the range is fringed by extensive alpine meadows and highland forests of Engelmann spruce, subalpine fir and the rarer white fir, with sporadic stands of graceful aspen.

The beauty and accessibility of the wilderness has led to great popularity. Controlling the environmental impact of the huge number of visitors is one of the primary tasks of the local forestry service.

PLANNING
Information Sources
Information about Maroon Bells–Snowmass Wilderness can be obtained from Aspen Ranger Station (☎ 970-925-5277; 806 W Hallam St, Aspen, CO 81611), or Ⓦ www.fs .fed.us/r2/whiteriver and Ⓦ www.fs.fsd.us/ r2/gmug.

Permits & Regulations
Permits are not necessary for hiking in the Maroon Bells–Snowmass Wilderness, but anglers must have a state fishing license. Always use the designated campsites established at some of the most popular camping areas (including Crater and Geneva Lakes on the Maroon Bells Loop, and at Conundrum Hot Springs). Camps are not allowed within 100ft of trails, streams and lakes (in certain cases within 0.25mi of lakes); fires must be at least 0.5mi below tree line.

Maroon Bells Loop

Duration	4 days
Distance	29.1mi (46.8km)
Standard	moderate
Start/Finish	Maroon-Snowmass Trailhead
Nearest Town	Aspen
Transport	car, bus

Summary A classic hike that circumnavigates the Maroon Bells, giving constantly changing views of these remarkable peaks.

This very high-level route (also known as the 'Four Passes Loop') is largely above 11,000ft and crosses four passes exceeding 12,000ft. The centerpoint of the hike, the majestic twins of Maroon Peak (14,156ft) and North Maroon Peak (14,014ft), are composed of reddish-brown sedimentary rock and have a stratified appearance more typical of the northern Rockies. Despite a few steep sections, the ascents on this hike are generally mild; however, hikers should be acclimated to the high altitude. Hiking in a clockwise direction is slightly easier and more scenic.

PLANNING
When to Hike
Lingering winter snow may keep this route closed well into July, while new falls could hamper hikers from late September. In June some of the streams are serious fords. From June through August powerful electrical storms are common in the early afternoon. Hikers seeking solitude should avoid the Maroon Bells area on summer weekends.

Maps
Trails Illustrated's 1:40,680 map No 128 *Maroon Bells Redstone, Marbles* covers the hike. Otherwise use USGS' 1:24,000 quads, *Maroon Bells* and *Snowmass Mountain*.

NEAREST TOWN
See Aspen (p253).

GETTING TO/FROM THE HIKE
The loop begins and ends at the Maroon-Snowmass Trailhead, near Maroon Lake, at the end of the Maroon Creek Rd. To use the trailhead car park (below the large picnic/parking area) you must pick up a pass at the USFS entrance gate. Due to the popularity of the Maroon Lake area, the road is closed to private traffic above the T-Lazy-7 Ranch between 8:30am and 5pm from June 19 to September 6 (plus weekends in September). During road closures, RFTA (☎ 970-925-8484) runs half-hourly shuttles between Aspen and Maroon Lake ($5 round-trip). The last bus leaves Maroon Lake at 5pm.

THE HIKE
Day 1: Maroon-Snowmass Trailhead to Upper West Maroon Creek
2¼–3 hours, 4.6mi, 1270ft ascent
It is a minute's walk from the trailhead to the shallow **Maroon Lake**, which, set before the majestic backdrop of the Maroon Bells, is one of the most picturesque tarns anywhere in the Rockies. Head past large beaver mounds to the western shore, where you can take any of several diverging trails; these lead along the north side of West Maroon Creek (the inlet), or cross and follow the creek's south side to converge roughly 0.5mi past Maroon Lake.

Climb through mixed conifer forest over a rocky crest to a trail junction in an aspen grove, then turn left and follow the West Maroon Creek Trail directly to **Crater Lake**, around one hour from the trailhead. This lake fills a trough (drained only by subterraneous seepage) right below North Maroon Peak and Pyramid Peak. To minimize impact on the environment, hikers should only camp at the 11 designated *campsites* (marked by numbered posts) around the lake's eastern shore. Fires are prohibited at Crater Lake.

Head south into the upper valley of West Maroon Creek. The trail climbs over sweeping scree slides and avalanche slopes, strewn with Colorado columbines and blue gentians,

as it rises below sheer terraced cliffs on the east face of Maroon Peak. Cut up through the forest where it fringes with raspberry thickets colonizing the talus slopes on your right, crossing the creek and following its eastern side before you recross it near tree line, around 1½ hours from Crater Lake. Pleasant *campsites* can be found along much of the upper valley, mostly on the creek's eastern side.

Day 2: Upper West Maroon Creek to Hasley Basin Turnoff
4½–6 hours, 8.5mi, 1975ft ascent
Head up over the rolling tundra slopes scattered with willow heath into the valley head, before making a long, sidling ascent southwest to reach **West Maroon Pass** (12,495ft) after about 1½ hours. From here you get an uplifting view of the ranges to the west, as well as a final look back down the spectacular upper valley of West Maroon Creek.

The muddy trail drops steeply into the open basin below the pass, then cuts right over glorious wildflower meadows to a junction marked only by a cairned pole. (The left turnoff goes down to the East Fork of West Maroon Trailhead on the Schofield Pass Rd.) Turn right along the North Fork Fravert Basin Trail, traversing gently northwest over extensive alpine-wildflower meadows surrounding the East Fork of the Crystal River, to reach a tarn on a small shelf.

Make a very steep, direct climb east to reach **Frigid Air Pass** (12,410ft), 1½ to two hours from West Maroon Pass. Pikas and marmots scamper around this spectacular spot, which looks directly across the grassy bowl of Fravert Basin to the staggered, 2000ft western face of Maroon Peak. The slight point of Snowmass Mountain can be made out to the northwest.

Drop down several switchbacks, then begin a descent left into the spruce forest to meet the meandering North Fork of Crystal River. The trail leads gently past streamside meadows, visited by flocks of mountain chickadees, getting increasingly steeper as the North Fork cascades and plunges over an escarpment into beaver ponds. There are *campsites* on the forested hillock below the

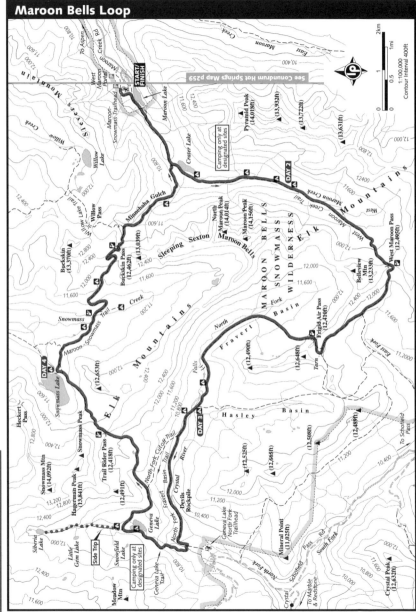

Maroon Bells Loop

Top: Dwarfed by the dramatic bluffs below Utah's Mt Timpanogos, hikers head for a shelter near Emerald Lake. **Bottom Left:** Little Matterhorn towers above Odessa Lake in Rocky Mountain National Park, Colorado. **Bottom Right:** Gilpin Lake, sited dramatically in the hollow of a deep glacial cirque, in Colorado's Mt Zirkel Wilderness.

CLEM LINDENMAYER

CLEM LINDENMAYER

GARETH McCORMACK

Top: The majestic twins of Maroon Peak and North Maroon Peak dominate Colorado's Maroon Bells–Snowmass Wilderness. **Bottom Left:** A partially-frozen tarn in the large, glacial Missouri Lakes basin, a popular hiking destination in Colorado's Holy Cross Wilderness. **Bottom Right:** Hiking above Silver Dollar Pond on the trail to Conundrum Hot Springs in the Maroon Bells–Snowmass Wilderness.

falls. Continue more gently through the forest to an unsigned, left (south) turnoff to Hasley Basin, just before the trail crosses the stream, 1½ to two hours from Frigid Air Pass. Many good *campsites* can be found here at the edge of the meadows.

Day 3: Hasley Basin Turnoff to Snowmass Lake
4½–6 hours, 8.4mi, 2526ft ascent
Cross the North Fork and pass more *campsites* in the trees to reach a trail junction. (Here hikers with less time can take the North Fork Cutoff Trail on the right, which switchbacks up the slope to join the Geneva Lake Trail after one to 1½ hours.) The trail continues down through meadows fringed by raspberry shrubs and stands of aspen, crossing a small torrent (which may be tricky to cross in early summer) to intersect with the Geneva Lake Trail. (The left branch leads 0.3mi down to the Geneva Lake North Fork Trailhead.)

Turn right and climb steep, tight switchbacks up slopes facing southwest toward tiny remnant glaciers on Treasury Mountain. The trail levels out shortly before you reach **Geneva Lake**, a pleasant, greenish tarn tucked into a hanging terrace high above the North Fork valley, around two hours from the Hasley Basin turnoff. There are several designated *campsites* above the steep western shore (no fires – camping otherwise not permitted within 0.25mi of the lake).

Skirt around to a stand of fir and spruce, where a route departs (left) to Siberia Lake (see Side Trip). The main trail cuts around Geneva Lake's northern shore and up southeast to a little saddle, where Maroon Peak reappears, before continuing upward, high above the North Fork to meet the incoming cutoff trail. Climb over grassy hillocks past a reedy pond, then make a final ascent to arrive at **Trail Rider Pass** (12,418ft), 1¾ to 2½ hours from Geneva Lake. Marked by a thin band of powdery limestone separating the gray and red rock strata, this dip in the ridge offers an excellent overview of the Snowmass basin ahead.

Drop over several broad switchbacks before beginning a high descent to reach the northeastern end of **Snowmass Lake**, around one hour from the pass. There are some ideal *campsites* near the lake outlet. At the lake head vast scree fields sweep down from a mighty trio of semidetached summits: Snowmass Peak (south), Hagerman Peak (middle) and Snowmass Mountain.

Side Trip: Siberia Lake
2½–3½ hours, 3mi, 916ft ascent
This side trip takes you up into the head of a wild alpine valley at the western foot of Snowmass Mountain. The mostly prominent trail (not shown on maps) leads north along the slopes high above the western side of the Geneva Lake inlet. After passing the shallow Little Gem Lake, follow the tiny valley stream to **Siberia Lake**, a raw tarn at the upper vegetation line. A rougher route continues over the rocky pass at the head of the valley into the drainage of Avalanche Creek.

Day 4: Snowmass Lake to Maroon-Snowmass Trailhead
3¾–5½ hours, 7.6mi, 1482ft ascent
Follow the muddy Maroon-Snowmass Trail gradually southeast through the forest, passing *campsites* beside the marshy meadows just before crossing Snowmass Creek. There are good views south to the west faces of the Sleeping Sexton (ridge) and the Maroon Bells. The trail soon passes a right turn (going to *campsites* on the creek's east side) and winds up past several more *campsites* at tree line, before heading across wildflower meadows and moraine dotted with shrub willow. A long, sweeping switchback over the alpine tundra brings you up to **Buckskin Pass** (12,462ft), two to three hours from Snowmass Lake. The pass gives uplifting views in both directions, including the mighty Pyramid Peak ahead.

Descend in steep curves past the Willow Lake Trail turnoff, continuing (right) down over alpine meadows into the forest. The trail winds down through Minnehaha Gulch, crossing the stream to pass *campsites* under the eastern walls of the Sleeping Sexton. Descend through groves of aspen to arrive back at the West Maroon Creek Trail junction near Crater Lake, one to 1½ hours from the pass. The hike back down to the trail-head at Maroon Lake (see Day 1, p255) takes 45 minutes to one hour.

Conundrum Hot Springs

Duration	2 days
Distance	17mi (27.4km)
Standard	moderate
Start/Finish	Conundrum Creek Trailhead
Nearest Town	Aspen
Transport	car

Summary A hot soak beneath 14,000ft peaks is the reward for a long and sometimes tedious approach.

This route makes a long and gradual ascent up the deep Conundrum Creek valley to reach Conundrum Hot Springs, perhaps the best undeveloped thermal pools in Colorado. Set under the 13,943ft Cathedral Peak and the 14,022ft Conundrum Peak, and looking out across the Conundrum valley, a warm evening or morning soak with this kind of view could not be more sublime and is ample reward for the tough hike up. Unfortunately the area around the hot springs has suffered some degradation from heavy use. Please observe regulations on camping and campfires, and try to keep to trails wherever possible.

Recommended alternatives to backtracking include continuing south from Conundrum Hot Springs across 12,900ft Triangle Pass (with minor side trips to Copper Pass and Copper Lake) to Gothic, a small town 7mi from Crested Butte. This results in a total hike of around 16mi. Alternatively, from Triangle Pass hike northwest to East Maroon Pass, and then north down East Maroon Creek Trail. This 20mi route exits at East Maroon Portal on the Maroon Creek Rd, where you can pick up a RFTA shuttle bus to Aspen (see Getting to/from the Hike, p255).

PLANNING
When to Hike
The trail is normally clear of snow by late June. To avoid crowds hike outside weekends and holiday periods.

Warning

Although the trail is popular with snowshoers and cross-country skiers you should be especially cautious about making spring or winter trips in the Conundrum Creek valley, as the area is prone to huge avalanches.

Maps
Use two Trails Illustrated 1:40,680 maps, No 127 *Aspen Independence Pass* and No 128 *Maroon Bells Redstone, Marble*; or three USGS 1:24,000 quads: *Highland Peak*, *Maroon Bells* and *Gothic*.

NEAREST TOWN
See Aspen (p253).

GETTING TO/FROM THE HIKE
The trailhead is at the end of Conundrum Creek Rd, which is signed to the right off Castle Creek Rd 5mi south of Aspen.

Rocky Mountain High

And the Colorado Rocky Mountain high,
I've seen it raining fire in the sky...
He climbed cathedral mountains,
he saw silver clouds below...
the serenity of a clear blue mountain lake...
Friends around the campfire and everybody's high...

John Denver

Rocky Mountain High is one of John Denver's most famous songs and rumor has it that he wrote it while soaking in Conundrum Hot Springs during the psychedelic 1960s. The words of the song are certainly suggestive of the location, and Denver was a known hiker and conservationist who later moved to Aspen (*Aspenglow* was one of his later releases). It is also something of a tradition to visit the springs during night-time meteor showers, which might explain the reference to raining fire. Whatever the truth, as you lie back in the hot water of the springs and watch steam rising toward Cathedral Peak, it is certainly easy to see where he might have got his inspiration from.

THE HIKE
Day 1: Conundrum Creek Trailhead to Conundrum Hot Springs
4–5 hours, 8.5mi, 2500ft ascent

The first 1mi of trail crosses lush meadows, which were forested until a few years ago. A recurring theme of the approach to the springs is huge avalanche tracks – these meadows are the result of one such avalanche that swept down from the western slopes with such force that it also flattened the forest for hundreds of feet up the eastern slopes.

Beyond the meadows the trail continues into beautiful aspen woodland, passing the remains of an old cabin and reaching the first bridge after 2.5mi. Continue through more aspen forest and then climb steadily across meadows marking another avalanche track. Once back in the trees, the trail climbs steeply for 1mi along the flanks of a steep gorge. The gradient then slackens as the trail continues through a mixture of pine forest, open meadow and low scrub to reach the second bridge, 6mi and three to 3½ hours from the start. Climb past **Silver Dollar Pond**, which often has striking reflections, then pass more ponds to reach the third crossing of Conundrum Creek; this time achieved by balancing on felled tree trunks.

The trail climbs steadily from here to the first established *campsites* some 2mi further up the valley. The first site is down on the left on the edge of an avalanche track. Continue up the trail for a few minutes and you'll reach a signed trail leading to this site and several others hidden in thick forest above the creek. Campfires are permitted at these sites.

Climb alongside a small gorge for a few hundred feet, passing more *campsites* and a disused cabin (campfires are prohibited at these sites and those closer to the springs). Cross the creek once more and climb the short distance to the **hot springs**. There is one main pool, with an overflow feeding into two smaller and cooler pools. Enjoy!

Day 2: Conundrum Hot Springs to Conundrum Creek Trailhead
3–4 hours, 8.5mi, 2500ft descent

Retrace the Day 1 hike back to Conundrum Creek Trailhead.

Sawatch Range

Running northwest-southeast alongside the Arkansas valley in the center of Colorado, the Sawatch Range overflows with superlatives. It includes 15 mountains over 14,000ft (more than in any other range of the contiguous US), hosts the three highest peaks in the Rockies and marks the highest point on the Continental Divide. It is little wonder that the range has been dubbed the 'backbone of the country'.

While the physical presence of the mountains is undeniable, the range is largely characterized by rounded rather than serrated peaks; size outreaches ruggedness here. Geologically, the mountains were formed in the Precambrian era by a faulted anticline, with a high level of tertiary activity that included the mineralization of much of the range. Gold, silver and lead all formed in large

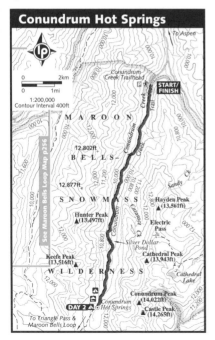

Conundrum Hot Springs

Long Hike – Colorado Trail

Duration	28 days
Distance	500mi (805km)
Standard	moderate
Start	Denver
Finish	Durango

Crossing eight mountain ranges, seven national forests, six wilderness areas and five river systems, the Colorado Trail is as diverse as it is demanding. It explores some of the most beautiful areas in the state. The 500mi trail (more if you include various side trips) is split into 28 stages. Each of these stages is a challenge – the easiest is 12mi long and involves 1040ft of ascent, while the most difficult is 32mi long, with 4520ft of ascent! Together they make up a formidable route, which most people chose to hike in several segments.

Much of the trail is remote (there are no shelters) and towns are usually some distance away. This means carrying a large pack of supplies, and the high altitude of the route necessitates extra gear for unpredictable weather (the trail's high point is 13,334ft and most day stages reach well over 11,000ft). For those for whom this is not enough of a challenge, several of Colorado's 14,000ft peaks can also be accessed from the trail, and numerous other side-trip permutations are possible.

The trail was originally developed as a high mountain route to serve both recreational and educational purposes, and it is maintained by the nonprofit Colorado Trail Foundation. This group can provide further information and also offers week-long supported treks along the trail, where hikers need only carry a day-pack.

Contact Colorado Trail Foundation (☎ 303-384-3729, ext 113; ⓦ www.coloradotrail.org; 710 10th St, Suite 210, Golden, CO 80401-5843). *The Colorado Trail: The Official Guidebook* by Randy Jacobs ($22.50) is also a mine of information and includes topographic maps of the entire route, as well as resupply and access details for both through- and segment-hikers. A full set of 29 waterproof 1:50,000 topographic maps is also available from the Foundation for $17.50.

quantities in fissures in the rocks, and the area was subject to a fortune-rush during the latter half of the 1800s. Many of the first ascents in the area can undoubtedly be attributed to miners around this time. The Sawatch name appears as early as 1853 and has been linked to an Indian word meaning 'water of the blue earth'.

Today the range is almost entirely protected and encompasses numerous designated wilderness areas. To the north of the mountain range, the Holy Cross Wilderness covers 190 sq miles. It is sometimes referred to as a 'water wilderness', in reference to the numerous streams, cascades and lakes that dot its alpine landscape. To the south, the Mt Massive Wilderness protects the lowland forest and high rocky summits of the biggest mountains (in terms of mass) in the Lower 48. Mt Elbert, the Sawatch's highest peak and second highest point in the Lower 48, actually lies outside all these wildernesses. Just to the south again is the 263-sq-mile Collegiate Peaks Wilderness. This area boasts the Rockies' most clustered concentration of 14ers (eight in total), most of which bear the names of eminent universities.

PLANNING
Information Sources
Leadville ranger station (☎ 719-486-0749; 2015 N Poplar St, Leadville, CO 80461) has information on local wilderness areas or see ⓦ www.fs.fed.us/r2/psicc/leadvile.

Permits & Regulations
No permits are required for hiking or camping in the Sawatch Range, although anglers must have a state fishing license. Designated campsites have been established at some of the popular camping areas. Camps are not allowed within 100ft of trails, streams and lakes (sometimes within 0.25mi of lakes); fires must be at least 0.5mi below tree line.

GETTING AROUND
High Country Jeep Tours (☎ 719-395-6111) offers hiker shuttles to trailheads around Buena Vista. However, the charge is likely to be at least $50 so it is only an economical option when shared between several hikers.

ACCESS TOWN
Buena Vista

Buena Vista occupies the flat land of the Arkansas valley, set against the sharp backdrop of Collegiate Peaks Wilderness. There is a small but friendly visitor center (☎ 719-395-6612, Ⓦ www.buenavistacolorado.org, 343 US 24 S). The Trailhead (☎ 719-395-8001, 707 US 24 N) is the best outdoor store in town.

Places to Stay There are six USFS campgrounds in the area, all costing $10. The *Collegiate Peaks campground* (☎ 877-444-6777), 11mi west of Buena Vista on CR 306, is the largest and best located. *Cottonwood Hot Springs Inn* (☎ 719-395-6434), 5mi up the same road, has a range of accommodations, with a dorm bed or a spot in a teepee for $35 (soaks in the hot springs included).

Getting There & Away There is no public transportation between Buena Vista and neighboring towns. By car Buena Vista is 30mi south of Leadville via US 24 and 115mi southwest of Denver via I-70, Hwy 91 and US 24.

Missouri Lakes

Duration	4–5 hours
Distance	6.5mi (10.5km)
Standard	easy–moderate
Start/Finish	Missouri Lakes Trailhead
Nearest Towns	Redcliff, Minturn, Leadville
Transport	car
Summary	A pleasant out-and-back hike to a scenic alpine basin holding several beautiful lakes.

The Missouri Lakes Trail is one of the most popular hikes in the Holy Cross Wilderness. A pretty, winding trail with only a few steep climbs along Missouri Creek to reach the Missouri Lakes basin, a large glacial basin dotted with several beautiful lakes and tarns. The out-and-back hike is the most popular option, especially early in the season, with many hikers choosing to camp near the lakes. Watch out for marmots around the lakes.

Holy Cross Under Threat

Water is essential to any ecosystem, but it is the heart and soul of the Holy Cross Wilderness. Here a network of mountain creeks feeds 87 alpine lakes. Extensive wetlands cover the floors of the area's five glaciated valleys, where fish, mammals and several rare plants thrive in the aquatic environment. The flow of water from peak to valley, particularly during spring snowmelt when the lowlands are often completely flooded, is an integral part of this water-based ecology.

But this ecology is under threat. A scheme to divert water from the wilderness to supply the cities of Aurora and Colorado Springs has been developing since 1962. Phase one of this scheme (Homestake Phase I) was completed in 1967, when 6ft-diameter diversion pipes were laid to feed water from several creeks on the east of the mountains into the Homestake Reservoir. As a result many of these creeks are a trickle of their former selves (including Missouri and Fancy Creeks, as explored on the Missouri Lakes hike). Homestake Phase II is now under debate. This stage involves tunneling 10mi under the Holy Cross Ridge to place diversion dams on creeks on the west side, and remove up to 90% of their water.

The USFS has sanctioned the scheme, citing the 1980 Colorado Wilderness Act, which specifically prevents any intervention in matters relating to the water rights of the two cities. Reports commissioned by the USFS also claim that water diversion would have a 'minimal' impact on the ecology of the area. However, the Holy Cross Wilderness Defense Fund, set up in the early 1980s, is fighting the development of the project, also citing scientific studies to back its claims of potential damage to the area.

Despite failed attempts to have the USFS decision overturned in the courts, the Homestake Phase II project has still not commenced and may die a slow death. Currently the Eagle County Commissioner has still not approved the scheme and attempts have recently been made to establish water sources outside the wilderness boundary, although at the time of research the issue is far from concluded.

For more information contact the Holy Cross Wilderness Defense Fund (☎ 303-447-1361; 1130 Alpine, Boulder, CO 80302).

CENTRAL COLORADO

PLANNING

When to Hike

The trail is normally clear of snow by mid-June, but small patches may persist in the lake basin and on Missouri Pass into July.

Maps

Use the Trails Illustrated 1:40,680 map No 126 *Holy Cross Reudi Reservoir*.

NEAREST TOWNS & FACILITIES

See Leadville (p253).

Redcliff

A few miles north of the Homestake Rd turnoff on US 24, this small town has no accommodations but *Mango's Mountain Grill* serves killer 'backcountry breakfasts'.

Minturn

Situated 6mi north of Redcliff on US 24, Minturn is a larger town with accommodations, although none are budget. *Minturn Inn* (☎ 800-646-8876, Ⓦ *www.minturninn.com, 442 Main St*) is a delightful and beautifully furnished B&B housed in a restored 1915 home along the Eagle River. Rates range from $79 to $189 from April 1 to December 21, and $99 to $269 during ski season.

Cougar Ridge Cafe (☎ 970-827-5609, 132 Main St) is a good spot for a meal. *Turntable Restaurant (☎ 970-827-4164, 160 Railroad Ave)*, open 5:30am to 10:30pm, is on the site of an old engine turntable and the restaurant is decorated with railroad memorabilia. It dishes up hearty breakfasts, as well as burgers, tacos and burritos. Most meals cost from $5 to $8.

Homestake Creek Campgrounds

Strung out along Homestake Rd there are several *USFS campgrounds* ($10), which could make a convenient base for the hike.

GETTING TO/FROM THE HIKE

Missouri Lakes Trailhead is tucked away at the head of the Homestake valley. Follow the gravel Homestake Rd for 7mi, turning left and following Missouri Creek Rd for another 4mi. Homestake Rd is signed to the left (west) of US 24, 21mi north of Leadville.

THE HIKE

From the trailhead follow a broad trail for 0.5mi until it narrows and steepens at the base of a stony slope. Climb this slope to reach a **small lake** where Missouri Creek has been dammed as part of the Homestake project (see the boxed text 'Holy Cross Under Threat', p261). Continue past this, crossing the boundary of the Holy Cross Wilderness, and climb steeply on a rough and rocky trail. Cross Missouri Creek on a footbridge, where the water tumbles noisily through a steep gorge. Continue on the rocky trail, climbing steadily away from the noise of the creek and into an area of waterlogged meadows. The trail skirts these wet areas, using drier ground to the north, and then gradually swings back to the creek, following beside it in a very pleasant section of trail along the bottom of a small gorge.

Emerge from the top of the gorge and the angle of the climb eases, with the trail soon crossing more patches of meadow as it winds gently upwards. Crossing a tributary of Missouri Creek you catch better views of the mountains ahead and, in another 15 minutes, the trees thin and small tarns appear beside the trail. Climb over a small

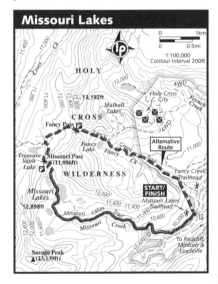

spur, and the first of the **Missouri Lakes** comes into view, backed by the almost sheer flanks of the mountains behind.

The trail skirts the eastern shore of this lake and then climbs over another rocky spur to reveal another charming lake set at a slightly higher elevation. The route continues in this vein with every few minutes of walking revealing yet another hidden lake, all connected by small streams. The final lake (2½ to three hours from the trailhead) sits darkly in a steep, glacial cirque just southeast of Missouri Pass and is often ice-covered well into summer. This is a good spot to sit and wait for the many marmots that inhabit the area to show themselves.

Retrace your steps to the trailhead.

Alternative Route
6 hours, 8mi, 2500ft ascent
As the snow melts off Missouri Pass from mid-July on, it is possible to extend this hike into a circular route. Cross Missouri Pass and then contour north to Fancy Pass before descending steeply along Fancy Creek Trail and finishing back at Missouri Lakes Trailhead. This rewarding loop provides great views and an extra physical challenge, and will take around six hours at a moderate to moderate–hard standard depending on snow.

Mt Elbert

Duration	5½–7 hours
Distance	7.6mi (12.2km)
Standard	moderate–hard
Start/Finish	Mt Elbert Trailhead
Nearest Town	Leadville
Transport	car

Summary A strenuous ascent of 4400ft leads to superlative views at the summit of the highest mountain in the Rockies.

Second in height in the contiguous US only to Mt Whitney (by a mere 63ft), Mt Elbert (14,433ft) is something of a monument for hikers. Walkers who ignore all other 14ers are still tempted by the challenge of standing on the highest summit in the Rockies,

and this is undoubtedly the most popular peak in the Sawatch Range. Unless you are making the climb out of season, don't expect to have the summit to yourself!

Despite its status, there is nothing subtle or technically demanding about the hike to Mt Elbert's top. If you are properly acclimated (many visitors are less than prepared and suffer for it) and if the idea of three or four hours of continuous uphill slog doesn't put you off, then several fairly straightforward trails lead to the summit. The route described here is the shortest and quickest, but is also steep. For a more gradual ascent the slightly longer (12.4mi) South Mt Elbert Trail from Twin Lakes Trailhead is recommended.

PLANNING
When to Hike
The northeastern and eastern ridges of Mt Elbert (which the North and South Mt Elbert Trails follow respectively) are easily visible from US 24, just south of Leadville. This is a great help because the amount of snow lying on each trail can be seen before you hike; there is likely to be snow cover until mid-June. Start your hike early to avoid afternoon thunderstorms.

What to Bring
No water is available on the trail, so enough for the return trip must be carried from the outset. The wind is cold and the weather is also notoriously changeable at these altitudes, so bring plenty of warm and waterproof clothing.

Maps
Use Trails Illustrated 1:40,680 map No127 *Aspen Independence Pass* or the USGS 1:24,000 quad *Mt Elbert*.

NEAREST TOWN
See Leadville (p253).

GETTING TO/FROM THE HIKE
Mt Elbert Trailhead is situated 10mi southwest of Leadville, along the gravel Halfmoon Rd. This road is signed west from US 24 on the southern edge of Leadville.

CENTRAL COLORADO

THE HIKE

Within a minute of leaving Mt Elbert Trailhead the path joins the Colorado Trail.

Turn left along this, cross a stream and begin climbing. After 20 minutes of ascent a corner is rounded and the terrain flattens for around 0.5mi, up to and past the point where the North Mt Elbert Trail turns right off the Colorado Trail (the junction is signed). Make the most of the even ground – it is in short supply from this point!

The trail then winds up through the pine trees, to exit them abruptly around 1½ hours from the start. From tree line the path can be seen winding up the rounded rocky shoulder ahead, although the summit itself is hidden from sight.

A couple of rises are mounted (from where the silhouettes of hikers on the south ridge will probably be visible) before the trail leads up and to the right of a steep cliff at the headwall of Box Creek cirque. The terrain here is steep, with a mixture of dirt and stones making the ground loose underfoot, and this is the most difficult section of the route.

From the cairn at the top of this rise it is still a 30-minute climb over several false summits to the top, with the last 200yds leading over a rocky but not overly exposed ridge. The **summit** is reached three to four hours from the start, depending on your aptitude for continuous ascents.

The view from the top is everything that might be expected, with peaks stretching in all directions as far as the eye can see. The sight is very impressive but also humbling, bringing the realization that it would take a lifetime to explore all that is laid out before you. There is a signature canister on the summit where you can register your achievement before returning to the trailhead via the same route.

Leadville 100

It was around the second week in August, and we were planning to spend a couple of nights in Leadville. It was a shock to discover the town full of people and accommodations scarce. After managing to secure one of the last spots in the hostel, I got chatting to one of the other guests, a sprightly looking older man with gray hair. In response to his inquiry about my purpose for visiting the area, I told him I was doing a bit of hiking. He was interested, and suggested a route to encompass the summits of both Mt Elbert and Mt Massive in a single day. I laughed: I had already been up Mt Elbert and the suggestion that it could be combined with Mt Massive, in such a short time frame, had to be a joke.

As it turned out he was not trying to be funny. He and many of the others in the area were acclimating for the Leadville 100; an annual 100mi mountain race run at elevations between 9200ft and 12,600ft. It starts at 4am and has a completion time limit of 30 hours. The current course record stands at 17 hours, 30 minutes, 42 seconds. I couldn't believe it! I like a challenge but this sounded like true masochism. Yet many of the incredibly fit-looking competitors were at least a generation older than me, if not two. It certainly put my trip up Mt Elbert in context!

Helen Fairbairn

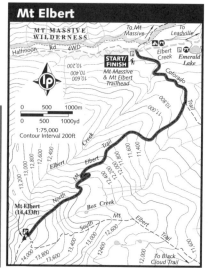

Mt Belford

Duration	6–7 hours
Distance	9mi (14.5km)
Standard	moderate–hard
Start/Finish	Missouri Gulch Trailhead
Nearest Town	Buena Vista
Transport	car

Summary A scenic circuit that winds through alpine moraine to a high pass before summiting another of Colorado's 14,000ft peaks.

The lofty panoramic summit of Mt Belford (14,197ft), on the northern edge of the Collegiate Peaks Wilderness, can be reached most directly via an out-and-back route along its northwest ridge from the Missouri Gulch Trailhead. The terrain on this ridge is steep and loose, however, and consists almost entirely of sharp switchbacks – not the most pleasant hiking for anybody wanting more than to reach the top as quickly as possible.

A route of far higher scenic quality, that also offers a more gradual ascent, includes a loop via Elkhead Pass. While preferable, this option is about 1.5mi longer than the direct route but still involves about 4557ft of ascent, so makes for a fairly strenuous day hike. Camping is available in the Missouri valley for those who want to make a longer trip of it and, for peak-baggers, an optional 2.5mi side trip leads from the summit of Mt Belford to the adjacent 14,153ft Mt Oxford.

PLANNING
When to Hike
This route should be free of snow by late June, but be wary of afternoon thunderstorms and try to summit by 1pm.

Maps
Use the Trails Illustrated 1:40,680 map No 129 *Buena Vista Collegiate Peaks*, or two USGS 1:24,000 quads, *Mount Harvard* and *Winfield*.

NEAREST TOWN
See Buena Vista (p261).

GETTING TO/FROM THE HIKE
Missouri Gulch Trailhead is on Clear Creek Rd, 8mi west of the turnoff on US 24, 15mi north of Buena Vista.

THE HIKE
A bridge leads across Clear Creek and the trail immediately begins to climb the steep, pine-forested slope to the west of Missouri Gulch. Half a mile of switchbacks leads to a slight easing of the gradient, before a stream crossing marks another steepening of terrain that lasts to tree line. A former miner's cabin, dated from around 1879, marks the end of the trees, one hour from the trailhead. There is *camping* around this cabin, although signs ask for compliance with regeneration work that is in progress.

Once onto open terrain the bulk of Mt Belford looms ahead, with the path that zigzags up its northwest ridge clearly visible. A trail junction indicates a left turn for Mt Belford, but only take this if you want to

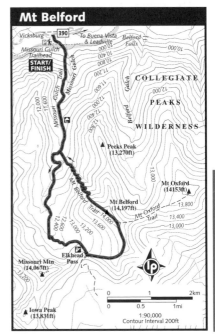

follow the steep ridge directly to the summit. Veer right for Elkhead Pass and you will soon cross the upper reaches of Missouri Gulch via stepping stones between two large cairns. The trail then winds up the impressive valley, passing between rolling moraine and alpine tundra, and beneath the jagged spires of Missouri Mountain. Jumbles of rock confuse the path in places but small cairns always mark the way. **Elkhead Pass** (marked by a cairn but no signs) is reached around 1½ hours from tree line, and allows a spectacular view into Missouri Basin to the south.

Turn left (east) at the pass and follow small cairns up the sweeping southwest shoulder of Mt Belford. The trail is indistinct at first, but soon consolidates and becomes more obvious. The summit ridge is attained from the south, where a side trail leads off east across a steep saddle to Mt Oxford. Continue along the ridge to find the summit of **Mt Belford**, set in a jagged ridge of orange rock, 3½ hours from the trailhead.

The steep, loose descent heads northwest down switchbacks to the valley floor. Short flights of rock steps have been formed in places to ease the passage down the delicate terrain. The trail joins the ascent route in the valley floor, where a right turn will lead you back through the trees to the trailhead.

Brown's Pass

Duration	5–7 hours
Distance	8mi (12.9km)
Standard	moderate
Start/Finish	Denny Creek Trailhead
Nearest Town	Buena Vista
Transport	car

Summary A pleasant and straightforward ascent to a pass with surprising views into the heart of Collegiate Peaks Wilderness.

During summer, Brown's Pass is a riot of color with the glorious alpine sunflowers especially prominent. The trail leading to the pass from Denny Creek Trailhead is well maintained and not overly strenuous, offering a variety of views and terrain. The pass itself is an important portal to some of the more remote areas in Collegiate Peaks Wilderness, and the route described here could easily be used as a starting point for an extended backpacking trip into the Texas Creek valley and beyond. However, the view from the pass will be enough for many and the scenic Hartenstein Lake can be added as a side trip for good measure.

PLANNING
When to Hike
This route should be free of snow by late June.

Maps
Use the Trails Illustrated 1:40,680 map No 129 *Buena Vista Collegiate Peaks*.

NEAREST TOWN
See Buena Vista (p261).

GETTING TO/FROM THE HIKE
Denny Creek Trailhead is 12mi west of Buena Vista on Hwy 306 and 1mi west of the Collegiate Peaks campground. See Getting Around (p260) for hiker shuttle details.

THE HIKE
Leave Denny Creek Trailhead along a series of steep switchbacks. The trail then flattens out and climbs gently to a log bridge crossing Denny Creek about 20 minutes from the start. More steep ascent leads through pleasant pine forest, passing the Mt Yale Trail (see Other Hikes, p267), continuing up to a rocky clearing with groves of young aspen and good views of Turner Peak. Shortly after, and about halfway to Brown's Pass, the junction with the Hartenstein Trail is reached (see Side Trip, p267).

Continue past the junction and cross North Fork via a log bridge, climbing through thick pine forest. Just below tree line the trail steepens through a couple of switchbacks, and then emerges onto open slopes about 0.5mi from Brown's Pass. Climb to the **pass**, where superb views north across the Texas Creek valley to the Three Apostles and Emerald Peak are revealed. To the northwest the remains of Brown's Cabin are

Brown's Pass

To Texas Creek Trail
Kroenke Lake
Kroepke Lake
COLLEGIATE
Brown's Cabin
Brown's Pass
▲(12,955ft)
(12,524ft)▲
North Fork
Brown's Pass Trail
PEAKS
Mt Yale (14,196ft)
(12,956ft) Side Trip
Hartenstein Trail
Denny
Hartenstein Lake
Denny Gulch
Turner Peak (13,233ft) ▲
▲(12,739ft)
WILDERNESS
START/FINISH
Denny Creek Trailhead
To Buena Vista
306
Collegiate Peaks

0   1   2km
0   0.5   1mi
1:120,000
Contour Interval 200ft

visible. Although it was once used as a shelter, the cabin is now in a poor state of repair and not suitable for human use.

Retrace your steps to the trailhead.

Side Trip: Hartenstein Lake
45 minutes–1½ hours, 2mi, 400ft ascent
Hartenstein Lake is hidden beneath Turner Peak and is a pleasant, scenic side trip if you want to lengthen your hike. Cross North Fork on logs or rocks and climb through trees onto an open shoulder. Climb steadily along this and then drop steeply down into the trees, to emerge at the shores of **Hartenstein Lake** beneath Turner Peak. This lake and the wetlands surrounding it are a valuable habitat for the rare boreal toad, which you are unlikely to see. Return along the approach route to rejoin Brown's Pass Trail.

Other Hikes

MAROON BELLS–SNOWMASS WILDERNESS
Cathedral Lake & Electric Pass
This route passes one of the prettiest alpine lakes in the Maroon Bells–Snowmass Wilderness on its way to the highest pass in Colorado (13,500ft). The

trip to Cathedral Lake (see map, p259) is very popular, so avoid hiking over weekends and holiday periods. Water is limited, so make sure you carry plenty, and avoid the pass during thunderstorms (it is called Electric Pass for a reason!).

The 11mi out-and-back trip from Cathedral Lake Trailhead to the pass involves 3600ft of ascent (6.4mi and 1980ft ascent to Cathedral Lake only). Use Trails Illustrated's waterproof 1:40,680 map No 127 *Aspen Independence Pass*.

SAWATCH RANGE
Mount of the Holy Cross
At 14,005ft, this peak is renowned not for its height but for the myths that surround the towering snow cross that adorns its northeast face. The 10mi out-and-back trip to this relatively isolated summit entails a total ascent of 5500ft, so this is a strenuous hike and not for the unfit.

From Half Moon campsite there is a 2mi climb to Half Moon Pass, and a 900ft descent to East Cross Creek (where permits are needed for camping), before the final climb along the mountain's broad north ridge to the summit.

Allow one to two days for this hike and use the Trails Illustrated 1:40,680 map No 126 *Holy Cross Reudi Reservoir*, or the USGS 1:24,000 quad *Mt of the Holy Cross*.

Mt Massive
The second highest peak in the Rockies, Mt Massive stands at 14,421ft. It is the mountain's bulk that gives it its name – the massif boasts a 3mi summit crest encompassing five main summits above 14,000ft. The trailhead is the same as that used for Mt Elbert (p263), but the route begins by heading north along the Colorado Trail. After 3mi the Mt Massive trail turns left and begins the steep climb up to the saddle between the main summit and South Massive, where a series of small rocky steps leads north to the true summit.

The 12.8mi hike involves 4300ft of ascent and should take eight hours. Use the Trails Illustrated 1:40,680 map No 127 *Aspen Independence Pass* or the the USGS 1:24,000 quad *Mt Massive*.

Mt Yale
The summit of Mt Yale (14,196ft) can be reached in a 7mi out-and-back trip from the Denny Creek Trailhead (*not* Denny Gulch, which is just east). The route makes a winding ascent of around 4300ft via Yale's southwest slopes (see the Brown's Pass hike, p266, for a description of the initial stages).

Use the Trails Illustrated 1:40,680 map No 129 *Buena Vista Collegiate Peaks* or the USGS 1:24,000 quad *Mount Yale*.

Southern Colorado

The Rockies of southern Colorado are dominated by two unique and contrasting ranges. In the southwest of the state are the San Juan Mountains, a collective term for the vast swathe of jagged summits and sweeping ridges that straddle the Continental Divide. The San Juans command the devoted attention even of many northern Coloradans. Well to the east, the Sangre de Cristo Mountains stretch along a high narrow spine with seven 14er (14,000ft) peaks. These two ranges are separated by the broad San Luis Valley, the largest and widest valley at such a height (averaging almost 8000ft) anywhere in the world. With its many superb wilderness areas, abundant wildlife and an intricate system of backcountry trails, the southern Colorado area offers one of the Rockies' truly great hiking experiences.

CLIMATE

Most of southern Colorado's mountain ranges are far enough west to receive plenty of precipitation delivered by winds from the Pacific Ocean in winter, and far enough south to intercept tropical air masses moving north from the Gulf of California in summer. With

---

Warnings

- Heavy cloud build-up above the high ranges, especially in July and August, almost guarantees daily thunderstorms and lightning – something to be aware of on high-level routes along the Continental Divide.

- Many of the hikes in southern Colorado involve driving from a relatively low valley base to a much higher trailhead, then climbing on foot to a peak or high ridge – a total ascent of perhaps 5000ft on the one day. While well-acclimated hikers (generally locals) may hardly notice the ill effects of this elevation gain, most will find the going rather more difficult and some may even experience symptoms of altitude sickness. See Altitude (p66) for more details on the causes and prevention of altitude sickness.

Highlights

CLEM LINDENMAYER

Abandoned mine workings are still evident at Kite Lake in the Needle Mountains.

- Inspecting historic mine workings below towering 14,000ft peaks in the Needle Mountains (p275)

- Lying in a natural thermal tub beside a rushing stream at Rainbow Hot Springs (p279)

- Identifying alpine wildflowers around spectacular Phantom Terrace on the Comanche-Venable Loop (p282)

- Surveying the vast, flat floor of the San Luis Valley from the summit of beautiful Blanca Peak (p285)

---

winter snowfalls that can exceed 200 inches on upper slopes, southern Colorado attracts countless (backcountry) skiers until late spring – shaded ridges and high passes sometimes don't even melt out until late July.

Despite high elevations, midsummer temperatures well above 90°F are common in the valleys (especially the semiarid San Luis Valley) but low humidity levels tend to

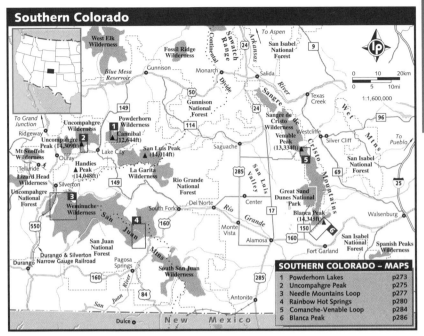

Southern Colorado

SOUTHERN COLORADO – MAPS	
1 Powderhorn Lakes	p273
2 Uncompahgre Peak	p275
3 Needle Mountains Loop	p277
4 Rainbow Hot Springs	p280
5 Comanche-Venable Loop	p284
6 Blanca Peak	p286

make the heat more bearable. Moving a few thousand feet higher generally brings cooler relief – above 10,000ft midsummer temperatures never go much above 70°F and night frosts are common.

INFORMATION
Maps & Books
The GTR Mapping 1:800,000 *Recreational Map of Colorado* ($3.95) is useful for a general overview of the state.

Dawson's Guide to Colorado's Fourteeners, Volume 2 by Louis Dawson II ($19.95) is tailored to peak-baggers in the south of the state. *The Complete Guide to Colorado's Wilderness Areas* by John Fielder & Mark Pearson ($24.95) and Altitude Guide's *Best Hikes in Colorado* by Christina Williams ($29.95) include selected routes in southern Colorado. *Colorado's Continental Divide Trail* ($24.95) by Tom Lorang Jones includes, arguably, the trail's wildest section through the San Juan Mountains.

Information Sources
Online information on Colorado can be found at W www.colorado.com (tourism) or W www.colorado.gov (general). Also check W www.hikingincolorado.org and the Bureau of Land Management's (BLM) state website at W www.co.blm.gov.

GATEWAYS
Durango
A major outdoor recreation center at the southwestern edge of the San Juan Mountains, Durango (population 15,000) is on the intersection of US 160 and US 550, roughly 60mi west of Pagosa Springs. For information contact the visitor center (☎ 970-247-0312, W www.durango.org, 111 S Camino del Rio). The San Juan Public Lands Center (☎ 970-247-4874, 15 Burnett Court) gives advice, as well as selling books and forest maps (but not USGS quads). Backcountry Experience (☎ 970-247-5830 e fungear@ bcexp.com, 1205 Camino del Rio) has a good

range of gear and quads. In the same building is Southwest Adventures (☎ 970-259-0370, 800-642-5389, W www.mtnguide.net), which operates hiker shuttles.

Places to Stay & Eat Several nearby US Forest Service (USFS) campgrounds, *Junction Creek*, a few miles west of town, *Purgatory*, on US 550 opposite the Purgatory Ski Area turnoff, and *Sig Creek*, on Forest Rd (FR) 578 about 7mi west of the ski area, have basic sites for around $10. *Durango East KOA (☎ 970-247-0783)*, 5mi east of town on US 160, charges $20. *Durango Hostel (☎ 970-247-9905, 543 E 2nd Ave)* has dorm beds for $13/15 members/nonmembers. *End O' Day Motel (☎ 970-247-1722, 350 E 8th Ave)* offers singles/doubles for $34/42. *Silver Spur Motel (☎ 970-247-5552, 800-748-1715, 3416 Main Ave)* charges $65/85. *Nature's Oasis (☎ 970-247-1988, 1123 Camino del Rio)* has natural and bulk foods ideal for backpacking.

Getting There & Away The historic Durango & Silverton Narrow Gauge Railroad (D&SNGRR; see Getting to/from the Hike, p276) runs to Silverton. Greyhound/TNM&O (☎ 970-259-2755) runs daily buses to Grand Junction and Albuquerque. There are daily flights to Denver, Phoenix and Albuquerque.

Pueblo
Pueblo (population 104,000) is 112mi south of Denver at the I-25/US 50 intersection. For information contact the chamber of commerce (☎ 719-542-1704, 800-233-3446, W www.pueblo.org, 302 N Santa Fe Ave) or the USFS office (☎ 719-545-8737, 1920 Valley Dr).

Places to Stay *Lake Pueblo State Park (☎ 719-561-9320)*, at the Northern Plains park north of Hwy 96 (13mi west of I-25 exit 101), has tent/RV sites for $6/14 (plus $4 daily admission). The cheerless *Travelers Motel (☎ 719-543-5451, 1012 N Santa Fe Ave)* has singles/doubles for $31/36. The *Rambler Motel (☎ 719-543-4173, 4400 N Elizabeth St)* and *USA Motel (☎ 719-542-3268, 414 W 29th St)* charge around $45/50.

Getting There & Away Greyhound/TNM&O buses (☎ 719-543-2775) between Denver and New Mexico and Texas stop frequently in Pueblo. United Express has daily flights to Denver and Alamosa.

San Juan Mountains

Formed by a 50mi-wide arc of high ranges that extend more than 100mi southeast from Mt Sneffels to Cumbres Pass, the San Juan Mountains have long been called the 'Alps of America'. The San Juans lie mostly inside San Juan National Forest, although the Gunnison, Uncompahgre and Rio Grande National Forests, as well as BLM lands, account for sizeable areas. The enormous 770-sq-mile Weminuche Wilderness fills the wild heart of the San Juans, but six smaller wildernesses – Lizard Head, Mt Sneffels, Uncompahgre, Powderhorn, La Garita and South San Juan – surround the Weminuche (pronounced **wem**-a-nooch).

The San Juans are the most consistently high mountain chain in the Lower 48, with more than a dozen 14er summits scattered through their (western and northern) ranges, as well as hundreds of peaks that break the 13,000ft barrier. These mountains are characterized by a diverse topography ranging from extensive highland plateaus, profoundly deep valleys and abrupt, faulted peaks with massive rock walls – summits sometimes rise 1mi above the valley floor.

Arguably the most scenic section of the entire Continental Divide Trail follows the divide's erratic, winding course through the center of the San Juans. Other trails take you across tundra wildflower meadows or to secluded hot springs. While the high elevation and remoteness of some backcountry routes require better physical condition and backcountry skills, the San Juans also offer a wide assortment of hikes for beginners.

HISTORY
The ancient Puebloans, or Anasazi people, inhabited the canyons, valleys and mesas at

the western and southern fringe of the San Juans, at times journeying into the mountains to hunt, cut wood or bathe in the hot springs. The Anasazi moved away sometime around AD 1200 but several centuries later the Ute people (recent adopters of a horse-based culture) began arriving from the northwest. Several Ute tribes, the Capote, Tabeguache and Weminuche, became established in the San Juan Mountains region.

The first Spanish settlers arrived in the region in the second half of the 16th century, naming the San Juan (Saint John) Mountains and adding their – still widespread – nomenclature to land features. In the 1760s the Spaniard Juan Maria Antonio de Rivera, prospected for silver in the San Juans. In 1848 an expedition led by John C Fremont transited the mountains, but he almost perished (and a third of his party died) while trying to make a winter crossing of La Garita Range.

Anglo-American gold prospectors ventured into the San Juans in the early 1860s, but hostile Ute tribes resisted these white encroachers and a treaty in 1868 granted the San Juan Mountains to the Ute people. As miners continued to push into the mountains, however, the new Brunot Treaty of 1873 was negotiated, tricking the Ute people into ceding all of the San Juans to the US Government. Subsequent Ute attacks on federal troops led to the forced relocation of all remaining Ute people to a narrow strip of land in southwest Colorado.

The gold and (later) silver rushes brought thousands of prospectors into the San Juans and led to the founding of dozens of towns (few of which exist today). Narrow-gauge railroads were pushed deep into the mountains as far as Lake City, Ouray, Silverton and Telluride. The mining boom gradually declined and finally petered out in the 1930s.

In 1905 President Theodore Roosevelt created the first San Juan National Forest, which was enlarged to 2970 sq miles in 1947. In 1974 a long campaign by conservationists finally came to fruition with the establishment of the Weminuche Wilderness, still the largest wilderness in the southern Rockies.

NATURAL HISTORY

The San Juan Mountains began to form around 35 million years ago as lava flows laid down a 4000ft-thick shield. From around 27 million years ago, this shield was pushed up by 5000ft, tilting east as it faulted and folded. Relatively soon after the rock was overlaid with molten basalt. Today volcanic rocks strongly characterize the San Juans and enduring (minor) volcanic activity nourishes many thermal springs.

The San Juans' rich montane and subalpine forests contain lodgepole pine, Engelmann spruce and subalpine fir, along with the less common white fir and blue (Colorado) spruce. On high plateaus and ridge tops exposed to strong winds, spruce grows as low 'banner trees', with branches only on the leeward side. The San Juans are famous for their extensive tundra meadows, which in early summer produce garish displays of alpine sunflowers, avens, arnicas, forget-me-nots, paintbrush, saxifrage and countless other wildflowers.

Hikers may encounter gray jays flitting about the branches looking for morsels (like camp scraps). Two rodents endemic to the southern Rockies are Abert's squirrel, a gray, tuft-eared squirrel that builds large, round tree nests in coniferous forests, and Gunnison's prairie dog, which, more like a ground squirrel, inhabits mountain meadows. Bighorn sheep, elk, deer and mountain goats are often spotted in the San Juans, but the only large predators are the cougars (mountain lions) and black bears. Some locals maintain that shy grizzlies continue to roam the remote Weminuche country and conservationists hope the San Juan Mountains will one day again support a strong population of wolves.

PLANNING
Maps & Books

The Trails Illustrated metric 1:125,000 bike map No 504 *Durango Area/Southwest* ($9.95) covers most of the San Juan Mountains and shows the main hiking trails. The USFS 1:126,720 map *San Juan National Forest* ($6.50) provides a good overview of the San Juans.

Covering the whole region are *Hiking Trails of Southwestern Colorado* by Paul Pixler ($16.95) and *San Juan Adventure Guide* by Jeff La Frenierre ($25), which also includes biking and skiing routes. *A Backpacker's Guide to the Weminuche Wilderness* by Dennis Gebhardt ($12.95) and Falcon Guide's *Hiking Colorado's Weminuche Wilderness* by Donna Ikenberry ($14.95) cover routes in the San Juans' wild heart. Falcon's *Climbing Colorado's San Juan Mountains* by Robert Rosebrough ($14.95) has both walk-up and technical ascents of all the great San Juans summits.

Information Sources

San Juan Mountains Association (☎ 970-385-1210; [W] www.sanjuanmountainsassociation .org; San Juan Public Land Center, 15 Burnett Court, Durango) runs courses on wildlife, geology and history, as well as organizing hikes and llama treks in the San Juans. For general information on the region check the USFS and BLM websites at [W] www.fs.fed .us/r2/sanjuan and [W] www.co.blm.gov/sjra/ index.html.

Permits & Regulations

Permits are not required to hike or camp anywhere on public land in the San Juans. Camping is not permitted within at least 200ft (often 300ft) of lakes and streams in all wilderness areas. Campfires are prohibited in many popular areas, such as Chicago Basin in the Needle Mountains. At a few trailheads (eg, Yankee Boy Basin in Mt Sneffels Wilderness) vehicles must display a parking pass.

ACCESS TOWN
Pagosa Springs

Locally famous for its hot mineral springs, Pagosa Springs (population 1900) is at the intersection of US 84/160. For information contact the chamber of commerce (☎ 970-264-2360, [W] www.pagosaspringschamber .com), across the bridge from US 160, or the local USFS office (☎ 970-264-2268, cnr 2nd St & Pagosa St). Ski & Bowrack (354 E Pagosa St) has a range of backpacking equipment, and sells regional quads and hiking maps.

The *San Juan Motel & RV Park* (☎ 970-264-2262, 191 E Pagosa St) offers singles/ doubles from $48/55, cabins for $65 and camping for $15/25 per tent/RV site.

Pagosa Rafting Outfitters (☎ 970-731-8060, [W] websites.pagosa.net/pagosarafting) operates shuttles from Pagosa Springs to Durango airport ($87, up to four people) and can shuttle hikers to trailheads.

Powderhorn Lakes

Duration	3¾–5¼ hours
Distance	8.8mi (14.2km)
Standard	easy
Start/Finish	Terminus of Indian Creek Rd (CR 58)
Nearest Towns	Gunnison, Lake City
Transport	car
Summary	A short hike to a remarkable lake basin under a basalt plateau.

The Powderhorn Lakes are the main attraction of the 96-sq-mile Powderhorn Wilderness, which is situated northeast of Lake City. Designated only in 1993, most of the wilderness (including the Powderhorn Lakes) lies on BLM land, although the area's southern section is part of the Gunnison National Forest.

The hike follows a straightforward route with a total ascent of less than 900ft. The round-trip can be done comfortably in a single day, but many visitors camp at the Powderhorn Lakes to better enjoy and explore the area. A popular side trip goes up to the Cannibal – a minor outcrop that was named after the exploits of the notorious Alferd Packer. Not far from the outcrop he murdered and ate five companions during a desperate winter journey in 1874.

PLANNING
Maps

USGS' 1:24,000 quad, *Powderhorn Lakes*, covers the hike but does not accurately show the main access trail. The side trip to the Cannibal is on the adjoining *Cannibal Plateau* map.

NEAREST TOWNS

Gunnison

Gunnison (population 5000) is on US 50, 65mi east of Montrose and 34mi west of Monarch Pass. For information contact the visitor center (☎ 970-641-1501, W www .gunnison-co.com, 500 E Tomichi Ave) or the USFS office (☎ 970-641-0471, 216 N Colorado Ave). Rock n' Roll Sports (☎ 970-641-9150, 608 W Tomichi Ave) sells outdoor gear and maps.

The *Cattleman Inn* *(☎ 970-641-1061, 301 W Tomichi Ave)* has singles/doubles for $32/39 but ring ahead. The *Hylander Inn* *(☎ 970-641-0700, 412 E Tomichi Ave)* offers better rooms for $62/68.

TNM&O buses connecting Pueblo with Grand Junction stop at the Gunnison County airport terminal (☎ 970-641-0060, 711 Rio Grande Ave).

Lake City

The tiny, remote town of Lake City (population 380) lies on Hwy 149, about 50mi north of Creede (or 47mi south of the US 50 intersection), amid 14ers that include the Uncompahgre Peak 10mi to the northwest. The chamber of commerce (☎ 970-944-2527, W www.lakecityco.com, 800 N Gunnison Ave) also acts as the USFS and BLM visitor center; it offers free trail information but sells only USFS maps. The Sportsman (☎ 970-944-2526, W www.lakecitysportsman.com, 238 S Gunnison Ave) sells backpacking gear and USGS quads.

Lake City Campground (☎ 970-944-2920, Bluff St) offers tent/RV sites for $12/15. The *Matterhorn Mountain Motel (☎ 970-944-2210, 409 Bluff St)* has singles/doubles for $38/48. The *Silver Spur Motel (☎ 970-944-2231, 800-499-9701, 301 Gunnison Ave)* offers rooms from $59.

GETTING TO/FROM THE HIKE

From its intersection with US 50, drive 20mi south on Hwy 149 and turn left along the Indian Creek Rd (County Road 58). Alternatively, drive 25mi north on Hwy 149 from Lake City and turn right. Follow the Indian Creek Rd south for about 10mi until it dead-ends at the trailhead parking area

(by an old clear-cut logging site); there is space here for around 15 cars but no water is available.

THE HIKE

Take Trail 3030 southwest for 0.5mi up through spruce forest to cross the wilderness boundary, where hikers should register their details in the logbook provided. The trail continues rising steadily for 1mi to a broad, grassy meadow (where elk and deer may be seen browsing), around 40 to 50 minutes from the trailhead. Skirt down along the edge of the clearing, then begin a long, undulating sidle south through the trees past two murky, reedy ponds to reach a trail junction in a little meadow at the entrance to the upper valley of the West Fork Powderhorn Creek, a further 45 minutes to one hour on. From here a little-used trail leads left down the creek to the elusive Hidden Lake.

Continue upvalley past large beaver dams below raw eroding ridges on your left. The trail rises 0.5mi to the pleasant **lower Powderhorn Lake**, heading around past *campsites* on its northern shore before it climbs over forested moraine and negotiates a soggy clearing to arrive at the **upper Powderhorn**

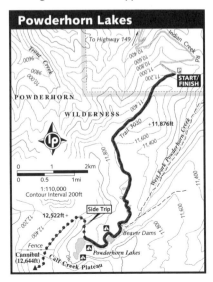

Lake, 40 to 50 minutes from the trail junction. This unique alpine tarn lies inside a horseshoe-shaped cirque rimmed by a high, flat-topped escarpment that falls away in cliffs and rubbly scree slides. The upper lake offers good trout fishing and wonderful *camping* among the open stands of spruce on its eastern shore.

Return to the trailhead via the same route (1¾ to 2½ hours)

Side Trip: Calf Creek Plateau & the Cannibal

2½–3 hours, 3.6mi, 785ft ascent

This interesting, moderate route takes you up to **Calf Creek Plateau**, part of the largest expanse of alpine tundra in the Lower 48 states. There is no water on this porous, volcanic tableland, so carry something to drink. Watch for thunderstorms and lightning in the afternoon.

From the upper Powderhorn Lake follow obvious livestock pads up the steep grassy slopes onto the plateau and continue left around the escarpment rim. After climbing over a wire stock fence you head southwest across the bleak basalt to the **Cannibal** (12,644ft), a vague 'summit' marked by a mast-like cross fixed by wires. The whole plateau offers a virtual 360-degree panorama of the surrounding Elk, Sawatch and San Juan Mountains, including (west-southwest) the mighty east face of Uncompahgre Peak. Return via your ascent route.

Uncompahgre Peak

Duration	4½–6½ hours
Distance	8.8mi (14.2km)
Standard	hard
Start/Finish	Uncompahgre Peak Trailhead
Nearest Town	Lake City
Transport	car
Summary	An ascent of the most outstanding lookout summit in the San Juan Mountains.

With its striking slanted form, Uncompahgre Peak (14,309ft) is the highest point in the San Juan Mountains. The hike is quite strenuous,

involving an ascent of around 2800ft, but follows a nontechnical route from a very high trailhead (around 11,200ft). Being reachable in a not-too-lengthy day, Uncompahgre Peak is popular among casual ramblers and dedicated peak-baggers alike. The climb leads through some glorious alpine terrain and is recommended to all fit, acclimated hikers.

PLANNING
Maps

One USGS 1:24,000 quad, *Uncompahgre Peak*, covers the route. Otherwise use Trails Illustrated's 1:66,667 map No 141 *Silverton, Ouray, Telluride, Lake City*.

NEAREST TOWN & FACILITIES

See Lake City (p273).

Slumgullion USFS Campground

This basic *campground*, 9mi southwest of Lake City below Slumgullion Pass, has sites for $9.

GETTING TO/FROM THE HIKE

From Lake City turn off Gunnison Ave (Hwy 149) along 2nd St (signposted 'Engineer Pass') and go left after just 150ft (at the bluff face). Continue for 5.6mi on Henson Creek Rd before you turn right (north) along the rough narrow Nellie Creek Rd (FR 877). This climbs steadily, fording and refording the creek to reach the Uncompahgre Peak Trailhead after 4mi; there is space for around 15 cars here. Drivers of non-4WD vehicles should park along the lower Nellie Creek and hike from there – which increases the ascent by 2000ft and adds three to four hours round-trip. There is limited parking space along a short turnoff between the two fords on Nellie Creek Rd.

> ### Warning
>
> Intense electrical thunderstorms occur on Uncompahgre Peak almost daily (from around noon) throughout the summer, bringing a real danger of lightning strike. Try to get an early start, and be prepared to retreat if the weather looks like turning bad.

THE HIKE

Sign the trailhead register and take Trail 239 directly into the wilderness through meadows of bluebells and yellow groundsels among stands of spruce. The trail follows the northeast side of tiny Nellie Creek for 1mi, rising out of the forest – there are scenic *campsites* on the creek's opposite bank, where tree line is higher – to give a clear view of the east face of Uncompahgre Peak ahead. Climb away from the stream to join Trail 233 (entering from the right) on lovely grassy meadows dotted with purple fringe (scorpionweed), white mountain avens and alpine sunflowers. Trail 233/239 rises opposite a fin-like ridge with eroding red talus slopes, sweeping around southwest into the rolling tundra bowl at the valley head to where Trail 233 diverges left (southwest), one to 1½ hours from the trailhead.

Double back right (northwest), traversing and switchbacking your way up the right side of Uncompahgre's southeast ridge to reach a minor saddle at around 13,800ft. (It may be necessary to skirt right to avoid a snow cornice early in the season.) Move 50yd left to avoid crags above the saddle, then cut up right through a steep gully of loose scree (your return descent through this section will require some care) back onto the ridge top. The trail ascends steadily through wheezy thin air, crossing the broad summit plateau to arrive at the highest point of **Uncompahgre Peak**, 1½ to two hours after leaving the upper Trail 233/239 junction.

This tilted stony platform drops away abruptly on its eastern side and offers a full panorama spreading in all directions across southwestern Colorado. Other San Juan 14ers are visible – including nearby Wetterhorn Peak (14,015ft), somewhat south of due west, Handies Peak (14,048ft) to the southwest, Redcloud Peak (14,034ft) to the south and San Luis Peak (14,014ft), slightly south of due east – but none is quite as high (or as majestic) as where you are standing.

The hike back to the trailhead car park takes two to three hours.

Needle Mountains Loop

Duration	4 days
Distance	35.2mi (56.7km)
Standard	moderate–hard
Start	Needleton
Finish	Elk Park
Nearest Towns	Durango, Silverton
Transport	train
Summary	A classic adventure through the majestic ranges of the western Weminuche Wilderness.

With the highest summits in the Weminuche Wilderness – including several 14ers – the Needle Mountains are a compact massif fronting the canyon of the Animas River at the western edge of the Weminuche. The Needles are composed of six jagged, lateral ranges separated by deep, narrow side valleys. Crossing several passes well above 12,000ft and following sections of the Continental Divide Trail and the Colorado Trail, the loop (the circuit is completed with a train ride out) leads through a wonderfully scenic and constantly changing alpine landscape. In the late 19th to the early 20th centuries, hives of prospectors swarmed through the

Uncompahgre Peak

Needles, and the route repeatedly passes traces of old mine workings.

PLANNING
When to Hike
The high passes are likely to be snowed over before July and after mid-October. Watch the sky for brewing thunderstorms, which can bring heavy rain and lightning that may endanger hikers on high exposed ridges.

Maps
Recommended are either Trails Illustrated's 1:66,667 map No 140 *Weminuche Wilderness* or Drake Mountain Maps' 1:60,000 *Mountains between Silverton and Durango*. For greater detail use four USGS 1:24,000 quads: *Snowdon Peak*, *Storm King Peak*, *Mountain View Crest* and *Columbine Pass*.

NEAREST TOWNS & FACILITIES
See Durango (p269).

Silverton
The historic mining town of Silverton (population 400) stands among eroding orange-red ranges on US 550, at the northern terminus of the Durango & Silverton Narrow Gauge Railroad (D&SNGRR; see Getting to/from the Hike). For information try the visitor center (☎ 970-387-5654, W www.silverton.org, cnr Greene St & US 550).

The **Silverton Hostel** *(☎ 970-387-0115, 1025 Blair St)* offers dorm beds for $10/12 members/nonmembers and private rooms for $24/28. **Triangle Motel** *(☎ 970-387-5780, 848 Greene St)* has singles/doubles for $50/60.

South Mineral USFS Campground
This basic *campground*, accessible via FR 585 (off US 550, 2mi west of Silverton) has sites for $10.

GETTING TO/FROM THE HIKE
The D&SNGRR provides access to this hike. Its beautifully restored steam locomotives run between Durango and Silverton via Needleton (8212ft) and Elk Park (8870ft) – 15mi and 8mi south of Silverton respectively

– two water stops along the Animas River. Trains run from early May to late October, and round-trip fares (all stops) from Durango or Silverton are $30/60 children (under 12)/adults in peak season (mid-June to mid-August), or $27/55 off-peak. In the peak season four trains depart daily from Durango between 7:30 and 9:45am. The trip from Durango to Needleton takes a little over 2½ hours and is very scenic and enjoyable.

Tickets can be purchased by phone, online (at least one week beforehand) or in person from the D&SNGRR (☎ 970-247-2733, 888-872-4607; W www.durangotrain.com; 479 Main Ave, Durango), or at the Silverton Depot (☎ 970-387-5416). As the trains are extremely popular, it's advisable to book early (especially in July and August). When buying your ticket advise railroad staff of your intended jumping-off/on points.

THE HIKE
Day 1: Needleton to Chicago Basin
2¾–3½ hours, 6.3mi, 2963ft ascent
The train drops you off at the Needleton water stop on the west bank of the Animas River. Cross the river on a long suspension footbridge and walk 0.7mi south (downvalley) to take the Needle Creek Trail (No 504) left. The trail climbs steadily southeast along the narrow forested drainage of the small Needle Creek, passing *campsites* (on the leveled site of a long gone prospector's hut) just before it crosses **New York Creek**, one to 1¼ hours from Needleton.

Continue up over avalanche chutes opposite ravines coming off the steep, rugged slopes to the south. The valley gradually broadens as you rise past Mt Kennedy and Aztec Mountain through beautiful subalpine meadows. Continue over grassy lawns dotted with blue gentians and fringed by stands of spruce to reach a cairned turnoff (left) to Twin Lakes Basin (see Side Trip, p277) in the **Chicago Basin**, 1¾ to 2¼ hours from New York Creek. Many hikers spend an extra day or more exploring this beautiful location. A herd of (salt-addicted – see Dangers and Annoyances, p57) mountain goats hangs around the Chicago Basin in summer.

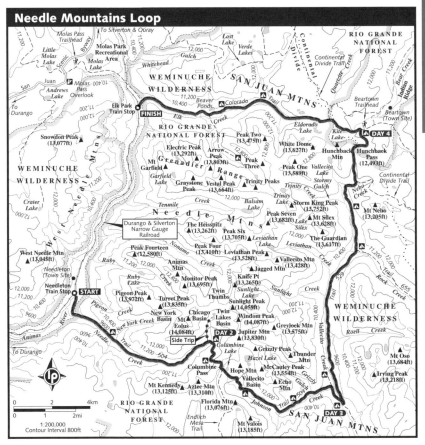

Needle Mountains Loop

Scenic **campsites** can be found back from the creek throughout the upper valley, which is enclosed by the towering trio of Mt Eolus (14,084ft), Sunlight Peak (14,059ft) and Windom Peak (14,087ft). Hikers must give maximum attention to minimizing their impact in this heavily visited area – don't light campfires and bury your feces thoughtfully.

Side Trip: Twin Lakes Basin
1¾–2¼ hours, 1.7mi, 1375ft ascent
Twin Lakes Basin is a small cirque (around 12,550ft), with two lovely tarns, perched high above Chicago Basin. It can be reached by

taking the social trail (left) steeply up beside the tumbling northern branch of the Needle Creek. Rougher routes go up in several directions to the surrounding 14er summits, which present no technical difficulties but require a good level of acclimation and fitness. Camping is not allowed at Twin Lakes Basin.

Day 2: Chicago Basin to Johnson Creek/Vallecito Trail Junction
4–5¼ hours, 8mi, 1540ft ascent
Head on (right) from the Twin Lakes Basin turnoff, jumping the tiny upper branches of Needle Creek before you begin a winding,

upward sidle southward past abandoned mines and a ruined log cabin to cross above a red eroding gully. The trail rises on steadily past *campsites* among stout old spruce, switchbacking up through coarse rubble to reach **Columbine Pass** (12,715ft), 1¼ to 1¾ hours from Chicago Basin. This rocky gap offers a fine view ahead to the row of neat peaks fronting the southern side of Johnson Creek, as well as back toward the Needle Mountains.

Cut down left, directly past the Endlich Mesa Trail (leading south over Trimble Pass), to **Columbine Lake**, an emerald-green tarn in a sparse, glacier-smoothed basin. Ignoring a social trail going left around the west shore, follow Trail 504 (now called the Johnson Creek Trail) down across the deeply eroded outlet, then spiral down past the first *campsites* in the Vallecito Basin, 45 minutes to one hour from the pass.

The Johnson Creek Trail continues down through fir-spruce forest and occasional meadows sprinkled with columbines and paintbrush along the north bank of Johnson Creek. Further on the creek plummets through a canyon (where a bizarre 50ft pinnacle juts out of the water). Proceed more gently down past *campsites* under the imposing red crags of Amherst Mountain (13,165ft) and Organ Mountain (13,032ft), whose 2500ft north walls are dissected by long deep couloirs (snow gullies) and natural cavities that – this being the San Juans – strangely resemble mine shafts bored into the cliff face.

The trail leads down across the small Grizzly Gulch and through aspen groves before coming out into the long valley of Vallecito Creek. A left turnoff here (marked by an 'F' on an aspen trunk) goes 500yd up-valley to some lovely *campsites* on grassy stream flats. Head downvalley (south) between mossy lawns along the creek's west bank, quickly fording Johnson Creek (or using an improvised log bridge). The Johnson Creek Trail passes more attractive *campsites* before it crosses Vallecito Creek on a sturdy footbridge to intersect with the Vallecito Trail (No 529), two to 2½ hours from Vallecito Basin.

Day 3: Johnson Creek/ Vallecito Trail Junction to Beartown Trailhead

5–6½ hours, 11.2mi, 3293ft ascent

Follow the more heavily used Vallecito Trail north along the east side of the creek, rising at a steady but comfortable gradient through mixed forest and meadows in the long, almost straight valley to make an easy ford of Roell Creek. The trail passes the prominent summits of Vallecito Mountain (13,428ft) and the Guardian (13,617ft), fronting the interesting side valleys of Sunlight Creek and Leviathan Creek (accessible via rough social trails leading off left). Cross the reddish **Rock Creek** on stepping stones just before passing the Trail 655 turnoff (going right to Rock Lake), 2¼ to 2¾ hours (6mi) from the Vallecito Creek footbridge. Very pleasant *campsites* can be found on stream flats down to the left.

Continue gently up across two unnamed side streams past *campsites* on grassy meadows opposite Stormy Gulch, a remarkable side valley dominated by Mt Silex (13,628ft) and Storm King Peak (13,752ft). The trail steepens to ford the cascading **Nebo Creek**, which it follows up northeast in switchbacks through spruce forest carpeted with shin-high whortleberry heath, crossing a side stream and climbing to meet the **Continental Divide Trail** (CDT).

Follow the CDT left out of the trees, refording the side stream as you head up north into the tiny upper valley covered in shrub willow. Cut across the stream near the valley head then ascend via a shale embankment onto tundra slopes that lead up to **Hunchback Pass** (12,493ft), 2¼ to three hours (4.6mi) from Rock Creek. These open tops on the Continental Divide give good views of the Needle Mountains to the southwest as well as the lower ranges around upper Bear Creek.

The trail exits the Weminuche Wilderness as it skirts 0.6mi down left above a grassy basin and past old mine shafts to reach a narrow 4WD road (FR 506) at Beartown Trailhead, about 30 to 40 minutes on. This serene valley head offers sheltered *camping* in a stand of spruces at tree line beside the trailhead register.

Day 4: Beartown Trailhead to Elk Park

4½–6 hours, 9.7mi, 1080ft ascent

Leave the CDT and follow the increasingly rough road 0.5mi up west almost to **Kite Lake**, with an old hut and disused mine on its shore. About 100yd before this forlorn little tarn, break away right (northwest) on an unsignposted trail leading up into a false saddle, then ascend rightward along a vague spur to meet the Continental Divide again. This sparse talus ridge (12,825ft) overlooks Eldorado Lake, nestled in an enchanting grassy bowl under the 13,627ft White Dome, and offers marvelous vistas toward high 13er peaks beyond Silverton. Walk 0.4mi right (north) along the ridge top to intersect with the **Colorado Trail** down in a grassy saddle (12,650ft), one to 1½ hours from Beartown Trailhead.

Here take the Colorado Trail down left (west) – its northbound branch continues 0.4mi along the ridge to intersect with the CDT – back into Weminuche Wilderness. The trail drops in numerous tight switch-backs over alpine slopes ablaze with wild-flowers along the north side of Elk Creek. Descend past more traces of old mine work-ings into a narrow gorge with impressive overhanging cliffs, before beginning a winding traverse into the subalpine forest opposite waterfall streams coming off the northern rim of Grenadier Range.

After crossing a larger side stream, pro-ceed through a cool, quiet spruce forest into a long flat meadow offering many excellent *campsites*. The Colorado Trail picks its way through a boulder field, from where views develop south to the sensational slab-sided summits of Electric Peak (13,292ft), Arrow Peak (13,803ft) and Vestal Peak (13,664ft), to reach more scenic *campsites* by clear, mossy beaver ponds, two to 2½ hours (5mi) from the trail junction on the Continental Divide. From here a social trail leads south across Elk Creek into the deep sided valley to a climbers' *base camp* (11,400ft) below these summits (three hours, 3.5mi round-trip).

Continue west on the main trail, mostly well above the valley but in places dropping to the rushing creek, to exit the wilderness at the very foot of the valley. (There is a trail register on the boundary.) About 150yd on leave the Colorado Trail (which contin-ues northwest to Molas Pass Trailhead on US 550) and cut down left across meadows to arrive at **Elk Park**, 1½ to two hours (3.3mi) from the beaver ponds. If you miss the last train, make a *camp* well back from the Animas River.

Rainbow Hot Springs

Duration	2 days
Distance	8.6mi (13.8km)
Standard	easy–moderate
Start/Finish	West Fork (San Juan River) Trailhead
Nearest Town	Pagosa Springs
Transport	car

Summary An invigorating hike to undeveloped thermal pools.

Rainbow Hot Springs (also known as West Fork Hot Springs) lie near the headwaters of the San Juan River in the eastern Weminuche Wilderness. They are a popular destination for day hikers and can become crowded. Backpackers often camp by the springs, al-lowing them to take a more leisurely evening bath. The route follows the small West Fork San Juan River, which offers good trout fish-ing. The first section of the hike passes through Borns Lake Ranch, where hikers should respect private property.

PLANNING
When to Hike

This low-level route can normally be hiked from late May until late October. Rainbow Hot Springs are particularly heavily visited on weekends in July and August – for greater enjoyment do the hike midweek out of season.

Maps

Use either two USGS 1:24,000 quads, *Sad-dle Mountain* and *South River Peak*, or Trails Illustrated's 1:66,667 map No 140 *Weminuche Wilderness*.

NEAREST TOWN & FACILITIES
See Pagosa Springs (p272).

Near the Trailhead
The **Bruce Spruce Ranch** (☎ *970-264-5374*, **W** *www.brucespruceranch.com*), along the West Fork Rd, has two-person cabins from $40 and tent/RV sites from $14.50/18. Further on are the basic **Wolf Creek** and **West Fork USFS campgrounds** (the latter 1mi before the trailhead) with sites for $8.

GETTING TO/FROM THE HIKE
Drive 15.2mi northeast from Pagosa Springs (or 8.7mi southwest from Wolf Creek Pass) on US 160, then turn left (right from Wolf Creek Pass) along West Fork Rd (FR 648). Proceed past Bruce Ranch and Wolf Creek USFS campground to a fork, then bear left past the West Fork USFS campground to the West Fork (San Juan River) Trailhead, 3mi from US 160; there is space for around 30 cars.

THE HIKE
Day 1: West Fork Trailhead to Rainbow Hot Springs
2½–3 hours, 4.3mi, 940ft ascent
Sign the trailhead register and head through a locked gate. The narrow road climbs 0.5mi through the property of Borns Lake Ranch to the (right) **Rainbow Trail** (No 561), just after a vacation house. (Note that there is no public access to Borns Lake itself, which hikers do not see.) Take the Rainbow Trail through Douglas and white firs along the west side of the **West Fork San Juan River**, which rushes through a canyon below overhanging bluffs. The trail enters the Weminuche Wilderness, crossing the churning **Burro Creek** before it descends past **campsites** to cross the small West Fork on a footbridge, 1¼ to 1½ hours from the trailhead.

Continue along the now gentler (east) bank of the wild river over the **Beaver Creek** footbridge, briefly following this side stream, before you climb away left (north) over low ridges back to the West Fork. The trail rises steadily past the (right) Beaver Creek Trail (No 560) to arrive at **campsites** among the open spruces above **Rainbow Hot Springs**

(9000ft), 1¼ to 1½ hours from the West Fork footbridge. The springs emerge from beside the stream – a slight down-climb is required to reach them – and flow into two tiny makeshift 'tubs' that are seldom unoccupied on midsummer days. Clothing is optional but soap and any other agents are not – please don't use them.

As the Rainbow Hot Springs area receives very heavy use, campers are requested to strictly observe Leave No Trace principles (p56) – pay special attention to proper disposal of bodily wastes. Fires are prohibited around the springs.

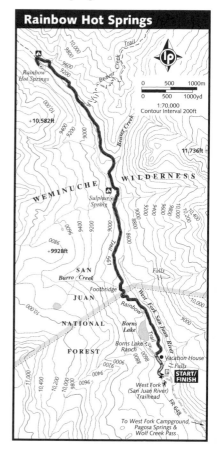

Day 2: Rainbow Hot Springs to West Fork Trailhead

2¼–2¾ hours, 4.3mi
Return to the trailhead as described on Day 1.

Sangre de Cristo Mountains

The Sangre de Cristo Mountains extend from just south of Salida to Santa Fe in New Mexico. They are often considered one of North America's longest continuous mountain ranges, although the Sangres of Colorado are actually linked to their New Mexico namesakes only by the short Culebra Range (south of La Veta Pass) and have a rather different character to the southern Sangre de Cristo Mountains (see the Northern New Mexico chapter, p288).

The Sangres run for 80mi in a slight bow-shape that divides the immense San Luis Valley from the Wet Mountains Valley to their east. The range is remarkable for its combination of great height and narrow width, with many valleys rising for little more than 6mi before they end at a cirque or high pass on the Sangres crest. Most of the Sangres lie within the 354-sq-mile Sangre de Cristo Wilderness, itself part of the Rio Grande and San Isabel National Forests.

The range contains nine 14,000ft peaks, arranged in two separate clusters. The Crestone group (Crestone Peak, Crestone Needle, Kit Carson Mountain, Challenger Point and Humboldt Peak), in the midsection of the range, are all technical climbs except for Humboldt Peak; the two Crestones are Colorado's most challenging 14ers. The Blanca group (Blanca Peak, Ellingwood Peak, Mt Lindsey and Little Bear Peak) are all accessible to (hardy) hikers willing to do some minor scrambling. The Sangres' almost 200mi of hiking trails lead to some extraordinary, yet accessible, scenery.

HISTORY

It is uncertain how these mountains acquired their name, although Sangre de Cristo (which means 'Blood of Christ' in Spanish) clearly originates from the early colonial period. When the Spaniards arrived in the late 16th century, Apache tribes had already occupied the Sangres and surrounding plains for centuries. From the 17th century the Ute people began migrating east into the region. They were later followed by the more warlike Comanche, whose eventual expulsion by the Spanish in 1779 left the Ute in possession of most of the northern Sangre de Cristo Mountains area.

From the 1820s isolated pockets of French, Anglo and Hispanic settlers moved into the region, sometimes grazing sheep in the Sangres' high valleys in summer. From the late 1860s gold and silver attracted a large number of prospectors into the adjacent Wet Mountains, although less ore was found in the Sangres. The following decades brought a major influx of settlers, including a young Englishman, Theodore Cockerell (later professor of botany at Boulder), who compiled the first natural history of the area.

From the 1880s foundries in nearby Pueblo stripped the Sangres' forests for furnace fodder, devastating the mountain ecology and causing appalling erosion in the valleys. In 1902 – just before the last grizzly bear was shot – the Sangres were finally made a forest reserve (renamed San Isabel National Forest in 1907). Decades of reforestation efforts – most notably by the Civilian Conservation Corps in the 1930s – and the reintroduction of locally exterminated wildlife gradually rehabilitated the Sangres' ecosystem. In 1993 Congress passed legislation establishing the Sangre de Cristo Wilderness.

NATURAL HISTORY

The Sangres have a unique and complex geological history, beginning with the formation of numerous low-angle thrust faults as the Rockies were compressed during the so-called Laramide deformation (around 65 million years ago). Faults either side of the range were reactivated from around 35 million years ago, uplifting the Sangres as a single massive block (known as a horst) and forcing down blocks (called grabens) on either side to create the San Luis and Wet Mountain Valleys.

The Sangres' lower slopes are covered in ponderosa pine, with gambel oak scrub or lodgepole pine forest interspersed with extensive aspen groves. The moister higher elevations support mainly Engelmann spruce and, along moist subalpine streams, pockets of white fir. Beautiful stands of limber and bristlecone pine spread along the slopes of the upper valleys. These coniferous forests are alive with buzzing flocks of pine siskins, which work over the trees systematically in search of insects and pine nuts. Black bears and a few cougars inhabit the Sangres, along with elk, mule deer and bighorn sheep. Marmots and pikas shelter in talus fields in the high tundra.

PLANNING
Maps & Books
The 1:60,000 plastic hiking map *Sangre de Cristo Wilderness Great Sand Dunes National Park* ($11.95), published by Sky Terrain, covers the entire range at a practical scale. The USFS 1:126,720 map *San Isabel National Forest* ($7) provides a fair regional overview but is unsuitable for serious navigation. *The Colorado Sangre de Cristo: A Complete Trail Guide* ($12.95) by Michael O'Hanlon includes hikes in the nearby Spanish Peaks and Culebra Range.

Information Sources
The USFS ranger stations at Canon City (☎ 719-269-8500) and La Veta (☎ 719-742-3681) give advice on San Isabel National Forest and Sangre de Cristo Wilderness, or take a look at [W] www.fs.fed.us/r2/riogrande.

Permits & Regulations
Permits are not required to hike or camp in the Sangres. However, in the Sangre de Cristo Wilderness camping is not permitted within 300ft of lakes or 100ft of streams, and dogs must be kept under control at all times. Campfires should be avoided or kept small.

ACCESS TOWN
Alamosa
Alamosa (population 8775) lies in the heart of the San Luis Valley, at the intersection of US 160 and US 285. For information contact

the visitor center (☎ 719-589-4840; [W] www.alamosa.org; Cole Park, 3rd St) or the BLM San Luis office (☎ 719-589-4975, 1921 State St). Spencer Sporting Goods (☎ 719-589-4361, 616 Main St) stocks hunting supplies but has USGS quads. Kristi Mountain Sports (☎ 719-589-9759, [e] kmn@slvoutdoor.com, 7565 W Hwy 160) sells gear (no quads).

KOA (☎ 719-589-9757, 800-562-9157, 6900 Juniper Lane), 3mi east of Alamosa, has tent/RV sites for $18/25. *Sky-Vue Motel (☎ 719-589-4945, 250 Broadway Ave)* has basic singles/doubles for $36/46. *Alamosa Lamplighter Motel (☎ 719-589-6636, 425 Main St)* charges $52/60. Next door to Kristi Mountain Sports, *Valley Food Co-op (☎ 719-589-5727)* has natural and bulk foods ideal for backpacking.

United Express (☎ 719-589-9446) has daily flights to Denver. Greyhound/TNM&O (☎ 719-589-4948) buses service Denver, Durango and into New Mexico.

Comanche-Venable Loop

Duration	2 days
Distance	12mi (19.3km)
Standard	moderate
Start/Finish	Comanche-Venable Trailhead
Nearest Towns	Westcliffe/Silver Cliff
Transport	car
Summary	A varied circuit connecting two enchanting little valleys.

One of the few viable circuits on the Sangres' eastern slope, the Comanche-Venable Loop is deservedly popular. The hike leads past several beautiful alpine lakes and over two scenic passes just north of the Crestone group of 14ers. Another highlight of the hike is the spectacular Phantom Terrace, where the trail is cut into cliffs. The route is normally passable at least from mid-June until late September.

PLANNING
What to Bring
Carry fluids on the first day as there is little water until shortly before Comanche Lake.

Maps
Sky Terrain's 1:60,000 map *Sangre de Cristo Wilderness Great Sand Dunes National Park* is recommended. Otherwise there are two USGS 1:24,000 quads that cover the route: *Horn Peak* and *Rito Alto Peak* – not *Electric Peak*, as wrongly indicated at the margin of the former sheet.

NEAREST TOWNS & FACILITIES
Westcliffe/Silver Cliff
These twin villages lie 1mi apart on Hwy 96, around 55mi west of Pueblo in the Wet Mountain Valley. The chamber of commerce (☎ 719-783-9163, **W** www.custerguide.com, 101 N 3rd St) is in Westcliffe. Valley Ace Hardware, south of Westcliffe on US 69 (toward Walsenburg), sells USGS quads and other topos.

Kleine's Trailer Park (☎ 719-783-2295, 320 Cliff St) has RV and tent sites (both $12). In Westcliffe, *Antler Motel (☎ 719-783-9305, cnr Main St & S 6th St)* has singles/doubles from $31/35. Silver Cliff's *Yoder's High Country Inn (☎ 719-783-2656, 700 Ohio St)* offers rooms for $37/44.

USFS Campgrounds
The basic *Alvarado campground* near the trailhead has 47 sites for $8. The *Middle Taylor Creek* and *DeWeese campgrounds* are just northeast of Westcliffe.

GETTING TO/FROM THE HIKE
From Westcliffe drive 3.4mi south on Hwy 69, then turn right (west) along CR 302 (Schoolfield Rd). Continue for 7mi (just past the Alvarado USFS campground turnoff) to the Comanche-Venable Trailhead. There is space for around 20 cars here, as well as drinking water and a privy.

THE HIKE
Day 1: Comanche-Venable Trailhead to Comanche Lake
2¼–3 hours, 4.1mi, 2620ft ascent
From the trailhead parking area, take the **Comanche Trail** (No 1345) leading up left (southwest). Trail 1345 passes a short social trail coming in from the Alvarado USFS campground (just down to the left), then

continues through Douglas fir and aspen over the Rainbow Trail before it crosses the wilderness boundary. Note details of your party in the register book here. Begin a steady climb into spaced lodgepole forest scattered with juniper, crossing the (normally dry) Alvarado Creek before you switchback up to reach a ridge top (11,040ft), 1½ to two hours from the trailhead.

The Comanche Trail sidles over rocky, avalanche-prone slopes strewn with graceful old bristlecone and limber pines high above the rushing Hiltman Creek. Skirt above moist meadows colonized by Indian hellebore (where idyllic **campsites** can be found among stands of spruce) to reach a short turnoff (left) leading down to **Comanche Lake**, 45 minutes to one hour from the ridge top. This lonely alpine tarn lies just below tree line under sweeping heath-covered mountainsides and the looming northeast face of Comanche Peak (13,277ft). There are **campsites** back from the shore or further upvalley by some beaver ponds.

Day 2: Comanche Lake to Comanche-Venable Trailhead (via Venable Lakes)
3¼–4¾ hours, 7.9mi, 1120ft ascent
Return to the Comanche Trail and cut up (southwest) out of the trees to a grassy shelf, then make a high winding traverse over scrubby tundra slopes to reach **Comanche Pass** (12,700ft) after 50 minutes to 1¼ hours. (If the final section of the trail is snowed-in or corniced, use a slightly higher detour.) This narrow pass is sprinkled with delicate yellow cinquefoils and pale-blue forget-me-nots. It offers classic vistas west across the wild drainage of North Crestone Creek into the level floor of the San Luis Valley, as well as back down Hiltman Creek to Westcliffe. To the south, behind Comanche Peak, lurks Mt Adams (13,931ft) with its impressive, craggy west ridge.

Follow the Comanche Trail northwest directly past the Trail 746 turnoff (leading down along Middle Fork North Crestone Creek) and sidle 1mi above sweeping tundra slopes into a small gap (12,780ft) just below Venable Peak (13,334ft). From here you get

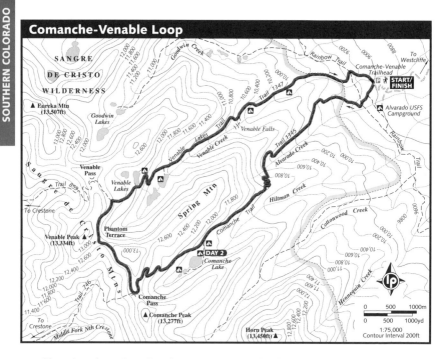

Comanche-Venable Loop

a sudden view down into the picturesque valley of Venable Creek, adorned by the two pairs of (upper and lower) Venable Lakes.

Skirt down northeast along **Phantom Terrace**, where the trail is cut into a precipitous 'rock garden' slope that nurtures a multitude of high-elevation wildflowers, including alpine avens, yellow arnicas, stoloniferous saxifrage and purplish subalpine fleabane. Continue down to a trail junction (where Trail 859 cuts up left over Venable Pass) among shrub willow meadows swarming with marmots, then bear right along the Venable Lakes Trail (No 1347) to reach the larger of the two upper **Venable Lakes**, 50 minutes to 1¼ hours from Comanche Pass. This lovely tarn sits on a terrace looking out on the eroding reddish ridge of Spring Mountain; there are semisheltered *campsites* among the battered scrub on its southeast side. The uppermost lake can be reached in five minutes by climbing beside the tumbling inlet stream.

Switchback down into the spruces above the meandering creek, passing the remains of a log cabin near the lowest of the Venable Lakes. There are better *campsites* among the bristlecone and limber pines edging meadows on the valley floor. Trail 1347 now begins a steady descent through small avalanche chutes in the spruce forest past **Venable Falls** (accessible via a short side trail), 45 minutes to one hour from the upper Venable Lakes. Here the small creek drops 100ft in a series of overlapping cascades before entering a chasm. Mule deer can sometimes be spotted in the vicinity.

Head down through aspen woodland scattered with yellow lupines past sporadic *campsites* near the creek. Continue across the Rainbow Trail into stands of Douglas fir and ponderosa pine (some killed by bark beetle infestation) to cross Venable Creek on a footbridge just before you arrive back at the Comanche-Venable Trailhead, 50 minutes to 1¼ hours from Venable Falls.

Blanca Peak

Duration	3 days
Distance	17mi (27.4km)
Standard	hard
Start/Finish	Lower Lake Como Rd
Nearest Town	Alamosa
Transport	car

Summary A challenging ascent of one of the Rockies' most beautiful and interesting 14,000ft summits.

The Sangres' highest point (and the fourth highest summit in the Rockies), the 14,345ft Blanca Peak was sacred to the Dineh (Navajo) people. This 'blunt tooth' mountain stands at the southernmost end of the range, and is part of a quartet of 14ers – known as the Blanca group – that give rise to six lovely alpine valleys. The normal summit approach route is from Lake Como, in the upper valley of Holbrook Creek. The climb is very strenuous but does not normally require specialized equipment (which increases its popularity). Although not every hiker makes it to the summit, all find the route scenic and enjoyable.

PLANNING
When to Hike
The route is likely to be excessively snowy before July and may be out of condition due to fall snowfalls as early as mid-September.

Maps
The route is best covered by Sky Terrain's 1:60,000 map *Sangre de Cristo Wilderness Great Sand Dunes National Park* or two USGS 1:24,000 quads, *Blanca Peak* and *Twin Peaks*. A USGS 1:100,000 metric map, *Blanca Peak*, provides a good overview of the area.

Warning

Electrically charged clouds build up on Blanca Peak almost every day in July and August, and hikers should plan to be off-summit by no later than 1pm – get an early start.

NEAREST TOWN
See Alamosa (p282).

GETTING TO/FROM THE HIKE
From Alamosa drive 14mi east on US 160, then turn off left (north) along Hwy 150 (signposted 'Great Sand Dunes National Park') and proceed 3.1mi before taking the (right) Lake Como Rd. The road is unmaintained after about 2mi. The remaining (5.7mi) section to Lake Como is extremely rough, persuading all but the most determined 4WD drivers to park and continue on foot (or by ATV).

THE HIKE
Day 1: Lower Lake Como Rd to Lake Como
4½–6 hours, 5.7mi, 3780ft ascent
The road deteriorates dramatically around the 8000ft contour. If you hike from here in the heat of the day, carry some water for the thirsty first section. The very rough 4WD track winds up through the pinyon-juniper scrub past *campsites* in Chokecherry Canyon. After cresting a ridge it fords and follows Holbrook Creek to arrive at **Lake Como**. The lake lies at the western foot of the 14,037ft Little Bear Peak. There is excellent *camping* here, especially around the east shore among the spruces.

Day 2: Como Lake return, via Blanca Peak
4½–6 hours, 5.6mi, 2565ft ascent
Continue around the north side of the lake under large talus fields descending the valley sides. The 4WD track gradually tapers into a foot trail as it climbs through marmot meadows interspersed with stands of low spruce that offer sheltered *camping*. Head around the lower of the **Blue Lakes**, then ascend beside the inlet waterfall, past shallow stream pools. The trail skirts the west side of **Crater Lake**, in a dramatic moraine basin, before it peters out at the very head of the valley near the remains of an old mine shack, 1½ to two hours from Lake Como.

A rough but well-trodden (sometimes cairned) route picks its way up 35 minutes to 50 minutes northeast over steep, broken

SOUTHERN COLORADO

rock into a high saddle (13,550ft) that drops away 2500ft into the lovely Huerfano Basin. The final ascent leads southeast through more bouldery rubble on the right-hand side of the ridge to arrive on **Blanca Peak**, 30 to 45 minutes from the saddle. The small summit offers stupendous views taking in a broad swathe of the southern Rockies, including the adjacent Ellingwood Peak (14,043ft), Mt Lindsey (14,042ft) and Little Bear Peak (14,037ft), as well as the far-off Uncompahgre, Wheeler and Pikes Peaks. More than 6000ft below you, the vast, pan-flat San Luis Valley stretches out to the southwest. There is a log book sealed in a pipe. Return to Lake Como via your ascent route (two to 2½ hours).

Day 3: Lake Como to Lower Lake Como Rd
4–5 hours, 5.7mi
Retrace your Day 1 steps. Hikers often opt to return on Day 2 after climbing Blanca Peak.

Other Hikes

SAN JUAN MOUNTAINS
Mt Sneffels
The striking 14,150ft Mt Sneffels rises just 7mi west of Ouray within the small Mt Sneffels Wilderness. This isolated peak gives stunning vistas of the western San Juans. From Yankee Boy Basin (11,200ft) it is a strenuous five- to 6½-hour (5mi) round-trip climb with many steep and/or rocky sections. The route follows Trail 201 almost to Blue Lake Pass, then cuts to the right up through steep rubble couloirs and along the southeast ridge to the summit.

Two USGS quads cover the route, *Mount Sneffels* and *Telluride*. To reach Yankee Boy Basin, turn west off US 550 along the Camp Bird Rd just south of Ouray and continue 7mi; above Camp Bird (about halfway) the road is passable only to high-clearance vehicles. A trailhead parking pass ($7.50/15 for ATVs and motorcycles/cars) is required at Yankee Boy Basin.

Handies Peak
The 14,048ft Handies Peak, 15mi southwest of Lake City, is a fairly easy 14er. Its panoramic summit can be reached in an enjoyable four- to 5½-hour round-trip climb from the trailhead at American Basin (11,600ft), a magnificent cirque at the headwaters of West Fork Gunnison River. The trail leads up past Sloan Lake to a saddle at 13,140ft, then climbs the west slopes to the summit. The USGS 1:24,000 quad *Handies Peak* covers the climb. American Basin is reached via the Lake Fork Gunnison River road turnoff from Hwy 149, 2.5mi south of Lake City. Drive 12.5mi (past Lake San Cristobal) to a fork, then continue right for 8.5mi. The final road section is very rough.

Weminuche Continental Divide Trail
One of the wildest and most spectacular sections in the entire 3100mi CDT leads 85mi through the Weminuche Wilderness in the San Juan Mountains. Taking around 10 days to complete, this classic hike leads northwest from Wolf Creek

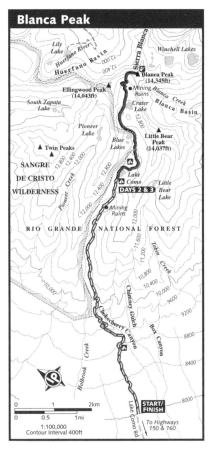

Blanca Peak

Lily Lake
Huerfano River
Huerfano Basin
Sierra Blanca
Winchell Lakes
Blanca Peak (14,345ft)
Mining Ruins
Blanca Creek
Ellingwood Peak (14,043ft)
Crater Lake
Blanca Basin
South Zapata Lake
Pioneer Lake
Blue Lakes
Little Bear Peak (14,037ft)
Twin Peaks
Lake Como
Little Bear Lake
SANGRE DE CRISTO WILDERNESS
Pinero Creek
DAYS 2 & 3
Mining Ruins
RIO GRANDE NATIONAL FOREST
Tobin Creek
Chimney Gulch
Box Canyon
Chokecherry Canyon
Holbrook Creek
START/FINISH
Lake Como Rd
To Highways 150 & 160

0   1   2km
0   0.5   1mi
1:100,000
Contour Interval 400ft

Pass (on US 160, 22.5mi northeast of Pagosa Springs) to Silverton or Elk Park. It is a high-level route (with many sections well above 12,000ft) that requires good acclimation and fitness as well as constant weather vigilance – electrical storms with lightning build up on an almost daily basis. The Weminuche CDT is usually impassable outside July, August and September.

To avoid making your own lengthy car shuttle, consider organizing a hiker shuttle from Durango (p269) then riding on the Durango & Silverton Narrow Gauge Railroad (see Getting To/From the Hike, p276) from Silverton (or Elk Park) back to Durango.

The Trails Illustrated 1:66,667 map No 140 *Weminuche Wilderness* and map No 141 *Silverton, Ouray, Telluride, Lake City* cover the route to Silverton (only the first map is needed if you hike to Elk Park). Rocky Mountain Adventure Maps' 1:100,000 *Weminuche Wilderness* map is an alternative. Otherwise use the following USGS 1:24,000 quads: *Wolf Creek Pass*, *Mount Hope*, *South River Peak*, *Palomino Mountain*, *Cimorrona Peak*, *Little Squaw Creek*, *Granite Lake*, *Weminuche Pass*, *Rio Grande Pyramid*, *Storm King Peak* and *Howardsville*.

South San Juan Wilderness

Characterized by broad alpine plateaus, the 248-sq-mile South San Juan Wilderness is smaller, but no less wild, than the adjacent Weminuche Wilderness. A moderate two-day (23mi) backpacking trip leaves from Cumbres Pass (10,000ft), on both Hwy 17 and the Cumbres & Toltec Scenic Railroad (☎ 719-376-5483, W www.cumbrestoltec.com). The route follows the CDT northwest to meet Trail 733, before heading southwest across the rolling tundra to Red Lake. It then leads down the Rio de los Pinos to the Trujillo Meadows USFS campground, from where a dirt road (FR 118) climbs back to Cumbres Pass.

Use either Trails Illustrated's 1:66,667 map No 142 *South San Juan/Del Norte* or two USGS 1:24,000 quads: *Archuleta Creek* and *Cumbres*.

Northern New Mexico

Often overlooked by out-of-state hikers (many imagining all of New Mexico to be a searing desert), the mountains of northern New Mexico offer surprisingly wild and varied hiking. Although the Continental Divide runs through western New Mexico, the principal mountain ranges are in the central region of the state.

Most spectacular are the Sangre de Cristo Mountains, one of the Rockies' longest and highest mountain chains. This varied range extends for some 200mi from Salida in Colorado before finally petering out just north of Sante Fe. The New Mexican half of the range includes the justifiably popular Pecos and Wheeler Peak Wilderness areas, where the state's highest summits are found.

CLIMATE

Elevation largely determines the climate in northern New Mexico – the contrast as you move from the arid, sweltering lowlands into the crisp, fresh atmosphere of the high ranges is remarkable.

While the annual precipitation in the low basins and valleys is often well under 10 inches, the higher ranges typically receive around 40 inches – roughly half falling as summer rain and half as winter snow. The first major snowfalls usually occur in mid-October. Mountain temperatures may reach 80°F in summer, plummeting when a storm moves in, while nights are cool, occasionally below freezing

INFORMATION
Maps & Books

GTR Mapping's 1:800,000 *Recreational Map of New Mexico* ($3.95) gives a good general overview of the state's national forest and wilderness areas.

The Hiker's Guide to the Enchanted Circle by Kathy Kalen ($11.95) and *Hiking The Wilderness* by Kay Matthews ($12.95) cover backpacking routes in the main wilderness areas of northern New Mexico. *Hiking New Mexico* by Laurence Parent ($14.95) along

Highlights

Typical adobe architecture in Taos, access town for those heading to Wheeler Peak.

- Admiring superb stands of whispering aspen on the Cruces Basin Loop (p291)
- Marveling at the panorama from the summit of Wheeler Peak (p294)
- Savoring the sweet pine-scented air in the high forests around Chimayosos Peak (p297) in the Pecos Wilderness.

with *50 Hikes in New Mexico* by Harry Evans ($12.95) feature hikes throughout the state. The larger-format *Guide to Hiking Areas of New Mexico* by Mike Hill ($29.95) is even more comprehensive.

Information Sources

The New Mexico Department of Tourism (☎ 575-827-7400, 800-545-2040; Ⓦ www .newmexico.org; 491 Old Santa Fe Trail, Santa Fe) produces the very useful (and free) *New Mexico Recreation and Heritage Guide*. Also in Santa Fe, contact the public lands

NORTHERN NEW MEXICO

Top Left: A high-level trail gives panoramic views of the rusty ranges of Colorado's Weminuche Wilderness. **Top Right:** A footbridge over Vallecito Creek on the Needle Mountains Loop in Weminuche Wilderness. **Bottom:** Alpine wildflowers dot the slopes of Handies Peak in the northern San Juan Mountains, Colorado.

CLEM LINDENMAYER

CLEM LINDENMAYER

CLEM LINDENMAYER

Top Left: Alpine meadows below Puerto Nambe on the Winsor-Skyline Loop in New Mexico's Pecos Wilderness. **Top Right:** New Mexico's capital, Santa Fe provides plenty of fresh produce and access to spectacular hiking trails. **Middle Right:** A makeshift bridge in the Pecos Wilderness. **Bottom:** The easy Frijoles Canyon Trail, in the Bandelier Wilderness, leads past ancient Pueblo sites.

CLEM LINDENMAYER

JOHN HAY

ROBERTO SONCIN GEROMETTA

BEN DAVIDSON

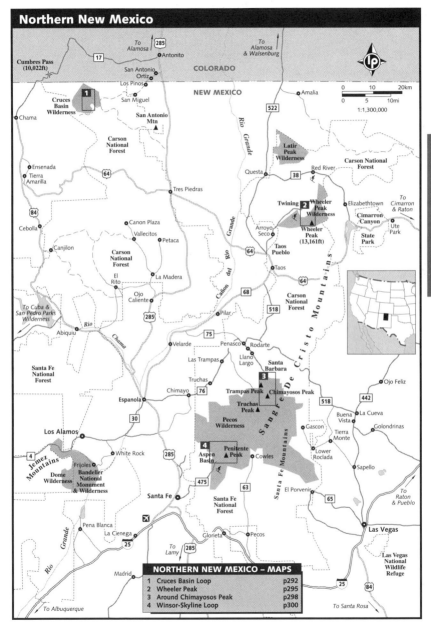

Northern New Mexico

To Alamosa

285

17

Cumbres Pass
(10,022ft)

Antonito

San Antonio

Ortiz

Los Pinos

San Miguel

COLORADO

NEW MEXICO

To
Alamosa
& Walsenburg

Chama

1 Cruces
Basin
Wilderness

San Antonio
Mtn

Carson
National
Forest

Amalia

522

Rio Grande

Latir
Peak
Wilderness

Carson National
Forest

Ensenada

Tierra
Amarilla

64

Tres Piedras

Questa

Red River

38

To
Cimarron
& Raton

84

Cebolla

Canon Plaza

Vallecitos

Petaca

Canjilon

Carson
National
Forest

El
Rito

La Madera

Ojo
Caliente

Twining

2 Wheeler
Peak
Wilderness

Wheeler
Peak
(13,161ft)

Elizabethtown

Cimarron
Canyon
State
Park

Ute
Park

Arroyo
Seco

64

Taos
Pueblo

Taos

64

Rio Grande

Cañon del Rio Grande

285

To Cuba &
San Pedro Parks
Wilderness

Abiquiu

Rio Chama

68

518

Carson
National
Forest

75

Velarde

Penasco

Rodarte

Santa Fe National Forest

Las Trampas

Llano
Largo

Santa
Barbara

Sangre De Cristo Mountains

Ojo Feliz

Truchas

76

3

Trampas Peak

Chimayosos Peak

518

442

Chimayo

Pecos
Wilderness

Truchas
Peak

Buena
Vista

La Cueva

Golondrinas

Espanola

30

Gascon

Tierra
Monte

Los Alamos

4

White Rock

285

Aspen
Basin

Penitente
Peak

Cowles

Lower
Roclada

Sapello

Jemez
Mountains

4

Frijoles

Dome
Wilderness

Bandelier
National
Monument
& Wilderness

475

63

El Porvenir

65

To
Raton
& Pueblo

Santa Fe

Santa Fe
National
Forest

Santa Fe Mountains

Las Vegas

Pena Blanca

La Cienega

25

Glorieta

Pecos

Las Vegas
National
Wildlife
Refuge

Madrid

To
Lamy

285

To Albuquerque

25

To Santa Rosa

84

Rio Grande

NORTHERN NEW MEXICO – MAPS

0   5   10mi
0   10   20km
1:1,300,000

NORTHERN NEW MEXICO

information center (☎ 575-438-7542, W www .publiclands.org/html/explore/about_NM.asp, 1474 Rodeo Rd) for camping and recreation information on all New Mexico public lands.

GATEWAY
Albuquerque

New Mexico's main transportation hub, Albuquerque (population 450,000) is an interesting melting pot of indigenous, Hispanic and Anglo cultures. For information contact the visitor bureau (☎ 575-842-9918, 800-284-2282; W www.abqcvb.org; 20 First Plaza Building, Suite 601) in the Galleria. Cibola National Forest office (☎ 575-842-3292; 5th floor, Federal Building, 517 Gold Ave SW) sells books and US Forest Service maps.

Places to Stay & Eat The *Palisades RV Park (☎ 575-831-5000, 9201 Central Ave NW)* has tent sites from $10. *Route 66 Hostel (☎ 575-247-1813, E ctaylor939@aol.com, 1012 Central Ave SW)* offers dorm beds for around $15 and singles/doubles from $20/25. The classic *El Vado Motel (☎ 575-243-4594, 2500 Central Ave SW)* charges from $28/38.

Double Rainbow (☎ 575-255-6633, 3416 Central Ave SE) has delicious, homemade fare and *Los Cuates (☎ 575-255-5079, 4901 Lomas Blvd NE)* serves regional specialties.

Getting There & Away Several large airlines fly to Albuquerque, including Southwest Airlines and America West. Mesa Airlines (☎ 575-842-4218, 800-637-2247) flies to many regional cities in New Mexico, as well as Durango, Colorado Springs and Dallas.

Warning

While elevations never quite reach those of central and southern Colorado, many hikes in New Mexico take you well into the danger zone for acute mountain sickness (AMS). If you have just arrived from a lower elevation, make sure you spend at least a day or two sightseeing in order to acclimate before you head into the mountains. See Altitude (p66) for more information on the causes and prevention of AMS.

Greyhound (☎ 575-243-4435, 800-231-2222) has four daily buses to Santa Fe ($12) and two to Taos ($24). Amtrak's (☎ 800-872-7245) *Southwest Chief* train between Los Angeles and Chicago stops daily in Albuquerque (both east and west services).

Cruces Basin Wilderness

Compact 18,902-acre Cruces Basin Wilderness is in Carson National Forest, straddling the New Mexico/Colorado state line.

Despite its size, the Cruces is one of New Mexico's great pristine areas. Long travel times from the regional centers, rough access roads and lack of a developed trail system mean that the Cruces tends to attract the more dedicated visitor.

With a gentle topography that makes navigation straightforward, the wilderness offers easy hiking suited to families. Numerous unmaintained trails lead along its beautiful grassy valleys. Visitors with minimal backcountry experience can explore the basin without worrying about getting (too) lost.

NATURAL HISTORY

The Cruces Basin is an undulating tableland measuring roughly 6mi across and ranging in elevation from 8600ft to almost 11,000ft. The basin is dissected by ridges or abrupt outcrops of pink granite largely covered in fir-spruce forest. A more striking feature of the Cruces is its beautiful stands of aspen, where the persistent tapping of the red-naped sapsucker may be heard. This woodpecker species pierces the bark of the aspen, releasing sticky sap to attract – and entrap – the insects on which it feeds.

The Cruces is an important summer pasture for elk, which browse the moist grasslands and forests. Deer and black bears also inhabit the wilderness and, although you will see plenty of signs, regular fall hunting makes the animals cautious and difficult to spot. The most common animals you'll see are cattle and sheep, which are grazed in the basin during the summer months.

PLANNING
Maps
The USGS 1:24,000 quad *Toltec Mesa* covers the entire Cruces Basin Wilderness. A better option is the USFS 1:24,000 quad *Cruces Basin Wilderness* ($7), a slightly modified version of this map.

Information Sources
The USFS office (☎ 505-758-8678) in tiny Tres Piedras, at the US 64/285 intersection, can give useful information on the Cruces, but sells only USFS maps.

Permits & Regulations
Permits are not required to hike or camp in Cruces Basin Wilderness, but anglers should have a valid New Mexico fishing license.

ACCESS TOWN
Antonito
Inside Colorado, Antonito is 5mi north of the New Mexico border. The visitor center (☎ 719-376-2049, 800-835-1098) is on US 285 opposite the railroad depot.

The ***Narrow Gauge Railroad Inn*** (*☎ 719-376-5441, 800-323-9469*) has singles/doubles for $44/54. The ***Dutch Mill*** *(401 Main St)* menu includes Mexican dishes.

TNM&O (☎ 719-376-5949) buses run regularly to Albuquerque and Denver.

Cruces Basin Loop

Duration	4¼–5¼ hours
Distance	7.7mi (12.4km)
Standard	easy–moderate
Start	Osha Creek Trailhead
Finish	Corral on FR 871
Nearest Towns	Antonito
Transport	car
Summary Explore several small and trout-filled tributaries of Beaver Creek.	

Entering the wilderness via the main (but unofficial) access trail down Osha Creek, this hike explores a number of tributaries of Beaver Creek, which drains the basin via a spectacular canyon at its northeast rim.

Small, wild (ie, nonhatchery) brook trout inhabit the creeks and are quite a challenge to hook. This short, gentle route can be extended by a day or two by exploring side valleys of Beaver Creek.

PLANNING
When to Hike
The Cruces Basin normally melts out by early June and the first snowfalls usually occur in late September. Weather conditions suitable for hiking often continue well into October but at that time the Cruces is also popular with elk hunters.

Maps
Recommended is the USFS 1:24,000 quad *Cruces Basin Wilderness* but the standard USGS 1:24,000 map *Toltec Mesa* will also do.

NEAREST TOWN & FACILITIES
See Antonito (this page).

Campgrounds
The free, but very popular, ***Rio de Los Pinos USFS campground***, on Forest Rd (FR) 87-A, is several miles west of San Miguel. There are two free USFS campgrounds, ***Upper*** and ***Lower Lagunitas***, approximately 5mi on from the NM 87-A/87 intersection near the trailhead; both have around 12 basic sites. Primitive ***campsites*** can also be found along FR 572, just outside the Cruces Basin Wilderness area.

GETTING TO/FROM THE HIKE
The trailhead is accessible to conventional vehicles with good clearance unless road conditions are very muddy or snowy.

From Antonito drive south on US 285, then turn right and follow NM 87-A for 20mi along the Rio de Los Pinos valley, via San Miguel, to the NM 87-A/87 intersection (where there is a USFS information board). Here go right (west) along NM 87 for 0.8mi, then turn right (north) and follow FR 572 for 1.8mi to the trailhead parking area.

The hike ends at a corral just off FR 87, 0.6mi southwest of the trailhead turnoff (FR 572). Hiking parties with two vehicles can do a minor shuttle.

THE HIKE

Pick up a well-trodden path below the parking area and follow it steeply down northwest through a forest of Douglas fir, whitebark pine, Engelmann spruce and aspen, crossing diminutive Osha Creek. Head down beside the largely open stream through a small gap overlooking the tiny valleys of Cruces Basin, then drop west to meet small Diablo Creek above its confluence with Beaver Creek, 25 to 30 minutes from the start. See Side Trips for other interesting options from here.

Ford Diablo and head upstream (southwest) for 0.6mi over open meadows before recrossing. The faint trail leads on past an outcrop that juts into the valley, forcing the creek to make a sharp curve. Climb slightly to cross a wire fence and make your way upvalley through forest patches (where you may spot mule deer or elk) until you reach Escondido Creek, 45 minutes to one hour from the Diablo/Beaver Creeks confluence. There is pleasant *camping* here.

From this point you may prefer to follow trails that lead up Diablo Creek to the Lagunitas campgrounds or to backtrack to the Osha Creek Trailhead via your approach route.

Otherwise, a horse trail climbs gently away southeast up the largely open northern side of Escondido Creek. Just before the creek turns southwest, break away left (east) to arrive at a **corral** at the end of FR 871, about one hour from the Diablo/Escondido Creeks junction. From here it's a 2.4mi (1¼ to 1½ hours) hike back to Osha Creek Trailhead.

Side Trip: Beaver Creek Cascades
1–1¼ hours, 2mi
This short, but worthwhile, side trip leads from the tiny gap downstream (northeast) along the often soggy banks of the gently meandering Beaver Creek. Avoiding occasional cliffs by skirting the valley's edge, the route ends at the basin rim where the stream abruptly spills into a bouldery gorge.

Side Trip: Cruces Creek
3–4½ hours, 7mi
This longer excursion explores the upper Cruces Creek. Ford Diablo Creek then immediately cross Beaver Creek. Head upstream for five to 10 minutes over the soggy meadows of Beaver Creek, then continue northwest into the drainage of the meandering Cruces Creek to cross a wire stock fence. The mostly obvious trail rises gradually through tussock-grass meadows with lively ground squirrels and past occasional beaver dams along the stream into high pastures at the head of Cruces Creek. There is *camping* all along the valley. Adventurous hikers can climb on to Toltec Mesa.

Wheeler Peak Wilderness

The 19,661-acre Wheeler Peak Wilderness lies northeast of Taos in the Sangre de Cristo Mountains. The Wheeler is centered around – and dominated by – 13,161ft Wheeler Peak, the highest point in New Mexico.

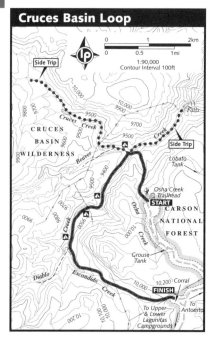
Cruces Basin Loop

HISTORY

Wheeler Peak honors George M Wheeler (1832–1909), a naturalist and surveyor of the US southwest. Descendants of the ancestral Pueblo people inhabited the area, and their first white contact was through French trappers in the 1730s. Gold and copper prospectors, including the legendary Kit Carson, established (ultimately unsuccessful) mines around Twining in the 1880s, and their abandoned mine workings are still visible. From the late 1950s, Twining was transformed into the Taos Ski Valley resort.

NATURAL HISTORY

The Wheeler is a rugged alpine landscape mostly well above 10,000ft with an ecosystem typical of the high ranges of northern New Mexico. Aspen, Engelmann spruce and subalpine fir are the dominant tree species, while ancient bristlecone pines grow on high ridges.

Bighorn sheep, which locally had been hunted to extinction, were successfully reintroduced in the Wheeler in 1993. Elk and mule deer frequent the area in summer, gorging on protein-rich alpine grasses and tender aspen shoots. Graceful golden eagles may be spotted gliding around the high peaks watching out for prey such as pikas or marmots. The streams are stocked yearly with rainbow trout and native cutthroat fry are released (by helicopter) every few years into several of the alpine lakes.

PLANNING

Maps

The USFS 1:63,360 *Latir Peak & Wheeler Peak Wilderness* map ($7) covers the entire wilderness.

Information Sources

Contact the USFS Carson National Forest office in Taos (☎ 505-758-6200, fax 505-758-6213, 208 Cruz Alta) or visit the USFS website at W www.fs.fed.us/r3/carson/html_trails/trail_wilderness_wheeler.htm.

Permits & Regulations

No permit is required to hike in Wheeler Peak Wilderness but, as this fragile alpine environment is heavily visited, hikers should aim to minimize their impact. All access trails pass through private land; hikers should respect property rights and camp only inside the national forest and/or wilderness boundary. Anglers require a New Mexico fishing license plus a trout stamp.

ACCESS TOWN

Taos

The old Spanish settlement of Taos is at the western foot of the mighty Sangre de Cristo Mountains. The visitor center (☎ 505-758-3873, 800-732-8267, fax 505-758-3872, cnr Paseo del Pueblo Sur & Paseo del Cañon) is open daily. Next to the USFS office (☎ 505-758-6200, fax 505-758-6213, 208 Cruz Alta) is the Bureau of Land Management (BLM) office (☎ 505-758-8851, 224 Cruz Alta).

Native Sons Adventures (☎ 505-758-9342, 800-753-7559, fax 505-751-4610, 1033A Paseo del Pueblo Sur) rents out backpacking gear and does guided trips. Taos Mountain Outfitters (☎ 505-758-9292), on the Plaza, sells hiking supplies.

Places to Stay & Eat The *Taos Valley RV Park & Campground (☎ 505-758-4469, 800-999-7571; 120 Estes Rd, Ranchos de Taos)* has sites for $15. The *Abominable Snowmansion (☎ 505-776-8298, fax 505-776-2107)*, north of Taos Arroyo Seco, has dorm beds ($17), tepees ($13), camping ($8) and double rooms ($45). The *Sun God Lodge (☎ 505-758-3162, 800-821-2437, 909 Paseo del Pueblo Sur)* offers rooms from $50.

El Pueblo Café (☎ 505-758-2053, 625 Paseo del Pueblo Norte) serves no-frills New Mexican fare. *Amigos Natural Foods Cafe (☎ 505-758-8493, 326 Paseo del Pueblo Sur)* does tofu burgers and stir-fry. *Cid's Food Market (☎ 505-758-1158, 623 Paseo del Pueblo Norte)* has organic and bulk foods ideal for backpacking.

Getting There & Away Rio Grande Air (☎ 877-I-FLY-RGA, e rga@newmex.com) has flights between Albuquerque and Taos ($150 return). TNM&O/Greyhound (☎ 505-758-1144, 800-231-2222, Paseo del Pueblo Sur) runs daily buses to/from Albuquerque

($22) and Santa Fe ($17). Both Faust (☎ 505-758-3410, 800-535-1106) and Pride of Taos (☎ 505-758-8340, 800-273-8340) run daily shuttles from Albuquerque airport to Taos for $35/65 one-way/return and from Santa Fe to Taos for $25/45. Both companies run regular shuttles to Red River (from $45 one-way).

Wheeler Peak

Duration	7–10 hours
Distance	13mi (20.9km)
Standard	moderate
Start/Finish	Taos Ski Valley
Transport	car, bus

Summary This hike follows the most popular of the three ascent routes to the 13,161ft summit of Wheeler Peak, New Mexico's highest point.

Wheeler Peak is a superb panoramic summit offering marvelous views of the surrounding Sangre de Cristo Mountains and the broad steppes of northern New Mexico. The climb presents no technical difficulty, but, due to the high altitude and a total ascent of 3921ft, it is quite demanding. Most hikers will take at least four hours to reach the summit and little less for their descent.

PLANNING
When to Hike
Wheeler Peak can be climbed from June through September. Trails can be rather busy in July and August.

What to Bring
Hikers must carry proper wet-weather gear. Bring enough water for the whole trip or a pump filter.

Warning

The ascent of Wheeler Peak is a high-altitude route best undertaken after at least a few days acclimation. The route leads over high ridges exposed to thunderstorms with severe lightning – plan to be off the summit before lightning activity gets threatening.

Maps
Use either the USGS 1:24,000 quad *Wheeler Peak* or the USFS 1:63,360 map *Latir Peak & Wheeler Peak Wilderness*.

NEAREST TOWN
Taos Ski Valley (Twining)
The Taos Ski Valley resort fronts the southern boundary of the wilderness, and provides the main trailhead access. This compact alpine village is 20mi from Taos. For information contact the Taos Valley Resort Association (☎ 505-776-2291, 800-776-1111, W www .taosskivalley.com/summer.html). A small range of hiking gear is available from Cottam's Ski & Summer Shop (☎ 505-776-8719 e cottams@alpine-suites.com).

The *Hotel Edelweiss (*☎ *505-776-2301,* e *edelweiss@taosnm.com)* and *Snakedance Inn (*☎ *505-776-2277,* e *snakednc@taos .newmex.com)* provide rooms from $65/75 singles/doubles. The *Amizette Inn (*☎ *505-776-2451, 800-446-8267)*, just below the village, and *Austing Haus (*☎ *505-776-2649,* e *austing@newmex.com)*, 2mi downvalley, charge from around $45. *Tim's Stray Dog Cantina (*☎ *505-776-2894)* has the typical pub fare.

GETTING TO/FROM THE HIKE
The hike begins directly from the Taos Ski Valley (Twining) parking area, on the north side of the Hondo River opposite the ski village. Parking is free of charge.

Faust (☎ 505-758-3410, 800-535-1106) operates hiker shuttles from Taos to Taos Ski Valley ($40 for two people, $5 for each additional person).

THE HIKE
From the upper side of the parking area take the trail variously signposted as 'Columbine-Twining National Recreation Trail' and 'Bull-of-the-Woods/Wheeler Peak Trail'. This climbs 1.9mi northeast beside a stream (which forms the national forest boundary) through aspen and spruce. Following a disused old road in places, the trail passes the (left) Long Canyon Trail (No 63) to reach a junction at **Bull-of-the-Woods Pasture** (10,880ft) after one to 1½ hours. From here the Gold Hill

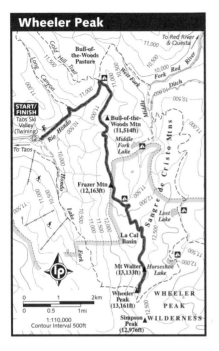

Wheeler Peak

Bull-of-the-Woods Pasture

To Red River & Questa

Cold Hill Trail

Long Canyon

West Fork

Red River

Fork

Ditch

START/FINISH
Taos Ski Valley (Twining)

Río Hondo

▲ Bull-of-the-Woods Mtn (11,514ft)

Middle Fork Lake

To Taos

Hondo

Lake

Frazer Mtn (12,163ft)

Sangre de Cristo Mtns

Lost Lake

La Cal Basin

Mt Walter (13,133ft)

Horseshoe Lake

Wheeler Peak (13,161ft)

WHEELER PEAK WILDERNESS

Simpson Peak ▲ (12,976ft)

0   1   2km
0   0.5   1mi
1:110,000
Contour Interval 500ft

Trail leads left (northwest) and some *campsites* can be found in the woods around the soggy meadow.

Continue to the right (southeast) past a tiny stream pond along a 4WD track (No 90) passing a turnoff to old mine workings to reach a stand of fragrant old bristlecone pines on a saddle on the north side of **Bull-of-the-Woods Mountain**. Head south along the ridge and traverse steadily up out of the forest over open slopes overlooking Taos Ski Valley. The path contours the east side of **Frazer Mountain** (12,163ft) before dropping left (southeast) into the **La Cal Basin** to cross the tiny upper streamlet of the Middle Fork Red River, about two hours from Bull-of-the-Woods Pasture. There are some *campsites* here among the Engelmann spruce.

Climb again southeast in a series of long switchbacks – please avoid the temptation to short-cut – then follow the ridge south over the false summit of **Mt Walter** (13,133ft). A gentle undulating climb along the ridge top

brings you to the summit of **Wheeler Peak** (13,161ft), around 1½ to two hours from La Cal Basin.

Towering above Williams and Horseshoe Lakes, Wheeler Peak offers marvelous views across the high rounded ranges of the Sangre de Cristos. On the summit are a commemorative plaque to GM Wheeler and a visitor log book sealed in a cylinder. Previous hikers have built a low rock shelter as protection against the often fierce winds.

Most hikers return via the main ascent route (allow three to 4½ hours), but experienced parties can cut down steeply from the ridge just north of the summit to Williams Lake, from where a good trail leads back to Taos Ski Valley.

Pecos Wilderness

New Mexico's largest wilderness area, the 350-sq-mile Pecos Wilderness, is at the southern end of the Sangre de Cristo Mountains. The Pecos is mainly within Santa Fe National Forest but the smaller northern section is inside Carson National Forest.

With a trail network totaling more than 1000mi, the Pecos offers a great variety of routes – from short day hikes to multiday backpacking trips. The 47mi Skyline Trail leads through the wilderness and forms the backbone of the trail system.

NATURAL HISTORY
The Pecos offers a cool respite from the surrounding hot, semiarid plains that are more typical of the New Mexico landscape. With elevations ranging from 8400ft to above 13,000ft, the Pecos is a collection of waterfalls, raw talus slides and impressive mountain walls of granite. Its 15 alpine lakes have good trout fishing. Both the Pecos River, the largest tributary of the Rio Grande, and the smaller Santa Fe River have their sources in the wilderness.

There is considerable altitudinal variation in forest types, which range from pinyon pine in the drier and lower elevations, to ponderosa pine and Douglas fir with increasing altitude. Vast, almost pure-stand forests of whispering aspen cloak the middle slopes of the ranges, although the main forest belt is formed by Engelmann spruce in association with subalpine fir. Stands of whitebark pine and bristlecone pine form tree line in many areas; the latter species is especially common on steep, dry slopes exposed to the sun. Alpine tundra, otherwise rare in the US southwest, covers the high, open mountaintops, forming dense mats of colored flowers.

The diverse Pecos wildlife includes pikas, marmots, squirrels, elk, mule deer, black bears, cougars (mountain lions) and bighorn sheep (which may even visit your camp). You are likely to spot ptarmigans flapping about the high forests or alpine meadows and golden eagles soaring above.

PLANNING
Maps & Books
The USFS 1:63,360 map *Pecos Wilderness* ($11.95) covers the wilderness area.

One Day Walks in the Pecos Wilderness by Carl Overhage describes six energetic routes. *Day Hikes in the Santa Fe Area* by the Sierra Club includes hikes in Pecos Wilderness.

Information Sources
Contact the USFS office in Taos (p293) or the Public Lands Information Center in Santa Fe. Ask for the *Visitor's Guide to the Pecos Wilderness*, which is available free at the USFS offices. You can also check out the USFS website at W www.fs.fed.us/r3/carson/html_trails/trail_wilderness_pecos.htm.

Permits & Regulations
Permits aren't required to hike or camp in Pecos Wilderness, but camping or campfires are prohibited within 200ft of any lake or within 50ft of any trail or stream. All lake basins are closed to camping and campfires – this includes on any slope that drains into a lake.

ACCESS TOWN
Santa Fe
The state capital, Santa Fe is the most southerly city in the Rocky Mountains. For

information contact the Santa Fe Convention and Visitors' Bureau (☎ 575-984-6760, 800-777-2489, W www.santafe.org, 201 W Marcy). The Public Lands Information Center (☎ 575-438-7542, 147 Rodeo Rd) sells topographic maps and books. Base Camp (☎ 575-982-9707, 322 Montezuma Ave) and Alpine Sports (☎ 575-983-5155, W www.alpinesports-santafe.com, 121 Sandoval) sell hiking gear.

Places to Stay & Eat The *Los Campos RV Park* (☎ 575-473-1949, 3574 Cerrillos Rd) charges $11 for tent sites. The *Santa Fe International Hostel* (☎ 575-988-1153, e hostel@trail.com, 1412 Cerrillos Rd) offers dorm beds for $15 and rooms from $25 per person. *Motel 6* (☎ 575-471-4140, 3695 Cerrillos Rd) has singles/doubles from around $47/53.

Josie's Casa de Comida (☎ 575-983-5311, 225 E Marcy) offers simple, home-style New Mexican fare. *Paul's* (☎ 575-982-8738, 72 W Marcy) serves more accomplished meals. *Wild Oats Community Market* (☎ 575-983-5333, 1090 St Francis Dr) has a range of whole foods ideal for backpacking.

Getting There & Away United Express (☎ 800-241-6522, 800-822-2746) has flights to/from Denver. Aspen Mountain (☎ 800-877-3932) flies to/from Dallas.

TNM&O/Greyhound (☎ 575-471-0008, cnr St Michael's Drive & Calle Lorca) runs four buses daily to/from Albuquerque ($12) and two services daily to/from Taos ($17). Shuttlejack (☎ 575-982-4311) operates a shuttle 10 to 12 times daily to/from the Albuquerque international airport and charges $20 one-way.

Amtrak (☎ 800-872-7245) trains stop every afternoon at Lamy; from here buses continue the 17mi to Santa Fe. Trains go to Los Angeles and Chicago.

Warning
Vehicle break-ins have occurred at Pecos Wilderness trailhead parking areas in recent years. Avoid leaving valuables in your car.

Around Chimayosos Peak

Duration	3 days
Distance	28.8mi (46.3km)
Standard	moderate
Start/Finish	Santa Barbara Trailhead
Nearest Town	Penasco, Taos
Transport	car

Summary An energetic lollipop loop that takes you close to the highest summits in the Pecos Wilderness.

This hike leads through wild valley forks of the upper Rio Santa Barbara to the foot of New Mexico's second highest summit, the 13,103ft Truchas Peak (which experienced hikers can climb). The route leads over extensive, flat-topped ridges of the Santa Barbara Divide that afford superb vistas around the less visited northern section of the Pecos.

PLANNING
When to Hike
Weather conditions can deteriorate rapidly in the mountains and thunderstorms with intense lightning are very common in summer, particularly after 11am, so keep a wary eye on the weather. Higher trails normally remain snowbound through May.

Maps
Recommended is the USFS 1:63,360 *Pecos Wilderness* map. For more detail use the USGS 1:24,000 quads: *Jicarita Peak*, *Pecos Falls* and *Truchas Peak*; the adjoining sheet, *El Valle*, is also useful for orientation.

NEAREST TOWNS & FACILITIES
See Taos (p293).

Penasco
This unattractive village is around 22mi south of Taos. There is nowhere to stay, although it has a small *supermarket*.

Campgrounds
The recently reconstructed *Santa Barbara USFS campground* (open from May through September), by the trailhead, has 29 basic tent sites ($9). Some people also *camp* near the Rio Santa Barbara road bridge, which is 1.3mi before the campground.

GETTING TO/FROM THE HIKE
From Penasco take Hwy 73 east for 2.4mi to Llano Largo, then turn left along FR 116 and continue for 4.9mi south along the Rio Santa Barbara to the trailhead parking area. Free parking is available here for around 20 vehicles.

THE HIKE
Day 1: Santa Barbara Trailhead to Truchas Lakes
5–6½ hours, 10.4mi, 2885ft ascent
From the upper end of the campground road loop, follow the Middle Fork Trail (No 24) up the west bank of the Rio Santa Barbara through pinyon pine and gambel oak scrub, and light meadows of wild roses among mixed forests of aspen, Douglas fir and Engelmann spruce. The trail leads south into Pecos Wilderness before crossing the small river on a footbridge and rising gently up its east side to a junction.

Take the (left) West Fork Trail (No 25) and continue upvalley to ford the Middle Fork Rio Santa Barbara – an easy wade after June or a log jam may even serve as a makeshift bridge – about one hour from the trailhead. There are *campsites* on the other side. Proceed up the West Fork opposite the steep, craggy ridge of Trampas Peak, then transit long hellebore meadows fringing beaver dams in the meandering stream. Some attractive *campsites* can also be found along here.

Ford the small West Fork and begin a long, winding traverse high above the steep-sided upper valley. The trail climbs through avalanche chutes and a forest of fir and whitebark pine, scattered with many tiny red-yellow columbines and low whortleberry heath, to pass some *campsites* just up from a derelict miner's cabin. Climb past **No Fish Lake**; this greenish tarn is visible only from above. Continue switchbacking up over steep gravel slopes to reach the ridge top known as **Santa Barbara Divide** (11,830ft), about four hours from the Middle Fork ford.

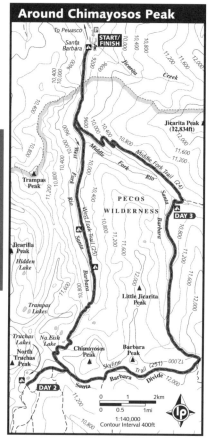

Around Chimayosos Peak

From here there are excellent views back downvalley and south across the pristine ranges of the Pecos Wilderness. Bighorn sheep can often be seen grazing on the open tundra. The summit of **Chimayosos Peak** (12,825ft) can be reached via a rough 0.9mi route along its sparse west ridge in two to 2½ hours round-trip.

Sidle down left along steep, dry slopes of bristlecone pine and juniper to meet the Skyline Trail (No 251). Turn right and skirt down southwest through a shallow glacial basin before rising up gently to the lower of the **Truchas Lakes**, 40 to 50 minutes from

Santa Barbara Divide. This beautiful tarn lies under the North and Middle Truchas Peaks, and the dramatic north wall of Truchas Peak (13,103ft) looms up directly to the southwest. The Truchas Lakes basin is closed to camping and campfires, but reasonable some *campsites* can be found on the approach to the lakes.

Day 2: Truchas Lakes to Middle Fork/East Fork Junction
4–5½ hours, 11.2mi, 184ft ascent
Return to the junction with the West Fork Trail and continue right (southeast), skirting around the southern side of Chimayosos Peak above the vast wooded basin formed by upper tributaries of the Pecos River. The Skyline Trail passes the Rito del Padre Trail turnoff (right) before rising into a saddle. Large cairns guide the way east along the panoramic open ridge top sprinkled with battered spruce and shrub willow gnawed by winter-foraging animals. Traverse past **Barbara Peak** and over a narrow and rocky section of the ridge bordered by grassy shelves to meet the Middle Fork Trail again in a broad saddle, two to three hours from the Truchas Lakes.

Cut down left (northwest) into the forest and make your way downvalley past soggy meadows grazed by mule deer and scree slides coming off the steep slopes to reford the Middle Fork Rio Santa Barbara (to its east bank). There are *campsites* just upstream from here. Continue 0.6mi to cross the tiny East Fork and climb to intersect with the East Fork Trail (No 26), two to 2½ hours from the junction saddle. There are several *campsites* around a meadow fringed by aspen.

Day 3: Middle Fork/East Fork Junction to Santa Barbara Trailhead
2¼–2¾ hours, 7.2mi
Proceed left and sidle downvalley high above the roaring stream to reach the junction of the West Fork/Middle Fork Trails again after 1¼ to 1½ hours. Retrace your steps as in Day 1 to arrive back at the trailhead after one hour.

Winsor-Skyline Loop

Duration	2 days
Distance	15.2mi (24.5km)
Standard	moderate–hard
Start/Finish	Santa Fe Ski Area
Nearest Town	Santa Fe
Transport	car

Summary This wonderfully scenic high-level hike combines the Winsor and Skyline Trails to link lovely lakes, panoramic passes and majestic mountains.

This loop hike winds through the Santa Fe Mountains that mark the southern end of the mighty Sangre de Cristo Mountains, making them the most southerly of all the Rockies' ranges. The bald summits of Lake and Penitente Peaks offer sweeping views across the surrounding ranges and down to the plains around Santa Fe. Gradients are generally moderate, but the route involves plenty of up-and-down and its high elevation may be a problem for some hikers. By taking the short-cut from Puerto Nambe it can be done as a less-inspiring, long day hike.

PLANNING
When to Hike
Before July and after mid- to late September, snow is likely to cover many trail sections above 11,000ft. The trails close to the ski area tend to be busy on summer weekends. Afternoon thunderstorms are a danger in July and August, so watch the weather.

Maps
Drake Mountain Maps' 1:50,000 *Mountains of Santa Fe and the Pecos Valley* shows the route most accurately. Otherwise use either the USFS 1:63,360 *Pecos Wilderness* map or the two USGS 1:24,000 quads, *Cowles* and *Aspen Basin*.

NEAREST TOWN & FACILITIES
See Santa Fe (p296).

USFS Campgrounds
Just below Hyde State Park, roughly 7mi from Santa Fe on Hwy 475 (Santa Fe Ski Area access road), **Black Canyon USFS campground** (☎ 505-982-8674) has 45 basic tent sites ($9). Uphill is the **Hyde State Park campground**, with sites and shelters for $10. **Big Tesuque**, several miles upvalley, and **Aspen Basin**, near the trailhead, each have six free sites. For more information call the Hyde Park USFS ranger station (☎ 505-983-7175).

GETTING TO/FROM THE HIKE
From the Plaza in Santa Fe drive north along Washington St then turn right into Artist Rd. Continue 7.5mi along what becomes Hyde Park Rd (Hwy 475) to Hyde State Park, then proceed a further 7.5mi to the large parking lot of the Santa Fe Ski Area. There's space for several hundred vehicles.

Capital City Cab (☎ 505-438-0000) can provide hiker shuttles to/from Santa Fe Ski Area for around $40.

THE HIKE
Day 1: Santa Fe Ski Area to Katherine Lake
3½–4½ hours, 6.2mi, 1480ft ascent
Find the trailhead near the toilet shed on the west side of the large parking lot and walk a few steps across a tiny stream to join the Winsor Trail (No 254). Turn right and head up through large firs and spruces, switchbacking briefly to enter the wilderness at a log fence on an open saddle (10,835ft) just east of Aspen Peak, 25 to 30 minutes from the trailhead. The Ravens Ridge Trail leads off right (east) from here.

Sign in at the USFS registry book here, then continue northeast down past Trail 403 (which leads left down to the Rio Nambe) through forest carpeted with low whortleberry shrubs. The Winsor Trail passes the Nambe Lake Trail (No 400) turnoff (right) to cross the tiny Rio Nambe, then sidles on past the Upper Nambe Trail (No 101), turnoff (left), one to 1¼ hours from the wilderness boundary.

Head gently uphill through tiny wildflower meadows giving views northeast to the open, rounded tops of Santa Fe Baldy (12,662ft). The trail passes the Rio Nambe Trail (No 160) turnoff (left) before fording

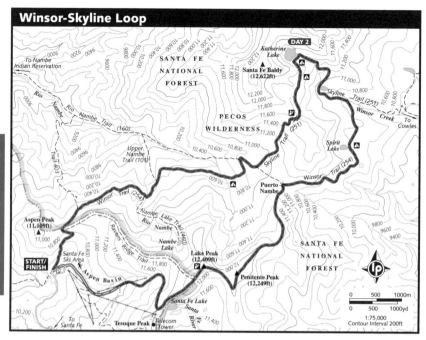

Winsor-Skyline Loop

two small streams – there are grassy *campsites* just after you cross the second streamlet. Climb steadily to reach a Y-junction on an attractive, grassy shelf scattered with spruce and Indian hellebore, 40 to 50 minutes from the Upper Nambe Trail turnoff.

Leave the Winsor Trail and continue left along the Skyline Trail (No 251), which gradually steepens and winds up northeast over fire-cleared slopes to reach a windy **pass** (11,620ft) after 40 to 50 minutes. From here there are sweeping views south to Lake Peak and Penitente Peak, and down across the broad Santa Fe plains. The Pecos Baldys stand out among the rolling expanse of forested hills to the northeast.

Descend in several steep, tight switchbacks into a small avalanche chute on the north side of the pass, then cut away left. (Before July the trail here may be corniced and snowbound, requiring a detour around the left (west) side of the pass.) The well-graded trail sidles on north through boulders

past a tiny tarn with *campsites* down to your right before it crosses Winsor Creek. Climb on through another rubble field to arrive at **Katherine Lake**, 45 minutes to one hour from the pass. This delightful tarn is enclosed within a small craggy cirque under Santa Fe Baldy. The lake basin itself is closed to camping and campfires, but legal *campsites* can be found well down from the lake.

Day 2: Katherine Lake to Santa Fe Ski Area
5–6½ hours, 9mi, 2374ft ascent
From the lake's northeast shore, drop in switchbacks to a small tarn in the bouldery forest. After quickly passing streamside *campsites*, the Skyline Trail sidles on east through regenerated fir and spruce forest to a ridge top. Follow this a short way, then cut down to the right to a trail junction.

Turn right to rejoin the Winsor Trail, which soon fords the small rushing Winsor Creek (the last running water until Aspen basin) near some *campsites*. A gentle rise over a broad spur brings you to **Spirit Lake**, a shallow tarn with a greenish algal tinge fringed by forested ridges. *Camping* is permitted only far back from the shore, well outside the lake basin. Cross the trickling outlet and begin a long sidle southwest along steep, dry slopes high above the upper basin of Holy Ghost Creek to reach a trail junction at the broad pass of **Puerto Nambe** (11,050ft), about two hours from Katherine Lake.

(The final section of the hike is a somewhat rougher and higher-level route. From Puerto Nambe, hikers with less time and/or experience may prefer to continue 0.5mi northwest to the Y-junction described in Day 1, then backtrack to the ski area parking lot.)

Turn left onto the Skyline Trail, rising south through the forest onto the ridge top, before climbing over open tundra and skirting the eastern slope of **Penitente Peak** (12,249ft) to a saddle on its south side.

Head about 10 minutes northwest into a narrow gap between lonely alpine basins. A snow cornice here may require some care to negotiate early in the season. The trail climbs along the rocky ridge (in places skirting briefly left or right) to reach the panoramic summit of **Lake Peak** (12,409ft), two hours from Puerto Nambe. From these lofty heights you get a cool view southwest to Santa Fe, which sprawls across the sweltering semi-arid plains 5000ft below. Nambe Lake is visible nestling in the cirque at Lake Peak's northwest flank.

Just below the summit, a much-traveled route picks its way southwest along the crest of the ridge to a tiny plateau area. A slightly lower route that traverses the east (right) side of the ridge avoids rock outcrops, but it is a rougher and more up-and-down alternative. (Cairns at the tiny plateau mark the start of the Ravens Ridge Trail. This popular 2.2mi alternative route – an unofficial trail not shown on most maps – turns down to the right into the forest and follows Ravens Ridge northwest to meet the Winsor Trail at the open saddle on the wilderness boundary (see Day 1) after about one hour.)

The now-improved trail dips back into the trees and proceeds southwest high above

Santa Fe Lake to ski facilities on the north side of Tesuque Peak (recognizable by telephone towers on its summit). Here take a winter ski run (initially a disused road) down diagonally to the right (north) for 0.5mi (past a short trail that cuts up directly to Ravens Ridge), then on through pleasant clearings into Aspen Basin to meet a rough dirt road. Follow this down under chairlifts to come out back at the top of the Santa Fe Ski Area parking lot, 1½ to two hours from Lake Peak.

Other Hikes

SAN PEDRO PARKS WILDERNESS
This 64-sq-mile wilderness area takes in most of the San Pedro Mountains – more a broad, rolling plateau with numerous natural, open 'parks' than a range proper – in the Santa Fe National Forest. The wilderness receives only a modest number of visitors and its most popular (and probably easiest) route is the Vacas Trail (No 51), a 17mi round-trip hike to the source of the Rio de las Vacas.

The trailhead is accessible from the town of Cuba, north of Albuquerque on Hwy 44. Drive 12mi east on Hwy 126 then turn off north and continue 2.8mi on FR 70. The USFS 1:63,360 *San Pedro Parks Wilderness Map* shows all trails in the wilderness. Otherwise use the two USGS 1:24,000 quads: *Nacimiento Peak* and *Gallina*.

BANDELIER WILDERNESS
The 42-sq-mile Bandelier Wilderness (which includes Bandelier National Monument and the adjoining Dome Wilderness) lies roughly 50mi northwest of Santa Fe in the Jemez Mountains. The Bandelier is an ancient caldera in which streams have cut out deep canyons in thick deposits of volcanic ash. Until the mid-1500s, the area was inhabited by the ancestral Pueblo people.

Most hikes start from the visitor center (☎ 505-672-3861, ext 517) in Frijoles Canyon, 3mi off Hwy 4. Backpackers must obtain a (free) backcountry permit here. Midsummer temperatures are often too hot for hiking, so come in spring or fall.

The easy (2mi) Frijoles Canyon Trail leads past ancient sites including a ceremonial kiva and cliff dwellings. A more challenging 21mi backcountry loop leads via the interesting Stone Lions rock carving and the prehistoric pictographs at Painted Cave, then back through the Capulin and Alamo canyons. Use two USGS 1:24,000 quads: *Frijoles* and *Cochiti Dam* (latter only needed for the loop).

Glossary

AAA – American Automobile Association; also called 'Triple A' or 'Auto Club'

alpine – all areas above *tree line*

Amtrak – national, government-owned passenger railroad company

andesite – fine-grained gray volcanic rock

ATV – all-terrain vehicle used for off-road transportation and recreation; see also *4WD*

avalanche slope – steep slope kept largely treeless by winter avalanches

backcountry – anywhere away from roads or other major infrastructure

backpacking – multiday hike requiring full camping gear

backtrack – to return via the approach route

bald – natural clearing below *tree line*

basalt – hard, dense and very common volcanic rock; solidified lava

batholith – mass of igneous rock, usually *granite*, formed from an intrusion of magma at great depth

bench – shelf or step-like area with steep slopes above and below it

BLM – Bureau of Land Management; government agency that controls large areas of *public land*

blowdown – instance of trees being blown down by the wind; a tree blown down

bouldering – hopping from one rock to the next; climbing boulders or small outcrops

box canyon – steep-sided valley with only one entrance

butte – prominent hill or mountain standing separate from surrounding ranges

cairn – pile or stack of rocks used to indicate the route or a trail junction

caldera – very large crater that has resulted from a volcanic explosion or the collapse of a volcanic cone

cascade – small waterfall

CDT – Continental Divide Trail

chamber of commerce – association of local businesses that commonly provides a tourist information service (does not provide information about nonmembers)

chinook – dry, warm, westerly wind on the east side of the *Continental Divide*

cirque – rounded, high ridge or bowl formed by glacial action

CO – abbreviation for Colorado

Continental Divide – major watershed separating east-flowing (to the Atlantic) from west-flowing (to the Pacific) streams

contour – to *sidle* around a hill at approximately the same altitude (or contour level); a line on a map connecting land points with the same elevation; see also *traverse*

cornice – potentially dangerous overhanging snowdrift on mountain passes and ridges

CR – county road

cutoff – shortcut trail

drainage – course of a creek or streamlet

drumlin – hill of glacial rubble (or till) with a streamlined or teardrop profile, shaped by advancing glacial ice

erratic – boulder carried by glacial ice and deposited some distance from its place of origin

esker – serpentine ridge of gravel and sand, formed by streams under, or in, glacial ice

fire blanket/fire pan – metal sheeting (mandatory in some *wilderness* areas) to protect the ground from campfires

foot – base of a mountain; lower end of a valley or lake; see also *head*

ford – to cross a river by wading

fork – branch or tributary of a stream or river

14er, 14-thousander – peak of 14,000ft or higher

4WD – Four-wheel-drive vehicle; see also *ATV*

FR – forest road

Front Range – prominent range marking the Rockies' outer (eastern or western) edge

gap – mountain pass or *saddle*; notch

geyser – spring that erupts intermittent jets of water and steam

glacier – extended mass of ice, formed from accumulating snow, that moves slowly down a mountain or valley

gorp – acronym for 'good old raisins and peanuts', commonly used when referring to *trail mix*

GPS – global positioning system; electronic, satellite-based network that allows for the calculation of position and elevation using a handheld receiver/decoder

graded – leveled (road or trail)

granite – coarse-grained, often gray, rock formed by the slow cooling of molten rock (magma) deep below the earth

Great Basin – semiarid plateau extending westward from western Idaho and Utah

Great Plains – vast prairies (steppes) east of the Rockies

green-up – resurgent spring growth after winter

guard station – *USFS* ranger station

gulch – narrow ravine cut by a river or stream

head – uppermost part of a valley; upper end of a valley or lake; see also *foot*

headwall – often very precipitous rocky cirque at the uppermost end of a valley

HI/AYH – Hostelling International/American Youth Hostels

hogback – steep, narrow ridge

hole – broad, flat valley floor (eg, Jackson Hole and Big Hole)

hookup – campground site with electricity

ID – abbreviation for Idaho

inlet – (principal) stream flowing into a lake

karst – a form of *limestone*

KOA – Kampgrounds of America; a private chain of campgrounds with substantial amenities

krummholz – wind-twisted, stunted trees found near *tree line*

limestone – sedimentary rock that is composed mainly of calcium carbonate

lollipop loop – circuit hike accessed via a long, straight section

Lower 48 – contiguous states of the US (ie, excluding Alaska and Hawaii)

meltwater – water derived from the melting of ice and snow

mesa – elevated tableland or plateau with steep edges

montane – lower forest zone

moraine – ridge, mound or irregular mass (mostly boulders, gravel, sand and clay) deposited at the snout or along the flanks of a *glacier*

mountain man – early trapper or explorer of the Rockies

MT – abbreviation for Montana

national forest – area of *public land* administered by the *USFS*

NM – abbreviation for New Mexico

NPS – National Park Service

NRA – National Recreation Area; similar to a *wilderness* area, but with some controlled development; also National Rifle Association

obsidian – black, glassy volcanic rock

old-growth – forest more than 200 years old and never altered by humans

outlet – stream flowing out of a lake

outlier – a diverging lateral range of a major mountain chain (eg, Bighorns and Sawtooths)

pads – well-trodden trail created by animal (or human) use

privy – pit toilet, usually at a campsite

public land – any federal or state land, especially that administered by the *BLM*, *NPS* or *USFS*

quad – 1:24,000 *USGS* topographic map

quartzite – white or gray *sandstone* composed primarily of quartz grains

radial hike – trip based at a *backcountry* camp, from where nearby areas are visited on day hikes

rhyolite – fine-grained volcanic rock

rut – fall (autumn) mating season, when male *ungulates* vie for mating rights

RV – recreational vehicle; motor home

saddle – low place in a ridge; see also *gap*

sandstone – sedimentary rock composed of sand grains

scree – weathered rock fragments at the foot of a cliff or on a hillside

sidle – to cut along a slope; to *contour*; see also *traverse*

slickrock – large expanse of exposed rock that has been sculpted and smoothed by erosion

snow line – level below which snow seldom falls and does not remain on the ground

snowpack – accumulation of slow-melting packed snow

social trail – non-official (unmaintained) trail created by the passage of many hikers

spur – small ridge that leads up from a valley to a main ridge; small branch of a main trail

subalpine – upper forest zone

switchback – route that follows a zigzag course on a steep grade

talus – large boulders accumulated on a slope, fanning out at its base

tarn – small mountain lake

timberline – upper limit of forest; see also *tree line*

topo – topographic map with *contour* lines

trail mix – snack-food mixture of nuts, dried fruit, seeds and/or chocolate; *gorp*

traverse – to cut along a slope (sometimes also along a ridge); see also *sidle* and *contour*

tree line – uppermost (natural) level to which tree cover extends on a mountainside; see also *timberline*

tundra – stunted *alpine* vegetation found at the uppermost level above *tree line*

ungulate – hoofed animal

USFS – United States Forest Service; manages the *national forest* system

USGS – United States Geological Survey; national cartographic organization

UT – abbreviation for Utah

wilderness – officially designated primitive area

wildland – roadless or primitive area (whether officially designated or not)

windthrow – uprooting and throwing of trees by the wind

WY – abbreviation for Wyoming

LONELY PLANET

You already know that Lonely Planet produces more than this one guidebook, but you might not be aware of the other products we have on this region. Here is a selection of titles that you may want to check out as well:

Rocky Mountains
ISBN 1 86450 327 0
US$24.99 • UK£14.99

USA phrasebook
ISBN 1 86450 182 0
US$6.99 • UK£4.50

Southwest: Arizona, New Mexico, Utah
ISBN 1 86450 376 9
US$24.99 • UK£14.99

British Columbia
ISBN 1 86450 220 7
US$16.99 • UK£10.99

Canada
ISBN 0 86442 752 2
US$24.95 • UK£14.99

Hiking in Alaska
ISBN 1 86450 038 7
US$19.99 • UK£12.99

Hiking in the Sierra Nevada
ISBN 1 74059 272 7
US$17.99 • UK£11.99

Hiking in the USA
ISBN 0 86442 600 3
US$24.99 • UK£14.99

Lonely Planet Unpacked Again
ISBN 1 86450 319 X
US$12.99 • UK£6.99

USA
ISBN 1 86450 308 4
US$24.99 • UK£14.99

Cycling USA - West Coast
ISBN 1 86450 324 6
US$21.99 • UK£13.99

Available wherever books are sold

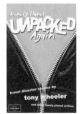

Index

Bold indicates maps.
For a list of hikes, see the
Table of Hikes (pp4–7).

Bold indicates maps.
For a list of hikes, see the
Table of Hikes (pp4–7).

Map Legend

BOUNDARIES

```
— — · — · — · — · —  International
— · — — · — — · —   Regional
— — — — — — —      Disputed
```

HYDROGRAPHY

```
.................... Coastline
.................... River, Creek
.................... Lake, Tarn
.................. Intermittent Lake
.................... Salt Lake
.................... Canal
⊙    ⤜⤜ ........ Spring, Rapids
⫟   ⫟ .............. Waterfalls
.................... Swamp
```

ROUTES & TRANSPORT

```
════════· ...... Interstate, Freeway
═══════════ ....... Highway
═══════════ .......... Major Road
═══════════ .......... Minor Road
= = = = = =· Unsealed Major Road
= = = = = =· Unsealed Minor Road
— — — — — — —· ............. Track
═══════════ .............. Lane
```

AREA FEATURES

```
█████  National Park, Wilderness
       Area (Regional Maps)
┌┄┄┄┐  National Park, Wilderness
└┄┄┄┘  Area (Hike Maps)
┌┄┄┄┐  National Forest,
└┄┄┄┘  Indian Reservation
▒▒▒▒▒  Glacier
```

MAP SYMBOLS

```
⊙  CAPITAL ............. State Capital
●  CITY ....................... City
●  Town ....................... Town
●  Village ............... Small Town

▲  ............. Camping Area
☐  ..................... Hut
☐  .... Overlook, Viewpoint
▼  ............. Place to Eat
■  ............. Place to Stay
●  .......... Point of Interest
☐  ..................... Shelter
⟒  .................... Trailhead
```

```
⇒═ ═ ═ ═ :. ............ Tunnel
├──┼──O──┼── .... Railroad & Station
⊢─⫟─⊢─⫟─⊢─⫟─ .. Cable Car or Chairlift
▬▬▬▬▬▬ .......... Described Hike
▬▬ ▬▬ ▬▬ ▬▬ ...... Alternative Route
● ● ● ● ● ● ● ● ● .......... Side Trip
— — — — — — — ....... Hiking Trail
· · · · · · · · · · · · · ... Undefined Route
```

ROUTE SHIELDS

```
═══⟨90⟩═══ ............... Interstate
═══⟨84⟩═══ ............... US Highway
═══⟨101⟩═══ ............. State Highway
◀1▬  ▬2▶ ......... Hike Number &
                   Direction of Hike
                   (one way; both ways)
```

```
☒  ..................... Airport
🚌  .................... Bus Stop
⌂  ....................... Cave
⛪  .................... Church
⌇⌇⌇  ........ Cliff or Escarpment
· · · · ·˙˙˙˙˙˙· Continental Divide
~500~  ................ Contour
❀  .................... Gardens
⋈  ...................... Gate
✛  .................... Hospital
▲  .......... Mountain or Hill
🏛  .................... Museum
☎  ............... National Park
```

```
🄿  ....Parking Lot/Car Park
)(  ....................... Pass
⊕  .............. Picnic Area
✚  ............. Police Station
✉  ............... Post Office
🛈  .................. Restroom
⊠  .......... Shopping Center
⛷  ..................... Ski Area
+(ft)  ............ Spot Height
☎  ................. Telephone
🛈  ...... Tourist Information
◓  ............. Transportation
△  ..... Trigonometric Point
```

Note: not all symbols displayed above appear in this book

LONELY PLANET OFFICES

Australia
Locked Bag 1, Footscray, Victoria 3011
☎ 03-8379 8000 fax 03-8379 8111
ⓔ talk2us@lonelyplanet.com.au

USA
150 Linden St, Oakland, CA 94607
☎ 510-893-8555 or ☎ 800-275-8555 (toll free)
fax 510-893-8572
ⓔ info@lonelyplanet.com

UK
10a Spring Place, London NW5 3BH
☎ 020-7428 4800 fax 020-7428 4828
ⓔ go@lonelyplanet.co.uk

France
1 rue du Dahomey, 75011 Paris
☎ 01 55 25 33 00 fax 01 55 25 33 01
ⓔ bip@lonelyplanet.fr
ⓦ www.lonelyplanet.fr

World Wide Web: ⓦ www.lonelyplanet.com *or* AOL keyword: lp
Lonely Planet Images: ⓔ lpi@lonelyplanet.com.au